Oxford
Practice
Grammar

Second edition

Oxford Practice Grammar

with answers

John Eastwood

Oxford University Press

OXFORD
UNIVERSITY PRESS

Oxford University Press is a department of the University of Oxford.
It furthers the University's objective of excellence in research, scholarship,
and education by publishing worldwide. Oxford is a registered trade mark of
Oxford University Press in the UK and in certain other countries

Published in Pakistan by
Ameena Saiyid, Oxford University Press
No.38, Sector 15, Korangi Industrial Area,
PO Box 8214, Karachi-74900, Pakistan

© Oxford University Press 1999

The moral rights of the author have been asserted

This edition published 2004

All rights reserved. No part of this publication may be reproduced, stored in
a retrieval system, or transmitted, in any form or by any means, without the
prior permission in writing of Oxford University Press, or as expressly permitted
by law, by licence, or under terms agreed with the appropriate reprographics
rights organization. Enquiries concerning reproduction outside the scope of the
above should be sent to the Rights Department, Oxford University Press, at the
address above

You must not circulate this work in any other form
and you must impose this same condition on any acquirer

ISBN 978-0-19-597835-3

Twenty-second Impression 2017

Printed on 55gsm Newsprint paper

Printed by Kagzi Printers, Karachi

Acknowledgements
Illustrated by Richard Coggan

This edition is licensed for sale in Pakistan only and not for export therefrom

Contents

Introduction *page vi*
Key to symbols *vii*
Starting test *viii*

Words and sentences

1. Word classes: nouns, verbs, adjectives, etc *2*
2. Sentence structure: subject, verb, object, etc *4*
3. Direct and indirect objects *6*

Verbs

4. The present continuous *8*
5. The present simple *10*
6. Present continuous or simple? *12*
7. State verbs and action verbs *14*
   Test 1: Present tenses *16*
8. The past simple *18*
9. The past continuous *20*
10. Past continuous or simple? *22*
    Test 2: Past simple and past continuous *24*
11. The present perfect (1) *26*
12. The present perfect (2): **just**, **already**, **yet**; **for** and **since** *28*
13. The present perfect (3): **ever**, **this week**, etc *30*
14. Present perfect or past simple? (1) *32*
15. Present perfect or past simple? (2) *34*
    Test 3: Present perfect and past simple *36*
16. The present perfect continuous *38*
17. Present perfect continuous or simple? *40*
18. The past perfect *42*
19. Review of the past simple, continuous and perfect *44*
20. The past perfect continuous *46*
    Test 4: Past and perfect tenses *48*
21. Review of present and past tenses *50*
    Test 5: Present and past tenses *54*
22. Introduction to the future *56*
23. **Will** and **shall** *58*
24. **Be going to** *60*
25. **Will** and **be going to** *62*
26. Present tenses for the future *64*
27. **When I get there, before you leave**, etc *66*
    Test 6: The future with **will, be going to** and present tenses *68*
28. **Will be doing** *70*
29. **Will have done** and **was going to** *72*
30. Review of the future *74*
    Test 7: The future *76*
31. The verb **have** *78*
32. Short forms, e.g **it's**, **don't** *80*
33. Emphatic **do** *82*

Questions, negatives and answers

34. Yes/no questions *84*
35. Short answers, e.g. **Yes, it is.** *86*
36. Wh-questions *88*
37. Subject/object questions *90*
38. Prepositions in wh-questions *92*
39. **Who, what** or **which**? *94*
    Test 8: Questions *96*
40. Negative statements *98*
41. Negative questions *100*
42. Question tags, e.g. **isn't it?** *102*
43. **So/Neither do I** and **I think so** *104*
    Test 9: Questions, negatives and answers *106*

Modal verbs

44. Ability: **can, could** and **be able to** *108*
45. Permission: **can, may, could** and **be allowed to** *110*
46. Possibility and certainty: **may, might, could, must**, etc *112*
47. Necessity: **must** and **have to** *114*
48. Necessity: **mustn't, needn't**, etc *116*
49. **Should, ought to, had better** and **be supposed to** *118*
50. Asking people to do things *120*
51. Suggestions, offers and invitations *122*
52. **Will, would, shall** and **should** *124*
53. **It may/could/must have been**, etc *126*
    Test 10: Modal verbs *128*

The passive

54. Passive verb forms *130*
55. Active and passive (1) *132*
56. Active and passive (2) *134*
57. Special passive structures *136*
58. **Have something done** *138*
59. **To be done** and **being done** *140*
    Test 11: The passive *142*

The infinitive and the ing-form

60 Verb + to-infinitive *144*
61 Verb + ing-form *146*
62 Verb + to-infinitive or verb + ing-form? *148*
63 **Like, start,** etc *150*
64 **Remember, regret, try,** etc *152*
Test 12: Verb + to-infinitive or ing-form *154*

65 Verb + object + to-infinitive or ing-form *156*
66 Question word + to-infinitive *158*
67 Adjective + to-infinitive *160*
68 **For** with the to-infinitive *162*
69 The infinitive with and without **to** *164*
70 Verb/Adjective + preposition + ing-form *166*
71 **Afraid to do** or **afraid of doing**? *168*
72 **Used to do** and **be used to doing** *170*
73 Preposition or linking word + ing-form *172*
74 **See it happen** or **see it happening**? *174*
75 Some structures with the ing-form *176*
Test 13: The infinitive and the ing-form *178*

Nouns and articles (**a/an** and **the**)

76 **Ship** and **water**: countable and uncountable nouns *180*
77 **A carton of milk, a piece of information,** etc *182*
78 Nouns that can be either countable or uncountable *184*
79 Agreement *186*
80 Singular or plural? *188*
81 Pair nouns and group nouns *190*
82 Two nouns together *192*
Test 14: Nouns and agreement *194*

83 **A/an** and **the** (1) *196*
84 **A/an** and **the** (2) *198*
85 **A/an, one** and **some** *200*
86 **Cars** or **the cars**? *202*
87 **Prison, school, bed,** etc *204*
88 **On Friday, for lunch,** etc *206*
89 **Quite a, such a, what a,** etc *208*
90 Place names and **the** *210*
Test 15: **A/an** and **the** *214*

This, my, some, a lot of, all, etc

91 **This, that, these** and **those** *216*
92 **My, your,** etc and **mine, yours,** etc *218*
93 The possessive form and **of** *220*
94 **Some** and **any** *222*
95 **A lot of, many, much, (a) few** and **(a) little** *224*
96 **All, half, most, some, no** and **none** *226*
97 **Every, each, whole, both, either** and **neither** *228*
Test 16: **This, my, some, a lot of, all,** etc *230*

Pronouns

98 Personal pronouns, e.g. **I, you** *232*
99 **There** and **it** *234*
100 Reflexive pronouns *236*
101 Emphatic pronouns and **each other** *238*
102 The pronoun **one/ones** *240*
103 **Everyone, something,** etc *242*
Test 17: Pronouns *244*

Adjectives and adverbs

104 Adjectives *246*
105 The order of adjectives *248*
106 **The old, the rich,** etc *250*
107 **Interesting** and **interested** *252*
108 Adjective or adverb? (1) *254*
109 Adjective or adverb? (2) *256*
Test 18: Adjectives and adverbs *258*

110 Comparative and superlative forms *260*
111 Comparative and superlative patterns (1) *264*
112 Comparative and superlative patterns (2) *266*
Test 19: Comparative and superlative *268*

113 Adverbs and word order *270*
114 **Yet, still** and **already** *274*
115 Adverbs of degree, e.g. **very, quite** *276*
116 **Quite** and **rather** *278*
117 **Too** and **enough** *280*
Test 20: Adverbs and word order *282*

Prepositions

118 Prepositions of place *284*
119 **In, on** and **at** (place) *288*
120 **In, on** and **at** (time) *290*
121 **For, since, ago** and **before** *292*
122 **During** or **while**? **By** or **until**? **As** or **like**? *294*
123 Preposition + noun, e.g. **on holiday** *296*
124 Noun + preposition, e.g. **trouble with** *298*
125 Adjective + preposition, e.g. **proud of** *300*
Test 21: Prepositions *302*

Verbs with prepositions and adverbs

126 Prepositional verbs, e.g. **wait for** *304*
127 Verb + object + preposition *306*
128 Phrasal verbs (1) *308*
129 Phrasal verbs (2) *310*
130 Phrasal verbs (3) *312*
131 Verb + adverb + preposition *314*
Test 22: Verbs with prepositions and adverbs *316*

Reported speech

132 Direct speech and reported speech *318*
133 Reported speech: person, place and time *320*
134 Reported speech: the tense change *322*
135 Reported questions *324*
136 Reported requests, offers, etc *326*
Test 23: Reported speech *328*

Relative clauses

137 Relative clauses with **who, which** and **that** *330*
138 The relative pronoun as object *332*
139 Prepositions in relative clauses *334*
140 Relative structures with **whose, what** and **it** *336*
141 The use of relative clauses *338*
142 Relative pronouns and relative adverbs *340*
143 Relative clauses: participle and to-infinitive *342*
Test 24: Relative clauses *344*

Conditionals and **wish**

144 Conditionals (1) *346*
145 Conditionals (2) *348*
146 Conditionals (3) *350*
147 Review of conditionals *352*
148 **If, when, unless** and **in case** *354*
149 **Wish** and **if only** *356*
Test 25: Conditionals and **wish** *358*

Linking words

150 **But, although** and **in spite of** *360*
151 **To, in order to, so that** and **for** *362*
152 Review of linking words *364*
153 Links across sentences *366*

Appendices

1 Word formation *368*
2 The spelling of endings *370*
3 Punctuation *372*
4 Pronunciation *374*
5 American English *377*
6 Irregular verbs *383*

Key to the starting test *385*

Key to the exercises *386*

Key to the tests *414*

Index *425*

Introduction

Who is this book for?

Oxford Practice Grammar is for students of English studying in undergraduate/graduate classes at college or university. This means students who have pre-intermediate or intermediate proficiency in English. The book is also suitable for those studying for the Cambridge First Certificate in English. It can be used by students attending classes or by someone working alone.

What does the book consist of?

The book consists of 153 units, each on a grammatical topic. The units cover the main areas of English grammar. Special attention is given to those points which are often a problem for learners: the meaning of the different verb forms, the use of the passive, conditionals, prepositions and so on.

Many units contrast two or more different structures such as the present perfect and past simple (Units 14–15). There are also a number of review units. The emphasis through the whole book is on the meaning and use of the forms in situations. Most units start with a dialogue, or sometimes a text, which shows how the forms are used in a realistic context.

There are also 25 tests. These come after each group of units and cover the area of grammar dealt with in those units.

Each unit consists of an explanation of the grammar point followed by a number of exercises. Almost all units cover two pages. The explanations are on the left-hand page, and the exercises are on the right-hand page. There are a few four-page units, with two pages of explanation and two pages of exercise.

The examples used to illustrate the explanations are mostly in everyday conversational English, except when the structure is more typical of a formal or written style (e.g. Unit 75B).

There are also appendices on a number of other topics, including word formation, American English and irregular verbs.

What's new about this edition?

There have been many changes in both the content and design of the book.

- The number of units has been increased from 120 to 153. There are more two-page units and fewer four-page units.

- The 25 tests are a new feature. There is also a Starting test to help students find out what they need to study.

- There are many more dialogues and illustrations on the explanation pages. Many of the examples and situation are new.

- There are many new exercises and more different types of exercise.

- The number of appendices has been increased from two to six.

- This new edition features a group of characters whose lives are the basis for many of the situations in both the explanations and the exercises. (But you can still do the units in any order.)

How should the book be used?

There are various ways of using the book. If you know that you have problems with particular points of grammar, then you can start with the relevant units. The contents list and index will help you find what you want. Or you can do the Starting test (see page *viii*) and then use the results to decide which parts of the book to concentrate on. Or you can start at the beginning of the book and work through to the end, although the grammar topics are not ordered according to their level of difficulty.

When you study a unit, start with the explanation page and then go on to the exercises. Often you can study a part of the explanation and then do one of the exercises. The letter after each exercise title, e.g. (A), tells you which part of the explanation the exercise relates to. If you have made mistakes in your answers to the exercises, look back at the explanation.

Key to symbols

What about the tests?

There are 25 tests at intervals through the book. You can do a test after you have worked through a group of units. At the beginning of each test you are told which units are being tested.

The tests do two things. Firstly, they enable you to find out how well you have mastered the grammar. (If you get things wrong, you can go back to the relevant unit or part of a unit.) Secondly, the tests give you practice in handling exam-type questions. Many of the test questions are similar to those used in the Cambridge First Certificate Use of English Paper.

What's the best way to learn grammar?

It is usually more effective to look at examples of English rather than to read statements about it. The explanations of grammar in this book are descriptions of how English works; they are a guide to help you understand, not 'rules' to be memorized. The important thing is the language itself. If you are learning about the present perfect continuous, for example, it is helpful to memorize a sentence like *We've been waiting here for twenty minutes* and to imagine a situation at a bus stop like the one in Unit 16A. The explanation – that the action happens over a period of time lasting up to the present – is designed to help towards an understanding of the grammar point. It is not intended that you should write it down or memorize it.

Active learning will help you more than passive reading, so it is important to do the exercises and to check your answers.

Another way of actively learning grammar is to write down sentences you see or hear which contain examples of the grammar you are studying. You may come across such sentences in English books or newspapers, on television or on the Internet. You may meet English speakers. For example, someone may ask you *How long have you been living here?* Later you could note down this sentence as a useful example of the present perfect continuous. It is also a good idea to collect examples with a personal relevance like *I've been learning English for three years*.

The symbol / (oblique stroke) between two words means that either word is possible. *I may/might go* means that *I **may** go* and *I **might** go* are both possible. In exercise questions this symbol is also used to separate words or phrases which need to be used in the answer.

Brackets ( ) around a word or phrase mean that it can be left out. *There's (**some**) milk in the fridge* means that there are two possible sentences: *There's **some** milk in the fridge* and *There's milk in the fridge*.

The symbol ~ means that there is a change of speaker. In the example *How are you? ~ I'm fine, thanks*, the two sentences are spoken by different people.

The symbol ▷ means that you can go to another place in the book for more information. ▷ 7 means that you can find out more in Unit 7.

The symbol ▶ in an exercise means an example.

For phonetic symbols see page 374.

Starting test

This test will help you to find out which parts of the book you need to spend most time on. You don't have to do the whole test at once – you could do numbers 2 to 22 first to test your knowledge of verbs. Choose the correct answer – a), b), c) or d).

Some of the questions are quite difficult, so don't worry if you get them wrong. This book was written to help you get them right in future!

Words and sentences

1 We gave .... a meal.
   a) at the visitors b) for the visitors c) the visitors d) to the visitors

Verbs

2 I'm busy at the moment. .... on the computer.
   a) I work b) I'm work c) I'm working d) I working

3 My friend .... the answer to the question.
   a) is know b) know c) knowing d) knows

4 I think I'll buy these shoes. .... really well.
   a) They fit b) They have fit c) They're fitting d) They were fitting

5 Where .... the car?
   a) did you park b) did you parked c) parked you d) you parked

6 At nine o'clock yesterday morning we .... for the bus.
   a) wait b) waiting c) was waiting d) were waiting

7 When I looked round the door, the baby .... quietly.
   a) is sleeping b) slept c) was sleeping d) were sleeping

8 Here's my report. .... it at last.
   a) I finish b) I finished c) I'm finished d) I've finished

9 I've .... made some coffee. It's in the kitchen.
   a) ever b) just c) never d) yet

10 We .... to Ireland for our holidays last year.
    a) goes b) going c) have gone d) went

11 Robert .... ill for three weeks. He's still in hospital.
    a) had been b) has been c) is d) was

12 My arms are aching now because .... since two o'clock.
    a) I'm swimming b) I swam c) I swim d) I've been swimming

13 I'm very tired. .... over four hundred miles today.
    a) I drive b) I'm driving c) I've been driving d) I've driven

14 When Martin .... the car, he took it out for a drive.
    a) had repaired b) has repaired c) repaired d) was repairing

15 Janet was out of breath because ....
    a) she'd been running b) she did run c) she's been running d) she's run

16 Don't worry. I .... be here to help you.
    a) not b) shall c) willn't d) won't

17 Our friends .... meet us at the airport tonight.
   a) are b) are going to c) go to d) will be to

18 .... a party next Saturday. We've sent out the invitations.
   a) We had b) We have c) We'll have d) We're having

19 I'll tell Anna all the news when .... her.
   a) I'll see b) I'm going to see c) I see d) I shall see

20 At this time tomorrow .... over the Atlantic.
   a) we flying b) we'll be flying c) we'll fly d) we to fly

21 Where's Robert? .... a shower?
   a) Does he have b) Has he c) Has he got d) Is he having

22 I .... like that coat. It's really nice.
   a) am b) do c) very d) yes

Questions, negatives and answers

23 What's the weather like in Canada? How often .... there?
   a) does it snow b) does it snows c) snow it d) snows it

24 Which team .... the game?
   a) did it win b) did they win c) won d) won it

25 What did you leave the meeting early ....? ~ I didn't feel very well.
   a) away b) because c) for d) like

26 Unfortunately the driver .... the red light.
   a) didn't saw b) didn't see c) no saw d) saw not

27 You haven't eaten your pudding. .... it?
   a) Are you no want b) Do you no want c) Don't want you d) Don't you want

28 I really enjoyed the disco. It was great, ...?
   a) is it b) isn't it c) was it d) wasn't it

29 Are we going the right way? ~ I think ....
   a) indeed b) it c) so d) yes

Modal verbs

30 The chemist's was open, so luckily I .... buy some aspirin.
   a) can b) can't c) did can d) was able to

31 Susan has to work very hard. I .... do her job, I'm sure.
   a) can't b) couldn't c) don't d) shouldn't

32 We had a party last night. .... spend all morning clearing up the mess.
   a) I must have b) I've been to c) I've had to d) I've must

33 There was no one else at the box office. I .... in a queue.
   a) didn't need to wait b) mustn't wait c) needn't have waited d) needn't wait

34 .... I carry that bag for you? ~ Oh, thank you.
   a) Do b) Shall c) Will d) Would

35 I've lost the key. I ought .... it in a safe place.
    a) that I put b) to be putting c) to have put d) to put

The passive

36 We can't go along here because the road is ....
    a) been repaired b) being repaired c) repair d) repaired

37 The story I've just read .... Agatha Christie.
    a) was written b) was written by c) was written from d) wrote

38 Some film stars .... be difficult to work with.
    a) are said b) are said to c) say d) say to

39 I'm going to go out and ....
    a) have cut my hair b) have my hair cut c) let my hair cut d) my hair be cut

The infinitive and the ing-form

40 The driver was arrested for failing .... an accident.
    a) of report b) report c) reporting d) to report

41 Someone suggested .... for a walk.
    a) go b) going c) of going d) to go

42 I can remember .... voices in the middle of the night.
    a) hear b) heard c) hearing d) to hear

43 The police want .... anything suspicious.
    a) that we report b) us reporting c) us to report d) we report

44 We weren't sure .... or just walk in.
    a) should knock b) to knock c) whether knock d) whether to knock

45 It was too cold .... outside.
    a) the guests eating b) for the guests to eat c) that the guests should eat d) that the guests eat

46 Did you congratulate Tessa .... her exam?
    a) of passing b) on passing c) passing d) to pass

47 I didn't like it in the city at first. But now .... here.
    a) I got used to living b) I'm used to living c) I used to live d) I used to living

48 They raised the money simply .... for it. It was easy.
    a) asking b) by asking c) of asking d) with asking

49 As we walked past, we saw Nigel .... his car.
    a) in washing b) to wash c) wash d) washing

Nouns and articles (**a/an** and **the**)

50 I need to buy ....
    a) a bread b) a loaf bread c) a loaf of bread d) breads

51 My father is not only the town mayor, he runs ...., too.
    a) a business b) a piece of business c) business d) some business

52 The .... produced at our factory in Scotland.
    a) good are b) good is c) goods are d) goods is

53 I'm looking for .... to cut this string.
    a) a pair scissors b) a scissor c) a scissors d) some scissors

54 I was watching TV at home when suddenly .... rang.
    a) a doorbell b) an doorbell c) doorbell d) the doorbell

55 I've always liked ....
    a) Chinese food b) food of China c) some food of China d) the Chinese food

56 In England most children go .... at the age of five.
    a) school b) to school c) to some schools d) to the school

57 We haven't had a holiday for .... time.
    a) a so long b) so a long c) such a long d) such long

58 Our friends have a house in ....
    a) a West London b) the West London c) West London d) West of London

This, my, some, a lot of, all, etc

59 It's so boring here. Nothing ever happens in .... place.
    a) that b) these c) this d) those

60 Is that my key, or is it .... ?
    a) the yours b) the your's c) your d) yours

61 Adrian takes no interest in clothes. He'll wear ....
    a) a thing b) anything c) something d) thing

62 There's .... use in complaining. They probably won't do anything about it.
    a) a few b) a little c) few d) little

63 I don't want to buy any of these books. I've got ....
    a) all b) all them c) everything d) them all

Pronouns

64 Let's stop and have a coffee. .... a café over there, look.
    a) Is b) It's c) There d) There's

65 Everyone in the group shook hands with ....
    a) each other b) one other c) one the other d) themselves

66 The washing-machine has broken down again. I think we should get ....
    a) a new b) a new one c) new d) new one

67 All the guests were dancing. .... having a good time.
    a) All were b) Every was c) Everyone was d) Someone were

Adjectives and adverbs

68 The house was .... building.
    a) a nice old stone b) a nice stone old c) a stone old nice d) an old nice stone

69 The government is doing nothing to help ....
    a) poor b) the poor c) the poors d) the poor ones

70 The young man seems very ....
    a) sensible b) sensiblely c) sensibley d) sensibly

71 I .... missed the bus. I was only just in time to catch it.
    a) mostly b) near c) nearest d) nearly

72 This detailed map is .... the atlas.
    a) more useful as b) more useful than c) usefuller as d) usefuller than

73 This place gets .... crowded with tourists every summer.
    a) always more b) crowded and more c) from more to more d) more and more

74 Yes, I have got the report. .... it.
    a) I just am reading b) I'm just reading c) I'm reading just d) Just I'm reading

75 I've read this paragraph three times, and I .... understand it.
    a) can't still b) can't yet c) still can't d) yet can't

76 We're really sorry. We regret what happened ....
    a) a bit b) much c) very d) very much

Prepositions

77 The village is .... Sheffield. It's only six miles away.
    a) along b) by c) near d) next

78 You can see the details .... the computer screen.
    a) at b) by c) in d) on

79 I've got a meeting .... Thursday afternoon.
    a) at b) in c) on d) to

80 We've lived in this flat .... five years.
    a) ago b) already c) for d) since

81 This car is ...., if you're interested in buying it.
    a) for sale b) in sale c) at sale d) to sell

82 Polly wants to cycle round the world. She's really keen .... the idea.
    a) about b) for c) on d) with

Verbs with prepositions and adverbs

83 I prefer dogs .... cats. I hate cats.
    a) from b) over c) than d) to

84 My father used the money he won to set .... his own company.
    a) forward b) on c) out d) up

85 Don't go too fast. I can't keep .... you.
    a) on to b) on with c) up to d) up with

Reported speech

86 Someone .... the tickets are free.
   a) said me b) said me that c) told me d) told to me

87 Last week Justin said 'I'll do it tomorrow.' He said he would do it ....
   a) the following day b) the previous day c) tomorrow d) yesterday

88 I don't know why Nancy didn't go to the meeting. She said she .... definitely going.
   a) be b) is c) was d) would

89 The librarian asked us .... so much noise.
   a) don't make b) not make c) not making d) not to make

Relative clauses

90 What's the name of the man .... gave us a lift?
   a) he b) what c) which d) who

91 What was that notice ....?
   a) at that you were looking b) you were looking at c) you were looking at it d) which you were looking

92 Susan is the woman .... husband is in hospital.
   a) her b) hers the c) whose d) whose the

93 York, ... last year, is a nice old city.
   a) I visited b) that I visited c) which I visited d) whom I visited

94 The accident was seen by some people .... at a bus stop
   a) waited b) waiting c) were waiting d) who waiting

Conditionals and **wish**

95 If .... my passport, I'll be in trouble.
   a) I lose b) I'll lose c) I lost d) I would lose

96 I haven't got a ticket. If .... one, I could get in.
   a) I'd have b) I had c) I have d) I've got

97 If the bus to the airport hadn't been so late, we .... the plane.
   a) caught b) had caught c) would catch d) would have caught

98 If only people .... keep sending me bills!
   a) don't b) shouldn't c) weren't d) wouldn't

Linking words

99 I just had to take the dog out .... of the awful weather.
   a) although b) despite c) even though d) in spite

100 Anna put the electric fire on .... warm.
    a) for getting b) in order get c) so she gets d) to get

Oxford
Practice
Grammar

1 Word classes: nouns, verbs, adjectives, etc

A Introduction

Look at the different kinds of word in this sentence.

Pronoun	Verb	Determiner	Adjective	Noun	Preposition	Noun	Adverb
I	*have*	*an*	*important*	*conference*	*at*	*work*	*tomorrow,*

Linking word	Pronoun	Verb	Adverb	Adjective
so	*I*	*am*	*rather*	*busy.*

B What kind of word?

There are eight different kinds of word in English. They are called 'word classes' or 'parts of speech'. Here are some examples from the conversations in the café. The numbers after the examples tell you which units in the book give you more information.

1. Verb: **have, am, is, would, like, come, are, sitting, look** ▷ 4–75
2. Noun: **conference, work, coffee, party, Saturday, Jessica, friends, corner** ▷ 76–82
3. Adjective: **important, busy, good, cheap** ▷ 104–109
4. Adverb: **tomorrow, rather, really, here** ▷ 113–117
5. Preposition: **at, to, on, in** ▷ 118–125
6. Determiner: **an, this, our, the** ▷ 83–97
7. Pronoun: **I, it, you** ▷ 98–103
8. Linking word: **so, and** ▷ 150–153

C Words in sentences

Some words can belong to different classes depending on how they are used in a sentence.

VERBS	NOUNS
Can I **look** at your photos?	I like the **look** of that coat.
We **work** on Saturday morning.	I'll be at **work** tomorrow.

1 Exercises

1 What kind of word? (B)

Read this paragraph and then say which word class each underlined word belongs to. To help you decide, you can look back at the examples in B.

Andrew didn't go to the café with the other students. Rachel told him they were going there, but he wanted to finish his work. Andrew isn't very sociable. He stays in his room and concentrates totally on his studies. He's an excellent student, but he doesn't have much fun.

- ▶ to   *preposition*
- ▶ café   *noun*
- 1 the
- 2 told
- 3 they
- 4 there
- 5 he
- 6 finish
- 7 sociable
- 8 in
- 9 and
- 10 totally
- 11 an
- 12 excellent
- 13 but
- 14 fun

2 What kind of word? (B)

Read this paragraph and then write the words in the spaces below. Write the first three verbs under 'Verb', and so on. Do not write the same word more than once.

Henry thinks Claire is wonderful. He loves her madly, and he dreams of marrying her, but unfortunately he is rather old for her. Today they are at a café with their friends Sarah and Mark, so Henry can't get romantic with Claire. But he might buy her some flowers later.

Verb	Noun	Adjective	Adverb
thinks	*Henry*		

Preposition	Determiner	Pronoun	Linking word

3 Words in sentences (C)

Is the underlined word a verb, a noun or an adjective?

- ▶ Shall we go for a walk?   *noun*
- ▶ Shall we walk into town?   *verb*
- 1 Laura wanted to talk to Rita.
- 2 Laura wanted a talk with Rita.
- 3 The windows aren't very clean.
- 4 Doesn't anyone clean the windows?
- 5 We went to a fabulous show in New York.
- 6 Laura wanted to show Rita her photos.
- 7 Henry thought Claire looked beautiful.
- 8 A strange thought came into Emma's head.
- 9 Sarah is feeling quite tired now.
- 10 Studying all night had tired Andrew out.

2 Sentence structure: subject, verb, object, etc

MIKE AND HARRIET ARE MOVING THEIR PIANO UPSTAIRS. TOM, MELANIE AND DAVID ARE HELPING THEM.

- My arms are aching.
- I need a rest.
- It's giving me backache.
- This piano is heavy.
- It's on my foot!

A Sentence structure

The parts of a sentence are the subject, verb, object, complement and adverbial. A statement begins with the subject and the verb. There are five main structures which we can use to make a simple statement.

1	SUBJECT	VERB
	My arms	are aching.
	Something	happened.

2	SUBJECT	VERB	OBJECT
	I	need	a rest.
	Five people	are moving	the piano.

The subject and object can be a pronoun (e.g. **I**) or a noun phrase (e.g. **the piano**).

3	SUBJECT	VERB	COMPLEMENT
	This piano	is	heavy.
	It	was	a big problem.

The complement can be an adjective (e.g. **heavy**) or a noun phrase (e.g. **a big problem**). The complement often comes after **be**. It can also come after **appear, become, get, feel, look, seem, stay** or **sound**. For adjectives and word order see Unit 104B.

4	SUBJECT	VERB	ADVERBIAL
	It	is	on my foot.
	Their house	is	nearby.

An adverbial can be a prepositional phrase (e.g. **on my foot**) or an adverb (e.g. **nearby**).

5	SUBJECT	VERB	OBJECT	OBJECT
	It	's giving	me	backache.
	David	bought	Melanie	a present.

We use two objects after verbs like **give** and **send** (see Unit 3).

B Adverbials

We can add adverbials to all the five main structures.

*My arms are aching **terribly**.* *I **really** need a rest.*
***Of course** this piano is heavy.* ***Fortunately** their house is nearby.*
***To everyone's surprise**, David **actually** bought Melanie a present **yesterday**.*

▷ 34, 36 Word order in questions ▷ 113 Adverbs and word order ▷ page 377 **Seem, look** etc in American English

2 Exercises

1 Parts of the sentence (A)
Mike and Harriet are on holiday. They have written a postcard to David and Melanie. Look at each underlined phrase and say what part of the sentence it is: subject, verb, object, complement or adverbial.
- ▶ We're having a great time.   *object*
1. The weather is marvellous. ....
2. We really enjoy camping. ....
3. It's great fun. ....
4. We're on a farm. ....
5. We like this place. ....
6. The scenery is beautiful. ....

2 Sentence structure (A)
After moving the piano, the five friends had a rest and a cup of tea.
Look at this part of their conversation and then write the letters a)– e) in the correct place.
- a) David: That was a difficult job.
- b) Tom: I agree.
- c) Mike: I'm on my deathbed.
- d) David: Someone should give us a medal.
- e) Harriet: I've made some more tea.

- ▶ Subject + verb   *b*
1. Subject + verb + object ....
2. Subject + verb + complement ....
3. Subject + verb + adverbial ....
4. Subject + verb + object + object ....

3 Word order (A)
Put the words in the correct order and write the statements.
- ▶ is / Melanie / very nice   *Melanie is very nice.*
1. football / likes / Tom
2. an accident / David / had
3. moved / the piano / we
4. a tall woman / Harriet / is
5. sat / on the floor / everyone
6. gave / some help / Mike's friends / him

4 Adverbials (B)
These sentences are from a news report. Write down the two adverbials in each sentence.
Each adverbial is a prepositional phrase or an adverb.
- ▶ Prince Charles opened a new sports centre in Stoke yesterday.   *in Stoke* / *yesterday*
1. He also spoke with several young people.
2. The sports centre was first planned in 1994.
3. Naturally, the local council could not finance the project without help.
4. Fortunately, they managed to obtain money from the National Lottery.

3 Direct and indirect objects

A Introduction

*Henry gave his **wife** some flowers.*
Here the verb **give** has two objects. **Wife** is the indirect object, the person receiving something. **Some flowers** is the direct object, the thing that someone gives.

*Henry gave **some flowers** to his wife.*
Here **give** has a direct object (**some flowers**) and a phrase with **to**. **To** comes before **Wife**, the person receiving something.

Here are some more examples of the two structures.

	INDIRECT OBJECT	DIRECT OBJECT		DIRECT OBJECT	PHRASE WITH TO/FOR
Emma gave	Rachel	a CD.	Emma gave	the CD	to Rachel.
I'll send	my cousin	a postcard.	I'll send	a postcard	to my cousin.
We bought	all the children	an ice-cream.	We bought	ice-creams	for all the children.

B To or for?

We give something <u>to</u> someone, and we buy something <u>for</u> someone.

We can use **to** with these verbs: **bring, feed, give, hand, lend, offer, owe, pass, pay, post, promise, read, sell, send, show, take, teach, tell, throw, write**

*Vicky paid the money **to** the cashier.* OR *Vicky paid the cashier the money.*
*Let me read this news item **to** you.* OR *Let me read you this news item.*
*We showed the photos **to** David.* OR *We showed David the photos.*

We can use **for** with these verbs: **book, bring, build, buy, choose, cook, fetch, find, get, leave, make, order, pick, reserve, save**

*They found a spare ticket **for** me.* OR *They found me a spare ticket.*
*I've saved a seat **for** you.* OR *I've saved you a seat.*
*Melanie is making a cake **for** David.* OR *Melanie is making David a cake.*

C Give + pronoun

Sometimes there is a pronoun and a noun after a verb such as **give**.
The pronoun usually comes before the noun.

*Henry is very fond of his wife. He gave **her** some flowers.*
We use **her** because his wife is mentioned earlier. **Her** comes before **some flowers**.

*Henry bought some flowers. He gave **them** to his wife.*
We use **them** because the flowers are mentioned earlier. **Them** comes before **his wife**.

3 Exercises

1 Give (A)

Look at the Christmas presents and write sentences about them.
Put one of these words at the end of each sentence: *necklace, scarf, sweater, tennis racket, watch*

▶ To Mike From Harriet   1 To Melanie From David   2 To Trevor From Laura   3 To Matthew From Emma   4 To Claire From Henry

▶ *Harriet gave Mike a watch.*
1 ....   3 ....
2 ....   4 ....

2 Indirect object or to? (A)

Write the information in one sentence. Put the underlined part at the end of the sentence. Sometimes you need *to*.

▶ Daniel lent something to Vicky. It was <u>his calculator</u>. → Daniel *lent Vicky his calculator.*
▶ Mark sent a message. It was to <u>his boss</u>. → Mark *sent a message to his boss.*
1 Emma sold her bike. <u>Her sister</u> bought it. → Emma ....
2 Tom told the joke. He told <u>all his friends</u>. → Tom ....
3 Melanie gave <u>some help</u>. She helped her neighbour. → Melanie ....
4 Ilona wrote to her teacher. She wrote <u>a letter</u>. → Ilona ....

3 To or for? (B)

Mark's boss at Zedco is Mr Atkins. He is telling people to do things. Put in *to* or *for*.

▶ Give these papers *to* my secretary.
▶ Could you make some coffee *for* us?
1 Book a flight .... me, could you?
2 Can you post this cheque .... the hotel?
3 Don't show these plans .... anyone.
4 Leave a message .... my secretary.
5 Fetch the file .... me, could you?
6 Write a memo .... all managers.

4 Give + pronoun (C)

Complete each answer using the words in brackets. Sometimes you need to use *to* or *for*.

▶ Matthew: Why is everyone laughing? (a funny story / us)
  Vicky: Daniel told *us a funny story.*
▶ Trevor: There's some fish left over. (it / the cat)
  Laura: I'll feed *it to the cat.*
1 Mark: What are you doing with those bottles? (them / the bottle bank)
  Sarah: I'm taking ....
2 Trevor: How are things with you, Daniel? (a job / me)
  Daniel: Fine. Someone has offered ....
3 David: What about those papers you found? (them / the police)
  Tom: Oh, I handed ....
4 Emma: It's pouring with rain, look. (my umbrella / you)
  Rachel: It's OK. I'll lend ....

4 The present continuous

A Introduction

The present continuous means that we are in the middle of an action.

SARAH'S TRAIN IS LATE, SO SHE IS PHONING MARK.

Mark? I'm at the station. I'**m waiting** for the train. Oh, I can hear it. It**'s coming** now.

B Form

The present continuous is the present tense of **be** + an ing-form.

I **am looking** OR **I'm looking**
you/we/they **are looking** OR you/we/they**'re looking**
he/she/it **is looking** OR he/she/it**'s looking**

NEGATIVE
I**'m not looking**
you/we/they **aren't looking**
he/she/it **isn't looking**

QUESTION
am I **looking**?
are you/we/they **looking**?
is he/she/it **looking**?

I**'m getting** the lunch ready.   The train **is coming**, look.
We**'re looking** for a post office.   Rachel **isn't wearing** her new dress.
What **are** you **doing**?   Who **is** Vicky **dancing** with?

For rules about the spelling of the ing-form see page 370.

C Use

We use the present continuous to say that we are in the middle of an action.
   I**'m waiting** for the train. (I'm at the station <u>now</u>.)
   I**'m getting** the lunch ready. (I'm in the kitchen <u>now</u>.)
I**'m waiting** means that I am in the middle of a period of waiting. The wait is not yet over.

We can also use the present continuous when we are in the middle of something but not actually doing it at the moment of speaking.
   I must get back to the office. We**'re working** on a new project.
   I'm quite busy these days. I**'m doing** a course at college.

We can use the present continuous when things are changing over a long period.
   The number of cars on the road **is increasing**.   The earth **is** slowly **getting** warmer.

For the future meaning of the present continuous see Unit 26A.
   I**'m playing** badminton with Matthew tomorrow.

▷ 6 Present continuous or simple?   ▷ 7 State verbs and action verbs

4 Exercises

1 Form (B)

Look at the pictures and say what people are doing.
Use these verbs: *carry, paint, play, ride, take*
Use these objects: *a bicycle, a parcel, a photo, a picture, basketball*

▶ *He's riding a bicycle.*
1 .... 3 ....
2 .... 4 ....

2 Form (B)

Rachel is in the computer room at college. Complete her conversation with Andrew.
Put in a present continuous form of the verb.

Andrew: What (▶) *are you doing?* (you / do)
Rachel: (▶) *I'm writing* (I / write) a letter to a friend. He's a disc jockey. Vicky and I
(1) .... (try) to organize a disco.
Andrew: That sounds a lot of work. How (2) .... (you / find) time for your studies?
Rachel: Well, as I said, Vicky (3) .... (help) me.
(4) .... (we / get) on all right. (5) .... (we / not / spend)
too much time on it. (6) .... (it / not / take) me away from my studies,
don't worry about that. Oh, sorry, (7) .... (you / wait) for this computer?
Andrew: Yes, but there's no hurry.
Rachel: (8) .... (I / correct) the last bit of the letter. I've nearly finished.

3 Use (C)

What can you say in these situations? Add a sentence with the present continuous.

▶ A friend rings you up in the middle of 'Neighbours', your favourite soap opera.
Is it important? *I'm watching 'Neighbours'.*
1 A friend is at your flat and suggests going out, but you can see rain outside.
I don't want to go out now. Look, ...
2 A friend rings you up at work.
Sorry, I can't talk now. ....
3 You want to get off the bus, but the man next to you is sitting on your coat.
Excuse me, ...
4 A friend wants to talk to you, but you have just started to write an important letter.
Can I talk to you later? ....
5 You have been ill, but you're better now than you were.
I'm OK now. ....

5 The present simple

*Yes, I **like** this supermarket. I **think** it's very nice. Yes, my husband **thinks** so, too. We always **shop** here. We **come** here every week. We **live** quite near, so it **doesn't take** long to get here.*

A Use

We use the present simple for
- thoughts and feelings: *I **think** so, I **like** it.*
- states, things staying the same, facts and things that are true for a long time: *We **live** quite near* (see Unit 7).
- repeated actions: *We **come** here every week.*

and also
- in phrases like **I promise, I agree**, etc: *I **promise** I'll pay you back.*
- in a negative question with **why** to make a suggestion: *Why **don't** we go out?*

For the future meaning of the present simple see Units 26 and 27.
*The new term **starts** next week.*

B Positive forms

I/you/we/they **get**
he/she/it **gets**

In the present simple we use the verb without an ending.
*I **get** the lunch ready at one o'clock, usually.* *We always **do** our shopping at Greenway.*
*Most children **like** ice-cream.* *You **know** the answer.*

But in the third person singular (after **he, she, it, your friend**, etc), the verb ends in **s** or **es**. For spelling rules see page 370.
*It **gets** busy at weekends.* *My husband **thinks** so, too.*
*Sarah **catches** the early train.* *She **faxes** messages all over the world.*

C Negatives and questions

NEGATIVE	QUESTION
I/you/we/they **do not get** OR **don't get**	**do** *I/we/you/they* **get**?
he/she/it **does not get** OR **doesn't get**	**does** *he/she/it* **get**?

We use a form of **do** in negatives and questions (but see Unit 37). We use **do** and **don't** except in the third person singular, where we use **does** and **doesn't**.
*We **don't live** far away.* *He **doesn't want** to go shopping.*
*Do you **live** here? ~ Yes, I do.* *What **does** he **want**? ~ Money.*

We do not add **s** to the verb in negatives and questions.
NOT *He doesn't gets* and NOT *Does he gets?*

▷ 6 Present continuous or simple? ▷ 7 State verbs and action verbs

5 Exercises

1 Use (A)

Look at each underlined verb and say what kind of meaning it expresses. Is it a thought, a feeling, a fact or a repeated action?

▶ Matthew <u>loves</u> sport.   *a feeling*
▶ Sarah often <u>works</u> late at the office.   *a repeated action*
1 I <u>hate</u> quiz programmes. ....
2 We <u>play</u> table tennis every Thursday. ....
3 The computer <u>belongs</u> to Emma. ....
4 These plates <u>cost</u> £20 each. ....
5 I <u>believe</u> it's the right thing to do. ....
6 I'm hungry. I <u>want</u> something to eat. ....
7 I usually <u>go</u> to work by bus. ....
8 It's OK. I <u>understand</u> your problem. ....

2 Forms (B–C)

Complete the sentences by putting in the verbs. Use the present simple. You have to decide if the verb is positive or negative.

▶ Claire is very sociable. She *knows* (know) lots of people.
▶ We've got plenty of chairs, thanks. We *don't want* (want) any more.
1 My friend is finding life in Paris a bit difficult. He .... (speak) French.
2 Most students live quite close to the college, so they .... (walk) there.
3 My sports kit is really muddy. This shirt .... (need) a good wash.
4 I've got four cats and two dogs. I .... (love) animals.
5 No breakfast for Mark, thanks. He .... (eat) breakfast.
6 What's the matter? You .... (look) very happy.
7 Don't try to ring the bell. It .... (work).
8 I hate telephone answering machines. I just .... (like) talking to them.
9 Matthew is good at badminton. He .... (win) every game.
10 We always travel by bus. We .... (own) a car.

3 Forms (B–C)

Complete the conversation. Put in the present simple forms.

Rita: (▶) *Do you like* (you / like) football, Tom?
Tom: (▶) *I love* (I / love) it. I'm a United fan. (1) .... (I / go) to all their games.
   Nick usually (2) .... (come) with me.
   And (3) .... (we / travel) to away games, too.
   Why (4) .... (you / not / come) to a match some time?
Rita: I'm afraid football (5) .... (not / make) sense to me — men running after
   a ball. Why (6) .... (you / take) it so seriously?
Tom: It's a wonderful game. (7) .... (I / love) it. United are my whole life.
Rita: How much (8) .... (it / cost) to buy the tickets and pay for the travel?
Tom: A lot. (9) .... (I / not / know) exactly how much.
   But (10) .... (that / not / matter) to me.
   (11) .... (I / not / want) to do anything else.
   (12) .... (that / annoy) you?
Rita: No, (13) .... (it / not / annoy) me.
   I just (14) .... (find) it a bit sad.

6 Present continuous or simple?

A Now or sometimes?

KITTY BEAMISH IS A TV REPORTER.

I'm speaking to you live from the White House.

KITTY IS ON GUY'S CHAT SHOW.

*I often **speak** live to the camera, Guy. I **love** that part of the job. News reporting **means** everything to me, you know.*

PRESENT CONTINUOUS	PRESENT SIMPLE

We use the present continuous for something happening now. *I am speaking to you live* means that Kitty is in the middle of a live broadcast. Here are some more examples.
    It's **raining** at the moment.
    I'm **watching** this programme.
    Look. That man **is taking** a photo of you.
	We use the present simple for repeated actions. *I often speak live to the camera* means that she does it again and again.
	
	    It always **rains** at the weekend.
	    I **watch** television most weekends.
	    He's a photographer. He **takes** lots of photos.

B Thoughts, feelings and states

We normally use the present simple to talk about thoughts and feelings.
    I **think** it's a good programme.   Kitty **likes** her job.
We also use it to talk about states (see Unit 7) and permanent facts.
    Reporting **means** a lot to her.   Paper **burns** easily.
We also use the present simple in **I promise, I agree, I refuse**, etc.
    I **promise** I'll write to you.   It's all right. I **forgive** you.

C Temporary or permanent?

PRESENT CONTINUOUS	PRESENT SIMPLE

We use the present continuous for a routine or situation that we see as temporary (for a short period).
    I'm **working** at a sports shop for six weeks.
    At the moment they're **living** in a very small flat.
	We use the present simple for a routine or situation that we see as permanent.
	
	    I **work** at a sports shop. It's a permanent job.
	    They **live** in a very nice flat.

D Always

PRESENT CONTINUOUS	PRESENT SIMPLE

We can use **always** with the present continuous to mean 'very often', usually with the added meaning of 'too often'.
    Tom **is always inviting** friends here.
    (= He invites them very often.)
    I'm **always making** silly mistakes.
    (= I make silly mistakes too often.)
	Always with the present simple means 'every time'.
	
	    Tom **always invites** us to stay at Christmas.
	    (= He invites us every Christmas.)
	    I **always make** silly mistakes in exams.
	    (= I make mistakes in every exam.)

6 Exercises

1 Present continuous or simple? (A–B)

At work Mark is talking to Alan in the corridor. Complete their conversation.
Put in the present continuous or simple of the verbs.

Mark: (▶) *Are you looking* (you / look) for someone?
Alan: Yes, (▶) *I need* (I / need) to speak to Neil. He isn't in his office.
Mark: (1) .... (he / talk) to the boss at the moment.
(2) .... (I / think) (3) .... (they / discuss) money.
Alan: Oh, right. And what about you? (4) .... (you / look) for someone too?
Mark: Yes, Linda. (5) .... (you / know) where she is?
Alan: Oh, she isn't here today. She only (6) .... (work) four days a week.
(7) .... (she / not / work) on Fridays. She'll be here on Monday.
Mark: Thank you. (8) .... (you / know) a lot about Linda.
Alan: Well, most days (9) .... (I / give) her a lift,
or (10) .... (she / give) me one. (11) .... (she / live)
quite close to me. (12) .... (it / save) petrol.
Mark: Yes, of course. Good idea. Yes, (13) .... (I / agree).
Well, (14) .... (I / waste) my time here then. I'll get back to my computer.

2 Present continuous or simple? (A–C)

Complete the sentences. Put in the present continuous or simple of the verbs.

▶ *I'm writing* (I / write) to my parents. *I write* (I / write) to them every weekend.
1 .... (it / snow) outside. .... (it / come) down quite hard, look.
2 Normally .... (I / start) work at eight o'clock,
but .... (I / start) at seven this week. We're very busy at the moment.
3 I haven't got a car at the moment, so .... (I / go) to work on the bus this week.
Usually .... (I / drive) to work.
4 The sun .... (rise) in the east, remember. It's behind us so
.... (we / travel) west.
5 I'm afraid I have no time to help just now. .... (I / write) a report. But
.... (I / promise) I'll give you some help later.
6 .... (I / want) a new car. .... (I / save) up to buy one.

3 Always (D)

Complete the sentences. Use *always* and the present continuous or simple.

▶ Melanie: Tom talks too much, doesn't he?
  Rita: Yes, and *he's always talking* about football.
▶ Laura: You forget your keys every time.
  Trevor: I try to remember them, but *I always forget*.
1 Claire: Sarah takes the train every day, doesn't she?
  Mark: Yes, ... the train.
2 Vicky: Rachel misses lectures much too often in my opinion.
  Emma: I agree. .... lectures.
3 Mike: Every time I drive along here, I go the wrong way.
  Harriet: But it's very simple, isn't it? Why .... the wrong way?
4 David: Trevor and Laura argue much too often, I think.
  Melanie: I know. ....

7 State verbs and action verbs

A States and actions

STATES	ACTIONS
A state means something staying the same. *The flat **is** clean.* *The farmer **owns** the land.* *The box **contained** old books.* State verbs cannot usually be continuous. NOT *The farmer is owning the land.*	An action means something happening. *I'm cleaning the flat.* *The farmer is buying the land.* *He put the books in the box.* Action verbs can be simple or continuous. *He put / He was putting everything away.*

Some state verbs: **be, believe, belong, consist of, contain, depend on, deserve, exist, hate, know, like, love, matter, mean, own, need, prefer, remember, resemble, seem, understand**

B I think/I'm thinking etc

Sometimes we can use a verb either for a state or for an action.

STATES (simple tenses)	ACTIONS (simple or continuous)
*I **think** you're right.* (= believe) *We **have** three cars.* (= own) *I **come** from Sweden.* (= live in)	*I'm **thinking** about the problem.* *We're **having** lunch.* (= eating) *I'm **coming** from Sweden.* (= travelling) *I usually **come** on the plane.*
*I **see** your problem.* (= understand) *Do you **see** that house?* (= have in sight) *This picture **looks** nice.* *She **appears** very nervous.* (= seems) *The bag **weighed** five kilos.* *The coat **fits**.* (= is the right size)	*Mark **is seeing** his boss.* (= meeting) *I **see** Daniel quite often.* *I'm **looking** at this picture.* *She **appeared/was appearing** in a film.* *They **weighed/were weighing** my bag.* *I'm **fitting** a lock to the window.*

These examples with the verb **be** are about how people behave.

PERMANENT QUALITY	TEMPORARY BEHAVIOUR
*Claire **is** a very sociable person.* *That man **is** an idiot.*	*Andrew **is being** very sociable today.* *You **are being** an idiot this morning.* (= You are behaving like an idiot.)

We use **am/are/is being** only to talk about behaviour, not about other things.
I'm better now, thanks.   *Are you ready?*   *Is anyone interested?*

C I like/I'm liking etc

We can use some state verbs in the continuous to talk about a short period of time.

PERMANENT STATE (simple tenses)	SHORT PERIOD (continuous)
*I **love/enjoy** parties.* *I **like** school.* *Holidays **cost** a lot of money.*	*I'm **loving/enjoying** this party.* *I'm **liking** school much better now.* *This trip **is costing** me a lot of money.*

Sometimes we can use either the simple or the continuous with no difference in meaning.
*You **look** well.* OR *You're **looking** well.*   *We **feel** a bit sad.* OR *We're **feeling** a bit sad.*

7 Exercises

1 States and actions (A)

Tom is on the Internet. He's telling people about himself.
Say which verbs express states and which express actions.

▶ I <u>surf</u> the Net most evenings.   *action*
1   My flat <u>is</u> in the town centre.   ....
2   I <u>drive</u> a taxi in the daytime.   ....
3   I <u>own</u> two cars.   ....
4   I <u>go</u> to lots of parties.   ....
5   I <u>love</u> football.   ....

2 I think/I'm thinking etc (B)

Complete the conversation. Choose the correct form of the verb.
Emma: Hi, Matthew. What (▶) <u>do you look</u>/<u>are you looking</u> at?
Matthew: Oh, hi. These are photos of me when I was a child.
Emma: Oh, look at this one. (1) <u>I think/I'm thinking</u> you look lovely, Matthew.
Matthew: (2) <u>I have/I'm having</u> some more photos here.
Emma: Look at this. Why such a big coat?
Matthew: It was my brother's. That's why (3) <u>it didn't fit/it wasn't fitting</u> properly.
Emma: Oh, (4) <u>I see/I'm seeing</u>. And (5) <u>you have/you're having</u> your tea here. And in this one
            (6) <u>you think/you're thinking</u> about something very serious.
Matthew: This is a photo of the village (7) <u>I come/I'm coming</u> from.
Emma: Oh, that's nice.
Matthew: And I caught this fish, look. (8) <u>It weighed/It was weighing</u> about half a kilo.
Emma: What a nice little boy! And what a sentimental old thing you are now!

3 The verb be (B)

Put in the correct form of *be*.
▶ Daniel is doing some of the work. He*'s being* very helpful at the moment.
▶ I*'m* tired. I want to go home.
1   The children .... very polite today. They don't usually behave so well.
2   I'm afraid Melanie can't come because she .... ill.
3   Of course you can understand it. You .... stupid, that's all.
4   We .... interested in doing a course here.
5   Vicky .... very lazy at the moment. She's done no work at all today.

4 I like/I'm liking etc (C)

Write a sentence which follows on. Choose from these sentences.
I think it's going to be perfect for me.   *And I've still got a chance to win.*
I've never wanted to change it.   *It uses so much petrol.*
It's too expensive to buy.   <u>*I play it every weekend.*</u>

▶ I enjoy the game. *I play it every weekend.*
1   I'm enjoying the game. ....
2   The car costs a lot of money. ....
3   The car is costing a lot of money. ....
4   I'm liking my new job. ....
5   I like my job. ....

Test 1   Present tenses (Units 4–7)

Test 1A

Read the conversation between two students. Then look at the answers below and write the correct answer in each space.

Lisa: Who (▶) *is* Michelle talking to?
Amy: I can't see Michelle.
Lisa: You (1) .... looking in the right place. She's over there.
Amy: Oh, that's Adrian. He's new here.
Lisa: Really? Where (2) .... he live? (3) .... you know?
Amy: No, I (4) .... know anything else about him.
Lisa: What (5) .... they talking about, I wonder?
Amy: Well, he (6) .... look very interested. He's got a very bored expression on his face. And he (7) .... saying anything.

▶ a) are   b) do   c) does   d) is
1 a) aren't b) doesn't c) don't   d) isn't
2 a) are   b) do   c) does   d) is
3 a) Are   b) Do   c) Does   d) Is
4 a) aren't b) doesn't c) don't   d) 'm not
5 a) are   b) do   c) does   d) is
6 a) aren't b) doesn't c) don't   d) isn't
7 a) aren't b) doesn't c) don't   d) isn't

Test 1B

Read Tessa's postcard to Angela and write the missing words. Use one word only in each space.

We're (▶) *having* a great time here. It's beautiful, and the sun (1) .... shining. Yesterday I went water-skiing! What (2) .... you think of that?

I'm (3) .... at a table in our hotel room and writing a few postcards. The room is fine, but we (4) .... like the food very much. But it (5) .... matter because we (6) .... out to a restaurant every evening.

We're both (7) .... very lazy at the moment. I (8) .... up quite late in the morning, and Nigel (9) .... up even later. You know of course how much Nigel's work (10) .... to him and how he's (11) .... talking about it. Well, the holiday is so good that he's forgotten all about work. So it's the perfect holiday. The only problem is that it's (12) .... us a lot of money. But we'll worry about that later.

Test 1C

Each of these sentences has a mistake in it. Write the correct sentence.
▶ ~~The children is doing their homework now.~~
   The children are doing their homework now.
1 ~~The girls are play tennis at the moment.~~
   ....
2 ~~Both my brothers likes sport.~~
   ....
3 ~~Anna wearing her new coat today.~~
   ....

Test 1

4 ~~What colour you like best?~~
....

5 ~~My suitcase is weighing ten kilos.~~
....

6 ~~At the moment I stay at a hotel.~~
....

7 ~~Robert catch the same bus every morning.~~
....

8 ~~What is this word here mean?~~
....

Test 1D

Complete the conversations. Put in the correct form of each verb.
Use the present continuous or the present simple.

▶ A: Is Janet in, please?
   B: Yes, but *I think* (I / think) she's busy at the moment. *She's washing* (she / wash) her hair.

1 A: .... (I / think) of buying a new computer.
  B: But computers .... (cost) so much money. What's wrong with the one we've got?
  A: .... (it / get) out of date now.

2 A: Your new trousers .... (look) nice.
  B: Thank you. The trouble is .... (they / not / fit) properly. .... (I / not / know) why I bought them, really.

3 A: What .... (you / do)?
  B: .... (I / weigh) this letter. .... (I / need) to know how many stamps to put on it.

4 A: .... (I / think) this road is really dangerous. Look how fast that lorry .... (go).
  B: .... (I / agree). People shouldn't go so fast.

5 A: .... (I / like) musicals. And this is a great show, isn't it? .... (you / enjoy) it?
  B: Yes, I am. .... (I / love) every minute of it.

6 A: .... (I / always / fall) asleep. I just can't keep awake.
  B: What time .... (you / go) to bed?
  A: About ten o'clock usually. But .... (it / not / make) any difference.

7 A: Could you post the goods to me, please?
  B: Yes, certainly.
  A: .... (I / live) at a guest house at the moment as .... (I / look) for a flat. So could you send it to my work address?
  B: Yes, of course. And you'll have the goods by the end of the week, ... (I / promise).

8 A: Why .... (you / want) to change the whole plan?
  B: I'm just not happy with it.
  A: And .... (I / not / understand) why .... (you / be) so difficult about it.

8 The past simple

A Introduction

> It all **happened** very quickly. The car **came** straight out of the side road, and the van **went** into the back of it. The van driver **didn't have** a chance. It **was** the car driver's fault.

B Positive forms

A regular past form ends in **ed**.
    It **happened** very quickly.   The van **crashed** into the car.
    I **posted** the letter yesterday.   We once **owned** a caravan.
For spelling rules, see page 370.

Some verbs have an irregular past form.
    The car **came** out of a side road.   Vicky **rang** earlier.   I **won** the game.
    I **had** breakfast at six.   The train **left** on time.   We **took** some photos.
For a list of irregular verbs, see page 383.

The past simple is the same in all persons except in the past tense of **be**.

| I/he/she/it **was** | I **was** ill last week. |
| you/we/they **were** | Those cakes **were** nice. |

C Negatives and questions

We use **did** in negatives and questions (but see Unit 37).

NEGATIVE	QUESTION
I/you/he/she/it/we/they **did not stop** OR **didn't stop**	**did** I/you/he/she/it/we/they **stop**?

    The car **did not stop**.   The driver **didn't look** to his right.
    What **did** you **tell** the police? ~ Nothing.   **Did** you **ring** home? ~ Yes, I did.

We do not use a past form such as **stopped** or **rang** in negatives and questions.
    NOT ~~The car didn't stopped~~ and NOT ~~Did you rang?~~

We also use **was** and **were** in negatives and questions.

NEGATIVE	QUESTION
I/he/she/it **was not** OR **wasn't**	**was** I/he/she/it?
you/we/they **were** OR **weren't**	**were** you/we/they?

    I **wasn't** very well last week.   The gates **weren't** open.
    Where **was** your friend last night?   **Was** your steak nice?

D Use

We use the past simple for something in the past which is finished.
    Emma **passed** her exam **last year**.   We **went** to the theatre **on Friday**.   Elvis Presley **died in 1977**.
    I **knew** what the problem **was**.   When **did** you **buy** this car? ~ About **three years ago**.

▷ 10 Past continuous or simple?   ▷ 14–15 Present perfect or past simple?

8 Exercises

1 Positive forms (B)

What did Claire do on holiday last month? Look at her photos and use these words:
go out dancing, have a picnic, lie on the beach, play volleyball, swim in the sea

▶ *She lay on the beach.*
1 ....
2 ....
3 ....
4 ....

2 Positive forms (B)

Complete the newspaper story about a fire. Put in the past simple forms of the verbs.

Two people (▶) *died* (die) in a fire in Ellis Street, Oldport yesterday morning. They (1) .... (be) Herbert and Molly Paynter, a couple in their seventies. The fire (2) .... (start) at 3.20 am. A neighbour, Mr Aziz, (3) .... (see) the flames and (4) .... (call) the fire brigade. He also (5) .... (try) to get into the house and rescue his neighbours, but the heat (6) .... (be) too great. The fire brigade (7) .... (arrive) in five minutes. Twenty fire-fighters (8) .... (fight) the fire and finally (9) .... (bring) it under control. Two fire-fighters (10) .... (enter) the burning building but (11) .... (find) the couple dead.

3 Negatives and questions (C)

Complete the conversation. Put in the past simple negatives and questions.
Claire: (▶) *Did you have* (you / have) a nice weekend in Paris?
Mark: Yes, thanks. It was good. We looked around and then we saw a show.
(1) .... (we / not / try) to do too much.
Claire: What sights (2) .... (you / see)?
Mark: We had a look round the Louvre. (3) .... (I / not / know) there was so much in there.
Claire: And what show (4) .... (you / go) to?
Mark: Oh, a musical. I forget the name. (5) .... (I / not / like) it.
Claire: Oh, dear. And (6) .... (Sarah / enjoy) it?
Mark: No, not really. But we enjoyed the weekend. Sarah did some shopping, too, but (7) .... (I / not / want) to go shopping.

9 The past continuous

A Introduction

The past continuous means that at a time in the past we were in the middle of an action.

*I had a wonderful dream last night. I **was sitting** in a park. The sun **was shining**, and the birds **were singing**. Children **were playing** and **laughing**. It was very peaceful. I didn't want to wake up.*

B Form

The past continuous is the past tense of **be** + an ing-form.

I/he/she/it **was playing**	
you/we/they **were playing**	
NEGATIVE	QUESTION
I/he/she/it **wasn't playing**	**was** I/he/she/it **playing**?
you/we/they **weren't playing**	**were** you/we/they **playing**?

Soft music **was playing**.   People **were walking** in the park.
I **wasn't dreaming**. I really was in New York City.
Why did you give our secret away? What **were** you **thinking** of?
Was Matthew already **waiting** for you when you got there?

C Use

Read this conversation.
Melanie: *I rang at about three yesterday afternoon, but you weren't in. I didn't know where you were.*
David: *Oh, I **was helping** Mike. We **were repairing** his car. It took ages. We **were working** on it all afternoon.*
Melanie: *It **was raining**. I hope you **weren't doing** it outside.*
David: *No, we were in the garage. So I didn't get wet. But I'm afraid I got oil all over my new trousers.*
Melanie: *Why **were** you **wearing** your new trousers to repair a car?*
David: *I don't know. I forgot I had them on.*

It was raining at three o'clock means that at three o'clock we were in the middle of **a period of rain**. The rain began before three and stopped some time after three. *We were working all afternoon* means that the action went on for the whole period. David is stressing the length of time that the work went on.

We use the continuous with actions. We do not normally use it with state verbs (see Unit 7). For states we use the past simple.
  I didn't know where you were. NOT *I wasn't knowing ...*

▷ 10 Past continuous or simple?

20 VERBS

9 Exercises

1 Form (B)

Today is the first of January, the start of a new year. Most people are feeling a bit tired.
What were they doing at midnight last night?
Use these verbs: *dance, drive, listen, watch, write*
Use these phrases after the verb: *an essay, his taxi, in the street, television, to a band*

▶ Claire *was listening to a band*.
1 Trevor and Laura ....
2 Vicky and Rachel ....
3 Tom ....
4 Andrew ....

2 Form (B)

Complete the conversation. Put in the past continuous forms.
Jessica: (▶) *I was looking* (I / look) for you, Vicky. I'm afraid I've broken this dish.
Vicky: Oh no! What (1) .... (you / do)?
Jessica: (2) .... (I / take) it into the kitchen.
          I bumped into Emma. (3) .... (she / come) out just as
          (4) .... (I / go) in.
Vicky: I expect it was your fault. (5) .... (you / not / look) where
          (6) .... (you / go).
Jessica: Sorry. I'll buy you another one as soon as I have some money.

3 Use (C)

What can you say in these situations? Add a sentence with the past continuous
to say that an action lasted a long time.
▶ You had to work yesterday. The work went on all day.
  I was working all day.
1 You had to make phone calls. The calls went on all evening.
  ....
2 You had to wait in the rain. The wait lasted for half an hour.
  ....
3 You had to make sandwiches. This went on all afternoon.
  ....
4 You had to sit in a traffic jam. You were there for two hours.
  ....
5 Your neighbour played loud music. This went on all night.
  ....

10 Past continuous or simple?

A Introduction

A reporter is interviewing Mike and Harriet.
Reporter: *Mike and Harriet, tell me what you **saw**.*
Harriet: *Well, when we **were driving** home last night, we **saw** a strange object in the sky.*
Mike: *As we **were coming** down the hill into town, it just suddenly **appeared** in front of us. We **stopped** the car and **got** out.*
Harriet: *It **was** a very clear night. The stars **were twinkling**.*
Mike: *It **was** a spaceship. It **seemed** quite big. It **had** some strange writing on the side. And a light **was flashing** on the top.*
Harriet: *As we **were watching** it, it suddenly **flew** away and **disappeared**.*

PAST CONTINUOUS	PAST SIMPLE
We use the past continuous for an action that we were in the middle of. *We **were driving** home.* (We were in the middle of our journey.) *A light **was flashing**.*	We use the past **simple** for a complete action in the past. *We **drove** home.* (We finished our journey.) *The spaceship **flew** away.*
We do not normally use the past continuous for states. See Unit 7. NOT *The spaceship was seeming ...* NOT *It was having writing ...* NOT *I wasn't knowing ...*	We also use the past simple (not normally the continuous) for states. See Unit 7. *The spaceship **seemed** quite big.* *It **had** writing on the side.* *I **didn't know** what it was.*

B It happened as I was driving

We often use the past continuous and simple together when one (shorter) action comes in the middle of another (longer) one.
*As we **were driving** down the hill, a strange object **appeared** in the sky.*
*While Laura **was sitting** in the garden, it suddenly **began** to rain.*
*You **drove** right past me when I **was waiting** for the bus.*

The appearance of the strange object comes in the middle of the longer action, the drive down the hill.
Longer action: *We were driving down the hill.*
Shorter action: *An object appeared.*

In the three sentences above, the past continuous comes after **as**, **while** or **when** (*As we **were driving** ...*). We can also use **when** before the past simple.
*We **were driving** down the hill **when** a strange object **appeared** in the sky.*
*David **was making** lunch **when** the phone **rang**.*

But we use two past simple verbs for one action after another.
*When we **saw** the spaceship, we **stopped** the car.* (= We saw it and then we stopped.)

C The sun was shining

PAST CONTINUOUS	PAST SIMPLE
We often use the past continuous to describe the background. *The sun **was shining**.* *The stars **were twinkling**.*	We use the past simple for actions in a story. *We **arrived** at the beach.* *The aliens **landed** quietly.*

10 Exercises

1 Past continuous or simple? (A–B)

David is always having accidents. His friend Henry is talking about some of the accidents. Write sentences from these notes. Each sentence has one verb in the past continuous and one in the past simple.

▶ when / he / carry / a suitcase / he / drop / it / on his foot
When he was carrying a suitcase, he dropped it on his foot.

▶ he / break / his leg / when / he / ski
He broke his leg when he was skiing.

1 he / sit down / on a chair / while / I / paint / it

2 as / he / run / for a bus / he / collide / with a lamppost

3 his hair / catch / fire / when / he / cook / chips

4 when / he / hold / a beautiful vase / he / suddenly / drop / it

5 he / sit / in the garden / when / a wasp / sting / him / on the nose

2 Past continuous or simple? (A–B)

Put in the correct form of the verb.

Rita: I hear the lights (▶) *went* (go) out in your flats last night.
Emma: Yes, (▶) *I was watching* (I / watch) a documentary on TV when suddenly
(1) .... (we / lose) all the power. But
(2) .... (it / come) on again after about ten minutes.
Vicky: Rachel (3) .... (come) down the stairs when the lights
(4) .... (go) out. She almost (5) .... (fall) over.
Daniel: Matthew and I (6) .... (play) table tennis at the time.
Andrew: (7) .... (I / work) on the computer.
(8) .... (I / lose) a whole hour's work. But this morning
(9) .... (I / get) up early and (10) .... (do) it again.

3 Past continuous or simple? (A–C)

Find the second part of each sentence. Put each verb into the correct form.

▶ Vicky (have) a beautiful dream   when she (touch) the wire.
▶ When Andrew (see) the question,   when I (find) a £10 note in it.
1 The train (wait)   when the alarm clock (ring).
2 I (read) a library book   the crowd (rush) in.
3 Sarah (have) an electric shock   he (know) the answer immediately.
4 When the doors (open),   they (see) that the sun (shine).
5 When the campers (wake),   when we (arrive) at the station.

▶ *Vicky was having a beautiful dream when the alarm clock rang.*
▶ *When Andrew saw the question, he knew the answer immediately.*

1
2
3
4
5

Test 2 Past simple and past continuous (Units 8–10)

Test 2A

Put in the past simple of the verbs in brackets.
► The car *stopped* (stop) at the lights.
1 We .... (leave) the cinema before the end of the film.
2 The streets .... (be) crowded with people.
3 My grandmother .... (die) last year.
4 Everyone .... (have) a marvellous time.
5 We .... (not / like) the food they gave us.
6 Claire .... (go) to Egypt last month.
7 The accident .... (happen) last weekend.
8 It .... (not / be) a very comfortable journey.
9 I .... (know) that ages ago.

Test 2B

Write a second sentence so that it has a similar meaning to the first. Use the word in brackets.
► There were lights on the spacecraft. (had)
   The spacecraft had lights on it.
1 I had my old coat on. (wearing)
   ....
2 I was on holiday, and you were on holiday, too. (we)
   ....
3 It isn't true that I made a mistake. (didn't)
   ....
4 The boys were in the middle of a game of cards. (playing)
   ....
5 No one told me about the change of plan. (know)
   ....
6 My friend was the winner of the competition. (won)
   ....
7 Is it a fact that the Romans built this wall? (did)
   ....

Test 2C

Lorna Bright is a long-distance walker. Look at this part of her diary describing a morning's walk along the coast. Write the missing words. Use one word only in each space.
It was a fine day (►) *when* I started out on the last part of my walk around the coast of Britain. The sun was (1) ...., and a light wind (2) .... blowing from the south-west. I was pleased that it (3) .... raining. I knew by now that I (4) .... like rain. In fact I (5) .... it.
I (6) .... along the cliff top and then down into the lovely little fishing village of Wellburn, past a café where people (7) .... having morning coffee. Three miles past Wellburn I (8) .... down for five minutes and (9) .... a drink.
Now it (10) .... getting warmer, so I (11) .... off one of my sweaters. I (12) .... stop for long because I (13) .... to reach Seabury by lunch-time. (14) .... I finally got there, it (15) .... just after half past twelve.

Test 2

Test 2D
Each of these sentences has a mistake in it. Write the correct sentence.
▶ ~~The hotel were very quiet.~~
The hotel was very quiet.

1 ~~It was peaceful, and the birds were sing.~~

2 ~~I washed my hair when the phone rang.~~

3 ~~You came not to the club last night.~~

4 ~~It taked ages to get home.~~

5 ~~We tried to keep quiet because the baby sleeping.~~

6 ~~As I was watching him, the man was suddenly running away.~~

7 ~~We pass a petrol-station two minutes ago.~~

8 ~~Everything was seeming OK.~~

9 ~~Where bought you that bag?~~

10 ~~When I heard the alarm, I was leaving the room immediately.~~

Test 2E
Complete the sentences. Put in the correct form of each verb. Use the past continuous or past simple.
▶ When Martin *arrived* (arrive) home, Anna *was talking* (talk) to someone on the phone. Martin *started* (start) to get the tea.

1 I .... (lie) in the bath when the phone .... (ring).
  It .... (stop) after a few rings.
2 It .... (be) cold when we .... (leave) the house that day, and
  a light snow .... (fall).
3 Your friend who .... (come) here the other day .... (seem)
  very nice. I .... (enjoy) meeting her.
4 When I .... (see) the man, he .... (stand) outside the bank.
  He .... (have) a black baseball cap on.
5 When I .... (open) the cupboard door, a pile of books ....
  (fall) out.
6 I .... (walk) along the street when I suddenly .... (feel)
  something hit me in the back. I .... (not / know) what it was.
7 We .... (go) to London yesterday, but on the way
  we .... (hear) about a bomb scare in Oxford Street. So
  we .... (drive) back home straightaway.
8 Something very strange .... (happen) to me on my way home from work
  yesterday afternoon. I .... (drive) along the bypass at the time. Suddenly
  I .... (see) my mother in the seat beside me. But she died three years ago.

11 The present perfect (1)

A Introduction

The aircraft has landed. They've opened the doors.

The present perfect tells us about the past and the present.
The aircraft has landed means that the aircraft is on the ground now.

B Form

The present perfect is the present tense of **have** + a past participle.

I/you/we/they **have washed** OR I/you/we/they**'ve washed**	
he/she/it **has washed** OR he/she/it**'s washed**	
NEGATIVE	QUESTION
I/you/we/they **haven't washed**	**have** I/you/we/they **washed**?
he/she/it **hasn't washed**	**has** he/she/it **washed**?

Regular past participles end in **ed**, e.g. **washed, landed, finished**.
   We**'ve washed** the dishes.   **Have** you **opened** your letter?
   The aircraft **has landed** safely.   How many points **has** Matthew **scored**?
   The students **haven't finished** their exams.

C Irregular forms

Some participles are irregular.
   I've **made** a shopping list.   We've **sold** our car.   I've **thought** about it a lot.
   Have you **written** the letter?   She hasn't **drunk** her coffee.
For a list of irregular verbs see page 383.

There is a present perfect of **be** and of **have**.
   The weather has **been** awful.   I've **had** a lovely time, thank you.

D Use

When we use the present perfect, we see things as happening in the past but having a result in the present.
   We**'ve washed** the dishes. (They're clean <u>now</u>.)   The aircraft **has landed**. (It's on the ground <u>now</u>.)
   We**'ve eaten** all the eggs. (There aren't any left.)   They**'ve learnt** the words. (They know the words.)
   You**'ve broken** this watch. (It isn't working.)

▷ 12–13 More on the present perfect   ▷ 14–15 Present perfect or past simple?   ▷ page 377 American English

11 Exercises

1 Form (B)

Add a sentence. Use the present perfect.

▶ I'm tired. (I / walk / miles) *I've walked miles.*
1. Emma's computer is working now. (she / repair / it) ....
2. It's cooler in here now. (I / open / the window) ....
3. The visitors are here at last. (they / arrive) ....
4. Mark's car isn't blocking us in now. (he / move / it) ....
5. We haven't got any new videos. (we / watch / all these) ....

2 Irregular forms (C)

Look at the pictures and say what the people have done.
Use these verbs: *break, build, catch, see, win*
Use these objects: *a film, a fish, a house, his leg, the gold medal*

▶ *She's won the gold medal.*
1. .... 3. ....
2. .... 4. ....

3 Review (A–D)

Trevor and Laura are decorating their house. Put in the verbs. Use the present perfect.

Laura: How is the painting going? (▶) *Have you finished?* (you / finish)
Trevor: No, I haven't. Painting the ceiling is really difficult, you know.
(1) .... (I / not / do) very much. And it looks just the same as before. This new paint (2) .... (not / make) any difference.
Laura: (3) .... (you / not / put) enough on.
Trevor: (4) .... (I / hurt) my back. It feels bad.
Laura: Oh, you and your back. You mean (5) .... (you / have) enough of decorating. Well, I'll do it. Where (6) .... (you / put) the brush?
Trevor: I don't know. (7) .... (it / disappear).
(8) .... (I / look) for it, but I can't find it.
Laura: You're hopeless, aren't you? How much (9) .... (you / do) in here?
Nothing! (10) .... (I / paint) two doors.
Trevor: (11) .... (I / clean) all this old paint around the window.
It looks much better now, doesn't it?
Laura: (12) .... (we / make) some progress, I suppose.
Now, where (13) .... (that brush / go)?
Oh, (14) .... (you / leave) it on the ladder, look.

12 The present perfect (2): just, already, yet; for and since

VICKY SEES RACHEL OUTSIDE THE CONCERT HALL.

I've just heard about the concert. Have you bought a ticket yet?

We're too late. They've already sold all the tickets.

Oh no!

A Just, already and yet

We can use the present perfect with **just**, **already** and **yet**.

Just means 'a short time ago'. Vicky heard about the concert not long ago. **Already** means 'sooner than expected'. They sold the tickets very quickly. We use **yet** when we are expecting something to happen. Vicky expects that Rachel will buy a ticket.

Just and **already** come before the past participle (**heard, sold**). **Yet** comes at the end of a question or a negative sentence.

Here are some more examples.
> We've **just come** back from our holiday.
> I've **just had** an idea.
> It isn't a very good party. Most people **have already gone** home.
> My brother **has already crashed** his new car.
> It's eleven o'clock and you **haven't finished** breakfast **yet**.
> **Has** your course **started yet**?

But for American English see page 377.

B For and since

We can use the present perfect with **for** and **since**.
> Vicky **has** only **had** that camera **for** three days.   Those people **have been** at the hotel **since** Friday.
> I've **felt** really tired **for** a whole week now.
> We've **lived** in Oxford **since** 1992. NOT ~~We live here since 1992~~.

Here something began in the past and has lasted up to the present time.

We use **for** to say how long this period is (**for** three days). We use **since** to say when the period began (**since** Friday).

We use **how long** in questions.
> **How long has** Vicky **had** that camera? ~ Since Thursday, I think.
> **How long have** Trevor and Laura **been** married? ~ Oh, for about three years.

We can also use the present perfect with **for** and **since** when something has stopped happening.
> I **haven't seen** Rachel **for** ages. She **hasn't visited** us **since** July.

▷ 11, 13 More on the present perfect ▷ 14–15 Present perfect or past simple?
▷ 17 Present perfect continuous or simple? ▷ 114 Yet, still and already ▷ 121 For, since, ago and before

12 Exercises

1 Just (A)

Write replies using the present perfect and *just*.
Use these past participles: *checked, eaten, made, remembered, rung, tidied*
▶ We must find out the address. ~ It's all right, *I've just remembered it.*
1. The children's room looks neat. ~ Yes, they've ....
2. Is Daniel making some coffee? ~ It's ready. ....
3. What happened to that chocolate? ~ Sorry, ...
4. Has Rachel got all the answers right? ~ Yes, ...
5. Have you told your sister? ~ Yes, I've ....

2 Just, already and yet (A)

Complete the dialogue. Use the present perfect with *just, already* and *yet*.
Vicky: (▶) *You haven't done your project yet* (you / not do / your project / yet), I suppose.
Rachel: No, I haven't. (1) .... (I / not / start / it / yet).
Vicky: (2) .... (I / just / see / Andrew), and he says
(3) .... (he / already / do) about half of it.
Rachel: Well, he works too hard.
Vicky: (4) .... (I / not / finish / my plan / yet).
Rachel: (5) .... (you / already / begin) to worry about it, haven't you?
Take it easy. There's plenty of time.
Vicky: (6) .... (we / already / spend) too long thinking about it.
(7) .... (I / not / do / any real work / yet)
and (8) .... (I / just / realize) that there are only four weeks
to the end of term.
Rachel: OK. (9) .... (I / just / decide) to start next week. Well, maybe.

3 For and since (B)

Andrew is a very hard-working student. It's midnight and he is still working at his computer.
Write sentences with the present perfect and *for* or *since*.
▶ be / at his computer / six hours   *He's been at his computer for six hours.*
1. not / have / any fun / a long time   ....
2. have / a cold / a week   ....
3. not / see / his friends / ages   ....
4. not / do / any sport / last year   ....
5. be / busy with his studies / months   ....

4 For and since (B)

Complete the sentences.
▶ You ought to wash the car. You haven't *washed it for* ages.
▶ I'd better have a shower. I haven't *had one since* Thursday.
1. I think I'll ring my friend. I haven't............................... the weekend.
2. We're going to see some old friends. We haven't .... five years.
3. Let's watch a video, shall we? We haven't .... quite a while.
4. We could have a barbecue. We haven't .... last summer.
5. Shall we play tennis? We haven't .... our holiday.

13 The present perfect (3): **ever, this week**, etc

A Gone to or been to?

Claire has **gone to** Australia.
Gone there means that she is still there.

Claire has **been to** Australia.
Been there means that the visit is over.

B Ever and never

Mark: Where have you been this time, Claire?
Claire: I've just come back from the States. Florida.
Mark: You get around, don't you? **I've never been** to Florida. Was it good?
Claire: It was OK. Not as good as Australia. I might go to Brazil next time. **Have** you **ever been** there?
Mark: No, I haven't.

We can use **ever** and **never** with the present perfect. We use **ever** in questions. In *Have you ever been to Brazil?* the word **ever** means 'in your whole life up to the present time'. **Never** means 'not ever'.

Here are some more examples.
Have you **ever played** cricket? ~ No, **never**. **Has** Andrew **ever had** any fun? ~ I don't think so.
I've never ridden a motor bike in my life. **You've never given** me flowers before.
This is the most expensive hotel **we've ever stayed** in.

C First time, second time, etc

After **It's/This is the first/second time**, we use the present perfect.
This is the **first time** we've **been** to Scotland, so it's all new to us.
This is the **second time** Rachel **has forgotten** to give me a message.
I love this film. I think it's the **fourth time** I've **seen** it.

D Today, this week, etc

We use the present perfect with **today** and phrases with **this**, e.g. **this morning, this week, this year**.
We've done quite a lot of work **today**.
I haven't watched any television so far **this week**.
Have you **had** a holiday **this year**? ~ No, not yet.
This year is the period which began in January and has lasted up to the present time.

▷ 14–15 Present perfect or past simple?

13 Exercises

1 Gone to or been to? (A)

Complete the conversation. Put in *gone* or *been*.
Emma: Hi. Where's Rachel?
Vicky: She's (▶) *gone* to the supermarket to get something for a meal.
Emma: But I've got some chicken for tonight. I've just (1) .... to a supermarket on my way home, that new place near the station.
Natasha: I haven't (2) .... to that one yet.
Vicky: Where's Jessica? Isn't she here?
Emma: No, she's (3) .... to London. She'll be back tomorrow.

2 Ever and never (B)

Write the questions and answers. Use the information in brackets.
▶ Matthew: (sailing?) *Have you ever been sailing?*
   Natasha: (no, windsurfing) *No, I've never been sailing*, but *I've been windsurfing*.
1 Laura: (San Francisco?) ....
   Mark: (no, Los Angeles) ...., but ....
2 Tom: (basketball?) ....
   Trevor: (no, volleyball) ...., but ....
3 Daniel: ('Hamlet'?) ....
   Vicky: (no, 'Macbeth') ...., but ....

3 First time, second time, etc (C)

What would you say in these situations? Use *time* and the present perfect.
▶ You are watching a cricket match. You have never seen one before.
  This is the first time I've seen a cricket match.
1 You have lost your bank card. It has happened once before.
  This is ....
2 The washing-machine has broken down. This has happened twice before.
  ....
3 You are in England for the first time in your life.
  ....
4 You are staying in a hotel where you once stayed before.
  ....
5 You have missed the bus. You've done the same thing about four times before.
  ....

4 Today, this week, etc (D)

Complete the sentences. Use the present perfect.
▶ Mark buys a newspaper most mornings, but *he hasn't bought one this morning*.
1 I see Vicky most days, but ....
2 We go to the club most weekends, but ....
3 We usually have a party each term, but ....
4 Someone usually rings in the evening, but no one ....

14 Present perfect or past simple? (1)

A I have done or I did?

The present perfect tells us about the past and the present. United have won the Cup, so it's theirs now.

The past simple tells us about the past, a time which is finished. Last year is in the past.

We use the past simple (not the present perfect) to talk about times in the past such as yesterday, last week, in 1994, a hundred years ago.

*We **watched** United last week.* NOT *We have watched United last week.*
*Long ago dinosaurs **lived** here.* NOT *Long ago dinosaurs have lived here.*

Here are some more examples.

PRESENT PERFECT	PAST SIMPLE
*Emma **has packed** her case.* (So her things are in the case now.)	*Emma **packed** her case last night.* (Her things may be unpacked now.)
*Mike **has repaired** the chair.* (So it's all right now.)	*Mike **repaired** the chair.* (It may be broken again now.)
*The plane **has just landed**.*	*The plane **landed** ten minutes ago.*
*I've **turned** the heating on.* (It's on now.)	*I **turned** the heating on earlier, but it's off again now.*
*I've **dropped** my calculator.* (It's on the floor now.)	*I **dropped** my calculator, but it seems to be OK.*

B I've done it. I did it yesterday.

Trevor: *We've **bought** a new car.*
Tom: *Oh, have you? What sort?*
Laura: *An Adagio. We **bought** it last week.*

We often give a piece of news in the present perfect, e.g. *We've bought a new car.* (The car is ours now.) We use the past simple, e.g. *We bought it last week*, to give details or to ask for details about things such as when and where it happened.

Here are some more examples.
*I've **found** my wallet.* ~ *Oh, good. Where **did** you **find** it?*
*Your parcel **has arrived**. The postman **brought** it at eight o'clock.*
*They've **closed** the factory.* ~ *Really? When **did** they **do** that?*

C Structures with for, since and last

PRESENT PERFECT	PAST SIMPLE
We can say that something hasn't happened <u>for</u> a long time or <u>since</u> a specific time in the past. *We **haven't had** a party **for** ages.* *We **haven't had** a party **since** Christmas.*	We can say that it is a long time <u>since</u> something happened or when was <u>the last time</u> it happened. *It's ages **since** we **last had** a party.* *Christmas was **the last time** we **had** a party.*

32 VERBS

14 Exercises

1 I have done or I did? (A)

Put in the correct verb form.
▶ *I've done* (I / do) all the housework. The flat is really clean now.
▶ A young couple *bought* (buy) the house next door. But they didn't live there long.
1 Our visitors .... (arrive). They're sitting in the garden.
2 There's still a problem with the television. Someone .... (repair) it, but then it broke down again.
3 .... (I / lose) my bank card. I can't find it anywhere.
4 The match .... (start). United are playing well.
5 My sister .... (run) away from home. But she came back two days later.
6 Daniel .... (earn) some money last week. But I'm afraid he's already spent it all.
7 .... (we / plant) an apple tree in the garden. Unfortunately it died.
8 Prices .... (go) up. Everything is more expensive this year.
9 Someone .... (turn) on the hi-fi. What's that song called?
10 .... (I / phone) the office at eleven to speak to the manager, but he isn't there today.
11 .... (I / make) a cake. Would you like a piece?
12 The runner Amos Temila .... (break) the world record for the 1500 metres in Frankfurt. Then two days later in Helsinki, Lee Williams ran it in an even faster time.

2 I've done it. I did it yesterday. (B)

Things that have happened today are on the radio and TV news.
Give the news using the present perfect and past simple.
▶ the Prime Minister / visit Luton University / speak to students there / earlier today
The Prime Minister has visited Luton University. He spoke to students there earlier today.
1 the train drivers / go on strike / stop work / at twelve o'clock
....
2 the Queen / arrive in Toronto / fly there / in an RAF aircraft
....
3 two men / escape from Parkhurst Prison / get away / during the night
....
4 the actor Howard Bates / die in a car accident / his car / crash into a wall
....
5 Linda Jones / win the women's marathon / run it / in 2 hours 27 minutes
....

3 Structures with for, since and last (C)

Complete the conversations.
▶ Mike: This car is filthy. I haven't been to the car wash for about a year.
   Tom: What! You mean it's twelve months *since you last went* to the car wash?
1 Laura: I haven't used my camera recently. June was the last time I took a photo.
   Trevor: Really? I'm surprised you .... June.
2 Rachel: I haven't seen Andrew for weeks.
   Daniel: Nor me. It's .... him.
3 Tom: What about a game of cards? We haven't played since your birthday.
   David: Really? You mean my birthday .... cards?
4 Emma: I feel terrible. It's three days since I ate anything.
   Vicky: What did you say? You .... three days?

15 Present perfect or past simple? (2)

A I've been or I was?

I've been in hospital for three weeks.

I was in hospital for six weeks.

PRESENT PERFECT	PAST SIMPLE
We use the present perfect for a state which has gone on up to the present. (David is still in hospital.) **We've lived here** for ten years. (And we still live here.)	We use the past simple for a state in the past, in a period which is finished. (David's stay in hospital is over.) We **lived there** for ten years. (We don't live there now.)

B Have you (ever) ...? and Did you (ever) ...?

PRESENT PERFECT	PAST SIMPLE
We use the present perfect for actions in a period of time up to the present. *This young director **has made** four films so far.* *He has made films* means that it is possible he will make more films.	We use the past simple for actions in the past, a period which is finished. *The director **made** many films in his long career.* *He made films* means that his career in films is over. He won't make any more.
Here are some more examples. *Have you **ever been** to America? ~ Yes, twice.* *I've **played** table tennis before.* *We've **never had** any money.*	*Did Churchill **ever go** to America? ~ Yes, I think so.* *I **played** table tennis at college.* *We **never had** any money in those days.*

C Today, this week, etc

PRESENT PERFECT	PAST SIMPLE
We use **today** and phrases with **this** for a period up to the present. *It **hasn't rained** today.* *Have you **seen** this week's magazine?*	We use **yesterday** and phrases with **last** for a past period. *It **rained** yesterday.* *Did you **see** last week's magazine?*

But sometimes **today** etc can mean a past period. Compare:

*I **haven't seen** Rachel today.* (It's still daytime.) *Has the post **come** this morning?* (It's still morning.)	*I **didn't see** Sarah at work today.* (The working day is over.) *Did the post **come** this morning?* (It's later in the day.)

15 Exercises

1 I've been or I was? (A)

Complete this letter to a newspaper. Put in the present perfect or past simple.

A few days ago I (▶) *learned* (learn) that someone plans to knock down the White Horse Inn. This pub (▶) *has been* (be) the centre of village life for centuries. It (1) .... (stand) at our crossroads for 500 years. It (2) .... (be) famous in the old days, and Shakespeare once (3) .... (stay) there, they say. I (4) .... (live) in Brickfield all my life. The villagers (5) .... (know) about the plans for less than a week and already there's a 'Save Our Pub' campaign. Last week we (6) .... (be) happy, but this week we're angry. We will stop them, you'll see.

2 Have you (ever) ...? and Did you (ever) ...? (B)

Look at each conversation and choose the best sentence, a) or b).
▶ Have you heard about the woman walking across the US? ~ Yes, she's reached the Rockies.
   a) ✓ The walk is continuing.   b) ☐ The walk has finished.
1 Have you ever played beach volleyball? ~ Yes, we played it on holiday.
   a) ☐ The holiday is still going on.   b) ☐ The holiday is over.
2 Did you know old Mr Green? ~ No, I never met him.
   a) ☐ Mr Green is probably alive.   b) ☐ Mr Green is probably dead.
3 Wayne Johnson is a great footballer. ~ Yes, he's scored 200 goals for United.
   a) ☐ Wayne Johnson still plays for United.   b) ☐ Wayne Johnson has left United.

3 Today, this week, etc (C)

Put in *this*, *last*, *today* or *yesterday*.
▶ *Last* month prices went up, but *this* month they have fallen a little.
1 It's been dry so far .... week, but .... week was very wet.
2 I went shopping earlier .... and spent all the money I earned ....
3 We didn't have many visitors .... year. We've had a lot more .... year.
4 I don't feel so tired now. We got up quite late .... morning. I felt really tired .... when we got up so early.

4 Present perfect or past simple? (Units 14 and 15)

Put in the verbs.
Tom: (▶) *Have you heard* (you / hear) the news about David?
Harriet: No. (1) .... (what / happen)?
Tom: (2) .... (he / have) an accident. He was walking down some steps.
   (3) .... (he / fall) and (4) .... (break) his leg.
Harriet: Oh, how awful! When (5) .... (it / happen)?
Tom: Yesterday afternoon. Melanie (6) .... (tell) me about it last night.
Harriet: Last night! (7) .... (you / know) about it last night, and
   (8) .... (you / not / tell) me!
Tom: Well, (9) .... (I / not / see) you last night. And
   (10) .... (I / not / see) you today, until now.
Harriet: I hope he's all right. (11) .... (he / have) lots of accidents, you know.
   (12) .... (he / do) the same thing about two years ago.

Test 3 — Present perfect and past simple (Units 11–15)

Test 3A

Put in the past participles of the verbs in brackets.
▶ We've *found* (find) all the answers.
1 Have you .... (wash) the car?
2 You haven't .... (eat) very much.
3 They've .... (open) a new supermarket.
4 You've .... (write) it in pencil.
5 I've .... (make) the sandwiches.
6 We've .... (have) our lunch.
7 United have .... (score) a goal.
8 The balloon has .... (land) in a field.
9 Who's .... (break) this glass?
10 It's warm because the heating has .... (be) on.
11 Have you .... (sell) your flat yet?
12 I've .... (finish) that job at last.

Test 3B

Complete the second sentence so that it follows on from the first. Use the present perfect.
▶ My hair is tidy now. I *'ve brushed* my hair.
1 The door is open. Someone .... the door.
2 This is Oliver's drawing, look. Oliver .... a picture.
3 The calculator is broken. Someone .... the calculator.
4 United are the winners. United .... the game.
5 There's no more wine in the bottle. We .... all the wine.
6 The floor is clean now. I .... the floor.
7 I know my number now. I .... my number by heart.
8 The guests are here now. The guests ....
9 I'm still working on the computer. I .... with the computer yet.

Test 3C

Decide which word is correct.
▶ I'd like to borrow this book. Has Anna read it *yet*?
   a) done   b) for   c) just   d) yet
1 Ben writes very quickly. He's .... finished his essay.
   a) already   b) been   c) for   d) yet
2 What are you going to do? ~ I don't know. I haven't decided ....
   a) just   b) long   c) since   d) yet
3 I've .... to London. I went there in June.
   a) been   b) gone   c) just   d) yet
4 Have you .... done any skiing?
   a) ever   b) for   c) just   d) long
5 My boyfriend hasn't rung .... week.
   a) for   b) last   c) since   d) this
6 I haven't seen that coat before. How .... have you had it?
   a) already   b) for   c) long   d) since
7 The girls have .... to the cinema. They won't be back until ten o'clock.
   a) already   b) been   c) gone   d) just

Test 3

8   I haven't seen my parents .... last Christmas.
    a) already   b) before   c) for   d) since
9   This is the first .... I've ever lived away from home.
    a) already   b) since   c) that   d) time
10 This programme must be new. I've .... seen it before.
    a) ever   b) never   c) since   d) yet

Test 3D

Some of these sentences are correct, and some have a word which should not be there. If the sentence is correct, put a tick (✓). If it is incorrect, cross the unnecessary *have* or *has* out of the sentence and write it in the space.

▶ Susan has lost her keys. She can't find them anywhere.   ✓
▶ Christopher has hurt his hand, but it's OK now.   *has*
1   The directors have arrived half an hour ago, but they didn't stay long.   ....
2   It's raining, and Peter has left his umbrella behind, look.   ....
3   It's a long time since your friends have last visited us.   ....
4   None of you have called me for weeks. Aren't we friends any more?   ....
5   We can play tennis now. The others have finished.   ....
6   The company has bought some land, but then it sold it.   ....
7   The computer isn't on now. Someone has turned it off.   ....
8   Tessa has posted the parcel. It's on its way to you.   ....
9   Several bombs have gone off in the city centre. It has happened
    an hour ago.   ....
10 Simon has left. He and Oliver have left after lunch.   ....

Test 3E

Put in the present perfect or past simple of the verbs in brackets.
▶ *I've had* (have) these shoes since my eighteenth birthday.
▶ I *tidied* (tidy) my desk, but now it's in a mess again.
1   The last time I .... (go) to Brighton was in August.
2   I'd like to meet a ghost, but I .... (never / see) one.
3   I've finished my homework. I .... (do) it before tea.
4   And the race is over! And Micky Simpson .... (win) in a record time!
5   I .... (work) for a computer company for a year. That was after college.
6   What time .... (you / get) to work this morning?
7   Martin .... (be) to Greece five times. He loves the place.
8   The President .... (come) out of the building and is going to make a speech.
9   You won't believe this, but I've got some tickets for the concert. ~ Oh, well done. How ....
    .... (you / get) them?
10 Of course I can ride a bike. But I .... (not / ride) one for years.
11 Marilyn Monroe .... (be) in about thirty films.
12 .... (you / ever / bake) your own bread? ~ No, but I might try it some time.
13 Janet .... (be) very ill three years ago.
14 Rupert has left a message for you. He .... (ring) last night.
15 .... (you / see) the news today? ~ No, not yet. I'll watch it at ten.
16 We moved here in 1993. We .... (be) here a long time now.

VERBS   37

16 The present perfect continuous

A Introduction

We use the present perfect continuous for an action (*waiting*). The action happens over a period of time (*for twenty minutes*). Here the period lasts up to the present – they are still waiting now.

B Form

The present perfect continuous is the present tense of **have** + **been** + an ing-form.

I/you/we/they **have been waiting** OR *I/you/we/they***'ve been waiting**
he/she/it **has been waiting** OR *he/she/it***'s been waiting**

NEGATIVE	QUESTION
I/you/we/they **haven't been waiting**	**have** *I/you/we/they* **been waiting?**
he/she/it **hasn't been waiting**	**has** *he/she/it* **been waiting?**

We've been standing here for ages.   *It has been raining all day.*
Have you been waiting long?   *Our team hasn't been doing very well lately.*

C Use

We use the present perfect continuous for an action over a period of time leading up to the present (see A). In these examples the action is still going on.
   We've been waiting here for twenty minutes. (We're waiting <u>now</u>.)
   Listen. That burglar alarm has been ringing since eight o'clock this morning.
We must use the perfect in these situations.
   NOT *We wait here for twenty minutes* OR *We're waiting here for twenty minutes.*

We can use the present perfect continuous to talk about repeated actions up to now.
   Natasha has been playing the piano since she was four.
We can also use it to talk about an action which ends just before the present.
   I've been swimming. That's why my hair is wet.

D For, since, how long and recently

We can use the present perfect continuous with **for** and **since** (see Unit 121).
   My sister has been staying with me for three weeks now.
   You've been playing on that computer since seven o'clock.
We use **how long** in questions.
   How long have you been waiting?

Note also **recently** and **lately**. These both mean 'in the last few days or weeks'.
   I haven't been feeling very well recently.   *What have you been doing lately?*

▷ 17 Present perfect continuous or simple?   ▷ 121 **For** and **since**

16 Exercises

1 Form (B)

Put in the verbs. Use the present perfect continuous.

Ilona: Sorry I'm late.
Emma: It's OK. (▶) *I haven't been waiting* (I / not / wait) long.
What (1) .... (you / do)?
Ilona: I've been with Mrs King. (2) .... (she / help) me with my English.
Emma: Your English is very good. You don't need lessons, surely.
How long (3) .... (you / study) English?
Ilona: Er, eight years now. But my accent wasn't so good before I came to England.
(4) .... (I / try) to improve it.
I think (5) .... (it / get) better lately.
Emma: Your accent is fine, Ilona. Honestly.

2 Use (C)

Say what these people have been doing. Use these verbs: *argue, cook, drive, wait, work*

▶ Andrew is tired because *he's been working* all day.
1 Trevor and Laura are upset because ....
2 David is hot because ....
3 Mark feels very stiff because .... all day.
4 Henry is annoyed. .... a long time for his wife.

3 Use (C–D)

What could you say in these situations? Write sentences with the present perfect continuous and a phrase with *for*. Use these verbs: *play, read, swim, talk, travel, work*

▶ A video is on. It began two hours ago, and it hasn't finished yet.
The video has been playing for two hours.
1 Matthew went into the water an hour ago. He doesn't want to come out yet.
....
2 Your friends started their journey around the world three months ago. They've gone about halfway now.
....
3 Mark got to the office early this morning. Ten hours later he's still there.
....
4 Melanie rang Rita forty minutes ago, and they're still on the phone.
....
5 Trevor has got an interesting book. He started it quite a long time ago. Ask him how long.
....

17 Present perfect continuous or simple?

A I have been doing or I have done?

Mike **has been repairing** the car.

We use the present perfect continuous for an action happening over a period of time (see Unit 16). We are thinking of Mike doing the repair and getting oil on his hands.

Mike **has repaired** the car.

We use the present perfect simple for a complete action (see Unit 11). We are thinking of the finished repair and the result of the repair – that the car is all right now.

Here are some **more examples**.

OVER A PERIOD (**have been doing**)

We've **been touring** Scotland.
A strong wind **has been blowing** all day.
Vicky is out of breath. She's **been running**.
I've **been writing** an essay. I'm tired now.

We normally use the continuous form when we say how long.
Rachel **has been playing** music **all day**.
I've **been ironing** shirts **since ten o'clock**.
How long have you **been learning** to drive?

COMPLETE (**have done**)

We've **finished** our tour of Scotland.
The wind **has blown** a tree over.
Vicky is here at last. She's **run** all the way.
I've **written** an essay. I can hand it in now.

We normally use the simple form when we say how much/many.
Rachel **has played** at least **twenty** CDs.
I've **ironed eight** shirts.
How many driving lessons **have** you **had**?

B States and actions

We cannot normally use the continuous form with a state verb (see Unit 7).
I've **known** the secret for a long time. NOT ~~I've been knowing the secret.~~
My parents **have had** this car for about ten years.
We've never **been** very happy here, I'm afraid.

Live and **work** (= have a job) can be continuous or simple, with no difference in meaning.
We've **been living** here since 1992. OR We've **lived** here since 1992.
Sarah **has been working** for the company for three years now. OR Sarah **has worked** for the company for three years now.

17 Exercises

1 I have been doing or I have done? (A)

Look at these conversations and put in the correct form of the verb.
Use the present perfect continuous or simple.

▶ Sarah: I feel really tired.
  Mark: It's because *you've been doing* (you / do) too much.
  Sarah: Well, at least *I've finished* (I / finish) that report now, and I can relax.
1 David: Someone .... (leave) the ladder outside, look.
  Harriet: I expect that's Mike. .... (he / clean) the windows. I don't think .... (he / finish) yet.
2 Laura: You've got mud on your shoes.
  Trevor: It's all right, I'll take them off. .... (I / work) in the garden.
  Laura: Yes, it looks a lot tidier. Well done. .... (you / do) a good job.
3 Tom: .... (I / hear) that you and Harriet are building a garage. How long .... (you / do) that?
  Mike: Oh, for about a month now. (we / do) .... about half of it.

2 I have been doing or I have done? (A)

What would you ask in these situations? Use the present perfect continuous or simple.
▶ Your friend is wearing glasses. You've never seen him with glasses on before. Ask him how long …
  How long have you been wearing glasses?
▶ Nick is playing computer games. Ask him how many …
  How many computer games have you played?
1 You meet a group of people walking across country. Ask them how many miles …
  ....
2 Some workmen are digging up the road outside Sarah's house. Ask her how long …
  ....
3 Laura is taking lots of photos of you and your friends. Ask her how many …
  ....
4 You have just woken up from an afternoon sleep and seen that it is raining. Ask your friend how long …
  ....

3 I have been doing or I have done? (A–B)

Complete the conversation. Put the verbs in the present perfect continuous or simple.
Laura: What are you doing, Trevor? (▶) *You've been* (you / be) in here for ages. You're making an awful mess.
Trevor: (1) .... (I / clear) out this cupboard most of the afternoon. There's a lot of old stuff in here. (2) .... (I / find) these, look.
Laura: (3) .... (you / sit) there staring at those old boots for the last five minutes. (4) .... (I / watch) you. (5) .... (you / be) in a dream.
Trevor: They're football boots. (6) .... (I / have) them since I was about sixteen. (7) .... (they / be) in here for years.
Laura: Well, throw them away. And what about that tennis racket? Is that yours?
Trevor: No, it must be yours. (8) .... (I / never / have) a tennis racket.

18 The past perfect

A Introduction

IN THE CANTEEN AT WORK, MARK IS TELLING A COLLEAGUE ABOUT THE DREADFUL DAY HE HAD YESTERDAY.

I felt really tired when I took the train to work yesterday because Sarah and I **had been** to a party the evening before. We **hadn't gone** to bed until after one. I **hadn't been** on the train long when I had a bit of a shock. I suddenly realized that **I'd left** my wallet at home. Then I began to wonder. **Had** I **left** it in the office the day before? I just couldn't remember. I wanted to go back to bed. I felt awful.

The situation is in the past (*I **took** the train ... I **felt** tired ...*). When we talk about things <u>before</u> this past time, we use the past perfect.

>Sarah and I **had been** to a party the evening before.
>**I'd left** my wallet at home.

We are looking back from the situation of the train journey to the earlier actions – going to a party and leaving home without the wallet.

Here are some more examples of the past perfect.
>It was twenty to six. Most of the shops **had** just **closed**.
>I went to the box office at lunch-time, but they **had** already **sold** all the tickets.
>By 1960 most of Britain's old colonies **had become** independent.

As well as actions, we can use the past perfect to talk about states.
>I felt better by the summer, but the doctor warned me not to do too much. **I'd been** very ill.
>The news came as no surprise to me. **I'd known** for some time that the factory was likely to close.

B Form

The past perfect is **had** + a past participle.
>He **had enjoyed** the party. OR He**'d enjoyed** the party.
>They **hadn't gone** to bed until late.   Where **had** he **put** his wallet?

For irregular past participles see page 383.

C Present perfect and past perfect

Compare these examples.

PRESENT PERFECT (before <u>now</u>)	PAST PERFECT (before <u>then</u>)
My wallet isn't here. I've **left** it behind.	My wallet wasn't there. I'd **left** it behind.
The match is over. United **have won**.	The match was over. United **had won**.
That man looks familiar. I've **seen** him somewhere before.	The man looked familiar. I'd **seen** him somewhere before.

▷ 19 Review of the past simple, continuous and perfect   ▷ 20 The past perfect continuous

18 Exercises

1 The past perfect (A)
Read about each situation and then tick the right answer.
▶ Two men delivered the sofa. I had already paid for it.
   Which came first, a) ☐ the delivery, or b) ☑ the payment?
1 The waiter brought our drinks. We'd already had our soup.
   Which came first, a) ☐ the drinks, or b) ☐ the soup?
2 I'd seen the film, so I read the book.
   Did I first a) ☐ see the film, or b) ☐ read the book?
3 The programme had ended, so I rewound the cassette.
   Did I rewind the cassette a) ☐ after, or b) ☐ before the programme ended?
4 I had an invitation to the party, but I'd arranged a trip to London.
   Which came first, a) ☐ the invitation, or b) ☐ the arrangements for the trip?

2 The past perfect (A–B)
Add a sentence with the past perfect using the notes.
▶ Claire looked very suntanned when I saw her last week.
   She'd just been on holiday. (just / be on holiday)
1 We rushed to the station, but we were too late.
   .... (the train / just / go)
2 I didn't have an umbrella, but that didn't matter.
   .... (the rain / stop)
3 When I got to the concert hall, they wouldn't let me in.
   .... (forget / my ticket)
4 Someone got the number of the car the raiders used.
   .... (steal / it / a week before)
5 I was really pleased to see Rachel again yesterday.
   .... (not see / her / for ages)
6 Luckily the flat didn't look too bad when my parents called in.
   .... (just / clean / it)
7 The boss invited me to lunch yesterday, but I had to refuse the invitation.
   .... (already / eat / my sandwiches)

3 Present perfect and past perfect (C)
Put the verbs in the present perfect (*have done*) or past perfect (*had done*).
▶ It isn't raining now. It*'s stopped* (stop) at last.
▶ We had no car at that time. We*'d sold* (sell) our old one.
1 The park looked awful. People .... (leave) litter everywhere.
2 You can have that newspaper. I .... (finish) with it.
3 There's no more cheese. We .... (eat) it all, I'm afraid.
4 There was no sign of a taxi, although I .... (order) one half an hour before.
5 This bill isn't right. They .... (make) a mistake.
6 I spoke to Melanie at lunch-time. Someone .... (tell) her the news earlier.
7 I was really tired last night. I .... (have) a hard day.
8 Don't you want to see this programme? It .... (start).
9 It'll soon get warm in here. I .... (turn) the heating on.
10 At last the committee were ready to announce their decision.
   They .... (make) up their minds.

VERBS   43

19 Review of the past simple, continuous and perfect

A Introduction
Read this true story. It happened some years ago.

> A young man **walked** into a supermarket in Southampton and **put** a few items of food in a basket. He **had chosen** a time when not many people **were shopping** in the store. He **found** a checkout where no one else **was waiting**. When the cashier **had checked** the goods, the man **gave** her a £10 note. When she **opened** the till, the man quickly **snatched** all the money from it and **ran** out of the store before she **realized** what **was happening**. At the time the security guard **was standing** at the other end of the store. When staff **checked** the records in the till, they **found** that the thief **had taken** only £4.37. As he **had left** the £10 note behind, the operation **had cost** him £5.63.

B Comparison of tenses
We use the past simple to talk about the past (see Unit 8).
> He **snatched** the money and **ran** away.

The past simple is used for the actions in the story, to tell us what happened next.

We use the past continuous (see Unit 9) for something <u>around</u> a past time or a past action.
> At the time of the incident, not many people **were shopping** in the store.

The few customers were in the middle of doing their shopping.

We use the past perfect (see Unit 18) for things <u>before</u> a past situation.
> Staff found that the thief **had taken** only £4.37.

The theft of the money happened before they found out how much.

C Past simple and past continuous
We often use these two forms together when a shorter action comes in the middle of a longer one (see Unit 10B).
> I **was waiting** at the checkout when I **noticed** a strange-looking man.

Seeing the man came in the middle of the wait.

D Past simple and past perfect
When we use these two forms together, we use the past perfect for what happened earlier.
> A man **walked** into a supermarket. He **had chosen** a quiet time.

The choice of the time came before the arrival in the supermarket.

In this example, one past action followed another.
> He **filled** the basket and **went** to the checkout.

We can also use either **when ... had done**, or **after ... did/had done**.
> **When** he **had filled** the basket, he **went** to the checkout.
> **After** he **had filled** (OR **After** he **filled**) the basket, he **went** to the checkout.

But when one short action comes straight after another, we use the past simple for both.
> When she **opened** the till, he **snatched** all the money out of it.

Note the different meanings.
> When I switched the TV on, the programme **started**. I was just in time.
> When I switched the TV on, the programme **had started**. I missed the beginning.

We can use the past perfect or the past simple with **before** or **until**. There is no difference in meaning.
> The man arrived at the store before it **had opened**/before it **opened**.
> The chairman didn't speak until he **had heard**/until he **heard** all the arguments.

19 Exercises

1 Past simple, continuous and perfect (A–D)

Look at these sentences and then tick the right answer.
▶ David and Tom were talking together when a young woman spoke to them.
Which took more time, a) ✓ what David and Tom said, or b) ☐ what the woman said?
1 Mike had put up the tent, but Harriet was still unloading things from the car.
Which finished first, a) ☐ putting up the tent, or b) ☐ unloading?
2 Mark went home and switched off the computer.
What did he do first, a) ☐ go home, or b) ☐ switch off the computer?
3 When Claire arrived, Henry was walking up and down.
Which started earlier, a) ☐ Claire's arrival, or b) ☐ Henry's walking?
4 When Sarah had phoned the office, she drove to the hotel.
Did she phone the office a) ☐ before, or b) ☐ after driving to the hotel?

2 Past simple and past perfect (D)

Write the two sentences as one. Use *when* and the past perfect in either the first or the second part of the sentence.
▶ I took the book back to the library. I read it.
I took the book back to the library when I'd read it.
▶ The students did the experiment. They wrote a report on it.
When the students had done the experiment, they wrote a report on it.
1 Nick saved enough money. He bought a motor bike.
   ....
2 Mark put all the dishes away. He dried them.
   ....
3 I looked both ways. I pulled out into the road.
   ....
4 The golfers went into the clubhouse. They played the last hole.
   ....

3 Past simple, continuous and perfect (A–D)

Daniel is telling the story of how he forgot his passport. Put the verbs into the correct form.

(▶) *It happened* (it / happen) last August at the airport. A few weeks before, a group of us
(1) .... (decide) to go to Greece together for a holiday.
(2) .... (we / wait) in the queue at passport control when suddenly
(3) .... (I / realize) that (4) .... (I / forget) my passport.
(5) .... (it / be) quite a shock. (6) .... (I / hurry) to a phone and
(7) .... (ring) my parents. (8) .... (they / work) in the garden,
but luckily my mother (9) .... (hear) the phone.
(10) .... (they / find) the passport and immediately
(11) .... (drive) to the airport with it. (12) .... (I / meet) them at
the information desk. (13) .... (we / have) no time to talk, but
(14) .... (I / say) goodbye to them earlier that morning.
(15) .... (I / run) all the way to the plane. I was just in time. When
(16) .... (I / get) there, the passengers (17) .... (sit) in their seats
ready for take-off. When (18) .... (they / see) me, everyone
(19) .... (start) clapping.

20 The past perfect continuous

A Introduction

I fell down the steps here and broke my leg. I'd taken a bus into town, and I'd been swimming in the pool here.

David is talking about a situation in the past (*I fell and broke my leg*). When we look back to something <u>before</u> this past time, we use the past perfect simple (see Unit 18) or the past perfect continuous.

Past perfect simple: I **had taken** a bus into town.
Past perfect continuous: I **had been swimming** in the pool.

We use the past perfect continuous for an action which happened over a period of time. The swimming went on for some time before David broke his leg.

B Form

The past perfect continuous is **had been** + an ing-form.
    I **had been waiting** ages. OR I'**d been waiting** ages.
    I **had not been paying** attention. OR I **hadn't been paying** attention.
    Was the ground wet? **Had** it **been raining**?

C I had been doing or I had done?

Compare the past perfect continuous and simple.

OVER A PERIOD (**had been doing**)	COMPLETE (**had done**)
*I found the calculator. I'**d been looking** for it for ages.* *Vicky felt tired because she'**d been working** all day.* We are thinking of Vicky's work going on as she got tired.	*I finally bought a new calculator. I'**d looked** everywhere for the old one.* *Vicky felt pleased because she'**d done** so much work.* We are thinking of Vicky's work as complete.

We normally use the continuous with a phrase saying <u>how long</u>.
    *When the company went bankrupt, it **had been losing** money for months.*
	We normally use the simple form with a phrase saying <u>how much/many</u>.
	    *When the company went bankrupt, it **had lost** over a million pounds.*

We do not normally use the past perfect continuous for states (see Unit 7).
    NOT *He had been seeming unwell.*
	We also use the past perfect simple for states (see Unit 7).
	    *The old man **had seemed** unwell for some time before he died.*

D Comparison with other continuous forms

Compare the <u>present</u> perfect continuous (**has/have been doing**) and the <u>past</u> perfect continuous.
   *Vicky looks very upset. I think she'**s been crying**.*
   *Vicky looked very upset. I thought she'**d been crying**.*
Compare the past continuous (**was doing**) and the past perfect continuous.
   *When I phoned, Natasha **was having** a piano lesson.* (I phoned <u>during</u> the lesson.)
   *When I phoned, Natasha **had been having** a piano lesson.* (I phoned <u>after</u> the lesson.)

20 Exercises

1 Form (B)

Complete the conversation. Put in the past perfect continuous of the verbs.

Rachel: How was your job interview?
Vicky: Awful. I felt terribly nervous. (▶) *I'd been worrying* (I / worry) about it all week. And I was tired because (1) .... (I / work) on my project the night before.
(2) .... (I / not look) forward to the interview at all.
Rachel: So what happened?
Vicky: The woman interviewing me was half an hour late because
(3) .... (she / deal) with an unexpected problem, she said.
(4) .... (I / wait) ages, and I'd got even more nervous.
Rachel: How did the interview go?
Vicky: Well, I tried to sound confident. (5) .... (I / read) a book that said that's what you have to do in job interviews. But I don't know if I gave the right answers.

2 Form and use (A–B)

Add a sentence with the past perfect continuous to explain why. Look at the pictures to find the reasons.

▶ lie / in the sun   1 cry   2 drive / too fast   3 play / with matches   4 stand / under a tree

▶ Claire got burnt. *She'd been lying in the sun.*
1 Vicky looked upset. ....
2 Henry was stopped by the police. ....
3 The children started a fire. ....
4 A young man was struck by lightning. ....

3 Comparison with other tenses (C–D)

Put in the correct form of the verbs.

▶ Tom could hear shouts from the flat next door. His neighbours *were arguing* (argue) again.
1 Emma went into the sitting-room. It was empty, but the television was still on. Someone .... (watch) it.
2 I .... (play) tennis, so I had a shower. I was annoyed because I .... (not win) a single game.
3 The walkers finally arrived at their destination. They .... (walk) all day, and they certainly needed a rest. They .... (walk) thirty miles.
4 When I saw Nick last week, he said he .... (stop) smoking. But when I saw him two days later, he .... (smoke) a cigarette. He looked rather ashamed.
5 I really must go and see the dentist. One of my teeth .... (ache) for weeks.
6 When Melanie arrived at David's place, he .... (lie) on the sofa reading a detective novel. He .... (buy) it at the second-hand bookshop, and he .... (read) it for most of the afternoon.

Test 4 Past and perfect tenses (Units 16–20)

Test 4A

Read the conversation. Then look at the answers below and write the correct answer in each space.

Tessa: Hello, Robert. I (▶) *haven't* seen you for ages.
Robert: Hello, Tessa. Great to see you. What have you (1) .... doing lately?
Tessa: (2) .... just started a new job in computer software.
Robert: You (3) .... working for Tuffex Plastics when we last met.
Tessa: That's right. I hadn't (4) .... working there long before I got fed up. I
(5) .... realized what a horrible job it would be. But what about you?
(6) .... you found a job?
Robert: Well, six months ago I (7) .... working for a car hire company, but then
they (8) .... bankrupt. So I'm out of work now.
(9) .... been looking around for another job.
Tessa: Well, I'm sure you'll find one soon.

▶ a) didn't b) hadn't c) haven't d) wasn't
1 a) been b) had c) has d) was
2 a) I'd b) I'll c) I'm d) I've
3 a) did b) had c) have d) were
4 a) be b) been c) done d) had
5 a) didn't b) hadn't c) haven't d) wasn't
6 a) Did b) Had c) Have d) Were
7 a) been b) had c) have d) was
8 a) go b) going c) gone d) went
9 a) I'd b) I'll c) I'm d) I've

Test 4B

Write a second sentence so that it has a similar meaning to the first. Use the word in brackets.

▶ Susan had a green dress on. (wearing)
   Susan was wearing a green dress.

1 The doctor began work at six o'clock and is still working. (has)
   ....

2 Rupert didn't have his credit card. (forgotten)
   ....

3 I didn't want to go without taking a photo. (until)
   ....

4 Nancy has been writing the report. It is finished now. (written)
   ....

5 My wait in the queue has lasted forty minutes so far. (I)
   ....

6 When we arrived, everyone was on the dance floor. (dancing)
   ....

7 The computer has been mine for four years. (had)
   ....

8 In the middle of our lunch there was a knock at the door. (when)
   ....

9 Nigel felt sick from eating too many cakes. (because)
   ....

Test 4

Test 4C

Write the sentences correctly.
▶ I like this CD. ~~I've been having it for ages~~.
I've had it for ages.

1 It was my first day back at work. ~~I was on holiday~~.

2 I'm quite tired now. ~~I play badminton~~.

3 I had to sit down. ~~I'd been having a shock~~.

4 You need a rest. ~~How much have you been working?~~

5 The robbery happened at midday. ~~Lots of people walked along the street~~ outside.

6 My sister speaks good English. ~~She is practising her English since last summer~~.

7 At last I have my qualification. ~~I've been passing my exam~~.

8 Michelle looked really sunburnt. ~~She'd lie in the sun for too long~~.

9 We got to the coach stop at nine yesterday. ~~But the coach has already gone~~.

Test 4D

Complete the conversations. Put in the correct form of each verb.
▶ A: *Did you buy* (you / buy) anything at the antiques sale yesterday?
B: No. *I wanted* (I / want) to buy some jewellery, but *I'd left* (I / leave) my credit card at home.

1 A: Are you still copying those addresses?
B: No, that's all of them. .... (I / finish) now.

2 A: The train is never going to get here.
B: How long .... (we / wait) now?
A: At least half an hour. .... (we / be) here since ten to five.

3 A: Did you have a nice chat with Tessa?
B: No, not really. When .... (we / drink) our coffee, ... (she / hurry) off home.

4 A: It's terrible about that plane crash, isn't it?
B: Yes, awful. .... (I / have) breakfast when .... (I / hear) the news.

5 A: So you sing in a rock band, do you? How long .... (you / do) that?
B: Oh, since I was sixteen. .... (we / do) about a dozen concerts.

6 A: Do you know what Polly was so upset about yesterday?
B: No, I don't. But I'm sure .... (she / cry). Her eyes looked red.
A: Perhaps .... (she / have) some bad news.

7 A: The shooting was very frightening, I suppose.
B: It certainly was. When we .... (hear) the shot, we all .... (throw) ourselves to the floor.

VERBS

21 Review of present and past tenses

A Introduction

Study the verb forms.

	Claire is ready to go on safari.
Present continuous:	She **is waiting** for her guide.
Present simple:	She **goes** on holiday a lot.
Present perfect:	She **has bought** a safari suit.
Present perfect continuous:	She **has been planning** her trip for months.
Past simple:	She **bought** the suit last week.
Past continuous:	She **was going** past Harrods when she saw it in the window.
Past perfect:	She **had** already **decided** that she needed a safari suit.
Past perfect continuous:	She **had been looking** for one for a week or two.

B I am doing or I do? (Unit 6)

PRESENT CONTINUOUS	PRESENT SIMPLE
We use the present continuous for an action now, something we are in the middle of. 　I **am writing** a letter. 　Claire **is wearing** a safari suit. 　We'**re getting** lunch now. We use the present continuous for a feeling over a short period of time. 　Vicky **is liking** her course much better this year. We use the present continuous for a temporary situation or routine. 　I'm very busy at the moment, so I'**m getting** up early this week.	We use the present simple for repeated actions, things that happen again and again. 　I **write** home every week. 　Tom never **wears** smart clothes. 　We usually **get** lunch at about one. We normally use the present simple for thoughts and feelings, and for states and permanent facts. 　Claire **likes** holidays. 　Four times twelve **makes** forty-eight. We use the present simple for a permanent situation or routine. 　I usually **get** up quite late.

C I have done or I did? (Units 14–15)

PRESENT PERFECT	PAST SIMPLE
The present perfect tells us about the past and the present. 　They **have locked** the door. No one can get in. We use the present perfect for a state which has gone on up to the present. 　I'**ve known** him for ages. He's an old friend. We use the present perfect for actions in a period of time up to the present. 　I **have seen** the carnival several times.	The past simple tells us about the past, a time which is finished. 　They **locked** the door at ten o'clock last night. We use the past simple for a state in the past. 　I **knew** him when we were at college together. We use the past simple for actions in the past. 　I **saw** the carnival several times as a child.

D I have been doing or I have done? (Unit 17)

PRESENT PERFECT CONTINUOUS	PRESENT PERFECT
We use the present perfect continuous for an action over a period of time leading up to the present. We are thinking of the action going on. 　Daniel's tired. He's **been working**. 　I've **been reading** all afternoon. 　We've **been staying** here for a week/since Thursday.	We use the present perfect simple for a complete action. We are thinking of the result. 　At least he's **earned** some money. 　I've **read** 200 pages.

E I was doing or I did? (Unit 10)

PAST CONTINUOUS	PAST SIMPLE
We use the past continuous for an action that we were in the middle of. 　I **was reading** the paper at half past ten.	We use the past simple for a complete action in the past or for a past state. 　I **left** the house at half past ten. 　Vicky **had** a headache.

We often use the past continuous and simple together when a shorter action (simple) comes in the middle of a longer one (continuous).
　We **were looking** for the coffee bar when we **met** Emma.
But we use two past simple verbs for one action after another.
　When we **saw** Rachel, she **waved** to us.

F I did or I had done? (Units 18–19)

We use the past simple to talk about a past situation and the past perfect for things that happened earlier.
　I **threw** the magazine away. I'd **finished** with it.
　When Sarah **found** the letter, someone **had** already **opened** it.
　When the new people **moved** in, the house **had been** empty for a year.

We can use **when ... had done** to say that one thing finished and then something else happened.
　When we'd **paid** the bill, we **left** the restaurant.
But when one short action comes straight after another, we use the past simple for both.
　When the firework **went** off, the dog **ran** away.

Compare these two sentences.
　When we arrived, the others all **left**. (We arrived and then they left.)
　When we arrived, the others **had** all **left**. (They left before we arrived.)

G I had been doing or I had done? (Unit 20)

We use these forms when we look back from a situation in the past.

PAST PERFECT CONTINUOUS	PAST PERFECT
We use the past perfect continuous for an action over a period of time. We are thinking of the action going on. 　Emma's hand ached because she'd **been using** the computer. 　When I finally served the meal, I'd **been cooking** for hours.	We use the past perfect simple for a complete action. We are thinking of the result. 　Her work looked really neat because she'd **used** the computer. 　I felt quite proud that I'd **cooked** a meal for eight people.

21 Exercises

1 Present tenses (A–D)

Complete the sentences using the notes in brackets. The verbs can be present continuous (*am doing*), present simple (*do*) or present perfect (*have done*).

▶ We bought this picture a long time ago. *We've had it* (we / have / it) for ages.
1 Sarah finds her mobile phone very useful. .... (she / use / it) all the time.
2 Vicky doesn't know where her watch is. .... (she / lose / it).
3 We're in the middle of decorating our kitchen, so we can't cook any meals. .... (we / get / them) from a take-away restaurant this week.
4 Claire is on a skiing holiday. .... (she / enjoy / it), she says on her postcard.
5 The colour of this paint is absolutely awful. .... (I / hate / it).
6 These figures certainly should add up. .... (I / check / them) several times already.
7 Trevor and Laura like Scrabble. .... (they / play / it) most evenings.
8 These flowers are dying. .... (you / not water / them) for ages.

2 Present tenses (A–D)

Read about each situation. What else do you say? Use the verb in brackets.

▶ You can't go out with a friend because you have a Saturday job. (work)
 I'm sorry. *I work on Saturdays.*
1 You have just met a friend you last saw months ago. (not see)
 Hello! How are you? ....
2 Someone has arranged to phone you at this time, and you're ready for the call. (wait)
 I have to stay by the phone. ....
3 Your friend is wearing a very nice jacket you haven't seen before. (like)
 Oh, that's nice. ....
4 You are watching the snow fall. It started yesterday and is still falling. (snow)
 I can't believe it. ....

3 Present and past tenses (A–F)

Read about each situation and then tick the right answer.

▶ When we were talking, Tom left the room.
 Which took longer, a) ☑ our conversation, or b) ☐ Tom's departure?
1 Mark has been a member of the golf club for two years.
 a) ☐ He joined the club two years ago and is still a member.
 b) ☐ He was a member of the club for two years but is not a member now.
2 Vicky is watching the weather forecast.
 The weather forecast a) ☐ hasn't started yet, b) ☐ has started but not finished, or c) ☐ is over.
3 I've switched off the burglar alarm.
 Do I think that the alarm a) ☐ is off, b) ☐ is on, or c) ☐ may be on or off?
4 I've been studying all afternoon, and I've got a headache.
 Am I thinking of a) ☐ how much I have learned, or b) ☐ the action going on for a long time?
5 We had already travelled some distance when the sun rose.
 Did our journey start a) ☐ before sunrise, b) ☐ at sunrise, or c) ☐ after sunrise?
6 I'm going to work by bus this week.
 a) ☐ I always go to work by bus. b) ☐ My routine is different for this week.

4 Present and past tenses (C–E)

Put in a pronoun and the correct form of the verb. Use the past continuous (*was doing*), the past simple (*did*) or the present perfect continuous (*have been doing*).

▶ Mark: I rang at one, but you weren't in your office.
   Sarah: No, *I was having* (have) lunch.
1. David: You look tired.
   Melanie: Yes, I expect I do. .... (work) all day.
2. Sarah: Is Laura at home?
   Trevor: No, ... (go) out about half an hour ago.
3. Vicky: I haven't finished this letter yet.
   Rachel: It must be a long letter. .... (write) it since lunch-time.
4. Harriet: I see you've got some new neighbours.
   Tom: Yes, a young couple. .... (move) in last month.
5. David: Did Tom drive you home?
   Melanie: Yes, ... (stop) and offered me a lift
   while .... (wait) for a bus outside the town hall.

5 Present and past tenses (A–G)

Complete the conversation. Choose the correct form.

Melanie: How (▶) are you getting/~~do you get~~ on in your new job, Nick?
Nick: Oh, so (1) you know/you're knowing about my job as a car salesman.
Melanie: (2) David's told/David told me yesterday.
Nick: Well, I (3) haven't been/wasn't in the job long. (4) I started/I've started on Monday.
Melanie: And how many cars (5) have you been selling/have you sold so far?
Nick: Well, none yet. Give me a chance. Up to now (6) I've been learning/I've learned all the time.
Melanie: David says you (7) had/were having a sports car once.
Nick: I've still got it. (8) I had/I've had it for about five years. (9) I don't often drive/I'm not often driving it because (10) I don't like/I'm not liking getting it dirty. Normally (11) I ride/I'm riding my motor bike. And the car is expensive to run. I (12) bought/had bought it on impulse. I (13) was working/worked on a building site at the time. For several months before I bought it, (14) I'd done/I'd been doing overtime, and when (15) I'd been earning/I'd earned enough to buy a car, it was a really magical moment. Maybe you'd like a ride in it some time?
Melanie: Oh, yes please. That would be lovely.

6 Present and past tenses (A–G)

Complete the radio news report. Put in the correct forms of the verbs.

Hello. This (▶) *is* (be) Kitty Beamish. (1) .... (I / speak) to you from Oxford, where the finals of the World Quiz Championships will be held tomorrow. The favourite is Claude Jennings of Cornwall, the man who (2) .... (know) everything. Twelve months ago no one (3) .... (hear) of Claude Jennings, although (4) .... (he / take) part in quiz competitions for years. Now suddenly he is a big star. So far this year (5) .... (he / answer) every single question correctly. And he is popular, too. When (6) .... (he / arrive) here two days ago, hundreds of fans (7) .... (wait) at the station to welcome him. Since his arrival Claude (8) .... (read) encyclopedias in his hotel bedroom. He is clearly the man to watch. And now back to the news desk.

Test 5 Present and past tenses (Unit 21)

Test 5A

Complete the conversations. Put in the correct form of each verb.
▶ A: Are you ready?
   B: I won't be a moment. *I'm doing* (I / do) my hair.
1 A: Could you tell me your address?
   B: Well, ... (I / live) in a friend's house at the moment.
      Luckily .... (I / find) a place of my own now, but I can't move in until next week.
2 A: Is this your CD?
   B: No, it isn't mine. .... (I / think) .... (it / belong) to Peter.
3 A: Can I borrow your calculator, please?
   B: Well, ... (I / use) it to work out these figures at the moment. .... (I / want) to finish doing them, now that .... (I / start).
4 A: Why can't you wash your dirty plates sometimes? .... (you / leave) them in the sink most of the time.
   B: OK, sorry. The last few weeks .... (I / have) so little time. .... (I / rush) around all the time.

Test 5B

Read the story and write the missing words. Use one word only in each space.

One day a man was (▶) *walking* past a house in Bournemouth when he (1) .... a woman's voice shouting for help. The man (2) .... someone (3) .... probably trying to murder her. He ran to a phone box and (4) .... the police. The police came quite quickly, but by now the shouting had (5) .... However, the man (6) .... quite sure that he (7) .... heard cries for help. When the police (8) .... on the door, there was no answer. So they broke down the door and went in. Inside the house was a woman who had just (9) .... out of the shower. She explained to the police that she had (10) .... singing along to the Beatles song 'Help!'.

Test 5C

Write a second sentence so that it has a similar meaning to the first. Begin with the word in brackets.
▶ Our trip to Africa was in October. (We ...)
  We went to Africa in October.
1 We've had ten hours of rain. (It ...)
   ....
2 It's the right thing to do in my opinion. (I ...)
   ....
3 Our sofa is in a different place now. (We ...)
   ....
4 It was breakfast-time when Susan rang. (I ...)
   ....
5 Their game of badminton is always on Tuesday. (They ...)
   ....

54 VERBS

Test 5

Test 5D

Write the correct answer in each space.
▶ This isn't my first visit to London. *I've been* here before.
  a) I'm   b) I've been   c) I was
1 I've got my key. I found it when .... for something else.
   a) I looked   b) I've looked   c) I was looking
2 Sorry, I can't stop now. .... to an important meeting.
   a) I go   b) I'm going   c) I've gone
3 I can't get Tessa on the phone. .... all afternoon.
   a) I'm trying   b) I try   c) I've been trying
4 The bank told me last week there was no money in my account. .... it all.
   a) I'd spent   b) I spent   c) I was spending
5 There's a new road to the motorway. .... it yesterday.
   a) They'd opened   b) They opened   c) They've opened

Test 5E

Some of these sentences are correct, and some have a word which should not be there. If the sentence is correct, put a tick (✓). If it is incorrect, cross the unnecessary word out of the sentence and write it in the space.

▶ Martin has changed his mind about next weekend.   ✓
▶ We ~~were~~ enjoyed the holiday very much.   were
1 Nancy is practising on the piano.   ....
2 It was lucky that we had been decided to buy our tickets in advance.   ....
3 We were riding our bikes when suddenly I was felt a pain in my leg.   ....
4 We are go camping for three weeks every summer.   ....
5 They have planted some new trees last year.   ....
6 I suddenly realized I had been walking in the wrong direction.   ....
7 Did you know that Anna has been won a prize?   ....
8 No one told me that the goods had arrived the week before.   ....

Test 5F

Complete the news report. Put each verb into the correct form.

The actress Vanessa Kemp (▶) *has disappeared* (disappear). Yesterday she (1) .... (fail) to arrive at the Prince Charles Theatre in London's West End for her leading role in the comedy 'Don't look now!'. Ms Kemp, who (2) .... (live) in Hampstead, (3) .... (leave) home at four o'clock yesterday afternoon for the theatre, a journey she (4) .... (make) several times the week before. Two people who (5) .... (walk) past her home at the time (6) .... (see) her leave. But no one (7) .... (see) her since then. At half past seven she still (8) .... (not / arrive) at the theatre. At eight o'clock the theatre manager had to break the news to the audience, who (9) .... (wait) patiently for the play to start. Since yesterday, theatre staff and friends (10) .... (try) to contact Ms Kemp, but they (11) .... (have) no success so far. The police (12) .... (take) the matter seriously, but they (13) .... (believe) that she is unlikely to be in any danger. Her friends all (14) .... (want) to hear from her soon.

22 Introduction to the future

A Present, past and future
Read this paragraph from Rachel's letter to her aunt and uncle.

> This is my last year at college, so I'll be leaving in June. And I've already got a job! In September I'm starting work at a bank in London. So I'll be free for most of the summer. I'm going to spend six weeks travelling around the US. My friend Vicky is coming with me. (She finishes college at the same time as me.) We're really looking forward to the trip. We might go to Canada too. Vicky has friends in Toronto.

When we talk about the present or the past, we use verb forms to say what <u>is happening</u> now, what <u>happened</u> yesterday, and so on.
Vicky **has** friends in Toronto.
We know about things in the present and in the past because they are already real. But talking about the future is more of a problem. There is no single form in English that we can always use for the future. There are many different ways of talking about the future, depending on how we see a future event. It may be something that is fairly sure to happen, but on the other hand it may be just a plan or an intention, or it may be something that you think will happen but you can't be sure about.

B Verb forms used for the future
Here are some examples of verb forms used to express the future.
Be going to   ▷ 24   *I'm going to spend* six weeks in the US. (an intention)
Will   ▷ 23A   *I'll be free* for most of the summer. (neutral future)
Present continuous   ▷ 26A   *I'm starting* work in September. (an arrangement)
Present simple   ▷ 26B   *She finishes* college at the same time. (a timetable)
Will be doing   ▷ 28   *I'll be leaving* in June. (in the course of events)

Very often there is more than one possible form that could be used.
She'll finish college in June.   *She finishes* college in June.
She's finishing college in June.   *She'll be finishing* college in June.
Rachel could use any of these in her letter.

C Will
We often use **will** as a neutral way of expressing the future, but it is not 'the future tense'. It is only one of the forms we can use. In some situations **will** is not the right word.
After college I'm going to travel around the US.
Here Rachel is saying what she intends to do in the future. We cannot use **will** here.

D Being sure and unsure
We cannot always be sure about the future. To show that we are unsure we can use **might** or **could** (see Unit 46).

> We **might** go to Canada.   It **could** snow soon.

To show how sure or unsure we are, we often use phrases like **I'm sure, definitely, I expect, I (don't) think** and **probably**.
I'm sure it'll be all right.   *We're definitely going to be at the meeting.*
I expect everyone will be going home.   *Rachel will probably be late.*
I think I'm going to sneeze.   *I don't think Tom's coming tonight.*

22 Exercises

1 Present, past and future (A–B)

Rachel has received a letter from a friend of hers who left college last year.
Find the sentences which refer to the future and write them below.

I'm really enjoying my work at the store. I'm learning lots about the job. Soon they're moving me to another store – in Birmingham. They told me about it last week. I'll be leaving here at the end of the month. I feel a bit sad about that. Luckily they'll find a flat for me.

The time is going very quickly. I've been here three months. The training programme finishes next summer. I like the work, and I want to stay with the company. They'll decide about that next year. I'm just hoping for the best.

▶ *Soon they're moving me to another store – in Birmingham.*
1 ....
2 ....
3 ....
4 ....

2 Present and future (A–D)

Say if the second sentence is about the present or the future.
Look at the phrases of time such as *at the moment* and *on Friday*.
▶ I'm busy. I'm cooking a meal at the moment.   *present*
1 I'm nervous. I'm cooking for ten people on Friday. ....
2 I don't want to go out. I might watch a video later. ....
3 There's football on TV tonight. I might watch it. ....
4 We're off at last. We arrive in New York at seven. ....
5 This train is never on time. We always arrive late. ....

3 Present and future (A–D)

Read each pair of sentences and then answer the question about them.
▶ a) I'll see you on Thursday.
   b) I saw you on Thursday.
   Which sentence is about the future? *a*
1 a) I'm going to Manchester. I'm waiting for a connecting train.
   b) I'm going to get a train to Manchester, changing at Birmingham.
   Which is spoken during the journey? ....
2 a) We'll know the results of the tests next week.
   b) We might know the results of the tests next week.
   Which sentence is more certain? ....
3 a) I'm doing two exams this year.
   b) I'm doing some work at the moment.
   In which sentence has the action already started? ....
4 a) What time do we arrive in Swansea?
   b) What time will we arrive in Swansea?
   Which question is more likely if you are travelling by car? ....
5 a) I'm eating at the Thai restaurant tonight.
   b) I'll eat at the Thai restaurant tonight.
   Which would you say if you've booked a table? ....

23 Will and shall

A Will for the future

*The world leaders **will arrive** here tomorrow. They **will have** plenty to talk about, but they **won't be** here for long – only 24 hours. You'**ll hear** live reports every hour.*

We use **will** to say what we know or think about the future. **Will** here has a neutral meaning. It does <u>not</u> express the idea that we have already decided to do something or that we are planning something.

B Will for instant decisions

We also use **will** for an instant decision, when we decide on something or agree to do it more or less at the moment of speaking.

*I'm thirsty. I think I'**ll make** some tea.*
NOT *I make some tea.*
*You've left your computer on. ~ Oh, I'**ll go** and switch it off.*
*We must celebrate. I know, we'**ll have** a party.*
*I don't think I'**ll do** any work tonight. I'm too tired.*

We also use it to order things.
*I'**ll have** the ham salad, please.*

We also use **will** in offers and invitations (see Unit 51).
Offer: *I'**ll peel** the potatoes. ~ Oh, thank you.*
Invitation: ***Will** you **come** to lunch? ~ Yes, thank you. I'd love to.*
Promise: *I'**ll pay** you back next week.*

C The form of will

The form is **will** or **'ll**.
*The west **will have** rain tomorrow.*   *You'**ll be** late if you don't hurry.*
***Will** you **be** at home this evening?*   *The world **will end** in the year 2050.*

The negative is **will not** or **won't**.
*The cost **will not be** more than £50.*   *I **won't have** time for a meal.*

D Shall

We can use **shall** for the future, but only in the first person, after **I** or **we**.
*I **will be**/I **shall be** on holiday in August.*
*We **will know**/We **shall know** the results soon.*
But NOT *Everyone shall know the results soon.*

I will and **I shall** have the same meaning here, but **shall** is a little formal. Both **I will** and **I shall** can be shortened to **I'll**, which is pronounced /aɪl/.
*I'**ll be** on holiday in August. (= I **will** OR I **shall**)*

Shall has other meanings. We can use it in offers and suggestions (see Unit 51).
Offer: ***Shall** I **pack** up your shopping for you? ~ Oh, thank you.*
Suggestion: ***Shall** we all **go** out together? ~ Good idea.*
We do not use **shall** in American English (see page 377).

▷ 25 **Will** and **be going to**   ▷ 28 **Will be doing**   ▷ 29 A **Will have done**   ▷ 144 **Will** in conditionals

23 Exercises

1 Will for the future and for instant decisions (A–B)

Read the conversations. Which replies are statements about the <u>future</u> and which are instant <u>decisions</u>?
▶ What would you like? ~ I'll have an orange juice, please.   *decision*
1. Shall we go out tonight? ~ I'll be too tired, I think.
2. We've lost a tennis ball. ~ I'll help you look for it.
3. I'm worried about the exam. ~ Oh, you'll be all right.
4. I haven't got any transport. ~ Oh, we'll give you a lift.
5. I must fix this shelf some time. ~ We'll be dead before then.

2 Instant decisions (B)

Say what your decision is in these situations, or what you offer to do.
Use these verbs: *answer, carry, have, post, <u>shut</u>*
▶ You and your friend have come into the room. The window is open, and it is cold.
I'll shut the window.
1. The phone is ringing. You are the nearest person to it.

2. The choice on the menu is fish or chicken. You hate fish.

3. You are meeting a friend at the station. He has two suitcases. There's a bag, too.

4. Your friend has written a letter. You are going to walk into town past the post office.

3 Will and won't for the future (C)

Use the notes to write about what will happen next weekend.
▶ it / be / warm / tomorrow   *It will be warm tomorrow.*
1. Tom / watch / the match
2. Harriet's party / be / fun
3. Trevor / not put up / the shelves
4. Laura / be / annoyed
5. Andrew / study / all weekend
6. Rachel / not do / any work

4 Will and shall (A, D)

Complete the conversation. Put in *will* or *shall*.
Rachel: What (▶) *shall* we do today?
Vicky: It would be nice to go out somewhere. The forecast says temperatures
          (1) .... rise to thirty degrees.
Jessica: (2) .... we go for a walk?
Rachel: That sounds a bit boring. What about the seaside? We could get a bus.
Jessica: How much (3) .... it cost? I haven't got very much **money**.
Vicky: It isn't far. It doesn't cost much.
Jessica: Everywhere (4) .... be so crowded today because it's a **holiday. The journey**
          (5) .... take ages.
Rachel: Come on, Vicky. (6) .... we leave Jessica behind if **she's going to be so**
          miserable?

24 Be going to

A Intentions

*I think the cat is stuck on the roof. **I'm going to climb** up and have a look.*

Be careful, David.

We use **be going to** to talk about something we have decided to do (an intention). David intends to climb up the ladder.

Here are some more examples.
   I'm going to watch the next programme.
   Emma **is going to do** an experiment this afternoon.
   Rachel and Vicky **are going to spend** six weeks in the States.
We can use **I'm not going to** for a refusal.
   I'm sorry, but **I'm not going to walk** half a mile in the rain.
   (= I don't want to/I'm not willing to walk.)

The present continuous can have a very similar meaning to **be going to**. We can often use either form (see Unit 26A).
   I'm going to visit my friend at the weekend.
   I'm visiting my friend at the weekend.
We do not use **will** here.

We can use **be going to** with the verb **go** (*We're going to go out this evening*), but the present continuous is more usual.
   We're going out this evening.

B Form

We use the present tense of **be** + **going to** + a verb.
   They're going to move house.   Matthew **is going to play** squash.
   Vicky **isn't going to have** any lunch.   We **aren't going to** complain.
   Is Daniel **going to apply** for the job? ~ I think he is.
   When **are** you **going to pay** this bill? ~ I don't know. I can't at the moment.
In informal speech 'going to' is often pronounced /ˈɡənə/.

C Predictions

We also use **be going to** for a prediction based on the present situation, when we can see that something is going to happen. The ladder is moving, so David is going to fall.

Here are some more examples.
   My sister **is going to have** a baby in March.
   It's nearly nine now. We**'re going to be** late.
   Do you think it**'s going to rain**?

Oh no! I'm going to fall!

▷ 25 **Will** and **be going to**   ▷ 29B **Was going to**

24 Exercises

1 Intentions (A–B)

Look at the pictures and say what is going to happen.
Use these verbs: *answer, catch, have, hit, light*
Use these objects: *the ball, a bath, a bus, the firework, the phone*

▶ *They're going to have a bath.*
1 ....
2 ....
3 ....
4 ....

2 Form (B)

Put in the verbs with *be going to*.
Laura: What are you doing with that camera?
Trevor: (▶) *I'm going to take* (I / take) it to work. (1) .... (I / lend) it to Phil.
 (2) .... (he / take) a few photos with it.
Laura: Why can't he buy his own camera?
Trevor: He's got one, but it isn't working properly. (3) .... (it / be) a while
 before he can get it repaired.
Laura: Well, how long (4) .... (he / keep) ours? When
 (5) .... (we / get) it back?
Trevor: (6) .... (he / have) it over the weekend.
 (7) .... (we / get) it back on Monday.
Laura: Well, I hope (8) .... (it / not / get) damaged.

3 Predictions (B–C)

What would you say in these situations? Use these words: *be sick, crash, get wet, lose, not stop, rain*
▶ The sky is full of dark clouds.
 It's going to rain.
1 Now it's starting to rain. There's nowhere to shelter, and you haven't got an umbrella.
 ....
2 You feel awful. There's a terrible feeling in your stomach.
 ....
3 You are playing Scrabble. The game is nearly over and you are 100 points behind.
 ....
4 You can see a plane coming down. It's out of control and falling to the ground.
 ....
5 You are waiting for a train. There's one coming, but you don't know if it's the one you want.
 It's travelling very fast.
 ....

25 Will and be going to

A Introduction

Emma: It's my birthday soon. **I'll be** twenty next Friday.
Aunt Joan: Oh, really? **Are** you **going to have** a party?
Emma: **I'm going to have** a meal in a restaurant with a few friends.
Aunt Joan: **That'll be** nice.

WILL	BE GOING TO
Will has a neutral meaning. We use it to talk about facts in the future. *I'll be twenty next Friday.* *The spacecraft will come down in the Pacific Ocean tomorrow morning.*	We use **be going to** for an intention, something we have already decided to do. *We're going to have a meal.* *Tom is going to sell his car.*

Will does <u>not</u> express an intention.
It's her birthday. She's going to have a meal with her friends. NOT *She'll have a meal.*

But we often use **be going to** for an intention and **will** for the details and comments.
We're all going to have a meal. There'll be about ten of us. ~ Oh, that'll be nice.

As well as **be going to**, we can use the present continuous (see Unit 26A).
We're going to drive/We're driving down to the South of France. ~ That'll be a long journey. ~ Yes, it'll take two days. We'll arrive on Sunday.

B Decisions and intentions

WILL	BE GOING TO
We use **will** for an instant decision or agreement to do something. *There's a postbox over there. I'll post these letters.* *You still haven't put those shelves up, Trevor. ~ OK, I'll do it tomorrow.* Trevor is deciding now.	**Be going to** means that we have already decided. *I'm going out. I'm going to post these letters.* *You still haven't put those shelves up, Trevor. ~ I know. I'm going to do it tomorrow.* Trevor has already decided.

C Predictions

WILL	BE GOING TO
We can use **will** for a prediction about the future. *I think United will win the game.* *One day people will travel to Mars.*	We use **be going to** for a prediction when we see from the present situation what is going to happen in the future. *There isn't a cloud in the sky. It's going to be a lovely day.* *This bag isn't very strong. It's going to break.*

It is often possible to use either form in a prediction. For example, we can also say *I think United are going to win* the game. Usually **be going to** is a little more informal and conversational than **will**.

25 Exercises

1 Will and be going to (A–B)

Complete the conversations. Put in *will* or *be going to* with the verbs.

▶ Vicky: Have you got a ticket for the play?
Daniel: Yes, I'*m going to see* (see) it on Thursday.
▶ Harriet: The alarm's going. It's making an awful noise.
Mike: OK, I'*ll switch* (switch) it off.
1 Daniel: Did you buy this book?
Matthew: No, Emma did. She _____ (read) it on holiday.
2 Laura: Would you like tea or coffee?
Sarah: Oh, I _____ (have) coffee, please.
3 Trevor: I'm going to miss a good film on TV because I'll be out tonight.
Laura: I _____ (video) it for you, if you like.
4 Rachel: I'm just going out to get a paper.
Emma: What newspaper _____ (you / buy)?

2 Will and be going to (A–C)

What would you say? Use *will* or *be going to*.
▶ You want to express your intention to look round the museum.
Your friend: Do you have any plans for this afternoon?
You: Yes, *I'm going to look round the museum.*
1 You hate dogs. Dogs always attack you if they get the chance.
Your friend: That dog doesn't look very friendly.
You: It's coming towards us. _____
2 You predict the landing of aliens on the earth in the next ten years.
Your friend: All this talk about aliens is complete nonsense, isn't it?
You: Is it? I think _____
3 You know that your friend's sister has decided to get married.
Your friend: Have you heard about my sister?
You: Well, I heard that _____
4 You suddenly decide you want to invite Ilona for a meal.
Your friend: Did you know Ilona will be in town next weekend?
You: No, I didn't. _____

3 Will and be going to (A–C)

Complete the news report about the village of Brickfield.
Use *will* or *be going to*. Sometimes either is possible.

We have learned this week that the local council has plans for Westside Park in Brickfield. The council (▶) *is going to sell* (sell) the land to a builder, Forbes and Son. The plans are all ready. '(1) _____ (we / build) fifty houses,' said Mr Forbes. 'In two years' time everything (2) _____ (be) finished. I'm sure people (3) _____ (like) the houses. Most of them (4) _____ (be) for young families. And we intend to take care of the environment. (5) _____ (we / not / cut) down all the trees, only a few of them.' But people living near the park are angry. 'This is a terrible idea. We're all against it,' said Mrs Mary Brent. '(6) _____ (we / have) a protest march on Saturday. I expect everyone in Brickfield (7) _____ (be) there. We've reached our decision. (8) _____ (we / stop) this plan.'

26 Present tenses for the future

A The present continuous for arrangements

Tom: **Are** you **doing** anything this evening?
Nick: Yes, **I'm going** to an ice hockey match.
The Tigers **are playing** the Kings.
I bought my ticket yesterday.

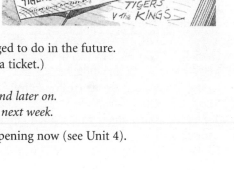

We use the present continuous for what someone has arranged to do in the future.
Here Nick has arranged to go to the match. (He has bought a ticket.)
Here are some more examples.

I'm meeting Harriet at six o'clock.   David **is coming** round later on.
We're having a party tomorrow.   Sarah **is going** to Paris next week.

We also use the present continuous to talk about things happening now (see Unit 4).
Present: **We're having** a party **at the moment**.
Future: **We're having** a party **tomorrow**.
Here the phrase of time shows whether we mean the present or the future. But sometimes there is no phrase of time, as when Nick says *The Tigers are playing the Kings*. Here it is clear from Tom's question that the conversation is about a future event.

The present continuous for the future and **be going to** (Unit 24A) have similar meanings.
We're having a party next week. (We have made the arrangements.)
We're going to have a party next week. (We intend / We have decided to have one.)
Often we can use either form.
I'm meeting/I'm going to meet Harriet at six o'clock.

B The present simple for a timetable

Mark: What time **does** your train **leave** tomorrow?
Sarah: Seven twenty-three in the morning.
It **gets** into Paris at eleven twenty-three.

We can use the present simple for the future when we are talking about a timetable, usually a public one such as a train timetable.

*The train **leaves** at seven twenty-three tomorrow morning.*
*The match **starts** at half past seven.*
*Next Friday **is** the thirteenth.*
*I've got the tour details here. We **spend** three days in Rome.*

Compare the present simple for repeated actions (see Unit 6A).
*The train **leaves** at seven twenty-three **every morning**.*

C Be to and be about to

We use **be to** for a future event that is officially arranged.
It is often used in news reports.
*The Queen **is to visit** Portugal in November.*
*The Student Games **are to take** place in Melbourne next year.*
We could also use the present continuous here.
*The Queen **is visiting** Portugal in November.*

We use **be about to** for the very near future.
*The plane is at the end of the runway. It **is about to take** off.*
*Do you want to say goodbye to our visitors? They're **about to leave**.*

64 VERBS

26 Exercises

1 The present continuous (A)

Read the conversation and say if the verb refers to the present or the future.
Mark: (▶) What <u>are</u> you <u>reading</u>, Claire?
Claire: Oh, it's a guidebook to Brazil. (1) <u>I'm going</u> there next month. (2) My sister and I <u>are having</u> a holiday there. (3) <u>I'm</u> really <u>looking</u> forward to it. (4) We<u>'re spending</u> three weeks in Rio. (5) So <u>I'm finding</u> out about all the things we can do there.

▶ present
1 ....
2 ....
3 ....
4 ....
5 ....

2 The present continuous for arrangements (A)

For each situation write a sentence with the present continuous. Use the verbs in brackets.
▶ Mike and Harriet have accepted an invitation to Tom's party next week. (go)
   They're going to Tom's party next week.
1 Laura has agreed to be in the office on Saturday. (work)
   ....
2 Claire has just bought a plane ticket to Cairo dated 15 May. (fly)
   ....
3 Mark has arranged a meeting with his boss at four o'clock this afternoon. (see)
   ....
4 Matthew and Daniel have booked a tennis court for tomorrow afternoon. (play)
   ....

3 Present tenses for the future (A–B)

Put the verbs into the present continuous or the present simple.
Emma: (▶) *Are you doing* (you / do) anything tonight?
Matthew: Yes, (1) .... (I / go) to the station to meet my friend Richard.
(2) .... (he / stay) here for the weekend, remember? His train
(3) .... (get) in at eight fifteen.
Emma: Oh, of course. I'd forgotten about that.
Matthew: Maybe we'll see you later. What (4) .... (you / do) tonight?
Emma: Oh, (5) .... (I / go) to the cinema with Vicky and Rachel and a couple of
other people. The film (6) .... (finish) quite early, so
(7) .... (we / go) to a pizza place afterwards.

4 Be to and be about to (C)

Complete these sentences on the news. Some are spoken by the newsreader in the studio and some by reporters on the spot. Use *be to* or *be about to* with the verbs in brackets.
▶ The new museum *is to open* (open) in the autumn.
▶ The Prime Minister is at the microphone now. He *is about to start* (start) speaking.
1 The leading runner is nearly there now. She .... (win) the race.
2 Taxes .... (go) up from next April.
3 The US President .... (visit) Ireland in the new year.
4 The riot isn't over yet, but the police are here. They .... (move) in.
5 The talks on world trade .... (take) place later this year.

27 When I get there, before you leave, etc

A Introduction

Mark: Did I tell you I've got a meeting in Glasgow at nine o'clock tomorrow morning? I'm driving up there overnight.

Sarah: You're going to drive all through the night? You're crazy. You'll be exhausted **before you arrive**. Why don't you take a train?

Mark: I'll be OK. I'll need the car **while I'm there**. I have to visit some companies in the area. I can sleep **when I get home**.

Study these examples.
   You'll be exhausted **before** you **arrive**. NOT *before you'll arrive*
   I'll need the car **while I'm** there. NOT *while I'll be there*
   I can sleep **when I get** home. NOT *when I'll get home*

Each of the sentences has a linking word of time, e.g. **before**, **while** or **when**. The sentences are about the future, about Mark's trip to Glasgow. But after the linking words we use the present simple (**arrive**, **am**, **get**), not **will**.

We can start the sentence with a linking word.
   When I get home, I can sleep.

B Linking words

We use the present simple for the future after these linking words of time:
after, as, as soon as, before, by the time, until, when, while.
   I'm starting a job in sales **after** I **finish** college.
   As soon as you **hear** any news, will you let me know?
   I must get to the bank **before** it **closes**.
   They'll have stopped serving meals **by the time** we **get** to the restaurant.

We also use the present simple for the future after **if** (see Unit 144).
   If you **come** in late tonight, please don't make a noise.

C Present perfect

After a linking word of time, we can often use the present perfect for the future.
   I'm starting a job in sales **after** I've **finished** college.
   As soon as you've **heard** any news, will you let me know?

Compare **after** I **finish** college (see B). The meaning is the same.

But sometimes there is a difference in meaning between the present simple and the present perfect.
   When I see the report, I'll make some notes. (I'll do both at the same time.)
   When I've seen the report, I'll make some notes. (I'll see it and then make notes.)

D Present continuous

We can also use the present continuous for the future, especially after **when** and **while**.
   When I'm boating along the canal next week, I might be able to relax.
   Mark is going to listen to music **while he's driving** to Scotland.

▷ 26 Present tenses for arrangements and timetables

27 Exercises

1 When I get there, before you leave, etc (A–B)

Comment on the situations. Start each sentence with *when* and the present simple.
▶ Claire: I have to call at the travel agency. I'm going to get some holiday brochures.
When Claire calls at the travel agency, she's going to get some holiday brochures.

1 Mark: I want to see the boss. I'm going to discuss my problem.
   ....

2 Rachel: I'm going to use the computer later. I'm going to send an e-mail.
   ....

3 Tom: I'm visiting David in hospital. I'm going to tell him about United's win.
   ....

4 Matthew: I'll be in town tomorrow. I might buy some new trainers.
   ....

2 When I get there, before you leave, etc (A–B)

Mark and Sarah are continuing the conversation in 27A. Put in the verbs. Use *will* or the present simple.
Sarah: If (▶) *you take* (you / take) a train, (▶) *it'll be* (it / be) much more comfortable. If
   (1) .... (you / need) a car, you can hire one when
   (2) .... (you / get) to Glasgow.
Mark: If (3) .... (I / hire) a car, (4) .... (it / be) too
   complicated. I'd rather take my own.
Sarah: It's too dangerous. You might fall asleep on the motorway.
Mark: I won't fall asleep. I can play loud music. Anyway, (5) .... (I / get) there
   much quicker when (6) .... (there / be) no traffic on the road. As soon as
   (7) .... (I / arrive), (8) .... (I / ring) you, I promise.
Sarah: (9) .... (I / be) worried until (10) .... (I / hear) from
   you. But don't ring before (11) .... (I / be) awake in the morning.
Mark: (12) .... (I / lie) down for a couple of hours before
   (13) .... (I / go).
Sarah: Good idea. (14) .... (you / be) exhausted tomorrow if
   (15) .... (you / not / get) some sleep this evening.

3 Present perfect and continuous (C–D)

Join each pair of sentences using the word in brackets.
▶ You can apply for a better job soon. But you need to have more experience first. (when)
   You can apply for a better job when you've had more experience.
▶ I'm going to listen to this tape. I'll be travelling on the motorway tomorrow. (as)
   I'm going to listen to this tape as I'm travelling on the motorway tomorrow.

1 You shouldn't decide now. You need to think about it first. (until)
   ....

2 I'll think of you next week. I'll be lying on the beach. (when)
   ....

3 We can leave in a minute. I need to pay the bill first. (as soon as)
   ....

4 We can discuss it later. We'll be sitting on the plane together. (while)
   ....

5 You can use the computer in a minute. I'll have finished with it soon. (when)
   ....

Test 6 The future with **will**, **be going to** and present tenses (Units 23–27)

Test 6A

Put in the missing words. Use one word only in each space.
▶ I don't want a steak. I think I'll *have* the chicken.
1 There's a fireworks display tomorrow. Janet is .... to watch it.
2 We're at that table in the corner. .... you join us?
3 I'm seeing the boss this afternoon. But I must study this report before I .... her.
4 There will be drinks at the reception, but there will .... be any food.
5 The European heads of state are .... meet in Brussels on 3 October.
6 It's a lovely day. .... we go for a walk?
7 My birthday .... on a Sunday next year.
8 My brother is engaged. He's .... married in June.
9 You won't be allowed to go to your seat after the play .... started.
10 Martin's got his coat on. I think he's .... to go out.

Test 6B

Write the sentences correctly.
▶ I'm hungry. ~~I think I have something to eat.~~
   I think I'll have something to eat.
1 You say you're getting a coach at nine. ~~What time is it getting to London?~~
   ....
2 I'll give Polly the news. ~~I'll tell her when I'll see her~~ evening.
   ....
3 Rupert looks really tired. ~~He's about falling asleep.~~
   ....
4 We've arranged to go out. ~~We meet in town later.~~
   ....
5 I'm going to Spain next week. ~~I send you a postcard.~~
   ....
6 I'm going to get to the airport early. ~~I can read a book while I'll be waiting.~~
   ....
7 I feel a bit tired. ~~I go to lie down.~~
   ....
8 Why not come to the party? ~~All your friends shall be there.~~
   ....
9 There's been a bomb warning. ~~No one can go into the building until the police will have searched it.~~
   ....

Test 6C

Read the news report and write the missing words. Use one word only in each space.

The Maxi-Shop company is (▶) *going* to build a huge new shopping centre on the edge of Millingham, it was announced yesterday. There (1) .... be at least three hundred shops, including some big department stores. When the project (2) .... complete, there (3) .... be hundreds of new jobs for local people. But not everyone is happy. 'We're (4) .... to fight this plan,' said a spokesperson for the local Environment Group. 'Just

Test 6

think what is going (5) .... happen to our countryside. When shopping malls (6) .... covered the whole country, there (7) .... be no green fields left. So we're (8) .... a protest meeting tomorrow evening at the town hall. It (9) .... at half past seven.' Owners of shops in the town centre are also unhappy. 'The new centre (10) .... take our customers away,' said one of them.

Test 6D

Look at the answers below and write the correct answer in each space.
▶ A: Let's go to the carnival, shall we?
   B: Yes, good idea. I expect *it'll be* fun.
   a) it'll be b) it's c) it's being

1 A: Could I have a word with you, please?
   B: Sorry, I'm in a big hurry. My train .... in fifteen minutes.
   a) is going to leave b) leaves c) will leave

2 A: Have you decided about the course?
   B: Yes, I decided last weekend. .... for a place.
   a) I apply b) I am to apply c) I'm going to apply

3 A: I'm trying to move this cupboard, but it's very heavy.
   B: Well, ... you, then.
   a) I help b) I'll help c) I'm going to help

4 A: Is the shop open yet?
   B: No, but there's someone inside. I think ....
   a) it opens b) it's about to open c) it will open

5 A: Do you mind not leaving your papers all over the table?
   B: Oh, sorry. I'll take them all with me when ....
   a) I go b) I'll go c) I'm going

6 A: It's a public holiday next Monday.
   B: Yes, I know. .... anything special?
   a) Are you doing b) Do you do c) Will you do

Test 6E

Write the sentences using a future form of the verb. Use the word in brackets.
▶ Express your instant decision to take a taxi. (I'll)
   I'll take a taxi.

1 Express your intention to have a rest. (going)
....

2 Express the idea that the timetable shows the start of term on 6 September. (starts)
....

3 Predict a world war in five years' time. (there)
....

4 Express the idea that you and Judy have arranged a game of tennis for tomorrow. (playing)
....

5 Give your prediction of a probable fall in prices. (probably)
....

6 Warn your passenger about the car crashing. (going)
....

VERBS 69

28 Will be doing

A Introduction

Rachel: *Would you like to come to our party tomorrow, Andrew?*
Andrew: *Er, thanks for the invitation, but I've got lots of work at the moment. I'**ll be working** all day tomorrow.*
Rachel: *You **won't be working** on Saturday evening, surely. Come on, Andrew, take a break. We'**ll be starting** at about ten o'clock.*

We can use **will be** + an ing-form (the future continuous) to talk about future actions. There are two different uses.

B Will be doing for continuous actions

We use the future continuous for an action over a period of time.
It means that at some time in the future we will be in the middle of an action.
   *Andrew can't go to the party. He'**ll be working** all day tomorrow.*
   *I'll be out at three o'clock. I'**ll be playing** golf.*
   *When the men leave the building, the police **will be waiting** for them.*
   *What **will** we **be doing** in ten years' time, I wonder?*

Compare the past continuous (Unit 9), present continuous (Unit 4) and future continuous.
Past: *This time **last week** we **were sitting** on the beach.*
Present: ***At the moment** we'**re sitting** on the beach.*
Future: *This time **next week** we'**ll be sitting** on the beach.*

Compare **will do** and **will be doing** in these sentences.
   *The band **will play** when the President enters.*
   (The President will enter and then the band will play.)
   *The band **will be playing** when the President enters.*
   (The band will start playing before the President enters.)

C Will be doing for single actions

We also use **will be** + an ing-form for an action which will happen in the course of
events because it is part of a plan or part of a schedule of future events.
   *The party **will be starting** at ten o'clock.* (part of the evening's events)
   *The ship **will be sailing** soon.* (part of our journey)

More than one form is often possible. **Will** (Unit 23) or the present continuous (Unit 26A) often have a
very similar meaning.
   *The visitors **will be arriving/will arrive/are arriving** later.*

We often use the future continuous for something that will happen as part of a routine.
   *I'll call in and see you tomorrow afternoon. I'**ll be passing** your house. It's on my way home from work.*
   *Trevor and Laura **will be cleaning** the house tomorrow. They always do it on Sunday.*

We can also use **will be** + an ing-form to ask about someone's plans.
   ***Will** you **be going** anywhere near a chemist's this morning? ~ Yes, why? ~ Could you get me some aspirin, please? ~ Yes, of course.*
   *How long **will** you **be using** this computer? ~ You can have it in a minute.*

28 Exercises

1 Will be doing (B)

Complete the conversation. Put in a pronoun and the future continuous form of the verb.

Daniel: I'm going to go into business when I leave college. Five years from now (▶) *I'll be running* (I / run) a big company. I expect (1) .... (I / earn) lots of money.
Vicky: I don't know what (2) .... (I / do). What about you, Natasha? What (3) .... (you / do), do you think?
Natasha: I'm too lazy to do any work. I intend to marry someone very rich.
(4) .... (I / give) dinner parties all the time. We'll have a cook (5) .... (who / do) all the work, of course. And you'll both get invitations.
Vicky: You're joking, aren't you, Natasha? I expect (6) .... (you / play) in an orchestra. That's what you really want to do, isn't it?

2 Will be doing (C)

Put in the answers. People are saying what they will be doing as part of their routine.

▶ David: When are you going to the club, do you know?
(Nick goes to the club every Friday.)
Nick: *I'll be going there next Friday.*
1 Vicky: Are you likely to see Ilona in the near future?
(Emma sees Ilona every day.)
Emma: .... tomorrow.
2 Claire: Are you going to France again soon?
(Henry goes to France every summer.)
Henry: ....
3 Jessica: When are you going to play badminton again?
(Matthew plays badminton every weekend.)
Matthew: ....
4 Andrew: When are you next having lunch in the canteen?
(Daniel has lunch in the canteen every day.)
Daniel: ....

3 Will be doing (C)

You want to ask a friend to do something for you or to let you do something.
Find out if it is convenient for your friend. Use the verbs in brackets.

▶ You want to have a look at your friend's magazine tonight. (read)
Will you be reading your magazine tonight?
1 You want your friend to take your library book back today. (go to)
....
2 You want your friend to send your best wishes to Vicky soon. (write to)
....
3 You want to use your friend's calculator this afternoon. (use)
....
4 You want your friend to give a photo to Daniel tomorrow. (see)
....
5 You want your friend to give you a lift to the festival. (drive)
....
6 You want your friend to give a message to her sister soon. (phone)
....

29 Will have done and was going to

A Will have done

We use **will have** + a past participle (the future perfect) for something that will be over in the future. Sarah is thinking of a future time (half past eight). At half past eight she will be able to say 'I have finished'.

Here are some more examples.
  I like looking at these pictures, but I'**ll have had** enough by lunch-time.
  Trevor and Laura **will have lived** here for four years next April.
  This chess game is going to last ages. They **won't have finished** it until midnight.
  Will you **have read** this book by the time it's due back to the library? ~ Yes. I'**ll have finished** it by then.
We often use the future perfect with expressions of time such as **by** lunch-time, **until** midnight, **before** then, **by the time** you have to take it back.

B Was going to

We can use **be going to** in the past tense to express an intention in the past. Trevor intended to put the shelves up yesterday. Often the intended action did not happen. In fact Trevor did not put the shelves up.

Here are some more examples.
  I **was going to tidy** the flat, but I didn't have time.
  Daniel **wasn't going to spend** any money, but he saw a jacket he just had to buy.
  The girls left early. They **were going to catch** the eight o'clock train.
  So you went to the airport without a ticket. Where **were** you **going to fly** to?
  The woman walked away just as I **was going to speak** to her. (just as = at the moment when)

We can also use **was going to** for a prediction in the past.
  I knew something **was going to go** wrong with the plan.
Would has a similar meaning (see Unit 134C).
  I knew something **would go** wrong with the plan.

72 VERBS

29 Exercises

1 Will have done (A)

Paul wants to be an artist. He's reading about a famous artist called Winston Plummer.

Winston Plummer was a great artist, who had a wonderful career. He won lots of prizes before he was twenty. By the age of twenty-five he had had his own exhibition. He was the subject of a TV documentary by the time he was thirty. By the age of thirty-five he had become world-famous. He made millions of pounds from his pictures before he was forty.

Paul is daydreaming about his own future career. What is he thinking?
► I hope *I'll have won lots of prizes* before I'm twenty.
1. Perhaps .... my own exhibition by the age of twenty-five.
2. I wonder if .... by the time I'm thirty.
3. Maybe .... by the age of thirty-five.
4. I hope .... by the age of forty.

2 Will have done (A)

How good is your maths? Can you work out the answers?
► It's quarter to six. Melanie is putting something in the oven.
   It needs to be in the oven for an hour and a half. When will it have cooked?
   It will have cooked at quarter past seven.
1. It's seven o'clock in the evening, and Andrew is starting to write an essay. He writes one page every fifteen minutes. He plans to finish the essay at midnight. How many pages will he have written?
   He will have written .... pages.
2. It's Monday morning, and Sarah is travelling to work. It's twenty miles from her home to the office. How far will she have travelled to and from work by the time she gets home on Friday?
   ....
3. Matthew is doing press-ups – one every two seconds. How many will he have done after five minutes?
   ....

3 Was going to (B)

Complete the sentences. They are all about being just too late.
Use *was/were going to* with these verbs: go, <u>get</u>, see, pick
► The train left just as Mike *was going to get* on it.
1. I'm afraid the shop closed just as we .... in.
2. The phone stopped ringing just as Melanie .... it up.
3. We .... a film about the Mafia, but the tickets were sold out.

4 Was going to (B)

Trevor is always making excuses for not doing things. Complete his sentences.
► put up the shelves / not have any screws
   Sorry. I was going to put up the shelves, but I didn't have any screws.
1. paint the door / not feel very well
   Sorry. ....
2. repair the lamp / forget
   Oh, yes. ....
3. wallpaper the bedroom / not have time
   Well, ...

30 Review of the future

A Introduction

CLAIRE IS TALKING TO SARAH OUTSIDE THE TRAVEL AGENT'S.

I'm going to New York next week. *I'm about to pick* up my ticket. *I'm going to do* some shopping on Fifth Avenue. I need some new clothes, and *I'll be buying* some Christmas presents, too. *I'm* only there for two days, so it*'ll be* a big rush.

There are many different ways of talking about the future in English. Often more than one form is possible.

I'll be buying some Christmas presents, too.
I'm going to buy some Christmas presents, too.

B Talking about the future

How we express future time depends on how we see a future event. Here are some ways of talking about what we think will happen in the future.

The neutral future	The sun **will rise** at 5.45 am tomorrow.	▷ 25A
A prediction	Claire's trip **will be** a big rush.	
	Claire's trip **is going to be** a big rush.	▷ 25C
A prediction based on the present	I'**m going to be** sick!	▷ 24C
A less certain prediction	I **think** it'**ll be** cold in New York.	
	It'**s probably going to be** cold in New York.	▷ 22D
The very near future	Claire **is about to pick** up her ticket.	▷ 26C
A future action over a period	Claire **will be shopping** non-stop for two days.	▷ 28B
Something that will be over in the future	The sales **will have finished** by Saturday.	▷ 29A

C Intentions and plans

We often want to talk about our decisions and intentions and what we plan to do in the future.

An instant decision (deciding <u>now</u>)	It's a lovely coat. It fits perfectly.	
	Yes, I'**ll buy** it.	▷ 23B
An intention (something <u>already</u> decided)	I'**m going to do** some shopping.	▷ 24A
A less certain decision or intention	I **think** I'**ll buy** this hat, too.	
	I **might go** to a show.	▷ 22D
A past intention	I **was going to buy** a guidebook, but I forgot.	▷ 29B
An arrangement	I'**m flying** to New York next week.	▷ 26A
In the course of events	I'**ll be buying** some presents, too.	▷ 28C
An official arrangement	The President **is to address** the nation tonight.	▷ 26C
A timetable	I'**m** in New York for two days next week.	▷ 26B

30 Exercises

1 Will, will be doing and will have done (B)

Complete the live news report. Put in *will* and the simple, continuous or perfect form of the verb.

The Quiz Marathon (▶) *will begin* (begin) in five minutes. (1) .... (it / be) a big test for the World Quiz Champion, Claude Jennings, (2) .... (who / answer) questions from a group of quiz writers. Claude (3) .... (answer) their questions for a very long time. In fact, (4) .... (he / still / give) answers when the rest of us are in bed tonight. Claude hopes that after 24 hours (5) .... (he / reply) to about seventeen thousand questions. No meal breaks are planned, so (6) .... (he / not / eat) anything. If all goes well, his name (7) .... (be) in the next Guinness Book of Records. Claude has also got a number of sponsors, and by tomorrow (8) .... (he / earn) at least £10,000 for charity. Well, (9) .... (we / return) this afternoon for news of how Claude is getting on. We think that by then (10) .... (he / get) some way past the five thousandth question.

2 The future (B–C)

What do these people say? Pay special attention to the underlined words.
▶ Tom is predicting a win for United in their next game.
   Tom: *United will win their next game.*
1 Andrew intends to get up early tomorrow.
   Andrew: I ....
2 Vicky's train timetable says 'Arrival 10.30'.
   Vicky: The train ....
3 Daniel has arranged to see his bank manager tomorrow.
   Daniel: ....
4 Rachel will go out in the very near future.
   Rachel: ....
5 There's a crowd of demonstrators in the main square of the capital. The police are arriving. Reporter Kitty Beamish is predicting trouble.
   Kitty: ....

3 The future (B–C)

Complete the conversation. In each sentence choose the best form of the verb to express the future. Usually more than one answer is possible.
Mark: Hello, Claire. Sarah tells me (▶) *you're going* (you / go) to New York.
Claire: Yes, (1) .... (I / spend) a couple of days there next week.
        (2) .... (I / look) round the shops.
Mark: (3) .... (that / be) exciting.
Claire: Exhausting, you mean. I think (4) .... (I / be) pretty tired when I get back.
Mark: (5) .... (you / stay) with friends?
Claire: No, (6) .... (I / stay) at a hotel near Central Park. But
        (7) .... (I / see) my friends. (8) .... (I / go) to their apartment for a meal one evening. And it isn't definite yet, but
        (9) .... (we / see) a show.
Mark: And when (10) .... (you / leave)?
Claire: My flight (11) .... (be) on Tuesday morning.
Mark: OK, (12) .... (I / see) you when you get back then.

Test 7 — The future (Units 23–30)

Test 7A

Read the telephone conversation. Then look at the answers below and write the correct answer in each space.

Amy: When (▶) *will* I see you again?
Simon: I don't know. I'm (1) .... to be busy this week. And I'll (2) .... going to London on Saturday.
Amy: Oh. But you (3) .... be here for my party, won't you?
Simon: No, I (4) .... get back until Sunday evening.
Amy: I (5) .... going to invite you.
Simon: Well, I'm sorry I can't come.
Amy: What (6) .... you doing in London?
Simon: Oh, I'm just going (7) .... see one or two people. Look, I must go. I'm cooking something that I think is (8) .... to boil over.

▶ a) am   b) do   c) going   d) will
1 a) being   b) going   c) shall   d) will
2 a) be   b) do   c) for   d) to
3 a) are   b) do   c) was   d) will
4 a) about   b) aren't   c) be   d) don't
5 a) be   b) have   c) was   d) will
6 a) are   b) going   c) to   d) will
7 a) be   b) for   c) is   d) to
8 a) about   b) might   c) probably d) will

Test 7B

Some of these sentences are correct, and some have a word which should not be there. If the sentence is correct, put a tick (✓). If it is incorrect, cross the unnecessary word out of the sentence and write it in the space.

▶ They're probably going to knock the building down.   ✓
▶ We are ~~be~~ going to get a dog soon.   *be*
1 The bus is leaves at eight twenty.   ....
2 The doors of the theatre are about to open.   ....
3 The meeting will be start at half past seven.   ....
4 The festival is for to take place in June.   ....
5 My friend will be calling here tomorrow morning.   ....
6 We were going to eat in the restaurant, but it was full.   ....
7 I have to register for my course before the classes will begin. ....
8 I will to have finished lunch by two o'clock.   ....

Test 7C

Put in a form of the verb. Use the future continuous (*will be doing*), the future perfect (*will have done*) or *was/were going to*.

▶ It's quite a long way, isn't it? We*'ll have walked* (walk) about five miles by the time we get back, I'd say.
1 It'll be better if you don't ring at one o'clock. We .... (have) lunch then.
2 I .... (drive) over and see you, but there's something wrong with the car.
3 I've got loads of work. I expect I .... (work) all night. And I'm not looking forward to it.
4 I'll have much more time next week because I .... (do) all my exams then.
5 We .... (buy) that computer game, but they don't make it for the kind of computer we've got.
6 I know you'll put on a wonderful show. You .... (have) so much practice by the time you perform it that it's sure to be brilliant.

Test 7

Test 7D
Complete the conversation. Use *will*, *be going to* or a present tense. Choose the best form. Sometimes more than one answer is correct.

Peter: Hello. Where are you going?
Polly: To my evening class. I'm learning Swedish. And next week (▶) *I'll have* (I / have) a chance to speak it for real. (1) .... (I / go) to Sweden for three weeks. (2) .... (I / leave) on Friday. (3) .... (I / visit) some friends there.
Peter: (4) .... (that / be) nice.
Polly: Well, I'd better hurry. My lesson (5) .... (start) at half past seven, and it's twenty-five past now.
Peter: OK. Come and see me when (6) .... (you / get) back from Sweden.
Polly: Thanks. (7) .... (I / send) you a postcard.

Test 7E
Write a second sentence so that it has a similar meaning to the first. Use the word in brackets.
▶ We have decided to help with the project. (going)
We are going to help with the project.

1 We're willing to wait for you. ('ll)
....

2 You can get off this train at Bath. (stops)
....

3 My friend intended to meet us. (going)
....

4 Adrian's job interview is on 17 October. (having)
....

5 Our meal will be over by eight o'clock. (finished)
....

6 I think I'm going to go on the trip. (might)
....

7 The fire hasn't gone out yet, but it will in a minute. (about)
....

Test 7F
Choose the correct form.
▶ A: I'd better go. I'm cycling home, and I haven't got any lights on my bike.
   B: Oh, yes. <u>It'll be</u>/~~It'll have been~~ dark soon.
1 A: I hear the rent on your flat is very expensive.
   B: Yes it is. <u>I'll move/I'm going to move</u>, I've decided.
2 A: I'd like a photo of Martin and me.
   B: <u>I'll take/I'm going to take</u> one with your camera, then.
3 A: Have you booked a holiday yet?
   B: Yes, <u>we go/we're going</u> to Spain.
4 A: What's that man doing up there?
   B: Oh no! <u>He'll jump/He's going to jump</u>!
5 A: Can I borrow your bike on Monday?
   B: I'm sorry, but <u>I'll be using/I'll have used</u> it. I always cycle to work.

31 The verb have

A Have and have got

Look at these examples.

HAVE	HAVE GOT
We **have** three cats.	We**'ve got** three cats.
Emma **has** toothache.	Vicky **has got** blue eyes.
Daniel **doesn't have** a car.	I **haven't got** any money.
Do you **have** the address? ~ Yes, I **do**.	**Have** you **got** a ticket? ~ No, I **haven't**.

Here **have** and **have got** mean the same thing. We can normally use either form. But **have got** is more informal. Note that we do not use **have got** in short answers (*No, I haven't.*).

B Forms

	PRESENT TENSE	
	have	**have got**
	I/you/we/they **have**	I/you/we/they **have got** OR I/you/we/they**'ve got**
	he/she/it **has**	he/she/it **has got** OR he/she/it**'s got**
NEGATIVE	I/you/we/they **don't have**	I/you/we/they **haven't got**
	he/she/it **doesn't have**	he/she/it **hasn't got**
QUESTION	**do** I/you/we/they **have**?	**have** I/you/we/they **got**?
	does he/she/it **have**?	**has** he/she/it **got**?
	PAST TENSE	
	I/you/he/she/it/we/they **had**	
NEGATIVE	I/you/he/she/it/we/they **didn't have**	
QUESTION	**did** I/you/he/she/it/we/they **have**?	

We do not often use **had got** in the past tense.

> Tom **had** several jobs to do.   We **didn't have** time to stop.   Why **did** you **have** that funny hat on?

C The action verb have

Here are some examples of **have** as an action verb.
> Mark **has** lunch around one.   I **have** a shower every morning.
> The children **had** a game of cards.   We **had** a wonderful holiday.

Have expresses an action. *Mark has lunch* means that he eats lunch.

With the action verb **have** we cannot use **got** and we cannot use a short form.
> NOT *Mark has got lunch around one* and NOT *I've a shower every morning*.

The action verb **have** can also be continuous.
> Mark **is having** lunch now.   We **were having** a conversation in English.
> What time **are** you **having** your driving lesson?

In negatives and questions in simple tenses, we use a form of **do**.
> We **didn't have** a very good time.   We **don't have** parties very often.
> Where **do** you **have** lunch?   How often **does** Vicky **have** strange dreams?

In English we often use expressions like **have a talk** instead of a verb like **talk**. Here are some examples.
> Shall we **have a swim**?   I usually **have a rest** in the afternoon.
> I **had a talk** with Daniel.   Trevor and Laura **are having an argument**.

31 Exercises

1 Have and have got (A–B)

Look at the pictures and write positive or negative sentences with *have* or *have got*.
Use these objects: *a car, a map, a rabbit, a ticket, an umbrella*

▶ *He's got a ticket.* OR *He has a ticket.*
1 ....   3 ....
2 ....   4 ....

2 Have and have got (A–B)

Complete the dialogue. Put in the negative or question forms.
Use *have got* for the present and *have* for the past.
David: (▶) *Have* you *got* a bike?
Mike: Yes, but I don't ride it very often.
David: (1) .... it .... lights on?
Mike: Yes, why?
David: Can I leave my bike here and take yours? Mine (2) .... any lights. It
        (3) .... any when I bought it. I meant to get some last week, but I
        (4) .... time.
Mike: But it's raining now. And you (5) .... a coat. I'll drive you home, David.

3 The action verb have (C)

What does *have* mean in these sentences? Choose from these verbs: *drink, eat, play, receive, spend*
▶ Mark never <u>has</u> breakfast.   has =   *eats*
1 We've just <u>had</u> a game of tennis.   had = ...
2 My father <u>has</u> a cup of cocoa every evening. has = ...
3 We've just <u>had</u> three weeks in Morocco.   had = ...
4 Claire <u>had</u> lots of presents on her birthday. had = ...

4 The verb have (A–C)

Complete the conversation. Use *have/have got* or the action verb *have*.
Claire: (▶) *You've got* (you / have) an empty plate, Henry. Would you like some more food?
Henry: Oh, yes please. I must say, (1) .... (we / have) a great time.
        Luckily (2) .... (you / have) lots of room in here.
Claire: Yes, it's a nice big flat, although (3) .... (it / not / have) a balcony.
Mark: How was Brazil? (4) .... (you / have) a good holiday?
Claire: Yes, (5) .... (I / have) a lovely time, thank you.
Henry: (6) .... (you / have) some photos here to show us?
Claire: Yes, you must (7) .... (have) a look at them some time. But I was so busy
        doing things (8) .... (I / not / have) time to take very many.

32 Short forms, e.g. it's, don't

A The use of short forms

I've lost my bank card. I don't know where it is.

I'll help you look for it. It's probably in your room somewhere.

A short form like **it's** or **don't** stands for the full form **it is** or **do not**. We leave out one or more letters and we write an apostrophe (') instead. We use short forms in conversational English and in informal writing such as a letter to a friend. Short forms are sometimes called 'contracted forms'.

We cannot use a short form when the word is stressed, in a short answer for example.
*Have you looked in this drawer? ~ Yes, I **have**.* NOT *Yes, I've*.
But we can use **n't** in a short answer: *No, I **haven't**.*

B The most common short forms

Some verbs can have short forms when they come after **I**, **you**, etc.

VERB	SHORT FORMS
am	I'm
are	you're, we're, they're
is/has	he's, she's, it's
have	I've, you've, we've, they've
had/would	I'd, you'd, he'd, she'd, it'd, we'd, they'd
will	I'll, you'll, he'll, she'll, it'll, we'll, they'll
shall	I'll, we'll

A short form can also come after a noun.
Vicky's lost her bank card. (Vicky **has** ...)   The **card'll** be in here. (The card **will** ...)

There are also some short forms with question words and with **here**, **there** or **that**.

who's, what's, where's, when's, how's, who'd, who'll, what'll
here's, there's, that's, there'll, that'll, there'd, that'd

There is a negative short form **n't** which can come after some verbs.

aren't, isn't, wasn't, weren't, haven't, hasn't, hadn't, don't /dəʊnt/, doesn't, didn't, won't (= will not), shan't (= shall not), can't /kɑːnt/, couldn't, mustn't /ˈmʌsnt/, needn't, mightn't, shouldn't, wouldn't, daren't

Sometimes we can shorten either **not** or the verb.
It is not funny. → *It **isn't** funny.* OR *It's not funny.*
You will not believe it. → *You **won't** believe it.* OR *You'll not believe it.*
But we cannot use **n't** after **I**.
I am not sure. → *I'm not sure.* NOT *I amn't sure.*

C 's and 'd

's can be **is** or **has**, and **'d** can be **had** or **would**.
She's short, and she's got fair hair. (She **is** short ... she **has** got ...)
If I'd known, I'd have told you. (If I **had** known, I **would** have ...)

32 Exercises

1 Short forms (B)

Write the sentences in a more informal style, with short forms.

In a business letter
▶ You are quite right.
1 It is a difficult problem.
2 I have seen the results.
3 I do not have any information.
4 We have not reached a decision.
5 I am very excited about it.
6 You need not decide now.
7 It is not yet certain.
8 We will be pleased to see you.
9 Do not worry.
10 I would like to buy a new computer.
11 We are willing to help.
12 We will not know the result for some time.

In a letter to a friend
You're quite right.
....
....
....
....
....
....
....
....
....
....
....
....

2 Short forms (B)

Complete the dialogues. Put in the short form of these phrases:
do not, he is, I am, is not, it is, what is, where is

▶ How are you? ~ *I'm* fine, thanks.
1 .... your luggage? ~ .... in Los Angeles.
2 Do you like this shirt? ~ No, I .... It .... my style.
3 .... that smell? ~ My husband. .... doing a chemical experiment.

3 's and 'd (C)

Write the forms in full. Use *is*, *has*, *had* or *would*.

▶ What's your name?   *What is your name?*
1 I'd like a coffee, please.   ....
2 There's been an accident.   ....
3 That's correct.   ....
4 I'd seen the film before.   ....
5 Who's got the key?   ....
6 We'd have stopped if we'd seen you. ....

33 Emphatic do

A Introduction

*Oh, that picture's new. It **is** nice. Yes, I **do** like it.*

Melanie wants to emphasize the idea that the picture is nice and that she likes it. She wants to say this in a strong and positive way.

NEUTRAL	EMPHATIC
It's nice.	It **is** nice.
I like it.	I **do** like it.

B Emphatic forms

Often we can be emphatic by using a full form like **is** or **have**, rather than a short form such as **'s** or **'ve** (see Unit 32). We stress the word when we speak it.

*Yes, it **is** late. It's half past one in the morning.*   *My goodness you **have** done a lot of work. Well done.*

We can also stress modal verbs such as **will** and **should**.

*You **will** write to me, won't you?*   *You really **should** drive more carefully. We almost had an accident.*

In the present simple we put **do** before the verb.

*You're so right. I **do** agree with you.*   *Your hair is much too long. You **do** need a haircut.*
*We **do** hope you can come to our barbecue.*   *I'm getting fed up with those dogs. They **do** make such a noise.*

In the third person singular we use **does**.

*The city centre **does** get crowded, doesn't it?*
*Emma says Matthew doesn't care about her, but he says he **does** care.*

We do not add **s** to the verb.

*It does **look** nice.* NOT *It does looks nice.*

In the past simple we use **did**.

*We **did** enjoy the concert. It was really good.*   *You shouldn't have forgotten. I **did** remind you.*
*Vicky is quite sure that she **did** see a ghost.*

We do not add **ed** to the verb.

*We did **enjoy** it.* NOT *We did enjoyed it.*

C The imperative with do

We can use **do** with an imperative for emphasis.

***Do** hurry up, or we'll be late.*   *Oh, **do** be quiet. I'm trying to concentrate.*

Here **do** makes the speaker sound more worried or annoyed. We use this structure only in an informal situation.

But we can also use **do** with an imperative in offers and invitations (see page 122).

***Do** have some more soup.*   ***Do** take a seat, won't you?*

Here **do** sounds very polite.

33 Exercises

1 Emphatic do (A–B)

Put in the emphatic forms of these sentences: *I like my new portrait. I'm smiling. It's foggy today. Yes, I'll be late home. Yes, I remembered the water.*

▶ *Yes, I will be late home.*
1 .... 3 ....
2 .... 4 ....

2 Emphatic do (A–B)

Complete the answers. Use a pronoun + emphatic *do* + a verb.
▶ Tom: Melanie is always helping people, isn't she?
  David: Yes, *she does help* a lot of people.
1 Trevor: How much did that dress cost?
  Laura: Well, ... rather a lot.
2 Jessica: Someone once told me I look like the singer Arlene Black.
  Natasha: Well, ... a bit like her, actually.
3 Daniel: This train doesn't stop at our station.
  Matthew: Are you sure? I think .... there.
4 Nick: Why didn't you go to the match on Saturday?
  Tom: What do you mean? .... to the match.
5 Vicky: Matthew and Emma never quarrel.
  Rachel: Oh yes, ... All the time, in fact.

3 Emphatic do (A–C)

What would you say? Use *do, does* or *did*.
▶ Tell your friend that you worry about your job prospects.
  You know, *I do worry about my job prospects.*
1 Say that you finished the crossword today.
  Actually, ...
2 Admit that your room needs tidying up.
  I'm afraid ....
3 Explain to your teacher that you find the work difficult.
  I'm afraid ....
4 Say that you wanted to give the course up.
  Actually, ...
5 Offer your friend a chocolate.
  Here you are. ....
6 Admit that this place depresses you.
  You know, ...

VERBS 83

34 Yes/no questions

A Use

A yes/no question is one that we can answer with **yes** or **no**.
Are you ready? ~ **Yes**, nearly./**No**, not quite.
Has anyone seen my bag? ~ **Yes**, it's on the chair./**No**, I don't think so.

These questions are asking for information. For example, Daniel wants to know if Vicky is ready or not.

Sometimes yes/no questions have other uses, especially questions with modal verbs. For example, when Matthew says *Shall we go then?* he is making a suggestion, not asking for information. Here are some examples of the different uses.

Making a suggestion:	**Shall** we eat out tonight?
Requesting:	**Can/Could** you write the address down for me, please?
Offering:	**Can** I carry something for you? ~ No, it's OK, thanks.
Inviting:	**Would** you like to come to a party? ~ Yes, I'd love to.
Asking permission:	**May** I use your phone? ~ Yes, of course.

B Form

A yes/no question begins with an auxiliary verb. An auxiliary verb is a form of **be** or **have** or a modal verb, e.g. **can**. The auxiliary verb comes before the subject.

AUXILIARY	SUBJECT			
Is	it	raining?	STATEMENT:	It **is** raining.
Has	David	got a car?		
Can	Emma	drive?	QUESTION:	**Is** it raining?

The main verb **be** also comes before the subject in a question.
   Is it cold out there?   *Are you ready?*   *Was it easy?*

If there is more than one auxiliary verb, only the first one comes before the subject.
   Have you been working?   *Could we have done better?*

In the present simple and past simple we use a form of **do**.

AUXILIARY	SUBJECT			
Do	the buses	run every day?	STATEMENT:	They **(do)** run every day.
Does	Mark	play golf?		
Did	you	like the concert?	QUESTION:	**Do** they run every day?

A question cannot begin with an ordinary verb such as *run, play* or *like*.
   NOT *Plays Mark golf?* and NOT *Liked you the concert?*
The verb after the subject does not end in **s** or **ed**.
   NOT *Does Mark plays golf?* and NOT *Did you liked the concert?*

▷ 35 Answers with **yes** and **no**

84   QUESTIONS, NEGATIVES AND ANSWERS

34 Exercises

1 Use (A)

Write down the use of each question. Choose from these uses:
asking for information (x3), *asking permission, inviting, making a suggestion, offering, requesting* (x2)

▶ Could you post this letter for me?   *requesting*
▶ Can we get a number 35 bus from this stop?   *asking for information*
1 Can I help you with those bags? ....
2 Shall we stop for a rest? ....
3 Is it Tuesday today? ....
4 Could you wait a moment, please? ....
5 Would you like to have tea with us? ....
6 Will your friend be here next weekend? ....
7 May I sit down? ....

2 Form (B)

Claude Jennings, the World Quiz Champion, is going to be on Guy's chat show.
Guy is wondering what to ask Claude. Read what Guy is thinking and write down his questions.

▶ (I expect Claude has won lots of prizes.) *Have you won lots of prizes?*
1 (I wonder if he's a rich man.) ....
2 (Perhaps quizzes are his only hobby.) ....
3 (I expect he worked hard at school.) ....
4 (I wonder if he's got any other interests.) ....
5 (I wonder if it's an interesting life.) ....
6 (Perhaps his wife asks him quiz questions.) ....
7 (And maybe he answers questions in his dreams.) ....

3 Yes/no questions (A–B)

What would you say in these situations?

▶ You want to know if Mark has been to Los Angeles. Ask Sarah.
 Has Mark been to Los Angeles?
1 You aren't sure if Rachel and Vicky are going to America. Ask them.
 ....
2 You want to know if Laura plays tennis. Ask Trevor.
 ....
3 You are wondering if Claire enjoyed her holiday. Ask her.
 ....
4 You want to suggest to Rachel that you both go for a walk.
 ....
5 You need to know if David will be at the club tonight. Ask him.
 ....
6 You want to know if the train is on time. Ask Mark.
 ....
7 You are wondering if Mike and Harriet go camping. Ask David.
 ....
8 You want to ask Matthew if you can borrow his squash racket.
 ....
9 You want to know if Nick has got a motor bike. Ask him.
 ....

35 Short answers, e.g. Yes, it is.

A Answering yes or no

Look at the answers to these questions.
*Is it raining? ~ **Yes**.   Are we going to be late? ~ **Yes, we are**.*
*Did you say something? ~ **No**.   Did you finish the crossword? ~ **No, I didn't**.*

We can sometimes answer a question with a simple **yes** or **no**, but we often use a short answer like **No, I didn't**. We usually put a comma after **yes** or **no**.

We do not normally use a full sentence, but we can do if we want to add emphasis to the answer.
*Did you open my letter? ~ **No, I didn't open your letter**.*

Sometimes, to be polite, we may need to add information.
*Did you get the tickets? ~ No, I didn't. **There wasn't time, I'm afraid. Sorry**.*

B Form

A positive short answer is **yes** + a pronoun + an auxiliary.

QUESTION		SHORT ANSWER		
Auxiliary			Pronoun	Auxiliary
Are	*you working tomorrow? ~*	*Yes,*	*I*	*am.*
Has	*Emma got a computer? ~*	*Yes,*	*she*	*has.*
Will	*I need my passport? ~*	*Yes,*	*you*	*will.*
Did	*they repair your phone? ~*	*Yes,*	*they*	*did.*

We can also use the main verb **be** in a short answer.
*Is it time to go? ~ **Yes, it is**. It's ten past eleven.*

Note that in the present simple and past simple we use a form of **do**.
***Do** you like classical music? ~ Yes, I **do**. NOT Yes, I like.*

A negative short answer is **no** + a pronoun + an auxiliary + **n't**.

QUESTION		SHORT ANSWER		
Auxiliary			Pronoun	Auxiliary + n't
Is	*the photocopier working now? ~*	*No,*	*it*	*isn't.*
Have	*the children gone to sleep? ~*	*No,*	*they*	*haven't.*
Will	*there be food at the party? ~*	*No,*	*there*	*won't.*
Does	*this train stop at Derby? ~*	*No,*	*it*	*doesn't.*

But note **No, I'm not**.
*Are you working tomorrow? ~ **No, I'm not**. NOT No, I amn't.*

C Answering requests, suggestions, offers and invitations

To answer a request, suggestion, etc, we normally use a phrase like **Yes, of course** or **Yes, please** rather than a short answer. If we answer in the negative, we have to give some explanation.

Request: *Could you help me move these chairs, please? ~ Yes, of course.* OR *I'm afraid I'm rather busy.*
Suggestion: *Shall we have a coffee? ~ Yes, OK.* OR *Sorry, I can't. I have to go.*
Offer: *Can I give you a hand? ~ Yes, please. That's very kind of you.* OR *It's OK, thanks. I can manage.*
Invitation: *Would you like to come to the barbecue? ~ Yes, please. I'd love to.* OR *I'd love to, but I'll be away.*

Short negative answers would sound strange or impolite here.

35 Exercises

1 Form (B)

It's eleven o'clock, and everyone has arrived at a party. Put in the short answers.

▶ Have you got a drink? ~ *Yes, I have*, thank you. I've just put it down somewhere.
1. Can you speak Arabic? ~ ...., but not very well.
2. Is it raining outside? ~ .... It's just started.
3. Has David come with you? ~ .... He's in hospital, actually.
4. Did you come by car, Tom? ~ .... It took ages because of all the traffic.
5. Are those people over there your friends? ~ .... I don't know them at all.
6. Do you like England? ~ .... I'm enjoying my stay here.
7. Is your brother here? ~ .... He's away on business at the moment.
8. Have you seen Nick recently? ~ .... I think he's moved away.

2 Form (B)

It's one o'clock in the morning, and the party is in full swing.
People are still talking. Put in the short answers.

▶ Are you French? ~ *No, I'm not*. I'm Italian. I'm from Milan.
1. Will you and Laura be here in August? ~ .... We're going to France.
2. Did you remember to bring the photos? ~ .... I'll give them to you in a minute.
3. Has Rita left her job? ~ .... It's all over, she told me.
4. Did you see that documentary about the ozone layer on television last night?
   ~ .... I was working late, unfortunately.
5. Does Laura like these old songs? ~ .... She loves Elvis Presley.
6. Are you and Mike staying the night here? ~ .... We have to get home tonight.
7. Can we afford a taxi? ~ .... It's quite a long way.
8. Are you OK, Vicky? ~ .... I feel really awful.

3 Answering questions (A–C)

Which would normally be the best answer?

▶ Are you busy today?
   a) ☐ Yes, busy.   b) ☑ Yes, I am.
1. Is it too hot in here for you?
   a) ☐ No, it isn't.   b) ☐ No, I'm fine, thanks.
2. Do you know Emma?
   a) ☐ Yes.   b) ☐ Yes, we live in the same building.
3. Tell me, did you steal my money?
   a) ☐ No.   b) ☐ No, I didn't steal your money.
4. Do you live on the campus?
   a) ☐ Yes, I do.   b) ☐ Yes, I live on it.
5. Would you like to come out with us for the day?
   a) ☐ Yes, I would like.   b) ☐ Yes, please.
6. Is it the eighteenth today?
   a) ☐ Yes, it is.   b) ☐ Yes, it is the eighteenth of November today.
7. Did you bring my CD?
   a) ☐ No.   b) ☐ No, sorry. I forgot it.
8. Can I carry your bags?
   a) ☐ No, you can't.   b) ☐ It's all right, thanks.

36 Wh-questions

A Introduction

Reporter Kitty Beamish is interviewing some guerrilla fighters.

Kitty:
Why are you fighting?
What can you do for the people?
When will the war be over?

Guerillas:
For our freedom.
We can help them.
Very soon.

A wh-question begins with a question word. Question words are **who**, **what**, **which**, **whose**, **where**, **when**, **why** and **how**. We use a wh-question to ask for information.

B Form

Most wh-questions begin with a question word + an auxiliary verb + the subject. (For another form of wh-question, see Unit 37.) An auxiliary verb is a form of **be** or **have** or a modal verb, e.g. **can**.

QUESTION WORD	AUXILIARY	SUBJECT	
What	is	Kitty	doing?
Where	have	you	put the map?
When	can	we	travel safely?

The main verb **be** also comes before the subject in questions.
　　Where **is** Kitty?　　How **are** you?　　What **was** that noise?
If there is more than one auxiliary verb, only the first one comes before the subject.
　　The guerrillas **have been** hiding. → Where **have** the guerrillas been hiding?
　　I **should have** said something. → What **should** I have said?

In the present simple and past simple we use a form of **do**.

QUESTION WORD	AUXILIARY	SUBJECT	
Where	do	people	meet?
How	does	the radio	work?
What	did	the guerrillas	say?

An ordinary verb such as **meet**, **work** or **say** cannot come before the subject.
　　NOT ~~Where meet people?~~ and NOT ~~How works the radio?~~
The verb after the subject does not end in **s** or **ed**.
　　NOT ~~How does the radio works?~~ and NOT ~~What did the guerrillas said?~~

C Question phrases

Look at these question phrases with **what** and **how**.
　　What time is your friend arriving? ~ Half past eight.　　**What colour** is your toothbrush? ~ Yellow.
　　What kind of/What sort of club is it? ~ A nightclub.　　**How old** is your sister? ~ She's twenty.
　　How often do you go out? ~ About once a week, usually.　　**How far** is the beach? ~ Only five minutes' walk.
　　How long will the meeting last? ~ An hour or so, I expect.　　**How many** televisions have you got? ~ Three.
　　How much money did you spend? ~ About a hundred pounds.

36 Exercises

1 Wh-questions (A–B)

What would you say in these situations?
▶ You are talking to a man at a party. Ask him where he works.
Where do you work?
1 You want to know what the date is today. Ask your friend.

2 You've forgotten when the course finishes. Ask your friend.

3 Your friend is having a party. You'd like to know who he has invited. Ask him.

4 Your favourite band are going to give a concert. Ask how you can get tickets.

5 You are in town with a friend, and you are wondering where the two of you are going to have lunch. What do you ask?

2 Question words and phrases (A–C)

Quiz champion Claude Jennings is answering questions. Put in these words and phrases:
how far, how long, how often, how many, what, what colour, what kind, when, where, who

Quiz-master: **Claude:**
▶ *What colour* is the Greek flag? Blue and white.
1 .... is Melbourne? It's in Australia.
2 .... centimetres are there in a kilometre? A hundred thousand.
3 .... did the Second World War end? In 1945.
4 .... did Romeo love? Juliet.
5 .... is Sirius? It's a star.
6 .... is it from Los Angeles to San Francisco? About 400 miles.
7 .... are the Olympic Games held? Every four years.
8 .... of food is Cheddar? It's cheese.
9 .... is a game of rugby? Eighty minutes.

3 Wh-questions (A–C)

Guy is interviewing a guest on his chat show. It's the actress Melissa Livingstone, who is in the TV soap opera 'Round the Corner'. Put in Guy's questions.

▶ Guy: *How often do you record 'Round the Corner'?*
   Melissa: Oh, we record it every day. It's a full-time job, you know.
1 Guy: And .... it?
   Melissa: In Birmingham, at the BBC studios.
2 Guy: ....
   Melissa: How many? Well, let me see, I think we've done a thousand programmes.
3 Guy: ....
   Melissa: I'm not going to tell you. How much money I earn is my business.
4 Guy: OK, I'm sorry. ....
   Melissa: Oh, a long time ago. I started acting when I was twelve.
5 Guy: ....
   Melissa: My plans for the future? I just want to go on with 'Round the Corner'.

37 Subject/object questions

A Who and what

Who is interviewing Kitty?

Who and **what** can be the subject of a question. The word order is the same as in a statement.

Who is Kitty interviewing?

Who and **what** can also be the object. An auxiliary (e.g. **did**, **will**) comes before the subject.

SUBJECT	OBJECT
Who rang you? (Someone rang you.)	*Who did you ring?* (You rang someone.)
Who is helping you? (Someone is helping you.)	*Who are you helping?* (You are helping someone.)
What will happen next? (Something will happen next.)	*What will they do next?* (They will do something next.)

Who and **what** can also be the object of a preposition, e.g. **to**, **with**.
(For prepositions in questions, see Unit 38.) Compare these sentences.

SUBJECT	OBJECT
Who was talking to you? (Someone was talking to you.)	*Who were you talking to?* (You were talking to someone.)
What wine goes with fish? (Some wine goes with fish.)	*What does this colour go with?* (This colour goes with something.)

B Which, whose, how many and how much

These words can also be either the subject or the object.

SUBJECT	OBJECT
Which program will work best? (One of the programs will work best.)	*Which program will you use?* (You will use one of the programs.)
Whose dog is barking over there? (Someone's dog is barking over there.)	*Whose dog is Melanie walking?* (Melanie is walking someone's dog.)
How many people came past? (Some people came past.)	*How many people did you see?* (You saw some people.)
How much oil got into the river? (Some oil got into the river.)	*How much oil did you buy?* (You bought some oil.)

37 Exercises

1 Who and what as subject and object (A)
Read about the situations and answer each question in a single phrase.

▶ The morning after his party, Tom was cleaning up. David came along and took away some empty bottles for him. Nick had just woken up after spending the night on Tom's sofa. He watched them for a while.
a) Who helped Tom? *David*   b) Who did Nick help? *no one*

1 Nick wants to marry Rita. She's been out with him a few times, but really she's in love with Tom. Unfortunately he isn't in love with her.
a) Who is Nick in love with? ....   b) Who is in love with Tom? ....

2 Mark met Sarah at the airport. The plane was two hours late. On the way out they passed Mike standing at a bus stop, but they didn't notice him.
a) Who met Sarah? ....   b) What was Mike waiting for? ....

3 There was an accident at the crossroads. A lorry crashed into a van that was waiting at the lights. The van slid forward and crashed into a car. The van driver had to go to hospital.
a) What hit the van? ....   b) What did the van hit? ....

2 Who and what as subject and object (A)
People aren't giving you enough information. Ask questions with *who* or *what*.

▶ Something has happened. ~ Oh? *What has happened?*
▶ I've invited someone to tea. ~ Well? *Who have you invited?*
1 Somebody is having a party. ~ Oh, really? ....
2 I was reading something. ~ Oh? ....
3 I've learnt something. ~ Go on, tell me. ....
4 We should do something. ~ Yes, I know, but ....
5 Someone is looking for you. ~ Oh? ....
6 I'm looking for someone. ~ Maybe I can help. ....
7 Rachel is planning something. ~ Is she? ....
8 Somebody has moved in next door. ~ Oh, really? ....
9 Something is worrying me. ~ Well, tell me. ....
10 I want to meet someone. ~ What do you mean? ....

3 Which, whose, how many and how much (B)
Harriet is visiting her grandmother, Mrs Evans. It's Mrs Evans's birthday. She can't hear very well, and she sometimes gets confused. Complete her questions.

Harriet: **Mrs Evans:**
▶ So ten people have sent cards.   Pardon? How many *people have sent cards?*
▶ I met David's friend yesterday.   What? Whose *friend did you meet?*
1 You can keep those photos.   Photos? Which ....
2 Those flowers look lovely.   Do they? Which ....
3 Fifty pounds went missing.   Missing? How much ....
4 I passed Mark's house earlier.   Pardon? Whose ....
5 The doctor has four children.   Really? How many ....
6 Doctors earn lots of money.   I don't know. How much ....
7 Mike's uncle has died.   What's that? Whose ....
8 Trevor's wife is coming later.   Oh? Whose ....

38 Prepositions in wh-questions

A Introduction

Daniel and Rachel each ask Vicky a question. In each question, the word **what** is the object of a preposition (**for**, **about**).
> **What** are you looking **for**?
> (You are looking **for something**.)
> **What** are you worrying **about**?
> (You are worrying **about something**.)

The preposition normally comes in the same place as in a statement: **looking for**, **worrying about**.
> NOT *For what are you looking?*
> NOT *About what are you worrying?*

But in more formal English, the preposition can come before the question word.
> **In which** warehouse were the goods stored?
> OR **Which** warehouse were the goods stored **in**?

In formal English we use a preposition + **whom** (not **who**).
> **From whom** did you obtain the information?
> OR **Who** did you obtain the information **from**?

Here are some more examples of prepositions in wh-questions.
> **Who** are we waiting **for**? ~ Rachel.
> **What**'s Nick laughing **at**? ~ Oh, one of Tom's jokes.
> **Where** are you **from**?/**Where** do you come **from**? ~ Bombay.
> **What kind of** holiday are you interested **in**? ~ A package holiday.
> **Who** did you go out **with** last night? ~ Just a friend.

B What ... for and what ... like

We can use a question with **what ... for** to ask about purpose.
> **What** did you buy this computer magazine **for**? ~ To read about business software.
> **What** are these bricks **for**? ~ We're going to build a wall.
> **What** are they digging the road up **for**? ~ They're repairing a gas pipe.

What ... for means the same as **why**.
> **Why** are they digging up the road? ~ They're repairing a gas pipe.

We can use **what ... like** to ask if something is good or bad, interesting or boring, etc.
> **What** was the party **like**? ~ Oh, we had a great time.
> **What**'s the place **like** where you live? ~ It's pretty quiet.

Note also **look like**.
> **What** does your friend **look like**? ~ She's very tall and blond.

But we use **how** to ask about someone's well-being.
> **How** are you? ~ I'm OK, thanks. And you?
> **How** are you getting on in your new job? ~ I'm really enjoying it.

Compare these two questions.
> **How**'s Melanie? ~ Oh, she's fine, thanks. (She is happy/in good health.)
> **What**'s Melanie **like**? ~ She's very nice. (She is a nice person.)

38 Exercises

1 Prepositions in wh-questions (A)

Ask these people questions with *what*.
Use these verbs and prepositions: *look at, look for, point at, talk about, wait for*

▶ *What are you looking for?*
1 ....
2 ....
3 ....
4 ....

2 Prepositions in wh-questions (A)

Put in the question. Use *what* and put the preposition in brackets at the end.
▶ Melanie: Tom is smiling. He's pleased. (about)
   David: Yes, he is. *What is he pleased about?*
▶ Laura: I'm busy today. I'm getting ready. (for)
   Trevor: *What are you getting ready for?*
1 Jessica: I've done something awful. I'm ashamed. (of)
   Andrew: ....
2 Trevor: Haven't you heard of Kitty Beamish? She's famous. (for)
   Ilona: No, I haven't. ....
3 Sarah: Mark is annoyed. He's going to complain. (about)
   Claire: ....
4 Matthew: Emma's in a hurry. She's going to be late. (for)
   Daniel: ....
5 Vicky: I don't feel very relaxed. I feel nervous. (about)
   Rachel: ....

3 What ... for and what ... like (B)

Trevor has just come home from work. Complete the conversation. Put in *for, how, like* or *what*.
Trevor: Hello, my love. (▶) *How* are you?
Laura: Hello. I'm all right, but I'm in a bit of a rush getting ready for the barbecue.
Trevor: Er, I forgot to tell you that I invited two more people.
Laura: (1) .... are you telling me now (2) .... ? I've bought all the food. I just hope there's enough. Anyway, who are these people? (3) .... are they (4) .... ?
Trevor: They're friends of Harriet's. They're very nice people. And after all, (5) .... are parties (6) .... ? To meet new people.
Laura: It isn't a party, it's a barbecue. (7) .... 's the weather going to be (8) .... ?
Trevor: The forecast said it's going to be perfect. Warm and dry.
Laura: Good. And (9) .... was your day?
Trevor: Oh, not too bad. Busy as usual.

39 Who, what or which?

A What or which?

We can use **what** or **which** before a noun.

WHAT	WHICH
What sport do you play? **What books** do you read? We use **what** when there is a wide choice of possible answers. We ask *What sport?* because there are lots of different sports.	**Which way** do we go here? **Which finger** did you break? We use **which** when there is a limited number of possible answers. We ask *Which way?* because there are only two or three ways to go.

What sport?
(Tennis or golf or football or hockey or … ?)

Which way?
(Right or left?)

After **which** we sometimes say the possible answers.
  Which café did you go to, **Snoopy's, the Coffee Pot or the Tea Gardens**?
  Which phone shall I use, **this one or the one in the office**?
Sometimes **what** and **which** are both possible.
  What day/**Which** day is your evening class?   **What** train/**Which** train will you catch?
  What platform/**Which** platform does the train go from?   **What** part/**Which** part of Italy are you from?

B Patterns with who, what and which

We can use **who, what** and **which** without a noun.
  Who sent the fax?   **What** do you think of our plan?   **Which** is quicker, the bus or the train?
We can use **what** and **which** before a noun, but not **who**.
  Which secretary sent the fax? NOT *Who secretary sent the fax?*

We can use **which** with **one** or **ones**, or with **of**.
  You can have a photo. **Which one** would you like?
  You can have some of the photos. **Which ones** would you like?
  Which of these photos would you like?
But we cannot use **who** or **what** before **of**.
  Which of the secretaries? but NOT *Who of the secretaries?*

Who always means a person.
  Who did you see? (a person)
What usually means a thing. It can mean a person only when it comes before a noun.
  What did you see? (a thing)   **What doctor/What film** did you see? (a person or a thing)
Which can mean a person or a thing.
  Which doctor/film did you see? (a person or a thing)

▷ 102 **One** and **ones**

39 Exercises

1 What or which? (A)

The questions you are asking have a number of possible answers.
If the list of answers is incomplete, ask a question with *what*. If the list is complete, use *which*.

▶ (Do you play the piano, or the violin, or the guitar, or …?)
   What musical instrument do you play?
▶ (Did you go to the Little Theatre or the Theatre Royal?)
   Which theatre did you go to?
1 (Did you take the morning flight or the afternoon flight?)
   ....
2 (Did you stay at the Grand Hotel or the Bristol?)
   ....
3 (Do you like classical music, or jazz, or rock music, or …?)
   ....
4 (Did you buy 'Time' magazine, or 'Newsweek', or a computer magazine, or …?)
   ....
5 (Do you work for EuroChemicals, or ICM, or SenCo, or …?)
   ....
6 (Are you learning English, or Spanish, or Arabic, or Japanese, or …?)
   ....

2 What or which? (A)

Rita is moving into a new flat. Trevor has come to see the flat and help her move in.
Complete his questions. Put in *what* or *which*.

▶ Trevor: *What* number is this building?
  Rita: Forty-two.
1 Trevor: I didn't realize there were only three floors. .... floor is your flat on?
  Rita: The first floor.
2 Trevor: It's a very nice flat. .... room will be your living-room?
  Rita: This one here, I thought.
3 Trevor: .... colour are you going to paint it?
  Rita: Oh, I don't know yet.
4 Trevor: .... time is your furniture arriving?
  Rita: Three o'clock, they said.
5 Trevor: I'll need some petrol. .... way is the nearest petrol station?
  Rita: Turn left at the end of the street.

3 Who, what or which? (B)

Detectives Wilson and Taylor are looking into the murder of Lord Weybridge at his country house.
Put in *who*, *what* or *which*.

Wilson: (▶) *Which* of the guests in this house is the murderer, do you think, Taylor?
Taylor: I don't know yet. (1) .... had the opportunity? (2) .... of the guests had the
         chance to do it?
Wilson: (3) .... happened after dinner last night? That's what we have to find out.
Taylor: There must be a motive for the murder. (4) .... motive could the murderer have?
Wilson: Love or money – they're the usual motives. (5) .... of them is it, I wonder?
Taylor: (6) .... did Lord Weybridge leave his money to? That's the question, Wilson.

Test 8 — Questions (Units 34–39)

Test 8A

Put the words in the right order and ask the question.
▶ everyone / is / ready
Is everyone ready?
1 been / have / where / you
2 do / postcards / sell / you
3 belong / calculator / does / this / to / who
4 are / here / how / long / staying / you
5 is / like / new / office / what / your
6 are / flights / full / of / the / which
7 carnival / does / start / the / time / what
8 decided / has / holiday / Nancy / on / what

Test 8B

Put in the correct question word or phrase.
▶ *What* did you buy? ~ A box of chocolates.
1 .... is this building? ~ It's about two hundred years old.
2 .... does your team play in? ~ Red.
3 .... bag are you carrying? ~ Judy's.
4 .... money do you earn? ~ About £250 a week.
5 .... hand do you write with? ~ My right hand.
6 .... of shop do you work in? ~ A toy shop.
7 .... first stepped on the moon? ~ Neil Armstrong, wasn't it?
8 .... is your mother? ~ She's much better, thank you.
9 .... is it to the post office? ~ About two hundred metres.
10 .... do you take a holiday? ~ Once a year.
11 .... name will you give the baby? ~ We haven't thought of one yet.

Test 8C

Write the sentences correctly.
▶ ~~Would like you to go sailing?~~   *Would you like to go sailing?*
1 ~~Do you be a student here?~~
2 ~~How many cakes have eaten you?~~
3 ~~Enjoyed you your walk?~~
4 ~~Where your friends have gone?~~
5 ~~What kind music do you like?~~
6 ~~Does Peter plays tennis?~~
7 ~~About what are you talking?~~
8 ~~What has it happened?~~

96 QUESTIONS, NEGATIVES AND ANSWERS

Test 8

Test 8D

Read about each situation and write down the question.
▶ You want to know if it is raining.
   Is it raining?
▶ You need to ask Polly where she lives.
   Where do you live?
1 You would like to ask Nancy where she bought her coat.
   ....
2 You want to ask Susan if Amy can swim.
   ....
3 You want to ask Simon which band he likes best.
   ....
4 On the phone you want to know who you are speaking to.
   ....
5 You need to know how much video recorders cost.
   ....
6 You are asking permission to come in.
   ....
7 You need to find out how long the journey takes.
   ....
8 You want to ask Adrian what he locked the door for.
   ....
9 You want to ask what happens next.
   ....
10 You want to suggest that you all go out together.
   ....

Test 8E

Write the questions to which the underlined words are the answers.
▶ Christopher is going to London by train.
   How is Christopher going to London?
1 The Smiths have got three cars.
   ....
2 Janet works at the supermarket.
   ....
3 Andrea is learning English because she will need it in her job.
   ....
4 The film was really romantic.
   ....
5 The meeting will take place next Tuesday.
   ....
6 Tessa switched off the computer.
   ....
7 Mr Johnson's burglar alarm was ringing.
   ....
8 Anna went to the dance with Martin.
   ....

QUESTIONS, NEGATIVES AND ANSWERS

40 Negative statements

A Use

Christopher Columbus
Christopher Columbus was a famous explorer. At one time people believed that he had 'discovered' America. We know now this **isn't** true. Columbus **was not** the first European to travel to the New World. We **don't** know who was, but the Vikings had sailed there around the year 1000, and probably others before them. In 1492 Columbus sailed to San Salvador in the Bahamas and to other islands, but he never reached the mainland of North America. He actually thought he was in Asia. He certainly **didn't** discover America.

We often use a negative statement to correct a mistaken idea, such as the idea that Christopher Columbus discovered America.

B Negative verb forms

	POSITIVE	NEGATIVE	
be:	*are* dancing	*are not* dancing	OR *aren't* dancing
have:	*have* seen	*have not* seen	OR *haven't* seen
Modal verb:	*must* stay	*must not* stay	OR *mustn't* stay

In a negative statement **not** or **n't** comes after the auxiliary verb.
The auxiliary verb is a form of **be**, **have** or a modal verb, e.g. **must**, **can**, **could**.
  *The girls **are not** dancing.*   *The modem **isn't** working properly.*
  *I **haven't** seen the new Disney film.*   *David **hasn't** got a car.*
  *I **mustn't** stay long.*   *You **can't** turn right here.*
  *I'**m not** feeling very awake today.*
We write **n't** without a space before it, e.g. **isn't**, **haven't**.

Not or **n't** also comes after the main verb **be**.
  *The photos **are not** ready yet.*   *It **isn't** very warm in here.*
If there is more than one auxiliary verb, we put **not** or **n't** after the first one.
  *This plate **hasn't** been washed.*   *You **shouldn't** have bothered.*

In the present simple and past simple, we use a form of **do**.

	POSITIVE	NEGATIVE	
Present simple:	work	*do not* work	OR *don't* work
	looks	*does not* look	OR *doesn't* look
Past simple:	enjoyed	*did not* enjoy	OR *didn't* enjoy

  *I **don't** work on Saturdays.* NOT *I work not on Saturdays.*
  *This part of town **doesn't** look very nice.*   *I'm afraid we **didn't** enjoy the day very much.*
The verb after **not** or **n't** does not end in **s** or **ed**.
  NOT *It doesn't looks very nice* and NOT *We didn't enjoyed the day*.

C No and not

We can use **no** before a noun or an adjective + noun. The verb is positive.
  ***No** music is allowed after eleven.* OR *Music is not allowed after eleven.*
  *There are **no** new houses in the village.* OR *There aren't any new houses in the village.*
We do not use **no** with a verb.
  NOT *Music is no allowed* and NOT *The shops are no open*.

40 Exercises

1 Use (A)

Read the information in A about Christopher Columbus.
Then choose a positive or a negative verb.
▶ Columbus discovered/didn't discover America.
1. The first European to sail to the New World was/wasn't Columbus.
2. Europeans had/hadn't been to the New World before Columbus.
3. We know/don't know definitely who first sailed to America.
4. Columbus landed/didn't land on the North American mainland.
5. People's opinion of Columbus has/hasn't changed over the last 500 years.
6. When Columbus landed on San Salvador, he knew/didn't know where he was.
7. It is/isn't true that Columbus travelled across the United States.

2 Negative verb forms (B)

Complete the conversation. Put in the negative forms of these words:
can, did, do, does, has, have, is, was, were

Rita: Does anyone live in that house next door?
Melanie: Yes, he's called Jake. He's rather strange. He (▶) *hasn't* got a job, but he (1) .... be short of money because he's just bought a new car.
Rita: The house (2) .... look very smart.
Melanie: The people who lived there before Jake (3) .... look after it very well. And they (4) .... very good at gardening. When Jake bought the house, it had been empty for a while. It (5) .... very expensive. But he (6) .... interested in doing anything to it, as you can see.
Rita: Is he a friend?
Melanie: No, we aren't really friends. I (7) .... know him very well. I say hello when I see him, that's all. I (8) .... seen him for a while, actually.

3 Negative verb forms (B)

Vicky and Rachel are good friends, but they are very different kinds of people.
Complete the sentences using a negative.
▶ Vicky gets upset, but Rachel *doesn't get upset*.
1. Vicky gets headaches. Rachel is lucky. She ....
2. Rachel can relax. Vicky is different. She ....
3. Rachel missed a lecture yesterday, but Vicky ....
4. Vicky is a nervous person, but Rachel ....
5. Vicky loses things. Rachel ....
6. Rachel was a happy child. Vicky ....
7. Rachel has decided on a career, but Vicky ....

4 No and not (C)

Complete this paragraph from a travel article. Put in *no* or *not*.
Metropolis is (▶) *not* an attractive town. There are (1) .... parks or gardens in the city centre.
I saw (2) .... interesting buildings, only factories, offices and blocks of flats.
The hotels are (3) .... very good, and there are (4) .... first-class restaurants.
(5) .... tourists visit Metropolis, and I certainly do (6) .... want to go there again.

41 Negative questions

A Introduction

Laura asks two negative questions. The first expresses surprise that Trevor hasn't put the shelves up yet. The second is a suggestion that he should put them up now.

B Form

We make a question negative by putting **n't** after the auxiliary (e.g **have**, **does**).

POSITIVE	NEGATIVE
Have you done it yet?	**Haven't** you done it yet?
What **does** the advert tell you?	What **doesn't** the advert tell you?
Who **eats** meat?	Who **doesn't eat** meat?
What **went** wrong?	What **didn't go** wrong?

C The use of negative yes/no questions

A negative yes/no question often expresses surprise.
   Haven't you put those shelves up yet? (= I am surprised that you haven't yet.)
   Don't the children want the ice-cream? (= I am surprised that they don't want it.)

A question with **can't** can be a complaint or an impolite request.
   Can't you sit down? You're blocking my view.

We can also use a negative yes/no question instead of a statement and a tag.
   Aren't you a friend of Harriet's? (= You're a friend of Harriet's, aren't you?)

D Yes/no answers

The answer **yes** means that the positive is true, and **no** means that the negative is true.
   Haven't you repaired the car yet? ~ **Yes**, I did it yesterday.
   Haven't you repaired the car yet? ~ **No**, sorry. I haven't had time.

E The use of negative wh-questions

We can use **Why don't** ...? for a suggestion.
   Why don't you put the shelves up now? ~ Well, all right.
   Why don't we sit on the balcony? ~ Good idea.

We can use **Why didn't** ...? to criticize.
   We'll have to stand now. **Why didn't** you book seats for us? (= You should have booked seats for us.)

We can also use a wh-question to ask for information.
   Who hasn't checked their baggage in? ~ Oh, I haven't. Sorry.
   What don't you understand? ~ This paragraph here.

41 Exercises

1 Negative yes/no questions (B–C)

What would you say in these situations? Use negative yes/no questions.
▶ You are surprised to learn that Rita doesn't like football.
Don't you like football, Rita?
1 You find it surprising that Melanie can't drive.
   ....
2 It's a surprise that Rachel won't be at the disco.
   ....
3 You find out that surprisingly Nick hasn't got a television.
   ....

2 Negative yes/no questions (B–C)

Complete the conversations using the words in the brackets.
▶ Mike: I walked home from the town centre. (take / bus)
   Harriet: You mean you walked all the way? *Didn't you take a bus?*
1 Vicky: I think I'd like to lie down for a while. (feel / well)
   Rachel: Oh, dear. ....
2 Matthew: I'm looking forward to getting the photos you've sent. (arrive / yet)
   Richard: I sent them a week ago. ....
3 David: I saw Rita, but she walked straight past me. (say / hello)
   Melanie: Without speaking to you? ....
4 Andrew: I never sit by the pool. I hate water. (swim)
   Emma: Really? ....

3 Yes/no answers (D)

Put in *yes* or *no*.
▶ Didn't Mike stop and give you a lift? ~ *No*, he didn't, but maybe he didn't see me.
1 Aren't you tired after working all day? ~ .... , I feel fine.
2 Didn't you write the number down? ~ .... , but I've lost the piece of paper.
3 Haven't you got an umbrella? ~ .... , it's here in my bag.
4 Couldn't you get in to the opera? ~ .... , we didn't have tickets.

4 Why not? (B, E)

Reporter Kitty Beamish is investigating an accident at the Magic World theme park. A ride crashed, and people were injured. This is what Kitty has found out.

▶ The people on the ride didn't get enough help.   3 They aren't trained in first aid.
1 The staff didn't know what to do.   4 The ambulance wasn't called immediately.
2 They couldn't stop the ride.   5 The doctor didn't have a mobile phone.

What questions beginning with *why* does Kitty ask?
▶ *Why didn't the people on the ride get enough help?*
1 ....
2 ....
3 ....
4 ....
5 ....

42 Question tags, e.g. isn't it?

A Use

Melanie: *It's a lovely day, **isn't it?***
Harriet: *Beautiful. We're having a glorious summer, **aren't we?***
Melanie: *You haven't heard a forecast for the weekend, **have you?***
Harriet: *No, I haven't, but I think it's going to stay sunny.*

A question tag is a short question added on to a statement. When a tag is spoken, the voice can go down or up.

FALLING	RISING
It's a lovely day, isn't it? ↘	*You haven't heard a forecast, have you?* ↗
With a falling intonation, the speaker thinks the statement is true. Melanie knows that it is a lovely day, and she is inviting Harriet to continue the conversation. The tag is not really a question.	With a rising intonation, the speaker is less sure. Melanie doesn't know if Harriet has heard a weather forecast or not. The tag is more like a real question.

B Form

POSITIVE STATEMENT + NEGATIVE TAG	NEGATIVE STATEMENT + POSITIVE TAG
*It **is** very warm, **isn't it?***	*It **isn't** very warm, **is it?***
A negative tag is an auxiliary verb + **n't** + pronoun.	A positive tag is an auxiliary verb + pronoun.
*You've played before, **haven't you?***	*David hasn't got a car, **has he?***
*The children can swim, **can't they?***	*I shouldn't laugh, **should I?***
*It'll be dark soon, **won't it?***	*You aren't ill, **are you?***
*There was a mistake, **wasn't there?***	*The answer wasn't right, **was it?***

The pronoun (**you**, **he**, etc) refers to the subject of the sentence, e.g. **you**, **David**.

In the present simple and past simple we use a form of **do**.

*You live near here, **don't you?***	*We don't have to pay, **do we?***
*This coat looks nice, **doesn't it?***	*The shower doesn't work, **does it?***
*I turned right, **didn't I?***	*Your horse didn't win, **did it?***

The answer **yes** means that the positive is true, and **no** means that the negative is true.
*Mark works for Zedco, doesn't he? ~ **Yes**, he does. (He **works** for Zedco.)*
*Melanie doesn't eat meat, does she? ~ **Yes**, I think she does. (She **eats** meat.)*
*Claire is married, isn't she? ~ **No**, of course she isn't. (She **isn't** married.)*
*Andrew hasn't got many friends, has he? ~ **No**. (He **hasn't** got many friends.)*

C Requests and suggestions

After a request with an imperative (e.g. **Wait** ...), we can use **can you?** or **could you?**
*Wait here a moment, **can you?*** *Give me an example, **could you?***
We can also use **You couldn't ..., could you?** or **You haven't ..., have you?** for a request.
*You couldn't help me, **could you?*** *You haven't got a pound, **have you?***
After **Don't** ... the tag is **will you?**: *Don't make any noise, **will you?***
After **Let's** ... we use **shall we?**: *Let's sit in the garden, **shall we?***

▷ page 379 Question tags in American English

42 Exercises

1 Use (A)

Look carefully at each statement and tag. Say if it is more likely to be a comment (with falling intonation) or a question (with rising intonation).

▶ This price list is up to date, isn't it? ~ Yes, it is.   *a question*
1 It was a super show, wasn't it? ~ Great. I really enjoyed it. ....
2 These sweaters are nice, aren't they? ~ I like this one. ....
3 We've got time for a coffee, haven't we? ~ A quick one maybe. ....
4 Let me see, the bus goes at ten past, doesn't it? ~ Quarter past. ....

2 Form (B)

You are at a barbecue. Add tags to help start a friendly conversation.

▶ These sausages are delicious, *aren't they*? ~ They certainly are.
▶ You haven't lived here long, *have you*? ~ No, only three months.
1 It's quite a big garden, ...? ~ Yes, there's plenty of room.
2 There aren't many people here yet, ...? ~ No, but it's still quite early.
3 You're Rachel's friend, ...? ~ Yes, I'm Vicky.
4 You came in a sports car, ...? ~ That's right.
5 These burgers look good, ...? ~ I can't wait to try them.
6 We can sit on the grass, ...? ~ I think it's dry enough.
7 The weather forecast wasn't very good, ...? ~ No, it wasn't.

3 Form (B)

Complete the conversation. Put in the question tags.

Emma: You don't really want to go out with me any more, (▶) *do you*?
Matthew: Of course I do. But I need a bit of time to myself sometimes.
Emma: You get plenty of time to yourself, (1) ....?
Matthew: Emma, you know what I feel for you.
I've told you enough times, (2) ....?
Emma: Yes, you have. And you're quite happy, (3) ....?
You don't mind, (4) ....?
The situation doesn't bother you, (5) ....?
Matthew: Why are we arguing? There's nothing to argue about, (6) ....?
Emma: You can't ever look at things from my point of view, (7) ....?

4 Requests and suggestions (C)

What would you say in these situations? Write sentences with a question tag. Use the word in brackets.

▶ You want to look at a newspaper. Daniel might have one, so ask him. (haven't)
   You haven't got a newspaper, have you?
1 Suggest to Vicky that you both listen to some music. (Let's)
   ....
2 Warn David not to do anything silly. (Don't)
   ....
3 You need a train timetable. Emma might have one, so ask her. (haven't)
   ....
4 Ask Rachel to pass you the salt. (Pass)
   ....

43 So/Neither do I and I think so

A So and neither

Vicky: I'm hungry.
Rachel: **So am I**. I haven't eaten anything all day.
Daniel: **Neither have I**. I didn't have time for breakfast.

We use **so** after a positive statement and **neither** after a negative one.
  I'm hungry. ~ **So** am I. (= And I'm hungry./I'm hungry, too.)
  I **haven't** eaten. ~ **Neither** have I. (= And I haven't eaten./I haven't eaten either.)

The structure is **so/neither** + an auxiliary + the subject.
The auxiliary is a form of **be** or **have** or a modal verb, e.g. **can**.
  We're really busy at work. ~ **So are we**.   Tom has gone to the match. ~ And **so has Nick**.
  David can't drive, and **neither can Melanie**.
The subject comes at the end. NOT *We're busy. ~ So we are.*
In the present simple and past simple we use a form of **do**.
  I love old cowboy films. ~ **So do I**.   This phone doesn't work. ~ **Neither does this one**.
  United won, and **so did Rangers**.

We can use **nor** instead of **neither**.
  Emma isn't here tonight. **Neither/Nor** is Matthew.

B I think so, etc

Vicky: It's 'Round the Corner' at half past seven, my favourite soap opera. Are we going to be back in time?
Daniel: **I think so**. We haven't got far to go now.
Rachel: We might miss the beginning.
Vicky: Oh, **I hope not**. I want to know if Bernard really did steal the money.

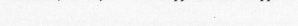

Here *I think so* means 'I think we'll be back in time', and *I hope not* means 'I hope we don't miss the beginning'.

We can use **so** after **be afraid, believe, expect, guess, hope, suppose** and **think**.
  Do you think you'll get the job? ~ Well, I **hope so**.
  Are you going on holiday this year? ~ Yes, I **expect so**.
  I don't know for sure if Henry is rich, but I should **think so**.
But we cannot use **so** after **know** or **be sure**.
  There's been an accident. ~ Yes, **I know**. NOT *I know so*.
  Are you sure you're doing the right thing? ~ Yes, **I'm sure**. NOT *I'm sure so*.

There are two negative structures.

NEGATIVE + **so**	POSITIVE + **not**
Is it raining? ~ I **don't think so**.	Is it raining? ~ **I hope not**.
Are you going to the concert? ~ I **don't expect so**.	Have we won a prize? ~ **I'm afraid not**.
With **expect** and **think**, we normally use the negative and **so**.	With **be afraid, guess** and **hope**, we use the positive and **not**.

We can use **believe** and **suppose** in either structure.
  Will there be any seats left? ~ I **don't suppose so**. OR *I suppose not*.

43 Exercises

1 So and neither (A)

Andrew has just met Jessica at a party. They are finding out that they have a lot in common.
Put in the structures with *so* and *neither*.

- Andrew: I haven't been to a party for ages.
- ▶ Jessica: *Neither have I.* I hate crowded rooms.
- ▶ Andrew: Yes, *so do I*. I'm not a party-goer, really.
- 1 Jessica: No, ... I can't make conversation.
- 2 Andrew: .... You know, I'm a quiet sort of person.
- 3 Jessica: And .... I lead a pretty quiet life.
- 4 Andrew: Well, ... I haven't got many friends.
- 5 Jessica: .... And I would really like a good friend.
- 6 Andrew: Oh, ...

2 So and neither (A)

Look at the table and complete the sentences.

	Mark	Claire	Melanie	Emma
Music	✓	✗	✗	✓
Travel	✓	✓	✗	✗
Skiing	✗	✓	✓	✗
Cooking	✗	✗	✓	✓

- ▶ Claire can ski, and *so can Melanie*.
- ▶ Mark isn't keen on cooking, and *neither is Claire*.
- 1 Melanie doesn't like travelling much, and ....
- 2 Mark has got lots of CDs, and ....
- 3 Emma can't ski, and ....
- 4 Claire isn't a music lover, and ....
- 5 Melanie cooks quite often, and ....
- 6 Mark travels quite a lot, and ....

3 I think so, etc (B)

Complete these short conversations. Put in structures with *so* or *not* and use the words in brackets.

- ▶ Laura: Does the library open on Saturdays? (think)
  Trevor: Yes, *I think so*. But I'm not absolutely certain.
- ▶ Harriet: You can't go out for an evening meal wearing shorts. (guess)
  Mike: *I guess not*. I'd better put some trousers on.
- 1 Sarah: Will there be a lot of people at the concert tonight? (expect)
  Mark: .... There aren't usually very many.
- 2 Daniel: Are you going to apply for the job? (suppose)
  Vicky: .... It's the only one available.
- 3 David: Do you think it's going to rain? (hope)
  Melanie: Well, ... I'm just about to go out.
- 4 Nick: Will the match take place in this weather? (think)
  Tom: .... In fact, I'm sure it won't.
- 5 Claire: Are my photos ready, please? (afraid)
  Assistant: .... We're having problems with the machine.

Test 9 Questions, negatives and answers (Units 34–43)

Test 9A

Read the conversation. Then look at the answers below and write the correct answer in each space.

Judy: (▶) *Shall* we go to the party tonight?
Lisa: (1) .... giving a party?
Judy: Susan. You know her, (2) .... you?
Lisa: I'm (3) .... sure. Has she got long dark hair?
Judy: Yes, she (4) .... And she's quite tall. (5) .... you spoken to her?
Lisa: No, I don't think (6) .... But I know who you mean. There are two sisters, Susan and Janet. They're twins, aren't (7) .... ?
Judy: Yes, that's right.
Lisa: (8) .... one is Susan?
Judy: Oh, I (9) .... know. They both look the same. I can't always tell them apart.
Lisa: No, (10) .... can I. In any case, I haven't been invited to the party.
Judy: That (11) .... matter.
Lisa: OK. (12) .... go to it then, shall we?

▶ a) Do   b) Shall   c) Would
1 a) What's   b) Who's   c) Whose
2 a) don't   b) know   c) so
3 a) isn't   b) no   c) not
4 a) got   b) has   c) so
5 a) Haven't   b) Having   c) Not
6 a) it   b) neither   c) so
7 a) it   b) not   c) they
8 a) What   b) Which   c) Who
9 a) don't   b) no   c) not
10 a) neither   b) not   c) so
11 a) doesn't   b) isn't   c) not
12 a) Could   b) Let's   c) Shall

Test 9B

What would you say? Use the word in brackets, and use a question form in each sentence.
▶ You want to suggest a game of cards. (have)
   Shall we have a game of cards?

1 You are asking Tessa where her house is. (live)
   ....

2 You want Janet to tell you what she is thinking. (about)
   ....

3 You are inviting a friend to come to your room. (like)
   ....

4 You are surprised that your friend missed the football match on television. (watch)
   ....

5 You are asking permission to take a photo. (may)
   ....

6 You are looking for Polly. You are asking her friend for information. (seen)
   ....

7 You are asking Nigel about the number of letters he has written. (how)
   ....

8 You are asking Nancy about the people coming to her party. (who)
   ....

9 You are asking Martin's wife if he cooks every day or once a week. (often)
   ....

10 You are asking about the weather tomorrow. (will)
   ....

Test 9

Test 9C

Each of these replies is wrong. Write the correct reply.
- ▶ Is it going to snow? ~ ~~I'm not thinking it.~~   *I don't think so.*
1. Has the computer arrived? ~ ~~No, not.~~
2. Don't you like curry? ~ ~~Yes, I hate it.~~
3. Will you be in tonight? ~ ~~Yes, I expect.~~
4. Horrible weather. ~ ~~It isn't very nice, isn't it?~~
5. Would you like a sweet? ~ ~~Yes, right.~~
6. I'm quite tired now. ~ ~~Too am I.~~
7. You might catch my cold. ~ ~~I don't hope to.~~
8. The first train didn't stop. ~ ~~Neither the second.~~

Test 9D

Rupert is at a job interview. Someone is asking him questions. Write the questions.
- ▶ Interviewer: *Where do you live?*
  Rupert: Oh, I live in Longtown.
1. Interviewer: ....
   Rupert: I'm twenty-three.
2. Interviewer: ....
   Rupert: Yes, I went to college.
3. Interviewer: ....
   Rupert: My interests? I don't have any, really.
4. Interviewer: ....
   Rupert: Which company? Oh, I work for BX Electric.
5. Interviewer: ....
   Rupert: Nothing. There's nothing I don't like about my job.

Test 9E

Put in the missing word.
- ▶ *How* does this phone work? ~ You press this button.
1. The new building looks awful. ~ I agree. It .... look very nice.
2. Could you give me a receipt, please? ~ Yes, of ....
3. This chair isn't very comfortable. ~ And .... is this bed.
4. Didn't you watch 'Frankenstein' last night? ~ .... , I hate horror films.
5. What's this wood .... ? ~ I'm going to make a table.
6. I didn't say the wrong thing, ... I? ~ Well, you weren't very polite.
7. Will there be any free gifts? ~ No, there ....
8. Have they sent you some money? ~ No, I'm afraid ....
9. Don't drop those plates, ... you? ~ OK, I'll be careful.
10. How .... is it to the station? ~ About half a mile.
11. Do those shoes fit you? ~ Yes, I think ....
12. Why .... we have a picnic? ~ Yes, good idea.
13. .... foot is hurting? ~ My right one.
14. I feel a bit cold actually. ~ Yes, ... do I.
15. Who .... eaten their ice-cream? ~ Oh, it's mine. I'm just going to eat it.
16. .... of these magazines would you like? ~ This one, please.

44 Ability: can, could and be able to

A Can and can't

Vicky: How many instruments **can** you play, Natasha?
Natasha: Three – the violin, the clarinet and the piano.
Vicky: That's terrific. You haven't got a piano here, though.
Natasha: No, but I **can** go to the music room in college and play the one in there.
Vicky: I'm not musical at all. I **can't** even sing.

We use **can** to say that something is possible: that someone has an ability (*Natasha **can** play the piano*) or an opportunity (*She **can** go to the music room*). **Can** is usually pronounced /kən/ but sometimes we say /kæn/. The negative is **cannot** /ˈkænɒt/ or **can't** /kɑːnt/.

B Can and be able to

In the present tense, **be able to** is a little more formal and less usual than **can**.
　　*Emma is good with computers. She **can** write/**is able to** write programs.*
But in some structures we always use **be able to**, not **can**.
To-infinitive:　　　　*It's nice **to be able to** go to the opera.* (NOT ~~to can go~~)
After a modal verb:　*Melanie **might be able to** help us.*
Present perfect:　　 *It's been quiet today. I've **been able to** get some work done.*

For the future we use **can** or **will be able to** but NOT ~~will can~~.
　　*If we earn some money, we **can** go/we'**ll be able to** go on holiday next summer.*
　　*I'm afraid I **can't** come/I **won't be able to** come to the disco on Friday.*
But to suggest a possible future action, we normally use **can**.
　　*Let's have lunch together. We **can** go to that new restaurant.*

C Could and was/were able to

For ability or opportunity in the past, we use **could** or **was/were able to**.
　　*Natasha **could** play (OR **was able to** play) the piano when she was four.*
　　*In those days we had a car, so we **could** travel (OR **were able to** travel) very easily.*

To say that the ability or opportunity resulted in a particular action, something that really happened, we use **was/were able to** but not **could**.
　　*The plane **was able to** take off at eleven o'clock, after the fog had lifted.*
　　*Luckily Mark **was able to** get (OR succeeded in getting) the work done in time.*
　　*The drivers **were able to** stop (OR managed to stop) before they crashed into each other.*

Compare these two sentences.

The children **could** swim when they were quite young. (a past ability)	The children **were able to** swim across the river. (a past action)

In negative sentences and questions, we can use either form.
　　*It was foggy, so the plane **couldn't/wasn't able to** take off.*
　　*The pool was closed, so they **couldn't/weren't able to** have a swim.*
　　***Could** you/**Were** you **able to** describe the man to the police?*

We normally use **could** (not **was/were able to**) with verbs of seeing etc, and with verbs of thinking.
　　*We **could see** the village in the distance.*
　　*As soon as Harriet opened the door, she **could smell** gas.*
　　*I **couldn't understand** what was happening.*

44 Exercises

1 Can and can't (A)

Look at the pictures and say what they can or can't do. Use these words: *climb trees, juggle, lift the weights, play the violin, walk on his hands*

▶ *He can walk on his hands.*
1 .... 3 ....
2 .... 4 ....

2 Can and be able to (B)

Harriet is visiting David, who hurt himself when he fell off a ladder. Complete the conversation using *can* or a form of *be able to*. Sometimes there is more than one possible answer.

Harriet: Hello, David. I'm sorry I haven't (▶) *been able to come* (come) and see you before.
I've been really busy lately. How are you?
David: I'm OK, thanks. (1) .... (I / walk) around now.
The doctor says (2) .... (I / go) back to work soon.
It'll be nice (3) .... (get) out again. I hate being stuck here like this.
I haven't (4) .... (do) anything interesting.

3 Could and was/were able to (C)

▶ Which is closer to the meaning of the sentence 'Years ago I could run a marathon'?
   a) ☐ I ran a marathon at one particular time in the past.
   b) ☑ I was once fit enough to run a very long way.
1 Which of these sentences is correct?
   I was ill, so I couldn't go to the party.
   I was ill, so I wasn't able to go to the party.
   a) ☐ Only the first one.   b) ☐ Only the second one.   c) ☐ Both of them.
2 Which is closer to the meaning of the sentence 'Sarah was able to leave work early yesterday'?
   a) ☐ Sarah left work early yesterday.
   b) ☐ Sarah had the opportunity to leave work early yesterday, but we don't know if she took it.

4 Could and was/were able to (C)

Put in *could* or *was/were able to*. Sometimes either is possible. Use a negative if necessary.
▶ Suddenly all the lights went out. We *couldn't* see a thing.
1 The computer went wrong, but luckily Emma .... put it right again.
2 There was a big party last night. You .... hear the music half a mile away.
3 I learnt to read music as a child. I .... read it when I was five.
4 People heard warnings about the flood, and they .... move out in time.
5 The train was full. I .... find a seat anywhere.

45 Permission: can, may, could and be allowed to

A Asking permission

We use **can**, **could** or **may** to ask for permission.
Can I use your pen?
Could we borrow your ladder, please? ~ Well, I'm using it at the moment.
May I see the letter? ~ Certainly.
Could often sounds more polite than **can**. **May** is rather formal.

B Giving and refusing permission

To give permission we use **can** or **may** (but not **could**).
You can wait in my office if you like.
Could I borrow your calculator? ~ Of course you can.
You may telephone from here. (a written notice)
May is formal and is not often used in speech.

You may telephone from here

Bicycles must not be left here

To refuse permission we use **can't** or **may not** (but not **couldn't**).
Could we picnic here? ~ I'm sorry. I'm afraid you can't.
Members may not bring more than two guests into the club.
We can also use **must not**.
Luggage must not be left unattended.

C Talking about permission

We sometimes talk about rules made by someone else. To do this we use **can**, **could** and **be allowed to**.

We use **can** to talk about the present, and we use **could** for the past.
Present: *Each passenger can take one bag onto the plane.*
Past: *In the 1920s you could drive without taking a test.*
We can also use **be allowed to**.
Present: *Passengers are allowed to take one bag onto the plane.*
Future: *Will I be allowed to record the interview on tape?*
Past: *We weren't allowed to look round the factory yesterday.*

For a general permission in the past we use either **could** or **was/were allowed to**.
I could always stay/I was always allowed to stay up late as a child.
But to say that the permission resulted in a particular action, something that really happened, we use **was/were allowed to** (but not **could**).
I was allowed to leave work early yesterday.
We were allowed to go into the control room when we looked around the power station.

Compare these questions with **may** and **be allowed to**.

ASKING FOR PERMISSION	ASKING ABOUT PERMISSION
May I take a photo of you? (= Will you allow it?)	Are we **allowed to** take photos? (= What is the rule?)

45 Exercises

1 Asking permission (A)

How would you ask for permission in these situations?
Use *Can I ...?*, *Could I ...?* or *May I ...?* and these verbs: *borrow, join, look at, use*

▶ You are at a friend's flat. You want to make a phone call.
   Can I use your phone?
1 You need a calculator. The person sitting next to you has got one.
   ....
2 You have gone into a café. Three people who you know from work are sitting at a table. You go over to the table.
   ....
3 You had to go to a lecture, but you were ill. Your friend went to the lecture and took notes. Next day you are well again and you see your friend.
   ....

2 Giving and refusing permission (B)

A policeman is telling you what the signs mean. What does he say?
Use *can* and *can't* and these verbs: *drop, go, have, park, play, smoke, turn*

Policeman:
▶ *You can't go this way.*
▶ *You can park here.*
1 ....
2 ....
3 ....
4 ....
5 ....

3 Be allowed to (C)

Put in the correct forms.
Rita: I hear you've moved into a new flat with a couple of friends.
Emma: Yes, it's a nice flat, but the landlady is really strict. (▶) *We aren't allowed to do* (we / not / allow / do) anything. It was my birthday last month, and
       (1) .... (I / not / allow / have) a party.
Rita: Oh, (2) .... (we / allow / have) parties at our place, luckily.
       (3) .... (we / allow / do) anything, more or less.
       We're hoping to have an all-night party soon, but I'm not absolutely sure if
       (4) .... (we / allow / hold) it.

4 May I ...? or Am I allowed to ...? (C)

Are you asking for permission, or are you asking what the rule is? Put in *May I ...?* or *Am I allowed to ...?*
▶ *May I* use your computer?
▶ *Am I allowed to* smoke in this cinema?
1 .... cross the road here?
2 .... ask you a personal question?
3 .... rollerblade in this park?
4 .... drive a car without insurance?
5 .... read your magazine?

46 Possibility and certainty: may, might, could, must, etc

A May, might and could

Rachel: *Whose bag is that?*
Daniel: *I don't know. It **may** belong to Maria's friend.*
Vicky: *It **might** be a bomb. It **could** explode at any moment.*

We use **may** or **might** to say that something is possible or that it is quite likely. We can use them for the present or the future.
   *It **may/might** be a bomb.* (= Perhaps it is a bomb.)
   *I **may/might** go to the disco tomorrow.* (= Perhaps I will go to the disco.)

We can use **could** to say that something is possible.
   *The story **could** be true, I suppose.* (= Possibly it is true.)
   *You **could** win a million pounds!* (= Possibly you will win a million pounds.)
Sometimes **could** means only a small possibility. It is possible (but not likely) that you will win a million pounds.

In some situations we can use **may**, **might** or **could**.
   *It **may/might/could** rain later.*

After **may**, **might** or **could** we can use a continuous form (**be** + an ing-form).
   *That man **may/might be watching** us.* (= Perhaps he is watching us.)
   *Sarah **may/might be working** late tonight.* (= Perhaps she will be working late.)
   *I'm not sure where Matthew is. He **could be playing** squash.* (= Possibly he is playing squash.)

B May, might and could in the negative

The negative forms are **may not**, **might not/mightn't**, and **could not/couldn't**.

MAY NOT AND MIGHT NOT	COULDN'T
Something negative is possible.	Something is impossible.
*Daniel **may not** get the job.*	*Vicky is afraid of heights. She **couldn't** climb onto the roof.*
*Tom **might not** be in.*	
*I **mightn't** finish the marathon tomorrow.*	*I'm completely unfit. I **couldn't** run a marathon.*
(It is possible that I will not finish it.)	(It is impossible for me to run it.)

C Must and can't

MUST	CAN'T
We use **must** when we realize that something is certainly true.	We use **can't** when we realize that something is impossible.
*She isn't answering the phone. She **must** be out.*	*We haven't walked far. You **can't** be tired yet.*
*I had my keys a moment ago. They **must** be here somewhere.*	*Life **can't** be easy when you have to spend it in a wheelchair.*
*Andrew isn't here. He **must** be working in the library.*	*Nick **can't** be touring Scotland. I saw him here this morning.*

▷ 53 **Might/could/must have been**   ▷ page 379 **Mustn't** in American English   ▷ 51A **Could** in suggestions

46 Exercises

1 Might be and might be doing (A)

Vicky and Rachel are at college. They're looking for their friend Natasha. Complete the conversation. Use *may* or *might* and the verb in brackets. Sometimes you need to use the continuous.

Vicky: I can't find Natasha. Have you seen her?
Rachel: (▶) *She might be* (she / be) in the music room. (▶) *She may be practising* (she / practise).
Vicky: No, she isn't there. I thought (1) .... (she / be) with you.
Rachel: It's a nice day. (2) .... (she / be) on the lawn.
(3) .... (she / sit) out there reading the paper.
Or (4) .... (she / have) a coffee.
(5) .... (you / find) her in the canteen.
Emma: No, I've looked there.
Rachel: Well, here comes Jessica. (6) .... (she / know).

2 May and might (A–B)

Add a sentence with *may* or *might* (both are correct).
▶ I'm not sure if it's going to rain. *It might rain.*
▶ I don't know if we'll see an elephant. *We may see one.*
1 I can't say whether Daniel will win. ....
2 I haven't decided if I'm having a holiday. ....
3 I don't know if we'll get an invitation. ....
4 I've no idea whether Sarah will be late. ....
5 I'm not sure if my friends are visiting me. ....

3 Mightn't and couldn't (B)

Put in *mightn't* or *couldn't*.
▶ I've got one or two things to do, so I *mightn't* have time to come out tonight.
▶ David *couldn't* work as a taxi driver. He can't drive.
1 We're going to need lots of glasses. We .... have enough, you know.
2 Mark .... be in the office tomorrow. He thinks he's getting a cold.
3 We .... possibly have a dog, living in a small flat like this.
4 How can you work with all this noise? I .... work in such conditions.
5 Don't ring tomorrow because I .... be in. I'm not sure what I'm doing.

4 Must, can't and might (A, C)

A reporter is interviewing Mrs Miles for a TV news programme.
Complete the conversation. Put in *must*, *can't* or *might*.

Mrs Miles: My name's Nora Miles, and I'm going to do a parachute jump.
Reporter: Mrs Miles, you're seventy-three, and you're going to jump out of an aeroplane.
You (▶) *must* be mad. You (1) .... be serious.
Mrs Miles: It really (2) .... be wonderful to look down from the sky.
I've always wanted to try it.
Reporter: But anything could happen. You (3) .... be injured or even killed.
I wouldn't take the risk.
Mrs Miles: Well, young man, your life (4) .... be much fun if you never take risks.
You ought to try it. You never know – you (5) .... enjoy it.
Reporter: Enjoy it? You (6) .... be joking!

47 Necessity: **must** and **have to**

A Present, past and future

We use **must** and **have to/has to** to say that something is necessary.
   You'll be leaving college soon. You **must** think about your future.
   We're very busy at the office. I **have to** work on Saturday morning.
   Mark **has to** get the car repaired. There's something wrong with the brakes.

When we use the past, or the future with **will**, we need a form of **have to**.
   Emma **had to** go to the dentist yesterday. NOT ~~She must go to the dentist yesterday~~.
   That wasn't very good. We'**ll have to** do better next time.
And in other structures we also use a form of **have to**, not **must**.
To-infinitive: I don't want **to have to** wait in a queue for ages.
After a modal verb: Emma has toothache. She **might have to** go to the dentist.
Present perfect: Mark **has had to** drive all the way to Glasgow.

For negatives and questions with **have to/has to** and **had to**, we use a form of **do**.
   I **don't have to** work on Sundays.   Why **does** Andrew **have to** study every evening?
   Did you **have to** pay for your second cup of coffee? ~ No, I didn't.
I don't have to work means that it is not necessary for me to work (see Unit 48B).

B Must or have to?

Both **must** and **have to** express necessity, but we use them differently.

MUST	HAVE TO

We use **must** when the speaker feels that something is necessary.
   You **must** exercise. (I'm telling you.)
   We **must** be quiet. (I'm telling you.)
	We use **have to** when the situation makes something necessary.
	   I **have to** exercise. (The doctor told me.)
	   We **have to** be quiet. (That's the rule.)

I/we must can also express a wish.
   I **must** buy a newspaper. I want to see the racing results.
   We **must** invite Claire. She's wonderful company.
	I **have to** buy a newspaper. The boss asked me to get one.
	   We **have to** invite Trevor and Laura. They invited us last time.

C Have got to

Have got to means the same as **have to**, but **have got to** is informal. We use it mainly in the present.
   I **have to/I've got to** make my sandwiches.   My father **has to/has got to** take these pills.
   Do we **have to** apply/**Have** we **got to** apply for a visa?

▷ 48 **Mustn't** and **needn't**

47 Exercises

1 Have to (A)

Complete the conversations. Use the words in brackets and a form of *have to*.

▶ Melanie: David's broken his leg. *He's had to go* (he's / go) to hospital.
  Harriet: Oh no! How long *will he have to stay* (will / he / stay) there?
  Melanie: I don't know.

1 Claire: I parked my car outside the hairdresser's, and while I was in there, the police took the car away. I've got it back now. But .... (I / pay) a lot of money.
  Henry: How much .... (you / pay)?
  Claire: Two hundred pounds!

2 Trevor: That door doesn't shut properly. .... (you / slam) it every time.
  Laura: .... (you / will / fix) it then, won't you?

3 Jessica: You're always taking exams. Why .... (you / take) so many?
  Andrew: .... (I / will / take) a lot more if I want a good job.

4 Mike: We're in a new house now. .... (we / move). The old place was too small.
  Nick: Did it take you long to find a house?
  Mike: No, we found one easily. .... (we / not / look) very hard. But it was in bad condition. .... (we've / do) a lot of work on it.

5 Nick: My brother .... (start) work at five o'clock in the morning.
  Melanie: That's pretty early. What time .... (he / get) up?
  Nick: Half past three.

2 Must and have to (B)

Write a sentence with *must*, *have to* or *has to*.

▶ The sign says: 'Passengers must show their tickets.'
  So *passengers have to show their tickets.*
▶ The children have to be in bed by nine.
  Their parents said: *'You must be in bed by nine.'*

1 Laura has to get to work on time.
  Her boss told her: ....
2 The police told Nick: 'You must keep your dog under control.'
  So Nick ....
3 The pupils have to listen carefully.
  The teacher says: ....
4 The new sign says: 'Visitors must report to the security officer.'
  So now ....

3 Must or have to? (B)

Put in *must* or *have to/has to*. Choose which is best for the situation.

▶ I *have to* go to the airport. I'm meeting someone.
1 You .... lock the door when you go out. There've been a lot of break-ins recently.
2 Daniel .... go to the bank. He hasn't any money.
3 I .... work late tomorrow. We're very busy at the office.
4 You really .... make less noise. I'm trying to concentrate.
5 I think you .... pay to park here. I'll just go and read that notice.
6 You really .... hurry up, Vicky. We don't want to be late.
7 I .... put the heating on. I feel really cold.

48 Necessity: mustn't, needn't, etc

A Mustn't or needn't?

We use **must** to say that something is necessary (see Unit 47).
> You **must** be careful with those glasses.   I **must** remember my key.

Now compare **mustn't** and **needn't**.

MUSTN'T	NEEDN'T

We use **mustn't** /ˈmʌsnt/ to say that something is a bad idea.
    You **mustn't** drop those glasses. They'll break.
    I **mustn't** forget my key, or I won't get in.
    You **mustn't** wear your best clothes. You'll get them dirty.
	We use **needn't** when something is not necessary.
	
	    You **needn't** wash those glasses. They're clean.
	    We **needn't** make sandwiches. There's a café.
	    You **needn't** wear your best clothes. You can wear what you like.

B Don't have to and don't need to

We can use **don't have to** and **don't need to** when something is not necessary.
The meaning is the same as **needn't**.
> You **don't have to** / **don't need to** wash those glasses. They're clean.
> Mark **doesn't have to** / **doesn't need to** finish the report today. He can do it at the weekend.

For American usage see page 379.

For the past we use *didn't*.
> The food was free. We **didn't have to** pay/We **didn't need to** pay for it.

C Didn't need to or needn't have?

> Daniel hadn't booked a seat, but luckily the train wasn't full. He **didn't need to** stand.

> Trevor and Laura booked a table for dinner. But the restaurant was empty. They **needn't have** booked a table.

DIDN'T NEED TO	NEEDN'T HAVE

We use **didn't need to** when something was not necessary. Standing was not necessary because there were seats.
    Mark **didn't need to** hurry. He had lots of time. He drove slowly along the motorway.
    We **didn't need to** go to the supermarket because we had plenty of food.
	We use **needn't have** + a past participle for something we did which we now know was not necessary, e.g. booking a table.
	    Mark **needn't have** hurried. After driving at top speed, he arrived half an hour early.
	    We **needn't have** gone to the supermarket. We already had a pizza for tonight.

Sometimes we can use **didn't need to** when the action happened, even though it was not necessary.
> Mark **didn't need to** hurry, but he drove at top speed. He likes driving fast.

48 Exercises

1 Must, mustn't or needn't? (A)

Put in *must, mustn't* or *needn't*.
▶ Laura: You *needn't* take an umbrella. It isn't going to rain.
  Trevor: Well, I don't know. It might do.
  Laura: Don't lose it then. You *mustn't* leave it on the bus.
1 Vicky: Come on. We .... hurry. We .... be late.
  Rachel: It's only ten past. We .... hurry. There's lots of time.
2 Claire: My sister and I are going a different way.
  Guide: Oh, you .... go off on your own. It isn't safe.
  We .... keep together in a group.
3 David: I'll put these cups in the dishwasher.
  Melanie: No, you .... put them in there. It might damage them.
  In fact, we .... wash them at all. We didn't use them.
4 Secretary: I .... forget to type this letter.
  Mark: Yes, it .... go in the post today because it's quite urgent.
  But the report isn't so important. You .... type the report today.

2 Don't have to (B)

An old woman is talking to a reporter from her local newspaper. She is comparing life today with life in the past. Complete her sentences using *don't have to, doesn't have to* or *didn't have to*.
▶ We had to make our own fun in the old days. There wasn't any television then. These days people *don't have to make their own fun.*
1 There's so much traffic now. You have to wait ages to cross the road. In those days you
  ....
2 I had to work long hours when I was young. But children today have it easy.
  They ....
3 My father had to work in a factory when he was twelve. Just imagine! Today a twelve-year-old child
  ....
4 There's so much crime today, isn't there? People have to lock their doors now. It was better in the old days when people ....
5 We had to wash our clothes by hand. There weren't any washing-machines, you know. Nowadays people ....

3 Didn't need to or needn't have? (C)

Write the sentences using *didn't need to* or *needn't have*.
▶ The previous owners had already decorated the flat, so *we didn't need to decorate it ourselves* (we / decorate / it / ourselves).
1 Luckily we were able to sell our old flat before we bought the new one,
  so .... (we / borrow / any money).
2 It was very hot yesterday, so I watered all the flowers.
  And now it's pouring with rain. .... (I / bother).
3 We've done the journey much more quickly than I expected.
  .... (we / leave / so early).
4 A friend had already given me a free ticket to the exhibition,
  so .... (I / pay / to go in).
5 Service was included in the bill, so .... (you / tip / the waiter).
  It was a waste of money.

MODAL VERBS 117

49 Should, ought to, had better and be supposed to

A Introduction

B Should and ought to

We use **should** and **ought to** to say what is the best thing or the right thing to do. There is no difference in meaning.

*You're not very well. Perhaps you **should** see a doctor.*
*Your uncle was very kind to me. I **ought to** write him a letter of thanks.*
*People **shouldn't** break/**oughtn't to** break their promises.*

We can also use **should** and **ought to** in questions to ask for advice.

*Where **should** I put this picture, do you think?*
*It's a difficult problem. How **ought** we **to** deal with it?*

After **should** or **ought to** we can use a continuous form (**be** + an ing-form).

*It's half past six already. I **should be cooking** the tea.*
*Why are you sitting here doing nothing? You **ought to be working**.*

C Had better

We use **had better** to say what is the best thing to do in a situation.

*It's cold. The children **had better** wear their coats.*
*The neighbours are complaining. We**'d better** turn the music down.*
*My wife is waiting for me. I**'d better not** be late.*

We could also use **should** or **ought to** in these examples, although **had better** is stronger. The speaker sees the action as necessary and expects that it will happen.

D Be supposed to

We use **be supposed to** when we are talking about the normal or correct way of doing things.

*The guests **are supposed to** buy flowers for the hostess.*
*Look at these cars. This area **is supposed to** be kept clear of traffic.*
*The bus driver needs to concentrate. You**'re not supposed to** talk to him.*
*How **am** I **supposed to** cook this? ~ It tells you on the packet.*

We can use **was/were supposed to** for the past.

*It's eleven o'clock. You **were supposed to** be here at ten thirty, you know.*

▷ 52D **Shall** used to ask for advice

49 Exercises

1 Should and ought to (B)

Put in *should*, *shouldn't*, *ought* or *oughtn't*. (Look for the word *to*.)

Vicky: I can't come out tonight, Rachel. I (▶) *ought* to do some more work.
I'm behind with everything. I've got so much to do.
Rachel: You (1) .... worry so much, Vicky. Don't panic.
You (2) .... to relax sometimes. You (3) .... take a break.
Vicky: I know I (4) .... panic, but I do. I can't help it.
Rachel: Anyway, you're doing OK, aren't you? Your results have been good.
You (5) .... be pleased. You (6) .... to invent problems for yourself.

2 Had better (C)

What would you say in these situations? Add a sentence with *'d better (not)* and the words in brackets.
▶ Vicky doesn't feel well. She's got a headache. What might you say to her? (an aspirin)
You'd better take an aspirin.
1 You and Daniel are meeting Rachel. You've both arrived, but she isn't there yet. She is usually late. (wait) ....
2 Ilona is leaving her bike outside the swimming-pool. You know it won't be safe if she leaves it unlocked. (lock) ....
3 Some friends are going to visit you today. Your room is in a mess. What do you think? (tidy) ....
4 Nick is giving you a lift in his old sports car. There's a speed limit, and there's a police car behind you. (too fast) ....
5 There's an exam tomorrow. Neither you nor Rachel have done any work for it. (some revision) ....

3 Be supposed to (D)

Add a sentence using *be (not) supposed to* and these verbs:
leave it outside, report to the police, stand in a queue, take two before meals, watch it
▶ You shouldn't bring your bike in here. *You're supposed to leave it outside.*
1 I've got some pills. ....
2 Foreign visitors can't travel freely here. ....
3 Be careful waiting for a bus in England. ....
4 This film isn't for under-sixteens. ....

4 Should, ought to, had better and be supposed to (A–D)

Complete the conversation. Use *should*, *ought to*, *had better* or *be supposed to* and the verbs in brackets. Usually there is more than one correct answer.

Vicky: What time (▶) *are we supposed to be* (we / be) at the coffee morning?
Rachel: The invitation says ten o'clock.
Vicky: Well, it's ten now. (1) .... (we / hurry).
(2) .... (we / not / be) late.
Rachel: Oh, it won't matter if we're a bit late.
Vicky: I think it would be rude, wouldn't it? I don't think people
(3) .... (arrive) late when they've been invited to something.
Rachel: You worry too much. (4) .... (you / not / take) everything so seriously, Vicky. It's a coffee morning, not a job interview.
(5) .... (we / not / get) there exactly on time.

MODAL VERBS 119

50 Asking people to do things

A Polite requests

We can use **can** or **could** in a request, when we ask someone to do something.
  Can *everyone be quiet for a minute, please?*
  Can *you keep me informed? ~ Yes, of course.*
  Could *you lend me ten pounds until tomorrow? ~ Sorry, I haven't got ten pounds.*
  I wonder if you **could** *explain something to me. ~ I'll try.*
Could is often more polite than **can**.

In a request we can also use **Do you mind …?** or **Would you mind…?** with an ing-form.
  Do you mind *waiting a moment? ~ No, I can wait.*
  Would you mind *sitting in the back? ~ No, not at all.*
We can also use **Would you like to …?**
  Would you like to *lay the table for me? ~ Yes, of course.*
We do not use **Do you like …?** for a request. NOT *Do you like to lay the table for me?*

It is always worth taking the trouble to use one of these request forms in English. We do not normally say *Lay the table for me*. This can sound very abrupt and impolite without a phrase like **Could you …?**

B The imperative

We can sometimes use the imperative form to tell someone what to do.
  Bring *another chair.*   **Hurry** *up or we'll be late.*
We form the negative with **don't**.
  Don't be *silly.*   **Don't make** *so much noise.*

We can use an imperative when we are with friends in an informal situation. But we do not use it to a stranger or in a more formal situation.
  Excuse me. **Could you** *tell me the way to Oxford Street, please?*
  NOT *Tell me the way to Oxford Street, please.*
  Would you mind *sending me a copy of your catalogue?*
  NOT *Send me a copy of your catalogue.*

Even people in authority often avoid using the imperative to give orders. Instead they can use **I want/I'd like you to …, You must …**, or a polite request form.
  Manager: **I want you** *all* **to** *be at the meeting.*
  Policeman: **You must** *wait until you see the green light.*
  Doctor: **Could you** *lie down on the bed, please?*

C Asking for things

We use **Can I/we have…?** and **Could I/we have …?** when we ask someone to give us something.
  Can we have *our room key, please?*   **Could I have** *a receipt, please?*
We can also say *Could you give me a receipt, please?* but we do not use the imperative.
  NOT *Give me a receipt.*

When we ask for something in a shop or a café, we can simply name what we want, but we must say **please**.
  A large white loaf, **please.**   *Two coffees,* **please.**
We can also use **I'd like …** or **I'll have …**
  I'd like *a chicken sandwich, please.*   **I'll have** *a coffee.*

▷ 45 **Can** and **could** for permission   ▷ 52B **Would like**

50 Exercises

1 Asking people to do things (A–C)

Complete these sentences and write them in: *Can I … a fork, please? Could … have a towel, …? Could you … the … for me? Would you … answering the phone?*

▶ *Could you open the door for me?*
1 ....
2 ....
3 ....

2 Asking people to do things (A–C)

Mr Atkins is the boss at Zedco. He tells everyone what to do. Complete his sentences. Use these words: *can, could, have, like, mind, must, want, wonder, would*

▶ Would you *mind* making some tea, Alan?
1 You .... inform me of any developments.
2 Could I .... the latest sales figures, please?
3 Would you .... to arrange a meeting some time next week, Fiona?
4 I .... everyone to read the report.
5 .... I see the file, please, Mark?
6 .... you mind putting this in writing?
7 I .... if you could translate this letter, Linda.
8 .... you meet our customer at the airport?

3 Asking people to do things (A–C)

Read about each situation and then make a request. Use the word in brackets.

▶ It is cold in the restaurant. Ask the waiter to shut the window. (could)
   Could you shut the window, please?
1 You are buying a coat. Ask the assistant for a receipt. (can)
   ....
2 You want to know the time. Ask someone in the street. (could)
   Excuse me. ....
3 You need someone to help you. Ask a friend. (can)
   ....
4 You have bought some food, but you haven't got a bag. Ask the assistant. (could)
   ....
5 You are carrying a tray. Ask someone to clear a space on the table. (mind)
   ....
6 You are on the phone. You want to speak to the manager. (could)
   ....

51 Suggestions, offers and invitations

A Suggestions

We can use **Shall we** ...? or **Let's** to make a suggestion.
*It's a lovely day. **Shall we** go for a walk? ~ Yes, OK.*
***Let's** play some music. ~ Good idea.*

We can also use **could** for a suggestion.
*We **could** watch this comedy on TV tonight. ~ Well, actually I've seen it before.*
*You **could** invite a few friends around. ~ Yes, why not?*

We can also use **Why don't** ...?
***Why don't** we have a look round the market?*

To ask for a suggestion we use **shall**, **should** or **can**.
*Where **shall/should** we go for our holiday? ~ What about Spain?*
*What **can** I get Claire for her birthday? ~ I've no idea.*

B Offers

We can use **will** or **can** to offer to do something.
I'll carry your bag. ~ Oh, thanks.
*We **can** give you a lift. ~ Oh, that would be great. Thank you.*

We can also use question forms with **shall** or **can**.
***Shall** we pay you the money now? ~ Oh, there's no hurry.*
***Can** I get a taxi for you? ~ Yes, please.*

To offer food or drink, we use **would like**.
***Would** you **like** one of these chocolates? ~ Yes, please. Thank you.*
***Would** anyone **like** more coffee? ~ No, thanks.*

We can also use **Will/Won't you have** ...?
***Will you have** a biscuit? ~ Thank you.*
***Won't you have** something to drink? ~ Not for me, thank you.*

In informal speech we can use the imperative.
***Have** a biscuit. ~ Thank you.*

C Invitations

The words we use in invitations are similar to those we use in offers of food and drink (see B).
To invite someone, we often use **Would you like to** ...?
***Would** you **like to** have lunch with us? ~ Yes, I'd love to. Thank you.*

Would like can have a verb with **to** after it, or an object with a noun.
*Would you **like to** stay the night. ~ Oh, that's very kind of you.*
*Would you **like a** bed for the night? ~ Are you sure it's not too much trouble?*

We can also use **Will/Won't you** ...?
***Will you** join us for coffee? ~ Yes. Thanks.*   ***Won't you** sit down?*

In informal speech we can use the imperative.
***Come** and have coffee with us.*   *Please **sit** down.*

▷ 52 **Will, would, shall** and **should**

51 Exercises

1 Suggestions, offers and invitations (A–C)

Put the words in the right order and write in the sentences:
post / for you / I'll / that letter
for a minute / shall / stop / we
have / one of these / won't / you
a game / like / would / you

▶ Won't you have one of these?
1 ....
2 ....
3 ....

2 Suggestions and offers (A–B)

Complete the conversation. Put in *could, shall, will* or *would*.
Daniel: Where (▶) *shall* we have our picnic, then?
Rachel: This looks all right. (1) .... we sit here?
Emma: Oh, I've forgotten the sausages. They're in the car.
Matthew: (2) .... I get them?
Emma: Oh, thanks, Matthew.
Vicky: We (3) .... sit by those trees. It looks nicer over there.
Rachel: No, it's fine here.
Daniel: Yes, it's better here, I think.
Emma: (4) .... you like a sandwich, Vicky?
Vicky: Oh, thank you.
Emma: (5) .... you have one, Rachel?
Matthew: And here are the sausages. (6) .... anyone like one?

3 Suggestions, offers and invitations (A–C)

What would you say? There is more than one correct answer.
▶ A friend has called at your flat. Invite him to come in.
  Would you like to come in?
1 Offer your visitor a cup of tea.
  ....
2 You don't know what to say in your letter. Ask your friend for a suggestion.
  ....
3 You are walking in town with a friend. Suggest having a cup of coffee.
  ....
4 A woman you know is afraid to walk home alone. Offer to walk home with her.
  ....
5 You are writing to a friend. Invite her to visit you one weekend.
  ....

52 Will, would, shall and should

A Will and would for predictions

We can use **will** for a prediction (see Unit 25C).
It's midnight, and Sarah is still working. She'll be tired tomorrow.
We're going to Cornwall for the weekend. ~ That'll be nice.
Wait a minute while I send this e-mail. It won't take long.

We use **would** for a past prediction or a prediction about a possible situation.
Past: *At midnight Sarah was still working. She would be tired the next day.*
Possible: *How about going to Cornwall next weekend? ~ That would be nice.*
I wouldn't enjoy a camping holiday.

We can use **shall** instead of **will**, and **should** instead of **would**, but only in the first person, after **I** and **we**.
I will/shall be twenty-five in June.
We would/should like to meet your family. But NOT *My friend should like …*
Shall and **should** are a little formal here.

B Would like

We can use **would like**, usually shortened to **'d like**, when we ask for something.
I'd like a brochure, please.   We'd like to order our drinks first.
This is a more polite way of saying *I want a brochure*, for example.

We also use **would like** in offers and invitations.
Would you like a free gift?   Would you like to visit the museum with us?

C Decisions and refusals

We can use **will** for an instant decision or for an offer.
Decision: *Tea or coffee? ~ I'll have coffee, please.* (see Unit 23B)
Offer: *I'll wait for you if you like. ~ Oh, thanks. I won't be long.*

We use **won't** and **wouldn't** for a refusal.
The strikers won't go back to work until they get a pay increase.
The key went in the lock, but it wouldn't turn.
I won't … is a strong refusal.
I won't listen to any more of this nonsense.

D Shall and should

We use **Shall I …?** in offers and **Shall we …?** in suggestions.
Offer: *Shall I wait for you? ~ Oh, thanks. I won't be long.*
Suggestion: *Shall we go to the park? ~ Good idea.*
We also use **shall** to ask for a suggestion.
What shall we have for lunch?

We use either **shall** or **should** to ask for advice.
I'm in terrible trouble. What shall/should I do?
We use **should** to say what is the best thing or the right thing to do.
People should exercise regularly.
You shouldn't spend all your money as soon as you've earned it.

▷ 23 **Will** and **shall** ▷ 49 **Should** ▷ 51 Suggestions, offers and invitations

52 Exercises

1 Will and would (A–B)

Complete the conversation. Put in *will, won't, would* or *wouldn't*.

Emma: We (▶) *won't* be here next September. It's hard to believe, isn't it?
In a few months our student days (1) .... be over.
Matthew: It (2) .... be long now. I wish I had a job.
Then I (3) .... know where I was going.
Emma: Who knows what the future (4) .... bring?
Matthew: Why don't we get married, Emma? Then at least we (5) .... be together.
Emma: I don't think so, Matthew. It (6) .... be a good idea.
Matthew: I couldn't live without you, Emma.
Emma: I really (7) .... like to believe you, Matthew.

2 Some other uses of will and would (B–C)

Complete the conversations. Put in *will, won't, would* or *wouldn't* with these verbs:
eat, give, go, help, let, like, open, stand

▶ Vicky: Have you noticed how thin Jessica has got?
Rachel: She's on a diet. She *won't eat* anything except carrots.
1 Harriet: Mike and I .... you get everything ready.
Mike: Yes, we're quite willing to lend a hand.
2 Laura: You're late. I thought you were going to leave work early today.
Trevor: Sorry. The boss .... me go.
3 Mark: Sarah and I .... you a lift, Mike.
Sarah: Yes, we're going your way.
4 Harriet: I heard Rita has quarrelled with her friend?
Melanie: That's right. If he's invited to the party, she ....
5 Vicky: I've had enough of table tennis for one day.
Rachel: OK. Maybe Daniel .... a game with me.
6 Trevor: What's wrong with the washing-machine?
Laura: When I tried to use it earlier, the door ....
7 Mike: This lamp is always falling over.
Harriet: It .... up properly.

3 Will, would, shall and should (A–D)

What would you say? Use *will, would, shall* or *should*.
▶ Offer to make the tea.
Shall I make the tea?
1 Suggest going to the swimming-pool.
....
2 Refuse to take any risks.
....
3 Say politely that you want a shower.
....
4 Tell someone it's best they don't decide in a hurry.
....
5 Predict the end of the world in the year 3000.
....

53 It may/could/must have been, etc

A Introduction

Vicky, Emma and Matthew are at a club in town.
Vicky: Where's Daniel? He **should have been** here half an hour ago.
Emma: He **may have got** lost. It isn't easy to find this place.
Matthew: He **could have forgotten** all about it, I suppose.
Emma: He **can't have forgotten**. We were talking about it this morning.
Matthew: Well, something **must have delayed** him.

We can use a modal verb with the perfect (**have** + a past participle).
We use this structure to talk about possible past events.

B May have, might have and could have

We use these forms to say that possibly something happened in the past.
  He **may have got** lost. (= Perhaps he has got lost.)
  You **might have left** your keys at work. (= Perhaps you left them at work.)
  Someone **could have stolen** them. (= It is possible that someone stole them.)
We also use **could have** for an opportunity that we didn't take or a possible result that didn't happen.
  We **could have gone** out somewhere, but we were too tired.
  You were very lucky. There **could have been** a terrible accident.

C May not have, might not have and couldn't have

Compare these different uses.

MAY/MIGHT NOT HAVE	COULDN'T HAVE
Possibly something did not happen.	It is impossible that something happened.
Daniel **may not have caught** the bus. I expect he missed it.	Daniel **couldn't have caught** the bus. It doesn't run on Sundays.
(Perhaps he didn't catch it.)	(It is impossible for him to have caught the bus.)
I **might not have locked** the door.	
(Perhaps I didn't lock it.)	

D Must have and can't have

Must and **can't** are opposites.

MUST HAVE	CAN'T HAVE
My watch says it's only ten past two. It **must have stopped**.	You've only spent five minutes on that job. You **can't have done** it properly.
I realize it is certainly true that my watch has stopped.	I realize it is impossible that you did the job properly.

E Should have and ought to have

We use these forms when someone didn't do the right thing.
  We didn't play very well. We **should have played** better.
  I got lost. ~ Sorry. I **ought to have drawn** you a map.
  It was a lovely old building. They **shouldn't have knocked** it down.

▷ 29A **Will have done** ▷ 46 **May, might, could, must, can't** ▷ 48C **Needn't have** ▷ 49 **Should, ought to** ▷ 146 **Would have**

53 Exercises

1 It may/could/must have been, etc (B–D)

Look at each conversation and choose the best sentence, a) or b).
▶ Has the car broken down? ~ Well, we may have run out of petrol.
   a) ☐ I'm sure there's no petrol left. b) ☑ I think there's no petrol left.
1 You could have had a free holiday. ~ Yes, we could, but the dates weren't convenient.
   a) ☐ We had a free holiday. b) ☐ We didn't have a free holiday.
2 Did you record the programme? ~ I can't remember. I might not have done.
   a) ☐ I'm not sure if I recorded it. b) ☐ I certainly didn't record it.
3 Can't you find that newspaper? ~ No, someone must have thrown it away.
   a) ☐ It was necessary to throw it away. b) ☐ I realize now that it was thrown away.

2 Should and ought to (E and Unit 49B)

Complete the replies. Use *should/ought to* or *should have/ought to have*.
▶ Rita: Tom's car was stolen. He hadn't locked it.
   David: I suppose it's his fault then. *He should have locked it.*
▶ Tom: I can't sleep sometimes. My neighbours play music all night.
   Melanie: That's a nuisance. *They shouldn't play music all night.*
1 Mark: The picnickers left litter everywhere.
   Sarah: That's awful. ....
2 Emma: Jessica isn't very friendly, is she? She never says hello to people.
   Matthew: I know. ....
3 Rachel: I don't think Daniel's going to get that job. He was late for the interview.
   Natasha: That can't have looked very good. ....
4 Daniel: Did you see Vicky crossing the road? She didn't look.
   Emma: She could have been killed. ....

3 It may/could/must have been, etc (B–E)

Complete the conversation. Use *can't have*, *might have*, *must have* and *shouldn't have*.
Harriet: There's a parcel outside. The postman (▶) *must have left* (leave) it.
Mike: Well, (1) .... (he / leave) it outside. He isn't supposed to do that.
         Someone (2) .... (take) it. Why didn't he ring the bell?
Harriet: He always rings. (3) .... (you / be) out when he came.
Mike: I haven't been out. So (4) .... (he / ring) the bell.

4 It may/could/must have been, etc (B–E)

Complete the sentences. The second person agrees with the first. Use *might have*, *couldn't have*, etc.
▶ Matthew: I'm sure the computer didn't make a mistake. That's impossible.
   Emma: No, of course *the computer couldn't have made a mistake.*
1 Mark: I can't see the letter here now. So clearly someone posted it.
   Alan: Yes, ...
2 Natasha: It's possible Emma didn't hear the alarm.
   Rachel: Well, I suppose ....
3 Sarah: Henry drove at 100 miles an hour. Don't you think that's dangerous?
   Mark: Yes, I do. ....
4 Daniel: I just don't believe that Andrew has failed the exam.
   Vicky: Andrew? Impossible! ....

Test 10 Modal verbs (Units 44–53)

Test 10A

Decide which word is correct.
▶ *Could* I have some more tea, please?
   a) Could b) Shall c) Will d) Would
1 Everyone's asleep. We .... make a noise.
   a) couldn't b) mustn't c) needn't d) wouldn't
2 .... you like to go for a ride with us?
   a) Do b) Should c) Will d) Would
3 I wonder if this is the right way. It .... not be.
   a) can b) could c) might d) must
4 I don't think I want to see this film. ~ Oh, I think you .... enjoy it.
   a) can b) shall c) will d) would
5 I'm quite happy to walk. You .... drive me home.
   a) don't b) haven't c) mustn't d) needn't
6 .... I show you the way? ~ Oh, thank you.
   a) Do b) Shall c) Will d) Would
7 It's late. I think we .... better go.
   a) had b) have c) should d) would
8 We all tried to push the van, but it .... move.
   a) can't b) couldn't c) won't d) wouldn't

Test 10B

Some of these sentences are correct, and some have a word which should not be there. If the sentence is correct, put a tick (✓). If it is incorrect, cross the unnecessary word out of the sentence and write it in the space.
▶ I won't be able to come to the meeting.   ✓
▶ We ~~didn't~~ needn't have watered the garden because it's raining.   *didn't*
1 Would you like to be in the team?
2 Did people have to bring their own sleeping-bags?
3 I could to ski when I was quite young.
4 Would you mind for checking these figures?
5 We may be go swimming tomorrow.
6 I knew that I would be sorry later.
7 If you had fallen, you could have been hurt yourself.
8 We're not supposed to use this entrance.
9 You don't have to do all the work yourself.
10 Anna wasn't be allowed to take photos.

Test 10C

Write a second sentence so that it has a similar meaning to the first. Use the word in brackets.
▶ Perhaps Susan knows the address. (may)
   Susan may know the address.
1 We should be careful. (ought)
   ....

2 I managed to finish all my work. (able)
   ....

Test 10

3   I realize that it was a terrible experience for you. (must)

4   It's against the rules for players to have a drink. (allowed)

5   The best thing for you to do is sit down. (better)

6   The report must be on my desk tomorrow morning. (has)

7   It is possible that Joanne did not receive my message. (might)

8   It's impossible for Martin to be jogging in this weather. (can't)

9   Tessa wants a cup of coffee. (like)

10 It was not necessary for Nancy to clean the flat. (didn't)

Test 10D

Say what the speaker is doing. After each sentence write one of the phrases from the box.

asking for advice	giving an order	making a suggestion	refusing permission
asking permission	inviting	offering food	
expressing a wish	making a request	offering to help	

▶   Will you have a piece of cake?   offering food
1   May I sit down?
2   You must report to me every day.
3   What jobs should I apply for?
4   Would you like to spend the day with us?
5   Shall I do the washing-up?
6   Shall we sit outside?
7   I'm sorry. You can't park here.
8   Could you fill in this form, please?
9   We really must have a nice big party.

Test 10E

Here is some information for visitors to New York City.
Write the missing words. Use one word only in each space.

Before you travel to the US, you (▶) *must* find out what documents you need. British people do not (1) .... to get a visa, but there are different rules for different nationalities. For example, you (2) .... need to show that you have enough money with you. But there's one rule you can be sure about: everyone (3) .... to show their passport. The roads in New York are very busy, but don't worry – you (4) .... get around cheaply and easily by subway. Remember that you are not (5) .... to smoke on public transport or in shops. And don't forget either that you are (6) .... to tip taxi drivers and waiters. New York is not the most dangerous city in the US, but you really (7) .... walk along empty streets at night. And it is safer if you are (8) .... to travel around in a group.

MODAL VERBS   129

54 Passive verb forms

A Introduction

A passive verb is a form of **be** + a passive participle, e.g. **is baked**, **was worn**. Some participles are irregular (see page 383).

B Summary of verb tenses

	ACTIVE	PASSIVE
Present simple:	We **bake** the bread here.	The bread **is baked** here.
Present continuous:	We **are baking** the bread.	The bread **is being baked**.
Present perfect:	We **have baked** the bread.	The bread **has been baked**.
Past simple:	We **baked** the bread yesterday.	The bread **was baked** yesterday.
Past continuous:	We **were baking** the bread.	The bread **was being baked**.
Past perfect:	We **had baked** the bread.	The bread **had been baked**.

We form negatives and questions in the same way as in active sentences.
   The bread **isn't baked** in a factory.   The jacket **hasn't been worn** for years.
   Where **is** the bread **baked**?   **Has** the jacket ever **been worn** by anyone else?

C The future and modal verbs in the passive

We use **be** + a passive participle after **will, be going to, can, must, have to, should**, etc.
   The gates **will be closed** this evening.   This rubbish **should be thrown** away.
   The machine **has to be repaired**.   The news **might be announced** soon.
   Seats **may not be reserved**.   How **can** the problem **be solved**?

	ACTIVE	PASSIVE
Future:	We **will bake** the bread next.	The bread **will be baked** next.
	We **are going to bake** the bread.	The bread **is going to be baked**.
Modal verb:	We **should bake** the bread soon.	The bread **should be baked** soon.
	We **ought to bake** the bread.	The bread **ought to be baked**.

D The passive with get

We sometimes use **get** in the passive instead of **be**.
   Lots of postmen **get bitten** by dogs.   I'm always **getting chosen** for the worst jobs.
   Last week Laura **got moved** to another department.
Get is informal. We often use it for something happening by accident or unexpectedly.

In negatives and questions in the present simple and past simple, we use a form of **do**.
   The windows **don't get cleaned** very often.   How **did** the painting **get damaged**?

We also use **get** in these expressions: **get dressed/changed, get washed** (= wash oneself), **get engaged/married/divorced, get started** (= start), **get lost** (= lose one's way).
   Emma and Matthew might **get married**.   Without a map we soon **got lost**.

54 Exercises

1 The present continuous passive (B)

Look at the pictures and say what is happening. Use these subjects: *the car*, *dinner*, *a flag*, *some houses*, *the seals*. Use these verbs: *build*, *feed*, *raise*, *repair*, *serve*.

▶ *The car is being repaired.*
1 ....
2 ....
3 ....
4 ....

2 Passive verb tenses (B)

Complete the information about Barford Hall. Put in the correct form of these verbs.

| ▶ *build* (past simple) | 2 *use* (past continuous) | 4 *not look* (past perfect) | 6 *use* (present simple) |
| 1 *own* (present simple) | 3 *buy* (past simple) | 5 *do* (present perfect) | |

The building at the end of the High Street is Barford Hall, which (▶) *was built* in 1827. Today the Hall (1) .... by Bardale Council. It (2) .... as a warehouse when it (3) .... by the Council in 1952, and it (4) .... after very well. Since then a lot of work (5) .... on it, and these days the Hall (6) .... as an arts centre.

3 The future and modal verbs in the passive (C)

A press conference is being held. Put in the correct form of the verbs.
▶ Reporter: Can this new drug prolong human life?
   Professor: Yes, we believe that human life *can be prolonged* by the drug.
1 Reporter: Are you going to do any more tests on the drug?
   Professor: Yes, further tests .... soon.
2 Reporter: What .... the drug .... ?
   Professor: It will be called Bio-Meg.
3 Reporter: Can people buy the drug now?
   Professor: No, it .... by the public yet.
4 Reporter: Do you think the company should sell this drug?
   Professor: Yes, I think Bio-Meg .... to anyone who wants it.

4 The passive with **get** (D)

Put in *get* or *got* and the passive participle of these verbs: *break*, *change*, *divorce*, *hurt*, *lose*.
▶ If we're going out to the theatre, I'd better *get changed*.
1 Daniel .... when he tried to break up a fight.
2 I know the way. We won't ....
3 You'd better wrap up the glasses, so they don't ....
4 They were only married a year before they ....

55 Active and passive (1)

A What is the sentence about?

Compare these two entries in an encyclopedia.

> **Alexander Graham Bell**
> A British inventor who went to live in Canada and then the USA. Bell invented the telephone.

> **Telephone**
> An apparatus with which people can talk to each other over long distances. The telephone was invented by Alexander Graham Bell.

Look at these two sentences.

ACTIVE	PASSIVE
Bell **invented** *the telephone*.	*The telephone* **was invented** *by Bell*.

The two sentences have the same meaning, but they are about different things. One sentence is about Bell, and the other is about the telephone. Each sentence begins with the subject. The subject is the starting-point of the sentence, the thing we are talking about. The new information about the subject comes at the end of the sentence.

We say *Bell invented the telephone* because we are talking about **Bell**, and the new information is that he invented **the telephone**.	We say *The telephone was invented by Bell* because we are talking about **the telephone**, and the new information is that it **was invented** by **Bell**.
When the subject is the person or thing doing the action (the agent), then we use an active verb.	When the subject is not the agent (is not doing the action), then we use a passive verb.

ACTIVE

Bell	invented the telephone.
Subject and agent	

The subject (**Bell**) is the agent.

PASSIVE

The telephone	was invented by	Bell.
Subject		Agent

The subject (**the telephone**) is not the agent. It is the thing that the action is directed at.

B The passive and **by the police, in 1876,** etc

In a passive sentence, when we want to say who or what did the action, we use **by**.
   On our way home we were stopped **by the police**.   The new hospital will be opened **by the Queen**.
   The paper was all blown away **by the wind**.

We can give other details about the action. For example, we can use a phrase saying when or where something happens.
   The telephone was invented **in 1876**.   The visitors will be driven **to the airport**.
   The concerts are usually held **at the university**.

Sometimes there is no phrase after the verb.
   A new swimming-pool **is being built**.   All the documents **have been destroyed**.

For more details see Unit 56.

55 Exercises

1 Active or passive verb? (A)
Choose the correct verb forms in this news report about a storm.

Millions of pounds' worth of damage (▶) has caused/has been caused by a storm which (1) swept/was swept across the north of England last night. The River Ribble (2) burst/was burst its banks after heavy rain. Many people (3) rescued/were rescued from the floods by fire-fighters, who (4) received/were received hundreds of calls for help. Wind speeds (5) reached/were reached ninety miles an hour in some places. Roads (6) blocked/were blocked by fallen trees, and electricity lines (7) brought/were brought down, leaving thousands of homes without electricity. 'Everything possible (8) is doing/is being done to get things back to normal,' a spokesman (9) said/was said.

2 By the police, etc (B)
In each of these sentences underline who or what is doing the action (the agent).

▶ The traffic was all heading out of town.
1 The photo was taken by my brother.
2 The water was pouring out of the hole.
3 A policeman has been murdered by terrorists.
4 We were woken by the alarm.
5 The guide led a group of tourists around the castle.
6 The dog has bitten several people.

3 Active and passive (A–B)
You are telling a friend some news. Use the notes and complete the second sentence.
Sometimes you need to use the active and sometimes the passive.

▶ (Past simple: Claire / go / to Florida / last month)
You remember Claire? She *went to Florida last month.*
▶ (Present perfect: send / our luggage / to Australia)
Bad news about our luggage. It's *been sent to Australia.*
1 (Past simple: Claude Jennings / win / the quiz competition)
Did you hear about the quiz competition? It ....
2 (Past simple: Mrs Miles / do / a parachute jump / last week)
You know Mrs Miles? She ....
3 (Present perfect: a bull / attack / David)
Have you heard about David? He's ....
4 (Present continuous: build / the house)
Trevor and Laura have bought a house. It's still ....
5 (Present simple: Andrew / like / Jessica)
Did I tell you about Andrew? He ....
6 (Present perfect: throw away / your stamp collection)
Bad news about your stamp collection. It's ....
7 (Present perfect: Martians / kidnap / my neighbours)
Did I mention my neighbours? They've ....
8 (Past simple: five people / see / the ghost)
Did you hear about the ghost? It ....

56 Active and passive (2)

A The passive and the agent

In a passive sentence, we sometimes mention the agent (the person or thing doing the action). We use **by** with the agent.

*The cheque must be signed **by the manager**.*
*The medals were presented **by Nelson Mandela**.*

But we mention the agent only if it is important for the meaning of the sentence. Sometimes we do not mention it.

1 We do not mention the agent if it does not add any new information.
All our money and passports were stolen.
A man was arrested last night.
We do not need to say that the money was stolen 'by a thief' or that the man was arrested 'by the police'.

2 We do not mention the agent if it is not important.
The streets are cleaned every day.
Oil has been discovered at the North Pole.
Who discovered the oil is less important than the fact that it is there.

3 It is sometimes difficult to say who the agent is.
This kind of jacket is considered very fashionable these days.
A number of attempts have been made to find the Loch Ness monster.

B Empty subjects (**they, people**, etc)

Compare these two sentences.

ACTIVE	PASSIVE
They clean the streets every day.	The streets are cleaned every day.

The new and important information is <u>how often</u> the streets are cleaned. We are not interested in saying who cleans them. In the active sentence we can use the 'empty subject' **they**. We sometimes use a sentence with an empty subject instead of the passive, especially in conversation.

We can also use the empty subjects **people**, **you**, **one** and **someone**.

ACTIVE	PASSIVE
People use this footpath all the time.	This footpath is used all the time.
You/One should check the details.	The details should be checked.
Someone took my purse.	My purse was taken.

C When do we use the passive?

We use the passive in both speech and writing, but it is more common in writing.
We see it especially in textbooks and reports. We use it to describe activities in industry, science and technology, and also for official rules.

*Bananas **are exported** to Europe.*   *The liquid **is heated** to boiling point.*
*Payment **can be made** at any post office.*   *Cars left here **will be towed** away.*

In these situations, it is often not important to say who is doing the action, or it is difficult to say.

The passive is also often used in news reports.
*A number of political prisoners **have been released**.*
*Talks **will be held** in London next week.*

56 Exercises

1 The passive and the agent (A)

Laura is writing to a friend. This is part of her letter.

Someone broke into our house at the weekend. The burglar took some jewellery. But luckily **he didn't do any damage**. A very nice young police officer interviewed me. Detectives found some fingerprints, **and the police computer identified the burglar**. Police have arrested a man and are questioning him. **But they haven't found the jewellery**.

Now complete the passive sentences in this conversation. Use a phrase with *by* only if it adds information.

Laura: Our house (▶) *was broken into at the weekend*
Melanie: Oh no!
Laura: Some jewellery (1) ....
But luckily no damage (2) ....
Melanie: Did the police come and see you?
Laura: Yes, they did. I (3) ....
Melanie: I don't suppose they know who did it.
Laura: Well, amazingly they do. Some (4) .... ,
and the (5) ....
A man (6) .... and (7) ....
Melanie: Wonderful.
Laura: There's only one problem. The (8) ....

2 Active or passive sentence? (A)

Write a paragraph from the notes about the first motor car. Some sentences are active and some are passive. Use a phrase with *by* only if it adds information.

▶ a Belgian called Etienne Lenoir / make / the first motor car
1 but / Lenoir / not produce / many cars / for sale
2 a German called Karl Benz / start / commercial production
3 people / now / see / Benz / as the father / of the motor car

The first *motor car was made by a Belgian called Etienne Lenoir.*
But Lenoir ....
....
Commercial ....
....
Benz ....
....

3 Empty subjects (B)

Reply to what people say. Use the subject in brackets.

▶ Daniel: The bus fares have been increased. (they)
Vicky: What? You mean *they've increased the bus fares* again!
1 Melanie: Bicycles should be used for short journeys. (people)
David: Yes, I agree. ....
2 Emma: A new source of energy has been discovered. (someone)
Daniel: What? Did you say that ....
3 Rachel: This building is going to be knocked down. (they)
Vicky: Well, no one told me that ....
4 David: Eggs shouldn't be kept in a freezer. (you)
Tom: Really? I didn't know ....
5 Vicky: Why isn't litter put in the bin? (people)
Emma: Exactly. Why don't ....

57 Special passive structures

A I was given ...

Look at these sentences.
   Henry gave some flowers to his wife.   *Henry gave his wife some flowers.*
An active sentence with a verb like **give** can have two different structures (see Unit 3).

If we use a passive sentence, either **some flowers** or **his wife** can be the subject.

> ***Some flowers*** *were given to Henry's wife.*
> This is about the flowers, and it tells us who received them.

> ***Henry's wife*** *was given some flowers* .
> This is about Henry's wife, and it tells us what she received

It is quite normal in English for a person to be the subject in a passive sentence like the one about Claire.
   Mike *was sent tickets for the concert.*   ***My wife*** *is paid more than I am.*
   Andrew *has been awarded a prize for his essay.*

We can use the following verbs in this structure: **allow, award, fed, give, grant, hand, leave** (in a will), **lend, offer, owe, pay, promise, sell, send, show, teach**

B It is said that ...

   It is said *that Rita is leaving her job.*
   (= People say that Rita is leaving her job.)

We can use the structure **it** + passive verb + clause with verbs of reporting. We use this structure when we cannot say or do not need to say who the speaker is, for example in news reports.
   It is thought *that the company is planning a new advertising campaign.*
   It was reported *that the President had suffered a heart attack.*
   It has been agreed *that changes to the scheme are necessary.*

Here are some verbs we can use in this structure: **agree, allege, announce, assure, believe, consider, decide, expect, explain, hope, know, report, say, suggest, suppose, think, understand**

C He is said to ...

We can also use subject + passive verb + to-infinitive.
   *Rita **is said to have** left her job.*
This structure is also used in news reports.
   *United **were expected to win**.* (= People expected that they would win.)
   *The company **is thought to be planning** a new advertising campaign.*
   (= Someone thinks that it is planning a new advertising campaign.)
   *The President **was reported to have suffered** a heart attack.*
   (= Someone reported that he had suffered a heart attack.)

We can use the following verbs in this structure: **believe, expect, find, know, report, say, think, understand**

We often use **be supposed to** for things that people say.
   *I might watch this programme. It's **supposed to be** very funny.*

57 Exercises

1 I was given ... (A)

Zedco managers are writing a report saying how well the company looks after its employees.
Write sentences from the notes. Put the important underlined information at the end of the sentence.

▶ useful work skills / they are taught to our staff
   Our staff are taught useful work skills.
▶ people with initiative / they are given opportunities
   Opportunities are given to people with initiative.
1 special training / it is given to new employees
   ....
2 staff who perform well / they are given extra payments
   ....
3 company shares / they are offered to most employees
   ....
4 six weeks' holiday / this is allowed to all Zedco staff
   ....
5 women who leave to have children / they are paid a full salary
   ....

2 It is said that ... (B)

Report these rumours. Instead of the active (e.g. *People say ...*) use the passive (e.g. *It is said that ...*).
▶ People say this.
   The quiz champion Claude Jennings has lost his memory.
   It is said that the quiz champion Claude Jennings has lost his memory.

1 Everyone expects this.
   The soap opera 'Round the Corner' will end next year.
   It is ....
   ....

2 Journalists suppose so.
   The footballer Wayne Johnson is earning £10 million a year.
   ....
   ....

3 Lots of people believe this.
   The Prime Minister and his wife have separated.
   ....
   ....

3 He is said to ... (C)

Now report the rumours in Exercise 2 like this.
▶ *The quiz champion Claude Jennings is said to have lost his memory.*
1 The soap opera 'Round the Corner' ....
2 ....
3 ....

58 Have something done

A Introduction
Compare these situations.

Claire decorated the room.
(She did the work herself.)

*Claire **had** the room **decorated**.*
(A decorator did the work.)

We can use **have** in a passive structure. *Claire had the room decorated* means that she arranged for a decorator to do it for her as a professional service.

B Form
Look at these examples.

	HAVE	SOMETHING	DONE	
You should	have	your car	serviced	regularly.
Mark usually	has	his suits	cleaned	at Superclean.
We	had	the television	repaired	only last year.
You've	had	your hair	cut.	
Our neighbours are	having	a new garage	built.	
Is Melanie	having	a new cooker	installed?	

Note that we can use the perfect or the continuous (**have had**, **are having**).

In negatives and questions in simple tenses, we use a form of **do**.
   Mark **doesn't have** his suits cleaned at Fastclean.
   We **didn't have** new windows put in because it was too expensive.
   Do you **have** your car serviced regularly?   Where **did** you **have** your hair cut?

C Get something done
We can also use **get something done**.
   We must **have** another key **made**. OR We must **get** another key **made**.
The sentences have the same meaning, but **get** is more informal than **have**.

Here are some more examples with **get**.
   Laura **got** her shoes **repaired**.   We're **getting** the carpet **cleaned**.
   Where **did** you **get** your hair **cut**?   Do you **get** your heating **checked** every year?

D Have meaning 'experience'
We can use **have** in this structure with the meaning 'experience something', often something unpleasant.
   We **had** all our money **stolen**.   The car **had** its mirror **pulled** off.

58 Exercises

1 Have something done (A–B)

Look at the pictures and say what people are doing or what they did.
Use these phrases: *her photo, his windows, his car, her eyes, his hair*
Use these verbs: *clean, cut, repair, take, test*

▶ At the moment Trevor *is having his hair cut.*
1 Last week Mike ....
2 At the moment Melissa ....
3 Yesterday David ....
4 At the moment Rachel ....

2 Have something done (A–B)

Read about each situation and write sentences with *have something done*.
▶ Melanie is paying the man who has repaired her bicycle.
  Melanie has had her bicycle repaired.
1 David went to the hospital. A nurse bandaged his arm.
  ....
2 Daniel is going to the dentist. She's going to fill his tooth.
  ....
3 Laura is walking around town while her photos are being developed.
  ....

3 Get something done (C)

Look again at Exercise 2. The jobs are all done now. Complete the questions using *get*.
▶ Mike: Where *did you get your bicycle repaired, Melanie?*
1 Harriet: Why ....
2 Emma: Where ....
3 Sarah: Where ....

4 Have meaning 'experience' (D)

Say what happened to these people.
▶ Claire (whose luggage was searched in customs)
  Claire had her luggage searched in customs.
1 Tom (whose car was stolen from outside his house)
  ....
2 Rita (whose rent was increased by ten per cent)
  ....
3 David (whose electricity has been cut off)
  ....

59 To be done and being done

A Active and passive forms

Compare the active and passive.

	ACTIVE	PASSIVE
to-infinitive:	I ought **to meet** Sarah at the airport.	I hope **to be met** at the airport.
ing-form:	I insist on **meeting** you at the airport.	I love **being met** at the airport.
	(I meet people.)	(People meet me.)

Here are some more examples.
   I want **to play** volleyball. I hope **to be chosen** for the team.
   The minister agreed **to answer** questions. He agreed **to be interviewed** on television.
   Why did Tom keep **making** jokes about me? I don't enjoy **being laughed** at.
   You say you remember **telling** me the news. But I certainly can't remember **being told**.

An ing-form sometimes comes after a preposition.
   The postman complained **about being attacked** by Nick's dog.
   Famous people get tired **of being recognized** everywhere they go.

B Active forms with a passive meaning

The active ing-form after **need** has a passive meaning.
   The bicycle **needs oiling**. (= The bicycle needs **to be oiled**.)
   The windows **need cleaning**. (= The windows need **to be cleaned**.)
We cannot use the passive ing-form here.
   NOT *The bicycle needs being oiled*.

We sometimes use an active to-infinitive when we talk about a job **to be done**.
   I've got some letters **to write** today.   We've got this bill **to pay**.
Here we use the active (**to write**) because the subject of the sentence (**I**) is the person who has to do the job.
But if the subject is <u>not</u> a person, then we use the passive infinitive.
   The letters are **to be written** today.   The bill is **to be paid** without delay.
   All this mess has **to be cleared** away.   The goods have **to be shipped**.

We can use the structure **be** + to-infinitive to give an order.
   The matter **is to be given** top priority.   You're not **to drive** too fast.

After the subject **there**, we can use either an active or a passive to-infinitive.
   There are some letters **to write/to be written** today.   There's a bill **to pay/to be paid**.

▷ 62 Verb + active to-infinitive or ing-form   ▷ 73 Preposition + active ing-form

59 Exercises

1 Passive forms (A)

Speech bubble: *I am asking the government to allow me into Britain. I am worried about them refusing me entry. I am afraid of your officials sending me away. I don't want you to misunderstand me. I hope someone in Britain will offer me a job. I don't mind them paying me low wages at first. I am willing for my employer to re-train me. I would like Britain to give me a chance.*

Caption: A REFUGEE HAS ARRIVED IN BRITAIN.

Report what the man says. Use the passive to-infinitive or ing-form.
▶ He's asking to be allowed into Britain.
▶ He's worried about being refused entry.
1 ....
2 ....
3 ....
4 ....
5 ....
6 ....

2 Active and passive forms (A)

TV reporter Kitty Beamish is interviewing some workers who are protesting about not being paid enough. Complete the workers' statements. Put in an active or passive to-infinitive or ing-form.
▶ We want *to be paid* (pay) better wages.
1 We don't enjoy .... (use) as cheap labour.
2 We're tired of .... (work) for low wages.
3 We expect .... (treat) like human beings.
4 We don't want .... (give) up all our rights.
5 We hope .... (invite) to a meeting with the management.
6 We insist on .... (take) seriously.

3 Active and passive forms (A–B)

Put in an active or passive to-infinitive or ing-form.
Jessica: Are you going to be busy today?
Andrew: Well, I've got a few things (▶) *to do* (do).
I've got an essay (1) .... (write). And this room ought
(2) .... (tidy) up a bit.
This carpet needs (3) .... (hoover).
Jessica: I've got some jobs (4) .... (do), too.
Most of my clothes need (5) .... (iron).
And I've got my project (6) .... (finish) off.
I'm worried about (7) .... (miss) the deadline.
It has (8) .... (hand) in tomorrow.
I don't want (9) .... (be) late with it.
Andrew: I don't remember (10) .... (tell) when the project was due in.
Jessica: Why? Haven't you done it yet?
Andrew: Oh, yes. I handed it in ages ago.

Test 11 The passive (Units 54–59)

Test 11A

Rewrite these sentences beginning with the underlined words.
▶ Thieves robbed a woman.
A woman was robbed.
1 They may ban the film.

2 They offered Nancy a pay increase.

3 We need to correct the mistakes.

4 Someone reported that the situation was under control.

5 They are testing the new drug.

6 We haven't used the machine for ages.

Test 11B

Read the story and write the missing words. Use one word only in each space.

During periods of terrorist activity by the IRA, people in Britain are always (▶) *being* warned to look out for bombs. Any bag or parcel without an owner (1) .... seen as a risk to the public. Some time ago a cardboard box was found at the entrance to Bristol Zoo one day. It was noticed (2) .... a visitor and reported to the director. Clearly, if it was a bomb and it went off, people might (3) .... killed. So army bomb experts (4) .... called in, and the box was safely blown up in a controlled explosion. Soon afterwards (5) .... was reported that the box had (6) .... left there by a boy wanting to find a new home for his pet rat. He was tired of the rat, he explained, but he was unwilling to (7) .... it put to sleep by a vet, so he left it in a box outside the zoo. The director of the zoo is thought (8) .... be unenthusiastic about looking after people's unwanted pets. No one knows what the rat thought about (9) .... blown up.

Test 11C

Write a second sentence so that it has a similar meaning to the first. Use the word in brackets.
▶ We have to test these products. (be)
These products have to be tested.
1 Pavarotti sang the song. (by)

2 Nigel's passport was stolen. (had)

3 They pay doctors a lot of money. (are)

4 I hope they'll interview me for the job. (to)

5 Someone was cleaning the floor. (being)

6 A mechanic is repairing Judy's car. (having)

Test 11

7 Tessa lost her way. (got)
....

8 Everyone agreed that the plan should go ahead. (it)
....

9 When did they decorate your kitchen? (get)
....

10 They say exercise is good for you. (be)
....

Test 11D

Which of the two sentences follows on best?
▶ There's going to be a big art exhibition.
   a) ☐ A lot of visitors will be attracted to it.   b) ✓ It will attract a lot of visitors.
1 Our neighbours have got a cat and a dog.
   a) ☐ A lot of mice are caught by the cat.   b) ☐ The cat catches a lot of mice.
2 Last night Martin dreamt he saw his dead grandmother.
   a) ☐ A white dress was being worn by the ghost.   b) ☐ The ghost was wearing a white dress.
3 We've bought a new computer.
   a) ☐ It can do the job much more quickly.   b) ☐ The job can be done much more quickly.
4 My grandfather is very ill.
   a) ☐ He's being looked after in the local hospital.   b) ☐ The local hospital is looking after him.
5 We've completed the experiment.
   a) ☐ The newspapers will publish the results.   b) ☐ The results will be published in the newspapers.

Test 11E

Each of these sentences is incorrect. Write the correct sentence.
▶ ~~Those nice glasses got break.~~
   Those nice glasses got broken.
1 ~~The story was written Agatha Christie.~~
....

2 ~~Baseball do play at this stadium.~~
....

3 ~~This shirt needs iron.~~
....

4 ~~I got cut my hair yesterday.~~
....

5 ~~It believes that there is going to be a war.~~
....

6 ~~My parents divorce themselves last year.~~
....

7 ~~I've got a report to be written.~~
....

8 ~~To the winner was given a prize.~~
....

9 ~~This man on TV supposes to be the tallest person in the world.~~
....

60 Verb + to-infinitive

A Introduction

*I've **decided to have** a round of golf. I've **arranged to play** with someone.*

*But you **promised to come** shopping this afternoon. I **want to look** for a new sofa.*

After some verbs we can use a to-infinitive, e.g. **decided to have**, **arranged to play**. Here are some more examples.
  *I **expect to get** my money back.*
  *Sarah **agreed to work** late at the office.*
  *We can't **afford to go** to Australia.*
  *Are you **hoping to get** a job in London?*
  *Melanie has **offered to help** us when we move house.*
We can put **not** before the to-infinitive.
  *Some people just choose **not to get** married.*
  *At least I managed **not to lose** my temper.*

With some other verbs we use an ing-form, not a to-infinitive (see Units 61 and 62).
  *Mark has **finished playing** golf.*

B Seem and appear

We can use a to-infinitive after **seem** and **appear**.
  *Sarah **seemed to be** quite annoyed.*   *The computer program **appears to have** a bug in it.*
  *The person I spoke to **didn't seem to know** anything about the company's products.*

We can use a continuous or a perfect to-infinitive.
  Continuous: *Andrew seems **to be studying** even harder these days.*
  Perfect: *David appeared **to have hurt** himself.*

C Tend, manage and fail

We use **tend to** for things that usually happen.
  *We **tend to get** up later at weekends.* (= We usually get up later at weekends.)
We use **manage to** for being able to do something.
  *Luckily I **managed to find** my way here all right.* (= I was able to find my way.)
We use **fail to** for things that don't happen.
  *David **failed to pay** his electricity bill.* (= David didn't pay his electricity bill.)

D He promised to go, his promise to go

Some nouns can come before a to-infinitive. Compare these sentences.
  Verb + to-infinitive: *Mark **promised to go** shopping.*
                          *But then he **arranged to play** golf.*
  Noun + to-infinitive: *Mark forgot about his **promise to go** shopping.*
                          *Sarah found out about his **arrangement to play** golf.*

Here are some nouns we can use: **agreement, arrangement, decision, demand, desire, failure, offer, plan, promise, refusal, tendency, threat**

▷ 61–62 Verb + ing-form   ▷ 65 Verb + object + to-infinitive

60 Exercises

1 Verb + to-infinitive (A)

Say what each speaker did. Use these verbs before a to-infinitive: *decide, demand, offer, promise, threaten*
▶ Henry: I really must speak to the manager.
Henry demanded to speak to the manager.
1 Trevor: I'll put the shelves up soon, I promise.
....
2 Claire: OK, I'll buy both the dresses.
....
3 Melanie: I'll cook the meal if you like.
....
4 Tom: If you don't control that dog, Nick, I'll shoot it.
....

2 Seem (B)

Complete the answers using *seem* and a to-infinitive.
(Some of the to-infinitives may be continuous or perfect.)
▶ Vicky: Have Matthew and Emma got over their quarrel?
  Daniel: I think so. *They seem to have got* over it.
▶ Rita: Is Claire in love with Henry?
  Sarah: Probably not. *She doesn't seem to be* in love with him.
1 Tom: Do Mike and Harriet really believe there's life on Mars?
  David: Well, yes. .... there is.
2 Victor: Has Ilona's English improved?
  Emma: Yes, ... quite a lot.
3 David: Does Rita like football?
  Tom: I don't think so. .... it much.
4 Natasha: Is Daniel working hard, do you think?
  Rachel: Yes, I think so. .... hard.
5 Sarah: Has Trevor made a good job of those shelves?
  Laura: Not really. .... a very good job of them.

3 Verb + to-infinitive (A–D)

Put in the to-infinitive form. (Some may be continuous or perfect.)
Use these verbs: *come, find, hang, have, invite, leave, take*
Harriet: Hello, Nick. You managed (▶) *to find* your way then?
Nick: Yes, in the end. It's a bit complicated, isn't it?
Harriet: Well you're here now. Do you want (1) .... your coat up?
Nick: Thank you.
Harriet: I'm glad you decided (2) .... to our party.
Everyone seems (3) .... a good time.
We tend (4) .... lots of people to our parties.
Nick: Is Tom here?
Harriet: No, he couldn't come. He'd already made an arrangement
(5) .... somebody somewhere in his taxi.
Nick: And Rita?
Harriet: Er, she was here, but she appears (6) .... early. I don't know where she's gone. She was with someone.

61 Verb + ing-form

A Introduction

After some verbs we can use an ing-form, for example, **suggested going**, **enjoy putting**.
 I usually **avoid driving** in the rush hour. We'll have to **practise throwing** the ball into the basket.
 Have you **finished typing** that letter? Nick says he's **given up smoking**.
We can sometimes put **not** before an ing-form.
 Imagine **not having** anywhere to live.

With some other verbs we use a to-infinitive, not an ing-form (see Units 60 and 62).
 I don't **want to put** up a tent in the rain.

B Mind

We use **mind** + an ing-form mostly in negative statements and in questions.
 Andrew doesn't **mind having** lots of work. He quite likes it.
 (= He doesn't dislike having lots of work.)
 Do you **mind waiting** a moment? ~ No, that's OK.
 I wouldn't **mind travelling** around the world some time.

C Verbs with can't

Note **can't** or **couldn't** with **help**, **resist**, **face** and **stand**. We can put an ing-form after these verbs.
 I think Tom is very amusing. I **can't help laughing** at his funny stories.
 The dress was so beautiful that Claire **couldn't resist buying** it.
 Let's eat out, shall we? I **can't face cooking** a meal today.
 I never go in the bank if it's busy. I **can't stand waiting** in a queue.

D Keep (on) and carry on

We use **keep** or **keep on** + an ing-form to talk about something continuing,
or when it happens again and again.
 Just **keep stirring** the mixture until it boils. Nick **keeps ringing** Rita and asking her out.
 The runners didn't mind the rain. They just **kept on running**.
For **continue** see Unit 63C.

Carry on means something continuing.
 Just **carry on stirring** the mixture until it boils.

▷ 65D Verb + object + ing-form

61 Exercises

1 Verb + ing-form (A)

Answer the questions using the notes in brackets.
- Mike: Is your car working now? (they / not / finish / repair / it)
  You: No, *they haven't finished repairing it* yet.
1. Laura: Have you done the crossword? (I / give up / try)
   You: No, ...
2. Daniel: There's a story here in the paper about a 110-year-old man. (I / can / not / imagine / be)
   You: Good Lord. .... so old.
3. Tom: Do you like football? (I / enjoy / watch / it / on TV)
   You: Well, ...
4. Rachel: Whose idea was it to invite all these people? (suggest / have / a party)
   You: I'm not sure. Someone ....

2 Verbs with **can't** (C)

Use three words from the table to complete each sentence.

1	2	3
can't	face	doing
couldn't	help	feeling
	resist	having
	stand	lying
		noticing

- Rita said she was OK, but I *couldn't help noticing* how upset she looked.
1. I hate holidays by the sea. I .... on a beach all day.
2. I feel really full. I'm afraid I .... a pudding with my lunch.
3. I was so tired yesterday I just .... any housework.
4. Tom's car was stolen, but, as he left it unlocked, I .... it's his own fault.

3 Verb + ing-form (A–D)

Some friends have had a meal together in a restaurant. Put in the ing-forms.
Use these verbs: *change, discuss, eat, get, miss, ring, try, wait, walk*

Vicky: Shall we go then?
Rachel: Daniel hasn't finished (▶) *eating* yet.
Daniel: It's OK. It's just a piece of chocolate.
Matthew: Chocolate? After that enormous meal?
Daniel: I know. I've eaten too much. When I find something new on the menu, I just can't resist (1) .... it.
Rachel: How are we getting home?
Vicky: I don't mind (2) .... I feel like some fresh air.
Rachel: You're crazy. It's miles. And we've just eaten.
Matthew: I suggest (3) .... for a taxi. It'll save (4) .... around for a bus.
Emma: Good idea. I couldn't face (5) .... cold again after being in the warm all evening.
Rachel: Yes, the bus journey is too complicated. It involves (6) .... buses in the centre. We don't want to risk (7) .... a bus and having to wait half an hour.
Daniel: Or we could take a taxi to the bus station and then get a bus from there.
Matthew: Well, you can carry on (8) .... the problem, but I'm going to ring for a taxi.

62 Verb + to-infinitive or verb + ing-form?

A Introduction

Some verbs are followed by a to-infinitive, and some by an ing-form.

VERB + TO-INFINITIVE (Unit 60)	VERB + ING-FORM (Unit 61)
Harriet **decided to have** a party. **Decide** takes a to-infinitive.	Harriet **suggested having** a party. **Suggest** takes an ing-form.

A few verbs take either a to-infinitive or an ing-form (see Units 63–64).
   Laura **started to paint/started painting** a picture.

B To-infinitive or ing-form?

+ TO-INFINITIVE	+ ING-FORM
These verbs are followed by a to-infinitive. *agree, aim, appear* (see 60B), *arrange, ask, attempt, beg, can't afford, can't wait* (see C), *choose, claim, decide, demand, desire, expect, fail* (see 60C), *guarantee, happen* (see D), *help* (see 69C), *hope, manage* (see 60C), *offer, plan, prepare, pretend, promise, prove* (see D), *refuse, seem* (see 60B), *tend* (see 60C), *threaten, turn out* (see D), *undertake, want, wish*	These verbs are followed by an ing-form. *admit, avoid, can't face* (see 61C), *can't help* (see 61C), *can't resist* (see 61C), *can't stand* (see 61C), *carry on* (see 61D), *consider, delay, deny, detest, dislike, enjoy, excuse, fancy* (see C), *finish, give up, imagine, involve, justify, keep* (*on*), (see 61D), *mention, mind* (see 61B), *postpone, practise, put off, resent, risk, save, suggest, tolerate*

C Can't wait and fancy

If you can't wait to do something, you are eager to do it.
   *I **can't wait to see** the photos you took.* (= I am eager/impatient to see the photos.)

If you fancy doing something, you want to do it.
   *Do you **fancy going** out for a meal?* (= Would you like to go out for a meal?)
Fancy is informal.

D Happen, turn out and prove

We use **prove to** or **turn out to** when experience shows what something is like.
   *In the end our forecast **proved to be** correct.*
   *Finding Harriet's house **turned out to be** more difficult than Nick had expected.*

Note the meaning of **happen to**.
   *I **happened to see** Sarah in town.* (= I saw Sarah by chance in town.)

E Two forms together

We can sometimes use more than one to-infinitive or ing-form together.
   *The government decided **to refuse to give** in to the terrorists.*
   *I want **to avoid hurting** anyone's feelings.*
   *The man denied **threatening to kill** a policeman.*

▷ 65 Verb + object + to-infinitive or ing-form   ▷ 70 Verb + preposition + ing-form

62 Exercises

1 To-infinitive or ing-form? (A–C)

Complete the conversation. Put in a to-infinitive or ing-form.

Matthew: Are we going to have a holiday this year?
Natasha: Didn't we all decide (▶) *to spend* (spend) our holidays on a Greek island?
Matthew: Lovely. I enjoy (▶) *lying* (lie) on the beach.
I might manage (1) .... (get) a suntan.
Daniel: I'd love a holiday. I can't wait (2) .... (leave) this place behind.
Emma: I don't fancy (3) .... (stay) in one place all the time.
I really dislike (4) .... (sit) on the beach all day.
Natasha: Well, I don't mind (5) .... (tour) around somewhere.
Emma: Matthew, you promised (6) .... (go) to Scotland with me.
We were planning (7) .... (hire) a car.
Matthew: Scotland? Are you sure? But I couldn't face (8) .... (drive) all the time.
Jessica: I'm afraid I can't afford (9) .... (spend) too much money.
Andrew: And I can't justify (10) .... (take) all that time off from my studies.

2 To-infinitive or ing-form? (A–D)

Complete this article from a magazine. Put in the to-infinitive or ing-form of these verbs:
accept, argue, be, find, have, insist, lose, plug, repair, say, take, wait

If you buy something from a shop, a new stereo for example, you usually can't wait (▶) *to plug* it in and put some music on. And of course, you expect (▶) *to find* the equipment in working order. But that doesn't always happen, unfortunately. If the thing doesn't work, you should take it straight back to the shop. If you delay (1) .... it back, you will risk (2) .... your rights as a customer. And you should prepare (3) .... on those rights. You may be one of those people who always avoid (4) .... with people, but in this case you should be ready for an argument. The assistant may prove (5) .... a true friend of the customer – it's not impossible – but first he or she will probably offer (6) .... the stereo for you. That's all right if you don't mind (7) .... a few weeks, but it isn't usually a good idea. What you should do is politely demand (8) .... your money back immediately. You may want to accept another stereo in place of the old one, but you don't have to. You should refuse (9) .... a credit note. Just keep on (10) .... that you want your money back.

3 Two forms together (E)

What might you say in these situations? Write a sentence with both a to-infinitive and an ing-form.
▶ Your decision to change your holiday arrangements might upset Vicky. You won't risk that. You don't want to. What do you say to Rachel?
I don't want to risk upsetting Vicky.

1 You and Melanie want to complain about your meal in a restaurant. You need to see the manager. Melanie won't ask, but you don't mind. What do you say to her?
....

2 Matthew doesn't like the idea of going to Scotland. But he promised. He admitted it. What do you tell Emma?
....

3 The band were playing. They finished just as you arrived. This was quite by chance. What do you tell your friends?
Just as I arrived, ...

63 Like, start, etc

A Like, love, prefer and hate

*I **like doing** parachute jumps. This is my third one. I **love to look** down at the fields below.*

After **like, love, prefer** and **hate**, we can use either a to-infinitive or an ing-form. The meaning is the same.
  Mrs Miles **likes to do/likes doing** parachute jumps.
  She **loves to look/loves looking** down at the fields below.
  We always **prefer to stay/prefer staying** in small hotels.
  I **hate to stand/hate standing** up while I'm eating.

But compare these two meanings of the verb **like**.

LIKE TO DO	LIKE DOING

Like takes a to-infinitive when it means that we prefer to do something even though we may not enjoy it.
  *I **like to check** my work carefully before I hand it in.*
	Like usually takes an ing-form when we use it to talk about hobbies and interests.
	  *Claire **likes skiing**.*
	  *I don't **like swimming** much.*

B Would like, etc

After **would like, would love, would prefer** and **would hate**, we use a to-infinitive but not usually an ing-form.
  *I'd **like to do** a parachute jump one day.* *My sister **would love to work** as an artist.*
  *Mark **would prefer to drive** rather than take the train.* *I'm glad I live here. I'd **hate to live** in a big city.*

Compare **would like** and **like**.

*I'd **like to lie** on the beach today. It's too hot to do anything else.* **I'd like** means 'I want', but it is more polite (see Unit 52B).	*I **like lying** on the beach. I always spend my holidays sunbathing.* **I like** means the same as 'I enjoy'.

C Start, intend, etc

We can use either a to-infinitive or an ing-form after these verbs:
begin, bother, continue, intend, propose (= intend), **start**

  *People **began to leave/began leaving** the theatre before the end of the play.*
  *Rachel didn't **bother to do/bother doing** the washing-up.*
  *Do you **intend to make/intend making** a complaint?*
The meaning is the same.

We do not usually have two ing-forms together.
  *It was **starting to get** dark.* NOT *It was starting getting dark.*

150 THE INFINITIVE AND THE ING-FORM

63 Exercises

1 Like and would like (A–B)

Write in the words. Begin *I like …* or *I'd like …*
Use these verbs: *buy, chase, drive, play, see*
Use these objects: *computer games, rabbits, the manager, this car, this tin*

▶ *I like playing computer games.*
1 ....
2 ....
3 ....
4 ....

2 Like, love, prefer and hate (A–B)

Complete the sentences using the words in brackets.
▶ Mark: I've always wanted to visit San Francisco.
  Sarah: Me too. *I'd love to visit* (I'd love) it some time.
1 Harriet: Tom seems to enjoy watching football matches.
  David: Yes, ... (he loves) United play.
2 Trevor: I'm glad I don't work as late as Sarah does.
  Laura: Me too. .... (I wouldn't like) such long hours.
3 Matthew: I think I'll go and see this new film.
  Emma: Can I go with you? .... (I'd like) it, too.
4 Rachel: Do you want to come with me or wait here?
  Vicky: .... (I'd prefer) with you if that's OK.
5 Laura: I think queuing is my least favourite activity.
  Tom: I agree. .... (I hate).
6 Claire: Does Mark cook for you?
  Sarah: No, not often. .... (he doesn't like).
7 Reporter: Have you ever flown in a hot-air balloon?
  Mrs Miles: No, but .... (I'd love) in one someday.
8 Rachel: Did you say you're having your teeth looked at today?
  Emma: Yes, ... (I like) them checked once a year.

3 Start, intend, etc (C)

Complete this news report about a stolen taxi. Put in the to-infinitive or the ing-form of these verbs:
drive, go, lock, make, search. Sometimes more than one answer is possible.

Kevin Paisley, 25, has lost his taxi. It was stolen on Friday afternoon. 'I just went into the newsagent's for a moment,' said Kevin. 'I didn't bother (▶) *to lock* the car.' Kevin started (1) .... his own taxi only six months ago. 'I was just beginning (2) .... a profit,' he said. 'I intend (3) .... on with my work as soon as I get my taxi back.' The police are continuing (4) .... for the stolen car.

64 Remember, regret, try, etc

With some verbs, the choice of a to-infinitive or an ing-form depends on the meaning.

A Remember and forget

I must **remember to post** this letter today. It's important.
The clothes are still dirty because I **forgot to switch** on the machine.
We use **remember/forget to do** for necessary actions. The remembering is before the action.

I can **remember posting** the letter. I posted it on Friday morning.
I'll never **forget flying** over the Grand Canyon. It was wonderful.
We use **remember/forget doing** for memories of the past. The action is before the remembering.

B Regret

We **regret to inform** you that we are not taking on any new staff at present.
Regret to do something means to be sorry for something you are doing, e.g. giving bad news.

I **regret spending** all that money. I've got none left.
Regret doing something means to be sorry because of something that happened in the past.

C Try

I'm **trying to run** this computer program.
Try to do something means to attempt something, to do your best.

I **tried clicking** on the box, but it doesn't work.
Try doing something means to do something which might solve a problem.

D Stop

An old man walking along the road **stopped to talk** to us.
Stop to do something means to stop so that you can do it.

There's too much noise. Can you all **stop talking**, please?
Stop doing something means to end an action, to finish doing it.

E Mean

I think Nick **meant to break** that glass. It didn't look like an accident.
Mean to do something is the same as to intend to do it.

I'm applying for a visa. It **means filling** in this form.
Means doing something expresses the idea of one thing resulting in another.

F Go on

The teacher introduced herself and **went on to explain** about the course.
Go on to do something means to do something else, to do the next thing.

The teacher told everyone to be quiet, but they just **went on talking**.
Go on doing something means to continue doing it.

G Need

I **need to clean** my shoes.
This means that I must clean my shoes, I have to clean them.

My shoes **need cleaning**.
This means that my shoes need to be cleaned (see Unit 59B).

64 Exercises

1 Remember and forget (A)

Put in the to-infinitive or the ing-form of the verbs.
Laura: Did you remember (▶) *to pick* (pick) up those photos today?
Trevor: What photos?
Laura: Oh, no. I can remember (1) .... (mention) it to you only this morning.
Trevor: I can't remember (2) .... (agree) to pick up some photos.
Laura: Well, don't forget (3) .... (call) at the shop for them tomorrow. You've got a terrible memory. Yesterday you forgot (4) .... (lock) the door.
Trevor: I'm sure I didn't forget (5) .... (lock) it.
I can clearly remember (6) .... (look) for my keys. They were in my pocket.
Laura: You ought to write notes to yourself to remind you.
Trevor: That wouldn't be any good. I'd never remember (7) .... (look) at them!

2 Remember, regret, try, etc (A–G)

Put in the to-infinitive or the ing-form of the verbs.

I used to like going to our local cinema. It was old and rather uncomfortable, but it had character. Now they've stopped (▶) *showing* (show) films there. The owner would like to go on (1) .... (run) the cinema, but he would need (2) .... (make) a lot of improvements, which would mean (3) .... (spend) tens of thousands of pounds. I remember (4) .... (watch) the last film at the cinema. It was a murder mystery. It was five minutes from the end, and we were trying (5) .... (work) out who the murderer was when suddenly all the lights went out and the film stopped. We sat in the dark for a few minutes, and then the owner appeared with a torch. 'I regret (6) .... (tell) you,' he said, 'that our electricity has failed. I don't mean (7) .... (disappoint) you, but I'm afraid we can't show you the end of the film. We've tried (8) .... (phone) the electricity company, but they say they can't help.' He went on (9) .... (explain) to the audience how the film ended. I didn't understand the story. But I don't regret (10) .... (go) to the cinema on that last evening.

3 Remember, regret, try, etc (A–G)

Write each pair of sentences as one. Use a to-infinitive or an ing-form.
▶ Trevor didn't ring Laura. He forgot.
Trevor forgot to ring Laura.
▶ Tom and Nick had been playing cards for hours. But they went on with the game.
Tom and Nick went on playing cards.

1 Harriet didn't think she could move the piano. She didn't even try.
    ....
2 Mike once saw a spaceship. He'll never forget it.
    ....
3 What about painting the walls? They need it.
    ....
4 Natasha was unkind to Jessica. But she didn't mean it.
    ....
5 Andrew was studying. He went on through the night.
    ....
6 When Mark was driving, he needed to make a phone call. So he stopped.
    ....

Test 12 Verb + to-infinitive or ing-form (Units 60–64)

Test 12A

Complete the conversations. Put in a to-infinitive or an ing-form.
- A: I hear you sometimes sail to France in your boat.
  B: That's right. I really enjoy *sailing*.
1. A: Are you going to organize our trip?
   B: Yes, of course. I've agreed .... it.
2. A: You wear a uniform at work, don't you?
   B: Yes, I have to, although I dislike .... it.
3. A: Do you think they'll approve the plan?
   B: Yes, I'm quite sure they'll decide .... it.
4. A: What time will you be back?
   B: Oh, I expect .... back some time around nine.
5. A: Did I remind you about the dinner tonight?
   B: Yes, thank you. You keep .... me.
6. A: Was your decision the right one, do you think?
   B: Yes, luckily. In the end it proved .... the best thing for everyone.
7. A: Do you still work at the post office?
   B: No, I gave up .... there last year.
8. A: Have ICM bought the company?
   B: Well, they've offered .... it.
9. A: I'm sorry you had to wait all that time.
   B: Oh, it's all right. I didn't mind ....

Test 12B

Make sentences from the notes.
- Tessa / want / buy / a new coat / soon
  Tessa wants to buy a new coat soon.
1. we / must / avoid / waste / so much time
2. sometimes / a country / refuse / take part / in the Olympics
3. I / like / see / the Rocky Mountains / some day
4. I / mean / give / Judy / a nice welcome / yesterday
5. I / always / like / see / my doctor / once a year
6. the buses / usually / stop / run / before midnight
7. I / can't face / get up / at five / tomorrow
8. last year / we / make / an agreement / work / together
9. yesterday / you / promise / carry on / shoot / the film
10. my father / seem / get / better / now

Test 12

Test 12C
Read the conversation and write the missing words. Use one word only in each space.

Anna: I hear you're preparing to (▶) *leave* for Australia.
Lisa: That's right. And I'm really looking forward to it. I can't (1) .... to get there. I'm hoping (2) .... see all my friends while I'm there. I'm going to enjoy (3) .... them again after so long.
Anna: Martin and I (4) .... like to go away, but we can't manage it this year.
Lisa: There's just one problem that I (5) .... to sort out. My tickets haven't arrived. I've tried to ring the travel agency, but I can't get through. I'm beginning to regret (6) .... going there myself to pick them up.
Anna: I expect they'll be here tomorrow.
Lisa: That's really leaving it to the last minute. It's such a worry.
Anna: Well, I know you. You can't (7) .... worrying, can you?
Lisa: No, I can't. I hope this holiday isn't going to turn out (8) .... be a disaster.
Anna: Of course it isn't. Just keep (9) .... trying to get through.

Test 12D
Each of these sentences has a mistake in it. Write the correct sentence.
▶ ~~The man kept ask us for money.~~   *The man kept asking us for money.*
1 ~~We've finished to decorate the flat.~~
2 ~~I regret say what I did.~~
3 ~~Tessa decided go not to work.~~
4 ~~Do you mind help me?~~
5 ~~I'm beginning getting worried.~~
6 ~~I can't afford buy a new car.~~
7 ~~I hope to avoid to make things worse.~~
8 ~~Peter seems gone away already.~~

Test 12E
Write a second sentence so that it has a similar meaning to the first. Use the word in brackets.
▶ I wish I hadn't sold my bike. (regret)
  I regret selling my bike.

1 The children were eager to see their presents. (wait)

2 I hate to get up in the dark. (stand)

3 By chance I saw your brother yesterday. (happened)

4 The shop usually opens ten minutes late. (tends)

5 Would you like to go for a walk? (fancy)

6 The police continued to watch the house. (carried)

7 Seeing Nelson Mandela will always stay in my memory. (forget)

65 Verb + object + to-infinitive or ing-form

A Introduction

Customer: *None of the things I ordered have arrived. They're three weeks late. I **expect the goods to arrive** on time.*

Mark: *I'm sorry we've **kept you waiting** so long. Can I find out what the problem is and then ring you back?*

Some verbs can take an object + a to-infinitive, and some take an object + an ing-form.

	VERB	OBJECT		
I	expect	the goods	to arrive	on time.
I'm sorry we've	kept	you	waiting	so long.

B Verb + object + to-infinitive

We **asked the doorman to let** us in.   Nick couldn't **persuade Rita to go** out with him.
The hot weather has **caused ice-cream sales to increase**.
It **took ages to download** the pictures from the Internet.
I didn't **mean my suggestion to be taken** seriously. (See Unit 59A.)

Here are some verbs we can use in this structure: **advise, allow, ask, beg, cause, enable, encourage, expect, force, help** (see Unit 69C), **intend, invite, mean** (= intend), **order, recommend, remind, take** (time), **teach, tell, warn**

C Want + object + to-infinitive

We can also use an object + a to-infinitive after **want, (would) like, (would) love, (would) prefer** and **(would) hate**.

Tom **wants United to win**.   We'd **hate the house to be left** empty.

We can use this structure to give an order (see Unit 50B).

I **want everyone to come** here.   I'd **like you to listen** carefully.

We cannot normally use a that-clause. NOT *I want that everyone comes here*.

D Verb + object + ing-form

Andrew is so serious. I can't **imagine him having** a good time.
Do you **remember Laura taking** our photo?   A new law has **stopped traffic going** into the city centre.

Here are some verbs we can use in this structure: **dislike, imagine, involve, keep, mind, prevent** (see Unit 70C), **remember, risk, stop** (see Unit 70C)

E Advise, allow, encourage and recommend

We can use these verbs with an ing-form or with an object + a to-infinitive.

+ ING-FORM	+ OBJECT + TO-INFINITIVE
They **allow fishing** here.	They **allow people to fish** here.
I wouldn't **recommend walking** home alone.	I wouldn't **recommend you to walk** home alone.

We do not use **suggest** + an object + a to-infinitive.

I **suggested** to Nick (that) he should leave. NOT *I suggested Nick to leave*.

65 Exercises

Verb + object + to-infinitive (B)
Report what people said. Use the verbs in brackets.
▶ Police to motorists: Take special care. (warn)
  The police warned motorists to take special care.
1 Guy to Kitty: Would you like to come on my chat show? (invite)
2 Sarah to Mark: Don't forget to get the theatre tickets. (remind)
3 Dentist to Daniel: You should give up eating sweets. (tell)
4 Police to gunman: Come out with your hands up. (order)

Want and would like (C)
Complete the sentences using *would like* or *don't/doesn't want*.
▶ Mike won't wear a tie. Harriet is annoyed.
  She *would like him to wear a tie* because they're going to a concert.
1 Mrs Miles is going to do a parachute jump, but her son and daughter don't like the idea.
  They .... because they think it's dangerous.
2 Henry is coming late to work and his wife is worried about this.
  She .... because she doesn't want him to lose his job.
3 Natasha may not go on holiday with her friends.
  They .... because she's always good fun to be with.

Verb + object + to-infinitive or ing-form (B, D)
Kitty Beamish is reporting what people have said to her. She combines the two sentences into one.
▶ 'The lorry skidded. The icy road caused it.'
  The icy road caused the lorry to skid.
▶ 'The workers might go on strike. The company can't risk that.'
  The company can't risk the workers going on strike.
1 'The suspects might leave the country. The police must stop that.'
2 'Congress opposed him. The President didn't expect that.'
3 'The hostages lay down. The terrorists forced them.'
4 'The pound is falling in value. The government doesn't mind that.'

Advise, allow, etc (E)
Complete this paragraph from a guidebook to London. Use the to-infinitive or the ing-form.
We wouldn't recommend (▶) *driving* (drive) into London in the rush hour.
We'd advise you (1) .... (travel) by train.
We'd recommend (2) .... (buy) a special saver ticket, which is cheaper than the full fare.
But the railway companies don't allow you (3) .... (use) saver tickets before ten o'clock.
This is to encourage people (4) .... (take) a later train, which will be less busy.

66 Question word + to-infinitive

A Introduction

Vicky uses a question word (**what**) and a to-infinitive (**to wear**). She is talking about the best thing to do. **I don't know what to wear** means that I don't know what I should wear.

B Structures with **what to do, where to go,** etc

Before the question word we can use a verb such as **ask, decide, discover, discuss, explain, find out, forget, know, learn, remember, say, think, understand, wonder.**
   *It was a real problem. I couldn't **think what to do**.*
   *We were **wondering where to park** the car.*
   *Matthew wants to **know how to work** the computer.*
   *Have Trevor and Laura **decided when to have** their barbecue?*

Sometimes there is a verb + object before the question word.
In this structure we can use **advise, ask, show, teach** and **tell**.
   *Tom **showed me how to change** a wheel.*
   *The guide didn't **tell the tourists when to be** back at the coach.*

Before the question word we can also use the adjectives **clear, obvious** and **sure** and the expressions **have an idea** and **make up your mind**.
   *I wasn't **sure who to ask** for help.*   *Claire doesn't **have much idea how to cook**.*

A preposition (e.g. **of**) can come before the question word.
   *There's the question **of who to invite** to the reception.*
   *You need to be informed **about what to do** in an emergency.*

C **Why, what, whose, which** and **whether**

We cannot use **why** before a to-infinitive.
   *No one could explain **why we had to wait**.* NOT *No one could explain why to wait.*

After **what, which, whose, how many** and **how much**, we can use a noun.
   *Sarah and Mark were discussing **what colour to paint** the walls.*
   *We wondered **whose story to believe** – both drivers said it wasn't their fault.*
   *It's difficult to know **how much luggage to take** with you.*

We can use **whether** but not **if**.
   *We'll have to decide **whether to go** ahead with the project (or not).*
   NOT *We'll have to decide if to go ahead.*
   *Melanie wasn't sure **whether to ring** the doctor or not.*
   *I was wondering **whether to order** some tea.*

158 THE INFINITIVE AND THE ING-FORM

66 Exercises

1 Structures with **what to do, where to go**, etc (B)

Comment on these situations.

 ▶ How do I switch the computer on?

 1 What should I say?

 2 Where shall we go?

 3 How do I stop?

▶ (not know) *He doesn't know how to switch the computer on.*
1 (can't think) ....
2 (not sure) ....
3 (not know) ....

2 Structures with **what to do, where to go**, etc (B)

Look at the questions and then complete the paragraph about a man coming out of prison.
Use a question word and a to-infinitive.

▶ How should he start a new life?
1 What can he expect?
2 Where should he go?
3 How can he find somewhere to live?
4 What should he do?
5 Who can he contact?

This man will have problems when he leaves prison. He needs advice on (▶) *how to start* a new life.
After a long time in prison, he isn't sure (1) .... in the outside world and he has
no idea (2) .... He doesn't know (3) .... a place to live either.
But he won't be completely alone. A social worker will advise him (4) .... ,
so he'll know (5) .... if he needs help.

3 Question word + to-infinitive (B–C)

You are finding it very difficult to make your mind up.
Complete your answers to the questions. Use a question word and a to-infinitive.

▶ Rachel: Are you going to buy that sweater?
  You: I don't know *whether to buy* it or not.
▶ Tom: What time do you think we should leave?
  You: I'm not really sure *what time to leave*.
1 Daniel: Do you want to do business studies?
  You: I'm wondering .... business studies or statistics.
2 Vicky: How much money should we spend on the present?
  You: I've no idea .... on it.
3 Matthew: Do you intend to join the sports club?
  You: I can't decide .... it or not.
4 Vicky: Which route should we take?
  You: It's difficult to know ....
5 Melanie: Which lottery numbers are you going to choose?
  You: I haven't decided ....

67 Adjective + to-infinitive

A Introduction

RACHEL IS HAVING A DRIVING LESSON.

It's **great to be** on the road. This car is **easy to drive**, isn't it?

It's **important to look** in the mirror sometimes. Don't forget to do that.

We can use a to-infinitive (e.g. **to be**) after an adjective (e.g. **great**).

B It is easy to drive the car

An adjective + to-infinitive often comes in this structure with **it** + **be**.
   It's **important to look** in the mirror.   It's **lovely to see** you.
   It's quite **safe to use** the ladder.   It was **silly to make** such a fuss.

The subject can also be a person.
   I'm **delighted to see** you.   We're **ready to start** now.

C The car is easy to drive

Compare these two sentences. They both mean the same thing.
   It is easy to drive **the car**.   **The car** is easy to drive.
We do not use **it** in the second sentence.
   NOT ~~The car is easy to drive it~~ and NOT ~~The car it is easy to drive.~~

Here are some more examples.
   Your writing is **difficult to read**.   A small car would be **cheap to run**.
   The parade was **fascinating to watch**.   The ladder is quite **safe to use**.

We can use this structure with adjectives meaning 'good' or bad', e.g. **awful**, **bad**, **exciting**, **fascinating**, **good**, **marvellous**, **nice**, **terrible**, **wonderful**. We can also use it with these adjectives: **cheap**, **convenient**, **dangerous**, **difficult**, **easy**, **expensive**, **impossible**, **safe**, **simple**.

D Certain, sure and likely

We can use a to-infinitive after **certain**, **sure**, **likely** and **unlikely**.
   United are **certain/sure to win**. (= They will certainly win.)
   Sarah is **likely to be** at work. (= She is probably at work.)

E For and of

After some adjectives we can use **for** + object + to-infinitive (see Unit 68).
   It's **important for drivers to take** care.   It isn't **safe for children to play** on ladders.

After an adjective describing how someone behaves (e.g. **polite**, **silly**), we can use **of**.
   It was **polite of Emma to write** and thank us. (Emma was polite.)
   It was **silly of me to forget** the tickets. (I was silly.)

▷ 68 **For** with the to-infinitive   ▷ 117 **Too** and **enough**

160   THE INFINITIVE AND THE ING-FORM

67 Exercises

1 It is easy to drive the car (B)

Sarah's job is to write advertisements. She is writing one for Compex computers.
Write sentences with *it* and an adjective followed by a to-infinitive.

▶ Buy a Compex computer. It isn't expensive.
  It isn't *expensive to buy a Compex computer.*

1 Using the computer is very simple.
   It's very ....
2 Understanding the handbook isn't difficult.
   It isn't ....
3 You can run any kind of software. It's easy.
   ....
4 Exploring the world of Compex is absolutely fascinating.
   ....
5 Try the ultimate computer experience. Are you ready?
   ....

2 The car is easy to drive (C)

Sarah isn't happy with her ideas for the Compex advertisement.
She is rewriting the first four sentences like this.

▶ A Compex computer *isn't expensive to buy.*
1 The computer ....
2 The handbook ....
3 ....
4 ....

3 Certain, sure and likely (D)

Complete the conversation. Make sentences from the notes in brackets.
Nick: Are you going to Mike and Harriet's party?
Tom: Yes, I am. (▶) *It's sure to be a good party* (it / sure / be / a good party).
Nick: Will there be a lot of people there?
Tom: Yes, (1) .... (it / likely / be / pretty crowded).
Nick: Has Rita been invited, do you know?
Tom: Oh, (2) .... (she / certain / be / there).
Nick: I don't know that part of town. Is the house easy to find?
Tom: No, it isn't. Take a map or (3) .... (you / unlikely / find / it).

4 For and of (E)

Vicky and Rachel are talking about two students they know called Gary and Steve.
Complete the conversation. Put in *for* or *of*.
Vicky: I can't believe that Gary and Steve had a fight in a pub. Don't you think that was very foolish (▶) *of* them?
Rachel: Yes, it was especially stupid (1) .... them to quarrel about which football team is the best. There must be something more interesting (2) .... them to talk about.
Vicky: I blame Steve. It wasn't very sensible (3) .... him to knock Gary's drink over.
Rachel: It was brave (4) .... Daniel to try to stop the fight. It was awful (5) .... him to get hit on the head with a chair.

68 For with the to-infinitive

A Introduction

Sarah: *I'll just ring the office. The boss is waiting **for me to ring** her back.*
Mark: *I don't think it was a good idea **for you to bring** that mobile phone on holiday with you, Sarah.*

We can use **for** + object + to-infinitive. Here are some more examples.

	FOR	OBJECT	TO-INFINITIVE
My mother has arranged	for	someone	to look after her dog next week.
It's difficult	for	unskilled people	to find work these days.
The crowd were impatient	for	the match	to begin.
It's a nuisance	for	you	to have to wait.

B For expressing purpose

We can use this structure to say why something is done (to express purpose). (See also Unit 151E.)
   *Mark photocopied the figures **for the Sales Manager to have** a look at.*
   (= He photocopied the figures so that the Sales Manager could have a look at them.)
   *The shop provides baskets **for the customers to put** their purchases in.*
   *I'd like to put forward a few suggestions **for you to think** about.*

C Too and enough

We can use **too** and **enough** with this structure.
   *The road is **too** busy **for the children to cross** safely.*
   *Unfortunately the table was **too** small **for all of us to sit** round.*
   *Fortunately the table was big **enough for all of us to sit** round.*
   *The guide didn't speak loudly **enough for everyone to hear** clearly.*

D For and of

FOR	OF

We often use **for** + object + to-infinitive after an adjective.
 	
   *Harriet was **anxious for** the party to be a success.*
   *Would it be **possible for** you to move your car, please?*
 	
Some of the adjectives we can use with **for**:
anxious, awful, cheap, convenient, dangerous, difficult, eager, easy, exciting, expensive, friendly, good, happy, horrible, impatient, important, interesting, marvellous, necessary, nice, normal, polite, possible, ready, safe, sensible, silly, stupid, terrible, useful, willing, wonderful, wrong
	After an adjective saying how someone behaves, we use **of** + object + to-infinitive.
	
	   *It's **kind of** Melanie to put you up for the night.* (Melanie is kind.)
	   *It was **clever of** you to work out the answer.* (You were clever.)
	
	Some of the adjectives we can use with **of**:
	brave, careless, clever, foolish, generous, good, helpful, honest, intelligent, kind, mean, nice, polite, sensible, silly, stupid, wrong

Compare these two sentences.
   *It was good **for** you to come jogging.*   *It was good **of** you to come jogging with me.*
   (= It was good for your health.)   (= It was a kind action by you.)

68 Exercises

1 For with the to-infinitive (A)

The second person agrees with what the first one says. Use *for* and a to-infinitive.
- Daniel: Andrew should take it easy. That would be best.
  Matthew: Yes, you're right. It *would be best for him to take it easy.*
1. Trevor: Our new computer should arrive soon. I just can't wait.
   Laura: Me neither. I ....
2. Rachel: Matthew shouldn't marry Emma. It would be a mistake.
   Vicky: I think so too. ....
3. Customer: Advertisements should tell the truth. It's important.
   Mark: I agree. ....

2 For expressing purpose (B)

Write the advertisement for a holiday centre.
Match the sentence pairs and write sentences with *for* and a to-infinitive.

| There are lots of activities. There's a fun pool. There are quiet areas. There are regular shows. There's a giant roller-coaster. | You can enjoy them. You can relax in them. Guests can take part in them. You can ride on it if you dare. Children can swim in it. |

- *There are lots of activities for guests to take part in.*
1. ....
2. ....
3. ....
4. ....

3 Too and enough (C)

Add a sentence with *too* or *enough* and: difficult, <u>funny</u>, <u>heavy</u>, high, hot, loud
- Mike and Harriet couldn't lift the piano. *It was too heavy for them to lift.*
- Tom won't repeat the joke. *It isn't funny enough for him to repeat.*
1. Emma can't reach the top shelf. ....
2. We can't understand the poem. ....
3. Not everyone could hear the music. ....
4. The tea had got cold. Daniel couldn't drink it. ....

4 For and of (D)

A Japanese company called Sanko is going to open a new factory in a town in England.
Write the sentences from the local newspaper.
- marvellous / the town / have / some new jobs
  It will be *marvellous for the town to have some new jobs.*
- clever / our local council / bring / Sanko / here
  It was *clever of our local council to bring Sanko here.*
1. difficult / the town / attract / new industry
   It has been ....
2. very generous / the council / give / the land / to Sanko
   It was ....
3. the company / eager / production / begin / soon
   The company ....

69 The infinitive with and without **to**

This is an overview of the different structures with a to-infinitive (e.g. **to do**)
and an infinitive without **to** (e.g. **do**).

A The to-infinitive

We use a to-infinitive:
1. After an adjective (see Unit 67)
    It's **nice to have** a place of your own.   The car is really **cheap to run**.
2. After a noun
    I must take a **book to read**. (= a book that I <u>can</u> read)
    We've got a few **jobs to do**. (= jobs that we <u>must</u> do)
3. With **be able to, be about to, be allowed to, be going to, have to, ought to** and **used to**
    We **aren't allowed to park** here.   The game **is about to start**.
    We**'re going to buy** a camcorder.   You **have to fill** in a form.
4. After some verbs, e.g. **decide, hope, manage, offer** (see Unit 60)
    Tom **decided to leave** early.   I **hope to see** you soon.
    Did you **manage to sort** out the problem?   Henry **offered to pay** for the meal.
5. After some verbs + object (see Unit 65)
    Laura **persuaded Trevor to put** up some shelves.
    I **want you to do** something for me.
6. After **for** + object (see Unit 68)
    We've arranged **for you to visit** our head office.
    It is important **for students to register** with a doctor.
7. After a question word (see Unit 66)
    We don't know **where to leave** our coats.
    This book tells you **how to train** race horses.
8. To say why (see Unit 151B)
    Mark went out **to play** golf.   I need the money **to pay** the phone bill.

B The infinitive without **to**

We use an infinitive without **to**:
1. After **can, could, may, might, must, needn't, shall, should, will**, and **would**
    We **could go** to a night club.   I **must speak** to the manager.
    It **might rain** later.   Sarah **will be** away for three days.
2. After **had better** and **would rather**
    It's cold. You**'d better wear** a coat.   I**'d rather listen** to Elvis than the Beatles.
3. After **make** + object and **let** + object
    That programme was funny. It really **made me laugh**.
    Trevor will be here at five. His boss is going to **let him leave** work early.
4. After **see** or **hear** + an object (see Unit 74)
    They **saw the lights come** on.   We all **heard the bomb go** off.

C Help

An infinitive after **help** can be with or without **to**.
    Can I **help (to) get** the tea?   Vicky **helped me (to) choose** a present.

69 Exercises

1 The to-infinitive (A)

Comment on these situations. Join each pair of sentences using a to-infinitive.

▶ Mike will give you a lift. He promised.
  You: Mike *promised to give me a lift.*

1. You want to eat. You must have something.
   You: I must ....
2. You are having a rest. It's nice.
   You: It's ....
3. Will Rita speak to Nick? He wants her to.
   Nick ....
4. Daniel can't repair the video. He doesn't know how to.
   ....
5. Claire and her sister are going to Bali. They have decided.
   ....
6. Melanie is visiting David. She has gone to the hospital.
   ....
7. Vicky is doing some studying. Unfortunately she has to.
   ....
8. Sarah must ring the office. It's important.
   ....

2 The infinitive without *to* (B)

Put in the missing verbs. Usually more than one answer is correct.

▶ I've been repairing the car. I really must *wash* my hands.

1. What's in the letter? Why won't you let me .... it?
2. Did you see that lovely old car .... past a moment ago?
3. It was a terribly sad story. It made me ....
4. I don't want to do anything energetic. I'd rather .... on the beach.
5. It's very cold. I think it might .... for the first time this winter.
6. I keep getting this pain in my leg. I think I'd better .... a doctor.

3 The infinitive with and without *to* (A–B)

Matthew and Emma are at the railway station. Emma is going away for the weekend.
Put in the infinitive of the verbs. You have to decide whether or not you need *to*.

Matthew: Are you sure you'll (▶) *be* (be) all right?
Emma: Yes, of course. I'm not a child. I can manage (▶) *to look* (look) after myself.
Matthew: OK, sorry.
Emma: Some friends have invited me (1) .... (visit) them. I'm not going to the North Pole.
Matthew: It'll be nice for you (2) .... (see) your old friends again. I just know you're going (3) .... (have) lots of fun. Let me (4) .... (buy) you a magazine (5) .... (read) on the train.
Emma: I can't (6) .... (read) when I'm travelling. It makes me (7) .... (feel) sick, even in a train. I'd rather just (8) .... (look) out of the window.
Matthew: OK. Well, you'd better (9) .... (get) in. I think it's about (10) .... (leave). Oh, did I remind you (11) .... (change) at York?
Emma: Yes, Matthew, you did. Don't worry, I won't (12) .... (forget). I know perfectly well how (13) .... (get) there.

70 Verb/Adjective + preposition + ing-form

A Introduction

Claire: I'm **thinking of going** to Turkey.
Travel agent: Are you **interested in travelling** around the country, or would you like to stay in one place?
Claire: I don't want to do a lot of travelling.

Some verbs and adjectives can have a preposition after them (see Units 125–126).
  I **apologized for** my mistake.   Laura is **keen on** photography.

Sometimes we can use an ing-form after the preposition.

		PREPOSITION	ING-FORM	
I	apologized	for	making	a mistake.
Laura is	keen	on	taking	photos.
I'm	thinking	of	going	to Turkey.
Are you	interested	in	travelling	around?
We're	tired	of	not having	a place to live.

We can use **not** before the ing-form, e.g. **not having**.

B Verb + preposition + ing-form

  Don't you **believe in discussing** things openly?   Laura doesn't **feel like cooking** tonight.
  Unfortunately Tom **insisted on telling** us all about United's win.
  I'm **looking forward to seeing** my friends again.
  I've **succeeded in getting** hold of the CD I wanted.
Also: **agree with, apologize for, concentrate on, object to, rely on, think of**

We can use **about** after **ask, complain, dream, speak, talk, think,** and **wonder**.
  They're **talking about building** a new swimming-pool.

C Verb + object + preposition + ing-form

After some verbs we can put an object (e.g. **Matthew**).
  Emma **accused Matthew of not caring** about her.
  Higher prices will **discourage customers from buying**.
  The fire-fighters **prevented/stopped the fire (from) spreading**.
  The club has **punished its players for fighting** during a match.
Also: **blame ... for, congratulate ... on, thank ... for**

We can use this structure in the passive.
  Matthew was accused of not caring.   **The customers will be discouraged** from buying.

D Adjective + preposition + ing-form

  People were **annoyed at not being** able to see properly.
  I'm **bored with waiting**.   Vicky is **excited about going** to America.
  I'm **fed up with living** in this awful place.   Tom is **good at telling** jokes.
  The man was found **guilty of stealing** from his employers.
  I'm **pleased about/at winning** a prize.
Also: **capable of, fond of, interested in** (see Unit 71B), **keen on, tired of**

▷ 125 Adjective + preposition   ▷ 126 Verb + preposition

70 Exercises

1 Verb + preposition + ing-form (A–B)

Complete the conversation between Claire and her sister Sophie.
Put in the verbs with these prepositions: *for, in, like, of, on*

Sophie: Where's that little radio of yours?
Claire: Oh, it got broken. Henry knocked it off the table.
Unfortunately he hasn't succeeded (▶) *in getting* (get) it to work again.
Sophie: Oh, what a pity.
Claire: It was only a cheap thing. In fact I'd been thinking (1) .... (buy) a new one.
But Henry not only apologized (2) .... (break) it, he
insisted (3) .... (buy) me a much nicer one. It's in the dining-room.
Sophie: Henry is such a gentleman.
Claire: He didn't really need to buy me a new one, but I didn't feel (4) .... (argue).

2 Verb (+ object) + preposition + ing-form (A–C)

Comment on these situations. Join each pair of sentences using a preposition and an ing-form.

▶ The police prevented the crime. It didn't take place.
The police *prevented the crime from taking place.*

1 Laura blamed Trevor. He forgot the tickets.
Laura ....

2 The doctors succeeded. They saved the driver's life.
The doctors ....

3 The customers complained. They didn't receive the goods.
....

4 Emma has accused Matthew. She says Matthew broke his promise.
....

5 Melanie is insisting. She's going to cook a meal for David.
....

6 A new traffic scheme has stopped cars. They can't go into the town centre.
....

7 Everyone congratulated Claude. He won the quiz competition.
....

8 Some football fans were arrested. They attacked a policeman.
....

3 Verb/Adjective + preposition + ing-form (A–D)

Complete Emma's letter to her friend Kirsty. Put in a preposition and an ing-form.

Thank you (▶) *for inviting* (invite) me to come and see you next month. I'm already excited
(1) .... (see) you again.

You must be very pleased (2) .... (get) the job you wanted. Congratulations. Personally,
I wouldn't be keen (3) .... (travel) forty miles to work.

I apologize (4) .... (not write) sooner, but a week in bed with flu has prevented me
(5) .... (do) anything. I haven't even felt (6) .... (write) letters
until today. I must be getting better because I'm starting to feel bored (7) .... (do)
nothing. I'm thinking (8) .... (go) back to work tomorrow.

71 Afraid to do or afraid of doing?

A Afraid

> David is **afraid to climb** the ladder.
> (= He <u>doesn't want to climb</u> the ladder because he is afraid.)

> David is **afraid of falling**.
> (= He is afraid <u>because he might fall</u>.)

Here are some more examples.

> I was **afraid to say** anything in front of all those people.
> Claire was **afraid to wander** too far from the hotel.

> I was **afraid of sounding** foolish, you see.
> She was **afraid of getting** lost.

B Anxious, ashamed and interested

Compare these examples.

> Zedco are **anxious to increase** their sales.
> (= They <u>want</u> to increase their sales.)

> Mark was **anxious about presenting** his report.
> (= He was worried because he had to present his report.)

> I'm **ashamed to tell** you what I scored in the test.
> (= I <u>don't want</u> to tell you because I'm ashamed.)

> I'm **ashamed of getting** such a low score.
> (= I'm ashamed because I got such a low score.)

> I'd be **interested to meet** Laura.
> (= I <u>want</u> to meet her.)

> Laura is **interested in painting**.
> (= It is an interest/a hobby of hers.)

> I was **interested to hear** Mike's story.
> (= I found his story interesting.)

C Structures with sorry

To apologize for something we are doing, we use a to-infinitive.
> I'm **sorry to tell** you this, but your test score is rather low.
> I'm **sorry to ring** so late, but it's important.

To express regret, we also use a to-infinitive.
> I was **sorry to hear** that Mike's uncle had died.

To apologize for something we did, we can use **about** + ing-form.
> I'm **sorry about making** all that noise last night.
> (OR I'm **sorry I made** all that noise last night.)

71 Exercises

1 Afraid (A)

Complete the sentences. Use these words and put the verb into the to-infinitive or ing-form:
dive into the water, drop them, fall, move

▶ He's afraid *to dive into the water.*
1 She's afraid ....
2 She's afraid ....
3 He's afraid ....

2 Afraid (A)

Look at what people say and write a comment about each person.
Rewrite the second sentence using *afraid to* or *afraid of*.
▶ Vicky: There's a large bull in the field. I don't want to open the gate.
   Vicky is afraid to open the gate.
▶ Claire: I arrived at the airport in good time. I thought I might get stuck in traffic.
   Claire was afraid of getting stuck in traffic.
1 Nick: I was going to do a bungee jump yesterday. But I couldn't jump.
....
2 Daniel: The policeman looked angry. I didn't want to argue with him.
....
3 Matthew: I'm keeping my shirt on. I might get sunburnt.
....

3 Afraid, anxious, ashamed and interested (A–B)

Complete the conversation. Put in a to-infinitive or a preposition + ing-form.
Laura: I'm ashamed (▶) *to admit* (admit) it, but aeroplanes terrify me. I get really anxious
(▶) *about flying* (fly). I'm afraid (1) .... (buy) a plane ticket. I can't stand being
on a plane. I'm afraid (2) .... (get) killed. I feel ashamed
(3) .... (be) so silly.
Sarah: Aren't there things you can do to overcome your fear?
Laura: Well, I was interested (4) .... (read) in the paper recently that you can go on a
course that helps you. I'm anxious (5) .... (book) a place on it very soon.

4 Sorry (C)

Complete the conversation. Use a to-infinitive or *about* + ing-form. Look at the information in brackets.
Alan: I'm sorry (▶) *to disturb you* (I'm disturbing you), but could I just say something? I'm sorry
(1) .... (I was so rude) last night. I didn't mean what I said.
Mark: Oh, that's OK. I'm sorry (2) .... (I lost my temper).
Alan: Right. OK. And, as I said, sorry (3) .... (I'm interrupting you).

72 Used to do and be used to doing

A Used to do

Used + to-infinitive means that something happened regularly or went on for a time in the past. *I used to travel* means that in the past I regularly travelled, but I no longer do so.

Here are some more examples.
> We **used to play** that game when we were younger.
> Nick **used to smoke**, but he gave it up.   I **used to like** fish, but I never eat it now.
> There **used to be** a dancehall here, but they knocked it down.

We cannot use this structure in the present tense.
> Claire **travels** a lot. NOT Claire uses to travel a lot.

We normally use **didn't use to** in negatives and **did ... use to** in questions.
> We **didn't use to have** computers. OR We **never used to have** computers.
> Where **did** people **use to buy** their food before the supermarket was built?
> **Did** you **use to live** in London?

B Be used to doing

Be used to + ing-form means that something is familiar and is no longer strange. *I'm used to travelling* means that travelling is no longer strange or difficult because I have done it for so long.

Here are some more examples.
> We**'re used to getting** up early. We do it every day. NOT We're used to get up early.
> Sarah **is used to working** late at the office.   Most visitors to Britain **aren't used to driving** on the left.
> I **wasn't used to wearing** glasses. It seemed very strange at first.

We can also say **get used to** to talk about things becoming more familiar.
> It was difficult at first, but Mike soon **got used to working** at night.
> After her husband died, the old woman had to **get used to living** on her own.

72 Exercises

1 Used to do (A)

Mrs Bell is a hundred years old. She's the oldest person in the village.
A radio reporter is interviewing her. Put in *used to* with the verb.

Mrs Bell: I've always lived in the village, but not always in this house.
Reporter: Where (▶) *did you use to live* (you / live)?
Mrs Bell: When I was a girl, we lived at Apple Tree Farm.
(1) .... (we / like) it there.
Reporter: But life was hard, wasn't it?
Mrs Bell: Oh, yes. Things (2) .... (be) different from the way they are now. In those days (3) .... (we / not / have) electricity.
Reporter: And (4) .... (you / help) with the farm work?
Mrs Bell: Yes, (5) .... (I / look) after the hens.

2 Used to do and be used to doing (A–B)

Look at the pictures and say what the people used to do or are used to doing.
Use these verbs: *climb, fly, paint, play, sign*
Use these objects: *autographs, badminton, mountains, pictures, planes*

▶ He *used to paint pictures.*
▶ She*'s used to signing autographs.*
1 She ....
2 They ....
3 He ....

3 Used to do and be used to doing (A–B)

Put in a to-infinitive or *to* + ing-form. Use the verbs in brackets.
▶ When I was a child, I used *to dream* (dream) of being an astronaut.
▶ I'm terribly nervous. I'm not used *to speaking* (speak) to a large audience.
1 It took us ages to get used .... (live) in a block of flats.
2 Lots of trains used .... (stop) here, but not many do now.
3 Didn't Nick use .... (work) on a building site?
4 There didn't use .... (be) so many soap operas on television.
5 I'll have an orange juice, please. I'm not used .... (drink) alcohol.
6 David doesn't seem to mind being in hospital. I suppose he's got used .... (be) there.
7 When Laura was at college, she used .... (have) a picture of Elvis Presley on her bedroom wall.

73 Preposition or linking word + ing-form

A Introduction

Rachel: *Shall we have some lunch?*
Jessica: *I usually go for a walk **instead of eating**. I'm on a diet.*
Rachel: *You're joking, aren't you? Since when?*
Jessica: ***Since discovering** I can't get into my old clothes.*
Rachel: *Well, just buy some new ones, then.*

We can use an ing-form after some prepositions (e.g. **instead of**) or linking words (e.g. **since**).
We cannot use an infinitive. NOT *instead of to eat*.

B Preposition + ing-form

Here are some more examples.
***As a result of losing** my passport, I had to fill in a complicated form.*
*Vicky and Rachel might go to Canada **as well as travelling** around the US.*
*You can get skin cancer **from being** in the sun too long.*
*You aren't **in favour of cutting** down trees, are you?*
*Sarah went to work **in spite of not feeling** well.*
*We can't have a party **without making** a bit of noise.*

We can use these prepositions before an ing-form: **against, as a result of, as well as, besides, by, despite, for, from, how about, in favour of, in spite of, instead of, on, what about, without**

We use **what about/how about** + ing-form to make a suggestion.
How about giving us some help?
We use **for** + ing-form to say what we use something for.
*This cloth is **for cleaning** the floor.*
We use **by** + ing-form to say how someone does something.
*The thief got in **by breaking** a window.*
We use **on** + ing-form to mean 'as soon as'.
***On hearing** the news of David's accident, Melanie burst into tears.*
(= As soon as she heard the news, ...)

C Linking word + ing-form

Here are some examples.
*I always have a shower **after playing tennis**.*
***Although hoping** to get the job, Rachel wasn't really expecting to.*
*Sarah wanted to finish the report **before going** to bed.*
*The man has been unemployed **since leaving** prison.*
*You should always lock the door **when leaving** your room.*
*Mark was listening to the car radio **while sitting** in a traffic jam.*

We can use these linking words before an ing-form: **after, although, before, since, when, while**

A linking word + ing-form can sometimes be a little formal. We can say the same thing like this.
*I always have a shower **after I've played** tennis.*
***Although she was hoping** to get the job, Rachel wasn't really expecting to.*

▷ 70 Verb/Adjective + preposition + ing-form

73 Exercises

1 Preposition + ing-form (B)

Complete the sentences using the words in brackets.
▶ Rachel: Do you want to walk? Vicky: Yes, let's not get a bus. (instead of)
Vicky wants to walk *instead of getting a bus.*

1 Sarah: Did you get through the work? Mark: Yes, I stayed up all night. (by)
Mark got through the work ....
2 Melanie: When do you take the pills? David: The minute I wake in the morning. (on)
David has to take the pills ....
3 Mike: So you got the answer? Harriet: Yes, and I didn't use a calculator. (without)
Harriet got the answer ....
4 Emma: Why the rucksack? Matthew: So I can carry the food. (for)
The rucksack is ....
5 Trevor: Sorry I forgot the sugar. Laura: Well, you had it on your list. (in spite of)
Trevor forgot the sugar ....
6 Mark: Do you have to do the typing? Secretary: Yes, and book some flights. (as well as)
The secretary has to book some flights ....

2 Linking word + ing-form (C)

This structure is often used in instructions (sentences which tell people what to do).
Put in *before* or *after* and the ing-form of the verb in brackets.
▶ Replace the top on the bottle *after taking* (take) the medicine.
1 Read the contract through carefully .... (sign) it.
2 You shouldn't have a bath straight .... (eat) a meal.
3 .... (leave) home ring the airport to check that your flight is on schedule.
4 Always put your skis away carefully .... (use) them.
5 Be sure to switch off the electricity .... (change) a fuse.
6 Make sure the safety chain is on .... (open) the door.

3 Preposition or linking word + ing-form (B–C)

Ron Mason owns a supermarket business. Write the sentences for a magazine article about his life.
Join two sentences into one using the words in brackets.
▶ He saw an empty shop. He was walking around town one day. (while)
He saw an empty shop while walking around town one day.

1 He thought carefully. He decided to buy it. (before)
....
2 He bought the shop. He had little money of his own. (despite)
....
3 He became successful. He gave the customers what they wanted. (by)
....
4 He put the profit back into the business. He didn't spend it on himself. (instead of)
....
5 He was happy. He was running his own business. (when)
....
6 He fell ill. He worked too hard. (as a result of)
....
7 He has made a lot of money. He bought his first shop ten years ago. (since)
....

74 See it happen or see it happening?

A Introduction

David fell down the steps.
Rachel **saw him fall**.

David was walking with a stick.
Rachel **saw him walking** across the road.

B See it happen

After some verbs we can use an object + an infinitive without **to**.

	VERB	OBJECT	INFINITIVE	
Rachel	saw	David	fall	down the steps.
Vicky	heard	someone	close	the door.
Let's	watch	the parade	go	past.
We all	felt	the house	shake.	

We can use this structure with these verbs: **feel, hear, listen to, notice, see, watch**

C See it happening

We can also use an ing-form after the object.

	VERB	OBJECT	ING-FORM	
Rachel	saw	David	walking	with a stick.
Can you	hear	someone	playing	the piano?
We	found	Matthew	exercising	in the gym.
I could	feel	an insect	crawling	up my leg.

We can use this structure with these verbs: **feel, find, hear, listen to, notice, see, smell, watch**

D See it happen or see it happening?

SEE IT HAPPEN	SEE IT HAPPENING
We saw Trevor **plant** the tree. (He planted the tree. We saw him do the whole job.) I watched Nick **light** a cigarette. We noticed a young man **sit** down and order a meal.	We saw Trevor **planting** the tree. (He was planting the tree. We saw him in the middle of the job.) I watched Nick **smoking** a cigarette. We noticed a young man **sitting** at the table eating a meal.

When we talk about a short action, it often does not matter which structure we use.
   They heard a car **turn/turning** the corner.   I didn't see anyone **leave/leaving** any litter.

74 Exercises

1 See it happen (B)

Henry is in court. He is answering questions about a Mr Lewis, who the police suspect of a number of crimes. Add a sentence using the verb in brackets.

▶ And you say a second man came into the restaurant? (see)
  Henry: That's right. *I saw him come in.*
1 Are you quite certain that Mr Lewis took the envelope? (see)
  Henry: Yes, absolutely. ....
2 Then Mr Lewis left the restaurant, did he? (watch)
  Henry: He left soon afterwards. ....
3 And he drove away. (hear)
  Henry: Yes, he did. ....

2 See it happening (C)

Look at the pictures and add a sentence with *I can see/hear/smell ...* and the ing-form of these verbs: *bark, burn, come, ring, wave*

▶ The postman is on his way. *I can see him coming.*
1 There's a phone upstairs. ....
2 There's a woman in the boat. ....
3 There are some dogs outside. ....
4 You've forgotten your lunch. ....

3 See it happen or see it happening? (D)

There has been a bomb explosion in the city centre. TV reporter Kitty Beamish is asking people about it. What did people see or hear?

▶ Man: The bomb exploded. I heard it. It was a shock.
  He heard the bomb explode.
▶ Woman: A man was lying in the road. I saw him. He was just lying there.
  She saw a man lying in the road.
1 Woman: The building shook. I felt it. I couldn't believe it.
  ....
2 Man: People were shouting. I heard them. There was panic.
  ....
3 Girl: An alarm was ringing. I could hear it. It went on and on.
  ....
4 Boys: The police arrived. We saw them. They were over there.
  ....
5 Man: I saw a woman. She was crying. She was in a terrible state.
  ....

75 Some structures with the ing-form

A Two actions at the same time

*All afternoon Claire **lay** in a hammock **reading** a magazine.*

When two things are happening at the same time, we can use a main verb (**lay**) and an ing-form (**reading**). Here are some more examples.
*We had to **stand** in a queue **waiting** for the bank to open.*
*You can't **sit watching** television all day.   All afternoon, Vicky **lay** on the sofa **thinking** about life.*

We can also use this structure when one action comes in the middle of another. We use the ing-form for the longer action.
*Matthew **injured** his knee **doing** gymnastics.* (= He injured his knee <u>while</u> he was doing gymnastics.)
*I **went** to sleep **listening** to the radio.*

B One action after another

When there are two short actions, one straight after the other, we can use an ing-form for the first action.
***Opening** the bottle, Mike poured the drinks.* (= He opened the bottle <u>and then</u> poured the drinks.)
***Turning** right into Madison Avenue, the car drove north for two blocks.*

We can also use the perfect ing-form.
***Having opened** the bottle, Mike poured the drinks.* (= <u>After opening</u> the bottle, Mike poured the drinks.)

If either of the actions is long, we must use the perfect.
***Having photocopied** all the papers, Sarah put them back in the file.*
***Having repaired** the car, Tom took it out for a road test.*
NOT *Repairing the car, Tom took it out for a road test.*

These patterns are typical of written English. In spoken English, to talk about one action after another we use a sentence like this.
*Tom repaired the car **and then** took it out for a road test.*

C The ing-form saying why

We can use the ing-form to give a reason.
*The fans queued for hours, **hoping** to get tickets.*
(= They queued for hours <u>because</u> they hoped to get tickets.)
***Being** the youngest child, Natasha was her father's favourite.*
***Not knowing** the way, I had to ask for directions.*

We can also use the perfect ing-form to give a reason.
***Having spent** all his money, Daniel couldn't afford a new jacket.*
*We decided not to travel, **having heard** the terrible weather forecast.*

75 Exercises

1 One action in the middle of another (A)

Say what accidents these people had. Use these phrases: *lift weights, light a fire, open a tin, run, ski*
Put the verbs describing the longer action in the -ing form.

▶ Harriet *burnt her hand lighting a fire.*
1 Matthew ....   3 Vicky ....
2 David ....   4 Trevor ....

2 One action after another (B)

Rewrite the sentences about a detective. Begin with an ing-form, e.g. *doing* or *having done*.

Mitchell picked up the phone and dialled a number. He let it ring for five long minutes and then slowly replaced the receiver. He took a gun out of the drawer and put it in his briefcase. He left the office and then had to wait a while for the lift. He reached the ground floor and hurried outside to a taxi. The taxi driver pulled out a gun and shot Mitchell.

▶ *Picking up the phone, Mitchell dialled a number.*
▶ *Having let it ring for five long minutes, he slowly replaced the receiver.*
1 ....
2 ....
3 ....
4 ....

3 The ing-form saying why (C)

Match the two parts and join them using an ing-form, e.g. *doing* or *having done*.

▶ Because she didn't want to be late,   Harriet turned on the heating.
▶ As she had worked hard all day,   Andrew took it back to the library.
1 Because he had studied the map,   Daniel found it hard to communicate.
2 She felt cold, so   Vicky ran to the bus stop.
3 Because he didn't know French,   Trevor knew which way to go.
4 He had finished the book, so   Sarah was exhausted.

▶ *Not wanting to be late, Vicky ran to the bus stop.*
▶ *Having worked hard all day, Sarah was exhausted.*
1 ....
2 ....
3 ....
4 ....

Test 13 The infinitive and the ing-form (Units 65–75)

Test 13A

Some of these sentences are correct, and some have a word which should not be there. If the sentence is correct, put a tick (✓). If it is incorrect, cross out the unnecessary word and write it in the space.

▶ I'm used to driving in heavy traffic every day. ✓
▶ Although ~~of~~ feeling tired, Polly didn't want to go to bed. *of*
1   It's important for to sign the form. ....
2   Peter broke his arm in playing rugby. ....
3   A woman accused Martin of stealing her money. ....
4   I wasn't sure whether to write a letter of thanks. ....
5   Do you remember a young man bumping into you? ....
6   The girl's parents wouldn't let her to stay out so late. ....
7   The book is too difficult enough for children to understand. ....
8   Police found the woman for lying dead on the floor. ....
9   Cars are always expensive to repair them. ....
10 The man died as a result of falling asleep while driving. ....

Test 13B

This is an advertisement for the book 'Winning in Business'. Put in the correct form of each verb.

Are you fed up with (▶) *being* (be) a failure in your job? Wouldn't you rather (▶) *succeed* (succeed)? Do you want (▶) *to earn* (earn) more money? Are you anxious (1) .... (get) ahead? Do you believe in (2) .... (make) the most of your talents? Do you sometimes dream about (3) .... (reach) the top? If the answer is yes, read on. Just imagine yourself (4) .... (run) a big successful company. And now you can do something about it instead of (5) .... (dream). It'll happen if you want it (6) .... (happen). Make it a reality by (7) .... (order) your copy of the best-selling 'Winning in Business'. It has a ten-point plan for you (8) .... (follow). Do it and you're certain (9) .... (be) a success. You'll know what (10) .... (do) in business. You can make other people (11) .... (respect) you and persuade them (12) .... (do) what you want. Experts recommend (13) .... (buy) this marvellous book. You'd better (14) .... (order) your copy today.

Test 13C

Combine each pair of sentences. Use a to-infinitive or an ing-form. Sometimes you also need a preposition.

▶   We've advised Nancy. She should get a lawyer.
    We've advised Nancy to get a lawyer.
▶   I'm getting bored. I've been sitting on the beach.
    I'm getting bored with sitting on the beach.
1   We saw Rupert. He was looking in a shop window.
    ....
2   I remember the clown. He fell over.
    ....
3   Tessa wasn't sure. Which way should she go?
    ....
4   The porter just stood there. He expected a tip.
    ....

Test 13

5 How about it? Shall we go to the barbecue?
....

6 Susan is used to it. She's always lived in the country.
....

7 I'm afraid. I might hurt myself.
....

8 Christopher apologized. He'd forgotten to pay.
....

9 The food was too cold. Michelle couldn't eat it.
....

10 Polly was silly. She gave away the secret.
....

Test 13D

Read the story and write the missing words. Use one word only in each space.

Calvin Coolidge was elected US President in 1924. He didn't believe (▶) *in* doing too much, and his slogan was 'Keep cool with Coolidge'. Soon (1) .... moving into the White House, Coolidge invited some old friends (2) .... have dinner with him there. They were all people he (3) .... to know in the old days, and they were simple country people. They were interested (4) .... see inside the White House, and they were looking forward to (5) .... dinner with the President. They thought it was nice (6) .... him (7) .... invite them. But there was one problem. They weren't used (8) .... attending formal dinners, and they were worried that they wouldn't know (9) .... to behave. They were afraid (10) .... looking foolish. So they decided it would be best (11) .... everyone to copy exactly what Coolidge did.

At last the day came. During the dinner, when Coolidge picked up his knife and fork, everyone did the same. When he drank, everyone drank, and so on. Finally Coolidge decided to amuse himself (12) .... playing a little trick on his visitors. He tipped some coffee into his saucer. Everyone did the same. (13) .... done this, he added a little cream and sugar. Everyone did the same. Then, horrified, they watched Coolidge bend down and (14) .... the saucer on the carpet for his cat.

Test 13E

Complete the conversations. Put in the correct form of each verb.
▶ A: I'm annoyed about *being* (be) late.
  B: Well, I told you *to set* (set) off in good time, didn't I?
1 A: Did you accuse Nigel of .... (break) a plate?
  B: Well, it was an accident, but he did break it. I saw him .... (knock) it off the table with his elbow.
2 A: I came here .... (see) Janet. She must have forgotten I was coming.
  B: It seems rather careless of her .... (forget).
3 A: Are you going to have a rest now after .... (do) all the cleaning?
  B: No, I've got some letters .... (write).
4 A: You say you need some advice?
  B: Yes, I'm sorry .... (bother) you, but I don't know who .... (ask).
5 A: Do you like Scrabble?
  B: Well, I used .... (play) it quite a lot, but I got fed up with it. I'd rather .... (watch) television, actually.

76 Ship and water: countable and uncountable nouns

A What is the difference?

a ship *two boats* *water*

COUNTABLE	UNCOUNTABLE
A countable noun (e.g **ship**) can be singular or plural. We can count ships. We can say **a ship/one ship** or **two ships**.	An uncountable noun (e.g. **water**) is neither singular nor plural. We cannot count water. We can say **water** or **some water** but NOT ~~a water~~ or ~~two waters~~.
Here are some examples of countable nouns. We could see a **ship** in the distance. Claire has only got one **sister**. I've got a **problem** with the car. Do you like these **photos**? I'm going out for five **minutes**.	Here are some examples of uncountable nouns. Can I have some **water**? Shall we sit on the **grass**? The **money** is quite safe. I love **music**. Would you like some **butter**?

B Nouns after the, a/an and numbers

There are some words that go with both countable and uncountable nouns. One of these is **the**. We can say **the ship** (singular), **the ships** (plural) or **the water** (uncountable). But other words go with one kind of noun but not with the other.

COUNTABLE	UNCOUNTABLE
A/an or **one** goes only with a singular noun. I need **a** spoon. Numbers above one go only with plural nouns. We eat **three** meals a day.	We do not use **a/an** with an uncountable noun. NOT ~~a water~~ and NOT ~~a music~~. We do not use numbers with an uncountable noun. NOT ~~three foods~~

C Nouns after some, many/much, etc

Some and **any** go with plural or uncountable nouns. We can also use plural and uncountable nouns on their own, without **some** or **any**.

PLURAL	UNCOUNTABLE
Tom told **some** jokes. Do you know **any** jokes? Tom usually tells jokes. But NOT ~~He told joke~~.	We had **some** fun. That won't be **any** fun. We always have fun.
Many and **a few** go only with plural nouns. There weren't **many** bottles. I made **a few** sandwiches.	**Much** and **a little** go with uncountable nouns. I don't drink **much** wine. There was only **a little** bread left.

▷ 79 Agreement ▷ 85 A/an, one and some ▷ 95 Many and much

76 Exercises

1 What is the difference? (A)
Look at the underlined nouns. Are they are countable or uncountable?

▶ There was a car behind us. countable
▶ I never eat meat. uncountable
1 Do you play golf? ....
2 I had to wait ten minutes. ....
3 Just tell me one thing. ....
4 Love makes the world go round. ....
5 Good luck in your new job. ....
6 Power stations produce energy. ....
7 I'm taking a photo. ....
8 Would you like an apple? ....

2 A and some (B–C)
Laura has been to the supermarket. What has she bought? Use *a* or *some* with these words: banana, biscuits, butter, cheese, eggs, flowers, lemon, light bulb, mineral water, magazine, soap, wine

▶ some flowers
▶ a magazine
▶ some cheese
1 ....
2 ....
3 ....
4 ....
5 ....
6 ....
7 ....
8 ....
9 ....

3 Countable and uncountable nouns (A–C)
Complete the conversation. Choose the correct form.

Jessica: What are you doing, Andrew?
Andrew: I'm writing (▶) essay/an essay.
Jessica: Oh, you've got (1) computer/a computer. Do you always write (2) essay/essays on your computer?
Andrew: Yes, but I'm not doing very well today. I've been working on my plan for about three (3) hour/hours now.
Jessica: You've got lots of books to help you, though. I haven't got as (4) many/much books as you. That's because I haven't got much (5) money/moneys. Quite often I can't even afford to buy (6) food/a food.
Andrew: Really? That can't be (7) many/much fun.
Jessica: I'd like to get (8) job/a job I can do in my spare time and earn (9) a/some money. I've got (10) a few/a little ideas, but what do you think I should do?
Andrew: I know someone who paints (11) picture/pictures and sells them. Why don't you do that?
Jessica: Because I'm no good at painting.

77 A carton of milk, a piece of information, etc

A

a **carton of** milk   two **tins of** soup   a **kilo of** sugar   a **piece/slice of** bread   a **loaf of** bread

Milk, soup, etc are uncountable nouns. We cannot use **a** or a number in front of them. We do not usually say ~~a milk~~ or ~~two soups~~. But we can say **a carton of milk** or **two tins of soup**. Here are some more examples.

CARTON, TIN, ETC	MEASUREMENTS	PIECE, SLICE, ETC
a **carton of** orange juice	a **kilo of** cheese	a **piece of** wood
a **tin of** paint	five **metres of** cable	a **piece/slice** of bread
a **bottle of** water	twenty **litres of** petrol	a **piece/sheet** of paper
a **box/packet of** cereal	half a **pound of** butter	a **bar of** chocolate
a **jar of** jam		a **loaf of** bread
a **tube of** toothpaste		
a **glass of** water		
a **cup of** coffee		

We can also use this structure with a plural noun after **of**.
   a **packet of** crisps   a **box of** matches   three **kilos of** potatoes   a **collection of** pictures

B A piece of information

Advice, **information** and **news** are uncountable nouns. We cannot use them with **a/an** or in the plural.
   Can I give you **some advice**? NOT ~~an advice~~
   We got **some information** from the tourist office. NOT ~~some informations~~
   That's wonderful **news**! NOT ~~a wonderful news~~

But we can use **piece of**, **bit of** and **item of**.
   Can I give you **a piece of/a bit of advice**?
   There are **two pieces/bits of information** we need to complete the questionnaire.
   There's **a bit of/an item of news** that might interest you.

These nouns are uncountable in English, although they may be countable in other languages:
accommodation, baggage, behaviour, equipment, fun, furniture, homework, housework, litter, luck, luggage, progress, rubbish, scenery, traffic, travel, weather, work

Some countable nouns have similar meanings to the uncountable nouns above.

COUNTABLE	UNCOUNTABLE
There aren't any **jobs**.	There isn't any **work**.
It's **a long journey**.	**Travel** can be tiring.
There were **sofas** and **chairs** for sale.	There was **furniture** for sale.
We've booked **a room**.	We've booked **some accommodation**.
I've got three **suitcases**.	I've got three pieces of **luggage**.

77 Exercises

1 A carton of milk (A)

What did Tom buy at the supermarket? Use *of*.

Milk	0.35
Milk	0.35
1 kilo flour	0.85
Jam	0.95
Matches	0.39
Bread	0.65
Bread	0.65
Chocolate	0.95
5 kilos potatoes	1.59
Breakfast cereal	1.38
Mineral water	0.74
Mineral water	0.74
Toothpaste	0.89
Total	£10.48

▶ *two cartons of milk*
▶ *a kilo of flour*
1 ....
2 ....
3 ....
4 ....
5 ....
6 ....
7 ....
8 ....

2 Countable and uncountable nouns (B)

Complete the sentences. Put in *a/an* or *some*.
▶ I really ought to do *some* housework.
1 The people who camped in the field have left .... rubbish.
2 I've been working on the business plan. I've made .... progress.
3 The visitors are here for two nights. They're looking for .... accommodation.
4 That shop has .... nice sofa.
5 You'll have to pay extra for the taxi because you've got .... luggage.
6 The flat is quite empty. I need .... furniture.
7 I can't possibly fit this guitar into .... suitcase.
8 You need .... luck to win at this game.

3 Countable and uncountable nouns (B)

You are talking about the holiday you had with a friend. Use these words:
accommodation, awful journey, beautiful scenery, chair, fun, good weather, meal.
You have to decide whether you need to put *a/an* or not.
▶ (It was quite easy to book a place to stay.)
  Booking *accommodation* was quite easy.
▶ (There was nothing to sit on in your room.)
  But my room wasn't very nice. It didn't even have *a chair* in it.
1 (You were in a beautiful part of the country.)
  It was a lovely place, though. There was .... all around us.
2 (The weather was good.)
  And we had .... while we were there.
3 (One evening you went to a restaurant with some other people.)
  One evening we had .... with some people we met.
4 (You enjoyed yourselves at the disco.)
  We went to a disco. We had .... there.
5 (Travelling home was awful.)
  We had .... home last Saturday.

78 Nouns that can be countable or uncountable

A A potato or potato?

Some nouns can be either countable or uncountable. For example, **a potato** is a separate, individual thing, but **potato** cannot be counted.

potatoes

potato

COUNTABLE	UNCOUNTABLE
I'm peeling the **potatoes**.	Would you like **some potato**?
Melanie baked **a cake** for David.	Have **some cake**/**a piece of cake**.
Vicky was eating **an apple**.	Is there **apple** in this salad?
Someone threw **a stone** at the police.	The house is built of **stone**.
There's **a hair** on your shirt.	I must brush my **hair**. NOT hairs

B A sport or sport?

Often the countable noun is specific, and the uncountable noun is more general.

COUNTABLE	UNCOUNTABLE
Rugby is **a sport**. (= a particular sport)	Do you like **sport**? (= sport in general)
That's **a nice painting** over there.	Paul is good at **painting**.
We heard a sudden **noise** outside.	Constant **noise** can make you ill.
John Lennon had **an interesting life**.	**Life** is complicated sometimes.

C A paper or paper?

Some nouns can be countable or uncountable with different meanings.

COUNTABLE	UNCOUNTABLE
I bought **a paper**. (= a newspaper)	I need **some paper** to write on.
I'll have **a glass** of orange juice, please.	I bought a piece of **glass** for the window.
Have you got **an iron**? (for clothes)	The bridge is made of **iron**.
I switched all the **lights** on.	There's more **light** by the window.
I've been to France many **times**.	I can't stop. I haven't got **time**.
The journey was **a great experience**.	He has enough **experience** for the job.
I run **a small business**. (= a company)	I enjoy doing **business**. (= buying and selling)
We finally found **a space** in the car park.	There's no **space** for a piano in here.
	There are hundreds of satellites out in **space**.

D A coffee or coffee?

Words for drink are usually uncountable: **Coffee** is more expensive than **tea**.
But when we are ordering or offering drinks, we can say either **a cup of coffee** or **a coffee**.
   Two coffees, please. (= two <u>cups of</u> coffee)   Would you like **a cold drink**? (= a glass/bottle/can)

Some nouns can be countable when we are talking about a particular kind or about different kinds.
   Chianti is **an Italian wine**. (= a <u>kind of</u> Italian wine)
   The use of **plastics** has greatly increased. (= the use of different <u>kinds of</u> plastic)

78 Exercises

1 A potato or potato? A sport or sport? (A–B)

Complete the conversations. Choose the correct form.

▶ Can I pick <u>an apple</u>/<s>some apple</s> from your tree? ~ Yes, of course.
1 I think <u>sport/a sport</u> is boring. ~ Me too. I hate it.
2 We ought to buy <u>some potato/some potatoes</u>. ~ OK, I'll get them.
3 I think <u>painting/a painting</u> is a fascinating hobby. ~ Well, you're certainly very good at it.
4 Did you hear <u>noise/a noise</u> in the middle of the night? ~ No, I don't think so.
5 Is there <u>cheese/a cheese</u> in this soup? ~ Yes, a little.
6 I had <u>conversation/a conversation</u> with Vicky last night. ~ Oh? What about?
7 Shall I put <u>a chicken/some chicken</u> in your sandwiches? ~ Yes, please.
8 Are you a pacifist? ~ Well, I don't believe in <u>war/a war</u>, so I suppose I am.
9 It isn't fair. ~ No, <u>life/a life</u> just isn't fair, I'm afraid.
10 What's the matter? ~ You've got <u>some egg/some eggs</u> on your shirt.

2 A paper or paper? (C)

Complete the conversations. Put in these nouns: *business* (x2), *experience* (x2), *glass, iron, light, paper, space, time*. Put *a/an* or *some* before each noun.

▶ Harriet: Did you manage to park in town?
  Mike: It took me ages to find *a space*. And all I wanted was to buy *some paper* to wrap this present in.
1 Sarah: Are you busy tomorrow?
  Mark: I'm meeting someone in the office. We've got .... to discuss.
2 Trevor: Do you think I need to take .... with me for my shirts?
  Laura: Oh, surely the hotel will have one.
3 Vicky: I was going to have some juice, but I can't find ....
  Rachel: If you turned .... on, you might be able to see properly.
4 Claire: I've never met your brother.
  Mark: Oh, he's usually very busy because he runs .... But he's been ill recently. The doctor has ordered him to spend .... resting.
5 Daniel: How did your interview go?
  Emma: Well, I didn't get the job. I think they really wanted someone with .... of the work, and that's what I haven't got. So it was a bit of a waste of time. And the train coming back was two hours late. That's .... I don't want to repeat.

3 Countable or uncountable? (A–D)

Complete Claire's postcard to her sister. Choose the correct form.

The island is very peaceful. (▶) <u>Life</u>/<s>A life</s> is good here. Everybody moves at a nice slow pace. People have (1) <u>time/a time</u> to stop and talk. It's (2) <u>experience/an experience</u> I won't forget for a long time. There aren't many shops, so I can't spend all my money, although I did buy (3) <u>painting/a painting</u> yesterday. Now I'm sitting on the beach reading (4) <u>paper/a paper</u>. The hotel breakfast is so enormous that I don't need to have lunch. I've just brought (5) <u>orange/an orange</u> with me to eat later. I've been trying all the different (6) <u>fruit/fruits</u> grown in this part of the world, and they're all delicious.

79 Agreement

A Subject and verb

Look at these examples of agreement between the subject (e.g. **the window**) and the verb (e.g. **is**).

SINGULAR	PLURAL
The **window is** open. She **was** upset. It **has** been raining. The **soup tastes** good. This **method doesn't** work.	The **windows are** open. The **door and** the **window are** open. Her **eyes were** wet. They **have** got wet. The **biscuits taste** good. These **methods don't** work.
After a singular or an uncountable noun and after **he**, **she** or **it**, we use a singular verb.	After a plural noun or **they**, and after nouns joined by **and**, we use a plural verb.

B Everyone, something, every, all, etc

After **everyone**, **something**, **nothing**, etc, we use a singular verb (see also Unit 103C).
   Everyone was pleased.   *Something is wrong.*

But compare these examples with **every**, **each** and **all**.

After a phrase with **every** or **each**, we use a singular verb. *Every seat has a number.* *Each door is a different colour.*	After **all** and a plural noun, we use a plural verb. *All the seats have a number.*

C One of, a number of and a lot of

After **one of** ..., we use a singular verb. *One of the photos is missing.*	After **a number of** ..., we normally use a plural verb. *A number of questions were asked.*

After **a lot of** ..., the verb agrees with the noun.
   *Every year a lot of **pollution is** created, and a lot of **trees are** cut down.*

D Any of, either of, neither of and none of

When a plural noun comes after **any of**, **either of**, **neither of** or **none of**, we can use either a singular or a plural verb.
   Is/Are any of these old maps worth keeping?
   I wonder if either of those alternatives is/are a good idea.
   Neither of these cameras works/work properly.
   None of the plants has/have grown very much.

E An amount + a singular verb

After an amount of money, a distance, a weight or a length of time, we normally use a singular verb.
   Eight pounds seems a fair price.   *A hundred metres isn't far to swim.*
   Ninety kilos is too heavy for me to lift.   *Five minutes doesn't seem long to wait.*
We are talking about the amount as a whole, not the individual pounds or metres.

79 Exercises

1 Subject and verb (A)

Mark and Sarah are in an antique shop. Complete the conversation by choosing the correct form of the verb.

Sarah: This table (▶) is/~~are~~ lovely.
Mark: Yes, the wood (1) is/are beautiful, isn't it?
Sarah: The style and the colour (2) is/are both perfect for what we want.
Mark: These chairs (3) looks/look very stylish, too, but they (4) is/are rather expensive.
Sarah: Can you see if the table (5) has/have got a price on?
Mark: Yes, it has. It says it (6) costs/cost £2,000. That's ridiculous.
Sarah: Don't you think prices (7) has/have gone up recently?
Those tables we saw last month (8) wasn't/weren't so expensive.

2 Everyone, every, etc and phrases with of (B–D)

Vicky has been to a very grand party. She is telling her parents about it. Put in *was* or *were*.

I really enjoyed the party. It (▶) *was* wonderful. Each guest (1) .... welcomed by the hostess in person. All the rooms (2) .... crowded with people. Everyone (3) .... enjoying themselves. A lot of people (4) .... dancing, and a number of people (5) .... swimming in the pool in the garden. All the people there (6) .... very smart. One of the guests (7) .... a TV personality– the chat show host Guy Shapiro. I didn't know many of the guests. None of my friends (8) .... there.

3 Agreement (A–D)

The BBC is making a documentary about police work. A policeman is talking about his job. Choose the correct form.

▶ Every policeman is/~~are~~ given special training for the job.
1 No two days are the same. Each day is/are different.
2 But the job isn't/aren't as exciting or glamorous as some people think.
3 Not all policemen is/are allowed to carry guns.
4 A number of police officers here works/work with dogs.
5 An officer and his dog has/have to work closely together.
6 One of our jobs is/are to prevent crime happening in the first place.
7 A lot of crime is/are caused by people being careless.
8 Sorry, I have to go now. Someone has/have just reported a robbery.

4 An amount + a singular verb (E)

Combine the questions and answers about travel and holidays into one sentence using *is* or *are*.

▶ Do you know the price of a room? ~ Fifty pounds.
Fifty pounds is the price of a room.
▶ How many public holidays are there? ~ Ten days in the year.
Ten days in the year are public holidays.

1 Are you going on a long walk? ~ Fifteen miles.
....

2 Who's travelling on the bus? ~ Eight students.
....

3 Was someone waiting for the museum to open? ~ Yes, three people.
....

4 Do you know the baggage allowance? ~ Twenty kilos.
....

80 Singular or plural?

A Clothes, etc

Some nouns have only a plural form (with **s**) and take a plural verb.
 The **clothes were** in the dryer. NOT ~~The clothe was~~ ...
 The **goods have** been sent to you direct from our factory. NOT ~~The good has~~ ...
 My **belongings are** all packed up in suitcases.

> PLURAL NOUNS
>
> *arms* (weapons), *belongings* (the things you own), *clothes*, *congratulations*, *contents* (what is inside something), *customs* (bringing things into a country), *earnings* (money you earn), *goods* (products, things for sale), *outskirts* (the outer part of a town), *remains* (what is left), *surroundings* (the environment, the things around you), *thanks*, *troops* (soldiers)

Some nouns have both a singular and a plural form with a difference in meaning.

SINGULAR	PLURAL
Our special price is £10 cheaper than normal. So don't miss this **saving** of £10.	My **savings** are in the bank. I'm going to take out all the money and buy a new car.
The storm did a lot of **damage** to buildings.	The newspaper had to pay £2 million in **damages** after printing untrue stories about a politician.
I've got a **pain** in my back. It really hurts.	I checked the figures carefully three times. I took great **pains** to get them exactly right.

B News, etc

Some nouns have a plural form (with **s**) but take a singular verb.
 The **news was** worse than I had expected. NOT ~~The news were~~ ...
 Economics is a difficult subject. NOT ~~Economics are~~ ...

> NOUNS TAKING A SINGULAR VERB
>
> The word *news*
> The subjects *economics*, *mathematics/maths*, *physics*, *politics* and *statistics*
> The activities *athletics* and *gymnastics*
> The games *billiards* and *darts*
> The illness *measles*

C Means, etc

Some nouns ending in **s** have the same singular and plural form.
 This means of transport **saves** energy.
 Both means of transport **save** energy.
 This species of insect **is** quite rare.
 All **these species** of insect **are** quite rare.

> NOUNS WITH ONE FORM
>
> *crossroads*, *means*, *series* (e.g. a **series** of TV documentaries), *species* (kind, type)

Works (a factory) and **headquarters** (a main office) take either a singular or a plural verb.
 The steel **works has/have** closed down.

80 Exercises

1 Clothes, etc (A)

Put in the nouns and add *s* if necessary.
▶ Claire had to take her luggage through *customs* (custom).
1 Please accept this gift as an expression of our .... (thank).
2 The woman is demanding .... (damage) for her injuries.
3 The .... (pain) was so bad I called the doctor.
4 The old man carried his few .... (belonging) in a plastic bag.
5 If we pay in cash, we make a .... (saving) of ten per cent.
6 More .... (good) should be transported by rail instead of by road.
7 The gas explosion caused some .... (damage) to the flats.
8 We're going to spend all our .... (saving) on a new car.
9 The company always takes .... (pain) to protect its image.

2 News, etc (B)

Look at each group of words and say what they are part of.
Start your answers like this: *ath..., eco..., geo..., his..., mat..., phy...*
▶ atoms, energy, heat, light — *physics*
1 algebra, numbers, shapes, sums ....
2 dates, nations, past times, wars ....
3 the high jump, the long jump, running, throwing ....
4 industry, money, prices, work ....
5 the climate, the earth, mountains, rivers ....

3 Clothes, news, etc (A–B)

Choose the correct verb form.
▶ The television news is/~~are~~ at ten o'clock.
1 These clothes is/are the latest fashion.
2 Maths is/are Emma's favourite subject.
3 The troops was/were involved in a training exercise.
4 The contents of the briefcase seems/seem to have disappeared.
5 Darts is/are often played in pubs in England.
6 The athletics we watched was/were quite exciting.
7 The remains of the meal was/were thrown in the bin.

4 Clothes, news, means, etc (A–C)

Complete this letter Rachel has received from her sister. Choose the correct forms.

(▶) ~~Thank~~/Thanks for your letter. Your news (1) was/were interesting. We must talk soon. What about us? Well, we're living on the (2) outskirt/outskirts of town, not far from the company (3) headquarter/headquarters, where Jeremy works. We've spent nearly all our (4) saving/savings on the house. That wouldn't matter so much if I hadn't crashed the car last week and done some (5) damage/damages to the front of it. More bills! But at least I wasn't hurt. The house is nice actually, but the surroundings (6) isn't/aren't very pleasant. We're on a very busy (7) crossroad/crossroads.

I'm doing the course I told you about. Statistics (8) is/are an easy subject, I find, but economics (9) gives/give me problems!

81 Pair nouns and group nouns

A Pair nouns

We use a pair noun for a thing made of two parts which are the same. Some pair nouns are **binoculars, glasses, jeans, pants, pyjamas, scissors, shorts, tights, trousers**.

A pair noun is plural and takes a plural verb.
*My **jeans need** washing.* NOT *my jean*
***These tights were** quite expensive.* NOT *this tight*
*We've got **some scissors** somewhere.* NOT *a scissor*

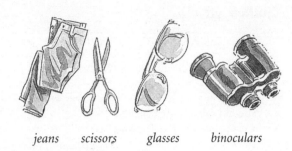

jeans   scissors   glasses   binoculars

We cannot use **a/an** or a number with a pair noun. But we can use **pair of**.
*I need **some jeans**.* OR *I need **a pair of jeans**.* NOT *a jean*
*Laura bought **four pairs of tights**.* NOT *four tights*

B Group nouns

A group noun can usually take either a singular or a plural verb.
*The **team was** playing well.* OR *The **team were** playing well.*
*The **government is** in crisis.* OR *The **government are** in crisis.*

The choice depends on whether we see the group as a whole or as individual people. Often it doesn't matter whether the verb is singular or plural. But sometimes one form is better than the other.

SINGULAR	PLURAL
*The **family is** a very old and famous one.* *The **orchestra consists** of eighty-six musicians.* When we mean the group as a whole, we use a singular verb.	*The **family are** delighted with their presents.* *The **orchestra don't** know what to play.* When we mean the individual people in the group, we normally use the plural.
We use **it** and **its**. *The **committee has** made **its** decision.*	We use **they, them** and **their**. *The **class** will miss **their** lessons because **they are** all going on a trip.*

Some group nouns: *army, audience, band, board, choir, class, club, committee, community, company, council, crew, crowd, family, government, group, management, orchestra, population, press* (= newspapers), *public, staff, team, union*
Also: *Harrods, the BBC, the United Nations,* etc and *England* (the England team), *Manchester United*

C Police, people and cattle

These nouns have a plural meaning and take a plural verb.
*The **police have** warned motorists to take extra care.*
***People don't** know what the future will bring.*
*The **cattle are** going to be sold with the farm.*

▷ page 379 Group nouns in American English

81 Exercises

1 Pair nouns (A)

Trevor and Laura are shopping for clothes. Choose the correct form.

Trevor: These trousers (▶) is/are a bit tight. They (1) doesn't/don't feel very comfortable. And I think the blue ones (2) goes/go better with the jacket.
Laura: That jacket (3) is/are too long.
Trevor: Well, the jeans (4) fits/fit all right. Perhaps I'll buy the jeans instead.
Laura: Yes, the jeans (5) looks/look good on you. I like the style. I think they (6) suits/suit you. Now you get changed while I look for (7) a/some shorts. And I might get (8) a/some skirt.

2 Pair nouns (A)

Complete what Rachel says to Vicky. Put one word in each space.

This old suitcase was in the corridor. I don't know who left it here. It's been here for about three days, so I'm having a look inside. There's a pair (▶) *of* pyjamas, (1) .... jeans, two (2) .... of tights and a (3) .... of sunglasses. There are (4) .... red shorts, too.

3 Group nouns (B)

Complete this TV news report. Choose the correct form of the verb.

Zedco (▶) have/has just announced that it made a loss of £35 million last year. The management (1) is/are well aware that they have made mistakes. The press (2) have/has all been printing stories and articles critical of the company. The Zedco board (3) knows/know that they now have some difficult decisions to take. Naturally, the staff (4) is/are worried about their jobs and (5) wants/want a meeting with management as soon as possible. But Chief Executive Barry Douglas says things aren't really so bad. He has said that the company still (6) has/have a great future ahead of it.

4 Group nouns (B–C)

Put in a group noun and *is* or *are*. Use these nouns:
cattle, choir, crew, crowd, orchestra, police, population, team

▶ The *crowd are* all enjoying the game.
1 This United .... the best one Tom has ever seen.
2 The .... hoping they can take part in a national singing contest.
3 The ship's .... all very tired after a long sea voyage.
4 The .... one of the biggest that has played at one of our concerts.
5 The .... installing cameras to photograph speeding motorists.
6 At the moment beef .... cheap because sales of beef are low.
7 The country's .... growing rapidly because of immigration.

82 Two nouns together

A Introduction
Look at these phrases.
> *a **bread knife*** = a knife for cutting bread
> *a **bus driver*** = someone who drives a bus
> *the **street lights*** = the lights in the street
> *a **cookery book*** = a book about cookery
> *my **birthday party*** = a party on my birthday
> *a **paper bag*** = a bag made of paper

In English we often use one noun before another like this.

The two nouns are often written as separate words, but we sometimes use a hyphen (-), or we write them as a single word.
> *a **tea break***   *at the **tea-table***   *a large **teapot***

There are no exact rules about whether we join the words or not. If you are unsure, it is usually safest to write two separate words.

B A souvenir shop, etc
Look at these examples.
> *a **souvenir shop*** = a shop selling souvenirs
> *an **animal hospital*** = a hospital for animals
> *through the **letter-box*** = a box for letters

The first noun is usually singular. There are some exceptions, e.g. *a **sports** club*, *a **goods** train*, *a **clothes**-brush*, *a **sales** conference*.

C A teacup and a cup of tea
Look at these pictures.

a teacup

a cup of tea

| **A teacup** is a cup for holding tea. | **A cup of tea** is a cup full of tea (see Unit 77A). |

Here are some more examples.

| *I picked up a **cigarette packet**.* | *Gary opened a **packet of cigarettes**.* |
| *I'll wash the **milk bottle**.* | *There's a **bottle of milk** in the fridge.* |

D An ing-form + a noun
We can use an ing-form with a noun.
> *a **sleeping-bag*** = a bag for sleeping in   *a **waiting-room*** = a room for waiting in
> *a **washing-machine*** = a machine for washing clothes

E Longer phrases
We can use more than two nouns.
> *a glass coffee-table*   *at Sydney Opera House*   *the bedroom carpet*
> *the winter bus timetable*   *our Assistant Computer Technology Manager*

82 Exercises

1 Two nouns together (A)

Say what these things are. For each picture use two of these nouns:
alarm, camera, chair, clock, cycle, luggage, motor, office, racket, television, tennis, trolley

▶ *an office chair*
1 ....
2 ....
3 ....
4 ....
5 ....

2 Two nouns together (A–D)

Can you say it a better way? Use two nouns together.
▶ (I read an interesting article in a newspaper yesterday.)
  I read an interesting newspaper article yesterday.
1 (Have you got any shirts made of cotton?)
  ....
2 (What shall I do with this bottle that had lemonade in it?)
  ....
3 (Have you got a bag to carry shopping in?)
  ....
4 (Is there a shop that sells shoes near here?)
  ....
5 (I'd like a table in the corner, please.)
  ....
6 (I'll need some boots to climb in.)
  ....
7 (Do you operate computers?)
  ....

3 Two nouns together (A–E)

Look at the definitions and write the words.
▶   a station from which trains leave   *a train station*
▶   a bottle once containing medicine and made of glass   *a glass medicine bottle*
1   a wall made of stone   ....
2   a centre where information is given to tourists   ....
3   a towel you use after having a bath   ....
4   clothes for working in   ....
5   a block of offices in the centre of a city   ....
6   a graph showing sales   ....
7   a card that gives you credit   ....
8   a race for horses   ....
9   the Director of Marketing   ....
10 a tour by bicycle at the end of the week   ....

NOUNS AND ARTICLES   193

Test 14 Nouns and agreement (Units 76–82)

Test 14A

Some of these sentences are correct, and some have a word which should not be there. If the sentence is correct, put a tick (✓). If it is incorrect, cross the unnecessary word out of the sentence and write it in the space.

▶ Would you like a piece of chocolate? ✓
▶ I like a~~ ~~classical music very much. a
1 That's a wonderful news! ....
2 Do you own a computer? ....
3 I heard an interesting piece of information today. ....
4 I saw your friend playing a golf. ....
5 There's some luggage in the car. ....
6 I bought a carton of some milk. ....
7 The gates were made of an iron. ....
8 You need an experience to run a business like this. ....

Test 14B

Tessa is talking about her shopping trip. Write the missing words. Use one word only in each space.

I spent (▶) *some* time looking round the shops in Oxford Street yesterday. I spent far too (1).................. money, of course. I bought some (2).................. : three dresses, a sweater, a blouse, two (3).................. of trousers and a skirt. I enjoyed myself – it was great (4).................. . The skirt is really nice. A hundred pounds (5).................. quite expensive, but I couldn't resist it. Anyway, it was reduced from a hundred and twenty pounds, so I made a (6).................. of twenty pounds. One of the dresses (7).................. fit, I've discovered, but I can take it back next time I go. I had a wonderful time and bought all these lovely things. But it was very crowded. Everyone (8).................. rushing about. And the traffic (9).................. terrible. I usually have a coffee and a (10).................. of cake, but the cafés were all full, so I didn't bother.

Test 14C

Complete the second sentence so that it has a similar meaning to the first. Use the word in brackets.

▶ Could I have some bread, please? (piece)
Could I have a piece of bread, please?

1 All the windows were broken. (every)
every window was broken

2 The money I earn isn't enough to live on. (earnings)
my earnings are not enough to live on

3 There were bits of paper everywhere. (litter)
There was litter every where

4 We went to the hotel to get a meal. (food)
....

5 Judy bought some binoculars. (pair)
....

6 I need a new book of cheques. (cheque)
....

7 I'll have some orange juice, please. (glass)
....

8 The reporter needed some information. (two)
....

194 NOUNS AND ARTICLES

Test 14

Test 14D
Each of these sentences has a mistake in it. Write the correct sentence.
▶ Can you lend me some pen to write this cheque?
Can you lend me a pen to write this cheque?
1 We can't sit here because the grass are wet.

2 Do you want a butter on your bread?

3 All my belonging was stolen.

4 Do you have any informations about hotels?

5 The police is questioning two men.

6 Can we have two coffee, please?

7 The news aren't very good, I'm afraid.

8 I just want to go into this shoes shop.

9 It's only a short travel by train.

Test 14E
Choose the correct form.
▶ The house is built of stone/a stone.
1 Each team wear/wears a different colour.
2 Let me give you an advice/a piece of advice.
3 Everyone was watching the football match/the match of football.
4 We had to take our luggage through customs/a customs.
5 The band is/are proud of their success.
6 I haven't got many/much friends.
7 Three hours is/are long enough to look round the museum.
8 I wear this glass/these glasses when I go out.
9 My father had a job at the steelwork/steelworks.
10 We couldn't find an/any accommodation.
11 Do you eat meat/a meat?
12 The contents of the box was/were thrown away.
13 Noise/A noise woke me up in the middle of the night.
14 Cattle was/were driven hundreds of miles by the cowboys.
15 One of the windows is/are open.
16 What would it be like to travel at the speed of light/a light?
17 Is there a sport club/sports club near here?
18 E-mail is a relatively new mean/means of communication.
19 We make furniture out of many different wood/woods.
20 Someone has/have kidnapped the President!

83 A/an and the (1)

A Introduction

Read this true story about an American tourist in Britain.

> **A man** from California was spending **a month** in Britain. One day he booked into **a hotel** in Cheltenham, **a nice old town** in **the West** of England. Then he went out to look around **the place**. But **the man** didn't return to **the hotel**. He disappeared, leaving **a suitcase** full of clothes behind. **The police** were called in, but they were unable to find out what had happened to **the missing tourist**. It was **a mystery**. But two weeks later **the man** walked into **the police station** in Cheltenham. He explained that he was very sorry, but while walking around **the town**, he had got lost. He had also forgotten **the name** of **the hotel** he had booked into. So he had decided to continue with his tour of **the country** and had gone to visit **a friend** in Scotland before returning to pick up **the case** he had left behind.

A/an goes only with a singular noun. With a plural or an uncountable noun we use **some**.
  *He left **a case**.* (singular)
  *He left **some cases**.* (plural)
  *He left **some luggage**.* (uncountable)
	The goes with both singular and plural nouns and with uncountable nouns.
	  *He needed **the case**.* (singular)
	  *He needed **the cases**.* (plural)
	  *He needed **the luggage**.* (uncountable)

B Use

When the story first mentions something, the noun has **a** or **an**.

> **A man** booked into **a hotel** in Cheltenham.

These phrases are new information. We do not know which man or which hotel.
But when the same thing is mentioned again, the noun has **the**.

> **The man** didn't return to **the hotel**.

These phrases are old information. Now we know which man and which hotel – the ones already mentioned earlier in the story. We use **the** when it is clear which one we mean.

A/AN	THE
*Would you like to see **a show**?* (I don't say which show.)	*Would you like to see **the show**?* (= the show we already mentioned)
*The cyclist was hit by **a car**.* (I don't say which car.)	*Whose is **the car** outside?* ('Outside' explains which car I mean.)
*In the office **a phone** was ringing.* (The office has lots of phones.)	*I was in bed when **the phone** rang.* (= the phone in my house)
*Has Melanie got **a garden**?* (We do not know if there is one.)	*She was at home in **the garden**.* (We know she has one.)
*The train stopped at **a station**.* (We don't know which station.)	*Turn left here for **the station**.* (= the station in this town)
*We took **a taxi**.*	*We went in **the car**.* (= my/our car)
*We could hear **a noise**.*	*We could hear **the noise** of a party.*
*I wrote the number on **an envelope**.*	*I wrote it on **the back** of an envelope.*

C A man/he and the man/someone

We use **a/an** + noun or **someone/something** when we aren't saying which one.
  ***A man/Someone** booked into a hotel.*
  *He left **a case/something** behind.*
	We use **the** + noun or **he/she/it** when we know which one.
	  ***The man/He** didn't return to the hotel.*
	  ***The case/It** contained clothes.*

196 NOUNS AND ARTICLES

83 Exercises

1 The use of a/an and the (A–C)

Complete this true story. Put in *a/an* or *the*.

(▶) A man decided to rob (1) ...a... bank in the town where he lived. He walked into (2) ...the... bank and handed (3) ...a... note to one of (4) ...the... cashiers. (5) ...The... cashier read (6) ...the... note, which told her to give (7) ...the... man some money. Afraid that he might have (8) ...a... gun, she did as she was told. (9) ...The... man then walked out of (10) ...the... building, leaving (11) ...the... note behind. However, he had no time to spend (12) .... money because he was arrested (13) .... same day. He had made (14) .... mistake. He had written (15) .... note on (16) .... back of (17) .... envelope. And on (18) .... other side of (19) .... envelope was his name and address. This clue was quite enough for (20) .... detectives on the case.

2 A man/he and the man/someone (C)

Replace the sentences which contain an underlined word. Use *a/an* or *the* with the word in brackets.

▶ We didn't have much time for lunch. David made something for us. (omelette)
David made an omelette for us.

1 They ran the race before they held the long jump. Matthew won it easily. (race)
....

2 The driver turned left. Suddenly someone ran into the road. (child)
....

3 Vicky was lying on the sofa. She was watching something on television. (film)
....

4 I had to take a train and then a bus. It was half an hour late. (bus)
....

5 A shoplifter tried to steal some clothes. The camera videoed her. (thief)
....

3 The use of a/an and the (A–C)

Complete the conversations. Put in *a/an* or *the*.

▶ Laura: Look outside. *The* sky is getting very dark.
  Trevor: I hope there isn't going to be *a* storm.
1 Mike: I'm going out for ...a... walk. Have you seen my shoes?
  Harriet: Yes, they're on ...the... floor in ...the... kitchen.
2 Melanie: Would you like ...a... tomato? There's one in ...the... fridge.
  David: Oh, yes, please. I'll make myself ...a... cheese and tomato sandwich.
3 Sarah: If you're going into ...the... city centre, can you post these letters for me?
  Mark: Yes, I'll take them to ...the... main post office.
4 Rita: I've got ...a... problem with my phone bill. Can I see someone about it?
  Receptionist: Yes, go to ...the... fifth floor. ...The... lift is along the corridor.
5 Tom: I didn't know Melanie had ...a... dog.
  David: It isn't hers. She's just taking it for a walk while ...the... owner is away.
6 Vicky: I've got ...a... headache. I've had it all day.
  Rachel: Why don't you go to ...the... health centre? It's open until six.
7 Andrew: Guess what. I found ...a... £50 note on the pavement this morning.
  Jessica: You really ought to take it to ...the... police station, you know.

NOUNS AND ARTICLES   197

84 A/an and the (2)

A Introduction

We use **a/an** and **the** when we aren't saying which one, and we use **the** when we know which one.
   A *tourist arrived in Cheltenham to look around* **the** *town*.
Look again at the story and the examples in Unit 83.

B The sun, etc

When there is only one of the things we are talking about, we use **the**.
   The sun *was going down*.   **The government** *is unpopular*.
   A drive in **the country** *would be nice*.   *We shouldn't pollute* **the environment**.
Normally there is only one sun or one government in the context.
We mean the government of our country and the sun in our solar system.

We normally say: **the country(side), the earth, the environment, the government, the moon, the ozone layer, the Prime Minister, the sea(side), the sky, the sun, the weather**

We also use **the** with **cinema, theatre** and **(news)paper**.
   Do you often go to **the cinema**?   *I read about the accident in* **the paper**.

Note that we say **a/the police officer** but **the police**.
   A police officer *came to the hotel*. NOT *A police came to the hotel*.
   The police *came to the hotel*. (= one or more police officers)

C A nice day, etc

A phrase which describes something has **a/an**.
   It was **a lovely day**.   *Cheltenham is* **a nice old town**.
   It's **a big hotel**.   *This is* **a better photo**.
But we use **the** with a superlative.
   It's **the biggest hotel** *in town*.   *This is* **the best photo**.

We also use **a/an** to classify something, to say what kind of thing it is.
   The play was **a comedy**.   *The man's disappearance was* **a mystery**.
We use **a/an** to say what someone's job is.
   My sister is **a secretary**.   *Nick is* **a car salesman**.

D A or an?

The choice of **a** or **an** and the pronunciation of **the** depend on the next sound.

a /ə/ or the /ðə/ + consonant sound			an /ən/ or the /ði/ + vowel sound		
a cup	/k/	the /ðə/ cup	an aspirin	/æ/	the /ði/ aspirin
a poster	/p/	the /ðə/ poster	an egg	/e/	the /ði/ egg
a shop	/ʃ/	etc	an Indian	/ɪ/	etc
a boiled egg	/b/		an old photo	/əʊ/	
a record	/r/		an umbrella	/ʌ/	

It is the sound of the next word that matters, not the spelling.

a one-way street	/w/	an open door	/əʊ/
a uniform	/j/	an uncle	/ʌ/
a holiday	/h/	an hour	/aʊ/
a U-turn	/j/	an MP	/e/

84 Exercises

1 The sun, etc (A–B)

Complete these sentences about pollution and the environment. Put in *a/an* or *the*.

▶ There was *a* programme on television about dangers to *the* environment.
1 There was also ...*an*... article about pollution in ...*the*... paper.
2 ...*The*... ozone layer will continue to disappear if we don't find ...*a*... way to stop it.
3 ...*The*... world's weather is changing. Pollution is having .... effect on our climate.
4 Last week ...*an*... oil tanker spilled oil into ...*the*... sea, damaging wildlife.
5 Some professors have signed ...*a*... letter of protest and have sent it to ...*the*... government.
6 If ...*the*... earth was ...*a*... human being, it would be in hospital.

2 The use of a/an and the (A–C)

Complete the conversations. Put in *a/an* or *the*.

▶ David: How was your trip to *the* coast?
  Trevor: Wonderful. *The* sun shone all day. We had *a* great time.
1 Henry: Would you like ...*a*... cigarette?
  Nick: No, thanks. I've given up smoking. It's ...*a*... bad habit.
2 Sarah: What's your brother doing now? Has he got .... good job?
  Laura: Yes, he's .... soldier. He's in .... army. He loves it.
          It's .... great life, he says.
3 Rita: I went to see Doctor Pascoe yesterday. She's .... best doctor I've ever had.
  Harriet: She's very nice, isn't she? You couldn't meet .... nicer person.
4 Rachel: You were .... long time at .... supermarket.
  Vicky: Yes, I know. There was .... enormous queue. I was thinking of complaining
          to .... manager.
5 Mark: Why were you late for your meeting?
  Sarah: Well, first I had to go to .... hotel I'd booked into. I took .... taxi
          from .... airport, and .... driver got completely lost.
          It was .... terrible nuisance. .... man was .... complete idiot.
6 Matthew: Is this ...*the*... book you were telling me about?
  Emma: Yes, it's ...*a*... really interesting story.
  Matthew: What did you say it's about?
  Emma: I knew you weren't listening to me. It's ...*a*... science fiction story.
          It's about ...*the*... beginning of ...*the*... universe.

3 A or an? (D)

Put in the abbreviations with *a* or *an*.

▶ a Personal Assistant   *a PA*
▶ a National Broadcasting Company reporter   *an NBC reporter*
1 a Disc Jockey   ....
2 a Very Important Person   ....
3 an Irish Republican Army member   ....
4 a Personal Computer   ....
5 a Los Angeles suburb   ....
6 an Unidentified Flying Object   ....
7 an Annual General Meeting   ....
8 a Member of Parliament   ....

85 A/an, one and some

A A/an and some

Look at this example.
> Trevor has found **some money** in his old trousers.
> There's **a note** and **some coins**.

We use **a/an** with a singular noun and **some** with a plural or an uncountable noun (see D).
A + singular noun: **a note**
Some + plural noun: **some coins**
Some + uncountable noun: **some money**

B A/an and one

A/an and **one** both refer to one thing. Using **one** puts more emphasis on the number.
> Henry gave the taxi driver **a note**. (not a coin)
> Henry gave the taxi driver **one note**. (not two)

We use **one** (not **a/an**) when we mean one of a larger number.
> **One question/One of the questions in the exam** was more difficult than the others.
> The team wasn't at full strength. **One player/One of the players** was injured.

C A dog = all dogs

We often use a plural noun on its own to express a general meaning (see Unit 86).
> **Dogs** make wonderful pets.   **Oranges** contain vitamin C.

Here **dogs** means 'all dogs, dogs in general'.

These sentences with **a/an** express the same general meaning.
> **A dog** makes a wonderful pet.   **An orange** contains vitamin C.
> **A butcher** is someone who sells meat.   **A video recorder** costs about £300.

A dog here is less usual than the structure with **dogs**, but we often use **a/an** when explaining the meaning of a word, e.g. **a butcher**.

D Some

Some with a plural noun means 'a number of', and **some** with an uncountable noun means 'an amount of'.
> Claire took **some photos**.   We went out with **some friends**.
> Henry bought **some flowers**.   I had **some chips** with my steak.
> Can you lend me **some money**?   Andrew is doing **some work**.
> Let's play **some music**.   There's **some milk** in the fridge.

Claire took some photos means that she took a number of photos, although we may not know the exact number.

We do not use **some** when we are describing something or saying what kind of thing it is.
> Vicky has **blue eyes**.   Is this **salt** or **sugar**?
> These are **marvellous photos**.   Those people are **tourists**.

Compare these sentences.
> I had **some chips** with my steak. (a number of chips)
> I had **chips** with my steak. (chips, not potatoes or rice)

▷ 76 Countable and uncountable nouns   ▷ 83–4 **A/an** and **the**   ▷ 94 **Some** and **any**   ▷ 96 **All**, **most** and **some**

85 Exercises

1 A/an and some (A)

Paul has painted some pictures for a competition. Say what is in the pictures.
Use *a* or *some* with these words: birds, cat, <u>fish</u>, flowers, fruit, luggage, <u>people</u>

▶ *some people*
▶ *a fish*
1 ....
2 ....
3 ....
4 ....
5 ....

2 A/an and one (B)

Put in *a/an* or *one*.
▶ Have you only got *one* bedroom? I thought you had two.
1 Melanie wanted something to drink. She was looking for .... café.
2 It was Sunday. .... shop was open, but all the others were closed.
3 .... of these photos is of you. Would you like it?
4 Shall I take .... photo of you two together?

3 A dog = all dogs (C)

Match each word with the right explanation and write sentences with *a/an*.

carrot	line of people	▶	*A carrot is a vegetable.*
violin	book of maps	1	....
queue	<u>vegetable</u>	2	....
atlas	tool for digging	3	....
spade	musical instrument	4	....

4 Some (D)

What would you say in these situations? Use a noun and decide if you need *some* or not.
▶ You and your friend would like a game of cards, but neither of you has a pack.
  We need *some cards*.
▶ You are describing Rachel to someone. Rachel's hair is dark.
  Rachel has *dark hair*.
1 You are eating nuts. Offer them to your friend.
  Would you like .... ?
2 You want a drink of mineral water. There's a jug on the table, but you don't know what's in it.
  Is there .... in this jug?
3 You've come home from a shopping trip with a few clothes. Tell your friend.
  I've bought ....
4 You are eating some bread that Melanie baked. It's lovely.
  Melanie, this is ....
5 The two women who live next door to you are both studying at the university.
  Tell your visitor. The women next door are ....

86 Cars or the cars?

A Introduction

We can use a plural noun (e.g. **cars**, **parties**) or an uncountable noun (e.g. **ice hockey**, **music**) without **the**. *I love parties* means that I love all parties, parties in general.

B General and specific meanings

GENERAL	SPECIFIC
A plural noun or an uncountable noun on its own has a general meaning.	**The** + plural noun or uncountable noun has a specific meaning.
Cars are expensive to buy.	**The cars** had both broken down.
Elephants are intelligent animals.	We saw **the elephants** at the zoo.
I don't understand **computers**.	**The computers** crashed at work today.
(= all computers, computers in general)	(= the specific computers at my workplace)
You always need **money**.	Laura put **the money** in her purse.
Glass is made from sand.	David swept up **the broken glass**.
I'm quite fond of **curry**.	**The curry** was delicious, thank you.
Natasha is studying **music**.	**The music** was too loud. (= the music at a specific time, at a party for example)
(= all music, music in general)	

A phrase or clause after the noun often shows that it is specific.
   Look at **the oil on your sweater**.   **The apples you gave me** were nice.
But the nouns in these sentences have a general meaning.
   I hate **people who never say hello**.   **Life in the old days** was hard.
Life in the old days is still a general idea, not a specific life.

A phrase with **of** usually takes **the**. Compare these two structures.
   a book on **Irish history**   a book on **the history of Ireland**

C Special uses of **the**

We use **the** + singular noun to make general statements about animals and about inventions and discoveries.
   The tiger can swim.   **The fly** is a common insect.
   Who invented **the camera**?   **The electron** is a part of every atom.
Here **the tiger** means all tigers, tigers in general. We use this structure mainly in written English. In speech, *Tigers can swim* is more usual.

We also use **the** with musical instruments. (But for American English see page 379.)
   Natasha can play **the piano**, **the violin** and **the clarinet**.
We do not use **the** with sports.
   Shall we play **tennis**? NOT *Shall we play the tennis?*
Note that we *listen to the radio* but normally *watch television*.

NOUNS AND ARTICLES

86 Exercises

1 He likes golf (A)

Look at the pictures and say what people like. Use these objects: *art, chemistry, chips, dogs, golf*

▶ *He likes golf.*
1 .... 3 ....
2 .... 4 ....

2 General and specific meanings (B)

Complete the conversations. Put in the nouns and decide if you need *the*.

▶ Tom: Did you see *the football* (football) on television last night?
    Melanie: No, I hate *football* (football). I was watching *the news* (news) on the other channel.

1 Rachel: Did your family have a dog when you were younger?
    Vicky: No, thank goodness. I'm afraid of .... (dogs). I didn't like .... (dogs) that were running around in the park yesterday. I was afraid they were going to attack me.

2 Melanie: You shouldn't drive so much, Mark. You know that .... (cars) cause .... (pollution), don't you?
    Mark: Yes, but .... (cars) these days are cleaner than they used to be. Isn't it .... (aeroplanes) that are mainly responsible for .... (pollution) of the atmosphere?

3 Melanie: I've put some bread out in the garden for .... (birds).
    Tom: You like .... (birds), don't you?
    Melanie: Yes, I do. I love .... (wildlife), in fact. I'd much rather live in the country if I could.

4 Laura: You're always reading books about .... (history), aren't you?
    Harriet: It was always my favourite subject. Do you know anything about .... (history) of this area?
    Laura: No, but if you like looking round .... (museums) and .... (old buildings), we could find out about it together.

3 Special uses of **the** (C)

Put in the correct noun and decide if you need *the*.
Use these nouns: *atom, football, guitar, radio, telescope, television*

▶ I was listening to a phone-in on *the radio*.
1 Rutherford split .... in 1911.
2 Tom and his friends played .... in the park.
3 Mike is quite musical. He can play ....
4 The children spend a lot of time watching ....
5 Galileo developed .... for use in astronomy.

87 Prison, school, bed, etc

A Prison or the prison?

Compare these situations.

*This man is in **prison**. He went to **prison** two years ago.*
We do not use **the** when we are talking about being **in prison** as a prisoner.

*The young woman is in **the prison**. She has gone to **the prison** to visit her father.*
We use **the** when we mean the prison as a specific building. The young woman is **in the prison** as a visitor.

Here are some examples with other buildings.

School is over at half past three.
(= school activities)
Vicky is at college.
(She is a student there.)
David is in hospital.
(He is a patient.)
Melanie is going to church.
(She is going to a service.)

The school is a mile from here.
(= the school building)
The meeting was at the college.

Melanie waited in the hospital for news.

We wanted to look round the church, but it was locked.

We can also use **jail** and **university** in this way. But we do not leave out **the** before other nouns for buildings, e.g. **the cinema, the factory, the house, the library, the office, the pub, the shop, the station**.

B Bed, home, etc

Here are some phrases with other nouns.

bed:	in bed, go to bed (to rest or sleep)	But *sit on the bed, make the bed*
home:	at home, go home, come home, leave home	But *in the house, to the house, in the home*
sea:	at sea (= sailing)	But *on the sea, by the sea, at/to the seaside,*
	go to sea (as a sailor)	*on/to the coast*
town:	in town, go into town, leave town	But *the town centre, the city, the village*
work:	at work, go to work, leave work	But *the office, the factory*

▷ page 379 American English

87 Exercises

1 Prison or the prison? (A)

Put in the words in brackets. Decide if you need *the*.

▶ The four members of the gang were sent to *prison* (prison). Their wives drove together to *the prison* (prison) every week to visit their husbands.

1. Not many people go to .... (church) regularly nowadays. I saw some tourists walking to .... (church) last week, but they only wanted to take photos of it.
2. A group of people came out of .... (cinema), crossed the road and went into .... (pub).
3. When my father was ill and had to go to .... (hospital), my sister went with him in the ambulance. She's a doctor, and she works at .... (hospital).
4. Mark has always known what he wanted to do in life. After leaving .... (school), he took a course in business studies at .... (college).

2 Prison, school, etc (A–B)

Complete this paragraph from a magazine article about Melissa Livingstone.
Put in the words with or without *the*.

Today Melissa Livingstone is a popular actress and star of the TV soap opera 'Round the Corner'. But as a child she was very unhappy. She didn't do well at (▶) *school* (school), and she never went to (1) .... (college). Her greatest pleasure was going to (2) .... (cinema). Her family lived in an unattractive town and their home was next to (3) .... (station). Melissa's father, Tom, was a sailor, and he spent months at (4) .... (sea). He was hardly ever at (5) .... (home) and when he was, he didn't do very much. Sometimes he spent all day in (6) .... (bed). Melissa's mother, Susan, had to get up at five o'clock every day to go to (7) .... (work). When Tom lost his job he stole a gold cup from (8) .... (church) Susan used to go to. He had to go to (9) .... (prison) for a year. Melissa's mother was horrified at the shame he had brought on the family.

3 Prison, school, etc (A–B)

Complete the sentences. Use *in*, *at* or *to* and these words:
bed, church, college, factory, home, hospital, library, prison, *shop*, *town*, work
Decide if you need *the*.

▶ We'll eat out tonight. I'll meet you *in town* later.
▶ This sweater was cheap. I bought it *at the shop* by the railway station.

1. The weather was awful. We stayed .... all weekend.
2. Melanie had an early night last night. She was .... at ten.
3. Emma's friend has just had a baby. Emma is going .... to visit her.
4. Vicky's parents are religious. They go .... every Sunday.
5. Laura doesn't like her job. She just goes .... to earn some money.
6. I've read these books. I'm taking them back ....
7. The man who did the robbery is no longer .... He was let out *last month*.
8. Jessica is a student. She's ....
9. It's very quiet .... when they've turned all the machines off.

88 On Friday, for lunch, etc

A Introduction

Henry: *Don't forget we're meeting on **Friday** for **lunch**.*
Sarah: *Of course I haven't forgotten. But remind me where we're eating.*
Henry: *The Riverside Restaurant. You've been there before. Claire was with us. It was **the Friday** before she went to Australia. We had **a** good **lunch**.*

Phrases of time are usually without **a/an** or **the**.	But we use **a/an** or **the** if there is a phrase or clause after **Friday, lunch**, etc.
*We're meeting on **Friday** for **lunch**.*	*It was **the Friday** before she went to Australia.* We normally use **a/an** or **the** if there is an adjective. *We had **a** good **lunch**.*

B Years, seasons and months

*I was born in **1974**.* *We play cricket in **summer**/in **the summer**.* *ced **Winter** always depresses me.* *I start the course in **September**.*	*That was **the year** I was born.* *It was **the winter** of 1995 when things started to go wrong for the company.*

C Special times

*We go away at **Christmas**.* *****Easter** is early this year.* *I'll be home for **Thanksgiving**.*	*We had **a** wonderful **Christmas**.* *I started work here **the Easter** before last.*

D Days of the week

*Yes, **Thursday** will be convenient.* *I'll see you on **Tuesday** evening.*	*The storm was on **the Thursday** of that week.* *We went surfing at **the weekend**.*

E Parts of the day and night

*I can't sleep at **night**.* *I prefer to travel by **day**/by **night**.* *I must get to bed before **midnight**.* *We were on the beach at **sunset**.* *I hope to get there before **dark**.*	*It's warmer in/during **the day**.* *Someone got up in/during **the night**.* *We're meeting in **the morning**.* *They arrived at the hotel in **the evening**.* *It was **a** beautiful **sunset**.* *I couldn't see in **the dark**.*

F Meals

*I'll see you at **breakfast**.* *We have **supper** at about eight.* *I'm going out after **lunch**.*	*We had **a** quick **breakfast**.* *****The supper** David cooked was excellent.* *****The meal** was very nice.* *We'll need **an** evening **meal**.*

NOUNS AND ARTICLES

88 Exercises

1 On Friday, etc (B–E)

Complete the conversations. Put in the words and use *a/an* or *the* if you need to.

▶ Rachel: Is it the pop festival on *Friday* (Friday)?
Vicky: I think it's *the Friday* (Friday) after that.

1 Henry: Will you be in America for .... (Thanksgiving)?
Claire: Oh no. That's in .... (November), isn't it?

2 Nick: Are you doing anything at .... (weekend)?
Tom: Well, I'm going to the match on .... (Saturday), of course.

3 Ilona: Does it snow here at .... (Christmas)?
Emma: Not often. We haven't had .... (white Christmas) for years.

4 Nick: How long have you lived here?
Harriet: We came here in .... (summer) of .... (1997).

5 Laura: I'd like to look round the castle in .... (afternoon).
Trevor: Well, it's just a ruin. The building dates from .... (year) 900.

6 Mark: I like driving at .... (night) when the roads are quiet.
Trevor: Oh, I don't like driving in .... (dark). I'd much rather travel during .... (day).

2 A/an or the with meals (F)

Laura is talking about the food she and Trevor had on holiday.
Put in the words and use *a/an* or *the* if you need to.

(▶) *The meals* (meals) we had weren't very good. We had (1) .... (breakfast) in the hotel, and that wasn't too bad. We usually went out for (2) .... (lunch) because (3) .... (lunch) they served in the hotel was always the same. And (4) .... (dinner) we had at the hotel on our first evening was pretty awful, so we tried a few restaurants. On our last evening we had (5) .... (marvellous meal) in a Chinese restaurant. I wish we'd discovered the place a bit sooner.

3 On Friday, for lunch, etc (A–F)

Put in the words. Decide if you need to use *the*.

Claire: Hello, Henry. Come in.
Henry: Oh, sorry. You're having (▶) *lunch* (lunch).
Claire: No, this is (1) .... (breakfast). I had a late night.
It was long after (2) .... (midnight) when I got in.
Henry: Someone told me you're going away after (3) .... (Christmas).
Claire: Yes, I'm going to the Seychelles on (4) .... (Wednesday).
Henry: What a life you lead, Claire. What time do you leave for the airport?
Claire: Oh, in (5) .... (morning) some time. About ten.
It's cheaper to fly at (6) .... (night), but I decided it would be easier during (7) .... (day).
Henry: I can drive you to the airport. I'm usually free on (8) .... (Wednesday) mornings. I'd like to see you off.
Claire: That's sweet of you Henry, but I can take a taxi.
Henry: I'll just check in my diary that it isn't (9) .... (Wednesday) of our next board meeting. No, it's OK. I can do it. And when will you be back?
Claire: At the beginning of (10) .... (February). The second, I think.

89 Quite a, such a, what a, etc

A Introduction

After **quite**, **such** and **what** we can use a phrase with **a/an**, e.g. *a game*. There is often an adjective as well, e.g. *such a good team*.

What a great win that was for United. They're such a good team.

Yes, it was quite a game, wasn't it?

B Very, quite, rather, etc

A/an goes before **very, fairly, really**, etc.
> It's **a very** old house.   It's **a fairly** long walk.
> I made **a really** stupid mistake.

But **a/an** usually goes after **quite**.
> It's **quite an** old house.   There was **quite a** crowd.

A/an can go either before or after **rather**.
> It's **a rather** old house. OR It's **rather an** old house.

We can also use **very, quite, rather**, etc + adjective + plural or uncountable noun.
> They're **very old** houses.   This is **quite nice coffee**.

C So and such a

SO	SUCH A/AN
The structure is **be + so + adjective**.	The structure is **such + a/an** (+ adjective) + noun.
*The test was **so easy**.*	*It was **such an easy test**.*
NOT *It was a so easy test.*	NOT *It was a such easy test.*
*The hill was **so steep**.*	*It was **such a steep hill**.*
*It's **so inconvenient** without a car.*	*It's **such a nuisance** without a car.*
	We can also use **such** + an adjective + a plural or uncountable noun.
*The weather is **so nice**.*	*We're having **such nice weather**.*
*Tom's jokes are **so awful**.*	*Tom tells **such awful jokes**.*
Note these sentences with **long, far, many/much** and **a lot of**.	
*It's **so long** since I saw you.*	*It's **such a long time** since I saw you.*
*Why are we **so far** from the beach?*	*It's **such a long way** to the beach.*
*There were **so many** people.*	*There were **such a lot** of people.*
*You waste **so much** time.*	*You waste **such a lot** of time.*
We can use this structure with **so ... (that)** or **such ... (that)**.	
*Emma was **so** angry with Matthew (that) she threw a plate at him.*	*Vicky got **such** a nice welcome (that) she almost cried.*
*I was **so** unlucky you wouldn't believe it.*	*I had **such** bad luck you wouldn't believe it.*

D What a

In an exclamation we can use **what a/an** with a singular noun and **what** with a plural or uncountable noun.
- singular noun: *What a goal!*   *What a good idea!*
- plural noun: *What lovely flowers!*   *What nice shoes you've got on!*
- uncountable noun: *What rubbish!*   *What fun we had!*

▷ 116 **Quite** and **rather**

89 Exercises

1 Very, quite, rather, so, etc (B–C)

What do you say in these situations?
▶ You're telling someone about the show you saw. It was quite good.
  You should go and see it. It's *quite a good show*.
▶ You are describing Harriet to someone who doesn't know her. She is fairly tall.
  Well, Harriet is *a fairly tall woman*.
1 You're talking about the Savoy Hotel, which is very grand.
  Yes, I know the Savoy. It's ....
2 You are talking about your journey. It was quite tiring.
  I travelled a long way. It was ....
3 You are telling someone about Claire's flat. It's really big.
  I've been to Claire's place. It's ....
4 You are telling a friend about your meal with Tom. It was quite nice.
  We went to that new restaurant. We had ....

2 So and such (C)

Complete the conversation. Put in *so* or *such*.
Sarah: Sorry I'm (▶) *so* late. We had (▶) *such* a lot to do at work.
Mark: You shouldn't do (1) .... much.
Sarah: The boss gets in (2) .... a panic about things. She makes (3) .... a big fuss.
Mark: Well, you shouldn't be (4) .... willing to work (5) .... long hours. No wonder you're (6) .... tired. You'll make yourself ill, you know.

3 So ... that and such ... that (C)

Match the sentences and combine them using *so* or *such*.
▶ Sarah was late home.   All the tickets sold out.
▶ Mike hadn't cooked for a long time.   He wouldn't speak to anyone.
1 The piano was heavy.   He'd almost forgotten how to.
2 Tom was annoyed about United losing.   It kept all the neighbours awake.
3 The band was a big attraction.   Mark had already gone to bed.
4 Vicky had a lot of work to do.   Mike and Harriet couldn't move it.
5 The party made a lot of noise.   She was sure she'd never finish it.

▶ *Sarah was so late home that Mark had already gone to bed.*
▶ *Mike hadn't cooked for such a long time that he'd almost forgotten how to.*
1 ....
2 ....
3 ....
4 ....
5 ....

4 What (D)

Put in *what* or *what a*.
▶ Come into the sitting-room. ~ Thank you. Oh, *what a* nice room!
1 Vicky believes in ghosts. ~ Oh, ... nonsense she talks!
2 Let's go for a midnight swim. ~ .... suggestion!
3 I think about you all the time, Emma. ~ .... lies you tell me, Matthew.

90 Place names and **the**

A Introduction

Man: *Could you tell me where **the Classic Cinema** is, please?*
Rachel: *Yes, it's in **Brook Street**. Go along here and take the second left.*

Whether a name has **the** depends on the kind of place it is – for example, a street (*Brook Street*) or a cinema (*the Classic Cinema*), a lake (*Lake Victoria*) or a sea (*the North Sea*).

Most place names do not have **the**.	Some place names have **the** – for example, a name with the word **cinema** or **sea**.
Europe California Melbourne *Brook **Street** **Lake** Victoria*	*the Classic **Cinema** the North **Sea***

Whether we use **the** can also depend on the structure of the name.

| We do not use **the** with a possessive (**'s**).

*at **Matilda's** Restaurant* | We often use **the** in structures with **of**, with an adjective and with plural names.
With **of**: *the Avenue **of** the Americas*
With an adjective: *the **White** House*
With a plural: *the **Bahamas*** |

B Continents, countries, islands, states and counties

| Most are without **the**.
*travelling through **Africa***
*a holiday in **Portugal***
*on **Jersey**   to **Rhode Island***
*from **Florida**   in **Sussex*** | Words like **republic** and **kingdom** have **the**.
*the Irish **Republic***
*the United **Kingdom** (the UK)*
Plural names also have **the**.
the Netherlands   the USA
the Canary Islands |

C Regions

| Regions ending with the name of a continent or country are without **the**.
*Central **Asia**   South **Wales***
*Western **Australia*** | Most other regions have **the**.
the West   the Middle East
the Riviera   the Midlands
Phrases with **of** have **the**.
*the South **of** France* |

D Hills and mountains

| Most are without **the**.
*She climbed (Mount) **Everest**.*
*down **North Hill*** | Hill ranges and mountain ranges have **the**.
*skiing in the **Alps***
*over the **Rockies*** |

E Lakes, oceans, seas, rivers and canals

| Only lakes are without **the**.
*near **Lake Michigan***
*beside **Coniston Water*** | Seas, oceans, rivers and canals have **the**.
the Mediterranean (Sea)
across the Atlantic (Ocean)
the (River) Thames   the Suez Canal |

F Cities, towns, suburbs and villages

Most are without **the**.
Harehills is a suburb of Leeds.
Houston is west of New Orleans.
We live in North London.

Exceptions are **The Hague** and **The Bronx**.
Note also **the West End** (of London).

G Roads, streets, squares and parks

Most are without **the**.
along Morden Road
in Church Street
on Fifth Avenue
near Berkeley Square
through Central Park

There are a few exceptions.
the High Street **The Avenue**
The Strand **The Mall**
Main roads and numbered roads have **the**.
the Bath road (= the road to Bath)
the A5 **the M6** (motorway)

H Bridges

Most are without **the**.
over Tower Bridge
on Brooklyn Bridge

But there are many exceptions.
across **the Golden Gate Bridge**
the Severn Bridge (= the bridge over the River Severn)

I Stations and airports; important buildings

We do not use **the** with most stations and airports; with religious, educational and official buildings or with palaces and houses.
to Waterloo (Station)
at Orly (Airport)
near St Mary's Church
Merton College   Norwich Museum
Lambeth Palace   Ashdown House

Exceptions are names with **of** or with a noun (*science*) or adjective (*open*).
at **the University of York**
in **the Palace of Westminster**
the Science Museum
the Open University
past **the White House**

J Theatres, cinemas, hotels, galleries and centres

A possessive form (**'s**) is without **the**.
St Martin's (Theatre)
at Durrant's (Hotel)
In the US, names with **center** are without **the**.
near Lincoln Center

But usually theatres, cinemas, etc have **the**.
at **the Globe** (*Theatre*)
the Plaza (*Cinema*)
outside **the Dorchester** (*Hotel*)
in **the Tate** (*Gallery*)
the Brunel shopping centre

K Shops and restaurants

Most shops and restaurants are without **the**.
shopping at Bloomingdale's
at Matilda's Restaurant

Names with a noun (*body, studio*) often have **the**.
at **the Body Shop**
The Studio Café

90 Exercises

1 Place names and **the** (B–F)

How much do you know about geography? Put in these names: *Andes, Brussels, Irish Republic, Italy, Lake Michigan, River Nile, North, Pennsylvania, Tasmania, United Kingdom, West Indies*
Decide if you need *the*.
▶ Harrisburg is the capital of *Pennsylvania*.
▶ Dublin is in *the Irish Republic*.
1 Chicago lies on the shore of ....
2 Sicily is a part of ....
3 .... are a mountain range in South America.
4 .... is England, Scotland, Wales and Northern Ireland.
5 .... is an island to the south of Australia.
6 Jamaica is an island in ....
7 .... flows through Egypt.
8 .... is the capital of Belgium.
9 Manchester is in .... of England.

2 Roads, buildings, etc (E–J)

Complete these sentences from a guide to London. Put in the words and decide if you need *the*.
▶ The train to Paris leaves from *Waterloo Station* (Waterloo Station).
▶ *The National Theatre* (National Theatre) is south of the river.
1 You can take a trip by boat along .... (Thames).
2 The Serpentine is a lake in .... (Hyde Park).
3 You can get to .... (Heathrow Airport) by underground.
4 Nelson's Column is in .... (Trafalgar Square).
5 Walk a little way along .... (Westminster Bridge).
6 From there you get a view of .... (Houses of Parliament).
7 The Queen lives at .... (Buckingham Palace).
8 Earl's Court is in .... (West London).
9 .... (M1 motorway) goes north from London.
10 .... (Ritz) is a very elegant hotel.

3 Roads, buildings, etc (F–K)

Complete the conversation. Put in the words and decide if you need *the*.
Sarah: We've just been to (▶) *the States* (States) – to (1) .... (New York).
Claire: Oh, really? I was there at Christmas. Were you on holiday?
Sarah: Yes, and we really needed a break. It was wonderful. We saw
(2) .... (Statue of Liberty), and we walked in
(3) .... (Central Park). We did all the sights. We spent a day in
(4) .... (Metropolitan Museum of Art).
And we walked along (5) .... (Broadway) and around
(6) .... (Macy's) department store.
Claire: Where did you stay?
Sarah: In a small hotel near (7) .... (Washington Square), not far from
(8) .... (New York University).
Claire: Last time I was there I stayed at (9) .... (Paramount). It's a nice hotel close to (10) .... (Broadway).

4 Roads, buildings, etc (I–J)

A woman is asking Trevor the way. Put in the words and decide if you need *the*.
Woman: Excuse me, can you tell me the way to (▶) *Millthorpe Station* (Millthorpe Station)?
Trevor: Yes, go along here and turn left by (1) .... (Little Theatre) opposite a
building called (2) .... (Kingston House).
The road is (3) .... (Wood Lane).
Go along there, straight across (4) .... (High Street),
past (5) .... (Royal Hotel), and you'll see the station in front of you.
Woman: Thank you very much.

5 Roads, buildings, etc (G–K)

Look at the addresses and write the sentences.

Useful addresses for visitors to Seaport	
Seaport Bus Station, Queen's Road	King Edward College, College Road
Grand Theatre, George Street	St John's Church, South Street
Odeon Cinema, The Avenue	Webster's department store, High Street
Clarendon Art Gallery, Newton Lane	Bristol Hotel, Westville Way

▶ Seaport Bus Station *is in Queen's Road.*
1 The Grand Theatre ....
2 ....
3 ....
4 ....
5 ....
6 ....
7 ....

6 Place names and **the** (B–K)

Write the headlines of the articles in this month's edition of 'Holiday', a travel magazine.
▶ walk / along / Princes Street   *A walk along Princes Street*
▶ holiday / in / Bahamas   *A holiday in the Bahamas*
1 day / at / Blenheim Palace
2 train journey / in / North Wales
3 tour / of / White House
4 beach / on / Riviera
5 shopping trip / to / Harrods
6 small town / in / France
7 trip / across / Severn Bridge
8 walk / around / Lake Windermere
9 visit / to / Tower Bridge
10 journey / across / Rockies
11 look / around / National Gallery
12 boat trip / along / Oxford Canal

Test 15 A/an and the (Units 83–90)

Test 15A

Complete the story about the theft of a river barge. Put in *a*, *an*, *one* or *the*.
This is (▶) *a* true story about (1) .... man who chose (2) .... worst possible time for his crime. It happened in London in (3) .... summer of 1972. (4) .... man stole a barge on (5) .... River Thames (in case you don't know, (6) .... barge is a river boat used for carrying goods). (7) .... owner of (8) .... barge soon discovered that it was missing and immediately informed (9) .... police so that they could look for it. Normally (10) .... river is quite (11) .... busy place, and it would be difficult to find what you were looking for. On this day, however, there was (12) .... dock strike, and so there was only (13) .... barge on (14) .... river. (15) .... thief was quickly found and arrested.

Test 15B

Decide which word or words are correct.
▶ I think that's *an awful* thing to say.
   a) a awful   b) an awful   c) awful
1 Judy goes to .... on the bus.
   a) work   b) a work   c) the work
2 I don't know what to do. It's .... problem.
   a) quite difficult   b) a quite difficult   c) quite a difficult
3 .... is my favourite sport.
   a) Golf   b) A golf   c) The golf
4 .... starts at nine o'clock.
   a) School   b) A school   c) The school.
5 We had .... time at the disco yesterday.
   a) really nice   b) a really nice   c) really a nice
6 Nigel opened a drawer and took out ....
   a) photos   b) a photos   c) some photos
7 Did you learn to play .... ?
   a) violin   b) a violin   c) the violin
8 We can finish the rest of the bread for ....
   a) breakfast   b) a breakfast   c) the breakfast
9 While I was in hospital, they gave me ....
   a) X-ray   b) a X-ray   c) an X-ray
10 I might listen to ....
   a) radio   b) radios   c) the radio
11 We need to protect .... from pollution.
   a) environment   b) some environment   c) the environment
12 Why do they always play .... music?
   a) so terrible   b) such terrible   c) such a terrible

Test 15C

Read the story about a silly mistake and decide if a word needs to go in the space.
If a word is missing, write the word. If no word is missing, write ✗.
This is also (▶) *a* true story. It shows how (▶) ✗ plans can sometimes go wrong and how (1) .... people can make silly mistakes. This too happened quite (2) .... long time ago – in (3) .... 1979, in fact. The scene was (4) .... old people's home in (5) .... small town in (6) .... north of England called (7) .... Otley. The

214 NOUNS AND ARTICLES

Test 15

owners of the home wanted to put (8) .... fence around it to make it more private. The work began soon after (9) .... Christmas when (10) .... workmen arrived in (11) .... lorry with planks of wood which they put up around the building. 'It was (12) .... very nice fence,' said (13) .... of the old people. But there was (14) .... problem. The workmen forgot to leave a gap for the lorry to drive out through. They had to come back the next day to knock down part of (15) .... fence. '(16) .... a silly mistake!' said another resident. 'It was (17) .... funny we had to laugh. In fact it was (18) .... most fun we've had for a long time.'

Test 15D

Some of these sentences are correct, and some have a word which should not be there. If the sentence is correct, put a tick (✓). If it is incorrect, cross the unnecessary word out of the sentence and write it in the space.

▶ The space capsule came down in the Pacific. ✓
▶ My new job starts in ~~the~~ April. *the*
1 I was so tired I went to bed at nine. ....
2 We had a very good lunch in the company canteen. ....
3 The life just isn't fair sometimes. ....
4 What the clever children you have! ....
5 We went out and bought some pictures. ....
6 Tessa was still working at the midnight. ....
7 I drive past the hospital every morning. ....
8 A one boy was much taller than all the others. ....
9 It costs such a lot of money, you know. ....
10 I'll meet you outside the National Gallery. ....
11 Have you any idea who invented the fridge? ....

Test 15E

Complete the conversation. Put in the words and decide if you need *a, an, some* or *the.*

Martin: I think we ought to book (▶) *a holiday* (holiday). Where shall we go?
Anna: What about (▶) *Scotland* (Scotland)?
  I think Edinburgh is (1) .... (beautiful city). I love going there.
Martin: (2) .... (weather) might not be very good.
  We went there at (3) .... (Easter), and it was freezing, remember.
Anna: We could have a walk along (4) .... (Princes Street) and up to the castle. And I wanted to go to (5) .... (Royal Scottish Museum), but we never found time.
Martin: Can't we go somewhere different?
Anna: We could spend some time in (6) .... (Highlands), I suppose.
Martin: When I go on holiday, I want to do something more relaxing than climbing (7) .... (mountains). And I find it pretty boring.
Anna: How can you say such (8) .... (thing)?
Martin: Actually, I'd prefer somewhere warmer and by (9) .... (sea).
  I think (10) .... (Corfu) would be nice.
  We might get (11) .... (sunshine) there. I just want to lie on a beach.
Anna: Martin, you know I'm not at all keen on (12) .... (beach holidays).

91 This, that, these and those

A Introduction

We use **this** and **these** for things near the speaker (**this** printout here). **This** goes with a singular or uncountable noun, e.g. **this** report. **These** goes with a plural noun, e.g. **these** results.

We use **that** and **those** for things further away (**that** table there). **That** goes with a singular or uncountable noun, e.g. **that** furniture. **Those** goes with a plural noun, e.g. **those** curtains.

We can leave out the noun if the meaning is clear.
   *I'm just having a look at **this**.*   *That's nice, isn't it?*
   *Last month's figures were bad, but **these** are worse.*

B Places and people

When we are in a place or a situation, we use **this** (not **that**) to refer to it.
   *There's a wonderful view from **this** office. Just come to the window.*
   ***This** party isn't much fun, is it? Shall we go home?*

We can use **this** to introduce people and **that** to identify people.
   *Jake, **this** is my friend Rita.*   *That's Andrew over there.*

On the phone we can use **this** to say who we are and **this** or **that** to ask who the other person is.
   *Hello? **This** is Laura speaking. Who's **this/that**, please?*

C Time

This/these can mean 'near in time' and **that/those** 'further away in time'.
   *I'm working as a tourist guide **this** summer. I'm pretty busy **these** days.*
   *Do you remember **that** summer we all went to Spain? **Those** were the days.*
   *I can't see you on the third of July. I'm on holiday **that** week.*

To refer back to something that has just happened or was just mentioned, we normally use **that**.
   *What was **that** noise? ~ I didn't hear anything.*
   *Jessica is on a diet. **That's** why she doesn't want to eat out with us.*
   *I've lost my key. ~ Well, **that's** a silly thing to do.*

To refer forward to something that is just going to happen or something that we are going to say, we use **this**.
   ***This** next programme should be quite interesting.*
   *I don't like to say **this**, but I'm not happy with the service here.*

▷ 13D **this week, this year**, etc

91 Exercises

1 This, that, these and those (A)

Write each of the words (*this*, *that*, *these*, *those*) in the correct place.

	Near	Further away
Singular	*this*	
Plural		

2 This, that, these and those (A)

Complete the sentences. Use *this*, *that*, *these* and *those*, and these nouns:
<u>car</u>, *dog, flowers, parcel, trees*

▶ *That car* has crashed.
1 Would you like ....?
2 I must post ....
3 The house is behind ....
4 Whose is ....?

3 This, that, these and those (A–C)

Complete the conversations. Use *this, that, these* and *those*.
▶ Mark: Are we going out *this* evening?
   Sarah: I can't really. I'll be working late at the office.
1 David: I hear you've got a new flat.
   Rita: ....'s right. I've just moved in.
2 Mike: What's the matter?
   Harriet: It's .... boots. They don't fit properly. They're hurting my feet.
3 Jessica: It's so boring here.
   Rachel: I know. Nothing ever happens in .... place.
4 Emma: What's happened? You look terrible.
   Vicky: You won't believe ...., but I've just seen a ghost.
5 Laura: What kind of planes are ....?
   Trevor: I don't know. They're too far away to see properly.
6 Matthew: The match is three weeks from today.
   Daniel: Sorry, I won't be able to play for the team. I'll be away all .... week.
7 Mark: Zedco. Can I help you?
   Alan: Hello. .... is Alan. Can I speak to Fiona, please?
8 Daniel: I've had .... bump on my head ever since someone threw a chair at me.
   Natasha: Someone threw a chair at you? .... wasn't a very nice thing to do.
9 Mark: .... seats aren't very comfortable, are they?
   Sarah: No, I don't think I'll want to sit here very long.

92 My, your, etc and mine, yours, etc

A Introduction

Mark: Why have you brought **your** work home? We're going out.
Sarah: I'll do it later. Let's go now. Shall we take **my** car?
Mark: Well, I'd rather not take **mine**. I think there's something wrong with it.

My, **mine**, **your**, etc express possession and similar meanings. **My car** means the car belonging to me; **your work** means the work you are doing. **My** comes before a noun, e.g. **my car**. We use **mine** on its own.

	MY, YOUR, ETC	MINE, YOURS, ETC
First person singular:	It's **my** car.	It's **mine**.
Second person singular:	Here's **your** coat.	Here's **yours**.
Third person singular:	That's **his** room.	That's **his**.
	It's **her** money.	It's **hers**.
	The dog's got **its** food.	
First person plural:	That's **our** table.	That's **ours**.
Second person plural:	Are these **your** tickets?	Are these **yours**?
Third person plural:	It's **their** camera.	It's **theirs**.

B Its and it's

We use **its** before a noun to express the idea of belonging.
   The street is around here somewhere, but I've forgotten **its** name.

It's is a short form of **it is** or **it has**.
   I think **it's** time to go. (= it is)   **It's** got a lot colder today, hasn't it? (= it has)

C My, your with parts of the body and clothes

We normally use **my**, **your**, etc with parts of the body and with someone's clothes.
   Emma shook **her** head sadly. NOT Emma shook the head sadly.
   Someone came up behind me and grabbed **my** arm.
   You must take off **your** shoes before you enter a mosque.
But we usually use **the** in the following structure with a prepositional phrase.

	VERB	PERSON	PREPOSITIONAL PHRASE
Someone	grabbed	me	by **the** arm.
The stone	hit	Mike	on **the** head.

D Own

We use **own** after **my**, **your**, etc to say that something belongs to us and to no one else.
   Rachel has got **her own** calculator. She doesn't borrow mine. NOT an own calculator
   I don't share any more. I've got a flat of **my own**. NOT of mine own

E A friend of mine

Look at these examples.
   Tom is **a friend of mine**. (= one of my friends) NOT a friend of me
   Rachel came to the party with **a cousin of hers**. (= one of her cousins)
   I borrowed **some magazines of yours**. (= some of your magazines)
Note also **'s** in this example: Rita is a friend of **Melanie's**.

218   THIS, MY, SOME, A LOT OF, ETC

92 Exercises

1 My, your, etc and mine, yours, etc (A)

Complete the conversation. Put in the missing words.
- Laura: Did you and (▶) *your* friends have a nice holiday?
- Emma: Yes, it was wonderful. We had the best holiday of (1) .... lives. It didn't start very well, though. Daniel forgot to bring (2) .... passport.
- Laura: Oh, dear. So what happened?
- Emma: Well, luckily he doesn't live far from the airport. He rang (3) .... parents, and they brought the passport over in (4) .... car, just in time.
- Laura: You remembered (5) ...., I hope.
- Emma: Yes, I had (6) ...., even though I'm usually the one who forgets things. Actually Rachel thought for a minute that she'd lost (7) .... Luckily it was in (8) .... suitcase. Anyway, in the end we had a marvellous time.

2 Its and it's (B)

Put in the correct form.
- ▶ Unfortunately, the town has lost *its* only cinema.
- ▶ The meeting won't last long. I'll see you when *it's* over.
1. You should return the book to .... owner immediately.
2. We'd like to go out for a walk, but .... raining.
3. I'm not buying this tablecloth because .... got a hole in it.
4. The board has decided that Zedco needs to improve .... image.

3 Parts of the body and clothes (C)

Put in *my, your,* etc or *the*.
- ▶ I was doing keep-fit exercises when I fell down and hurt *my* leg.
- ▶ Matthew served, and the ball hit Daniel on *the* knee.
1. A wasp stung me on .... neck. It really hurt.
2. The mother put both .... arms around the child.
3. Aunt Joan kissed Emma on .... cheek.
4. The fans were all shouting at the top of .... voices.
5. Don't just stand there with .... hands in .... pockets.

4 My own, a friend of mine, etc (D–E)

Correct the sentences which have a mistake.
- ▶ We're lucky. ~~We've got an own garden.~~
   We've got our own garden.
1. I met some nice people. ~~Harriet introduced me to a friend of herself.~~
   ....
2. My friends swim every day. ~~They've got their only pool.~~
   ....
3. I enjoy rock-climbing. ~~It's a favourite hobby to me.~~
   ....
4. I hope Matthew will be here. ~~I've got some CDs from his.~~
   ....
5. I don't want to share. ~~I'd like my very room.~~
   ....

93 The possessive form and **of**

A Form

We use the possessive of a noun in phrases like *the boy's name* and *Vicky's room*.
We form the possessive like this.

Singular noun:	**'s**	boy → boy**'s**	Vicky → Vicky**'s**
Plural noun ending in **s**:	**'**	boys → boys**'**	tourists → tourists**'**
Plural noun <u>not</u> ending in **s**:	**'s**	men → men**'s**	children → children**'s**

We can use the possessive form with another noun or on its own.
　*I've met **Rachel's family**, but I haven't met **Vicky's**.* (*Vicky's* = Vicky's family)

B The **boy's** name or the **name of the boy**?

Compare these structures.

THE POSSESSIVE FORM	PHRASE WITH **OF**
the **boy's** name	the name **of the boy**
the **boys'** names	the names **of the boys**
the **men's** names	the names **of the men**

Sometimes we can use either the possessive (*the boy's name*) or a phrase with **of** (*the name of the boy*), but often only one is possible. We normally use the possessive with people and animals.
　my friend's house　　**Claire's** idea　　**Daniel's** brother　　**our neighbour's** garden　　**the dog's** owner
　the policemen's uniforms　　**the women's** changing room　　**the Parkers'** car

We normally use **of** with things, and not the possessive form.
　*the side **of the house*** NOT *the house's side*
　*the result **of the match*** NOT *the match's result*
　*the day **of the meeting*** NOT *the meeting's day*

But we use **of** with people when there is a long phrase.
　*the house **of one of our teachers at college***
　*the address **of those people we met in Spain***
　NOT *those people who we met in Spain's address*

We can use both structures for places and organizations.
　London's museums OR *the museums **of London***
　the earth's atmosphere OR *the atmosphere **of the earth***
　the company's future OR *the future **of the company***
　the government's intentions OR *the intentions **of the government***

C The possessive of time

We can use the possessive to say 'when' or 'how long'.
　last week's concert　　**today's** TV programmes　　**yesterday's** news
　about **a month's** work　　**a moment's** silence　　**ten minutes'** walk

Note also:
　*in **two months'** time* (two months from now)
　***a week's** wages* (wages for a week)

93 Exercises

1 The possessive form (A)

Write descriptions of the things in the photos. Use *boy*, *girl* and *children* and these words:
bike, cat, <u>dog</u>, skateboards, tent, trophies

▶ *the children's dog*
1 ....
2 ....
3 ....
4 ....
5 ....

2 The possessive form (A)

Laura is showing Melanie her photos. Put in the possessive form of the nouns.

Laura: This was taken in (▶) *my friend's* (my friend) garden.
It was (1) .... (the twins) birthday party.
This is Kerry, (2) .... (Luke) cousin.
And that's (3) .... (Jason) sister Emily.
Melanie: And who are these two?
Laura: That's (4) .... (Debbie) mother.
She's talking to Monica Davis, (5) .... (her children) teacher.
And that's (6) .... (the Lanskys) dog
sitting on (7) .... (Olivia) foot.

3 **The boy's name** or the **name of the boy**? (B)

Ed Buckman writes detective stories. Here are the titles of some of his stories.
Write the titles using either *of* or a possessive form (with *'s* or *s'*).

▶ the mistake / the policeman   *The Policeman's Mistake*
▶ the bottom / the bottle   *The Bottom of the Bottle*
1 the gun / Mr Hillman   ....
2 the smell / blood   ....
3 the car / the terrorist   ....
4 the middle / the night   ....
5 the death / someone important   ....
6 the money / the gangsters   ....

4 The possessive of time (C)

Rewrite the <u>underlined</u> phrases using a possessive form.

▶ <u>The prices this year</u> are even lower.   *This year's prices*
▶ From here it's <u>a drive of two hours</u>.   *a two hours' drive*
1 I read about it in <u>the paper yesterday</u>.   ....
2 I just want <u>a rest for five minutes</u>.   ....
3 It's <u>the special offer for this month</u>.   ....
4 I'll see you <u>in a week</u>.   ....

94 Some and any

A Basic use

Some and **any** go before a plural or uncountable noun (see Unit 85A).
　*There was a bowl and **some** cornflakes on the table, but there wasn't **any** milk.*
We can also use **some** and **any** without a noun.
　Trevor wanted some milk, but he couldn't find any.

We normally use **some** in positive sentences and **any** in negative sentences or ones with a negative meaning.

POSITIVE	NEGATIVE
There's **some** milk in the fridge.	I haven't **any** milk. (= I have <u>no</u> milk.)
I need **some** stamps. ~ There are **some** in the drawer.	I haven't got **any** stamps. Have you got **any**?
I met **some** interesting people last night.	I never meet **any** interesting people nowadays.
We'll have **some** fun at Disneyland.	We won't have **any** fun without you.

We can also use **any** in a sentence with **if**.
　***If** you have **any** problems, you can discuss them with your group leaders.*
　*I can answer **any** questions. (= <u>If</u> there are any questions, ...)*

In questions we can use either **some** or **any**, but **any** is more common.
We don't know whether the answer will be yes or no.
　*Have we got **any** butter?　　Will there be **any** food for the guests?　　Did you buy **any** clothes?*

We normally use **some** in offers and requests to make them sound more positive.
　*Would you like **some** coffee?　　Could you post **some** letters for me?*
We can use **some** in questions when we think the answer might be yes.
　*Did you buy **some** clothes?* (Perhaps I know that you went out to buy some.)

B Someone, anything, etc

We choose between **someone** and **anyone**, **something** and **anything**, and **somewhere** and **anywhere** in the same way as between **some** and **any**.

Someone has spilt water everywhere.	Did **anyone** see what happened?
Would you like **something** to eat?	We haven't got **anything** to eat.
Let's go out **somewhere**.	Is there **anywhere** we can go?

C Another use of any

We can use **any** in a positive sentence to mean 'it doesn't matter which'.
　*I'm free all day. Call **any** time you like.*
　***Any** student will be able to tell you where the college library is.*
　*You can buy these maps at **any** petrol station. They all have them.*
We say *any petrol station* because all petrol stations have the maps. It doesn't matter which one you go to. They are all equally good.

Look at these examples with **anyone**, **anything** and **anywhere**.
　*It's a very simple puzzle. **Anyone** could solve it. (= It doesn't matter who.)*
　*What shall we have for lunch? ~ Oh, **anything**. I don't mind.*
　*Where do we have to sit? ~ We can sit **anywhere**. It doesn't matter.*

▷ 85A **A/an** and **some**　▷ 103 **Everyone, something**, etc

94 Exercises

1 Basic use (A)

Look at the pictures and say what people have or haven't got. Use *some* or *any*.
Use these words: *cats, money, petrol, poison, sandwiches*

▶ *They've got some sandwiches.*
▶ *She hasn't got any money.*
1 ....
2 ....
3 ....

2 Basic use (A)

Justin Cooper is a radio disc jockey. Complete what he is saying. Put in *some* or *any*.

That was 'I can't find (▶) *any* love' by Arlene Black. Now, I've had (▶) *some* letters asking for something by Express. One listener says she hasn't heard (1) .... Express songs on this programme for months. Well, I'm going to put that right. And this will be our last track because there isn't (2) .... more time left. We've had (3) .... great songs tonight, and I'll be here next week to play (4) .... more. Now here's (5) .... music from Express – 'I never have (6) .... luck'.

3 Some, any, someone, anyone, etc (A–B)

Complete the conversations. Put in *some, any, anyone, someone, something* or *anything*.

▶ Trevor: We haven't got *any* bread.
  Laura: You'd better go to the shop, then. We need *some* tomatoes, too.
1 Claire: Would you like .... cheese and biscuits?
  Sarah: Oh, no thank you. That was delicious, but I couldn't eat .... else.
2 Harriet: There's .... at the door.
  Mike: Are we expecting .... visitors?
3 Melanie: Has .... offered to help you with the tea?
  Rita: No, but I'd be very grateful for .... help you can give.
4 Vicky: I was looking for ...., and now I can't remember what it was.
  Rachel: You said you were looking for .... matches.

4 Another use of any (C)

Put in *any* + noun, *anyone* or *anything*.

▶ The seats aren't reserved. You can have *any seat* you like.
▶ I don't mind what we do today. We can do *anything* you want.
1 If it's your party, you can invite .... you like.
2 All the buses go into the town centre. Take .... that comes along here.
3 This carpet is available in lots of colours. You can have .... you like.
4 My father has the television on all the time. He'll watch ....
5 It doesn't matter which day you phone. Ring .... you like.

95 A lot of, lots of, many, much, (a) few and (a) little

A Introduction

A lot of, **lots of**, **many** and **much** mean a large quantity.
   *Ron Mason owns a chain of supermarkets. He's made **a lot of** money.*
A few and **a little** mean a small quantity.
   *I'd better hurry. My bus goes in **a few** minutes.*

Many and **a few** go before plural nouns.	**Much** and **a little** go before uncountable nouns.
many places **many** problems	**much** money **much** trouble
a few people **a few** buildings	**a little** sunshine **a little** food

A lot of and **lots of** go before both plural and uncountable nouns.

a lot of tourists **lots of** games	**a lot of** sugar **lots of** fun

We use these words without a noun if it is clear what we mean.
   *I take photos, but not as **many** as I used to. At one time I took **a lot**.*
Note that we say **a lot** without **of**.

B A lot of, many and much

As a general rule, we use **a lot of** and **lots of** in positive statements and **many** and **much** in negatives and questions.
Positive: We get **a lot of** storms here.   We get **a lot of** rain here.
Negative: We don't get **many** storms here.   We don't get **much** rain here.
Questions: Do you get **many** storms here?   Do you get **much** rain here?
            How **many** eggs do we need?   How **much** salt do we put in?

We use **many** or **much** (not **a lot of**) after **too**, **so** and **as**.
   *There are **too many** cars.   I've got **so much** work.   I haven't got **as much** money as you.*

In formal English, we can sometimes use **many** and **much** in a positive statement.
   ***Many** students have financial problems.   There is **much** enthusiasm for the idea.*
But this is less usual in conversation, where we normally use **a lot of** or **lots of**.

In informal English, you may hear **a lot of** in a negative or a question.
   *I don't have **many** friends/**a lot of** friends.   Do you eat **much** fruit/**a lot of** fruit?*

C Few and little with and without a

With **a** the meaning is positive.	Without **a** the meaning is negative.
***A few** customers have come into the shop. It has been fairly busy.*	***Few** customers have come into the shop. It has been quiet.*
*Vicky has made **a little** progress and so is feeling quite pleased.*	*Vicky has made **little** progress and so is not feeling very pleased.*
A few customers = some customers, a small number of customers	**Few** customers = not many customers
A little progress = some progress, a small amount of progress	**Little** progress = not much progress

Few and **little** (without **a**) can be rather formal. In informal speech we can use these structures.
   ***Not many** customers have come in.   Vicky hasn't made **much** progress.*
   ***Only a few** customers have come in.   Vicky has made **only a little** progress.*

95 Exercises

1 A lot of, lots of, many, much, a few and a little (A)

Write the sentences correctly.
▶ Mark was only spending one night away. ~~He quickly put a little things into a bag.~~
   He quickly put a few things into a bag.
1 Rachel is learning to drive. ~~She hasn't had much lessons yet.~~

2 I'm making soup for twenty people. ~~I'll have to make a lot of.~~

3 I feel really tired. ~~I haven't got many energy.~~

4 The mixture looks rather dry. ~~Maybe you should add a few water.~~

5 We're having a big party. ~~We've invited a lots of friends.~~

2 A lot of, many and much (A–B)

Complete the conversation. Put in *a lot of*, *many* or *much*. More than one answer may be correct.
Matthew: There are (▶) *a lot of* athletes taking part in the International Games in London.
          There's been (1) .... coverage in the papers.
Daniel: Our runners haven't won (2) .... medals, have they?
Matthew: No, not as (3) .... as last time. But there's plenty of time.
          There are still (4) .... events to come. I'd like to go and see some
          of the track events, but I haven't got (5) .... time at the moment.
Daniel: No, not with exams coming up.
Matthew: I'm hoping to go at the weekend if I can get a ticket.
          Apparently there aren't (6) .... seats left.
Daniel: I've heard the cheapest tickets are £25. I think that's too (7) ....

3 A few, few, a little and little (C)

Put in *a few*, *few*, *a little* or *little*.
▶ I don't think I can lift this box on my own. I need *a little* help.
▶ *Few* tourists visited Northern Ireland in the 1980s because of the terrorism there.
1 The postman doesn't often come here. We receive .... letters.
2 The snow was quite deep. There seemed .... hope of completing our journey.
3 Trevor isn't finding it easy to fix the shelves. He's having .... trouble.
4 Sarah is exhausted. She's having .... days' holiday next week.
5 David quite likes golf, but unfortunately he has .... ability.
6 I can speak .... words of Swedish, but I'm not very fluent.

4 Many, few, much and little (B–C)

Complete this paragraph from a travel book. Put in *many*, *few*, *much* or *little*.

The main town on the island is very small and does not have (▶) *many* important buildings. The islanders do not have (1) .... money, and they have (2) .... contact with the outside world. There is not (3) .... chance of the place attracting large numbers of tourists. The roads are not very good. There are lots of bicycles but not (4) .... cars. And there are hardly any of the modern facilities which visitors expect. There are (5) .... shops, and there is (6) .... entertainment.

96 All, half, most, some, no and none

A All, most and some

We can use **all**, **most** and **some** before a plural or an uncountable noun.
  All plants need water.   **All matter** is made up of atoms.
  Most people would like more money.   **Some food** makes me ill.

All plants means 'all plants in general/in the world'. *Most people* means 'most people in this country/in the world'. *Some food* means 'some food but not all food'. Here **some** is pronounced /sʌm/.

B All of, half of, most of and some of

Laura: Why do you keep **all of these clothes**? You never wear **most of them**. You've had **some of your jackets** for ten years. Why don't you throw **them all** out? This one is completely out of fashion.
Trevor: Well, I thought if I waited long enough, it might come back into fashion.

All of these clothes has a specific meaning. Laura is talking about Trevor's clothes, not about clothes in general.

We can use **all (of)**, **half (of)**, **most of** and **some of**.
  Have **all (of) the plants** died? ~ No, not **all of them**.
  Most of the people who live around here are students.
  I've spent **most of my money** already.
  Half (of) the audience left before the end of the film.
  Some of that food from the party was all right, but I threw **some of it** away.

We can leave out **of** after **all** or **half**, but not before a pronoun.
  all of these clothes OR *all the clothes* BUT *all of them* NOT *all them*
  half of our group OR *half our group* BUT *half of us* NOT *half us*

We can also use **all** in mid position (see Unit 113B) or after a pronoun.
  These cups **are all** dirty. I'll have to clean **them all**.
  The guests **have all gone** now. I think **they all** enjoyed themselves.

We can use **most** and **some** on their own.
  The band sang a few songs. **Most** were old ones, but **some** were new.

C All meaning 'everything' or 'the only thing'

We can use **all** with a clause to mean 'everything' or 'the only thing'.
  Tell me **all** you know.   **All** I did was ask a simple question.

Here *you know* and *I did* are clauses. We do not normally use **all** without the clause.
  Tell me **everything**. NOT *Tell me all*.

D No and none

We use **no** with a noun.
  We've rung all the hotels, and there are **no rooms** available.
  I'm afraid I've got **no money**. (= I haven't got **any** money.)

We use **none** with **of** or on its own.
  None of my friends will be at the party.   Look at these clothes. **None of them** are in fashion now.
  I wanted some cake, but there was **none** left. NOT *There was no left*.

▷ 86 **Cars** or **the cars**?   ▷ 94 **Some** and **any**   ▷ 103 **Everyone**, etc

96 Exercises

1 All, most, half, some and none (B, D)

Read this advertisement for some new flats and then complete the sentences.
Put in *all of them, most of them, half of them, some of them* and *none of them*.

Hartley House is an old manor house which has been converted into thirty one-bedroom and two-bedroom flats. All the flats have a fitted kitchen, bathroom and large living-room. Ten of them have a separate dining-room. Twenty-five of the flats have a view of the sea, and fifteen have a private balcony. All thirty flats are still for sale. Ring us now for more details.

▶ The flats are modern. *All of them* have a fitted kitchen.
1 .... have two bedrooms.
2 From .... you can see the sea.
3 .... have a private balcony.
4 .... have a large living-room.
5 There's also a dining-room in ....
6 .... has been sold yet.

2 All, most, some and none (B, D)

There was a quiz evening yesterday. Six friends took part, and they all answered twenty questions.
Did they get all, most, some or none of them right?
▶ Natasha answered all twenty correctly. *She got all of them right.*
▶ Daniel's score was fifteen. *He got most of them right.*
1 Jessica had only eight correct answers. ....
2 Matthew got them all right except three. ....
3 Andrew gave twenty correct answers. ....
4 But poor Vicky didn't get a single one right. ....

3 All, most, no and none (A–D)

Complete the conversations. Use the word in brackets with *all, all the, most, most of the, no* or *none of the*.
▶ Andrew: I wonder where they make this milk.
  Jessica: It isn't made in a factory, Andrew. *All milk* (milk) comes from animals.
▶ Rita: What do you usually do on a Sunday?
  Mike: Not much. We spend *most of the time* (time) reading the papers.
1 Claire: In general, people aren't interested in politics, are they?
  Mark: I think .... (people) are bored by the subject.
2 Vicky: These new flats are supposed to be for students.
  Rachel: That's ridiculous. .... (student) in the world could possibly afford such a high rent.
3 Tom: Who's paying for the new ice-rink to be built?
  Nick: Well, ... (money) will come from the government, but the city has to pay a quarter of the cost.
4 Melanie: We should ban cars. .... (cars) pollute the air, don't they?
  David: Well, except electric ones, I suppose.
5 Vicky: What kind of fruit should you eat to stay healthy?
  Natasha: I don't think it matters. .... (fruit) is good for you, isn't it?
6 Tom: I knew there had been a power cut because it was so dark everywhere.
  Harriet: Yes, ... (lights) in our street went out.

97 Every, each, whole, both, either and neither

A Every and each

We use **every** and **each** before a singular noun to talk about a whole group.
   *The police questioned **every person/each person** in the building.*
   ***Every room/Each room** has a number.*
In many contexts either word is possible, but there is a difference in meaning.

EVERY	EACH
***Every** person* means 'all the people', 'everyone'.	***Each** person* means all the people seen as individuals, one by one.
*****Every** guest** watched as the President came in.* *I go for a walk **every day**.*	*****Each** guest** (in turn) shook hands with him.* *****Each** day** seemed to pass very slowly.*
Every means three or more, usually a large number.	***Each*** is more usual with smaller groups and can mean only two.
*There were cars parked along **every street** in town.* (= all the streets)	*There were cars parked along **each side** of the street.* (= both sides)

We can use **each** (but not **every**) on its own or with **of**.
   *There are six flats. **Each** has its own entrance.* NOT *Every has ...*
   ***Each of** the six flats has its own entrance.* NOT *Every of the ...*
We can also say ***Each one/Every one** has its own entrance.*

We can also use **each** in mid position (see Unit 113B) or after a pronoun.
   *We've **each got** our own desk.*   *They gave **us each** a desk.*

Compare **every** and **all** before **day, morning, week,** etc.
   *I travel **every day**.* (= Monday, Tuesday, Wednesday, ...)
   *I was travelling **all day**.* (= from morning till evening)

B Whole

We use **whole** before a singular noun. It means 'all' or 'complete'.
   *The baby cried **the whole time**.* (= all the time)
   *I've spent **my whole life** waiting for this moment.* (= all my life)
   *We'll need **a whole loaf** to make sandwiches for everyone.*

C Both, either and neither

We use **both, either** and **neither** for <u>two</u> things.
   *I've got two bicycles. **Both** of them are quite old. I've given up cycling, so I don't ride **either** of them any more. **Neither** of them is in very good condition, I'm afraid.*

Both means 'the one and the other'. We can use it in the following structures.
   *We had two letters this morning, and **both letters/both the letters/both of the letters/both of them** are bills.*
We can also use **both** in mid position (see Unit 113B) or after a pronoun.
   *The letters **are both** bills. I've opened **them both**.*

Either means 'the one or the other', and **neither** means 'not the one or the other'.
*I haven't met **either twin/either of the twins/either of them**.*
   ***Neither** shoe fits/**Neither of the shoes** fit(s)/**Neither of them** fit(s).*

We can use **both, either** and **neither** on their own.
   *The store has two lifts, and **both** are out of order/**neither** is working.*

97 Exercises

1 Every and each (A)

Complete the dialogue. Put in *every* or *each*. Sometimes both are possible.
Laura: It's a lot bigger than your last house, isn't it? Did you say there are four people living here?
Natasha: Yes, and we (▶) *each* have our own bedroom.
Laura: Does (1) .... person pay a quarter of the rent?
Natasha: That's right. On the first of (2) .... month.
Laura: It must be fantastic for parties.
Natasha: Yes, it is. We don't have one (3) .... week, but almost!
Laura: Isn't that rather expensive?
Natasha: Not if (4) .... guest brings something to eat or drink! Anyway, there'll be no more parties until our exams are over. We're spending (5) .... moment revising.

2 Every, all and whole (A–B)

Put in *every*, *all* or *the whole* and the word in brackets. Sometimes more than one answer is possible.
▶ Melanie is a religious person. She goes to church *every Sunday* (Sunday).
1 The weather has been awful today. It's been raining .... (day).
2 I just can't sleep. I spent .... (night) lying awake.
3 Sarah gets the train at half past seven .... (morning).
4 It's eleven o'clock. Are you going to lie in bed .... (morning)?
5 Last Saturday Trevor spent .... (day) putting up some shelves.
6 Why are you in such a hurry .... (time) I see you?

3 Both, either and neither (C)

There are two pubs in Brickfield, The White Horse and The Ship. Look at the information and then write the sentences. Use *both of them*, *one of them* or *neither of them*.

THE WHITE HORSE	THE SHIP
MEALS BAR SNACKS FAMILY ROOM	MEALS SEPARATE RESTAURANT BAR SNACKS NON-SMOKING AREA

▶ (serve meals) *Both of them serve meals.*
1 (have a separate restaurant) ....
2 (serve bar snacks) ....
3 (have a family room) ....
4 (allow pub games) ....
5 (have live music) ....
6 (have a non-smoking area) ....

4 Every, each, whole, both, either and neither (A–C)

Complete the conversation. Put in *every*, *each*, *whole*, *both*, *either* or *neither*.
Assistant: These plain sofas come in two different styles.
Sarah: I think (▶) *both* styles are rather old-fashioned. (1) .... of them is really what I want. I don't like (2) .... of them, I'm afraid.
Assistant: What about a patterned fabric? There are some lovely colours here.
Sarah: I feel more and more unsure with (3) .... new fabric I look at.
Mark: We haven't got time to look at (4) .... fabric in the shop. We've been in here a (5) .... hour already, you know.

Test 16 This, my, some, a lot of, all, etc (Units 91–97)

Test 16A

Look at what people are saying and choose the correct meaning.
▶ Polly: Let's sit under these trees, shall we?
   The trees are a) ☑ near Polly.   b) ☐ a long way away from Polly.
1 Martin: My friend and I ate a whole loaf.
   Martin and his friend ate a) ☐ part of the loaf.   b) ☐ all the loaf.
2 Nigel: The girls' dog has gone missing.
   The dog belongs to a) ☐ one girl.   b) ☐ more than one girl.
3 Tessa: My brother has got his own office.
   Tessa's brother a) ☐ works alone in the office.   b) ☐ shares the office with another person.
4 Nancy: The weather looks a little better, I think.
   How does Nancy feel about the weather? a) ☐ Hopeful.   b) ☐ Not very hopeful.
5 Ben: I can't answer either of these questions.
   How many questions is Ben talking about? a) ☐ One.   b) ☐ Two.   c) ☐ More than two.
6 Adrian: The children can keep any tennis balls they find.
   Will they find any tennis balls? a) ☐ Yes.   b) ☐ No.   c) ☐ Adrian doesn't know.

Test 16B

Decide which word is correct.
▶ What colour shall we have? ~ I don't mind. Pick *any* colour you like.
   a) any   b) some   c) that   d) what
1 Peter has two brothers, but he doesn't speak to .... of them.
   a) any   b) both   c) either   d) neither
2 .... has left a bicycle outside.
   a) Anyone   b) Anything   c) Someone   d) Something
3 I like .... pictures here. ~ Yes, so do I.
   a) that   b) these   c) this   d) those
4 Would you mind waiting .... minutes?
   a) a few   b) a little   c) few   d) little
5 .... countries still have a king or a queen, don't they?
   a) Any   b) Half   c) Part   d) Some
6 Safety should come first. .... lives shouldn't be put at risk.
   a) People   b) Peoples   c) People's   d) Peoples'
7 Nigel isn't very well. ~ Oh, I'm sorry to hear ....
   a) so   b) that   c) this   d) you
8 Mr Jones is an uncle of ....
   a) Polly   b) Pollys   c) Polly's   d) Pollys'

Test 16C

Tessa is walking along the street when she sees her old friend Angela.
Read the conversation and write the missing words. Use one word only in each space.
Tessa: Hello, Angela. How are you?
Angela: Tessa! Hello! Shall we have lunch together?
Tessa: I was just going to the bank to get (▶) *some* money. I have to be back at the office in
         (1) .... few minutes. My life's one mad rush.
Angela: So is (2) .... I'm working for Tuffex Plastics now. And my daughter has invited three

230   THIS, MY, SOME, A LOT OF, ETC

	friends (3) .... hers to stay. I wish I didn't have so (4) .... things to do at once.	
Tessa:	I'm glad I've run into you. I never see (5) .... else from our old gang. (6) .... of them seem to be around any more.	
Angela:	I think they've (7) .... moved away, except us two. Carol went to Japan.	
Tessa:	Angela, would you like to come for a meal some time?	
Angela:	Oh, that would be lovely. We'll certainly have a (8) .... to talk about.	
Tessa:	Maybe we'll need a (9) .... day. What about the Saturday after next?	

Test 16D

Each of the sentences has a mistake in it. Write the correct sentence.
▶ ~~Are you going on holiday that year?~~ *Are you going on holiday this year?*
1 ~~That was a very good idea of you.~~
2 ~~You've got a lot books, haven't you?~~
3 ~~I don't know the meeting's time.~~
4 ~~Nigel has hurt the leg.~~
5 ~~All rooms in the house were cold.~~
6 ~~Wear everything—it doesn't matter what.~~
7 ~~Every of the four doors was locked.~~
8 ~~I live my life, and my sister lives her.~~
9 ~~The both socks have got holes in them.~~
10 ~~Here's a copy of this week magazine.~~
11 ~~This sweater is losing it's colour.~~
12 ~~I want some paper, but there's no in here.~~

Test 16E

Write a second sentence so that it has a similar meaning to the first. Use the word in brackets.
▶ When I was on holiday, it rained all week. (whole)
When I was on holiday, it rained the whole week.
1 I've lived here more than half my life. (most)

2 All the hotels were full. (every)

3 The house on the corner is bigger than our house. (ours)

4 I've forgotten my doctor's name. (of)

5 We haven't had much warning of the changes. (little)

6 Such a large number of people have applied for the job. (so)

7 I met one of your old boyfriends at a party. (an)

8 Both the chairs are uncomfortable. (neither)

9 My holiday starts ten days from now. (time)

98 Personal pronouns, e.g. I, you

A The meaning of the pronouns

Vicky: Hello, Andrew. Have **you** seen Rachel?
Andrew: *I* don't think so. No, *I* haven't seen **her** today.
Vicky: **We**'re supposed to be going out at half past seven, and **it**'s nearly eight now.
Andrew: Maybe **she**'s just forgotten. **You** know Rachel.
Vicky: **We**'re going out for a meal. Matthew and Emma said **they** might come too. I hope **they** haven't gone without **me**.

I/me means the speaker, and **you** means the person spoken to.
We/us means the speaker and someone else. Here, **we** = Vicky and Rachel.
He/him means a male person and **she/her** a female person. Here, **she** = Rachel.
It means a thing, an action, a situation or an idea. Here, **it** = the time.
They/them is the plural of **he**, **she** and **it** and means people or things.

We can also use **they/them** for a person when we don't know if the person is male or female.
*If anyone calls, ask **them** to leave a message.*

B Subject and object forms

		FIRST PERSON	SECOND PERSON	THIRD PERSON
SINGULAR	Subject	I	you	he/she/it
	Object	me	you	him/her/it
PLURAL	Subject	we	you	they
	Object	us	you	them

We use the subject form (**I**, etc) when the pronoun is the subject and there is a verb.
*I don't think so.   Maybe **she**'s just forgotten.*
We use the object form (**me**, etc) when the pronoun is the object of a verb or preposition.
*I haven't **seen her** today.   I hope they haven't gone **without me**.*

The pronoun on its own or after **be** usually has the object form.
*Who spilt coffee all over the table? ~ **Me**./Sorry, it was **me**.*
Compare this answer.
*Who spilt coffee all over the table? ~ **I** did.*

C You, one and they

We can use **you** or **one** to mean 'any person' or 'people in general', including the speaker.
***You** shouldn't believe what **you** read in the newspapers.*
OR ***One** shouldn't believe what **one** reads in the newspapers.*
***You** don't like/**One** doesn't like to have an argument in public.*
You is normal in conversation. **One** is more formal.

We can use **they** for other people in general.
***They** say too much sugar is bad for you.*
We can also use it for people in authority.
***They**'re going to build a new swimming-pool here.*
They is informal and conversational. We use the passive in more formal situations.
*A new swimming-pool **is going to be built** here (see Unit 56B).*

▷ 99 **There** and **it**   ▷ page 380 **You** and **one** in British and American English

98 Exercises

1 The meaning of the pronouns (A)

Read the conversation between Melanie and Rita. Then say what the underlined pronouns mean.

Melanie: Have (▶)you been in that new shop?
Rita: No, not yet.
Melanie: Nor have I, but (▶)it looks interesting. There's a lovely dress in the window, and (1) it isn't expensive.
Rita: Laura bought some jeans there. (2) She said (3) they were really cheap.
Melanie: (4) You ought to go along there and have a look, then.
Rita: (5) We'd better not go now or we'll be late. (6) I told Mike and Harriet we'd meet (7) them at half past five.
Melanie: Oh, Tom said (8) he's coming too.

▶ you = *Rita*
▶ it = *the shop*
1 it = ...
2 she = ...
3 they = ...
4 you = ...
5 we = ...
6 I = ...
7 them = ...
8 he = ...

2 Subject and object forms (B)

Complete the conversation. Put in the pronouns.

Nick: Did (▶)*you* say that you and Harriet wanted some coloured lights for your party?
Mike: Yes, but (▶)*it*'s OK. Melanie's neighbour Jake has got some, and (1) ....'s going to lend (2) .... to (3) ....
Nick: Great. Is Rita coming to the party?
Mike: We've invited (4) .... of course, but (5) .... isn't sure if (6) .... can come or not. Her parents are flying somewhere on Saturday evening, and she might be taking (7) .... to the airport.
Nick: And what about Laura's friend Emily?
Mike: I expect (8) .... 'll be there. And her brother. (9) .... both came to our last party.
Nick: Do (10) .... mean Jason? I don't like (11) .... very much.
Mike: Oh, (12) .... 's OK. But (13) .... don't have to talk to (14) ....

3 Subject and object forms (B)

Put in the pronouns.

▶ There's no need to shout. I can hear *you*.
1 You and I work well together. .... 're a good team.
2 We've got a bit of a problem. Could .... help .... , please?
3 This is a good photo, isn't .... ? ~ Is Jessica in .... ? ~ Yes, that's .... , look. .... 's next to Andrew.
4 Who did this crossword? ~ .... I did .... this morning.
5 Is this Vicky's bag? ~ No, ... didn't bring one. It can't belong to ....
6 .... 'm looking for my shoes. Have .... seen .... ? ~ Yes, ... 're here.

4 You and they (C)

Complete the conversation. Put in *you* or *they*.

Trevor: I'm not going to drive in this weather. It's too icy.
Laura: (▶) *You* don't want to take any risks. (1) .... can't be too careful.
Trevor: I've just heard the weather forecast and (2) .... say there's going to be more snow. (3) .... 're better off indoors in weather like this.
Laura: I think (4) .... ought to clear the snow off the roads more quickly.

99 There and it

A There + be

Look at these examples.
> *I really ought to phone home.* ~ *Well, **there's** a phone box round the corner.*
> *Could I make myself an omelette?* ~ *Of course. **There are** some eggs in the fridge.*
> ***There's** an important meeting at work that I have to go to.*

To talk about the existence of something, we use **there + be**. We usually pronounce **there** /ðə/, like **the**. **There's** is /ðəz/ and **there are** is /ˈðərə/. **Be** agrees with the following noun.
> *There **is** a phone box.* BUT *There **are** some eggs.*

Here are some more examples.
> ***There's** a bus at ten to five.*   ***There'll be** a meal waiting for us.*
> ***Is there** a toilet in the building?*   ***Were there** any bargains in the sale?*
> ***There have been** some burglaries recently.*   ***There might have been** an accident.*

We also use **there** with words like **a lot of, many, much, more, enough** and with numbers.
> *There were **a lot of** problems to discuss.*   *There's too **much** noise in here.*
> *Will there be **enough** chairs?*   *There are **thirty** days in April.*

B Uses of it

We use **it** for a thing, an action, a situation or an idea.
> *You've bought a new coat. **It's** very nice.* (**it** = the coat)
> *Skiing is an expensive hobby, isn't **it**?*
> *You have to fill in all these stupid forms. **It's** ridiculous.*
> *I find astrology fascinating. I'm really interested in **it**.*

We use **it** to mean 'the unknown person'.
> *Did someone ring?* ~ ***It** was Vicky. She just called to say she's arrived safely.*

We use **it** for the time, the weather and distance.
> ***It's** half past five already.*   ***It's** Sunday tomorrow.*
> ***It** was much warmer yesterday.*   ***It's** fifty miles from here to Brighton.*

We also use **it** in structures with a to-infinitive or a that-clause (see also Unit 67B).
> ***It** was nice **to meet your friends**.*
> ***It** would be a good idea **to book in advance**.*
> ***It's** important **to switch off the electricity**.*
> ***It's** a pity **(that) you can't come with us**.*

This is much more usual than, for example, *To meet your friends was nice.*

C There or it?

We often use **there** when we mention something for the first time, like the picture in this example.
> ***There** was a picture on the wall. **It** was an abstract painting.*

We use **it** when we talk about the details. **It** means *the picture*.

Here are some more examples.
> ***There's** a woman at the door.* ~ *Oh, **it's** Aunt Joan.*
> ***There** was a dog in the field. **It** was a big black one.*
> ***There's** a new one-way traffic system in the town centre. **It's** very confusing.*

99 Exercises

1 There + be (A)

Look at the pictures and comment on what you see. Use these words: *a balloon, some boxes, the car, a dinosaur, an elephant, some flowers, the garden, her hat, the sky, the water*

   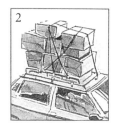 

▶ *There's a dinosaur in the water.*
▶ *There are some flowers on her hat.*
1 .... 2 ....
  3 ....

2 There + be (A)

Put in *there* and a form of *be*, e.g. *is, are, was, have been* or *will be*.
▶ Victor: *Are there* any restaurants here that open on a Sunday?
   Rachel: *There's* a café in the High Street which is open for lunch.
1 Alan: .... a train at twelve thirty, isn't there? Let's catch that one.
   Mark: OK. .... time to finish our discussion on the train.
2 Vicky: What's happened? Why .... so many police cars here?
   Daniel: .... a hold-up at the bank.
3 Tom: Last night .... a party next door. I couldn't get to sleep.
   Melanie: .... must .... a lot of people there.

3 Uses of it (B)

Rewrite the sentences in brackets using *it*.
▶ We sometimes go surfing. (Surfing is really good fun.) *It's really good fun.*
1 I bought a shirt in the market. (The shirt was very cheap.) ....
2 Someone rang. (The caller was Vicky.) ....
3 Our heating is out of order. (The situation is a nuisance.) ....
4 I've left my coat at home. (The weather is very warm.) ....
5 Don't lose your credit card. (To keep it somewhere safe is important.)
   ....

4 There or it? (C)

Put in *there* or *it*.
▶ Is *it* the fifteenth today? ~ No, the sixteenth.
1 The road is closed. ....'s been an accident.
2 Take a taxi. ....'s a long way to the station.
3 .... was a motor bike outside. .... looked very expensive.
4 Will .... be any delays because of the strike? ~ Well, ... would be a good idea to ring the airline and check.
5 .... was wet, and .... was a cold east wind. .... was after midnight, and .... were few people on the streets.

100 Reflexive pronouns

A Introduction

Myself is a reflexive pronoun. In the sentence *I've cut myself*, the words **I** and **myself** mean the same thing. **Myself** refers back to the subject, **I**.

B Form

	FIRST PERSON	SECOND PERSON	THIRD PERSON
SINGULAR	myself	yourself	himself/herself/itself
PLURAL	ourselves	yourselves	themselves

Compare **yourself** and **yourselves**.
  *Emma, you can dry **yourself** on this towel.*   *Vicky and Rachel, you can dry **yourselves** on these towels.*

C The use of reflexive pronouns

Here are some examples.
  *Mark made **himself** a sandwich.*   *Vicky had to force **herself** to eat.*
  *We've locked **ourselves** out.*   *The children watched **themselves** on video.*

We cannot use **me**, **you**, **him**, etc to refer to the subject. Compare these sentences.
  *When the policeman came in, the gunman shot **him**.* (**him** = the policeman)
  *When the policeman came in, the gunman shot **himself**.* (**himself** = the gunman)

We can use a reflexive pronoun after a preposition.
  *The children are old enough to look **after themselves**.*
But after a preposition of place, we can use **me**, **you**, **him**, etc.
  *In the mirror I saw a lorry **behind me**.*   *Mike didn't have any money **with him**.*
  *Laura thought she recognized the woman standing **next to her**.*

D Idioms with reflexive pronouns

Look at these examples.
  *We really **enjoyed ourselves**.* (= had a good time)
  *I hope the children **behave themselves**.* (= behave well)
  *Just **help yourself** to sandwiches, won't you?* (= take as many as you want)
  *Please **make yourself at home**.* (= behave as if this was your home)
  *I don't want to be left here **by myself**.* (= on my own, alone)

E Verbs without a reflexive pronoun

Some verbs do not usually take a reflexive pronoun, although they may in other languages.
  *We'd better **hurry**, or we'll be late.* NOT *We'd better hurry ourselves.*
  *Shall we **meet** at the cinema?*   *I **feel** uncomfortable.*   *Just try to **relax**.*

Some of these verbs are: **afford, approach, complain, concentrate, decide, feel** + adjective, **get up, hurry (up), lie down, meet, remember, rest, relax, sit down, stand up, wake up, wonder, worry**

We do not normally use a reflexive pronoun with **change** (clothes), **dress** and **wash**.
  *Daniel **washed** and **changed** before going out.* (See also Unit 54D.)
But we can use a reflexive pronoun when the action is difficult.
  *My friend is disabled, but she can **dress herself**.*

100 Exercises

1 Reflexive pronouns (A–C)

Look at the pictures and write sentences with a reflexive pronoun.
Use these words: *dry, introduce, look at, photograph, teach*

▶ *He's photographing himself.*
1 She .... 3 ....
2 They .... 4 ....

2 Reflexive pronouns (A–C)

Complete the conversations. Put in a reflexive pronoun (*myself, yourself*, etc).
▶ Matthew: I'll get the tickets, shall I?
   Emma: It's OK. I can pay for *myself*.
1 Olivia: I've got lots of photos of my children.
   Linda: Yes, but you haven't got many of ...., Olivia.
2 Rita: Did you have a good time at the Holiday Centre?
   Laura: Well, there wasn't much going on. We had to amuse ....
3 Emma: Why has the light gone off?
   Matthew: It switches .... off automatically.

3 Pronouns after a preposition (C and Unit 98B)

Put in the correct pronoun (e.g. *me* or *myself*).
▶ We looked up and saw a strange animal in front of *us*.
▶ Don't tell us the answer to the puzzle. We can work it out for *ourselves*.
1 It's a pity you didn't bring your camera with ....
2 Mark talked to the woman sitting next to ....
3 The old man is no longer able to look after ....
4 My mother likes to have all her family near ....
5 To be successful in life, you must believe in ....

4 Idioms with and without reflexive pronouns (D–E)

Rachel and Vicky are at Mike and Harriet's party. Complete the conversation.
Put in the verbs with or without a reflexive pronoun.
Mike: Have you two (▶) *met* (met) before?
Rachel: Yes, we have. Vicky and I are old friends.
Mike: Oh, right. Well, I hope you (▶) *enjoy yourselves* (enjoy) tonight.
Rachel: I'm sure we will. I (1) .... (feel) just in the mood for a party.
Mike: Well, please (2) .... (help) to a drink. Are you OK, Vicky?
Vicky: Sorry, I've got this awful feeling that I have to do something very important, and I can't
     (3) .... (remember) what it is.
Rachel: Vicky, you (4) .... (worry) too much. Come on, just
     (5) .... (relax).

101 Emphatic pronouns and **each other**

A Emphatic pronouns

*Trevor and Laura are decorating their living-room **themselves**.*

An emphatic pronoun is a word like **myself, yourself**.
It has the same form as a reflexive pronoun (see Unit 100B).

Here the emphatic pronoun means 'without help'. Trevor and Laura are decorating the room without help from anyone else. Compare *They're having the room wallpapered (by a decorator)* (see Unit 58A).

Here are some more examples.
*I built this boat **myself**.   My sister designs all these clothes **herself**.
Are you doing all the painting **yourselves**?*
When we say these sentences, we stress **self** or **selves**.

Now look at these examples.
*The manager **himself** welcomed us to the hotel.*
(= The manager welcomed us, not someone else.)
*Although she is very rich, the Queen **herself** never carries any money.
The house **itself** is small, but the garden is enormous.
Of course the children have been to the zoo. You **yourself** took them there last year.*
Here the emphatic pronoun comes after the noun or pronoun it relates to.

B Each other

Look at this example.
*Andrew and Jessica help **each other** with their work.*
This means that Andrew helps Jessica, and Jessica helps Andrew. Here are some more examples.
*Mark and Alan aren't really friends. They don't like **each other** much.
I'm still in touch with Kirsty. We write to **each other**.*
One another has the same meaning.
*We send **each other/one another** Christmas cards every year.*

We can also use the possessive form **each other's**.
*Tom and Mark wrote down **each other's** phone numbers.*
This means that Tom wrote down Mark's number, and Mark wrote down Tom's number.

Compare **each other** and **themselves**.

*They're laughing at **each other**.*

*They're laughing at **themselves**.*

101 Exercises

1 Emphatic pronouns (A)

Add a sentence with an emphatic pronoun, e.g. *myself*.
Use these verbs: *bake, clean, decorate, develop, grow, paint, service, type*
▶ I don't take the car to the garage. *I service it myself.*
▶ Laura didn't buy those pictures. *She painted them herself.*
1 Tom doesn't have his windows cleaned. ....
2 My bread doesn't come from a shop. ....
3 My friends eat lots of fresh vegetables. ....
4 We finished the dining-room yesterday. ....
5 Mark doesn't dictate his letters to a secretary. ....
6 I don't pay to have my photos done. ....

2 Emphatic pronouns (A)

Put in an emphatic pronoun, e.g. *myself, yourself*.
▶ Of course I know about Matthew and Emma. You told me *yourself*.
1 The princess .... visited the children in hospital.
2 The song .... wasn't very good, but the title of the song became a popular phrase.
3 The visitors were welcomed to the school by the headmaster ....
4 The pilots .... are nervous of flying because of terrorist threats.
5 You all know that no one can take your decisions for you. You .... will have to decide.

3 Each other (B)

Claire and Melanie are friends. Write sentences about them using *each other*.
▶ Melanie often writes notes to Claire. She also often writes notes to Melanie.
   They often write notes to each other.
1 Claire is always thinking about Melanie. She's just the same. She's always thinking about her.
   ....
2 Melanie has got lots of photos of Claire. She's got lots of photos of her, too.
   ....
3 They like being together. Claire enjoys Melanie's company, and she enjoys Claire's company.
   ....
4 Melanie is crazy about films. Claire feels the same way. She's crazy about films too.
   ....

4 Each other or a reflexive pronoun? (B and Unit 100)

Put in *each other, ourselves* or *themselves*.
▶ We could all do more to keep healthy. We don't look after *ourselves* properly.
▶ The hostess introduced the two guests to *each other*.
1 The two boxers did their best to knock .... out.
2 We talk to .... in French because it's the only language we both know.
3 People who talk to .... may get strange looks from other people.
4 We'd better set off early to give .... plenty of time to get there.
5 The guards who shot a gunman claimed that they were defending ....
6 Luckily we managed to get two seats next to ....

102 The pronoun **one/ones**

A Introduction

Trevor: Here's that bottle of mineral water you wanted.
Laura: Oh, no, you've got a small **one**. I wanted a big **one**.
Trevor: They didn't have any big **ones** at the shop on the corner.
Laura: That shop never has what I want. Why didn't you go to the **one** in the High Street?

Here *a small* **one** means 'a small bottle', *big* **ones** means 'big bottles', and *the* **one** *in the High Street* means 'the shop in the High Street'. We use **one** for a singular noun and **ones** for a plural noun. We use **one** and **ones** to avoid repeating a noun.

We cannot use **one** or **ones** with an uncountable noun, e.g. **water**.
   There was no hot water. I had to wash in **cold**.

B Structures with **one/ones**

Sometimes we can either put in **one/ones** or leave it out.
   These bowls are nice. What about **this (one)**?
We can do this after **this**, **that**, **these** and **those**; after **each** or **another**; after **which**; or after a superlative, e.g. **easiest**.
   I don't like these sweaters. I prefer **those (ones)** *over there.*
   I tried all three numbers, and **each (one)** *was engaged.*
   The product is available in all these colours. **Which (one)** *would you like?*
   The last question is the **most difficult (one)**.

Sometimes we cannot leave out **one/ones**.
   Our house is the **one** *on the left.* NOT *Our house is the on the left.*
We cannot leave out **one/ones** after **the** or **every** or after an adjective.
   The film wasn't as good as **the one** *we saw last week.*
   I rang all the numbers, and **every one** *was engaged.*
   I'd like a box of tissues. A **small one**, *please.*
   I threw away my old trainers and bought some **new ones**.

C **A small one** and **one**

We can say **a small one**, **a red one**, etc but NOT *a one*.
   I've been looking for a coat, but I can't find **a nice one**.
   I've been looking for a coat, but I can't find **one**.
Here we use **one** instead of **a coat**. Here are some more examples.
   We decided to take a taxi. Luckily there was **one** *waiting.*
   If you want a ticket, I can get **one** *for you.*

Now look at these examples with **one**, **some**, **it** and **them**.
   I haven't got a passport, but I'll need **one**.   (**one** = **a** passport)
   I haven't got any stamps, but I'll need **some**.   (**some** = **some** stamps)
   I've got my passport. They sent **it** *last week.*   (**it** = **the** passport)
   I've got the stamps. I put **them** *in the drawer.*   (**them** = **the** stamps)

One and **some/any** are like **a**, but **it** and **they/them** are like **the**. We use **one** and **some/any** when we aren't saying which, and we use **it** and **they/them** to be specific (when we know which).

102 Exercises

1 One (A)
Look at the pictures and complete the conversations.

▶ blue ✓ black ✗

1 smart ✗ casual ✓

2 big ✓ small ✗

3 white ✗ brown ✓

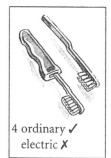
4 ordinary ✓ electric ✗

▶ Emma: Can you lend me a pen, please?
   Matthew: Do you want *a blue one or a black one*?
   Emma: Oh, *a blue one*, please.
1 Mark: I might buy a new jacket.
   Sarah: Do you mean ....?
   Mark: Oh, ... for when I go on holiday.
2 Jessica: Could you pass me one of those saucepans, please?
   Andrew: Do you need ....?
   Jessica: ...., please.
3 Sarah: Could I have a small envelope?
   Secretary: Yes, of course. ....?
   Sarah: ...., please. Thanks.
4 Vicky: I'm looking for a toothbrush, but I can't find any.
   Assistant: Do you mean ....?
   Vicky: Oh, ...

2 One and ones (A–C)
Rewrite the sentences in brackets so that the noun is not repeated. Use *one* or *ones*.
▶ These cups are nice. *Each one is hand-painted.* (Each cup is hand-painted.)
1 I need to fill in a form about my driving test, but .... (I haven't got a form.)
2 I've watched all these videos. .... (I must get some new videos.)
3 These photos are good. .... (Have you seen this photo?)
4 I need a dinner-jacket for the party, so .... (I've hired a dinner-jacket.)
5 Those socks are horrible. .... (Can't you find any nice socks?)
6 This map isn't very good. .... (The map in the car is better.)

3 One, some, it and them (C)
Put in *one, some, it* or *them*.
▶ I don't know if I'll need any money. I'd better take *some*, I suppose.
1 If you need an umbrella, I can lend you ....
2 The radio isn't working. Vicky dropped .... on the floor.
3 I'm having a biscuit. Would you like ...., too?
4 I had the matches a minute ago, and now I can't find ....
5 I haven't got any computer disks, but Emma has got ....

PRONOUNS 241

103 Everyone, something, etc

A Introduction

Look at these examples.
Everyone enjoyed the show. It was a great success.
The police searched the house but found *nothing*.
Let's find *somewhere* to eat.
Nobody came into the shop all afternoon.

With **every**, **some** and **no**, we can form words ending in **one**, **body**, **thing** and **where**.

everyone/everybody = all the people	everything = all the things	everywhere = (in) all the places
someone/somebody = a person	something = a thing	somewhere = (in) a place
no one/nobody = no person	nothing /'nʌθɪŋ/ = no things	nowhere = (in) no places

Words ending in **thing** can also mean actions or ideas.
Something awful has happened.   You must tell me *everything*.

B Someone and anyone, etc

We can also form words with **any**: *anyone, anybody, anything, anywhere*.
For **some** and **any** see Unit 94A.

Positive:	There's *some*one in the phone box.
Negative:	I looked round the shops, but I didn't buy *any*thing.
Question:	Has *any*one seen today's newspaper?
Offer/Request:	Could you do *some*thing for me, please?

We can also use words with **any** in a positive sentence.
This door is always left open. *Any*one could just walk in here.
Where shall we go? ~ *Any*where. I don't mind.

In these sentences **anyone** means 'it doesn't matter who', and **anywhere** means 'it doesn't matter where'. For more details about **any** see Unit 94C.

C Singular and plural

We use a singular verb after **everyone, something, anything**, etc.
Everywhere was very crowded.   *No one knows* how to start the motor.

After words with **one** or **body**, we normally use **they/them/their**, even though the verb is singular.
Everyone is having *their* lunch.   *Nobody* wants to have *their* coffee yet.

We can also use **he, she, him, her, his**, etc with **someone/somebody** when we know the person's sex.
Someone left *their/her* handbag behind.

D Other structures

After **everyone, something**, etc we can use an adjective.
Let's go *somewhere nice*.   Is there *anything interesting* in that magazine?

We can also use **else**.
We always play Scrabble. Let's play *something else*. (= a different game)
Henry wore a suit, but *everyone else* had jeans on. (= all the other people)

Words ending in **one** and **body** have a possessive form (with **'s**).
Someone's cat is on our roof.   I need to be informed about *everybody's* plans.

▷ page 380 **Someplace**, etc in American English

103 Exercises

1 Everyone, something, etc (A)

Complete the conversations. Put in the correct words.
- ▶ Melanie: Did you say you found *something* in the street?
  David: Yes, a diamond ring.
1. Nick: We all know the man is a thief, don't we?
   Tom: Yes, ... knows, but .... dares to say so publicly.
2. Mark: Were there any calls for me?
   Secretary: Yes, ... rang while you were out. It was rather strange. He refused to give his name, but he wants to discuss .... with you.
3. Melanie: Do you have any plans for the summer?
   Tom: I'd like to go away .... if I can. .... I know has invited me to his villa in Portugal, so I may go there.
4. Daniel: Has Matthew got a job yet?
   Emma: No, but he's looked .... He's been to all the job agencies. He hates the idea of sitting around doing ....

2 Someone and anyone, etc (B)

Put in *someone, anyone, something, anything, somewhere* or *anywhere*.
Rachel: Have you seen my calculator? I can't find it (▶) *anywhere*.
Vicky: No, I haven't. Perhaps (1) .... 's borrowed it.
Rachel: I haven't given (2) .... permission to borrow it.
It must be (3) .... in this room.
Vicky: Things are in such a mess. It could be (4) ....
Rachel: I know. I can never find (5) .... when I want it.
Vicky: We'll have to do (6) .... about this mess. We'd better tidy it up.

3 Singular and plural (C)

Choose the correct form.
- ▶ We had to wait because someone had lost its/their ticket.
1. One of the policemen had injured his/their arm.
2. One of the guests had brought something wrapped in brown paper. She put it/them on the table.
3. No one likes/like going to the dentist, do he/they?
4. Everyone have/has to leave his/their bags outside.

4 Other structures (D)

Rewrite the sentences using a phrase with *everyone, someone, something, nothing* and *somewhere* instead of the phrases in brackets.
- ▶ I'd like to buy (a nice thing). *I'd like to buy something nice.*
- ▶ Let's go (to another place), shall we? *Let's go somewhere else, shall we?*
- ▶ I'll try to remember (the name of everyone). *I'll try to remember everyone's name.*
1. I once met (a famous person). ....
2. (A person's car) is blocking me in. ....
3. I've got (a different thing) to tell you. ....
4. We know (the opinions of all the people). ....
5. (All the other people) except you are going. ....
6. (No exciting things) ever happen here. ....

Test 17 Pronouns (Units 98–103)

Test 17A

A group of friends are going on a coach trip together. They're meeting at the coach stop. Complete the conversation. Put in a personal pronoun (*I, me, you,* etc) or a reflexive pronoun (*myself, yourself,* etc).

Polly: Where's Martin?
Rupert: He's ill. I spoke to (▶) *him* yesterday. He was feeling a bit sorry for (1) ....
Polly: Oh, poor Martin. And what about the twins?
Peter: (2) .... came with Janet and me. (3) .... gave (4) .... a lift.
Janet: Yes, the twins came with (5) .... in the car.
Tessa: I hope they're going to behave (6) ....
Janet: Oh, I'm sure they will.
Rupert: (7) .... 'll be nice to have a day out. (8) .... say it's going to stay sunny.
Polly: I'm sure we'll all enjoy (9) ....
Peter: Where's Anna?
Tessa: Oh, she's here somewhere. I spoke to (10) .... a moment ago. She was standing right next to (11) ....

Test 17B

Decide which word is correct.

▶ I can't go to a party. I haven't got *anything* to wear.
   a) anything b) everything c) something d) nothing
1. Take care, won't you, Anna? Look after ....
   a) you b) your c) yours d) yourself
2. Yes, ... would be lovely to see you again.
   a) it b) that c) there d) you
3. If you want some apples, I'll get you .... at the shop.
   a) any b) it c) one d) some
4. We've brought some food with ....
   a) me b) ourselves c) us d) we
5. Who does this CD belong to? ~ .... I've just bought it.
   a) I b) Me c) Mine d) Myself
6. The shop doesn't sell new books. It only sells old ....
   a) of them b) ones c) some d) them
7. Is .... a post office near here, please?
   a) here b) it c) there d) this
8. The two girls often wear .... clothes.
   a) each other b) each other's c) themselves d) themselves'
9. Have you had enough to eat, or would you like something .... ?
   a) another b) else c) new d) other

Test 17C

Use a pronoun instead of the words in brackets.

▶ Michelle is in hospital. *She* (Michelle) isn't very well.
1. I lost my watch, but it was only a cheap .... (watch).
2. I have to make tea for .... (all the people).
3. Tessa took a photo of .... (Tessa).
4. My flat is the .... (flat) at the top.

5   The phone rang. .... (The caller) was Alex.
6   There was .... (a thing) worrying me.
7   I've got some sweets. Would you like .... (a sweet)?
8   .... (People in general) can't make an omelette without breaking eggs.
9   We decorated the whole house .... (without help).

Test 17D

Complete the text. Write the missing words. Use one word only in each space.

(▶) *It* was on 20 September 1973 that Bobby Riggs met Billie Jean King on the tennis court. Of all the tennis matches until then, this was probably the (1) .... that attracted the most attention. Riggs had once been a champion, but at 55 he was getting rather old for top-class tennis. But he considered (2) .... a better player than any woman. In fact, he thought women should go home and find (3) .... useful to do in the kitchen. Billie Jean King, on the other hand, was a 29-year-old star of women's tennis and a feminist. Riggs thought that (4) .... would be a good idea to play King. He was sure he could beat (5) .... King agreed to play. (6) .... was a lot of interest in the match, and more or less (7) .... in the country was looking forward to (8) .... On the night of the match, (9) .... were over 30,000 people in the Houston Astrodome. When Riggs and King came face to face with (10) .... other, they had 50 million people watching (11) .... on TV. The match didn't work out for Riggs, because Billie Jean King defeated (12) ...., 6–4, 6–3, 6–3.

Test 17E

Each of these sentences has a mistake in it. Write the correct sentence.
▶   ~~I didn't want the fridge, so I sold him.~~
    I didn't want the fridge, so I sold it.
1   ~~It's a train leaving in ten minutes.~~

2   ~~I think someone are coming up the stairs.~~

3   ~~Let's meet ourselves at eight o'clock, shall we?~~

4   ~~We haven't got a camcorder, but we'd like a.~~

5   ~~Let's do a different something today.~~

6   ~~One is going to build a new motorway through here.~~

7   ~~I'm afraid I haven't done something all day.~~

8   ~~Everyone enjoyed themselves at the barbecue.~~

9   ~~If you're buying a loaf, get a nice fresh.~~

10 ~~I've looked in all places for my credit card.~~

11 ~~The two friends still see themselves occasionally.~~

PRONOUNS   245

104 Adjectives

A Introduction

*Henry and Claire are having dinner in a **quiet** restaurant. It's a **warm** evening. The food is **delicious**. Henry is feeling **hungry**.*

An adjective is a word like **quiet, warm, delicious, hungry**. The word **quiet** describes the restaurant. It tells us what the restaurant is like.

B Word order

There are two places where we can use an adjective:
before a noun (*a quiet restaurant*) and after a linking verb (*feeling hungry*)

BEFORE A NOUN	AFTER A LINKING VERB
Claire's got a **new** car.	Claire's car is **new**.
It was a **dark** night.	It was getting **dark**.
This is **good** coffee.	This coffee tastes **good**.
	Some linking verbs are: **appear, be, become, feel, get, look, seem, smell, stay, taste**

We can use two or more adjectives together (see Unit 105).
   *It's a **quiet little** restaurant.*   *Mike was wearing a **dirty old** coat.*

We can put a word like **very** or **quite** before an adjective.
   *It was a **very dark** night.*   *Henry was feeling **quite hungry**.*
Very and **quite** are adverbs of degree (see Unit 115).

C Adjectives used in one position only

We can use most adjectives in both positions – before a noun or after a linking verb. But a few adjectives can go in one position but not in the other.

Here are some examples of adjectives which can only go before a noun.
   *Be careful crossing the **main** road.*   *The **only** problem is I've got no money.*
   *Chess is an **indoor** game.*   *The **former** footballer now trains young players.*

Some more examples are: **chief** (= main), **elder** (= older), **eldest** (= oldest), **inner, outdoor, outer, principal** (= main), **upper**

Here are some examples of adjectives which can only go after a linking verb.
   *At last the baby is **asleep**.*   *Emma's two brothers are very **alike**.*
   *I'm really **pleased** to see you.*   *Vicky looked **ill**, I thought.*

Some more examples are: **afraid, alone, ashamed, awake, alive, content** (= happy), **fine** (= in good health), **glad, unwell, well**

▷ 82 Two nouns together, e.g. **a colour photo**   ▷ 108 Adjective or adverb?

104 Exercises

1 Adjectives (A)

Look at the pictures and write a phrase with an adjective and noun.
Use these nouns: *building, car, cat, chairs, music, power, skirt, weather*

▶ long/short

▶ hot/cold

1 traditional/modern

2 black/white

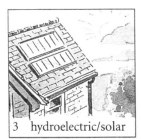
3 hydroelectric/solar

4 classical/pop

5 new/old

6 tall/low

▶ *a long skirt*
▶ *cold weather*
1 ....
2 ....
3 ....
4 ....
5 ....
6 ....

2 Adjectives (A–B)

<u>Underline</u> all the adjectives in this description of a hotel.

This <u>comfortable</u> hotel with its pleasant gardens is ideal for people who want a quiet holiday, yet it is only a short distance from the highly popular attractions of the area. There are lovely views from every room. The atmosphere is very friendly, and the staff are always helpful. A holiday here is very good value for money. You can eat your meals at the hotel, where the food tastes marvellous. Or you can of course try some of the excellent local restaurants.

3 Adjectives used in one position only (C)

Look at the notes and write the song titles. Sometimes the adjective comes before the noun, and sometimes you need to use *is* or *are*.

▶ your sister / elder   *Your elder sister*
▶ this boy / alone   *This boy is alone*
1 the world / asleep   ....
2 my desire / chief   ....
3 my heart / content   ....
4 the thing to remember / main ....
5 the night / alive   ....
6 secrets / inner   ....
7 the girl for me / only   ....

105 The order of adjectives

A Introduction

It's **beautiful sunny** weather.

Nick has got a **big black** dog.

We can use more than one adjective before a noun. There is usually one correct order.
We cannot say ~~sunny beautiful weather~~ or ~~a black big dog~~.

B Adjectives and nouns

We sometimes use two nouns together (see Unit 82).
   a glass door   a computer program
Here we use **glass** like an adjective, to describe the door. When we use another adjective as well (e.g. **heavy**), it comes before both the nouns.
   *a **heavy** glass door   a **useful** computer program*

C Word order

We order adjectives according to their meaning. This is the normal order:

	GROUP	EXAMPLES	
1	Opinion (how good?)	wonderful, nice, great, awful, terrible	Adjectives that say how good
2	Size (how big?)	large, small, long, short, tall	and how big come first.
3	Most other qualities	quiet, famous, important, soft, wet, difficult, fast, angry, warm	Most adjectives come next if they do not belong to another group.
4	Age (how old?)	new, old	
5	Colour	red, blue, green, black	
6	Origin (where from?)	American, British, French	
7	Material (made of?)	stone, plastic, steel, paper	Some of these are nouns.
8	Type (what kind?)	an **electric** kettle, **political** matters, **road** transport	
9	Purpose (what for?)	a **bread** knife, a **bath** towel	

Here are some examples.
   *a **small green** insect* (size, colour)   *Japanese industrial designers* (origin, type)
   *a **wonderful new face** cream* (opinion, age, purpose)   *awful plastic souvenirs* (opinion, material)
   *a **long boring train** journey* (size, quality, type)   *some **nice easy quiz** questions* (opinion, quality, purpose)
   *a **beautiful wooden picture** frame* (opinion, material, purpose)

We sometimes put commas between adjectives in Groups 1–3
   *a **horrible, ugly** building   a **busy, lively, exciting** city*

105 Exercises

1 The order of adjectives (A–C)

Describe the pictures. Use these words: *boots, building, car, seat, singer*

▶ They're leather. They're big.

1 It's small. It's white.

2 It's old. It's attractive.

3 It's wooden. It's for the garden. It's expensive.

4 He sings in the opera. He's Italian. He's famous.

▶ *big leather boots*
1 ....
2 ....
3 ....
4 ....

2 The order of adjectives (A–C)

Write a list of things to be sold at an auction.
▶ basin / sugar, antique, silver   *an antique silver sugar basin*
1 vase / glass, old, lovely   ....
2 mirror / wall, attractive   ....
3 desk / modern, office   ....
4 chairs / kitchen, red, metal   ....
5 boat / model, splendid, old   ....
6 stamps / postage, valuable, Australian ....
7 table / small, coffee, wooden   ....

3 The order of adjectives (A–C)

Look at each advertisement and write the information in a single sentence.
▶ This game is new. It's for the family. And it's exciting.
  This is an exciting new family game.
1 This computer is for business. It's Japanese. And it's powerful.
  ....
2 This fire is electric. It's excellent. And it's small.
  ....
3 This is a chocolate bar. It's new. And it's a big bar.
  ....
4 This comedy is American. It's for television. And it's terrific.
  ....
5 These doors are aluminium. They're for your garage. And they're stylish.
  ....
6 These shoes are modern. They're for sports. And they're wonderful.
  ....
7 This phone is a mobile. It's German. And it's very good.
  ....

106 The old, the rich, etc

A Introduction

*These people are protesting. They want equal rights for **the disabled** and more help for **the blind**.*

There are some adjectives that we can use with **the** to talk about groups of people in society, e.g. **the disabled, the blind**. Here are some more examples.

What can we do to feed **the hungry**?   **The rich** can afford to pay more taxes.
The young are usually keen to travel.   It is our duty to care for **the sick**.

B What adjectives can we use?

These are some of the adjectives and other words that we can use in a phrase with **the**.

> To do with social or economic position:
> *the disadvantaged, the homeless, the hungry, the poor, the privileged, the rich, the starving, the strong, the underprivileged, the unemployed, the weak*
>
> To do with physical condition or health:
> *the blind, the deaf, the dead, the disabled, the handicapped, the living, the sick*
>
> To do with age:
> *the elderly, the middle-aged, the old, the over-sixties, the under-fives, the young*

We can sometimes use an adverb before the adjective.
The very poor are left without hope.   **The severely disabled** need full-time care.
There are some adjectives in this structure that normally have an adverb.
The less fortunate cannot afford to go on holiday.
Should **the mentally ill** be allowed to live in the community?

C The young or the young people?

The young means 'young people in general'.
The young have their lives in front of them.
When we mean a specific person or a specific group of people, then we use **man, woman, people**, etc.
There was **a young man** standing on the corner.
I know **the young woman** in reception. She lives in our street.
None of **the young people** in the village can find jobs here.

106 Exercises

1 The old, the rich, etc (A)
Write in the missing words. Use *the* and these adjectives: *homeless, hungry, old, sick, unemployed, young*

▶ Better education for *the young*
1 Food for ....
2 Homes for ....
3 Better hospitals for ....
4 Jobs for ....
5 Better pensions for ....

2 The old, the rich, etc (A–B)
Rewrite the sentences using a phrase with *the* and an adjective instead of the underlined phrases.
▶ People who have lots of money have comfortable lives.
   The rich have comfortable lives.
1 We live near a special school for people who can't hear.
   ....
2 The old soldiers were holding a service for those who had died.
   ....
3 The government should do more for people who do not have enough money.
   ....
4 I'm doing a course on caring for people who are mentally handicapped.
   ....

3 The young or the young people? (C)
Complete these sentences from a newspaper. Use the adjectives in brackets.
Put in e.g. *the hungry* or *the hungry people*.
▶ Rich nations can afford to feed *the hungry* (hungry).
▶ *The homeless people* (homeless) whose story appeared in this paper last week have now found a place to live.
1 .... (sick) need to be looked after, so money must be spent on hospitals.
2 Some of .... (young) at the youth club here are running in a marathon.
3 Life must be hard for .... (unemployed) in our society today.
4 What is the government doing to help .... (poor)?
5 There was a fire at a nursing home in Charles Street, but none of .... (old) who live there were hurt.
6 .... (homeless) usually have great difficulty in getting a job.
7 There is a special television programme for .... (deaf) every Sunday morning.

107 Interesting and interested

A Introduction

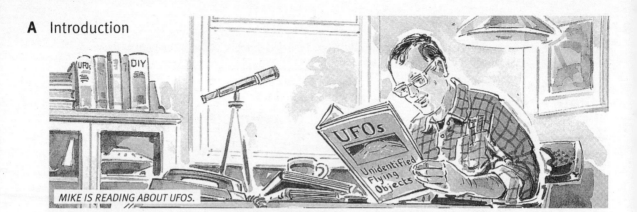

MIKE IS READING ABOUT UFOS.

INTERESTING	INTERESTED
The book is full of information. It's very **interesting**.	Mike is very **interested** in UFOs.
The word **interesting** tells us what the book does to Mike – it interests him. A book can be **interesting, boring, exciting** or **amusing**, for example.	The word **interested** tells us how Mike feels. A person can feel **interested, bored, excited** or **amused**, for example.

B Adjective pairs

Here are some more examples.

ING	ED
Tom told us an **amusing** story.	We were **amused** at Tom's story.
The two-hour delay was **annoying**.	The passengers were **annoyed** about the delay.
I didn't enjoy the party. It was **boring**.	I went to the party, but I felt **bored**.
This computer has some very **confusing** instructions.	I got very **confused** trying to make sense of the instructions.
This wet weather is so **depressing**.	This weather makes me so **depressed**.
It was very **disappointing** not to get the job.	I was very **disappointed** not to get the job.
The game was really **exciting**.	The United fans were **excited**.
Going for a jog with Matthew is **exhausting**.	I'm **exhausted** after jogging all that way.
I thought the programme on wildlife was **fascinating**.	I watched the programme on wildlife. I was absolutely **fascinated**.
For one **frightening/terrifying** moment I thought I was going to fall.	When I got onto the roof, I felt **frightened/terrified**.
I just don't understand. I find the whole thing rather **puzzling**.	I must say I'm **puzzled**. I just don't understand.
Lying in a hot bath is **relaxing**.	I feel **relaxed** when I lie in a hot bath.
I think the way Jessica behaved was quite **shocking**.	I was quite **shocked** to see Jessica behaving like that.
The test results were **surprising**.	I was **surprised** at the test results.
What **thrilling** news this is! Congratulations!	We were **thrilled** to hear your good news.
The journey took all day and night. They found it very **tiring**.	After travelling all day and night they were very **tired**.

107 Exercises

1 Interesting and interested (A–B)

What are they saying? Put in these words: *depressing, exciting, exhausted, fascinating, interested*

▶ This is a *depressing* place.
1 I'm absolutely ....
2 I'm .... in astronomy.
3 Chess is a .... game.
4 This is really .... !

2 Interesting and interested (A–B)

Complete the conversation. Write the complete word in each space.
Vicky: That was an (▶) *exciting* (excit...) film, wasn't it?
Rachel: Oh, do you think so? I'm (1) .... (surpris...) you liked it.
I thought it was rather (2) .... (disappoint...).
Vicky: Well, I was (3) .... (puzzl...) once or twice. I didn't understand the whole story.
It was (4) .... (confus...) in places. But the end was good.
Rachel: I was (5) .... (bor...) most of the time.
I didn't find it very (6) .... (interest...).

3 Interesting and interested (A–B)

Complete the conversations using a word ending in *ing* or *ed*.
▶ David: I'm surprised how warm it is for March.
  Melanie: Yes, all this sunshine is quite *surprising*.
▶ Vicky: I'm not very fit. I was pretty tired after climbing the mountain.
  Natasha: Yes, I think everyone felt *tired*.
1 Trevor: I think I need to relax.
  Laura: Well, lying by the pool should be ....
2 Vicky: It was annoying to lose my ticket.
  Emma: You looked really .... when you had to buy another one.
3 Sarah: The cabaret was amusing.
  Mark: Claire was certainly .... She couldn't stop laughing.
4 Daniel: The museum was interesting, wasn't it?
  Rachel: It was OK. I was quite .... in those old maps.
5 Matthew: I'm fascinated by these old photos.
  Emma: I always find it .... to see what people looked like as children.
6 Rachel: Was it a big thrill meeting Tom Hanks?
  Vicky: You bet. It was just about the most .... moment of my life.
7 Sarah: You look exhausted. You should go to bed.
  Mark: Driving down from Scotland was pretty ....

108 Adjective or adverb? (1)

A Introduction

Vicky: *I like that song that Natasha sang.*
Rachel: *Yes, it's a **nice** song. And she sang it **nicely**, too.*

> An adjective (**nice**) describes a noun (**song**).
> *The man had a **quiet** voice.*
> *Claire wears **expensive** clothes.*
> *The runners made a **slow** start.*
>
> An adverb (**nicely**) describes a verb (**sang**).
> *The man spoke **quietly**.*
> *Claire dresses **expensively**.*
> *They started the race **slowly**.*
> We do NOT say *She sang it nice.*

We can use adverbs in other ways. An adverb like **really** or **very** can be combined with an adjective (**hot**) or another adverb (**carefully**) (see Unit 115).
*It was **really** hot in the sun.*   *Andrew checked his work **very** carefully.*
An adverb like **fortunately** or **perhaps** says something about the whole situation.
***Fortunately** nothing was stolen.*   ***Perhaps** Sarah is working late.*

B The ly ending

We form many adverbs from an adjective + **ly**. For example **politely**, **quickly**, **safely**.
But there are some special spelling rules.

> 1 We do not leave out *e*, e.g. *nice* → *nicely*
>   Exceptions are *true* → *truly*, *whole* → *wholly*.
>
> 2 *y* → *ily* after a consonant, e.g. *easy* → *easily*, *lucky* → *luckily*
>   Also *angrily*, *happily*, *heavily*, etc.
>
> 3 *le* → *ly*, e.g. *possible* → *possibly*
>   Also *comfortably*, *probably*, *reasonably*, *sensibly*, *terribly*, etc.
>
> 4 *ic* → *ically*, e.g. *dramatic* → *dramatically*
>   Also *automatically*, *scientifically*, etc. (Exception: *publicly*)

C Looked nice and looked carefully

Compare these two structures.

LINKING VERB + ADJECTIVE	ACTION VERB + ADVERB
*Tom **was hungry**.* *The children **seemed happy**.* *My soup **has got cold**.* An adjective can come after a linking verb such as **be** (see Unit 104B).	*Paul **ate hungrily**.* *The children **played happily**.* *The man **stared coldly** at us.* We use an adverb when the verb means that something happens.

Some verbs like **look**, **taste** and **appear** can be either linking verbs or action verbs.

LINKING VERB + ADJECTIVE	ACTION VERB + ADVERB
*Mike **looked angry**.* *The medicine **tasted awful**.* *The man **appeared** (to be) **drunk**.*	*He **looked carefully** at the signature.* *Emma **tasted** the drink **nervously**.* *A waiter **appeared suddenly**.*

▷ page 380 American English

108 Exercises

1 Adverbs (A–B)

This is part of a story about a spy called X. Put in adverbs formed from these adjectives:
bright, careful, fluent, immediate, patient, punctual, quiet, safe, secret, slow

The journey took a long time because the train travelled so (▶) *slowly*. It was hot, and the sun shone (1) .... from a clear sky. X could only wait (2) .... for the journey to end. When the train finally arrived, he had no time to spare, so he (3) .... took a taxi to the hotel. Y was on time. She arrived (4) .... at three. No one else knew about the meeting – it was important to meet (5) .... 'I had a terrible journey,' said Y. 'But luckily the pilot managed to land (6) ....' Her English was good, and she spoke very (7) .... X was listening (8) .... to every word. They were speaking very (9) .... in case the room was bugged.

2 The ly ending (B)

Look at the information in brackets and put in the adverbs. Be careful with the spelling.
▶ (Emma's toothache was terrible.) Emma's tooth ached *terribly*.
1 (Henry was angry.) Henry shouted .... at the waiter.
2 (I'm happy sitting here.) I can sit here .... for hours.
3 (The switch is automatic.) The machine switches itself off ....
4 (The debate should be public.) We need to debate the matter ....
5 (Everyone was enthusiastic.) Everyone discussed the idea ....
6 (We should be reasonable.) Can't we discuss the problem .... ?
7 (The building has to be secure.) Did you lock all the doors .... ?

3 Adverb or adjective? (A–B)

Decide what you need to say. End your sentence with an adverb ending in *ly*.

▶ Tell the police that you can't remember the accident. It isn't very clear in your mind.
   I can't remember the accident very clearly.
1 Tell your friend that United won the game. It was an easy win.
   ....
2 Tell your boss that you've checked the figures. You've been careful.
   ....
3 Tell your neighbour that his dog barked at you. It was very fierce.
   ....
4 You are phoning your friend. Tell him about the rain where you are. It's quite heavy.
   ....

4 Adverb or adjective? (A–C)

Vicky is telling Rachel about a dream she had. Choose the correct forms.

I had a (▶) <u>strange/~~strangely~~</u> dream last night. I was in a garden. It was getting (1) <u>dark/darkly</u>, and it was (2) <u>terrible/terribly</u> cold. My head was aching (3) <u>bad/badly</u>. I was walking out of the garden when (4) <u>sudden/suddenly</u> I saw a man. He was sitting (5) <u>quiet/quietly</u> on a seat. He seemed very (6) <u>unhappy/unhappily</u>. He looked up and smiled (7) <u>sad/sadly</u> at me. I don't know why, but I felt (8) <u>curious/curiously</u> about him. I wanted to talk to him, but I couldn't think what to say. I just stood there (9) <u>foolish/foolishly</u>.

109 Adjective or adverb? (2)

A Friendly, likely, etc

The ending **ly** is the normal adverb ending (see Unit 108). But a few adjectives also end in **ly**.
  *Melanie was very **friendly**.*   *It was a **lively** party.*   *We had a **lovely** time.*

Some more examples are: **elderly, likely, lonely, silly, ugly**

The words are adjectives, not adverbs (NOT ~~She spoke to us friendly~~). And we cannot add **ly**. There is no such word as ~~friendlily~~. But we can say **in a friendly way/manner**.
  *She spoke to us **in a friendly way**.*
If we need to use an adverb, we often choose another word of similar meaning.
  *It was **lovely**. Everything went **beautifully**.*

B Hard, fast, etc

Compare these sentences.

ADJECTIVE	ADVERB
We did some **hard** work.	We worked **hard**.
I came on the **fast** train.	The train went quite **fast**.

We can use these words both as adjectives and as adverbs:
deep, early, fast, hard, high, late, long, low, near, right, straight, wrong (For **hardly, nearly**, etc, see C.)

In informal English, the adjectives **cheap, loud, quick** and **slow** can be adverbs.

ADJECTIVE	ADVERB
They sell **cheap** clothes in the market.	They sell things **cheap**/cheaply there.
Back already! That was **quick**.	Come as **quick**/quickly as you can.

C Hard, hardly, near, nearly, etc

There are some pairs of adverbs like **hard** and **hardly** which have different meanings.
Here are some examples.
  *I tried **hard**, but I didn't succeed.*
  *I've got **hardly** any money left.* (hardly any = very little, almost none)
  *Luckily I found a phone box quite **near**.*   *I **nearly** fell asleep in the meeting.* (nearly = almost)
  *Rachel arrived **late**, as usual.*   *I've been very busy **lately**.* (lately = in the last few days/weeks)
  *The plane flew **high** above the clouds.*   *The material is **highly** radioactive.* (highly = very)
  *We got into the concert **free**.* (free = without paying)
  *The animals are allowed to wander **freely**.* (freely = uncontrolled)

D Good and well

Good is an adjective, and **well** is its adverb. The opposites are **bad** and **badly**.

ADJECTIVE	ADVERB
Natasha is a **good** violinist.	She plays the violin very **well**.
Our test results were **good**.	We all did **well** in the test.
I had a **bad** night.	I slept **badly** last night.

Well can also be an adjective meaning 'in good health', the opposite of **ill**.
  *My mother was very **ill**, but she's quite **well** again now.*   *How are you? ~ Very **well**, thank you.*

109 Exercises

1 Friendly, hard, hardly, etc (A–C)

Decide if each underlined word is an adjective or an adverb.
- ▶ That new building is rather <u>ugly</u>.   *adjective*
- ▶ I'd like to arrive <u>early</u> if I can.   *adverb*
1. I haven't seen you for a <u>long</u> time. ....
2. Why are you wearing that <u>silly</u> hat? ....
3. Very young children travel <u>free</u>. ....
4. The temperature is quite <u>high</u> today. ....
5. We <u>nearly</u> missed the bus this morning. ....
6. Do you have to play that music so <u>loud</u>? ....

2 Friendly, hard, hardly, etc (A–C)

Complete the conversation. Decide if you need *ly* with the words in brackets.

Mark: How did you get on with Henry today?
Sarah: Oh, we had a nice lunch and some (▶) *lively* (live) conversation. Henry was charming, as usual. He gave me a lift back to the office, but it was (1) .... (hard) worth risking our lives to save a few minutes. He (2) .... (near) killed us.
Mark: What do you mean?
Sarah: Well, we'd sat a bit too (3) .... (long) over our meal, and we were (4) .... (late) getting back to work. Henry drove very (5) .... (fast). I tried (6) .... (hard) to keep calm, but I was quite scared. We went (7) .... (wrong) and missed a left turn, and Henry got annoyed. Then a van came round the corner, and it was coming (8) .... (straight) at us. I don't know how we missed it.
Mark: Well, I'm glad you did. And next time you'd better take a taxi.

3 Good and well (D)

Complete the conversation. Put in *good*, *well* (x2), *bad*, *badly* and *ill*.

Rachel: How did you and Daniel get on in your tennis match?
Matthew: We lost. I'm afraid we didn't play very (▶) *well*. Daniel made some (1) .... mistakes. It wasn't a very (2) .... day for us. We played really (3) ....
Andrew: I heard Daniel's in bed at the moment because he isn't very (4) ....
Matthew: Yes, I'm afraid he's been (5) .... for several days, but he's better now.

4 Friendly, hard, hardly, etc (A–D)

Complete the conversation. Choose the correct form.

Daniel: Is it true you saw a ghost last night?
Vicky: Yes, I did. I went to bed (▶) <u>late</u>/<s>lately</s>, and I was sleeping (1) <u>bad/badly</u>. I suddenly woke up in the middle of the night. I went to the window and saw the ghost walking across the lawn.
Daniel: Was it a man or a woman?
Vicky: A woman in a white dress. I had a (2) <u>good/well</u> view from the window, but she walked very (3) <u>fast/fastly</u>. She wasn't there very (4) <u>long/longly</u>. I'd (5) <u>hard/hardly</u> caught sight of her before she'd gone. I (6) <u>near/nearly</u> missed her.
Daniel: You don't think you've been working too (7) <u>hard/hardly</u>? You've been looking a bit pale (8) <u>late/lately</u>.
Vicky: I saw her, I tell you.
Daniel: It isn't very (9) <u>like/likely</u> that ghosts actually exist, you know. I expect you were imagining it.

Test 18 Adjectives and adverbs (Units 104–109)

Test 18A

Choose the correct word or phrase.
▶ We walked slow/<u>slowly</u> back to the hotel.
1 We could walk free/<u>freely</u> around the aircraft during the flight.
2 <u>The young/The young man</u> with dark hair is my sister's boyfriend.
3 I'm getting quite <u>hungry/hungrily</u>.
4 The man looked <u>thoughtful/thoughtfully</u> around the room.
5 Have I filled this form in <u>right/rightly</u>?
6 I think Egypt is a <u>fascinated/fascinating</u> country.
7 The two sisters do <u>alike/similar</u> jobs.
8 I'm pleased the plan worked so <u>good/goodly/well</u>.
9 She invented a new kind of wheelchair for <u>the disabled/the disabled people</u>.
10 I'm very <u>confused/confusing</u> about what to do.
11 They performed the experiment <u>scientifically/scientificly</u>.
12 The hostages must be very <u>afraid/frightened</u> people.

Test 18B

Put the words in the right order to form a statement.
▶ a / bought / coat / I / new / red
  I bought a new red coat.
1 a / is / nice / place / this
  ....
2 biscuit / can't / find / I / large / the / tin
  ....
3 a / behaved / in / silly / Tessa / way
  ....
4 coffee / cold / getting / is / your
  ....
5 a / house / in / live / lovely / old / stone / they
  ....
6 for / hospital / ill / is / mentally / the / this
  ....

Test 18C

Write the words in brackets and add *ly*, *ing* or *ed* only if you need to.
Janet: Is this the (▶) *new* (new...) car you've just bought?
Nigel: That's right. Well, it's second-hand of course.
Janet: It's (▶) *exciting* (excit...) buying a car, isn't it?
Nigel: Well, it was a bit of a problem actually because I didn't have much money to spend. But I managed to find one that wasn't very (1) .... (expensive...).
Janet: It looks very (2) .... (nice...), I must say.
Nigel: It's ten years old, so I was (3) .... (surpris...) what good condition it's in. The man I bought it from is over eighty, and he always drove it very (4) .... (careful...), he said. He never took it out if it was raining, which I find (5) .... (amus...).
Janet: I think (6) .... (elder...) people look after their cars better than young people.
Nigel: He was a (7) .... (friend...) old chap. He even gave me all these maps (8) .... (free...).

Test 18

Test 18D

Write a second sentence so that it has a similar meaning to the first. Use the word in brackets.
▶ Jonathan was stupid. (behaved)
Jonathan behaved stupidly.

1. The drink had a strange taste. (tasted)

2. Obviously, sick people need to be looked after. (the)

3. The dog slept. (asleep)

4. The young woman was polite. (spoke)

5. The train was late. (arrived)

6. The film's ending is dramatic. (ends)

7. Polly gave an angry shout. (shouted)

8. Billiards is a game for indoors. (indoor)

9. The clown amused people. (amusing)

10. There was almost no time left. (any)

Test 18E

Some of these sentences are correct, but most have a mistake. If the sentence is correct, put a tick (✓).
If it is incorrect, cross the sentence out and write it correctly.

▶ Your friend looked rather ill.   ✓
▶ ~~It was a steel long pipe.~~   *It was a long steel pipe.*
1. I tasted the soup careful.
2. It's a beautiful old English church.
3. Are they asleep children?
4. It's a school for the deaf people.
5. It's a leather new nice jacket.
6. The riches are very lucky.
7. You handled the situation well.
8. He used a green paper thick towel.
9. Our future lies with the young.
10. The course I started was bored.
11. I often talk to the two old next door.
12. The smoke rose highly into the air.
13. It feels warm in here.
14. We felt disappointing when we lost.
15. Everyone seemed very nervously.
16. Tessa drives too fastly.
17. This scenery is really depressing.

110 Comparative and superlative forms

A The comparison of adjectives

We form the comparative and superlative of short adjectives (e.g. **cheap**) and long adjectives (e.g. **expensive**) in different ways.

	COMPARATIVE	SUPERLATIVE
Short word, e.g. *cheap*:	cheaper	(the) cheapest
Long word, e.g. *expensive*:	more expensive	(the) most expensive

For **less** and **least**, see Unit 112A.
   *There are some **less expensive** ones here, look.*

B Short and long adjectives

One-syllable adjectives (e.g. **small, nice**) usually have the **er, est** ending.
   *Your hi-fi is **smaller**.   Emma needs a **bigger** computer.*
   *This is the **nicest** colour.   This room is the **warmest**.*

But we use **more, most** before words ending in **ed**.
   *Everyone was pleased at the results, but Vicky was the **most pleased**.*

We also use **more, most** with three-syllable adjectives (e.g. **ex·cit·ing**) and with longer ones.
   *The film was **more exciting** than the book.   This dress is **more elegant**.*
   *We did the **most interesting** project.   This machine is the **most reliable**.*

Some two-syllable adjectives have **er, est**, and some have **more, most**. Look at this information.

> TWO-SYLLABLE ADJECTIVES
> 1 Words ending in a consonant + *y* have *er*, *est*, e.g. *happy* → *happier*, *happiest*.
>   Examples are: *busy, dirty, easy, funny, happy, heavy, lovely, lucky, pretty, silly, tidy*
> 2 Some words have *er*, *est* OR *more*, *most*, e.g. *narrow* → *narrower*, *narrowest* OR **more** *narrow*, **most** *narrow*.
>   Examples are: *clever, common, cruel, gentle, narrow, pleasant, polite, quiet, simple, stupid, tired*
> 3 The following words have *more*, *most*, e.g. *useful* → *more useful*, *most useful*.
>   a Words ending in *ful* or *less*, e.g. *careful, helpful, useful; hopeless*
>   b Words ending in *ing* or *ed*, e.g. *boring, willing; annoyed, surprised*
>   c Many others, e.g. *afraid, certain, correct, eager, exact, famous, foolish, frequent, modern, nervous, normal, recent*

C Spelling

There are some special spelling rules for the **er** and **est** endings.

1. e → er, est, e.g. *nice* → *nicer, nicest, large* → *larger, largest.*
   Also *brave, fine, safe,* etc
2. y → ier, iest after a consonant, e.g. *happy* → *happier, happiest.*
   Also *lovely, lucky, pretty,* etc
3. Words ending in a single vowel letter + single consonant letter → double the consonant
   e.g. *hot* → *hotter, hottest, big* → *bigger, biggest.*
   Also *fit, sad, thin, wet,* etc (but w does not change, e.g. *new* → *newer*)

For more details, see page 371.

D The comparison of adverbs

Some adverbs have the same form as an adjective, e.g. **early, fast, hard, high, late, long, near.**
They form the comparative and superlative with **er, est**.
  *Can't you run **faster** than that?*   *Andrew works the **hardest**.*
Note also the spelling of **earlier** and **earliest**.

Many adverbs are an adjective + **ly**, e.g. **carefully, easily, nicely, slowly**.
They form the comparative and superlative with **more, most**.
  *We could do this **more easily** with a computer.*
  *Of all the players it was Matthew who planned his tactics the **most carefully**.*

In informal English we use **cheaper, cheapest, louder, loudest, quicker, quickest** and **slower, slowest** rather than **more cheaply, the most loudly**, etc.
  *Melanie reacted the **quickest**.*   *You should drive **slower** in fog.*

Note the forms **sooner, soonest** and **more often, most often**.
  *Try to get home **sooner**.*   *I must exercise **more often**.*

E Irregular forms

Good, well, bad, badly and **far** have irregular forms.

ADJECTIVE/ADVERB	COMPARATIVE	SUPERLATIVE
good/well	better	best
bad/badly	worse	worst
far	farther/further	farthest/furthest

  *You've got the **best** handwriting.*   *How much **further** are we going?*

We can use **elder, eldest** + noun instead of **older, oldest**, but only for people in the same family.
  *My **elder/older** sister got married last year.*

F Comparing quantities

We use **more, most** and their opposites **less** and **least** to compare quantities.
  *I haven't got many books. You've got **more** than I have.*   *The Hotel Bristol has the **most** rooms.*
  *Trevor spends **less** on clothes than Laura does.*   *Emma made the **least** mistakes.*

▷ 111–112 Comparative and superlative patterns

110 Exercises

1 The comparison of adjectives (A–B)

Complete the sentences. Use these adjectives: *beautiful, expensive, high, interesting, tall*

▶ The giraffe *is taller* than the man.
▶ The CD *is more expensive* than the cassette.
1   Detective stories .... than algebra.
2   The top of the mountain .... than the clouds.
3   The acrobat .... than the clown.

2 The comparison of adjectives (A–B)

Tom is a United fan. He never stops talking about them. Put in the superlative form of the adjectives.
▶ Everyone's heard of United. They're the *most famous* (famous) team in the world.
▶ They've got a long history. They're the *oldest* (old) club in England.
1   They've got lots of money. They're the .... (rich) club in the country.
2   Their stadium is new. It's the .... (modern) stadium in Europe.
3   United are wonderful. They're the .... (great) club in the world.
4   And what a team! It's the .... (exciting) team ever.
5   They've got lots of fans. They're the .... (popular) team in the country.
6   United have won everything. They're the .... (successful) team ever.
7   They're good to watch. They play the .... (attractive) football.
8   United fans are happy. We're the .... (happy) people in the world.

3 The comparison of adjectives (A–C)

Complete the advertisements with the comparative form of the adjective.
▶ Use Get-It-Clean and you'll get your floors *cleaner*
▶ Elegant Wallpapers simply look *more elegant*
1   Watch a Happy Video and you'll feel ....
2   Wear a pair of Fast Shoes and you'll be a .... runner.
3   Helpful Cookbooks are a .... guide to cooking.
4   Wash your hair with Lovely Shampoo for .... hair.
5   Try a Big-Big Burger and you'll have a .... meal.
6   Restful Beds give you a .... night.
7   Wear Modern Fashions for a .... look.

4 The comparison of adverbs (D)

Put in the comparative form of these adverbs: *carefully, early, easily, high, long, loud, often, smartly*
▶ I was too nervous to go *higher* than halfway up the tower.
▶ We could have found the place *more easily* with a map.
1 Do you have to wear those old jeans, Mike? Can't you dress ....?
2 You needn't go yet. You can stay a bit ....
3 There are lots of break-ins. They happen .... nowadays.
4 If you do it again ...., you won't make so many mistakes.
5 The film starts at eight, but we should get to the cinema a few
   minutes ....
6 We can't hear. Could you speak a bit ....?

5 Irregular forms (E)

Matthew and Emma are walking in the country. Put in *further, furthest, better, best, worse* and *worst*.
Emma: I'm not used to country walks. How much (▶) *further* is it?
Matthew: Not far. And it gets better. We've done the (1) .... part. Look, the path gets
         easier. It goes downhill from here. I hope you're feeling (2) .... now, Emma.
Emma: I feel dreadful, actually, (3) .... than before.
Matthew: Oh, dear. Do you want to have a rest?
Emma: No, the (4) .... thing would be to get home as soon as we can. I'm not very fit,
         you know. This is the (5) .... I've walked for a long time.

6 Comparing quantities (F)

Put in *more, most, less* (x2) and *least*.
Laura: Our new car is smaller, so it uses (▶) *less* petrol. They tested some small cars, and this **one costs**
         the (1) .... to run of all the cars in the test. It's very economical, so **Trevor likes**
         it. He wants to spend (2) .... on motoring.
Harriet: Can you get three people in the back?
Laura: Not very easily. We had (3) .... room in our old car. (4) ....
         cars take five people, but not this one.

7 Comparative and superlative forms (A–F)

Write the correct forms.
▶ You're the ~~luckyest~~ person I know.   *luckiest*
▶ The situation is getting ~~difficulter~~.   *more difficult*
1 I was ~~happyer~~ in my old job.   ....
2 I've got the ~~most small~~ office.   ....
3 This photo is the ~~goodest~~.   ....
4 Last week's meeting was ~~more short~~.   ....
5 Money is the ~~importantest~~ thing.   ....
6 Is Rachel ~~elder~~ than Vicky?   ....
7 This game is ~~excitinger~~ than the last one.   ....
8 Of all the students, Andrew does the ~~more~~ work. ....
9 This month has been ~~weter~~ than last month.   ....
10 The prices are ~~more low~~ here.   ....
11 I feel ~~more bad~~ than I did yesterday.   ....

111 Comparative and superlative patterns (1)

A Introduction

Claire, do you know Alison?

Yes, Henry, she's the **nicest** person I know. But she's twenty years **older than** me.

There are a number of different sentence patterns with comparative and superlative forms, e.g. **older than me, the nicest person I know**.

B The comparative and than

We often use a phrase with **than** after a comparative.
*This restaurant is **nicer than** the Pizza House.*
*I had a **bigger** meal **than** you.*
*The steak is **more expensive than** the fish.*

C The superlative

We normally use **the** before a superlative.
***The quickest** way is along this path.*   *The last question is **the most difficult**.*
Note the pattern with **one of**.
*Michael Jackson is **one of the most famous** pop singers ever.*

After a superlative we can use **in** or **of**. We use **in** with places and with groups of people, e.g. **team**.
*It's the **most expensive** hotel **in Oxford**.*   *Who is the **best** player **in the team**?*
*This question is the **most difficult of all**.*   *August is the **wettest** month **of the year**.*

We often use a clause after a superlative.
*That was the **most delicious** meal **(that) I've ever eaten**.*
*Melanie is the **nicest** person **you could meet**.*

D As ... as

We use **as ... as** to say that things are equal or unequal.
*Our house is **as big as** yours. They're the same size.* NOT *It is so big as yours*.
*It's warmer today. It isn't **as cold as** yesterday.*

In a negative sentence we can also use **so ... as**, but this is less common than **as ... as**.
*This flat isn't **as big as/so big as** our old one.*

Here are some more examples of **as ... as**.
*The chair is **as expensive as** the table.*   *We can't do crosswords **as quickly as** you do.*
*I don't earn **as much** money **as** I'd like.*

Note also **the same as**.
*The result of the match was **the same as** last year.*

E Than me/than I am

Compare **than me** and **than I am**. Both are correct, and they have the same meaning.

*You're twenty years older than **me**.*	*You're twenty years older than **I am**.*
*Harriet's husband isn't as tall as **her**.*	*Her husband isn't as tall as **she is**.*
After **than** or **as**, a personal pronoun on its own has the object form, e.g. **me**.	But if the pronoun has a verb after it, then we use the subject form, e.g. **I**.

111 Exercises

1 The comparative and **than** (B)

Comment on these situations. Write sentences with a comparative and *than*.
Use these adjectives: *big, expensive, long, old, popular, strong, tall*

▶ The film lasts two and a half hours, but the videotape is only two hours long.
The film is longer than the videotape.

▶ The water-colour is £85, and the oil-painting is £100.
The oil-painting is more expensive than the water-colour.

1 The church was built in 1878 and the library in 1925.

2 Daniel can lift 90 kilos, but Matthew can lift 120 kilos.

3 Mike is 1.7 metres tall, but Harriet is 1.8 metres.

4 Andrew hasn't many friends. Claire has lots of friends.

5 Mark's car has room for five people, but Sarah's has room for only four.

2 The superlative (C)

Write sentences from the notes. Use the superlative form of the adjective.
▶ Melanie / kind person / I know   *Melanie is the kindest person I know.*
1 Friday / busy day / week   .... of the week.
2 the Metropole / nice hotel / town
3 this watch / one / cheap / you can buy
4 this Beatles album / good / they ever made
5 Alan / successful salesman / company

3 As ... as (D)

Use the notes and add sentences with *isn't as ... as*.
▶ a car / a motor bike / expensive
Why don't you buy a motor bike? *A motor bike isn't as expensive as a car.*
1 metal / plastic / strong
I don't like these plastic screws.
2 the armchair / the stool / comfortable
Oh, don't sit there.
3 surfing / swimming / exciting
I prefer surfing to swimming.
4 the post / e-mail / quick
A letter will take two days.

4 Than me/than I am (E)

Choose the correct pronoun.
Tom: Why is Luke in our basketball team and not me? Aren't I as good as (▶) he/him? Is he taller than (1) I/me? Is he a better player than (2) I am/me am?
Nick: I don't know. I can't understand why I'm in the team. You and Luke are both better than (3) I/me.
Tom: Carl's in the team too, but I've scored a lot more points than (4) he has/him has.

112 Comparative and superlative patterns (2)

A Less and least

Less and **least** are the opposites of **more** and **most**. We use **less** and **least** with both long and short words.
   A bus is **less** expensive than a taxi.
   (= A bus is cheaper than a taxi./A bus isn't as expensive as a taxi.)
   I feel better today, **less** tired.   I'm the **least** musical person in the world, I'm afraid.
   We go out **less** often these days.   You should do **less** work. You do too much.

B Much faster

We can put a word or phrase (e.g. **much, far, a bit**) before a comparative
to say how much faster, cheaper, etc something is. Look at these examples.
   It's **much faster** by tube.   A bus is **far cheaper** than a taxi.
   This bed is **a bit more comfortable**.   Business is **rather better** this year.
   I got up **a little later** than usual.   This month's figures are **slightly less good**.
   I'll need **a lot more** water.   A computer will do it **much more efficiently**.
Before a comparative we can use **much, a lot, far; rather; slightly, a bit, a little**.

We can also use **no** and **any**. **No** has a negative meaning.
   Your second throw at the basket was **no nearer** than your first.
We can use **any** in negatives and questions and with **if**.
   Your second throw wasn't **any nearer** than your first.
   Are you sleeping **any better** since you've been taking the pills?
   If we leave **any later** than seven, we'll get caught in the rush hour.

C Faster and faster

We use expressions like **faster and faster** and **more and more expensive**
to say that something is increasing all the time.
   The caravan was rolling **faster and faster** down the hill.
   The queue was getting **longer and longer**.
   Prices go up and up. Everything gets **more and more expensive**.
   The crowd are becoming **more and more excited**.
   The country is rapidly losing its workers, as **more and more** people are emigrating.
The form depends on whether the comparative is with **er** (e.g. **louder**) or with **more** (e.g. **more expensive**) (see Unit 110B).

We can also use **less and less** for something decreasing.
   As each new problem arose, we felt **less and less enthusiastic**.

D The faster, the better

We use this pattern to say that a change in one thing goes with a change in another. Look at these examples.
   There's no time to lose. **The faster** you drive, **the better**.
   The higher the price, **the more reliable** the product.
   The more the customer complained, **the ruder** and **more unpleasant** the manager became.
   The sooner we leave, **the sooner** we'll get there.
   Are you looking for a cheap holiday? ~ Yes, **the cheaper the better**.

112 Exercises

1 Less (A)

Complete the sentences. Use *less* with these words: *attractive, busy, convenient, nervous, optimistic, painful, seriously*

▶ Laura once hated flying, but now she feels *less nervous* about it.
1 David says his leg really hurt at first, but now it's ....
2 Mark and Sarah normally have lots to do, but they're .... this week.
3 Rita's old flat was near the shops. Her new place is .... for shopping.
4 Claire used to think Henry was very handsome, but now she finds him ....
5 Matthew is always exercising. Maybe he should take his fitness ....
6 With United's best player injured, Tom feels .... about their chances.

2 Much faster (B)

Decide what to say. Use a phrase like *a bit better* or *a lot colder*.
▶ You were feeling unwell earlier. Say that you feel better now. A bit, anyway.
  I feel a bit better now.
1 Mention that yesterday was colder than today. A lot colder, in fact.
  ....
2 Say that your coat is longer than is fashionable. A bit, anyway.
  ....
3 You left work earlier than usual this afternoon. Slightly, anyway. Tell your friend.
  ....
4 Say that the shop is more expensive than the supermarket. Much more.
  ....
5 Ask if the new machine is reliable – any more so than the old one.
  ....

3 Faster and faster (C)

Vicky works very hard at her studies, but she's worried that she's making no progress. Complete her sentences.
▶ This subject gets *harder and harder* (hard) all the time.
▶ I'm just getting *more and more confused* (confused).
1 It's becoming .... (difficult) for me to keep up.
2 The textbook just gets .... (complicated).
3 I spend .... (more) time on my work.
4 My list of things to do gets .... (long).
5 My problems are just getting .... (bad).

4 The faster, the better (D)

Complete each sentence using the information in brackets.
▶ (The rent is high.) The bigger a flat is, *the higher the rent is.*
▶ (You learn quickly.) The younger you are, *the more quickly you learn.*
1 (The roads are quiet.) The earlier you leave, ...
2 (The choice is wide.) The bigger a supermarket is, ...
3 (I get confused.) The more I try to work this out, ...
4 (You can speak fluently.) The more you practise, ...
5 (The beaches get crowded.) The better the weather is, ...

Test 19 Comparative and superlative (Units 110–112)

Test 19A
Write the comparative form of the words in brackets.
- They've made these chocolate bars *smaller* (small).
- Sport is *more interesting* (interesting) than politics.
1. Can't you think of anything .... (intelligent) to say?
2. Well, the place looks .... (clean) now.
3. Janet looks .... (thin) than she did.
4. You need to draw it .... (carefully).
5. The weather is getting .... (bad).
6. The programme will be shown at a .... (late) date.
7. I can't stay .... (long) than half an hour.
8. A mobile phone would be a .... (useful) present.
9. I'll try to finish the job .... (soon).
10. It was .... (busy) than usual in town today.
11. I'll be even .... (annoyed) if you do that again.
12. Since the break-in I feel .... (nervous).

Test 19B
Write the superlative form of the words in brackets.
- It's the *shortest* (short) day of the year.
- It's the *most beautiful* (beautiful) building in the world.
1. That was the .... (funny) film I've ever seen.
2. It was the .... (horrible) feeling I've ever had.
3. Have you read her .... (recent) book?
4. It's the .... (large) company in the country.
5. It was the .... (boring) speech I've ever heard.
6. You've got the .... (far) to travel.
7. That's the .... (helpful) idea so far.
8. The factory uses the .... (modern) production methods.
9. This is the .... (early) I've ever got up.
10. It was the .... (sad) day of my life.

Test 19C
Some of these sentences are correct, and some have a word which should not be there. If a sentence is correct, put a tick (✓). If it is incorrect, cross the unnecessary word out of the sentence and write it in the space.
- I've got the least powerful computer in the world.   ✓
- London is ~~more~~ bigger than Birmingham.   *more*
1. Silver isn't as expensive as gold.   ....
2. Indian food is the nicer than Chinese, I think.   ....
3. The telephone is one of the most useful inventions ever.   ....
4. I feel a much better now, thank you.   ....
5. The longer you wait, so the harder it'll be.   ....
6. The piano is heavier than the sofa.   ....
7. This is the most quickest way to the hotel.   ....
8. You're taller than he is.   ....
9. Who is the cleverest student in of the class?   ....
10. The weather is getting hotter and more hotter.   ....

Test 19

Test 19D

Read this part of Tessa's letter to her friend Angela about her new job.
Then look at the answers after the letter and write the correct answer in each space.

My new job is great. I like it (▶) *much* better than my old one. The people here are (1) .... than I expected. Luckily my new boss isn't as rude (2) .... my old boss, Mrs Crossley, was. I hated her. She was the (3) .... friendly person I've ever met. Everyone here is older (4) .... In fact I'm the youngest person (5) .... the office. But I don't mind.

The good thing about the job is that I get a (6) .... more money, although not much more than I did before. The bad thing is that the journey isn't (7) .... simple as it was in my old job, where the bus took me straight there. Now I have to change buses. But I'm allowed to start work early. The earlier I leave home, (8) .... the journey is because the buses aren't so crowded.

▶ a) more   b) most   c) much   d) very
1 a) more nice b) most nice   c) nicer   d) nicest
2 a) as   b) so   c) than   d) that
3 a) least   b) less   c) less and less d) so
4 a) as I   b) as me   c) than I   d) than me
5 a) from   b) in   c) of   d) out of
6 a) bit   b) less   c) lot   d) much
7 a) as   b) less   c) more   d) same
8 a) more easier b) more easy c) the easier   d) the easy

Test 19E

Complete the second sentence so that it has a similar meaning to the first. Use the word in brackets.
▶ This train is more convenient than all the others. (most)
  This train *is the most convenient*.
1 The living-room isn't as big as the kitchen. (bigger)
   The kitchen ....
2 I'm not as fit as you. (am)
   You're ....
3 The table and the desk are the same size. (big)
   The table .... the desk.
4 Prices just get higher all the time. (and)
   Prices ....
5 The dress is cheaper than the skirt. (expensive)
   The skirt .... the dress.
6 This crossword is the easiest. (difficult)
   This crossword ....
7 Their excitement was increasing all the time. (excited)
   They were getting ....
8 I've never read a more romantic story. (most)
   It's the .... read.

113 Adverbs and word order

A Where do adverbs go?

There are three places in the sentences where an adverb can go. They are called front position (at the beginning of a sentence), mid position (see B) and end position (at the end of a sentence). (But for adverbs of degree see Unit 115.)

FRONT		MID		END
Then	the ship	**slowly**	sailed	**away**.
Outside	it was	**obviously**	raining	**hard**.

B Mid position

Mid position means close to the verb. Here are some examples of adverbs in mid position.

	AUXILIARY	ADVERB	AUXILIARY	MAIN VERB	
The visitors	are	**just**		leaving.	
Andrew	has	**always**		liked	Jessica.
We	don't	**often**		go	out in the evening.
You	should	**never**		take	unnecessary risks.
The pictures	have	**definitely**	been	stolen.	
I		**really**		hate	housework.
You		**probably**		left	the bag on the bus.

The adverb comes after the first auxiliary, e.g. **are, has, don't**.
If there is no auxiliary, then the adverb comes before the main verb, e.g. **hate, left**.

Note the word order in questions.
  *Has Andrew **always** liked Jason?*   *Do you **often** go out with him in the evening?*

When the verb **be** is on its own, the adverb usually comes after it.
  *The boss is **usually** in a bad temper.*   *You're **certainly** a lot better today.*

When there is stress on the main verb **be** or on the auxiliary, then the adverb usually comes before it.
  *You **certainly** are a lot better today.*   *I **really** have made a mess, haven't I?*

C Verb and object

An adverb does not usually go between the verb and the direct object.
We put it in end position, after the object.

	VERB	OBJECT	ADVERB		
Tom	ate	his breakfast	**quickly**.	NOT	~~Tom ate quickly his breakfast.~~
We	played	volleyball	**yesterday**.	NOT	~~We played yesterday volleyball.~~
I	like	classical music	**very much**.	NOT	~~I like very much classical music.~~

But an adverb can go before a long object.
  *Detectives examined **carefully** the contents of the dead man's pockets.*

D Adverbs of manner

An adverb of manner tells us how something happens, e.g. **noisily, quickly**. It usually goes in end position, but an adverb which ends in **ly** can sometimes go in mid position.
  *We asked permission **politely**.*   *We **politely** asked permission.*

E Adverbs of place and time

Adverbs and adverbial phrases of place and time usually go in end position.
*Is there a phone box **nearby**?*   *People didn't have cars **then**.*
*We're meeting **by the entrance**.*   *Trevor wasn't very well **last week**.*
*Did you have a nice time **in New York**?*   *I'll see you **before very long**.*
Sometimes they can go in front position.
*We're really busy this week. **Last week** we had nothing to do.*

Some short adverbs of time can also go in mid position.
*I'll **soon** find out.*   *The train is **now** approaching Swindon.*
For **yet**, **still** and **already** see Unit 114.

F Adverbs of frequency

An adverb of frequency tells us 'how often'. It usually goes in mid position (see B).
*Mark is **always** in such a hurry.*   *I **sometimes** feel depressed.*
*I've **often** thought about getting married.*   *Do you **usually** work so late?*
Normally, **usually**, **often**, **sometimes** and **occasionally** can also go in front or end position.
***Normally** Sarah goes by train.*   *I feel depressed **sometimes**.*

Phrases like **every day**, **once a week** or **most evenings** go in front or end position.
***Every day** we go jogging.*   *Rachel has a driving lesson **three times a week**.*
*There's a news summary **every hour**.*   *We watch television **most evenings**.*

G Sentence adverbs

A sentence adverb is a word or phrase like **certainly**, **perhaps**, **luckily**, **of course**. It says something about the situation described in the sentence. The adverb can go in front, mid or end position.
Sometimes we put a comma after or before the adverb, especially in front or end position.
***Fortunately**, the weather stayed fine.*   ***Maybe** you'll win a free holiday.*
*We'll **probably** have to queue for tickets.*   *Rachel was late, **of course**.*
In a negative sentence, **probably** and **certainly** come before **won't**, **didn't**, etc.
*We **probably** won't get there in time.*   *I **certainly** didn't expect a present!*

Also usually goes in mid position, but **too** and **as well** go in end position.
*Melanie bakes lovely cakes. She **also** makes bread./She makes bread, **too/as well**.*

H End position

There can be more than one adverb or adverbial phrase in end position. Usually a single-word adverb (e.g. **safely**) comes before a phrase (e.g. **on a small airfield**).
*They landed **safely on a small airfield**.*   *I always eat **here at lunch-time**.*

When there is a close link in meaning between a verb and an adverb, then that adverb goes next to the verb. For example, with verbs of movement like **go**, **come** and **move**, a phrase of place comes before time.
*I usually go **to bed early**.*
*Tom came **here yesterday**.*
*My parents moved **to London in 1993**.*

But often two adverbial phrases can go in either order.
*The concert was held **at the arts centre last night**.*
*The concert was held **last night at the arts centre**.*

Exercises

1 Adverbs (A–B)

Read each sentence and write down the word which is an adverb.

▶ I'm just finishing an interesting article in this magazine.   *just*
1. We have to leave our dirty shoes outside.
2. Perhaps you have to type a password into the computer.
3. Someone always leaves this door open.
4. Obviously we aren't going to go for a walk in the rain.
5. The car rolled silently down the hill.
6. Your friend Andrew works hard, doesn't he?

2 Adverbs and their position (A–B)

Read this true story. Some adverbs are underlined. Say if their position is front, mid or end.

<u>Once</u> a man called Alvin decided to rob a bank in Montgomery, Alabama. Alvin's parents had <u>often</u> told him that good manners were important. So Alvin went to the bank and stood in line. He waited <u>patiently</u>. <u>Soon</u> it was his turn. He <u>dramatically</u> pulled out a gun and threatened the cashier. She <u>politely</u> told him that he was in the wrong line and should go to another counter. Alvin <u>immediately</u> went to the correct place and stood in line <u>again</u>. <u>Suddenly</u> the police rushed in and arrested him. Alvin was amazed. They'd caught him before he'd <u>even</u> done the robbery. The moral of the story is that you shouldn't <u>always</u> do what your parents tell you.

	ADVERB	POSITION		ADVERB	POSITION
▶	once	front			
1	often		6	immediately	
2	patiently		7	again	
3	soon		8	suddenly	
4	dramatically		9	even	
5	politely		10	always	

3 Mid position (B)

Complete the conversations using the words in brackets. Put the adverbs in the best place.

▶ Emma: Did you know the man who tried to steal your bag? (certainly / recognize / would)
   Vicky: No, but I *would certainly recognize* him again.
1. David: That was a goal, wasn't it? (clearly / crossed)
   Tom: Yes, the ball .... the line.
2. Mark: The weather is a lot better today. (probably / rain / will)
   Sarah: It said on the radio it .... later.
3. Tom: How do we get to Mike's place? (didn't / fully / understand)
   Nick: I don't know. I .... the directions.
4. Harriet: It's quiet here today, isn't it? (usually / are)
   Laura: Yes, the neighbours .... out on a Sunday.
5. Emma: Have you been to this place before? (it / occasionally / visited)
   Matthew: Yes, I .... as a child.
6. Alan: Did the computers crash this morning? (soon / were / working)
   Mark: Yes, but they .... again.
7. Melanie: Your friend's late, Vicky. (forgotten / has / obviously)
   Vicky: Rachel .... that we arranged to go out.

4 Adverbs of frequency (B, F)

Look at what people are saying and write the information in one sentence.
Put the adverb or adverbial phrase in mid or end position. Choose the best position.

▶ Vicky: I lose my way in London. It always happens.
   Vicky always loses her way in London.
▶ Laura: The birds wake me up. It happens every morning.
   The birds wake Laura up every morning.
1 David: It rains when I'm on holiday. Well, usually.

2 Rita: My friend visits me. She comes most weekends.

3 Mark: I get a pay rise. I get one every year.

4 Rachel: I don't check my work. I never do that.

5 Adverbs and word order (A–G)

Put the words in the right order and write the statements. Sometimes there is more than one possible order.
▶ cleaned / every day / is / the office   *The office is cleaned every day.*
1 always / I've / known / your secret
2 afford / can't / certainly / a new car / we
3 didn't / far / the tourists / walk
4 carefully / cut / the paper / Tom
5 also / can / Natasha / play / the violin
6 I / most days / read / the newspaper

6 Adverbs in end position (H)

Complete these sentences from a newspaper. Put the words and phrases in the best order.
▶ The Queen has visited the show *regularly since 1985* (regularly / since 1985).
1 The President died .... (at his home / peacefully).
2 The protesters marched .... (through the streets / yesterday).
3 The Prime Minister went .... (last year / to Greece).
4 Henry likes Rome. He spent a week .... (in June / there).

7 Adverbs and word order (A–H)

Read the postcard from Olivia to her friend Kirsty and write the sentences. Put the adverbs in the best place.

(▶) Thank you for having us (last weekend). (1) We had a lovely time (in the country). (2) We arrived home at about eight (safely). (3) You must come and visit us (before too long). (4) It's nice to see you and Tony (always). (5) You'll be able to come in the new year (maybe). (6) We'll see you (sometime).

▶ *Thank you for having us last weekend.*
1
2
3
4
5
6

114 Yet, still and already

A Introduction

Yet means that we are expecting something. (It's the time to book a holiday.)
Still means 'going on longer than expected'. (It's late to be thinking about a holiday.)
Already means 'sooner than expected'. (It's early to have had a holiday.)

B Yet

Yet usually goes at the end of a negative statement or a question.
 Vicky has got a present, but she hasn't opened it **yet**.   Wait a minute. I'm not ready **yet**.
 Have they sent you your cheque **yet**? ~ No, not **yet**. I should get it next week.

C Still and already

In a positive statement, **still** and **already** usually go in mid position (see Unit 113B).
 Sarah isn't home yet. She's **still** at work.
 We wrote a month ago, and we're **still** waiting for a reply.
 I've only been at work an hour, and I'm **already** exhausted.
 There's no need to tell me. I **already** know.

We can also use **still** in a negative statement. It goes before **haven't**, **can't**, etc.
 It's nearly lunch-time, and you **still** haven't opened your mail.
 My friend is sixteen, and she **still** can't swim.
Compare these sentences. The meanings are similar.
 Rita hasn't booked a holiday **yet**.   Rita **still** hasn't booked a holiday.
Still is stronger than **yet**. It often expresses surprise that the situation has gone on for so long.

In a question **still** and **already** usually go after the subject.
 Are you **still** waiting after all this time?   Has Tom **already** been on holiday?

D No longer and any longer/any more

No longer means that something is finished. It goes in mid position (see Unit 113B).
 You can't buy these bikes now. They **no longer** make them.
 I used to belong to the sports club, but I'm **no longer** a member.

No longer can be a little formal. In informal speech we use **not ... any longer** or **not ... any more**.
 They don't make these bikes **any longer/any more**.
 Rita has moved. She doesn't live here **any longer/any more**.
Any longer/any more comes at the end.

▷ 12A **Yet** and **already** with the present perfect

114 Exercises

1 Yet, still and already (A)

Put in *yet, still* or *already*.
▶ Mark: I know it isn't lunch-time *yet*, but I'm really hungry.
　Sarah: It's only eleven. And you've *already* had two coffees since breakfast.
1 Vicky: You've .... got this library book, and it was due back ten days **ago**.
　Rachel: Well, I haven't finished it ....
2 Nick: Tom is a very slow eater, isn't he? He's .... having his soup.
　David: And we've .... started our pudding.
3 Trevor: Has the postman been ....? I'm expecting a letter from the bank.
　Laura: Yes, he has, but that letter .... hasn't arrived.

2 Word order with yet, still and already (A)

Put the word in brackets into one of the sentences.
▶ I've bought some CDs. I haven't played them. (yet)
　I haven't played them yet.
▶ This calculator works. I've had it for ages. (still)
　This calculator still works.
1 I owe Emma £20. I can't ask her for more. (already)
　..
2 We've spent all our money. And we're only halfway through our holiday. (already)
　..
3 I've cleaned this window. But it looks dirty. (still)
　..
4 Our friend took some photos. We haven't seen them. (yet)
　..
5 I can't understand the rules. I know you explained them to me. (still)
　..

3 Still and any more (C–D)

Two people are talking about the place they live in. Write the replies using *still* or *not ... any more*.
　Old man:　　　　　　　　　　　**Young man:**
▶ There was a church.　~　Well, *there's still a church.*
▶ You could see fields.　~　*You can't see them any more.* Now it's just houses.
1 Children played there.　~　Not now. ....
2 Boats came along the river.　~　Oh, ... Look at them.
3 The view was beautiful.　~　Well, ... It's **awful**.
4 It was our home.　~　And ....

4 Yet, still, already, no longer and any longer/any more (A–D)

Put in *already, any more, no longer, still* and *yet*.
▶ It's *still* raining, look. How much longer can it go on?
1 The railway closed down years ago, so there's .... a railway station here.
2 They want to build a new hotel here, but they haven't got permission ....
3 Rita isn't going out with Nick. She told him she didn't want to see him ....
4 Those people moved here only three months ago, and they're .... leaving.

115 Adverbs of degree, e.g. **very**, **quite**

A Very, quite, a bit, etc

*Laura is **a bit** tired. She's been working all morning.*

*Mark is **quite** tired. He's been working all day.*

*Sarah is **very** tired. She's had to work late at the office.*

An adverb of degree makes the meaning weaker or stronger. Here are some more examples.

SMALL DEGREE (weaker)	MEDIUM DEGREE	LARGE DEGREE (stronger)	
a little late	*fairly* unusual	*absolutely* sure	*really* ill
slightly complicated	*pretty* good	*completely* mad	
	rather nice	*extremely* cold	

B Very cold, quite quickly, etc

An adverb of degree (e.g. **very**) goes before an adjective (e.g. **cold**) or an adverb (e.g. **quickly**).

ADVERB + ADJECTIVE	ADVERB + ADVERB
*It's **very cold** today.*	*The time passed **quite quickly**.*
*Rita looked **rather upset**.*	*We go on holiday **fairly soon**.*
*This dress is **absolutely marvellous**.*	*United played **extremely well**.*

Before a comparative we can use **a bit, a little, a lot, far, much, rather** and **slightly**. See also Unit 112B.
   *I'm feeling **a lot better** today.*   *These new trains go **much faster**.*

C Really hurting, quite enjoys, etc

Some adverbs of degree can describe a verb.
They usually go in mid position (close to the verb — see Unit 113B).
   *My foot is **really hurting**.*   *Laura **quite enjoys** shopping.*   *I **rather like** this cake.*
Some adverbs of degree go at the end of a sentence when they describe a verb.
They are **a bit, a little, a lot, awfully, much** and **terribly**.
   *Mark travels **a lot**.*   *I'll open the window **a little**.*   *The animals suffer **terribly**.*

Absolutely, completely and **totally** can go in mid position or at the end.
   *We **completely** lost our way./We lost our way **completely**.*
   *I'm afraid I **totally** disagree./I'm afraid I disagree **totally**.*

D Much

Now look at these sentences.
Positive: *I like this town **very much**.* NOT *I like this town much.*
Negative: *I don't like this town **very much**.* OR *I don't like this town **much**.*
In a positive statement we use **very much**. In a negative statement we can use either **very much** or **much**.

▷ 116 More about **quite** and **rather**   ▷ 117 **Too** and **enough**

276 ADJECTIVES AND ADVERBS

115 Exercises

1 Very, quite, a bit, etc (A)
Write sentences using one of the phrases in brackets.

▶ (quite hungry or very hungry?) *He's quite hungry.* 3 (quite strong or very strong?) ....
1 (a bit busy or very busy?) .... 4 (fairly happy or extremely happy?) ....
2 (a bit thirsty or really thirsty?) ....

2 Very, quite and a bit (A)
Put in *very, quite* or *a bit*.

▶ The bus service is all right. The buses are *quite* frequent.
1 I couldn't sleep because of the awful noise. The disco was .... noisy.
2 The weather was OK – at least it didn't rain. It was .... good.
3 The train was almost on time. It was just .... late.
4 Someone paid a great deal of money for the house. It was .... expensive.
5 There were some very small traces of mud on the boots. They were .... dirty.
6 There was a medium amount of traffic on the road. It was .... busy.

3 Very cold, really hurting, etc (B–D)
Put the adverbs in the right place. Sometimes more than one answer is correct.

▶ These books are old (very).   *These books are very old.*
▶ I hate travelling by air (really).   *I really hate travelling by air.*
1 That radio is loud (a bit).
2 I like my new job (quite).
3 Why don't you slow down (a little)?
4 The rain spoilt our day (completely).
5 We did the job quickly (fairly).
6 I feel better now (a lot).
7 We enjoyed the concert (very much).
8 My arms ached (terribly).

4 Adverbs of degree (A–D)
Complete the advertisement for holiday apartments by choosing the correct words.

Why not take this opportunity to buy a wonderful Interlux Timeshare apartment in San Manila? These are (▶) a bit/rather/really luxurious apartments set in this (1) absolutely/slightly magnificent seaside resort, a (2) fairly/really beautiful and unspoilt place, which you'll like (3) much/very/very much. The apartments are (4) extremely/pretty/quite good value. And we are a company with a (5) fairly/quite/very good reputation. This is a (6) bit/slightly/totally safe way of investing your money. But hurry! People are buying up the apartments (7) a lot/very/very much quickly.

116 Quite and rather

A Quite meaning 'fairly'

Quite usually means 'fairly' or 'a medium amount' (see Unit 115A).
   I feel **quite** hungry now.   Repairing the machine is **quite** difficult.
   The talk was **quite** interesting.   We were **quite** surprised at the result.
(But see D for another meaning of **quite**.)

B Stress with quite

In speech, whether we stress **quite** or the adjective makes a difference to the meaning.

If we stress **quite**, it means 'fairly but not very'. The meaning is negative.	If we stress the adjective, the meaning is positive (but not as positive as **very**).
The exhibition was <u>quite</u> good, but I've seen better ones.	The exhibition was quite <u>good</u>. I enjoyed looking round it.
I get up <u>quite</u> early, but not as early as you do.	I got up quite <u>early</u>. I had a lot of jobs to do.

C Quite or rather?

When we make a favourable comment, we usually say **quite**, not **rather**.
   The book was **quite interesting**.   It's **quite warm** now.
   It was **quite nice** walking through the park.

In unfavourable comments, we usually say **rather**, but **quite** is possible.
   The book was **rather boring**/quite boring.
   It was **rather awkward**/quite awkward taking my suitcase on the underground.

Rather in a favourable comment means 'to a surprising or unusual degree'.
   It's **rather warm** for October. (It isn't usually so warm.)
   I didn't know David can cook. He's **rather good** at it.
   I expect Tom's jokes were awful. ~ Actually they were **rather funny**.

We can use **rather** with a comparative but not **quite**.
   The meal took **rather longer** than we expected.

For **quite** and **rather** with **a/an**, see Unit 89B.
   It was **quite an interesting** book.

D Quite meaning 'completely'

With some adjectives, **quite** means 'completely' or 'totally'.
   What you said is **quite wrong**. (= completely wrong)
   The idea is **quite absurd**. (= totally absurd)
   The situation is **quite hopeless**.

Quite means 'completely' with these adjectives: **absurd, alone, amazing, awful, brilliant, certain, dead, different, dreadful, extraordinary, false, hopeless, horrible, impossible, perfect, ridiculous, right, sure, true, useless, wrong**

Compare the uses of **quite**.

I'm **quite tired**. (= fairly)	I'm **quite exhausted**. (= completely)
The advice was **quite useful**. I got one or two tips.	The advice was **quite useless**. It was absolutely no good at all.

116 Exercises

1 Stress with quite (B)

Which word do we stress, *quite* or the adjective? Underline the stressed word.
- These pens are quite good but not as good as the ones I usually buy.
- This book is quite <u>exciting</u>. I can't put it down.
1. These fashions are quite new but not the very latest thing.
2. It's quite late. We'd better be going.
3. The sums are quite easy. I can do them in my head.
4. The music was quite good, but I wasn't really impressed.
5. The sun is quite bright. You'll need your sunglasses.

2 Quite or rather? (C)

Put in these adjectives: *better, busy, <u>nice</u>, noisy, popular*
Use *quite* or *rather* with each adjective. Sometimes either is possible.
Mark: I didn't like that meal very much.
Sarah: The soup was (▶) *quite nice* though, wasn't it?
Mark: The food was (1) .... the last time we came.
Sarah: It's (2) .... in here, isn't it? Everyone seems to be shouting.
Mark: I wasn't expecting the place to be so full. It's (3) .... for a **Monday evening**.
Sarah: This restaurant is (4) .... , you know.

3 Quite or rather? (C)

Add a sentence expressing the idea in brackets.
Use *quite* or *rather* in your sentence. Sometimes either is possible.
- (It's pleasant by the river.)
  Let's walk along by the river. *It's quite pleasant there.*
- (You think Nick is aggressive.)
  I don't like Nick much. *I think he's rather aggressive.*
1. (Changing trains twice is complicated.)
   We have to change trains twice. ....
2. (Your car is big.)
   I can give you all a lift. ....
3. (The show went on longer than you expected.)
   It was a good show, but ....
4. (You made your decision quickly.)
   It wasn't a difficult decision. ....

4 The meanings of quite (A, D)

Does *quite* mean 'fairly' or 'completely'?
- Try one of these sweets. I think they're <u>quite nice</u>. = *fairly nice*
- The driver walked away unhurt. It was <u>quite amazing</u>. = *completely amazing*
1. I couldn't agree to the idea. It was <u>quite ridiculous</u>. = ...
2. I need some help with this crossword. It's <u>quite difficult</u>. = ...
3. That isn't the same thing at all. It's <u>quite different</u>. = ...
4. I wasn't expecting to get a postcard. I was <u>quite surprised</u>. = ...
5. I bought this guidebook. It looks <u>quite useful</u>. = ...
6. Are you sure you want the job? ~ Yes, I'm <u>quite certain</u>. = ...

117 Too and enough

A Introduction

Too short and not long enough both mean the same thing.

B Word order with too and enough

Too goes before an adjective or adverb.
  Claire doesn't want to marry Henry. She thinks he's **too old**.
  Zedco are in trouble. The company reacted **too slowly** to the rise in prices.
Enough goes after an adjective or adverb.
  The water isn't **hot enough**. It needs to be boiling. NOT ~~enough hot~~
  You didn't put the screws in **tightly enough**. NOT ~~enough tightly~~

Too many, **too much** and **enough** go before a noun.
  No wonder you're tired. You've been going to **too many parties**.
  Andrew spends **too much time** working.
  There'll be fifteen people for coffee. Have we got **enough cups**?
  Everything is so expensive. Did you bring **enough money**?
We use **many** with a plural noun and **much** with an uncountable noun (see Unit 95A).

Compare these examples with **enough**.
After an adjective: The coffee isn't **strong enough**.
Before a noun: You didn't put **enough coffee** in.

We leave out the noun if the meaning is clear without it.
  Just add a little water. Not **too much**.   We'll need fifteen cups. Have we got **enough**?

C Other structures with too and enough

We can use a phrase with **for** after **too** or **enough**.
  These puzzles are **too** difficult **for children**.   This coat isn't warm **enough for winter**.
  Have we got **enough** cups **for everyone**?

We can also use a to-infinitive.
  It's **too** dangerous **to walk** home at this time of night.
  There are **too** many museums here **to visit** in a single day.
  Are you fit **enough to run** a marathon?
  I couldn't get close **enough to see** properly.
  Vicky didn't bring **enough** money **to buy** two CDs.

280 ADJECTIVES AND ADVERBS

117 Exercises

1 Too and enough (A–B)

Look at the pictures and write sentences with *too* and *enough*.
Use these nouns and adjectives: *big, gate, long, low, plane, sweater, ruler, warm, water, wide*

▶ *The sweater is too big.*
▶ *The ruler isn't long enough.*
1 ....
2 ....
3 ....

2 Too and enough (A–B)

Look at what people are saying and complete the sentences. Use *too, too many, too much* or *enough* with these words: *clearly, complicated, difficult, expensive, food, hastily, mistakes, rain, sweet, traffic*

▶ You should have stopped to think first. You acted *too hastily*.
▶ This quiz is rather easy. The questions aren't *difficult enough*.
1 Can I have some more sugar in my coffee, please? It isn't ....
2 I can't afford a new stereo. It would be ....
3 There's a water shortage. There just hasn't been ....
4 I can't read your writing. You don't write ....
5 Try to be more careful, please. You're making ....
6 The roads are very crowded. There's simply ....
7 I can't understand these instructions. They're ....
8 Thousands of people are starving because they can't get ....

3 Other structures with too and enough (C)

Comment on the situations. Use *too* or *enough* and a phrase with *for* or a to-infinitive.
▶ A taxi would have been best. But you didn't have the money.
  I didn't have enough money for a taxi.
▶ Sarah can't take a day off. She's very busy.
  Sarah is too busy to take a day off.
1 A picnic would be nice. But it's wet.
  ....
2 All your guests will need chairs. But you haven't got very many.
  ....
3 You couldn't carry the equipment. You had such a lot.
  ....
4 Natasha wants to be a professional musician. You think she's very good.
  ....

Test 20 Adverbs and word order (Units 113–117)

Test 20A

Put each word in brackets into the sentence.
▶ Anna arrives for work. (late)
  Anna arrives late for work.
1 I like old cowboy films. (quite)

2 Have you finished this magazine? (yet)

3 This coat is big. (too)

4 Have the children had their tea? (already)

5 You don't look ill. (certainly)

6 We don't go out. (much)

7 I think everyone works hard. (fairly)

8 I don't know the date of the meeting. (still)

9 The others are getting ready. (just)

10 I have to go to work. (on Saturdays)

Test 20B

Put the words in the right order to form a statement.
▶ I / love / really / these trousers
  I really love these trousers.
1 is / rather / silly / this game

2 already / I've / paid / the bill

3 enough / isn't / loud / the alarm

4 easily / Jonathan / passed / the test

5 a lot / cards / play / the children

6 didn't / enough / sell / they / tickets

7 ask / many / questions / too / you

8 a member / any more / of the club / I'm / not

9 enough / it's / outside / to sit / warm

Test 20

Test 20C
Read the conversation. Then look at the answers below and write the correct answer in each space.

Martin: Hello, Nancy. (▶) *How* are you? Have you found a job (1) .... ?
Nancy: No, I'm afraid not, but I'm (2) .... looking. It's taking (3) .... longer than I expected. The problem is there just aren't (4) .... jobs. And there are too (5) .... people looking for jobs.
Martin: I'm old enough (6) .... remember when there was plenty of work.
Nancy: There used to be lots of work, but there isn't (7) .... more. I'm afraid I'm (8) .... longer as optimistic as I was a few weeks ago. In fact I feel a (9) .... depressed about it sometimes.
Martin: Don't worry. You'll (10) .... find something, I expect.

▶ a) How b) What c) Who d) Why
1 a) longer b) soon c) still d) yet
2 a) already b) more c) still d) yet
3 a) more b) quite c) rather d) some
4 a) enough b) plenty c) right d) several
5 a) big b) lot c) many d) much

6 a) for b) of c) that d) to
7 a) any b) no c) now d) some
8 a) any b) never c) no d) not
9 a) bit b) piece c) quite d) slightly
10 a) already b) yet c) soon d) before very long

Test 20D
Each of these sentences has a mistake in it. Write the correct sentence.

▶ My friend calls always for me.   *My friend always calls for me.*
1 I didn't last night sleep very well.   ....
2 I think I need to rest little.   ....
3 I don't work for the company longer.   ....
4 The article is fair interesting.   ....
5 Tessa locked carefully the door.   ....
6 You aren't enough tall to play basketball.   ....
7 We went yesterday to town.   ....
8 I like this music much.   ....

Test 20E
Write a second sentence so that it has a similar meaning to the first. Use the word in brackets.

▶ It's probable that the strike will be over soon. (probably)
The strike will probably be over soon.

1 We often go to the cinema. (a lot)

....

2 Adrian wears jeans all the time. (always)

....

3 These shoes are too small. (big)

....

4 I don't live in Birmingham any more. (no)

....

5 Polly spent more money than she should have done in the sales. (too)

....

ADJECTIVES AND ADVERBS   283

118 Prepositions of place

A Meanings

The bird is **in/inside** the cage.

Sarah is diving **in/into** the water.

Tom is getting **out of** the car.

They're waiting **outside** the bank.

The jug is **on** the table.

The case is **on top of** the wardrobe.

Emma is putting her luggage **on/onto** the trolley.

Henry is falling **off** the horse.

Rachel is **at** the bus stop.

The table is **by/beside** the bed.

Jessica is sitting **next to** Andrew.

The airport is **near** Manchester.

The coach is going **to** London.

The letter is **from** Chicago.

Matthew is walking **towards** the sun.

Vicky is running **away from** the fire.

There's a bridge **over** the river.

Tom is **under** the car.

The plane is **above** the clouds.

The temperature is **below** zero.

The cyclist is **in front of** the bus.

The cyclist is **behind** the tractor.

Rita is going **up** the stairs.

Daniel is coming **down** the stairs.

Melanie is running **across** the road.

The cars are going **through** the tunnel.

Trevor is walking **along** the street.

The car is going **past** the house.

The house is **among** the trees.

Jackson is **between** Memphis and New Orleans.

Jessica is sitting **opposite** Andrew.

They're running **around/round** the track.

B Position and movement

Most of these prepositions can express either position (where something is) or movement (where it is going).
Position: *The coin **was under** the sofa.*
Movement: *The coin **rolled under** the sofa.*

Now look at these examples with **in** and **on** expressing position.
  *The manager was **in** the office.*   *The papers were **on** the floor.*
To express movement, we use **into** and **onto**, but we can also use **in** and **on**, especially in informal English.
  *The manager came **in/into** the office.*   *The papers fell **on/onto** the floor.*

At expresses position, and **to** expresses movement.
Position: *Vicky **was at** the doctor's.*
Movement: *Vicky **went to** the doctor's.*

▷ page 380 British and American English

118 Exercises

1 Prepositions of place (A)

Put in the prepositions. Sometimes more than one answer is correct.

▶ Sarah is getting *out of* the taxi.

1 David is going .... the ladder.

2 The furniture is .... the van.

3 My friend lives in a flat .... a shop.

4 The boss is coming .... the corridor.

5 There's a garage .... the house.

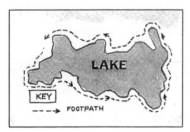

6 We walked .... the lake.

7 There's a statue .... the museum.

8 Tom and Nick are walking .... the stadium.

2 Prepositions of place (A)

Complete the conversations. Choose the correct preposition.
1 Vicky: I felt really afraid when I was walking home <u>from/off</u> the club. All the time I could hear someone <u>behind/in front of</u> me, but I didn't dare turn round.
   Rachel: I expect you were imagining it.
   Vicky: No, I wasn't. I saw him after I'd come in <u>across/through</u> the gate. He was wearing a long black coat that came down well <u>below/under</u> his knees.
2 Daniel: You know Adam, don't you? He's very strange. He walked right <u>along/past</u> me yesterday as I was coming <u>among/down</u> the stairs, but he didn't say hello.
   Matthew: The other day he was sitting <u>beside/opposite</u> me at lunch, so I couldn't help looking at him. I said hello, but he didn't speak.

3 Between, next to and opposite (A)

Look at the plan and explain where things are. Use *between*, *next to* or *opposite*.

- ▶ The bank is *next to* the gift shop.
- 1 The sports shop is .... the bank.
- 2 The travel agency is .... the sports shop and the art gallery.
- 3 The restaurant is .... the art gallery.
- 4 The gift shop is .... the bank and the restaurant.
- 5 The art gallery is .... the travel agency.

4 Prepositions of place (A–B)

Where did the fly go? Put in these prepositions: *around, into, on, out of, through, under, up*

- ▶ The fly came in *through* the door.
- 1 It flew .... the chair.
- 2 It crawled .... the chair leg.
- 3 It stopped .... the desk for a moment.
- 4 It went .... the telephone.
- 5 It flew .... the drawer.
- 6 It went .... the window.

5 Prepositions of place (A–B)

Put in the correct preposition.
- ▶ Rachel was lying *on* the grass reading a book.
- 1 It's my holiday next week. I'm going .... Spain.
- 2 There was a big crowd .... the shop waiting for it to open.
- 3 That man is an idiot. He pushed me .... the swimming-pool.
- 4 I went .... the chemist's just now, but I didn't notice if it was open.
- 5 David hurt himself. He fell .... his bike.
- 6 There's a café .... top of the mountain. You can have a coffee there before you go down.
- 7 The sheep got out .... a hole in the fence.
- 8 Pompeii is quite .... Sorrento. It's only a short train ride.
- 9 There's such a crowd. You won't find your friend .... all these people.

119 In, on and at (place)

A Meanings

Emma is **in** the phone box.

Nick's dog is **on** the rug.

There's someone **at** the door.

IN	ON	AT
in the phone box	sit **on** the floor	sit **at** my desk
in the kitchen	walk **on** the pavement	wait **at** the bus stop
work **in** the garden	a number **on** the door	**at** the crossroads
swim **in** the pool	egg **on** your shirt	wait **at** the traffic lights
In a town/country	**On** a floor (1st, 2nd, etc)	**At** a place on a journey
Kate lives **in** York.	**on** the first floor	Does this train stop **at** York?
Atlanta is **in** Georgia.		
In a street (GB)	**On** a street (US)	**At** a house/an address
in Shirley Road	**on** Fifth Avenue	**at** Mike's (house)
	On a road or river	**at** 65 Shirley Road
	a village **on** this road	**At** an event
	Paris is **on** the Seine.	**at** the party

B In and at with buildings

IN	AT
There are 400 seats **in** the cinema.	I was **at** the cinema. (= watching a film)
It was raining, so we waited **in** the pub.	We were **at** the pub. (= having a drink)
We use **in** when we mean inside a building.	But we normally use **at** when we are talking about what happens there.

C Some common phrases

IN	ON	AT
in prison/hospital	**on** the platform	**at** the station/airport
in the lesson	**on** the farm	**at** home/work/school
in a book/newspaper	**on** the page/map	
in the photo/picture	**on** the screen	
in the country	**on** the island/beach/coast	**at** the seaside
in the middle	drive **on** the right/left	**at** the top/bottom of a hill
in the back/front of a car	**on** the back of an envelope	**at** the back of the room
in a queue/line/row		**at** the end of a corridor

▷ 87 **In** bed, **at** home, etc ▷ 123C **In** the car, **on** the train, etc

119 Exercises

1 Meanings (A)

Look at the pictures and write the sentences. Use *in*, *on* or *at* and these words:
the bath, the disco, the lights, the roof, the table

▶ *He's on the table.*
1 ....
2 ....
3 ....
4 ....

2 In and at with buildings (B)

Complete each sentence. Use *in* or *at* and these words:
the petrol station, the restaurant, the stadium, the station, the theatre, the zoo

▶ There's a huge crowd *in the stadium* waiting for the Games to start.
1 Sarah's just rung. She's .... getting some petrol.
2 The children like wild animals. They'd love to spend an afternoon ....
3 It was so hot .... that I didn't really enjoy the play.
4 We're quite a large group. There may not be enough room .... for all of us to sit together.
5 I saw Daniel while I was .... waiting for a train.

3 In, on and at (A, C)

Put in the preposition *in*, *on* or *at*.

▶ We spent the whole holiday *on* the beach.
1 I read about the pop festival .... a magazine.
2 My parents' flat is .... the twenty-first floor.
3 Melanie was holding a small bird .... her hands.
4 I'll meet you .... the airport.
5 Natasha now lives .... 32 The Avenue.
6 I was standing .... the counter in the baker's shop, waiting to be served.
7 London is .... the Thames.
8 There weren't many books .... the shelves.
9 The passengers had to stand .... a queue.
10 The woman sitting next to me left the train .... Chesterfield.

120 In, on and at (time)

A Saying when
Look at these examples.

IN	ON	AT
We bought the flat **in** 1994.	The race is **on** Saturday.	The film starts **at** seven thirty.

In + year/month/season
  in 1988
  in September
  in winter
  in the 21st century
	On + day/date
	  on Wednesday
	  on 15 April
	  on that day
		At + clock time/meal time
		  at three o'clock
		  at lunch (-time)
		  at that time
		  at the moment

In + a week or more
  in the Easter holiday
  in the summer term
	On + a single day
	  on Easter Monday
	  on Christmas Day
		At + two or three days
		  at Easter/Christmas
		  at the weekend
		  (US: **on** the weekend)

In + part of day
  in the morning
  in the evening
	On + day + part of day
	  on Friday morning
	  on Tuesday evening	

Look at these examples with **night**.
  I woke up **in** the night.
  (= in the middle of the night)
  It happened **on** Monday night.
  I can't sleep **at** night.
  (= when it is night)

But we do not use **in**, **on** or **at** before **every**, **last**, **next**, **this**, **tomorrow** and **yesterday**.
  We go to Greece **every summer**.   My brother came home **last Christmas**.
  I'll see you **next Friday**.   I leave school **this year**.
  The party is **tomorrow evening**.   The group set off **yesterday morning**.

B In time or on time?

IN TIME	ON TIME

In time means 'early enough'.
  We'll have to hurry if we want to be **in time** for the show.
  We got to the airport **in time** to have a coffee before checking in.
  I was about to close the door when **just in time** I remembered my key. (= at the last moment)
	On time means 'at the right time', 'on schedule'.
	  The plane took off **on time**.
	  I hope the meeting starts **on time**.
	  Rachel is never **on time**. She's always late.

C Other uses of in

We can use **in** for the time it takes to complete something.
  I did the crossword **in** five minutes.   Could you walk thirty miles **in** a day?

We can also use **in** for a future time measured from the present.
  Your photos will be ready **in** an hour. (= an hour from now)
  The building will open **in** six weeks/**in** six weeks' time.

▷ 88 **On Friday**, etc without **the**

120 Exercises

1 Saying when (A)

Read the information about John F. Kennedy and then answer the questions.
Begin each answer with *in*, *on* or *at*.

John F. Kennedy was born into a famous American family. His date of birth was 29 May 1917. The year 1961 saw him become the 35th President of the US. Kennedy was killed as he drove in an open car through the streets of Dallas, Texas. Friday, 22 November 1963 was a sad day for America. It was 12.30 when a gunman opened fire and shot the President dead.

▶ When was John F. Kennedy born?   *On 29 May 1917.*
1 When did he become President? ....
2 When was he killed? ....
3 What time was he shot? ....

2 Saying when (A)

Mark is arranging a business meeting. Decide if you need *in*, *on* or *at*.
If you do not need a preposition, put a cross (✗).

Mark: I'm sorry I was out when you called (▶)✗ yesterday afternoon, Alice. Look, I'm free (▶)*on* the fifteenth of March. Can we meet then?
Alice: I'm pretty busy (1) .... next week, I'm afraid. I can't see you (2) .... Friday.
Mark: I'd like to have a meeting (3) .... this month if possible.
I'll be very busy (4) .... April.
Alice: I'm going away (5) .... Easter, so how about the week after?
Shall we meet (6) .... the twenty-seventh? That's a Wednesday.
Mark: I've got an appointment (7) .... the morning but nothing (8) .... the afternoon.
Let's meet (9) .... Wednesday afternoon (10) .... half past two.

3 In time or on time? (B)

Put in the right phrase: *in time* or *on time*.

▶ If the plane is late, we won't get to Paris *in time* for our connecting flight.
1 We were up very early, ... to see the sun rise.
2 How can the buses possibly run .... with all these traffic jams?
3 The post goes at five. I'm hoping to get this letter written ....
4 The coach will be here at 12.13 if it's ....

4 In, on or at? (A–C)

Complete the conversations using *in*, *on* or *at*.

▶ Andrew: You only bought that book *on* Saturday. Have you finished it already?
   Jessica: I read it *in* about three hours yesterday evening.
1 Vicky: Will the bank be open .... half past nine?
   Daniel: Yes, it always opens absolutely .... time.
2 Sarah: We're leaving .... half past, and you haven't even changed.
   Mark: It's OK. I can easily shower and change .... ten minutes.
3 Laura: Your mother's birthday is .... Monday, isn't it?
   Trevor: Yes, I just hope this card gets there .... time.
4 Harriet: If we ever go camping again, it's going to be .... summer, not autumn.
   Mike: Never mind. We'll be home .... two days, and then we'll be dry again.

121 For, since, ago and before

A Introduction

FOR	SINCE	AGO
Mark has spent three hours playing a computer game. He's been sitting there **for three hours**.	It was two o'clock when Mark started the game. He's been playing **since two o'clock**.	Three hours have passed since Mark and Sarah got up from the lunch table. They finished their lunch **three hours ago**.

B For and since with the present perfect

We often use **for** and **since** with the present perfect to talk about something continuing up to the present.

FOR	SINCE
We use **for** to say <u>how long</u> something has continued.	We use **since** to say <u>when</u> something began.
I've been waiting **for forty minutes**.	I've been waiting **since ten past six**.
We've known about it **for two days**.	We've known about it **since Monday**.
Melanie has been living here **for a year** now.	Melanie has been living here **since last year**.

We can also use **for** with other tenses.
   *I'm staying in England **for** a year.*   *We **swam for** quite a long time.*
We can often leave out **for** (but not from some negative sentences).
   *We've had this car (**for**) six months.*   *I haven't seen Vicky **for** a day or two.*

C Ago with the past

We can use the adverb **ago** to talk about a past time measured from the present.
Six months ago means six months before now.
   *I passed my driving test **six months ago**.* NOT *since six months*
   *Vicky wrote to the company **weeks ago**.*   *David first met Melanie **a long time ago**.*
   *Have you seen Emma? ~ Yes, just **a few minutes ago**.*
We put **ago** after the phrase of time. NOT *ago six months*

D Before with the past perfect

We use **before** (not ago) with the past perfect, e.g. **had done**.
   *I bought a car in August. I'd passed my driving test **three months before**.*
   (= in May, three months before August)
   *Vicky finally received a reply to the letter she had written **weeks before**.*

121 Exercises

1 For and since (A–B)

Put in *for* or *since*.
Daniel: How long have you been learning English?
Ilona: Well, I studied it (▶) *for* five years at school, and I've been having evening classes (1) .... last summer. That's when I left school.
Daniel: And you're staying here (2) .... three months?
Ilona: That's right. I've been here (3) .... the end of April. I'm going to London (4) .... a week before I go home.

2 For and since (A–B)

Look at the pictures and say how long people have been there.
Use these phrases: *at his desk, in bed, in the garden, in the shop, on the road*

▶ half an hour

1 three days

2 breakfast

3 nine o'clock

4 five hours

▶ *She's been in the shop for half an hour.*
1 ....
2 ....
3 ....
4 ....

3 For, since or ago? (A–C)

Put in a phrase with *for*, *since* or *ago*.
▶ I got here an hour ago. ~ What! You mean you've been waiting *for an hour*?
1 The phone last rang at four o'clock. ~ So you've had no calls .... ?
2 I haven't been to the dentist for ten years. ~ You last went to the dentist .... ?
3 I last saw Rachel on Monday. ~ Haven't you seen her .... ?
4 We've had six weeks without rain. ~ Yes, it hasn't rained ....
5 It's three years since Laura got married. ~ Really? Has she been married .... ?
6 It's eight months since my brother had any work. ~ He lost his job .... ?
7 Mrs Miles was taken ill three weeks ago. ~ You mean she's been ill .... , and nobody's told me!

4 Ago or before? (C–D)

Put in *ago* or *before*.
▶ This film looks familiar. Didn't we see it at the cinema about two years *ago*?
1 The road was wet when the accident happened. It had stopped raining only half an hour ....
2 My telephone is working now. They repaired it a week ....
3 A young man threw himself off this bridge last year. He had lost his job two days ago.................. .

122 During or while? By or until? As or like?

A During or while?

Compare these examples.

> I often read **during** a meal.
> It happened **during** the night.
> You'll have to be quiet **during** the performance.
> **During** is a preposition (like **in**). It comes before a phrase like **a meal** or **the night**.

> I often read **while** I'm eating.
> It happened **while** they were asleep.
> Were there any phone calls **while** I was out?
> **While** is a linking word (like **when**). It comes before a clause, e.g. **I'm eating**.

B By or until?

Compare these examples.

> I'm very busy this week. I have to finish this report **by** Thursday.
> Trevor will be home **by** half past six.
> They hope to build the new bridge **by** next July.
> The post should be here **by** now.

> I'll be busy for most of this week. I won't have any time **until** Friday.
> He'll be at work **until** half past five.
> We won't have another holiday **until** next summer.
> **Till** is more informal than **until**.
> I slept **till** ten o'clock.

We can use **by the time** or **until** before a clause, e.g. **we arrived**.

> There was no food left **by the time** we arrived.
> NOT *by we arrived*

> I'll wait **until** you're ready.
> See Unit 27B for the present simple after **until**, etc.

C As, like and as if

Compare these examples.

> She works **as** a fashion model.
> (= She is a model.)
> **As** a beginner you simply have to learn the basics.
> I'm using this tin **as** an ashtray.
> We use **as** to talk about a job or function.

> She dresses **like** a fashion model.
> (= Her clothes are similar to a model's.)
> Mark is a good golfer, but today he played **like** a beginner.
> You look **like** your brother.
> We use **like** to talk about things being similar.

We can also use **as** or **like** before a clause.
> We drive on the left here, **as/like** you do in Britain.
> Mike and Sarah are going to Paris for the weekend, **as/like** they did last year.

Like is more informal than **as** before a clause.

We also use **as** with verbs of speaking and knowing, e.g. **say, know, expect**.
> **As I said before**, I'm sorry. (= I'm sorry, and I said so before.)
> I haven't much money, **as you know**. (= I haven't much money, and you know it.)
> Rachel arrived late, **as we expected**. (= We expected her to arrive late, and she did.)

We use **as if** before a clause to say how something seems.
> Tom looks really awful. He looks **as if he's been up all night**.
> Nick can be a difficult person. He sometimes behaves **as if he's the only one with problems**.

122 Exercises

1 During or while? (A)

Put in *during* or *while*.
▶ Did you take notes *during* the lecture?
1 Shall we have a coffee .... we're waiting?
2 Try not to make any noise .... the baby is asleep.
3 The fire alarm rang .... yesterday's meeting.
4 Trevor tried to fix the shelves .... Laura was out shopping.

2 By or until? (B)

Rachel is talking to her teacher. Put in *by* or *until*.
Mrs Lewis: You'll need to hand your project in (▶) *by* the end of the week.
I'd like to have it (1) .... Friday, ideally.
Rachel: Well, I'm going on a three-day study trip tomorrow. I'll be away (2) .... Thursday.
The project will probably take me (3) .... the middle of next week.
I can't finish it (4) .... the end of this week.
Mrs Lewis: Well, let me have it (5) .... Wednesday of next week, please.

3 As or like? (C)

Put in *as* or *like*.
▶ Sarah works in here. She uses this room *as* her study.
1 Matthew worked .... a waiter last summer.
2 The way your sister plays the violin sounds .... two cats fighting.
3 Do you mind using this saucer .... a plate?
4 The body sank .... a stone to the bottom of the river.

4 As or as if? (C)

Put in *as* or *as if*.
▶ That poor dog looks *as if* it never gets fed.
1 Rachel failed her driving test, ... she expected.
2 Daniel spends money .... it grows on trees.
3 We shall deliver the goods on the twenty-seventh, ... we promised.
4 From what Emma said, it sounds .... she and Matthew are going to get married.

5 While, by the time, until, as and like (A–C)

Decide what to say. Use the word in brackets to join the two ideas together.
▶ Tell Matthew he needs to click on the box. You showed him. (like)
You need to click on the box, like I showed you.
1 Tell Tom that you arrived at his flat, but he'd left. (by the time)
....
2 Tell your friend that Rita went to the party with Tom. Your friend predicted this. (as)
....
3 Tell Claire that you saw her sister. You were shopping in London. (while)
....
4 Tell Vicky she can keep the book. She can finish it. (until)
....

123 Preposition + noun, e.g. **on holiday**

A Some useful phrases

on holiday, on business, on a journey/a trip/a tour
   *I'm travelling **on business**.*   *We're **on a** coach **tour** of Europe.*

in cash, by cheque/credit card
   *It's cheaper if you pay **in cash**.*   *Can I pay **by credit card**?*

in writing, in pen/biro/felt-tip/ink/pencil
   *Could you confirm that **in writing**?*   *I'll write the names **in pencil**.*

on television, on the radio/the phone/the Internet
   *I saw the programme **on TV**.*   *Mark is **on the phone** at the moment.*

for sale, on the market
   *The house next door is **for sale**.*   *It's the best hi-fi **on the market**.*

on the whole, in general
   ***On the whole** it's a good idea, but there are one or two problems.*
   *People **in general** aren't very interested in politics.*

in advance, up to date, out of date
   *The company wants us to pay for the goods **in advance**.*
   *Oh no! My passport is **out of date**.*   *These latest figures are **up to date**.*

in my opinion, from my point of view
   *All sport is silly **in my opinion**.*
   *Matthew never sees things **from Emma's point of view**.*

on purpose, by mistake/chance/accident
   *I didn't spill my drink **on purpose**.*   *I pressed the wrong button **by mistake**.*
   *We didn't arrange to meet. We met **by chance** in the street.*

B Way and end

On the way = during the journey.
   *I'm driving into town. I'll get some petrol **on the way**.*
	In the way = blocking the way.
	   *We couldn't get past because there was a parked car **in the way**.*

In the end = finally, after a long time.
   *It took Claire hours to decide. **In the end** she chose a long blue dress.*
	At the end = when something stops.
	   *We all left quickly **at the end** of the meeting.*

C Transport

We use **by** without a/the when we talk about a means of transport.
   *We decided to go to Brussels **by train**.* NOT ~~go by the train~~

We can also use **in** and **on**.
   *It'll be quicker to go **in the car**.*   *Richard came **on the train**.*

Note that **on foot** means 'walking'.
   *We came all the way **on foot**.* NOT ~~by foot~~

BY:	*air, bicycle/bike, boat, bus, car, coach, ferry, helicopter, hovercraft, plane, rail, sea, ship, taxi, train, tube*
IN:	*the/my/your car, a helicopter, a taxi*
ON:	*my bicycle/bike, the boat, the bus, the ferry, the hovercraft, the plane, the ship, the train*

123 Exercises

1 Preposition + noun (A–B)

Put in *by, from, in* or *on*.
▶ There's something I want to listen to *on* the radio.
1 They've promised me more money, but I haven't got it .... writing.
2 Why can't you look at the problem .... my point of view?
3 Would you mind moving? You're rather .... the way here.
4 I rang the wrong number .... mistake.
5 I booked our seats more than a month .... advance.
6 Sarah's mobile phone was stolen while she was away .... a business trip.
7 Could you be quiet for a minute, please? I'm .... the phone.
8 We've had a few nice days, but .... general it's been a poor summer.
9 I was lucky. I found the solution .... accident.
10 It's a long journey. Let's stop somewhere .... the way and have a meal.
11 I spent ages looking for a phone box. .... the end I found one.
12 Are you here .... holiday or .... business?

2 Preposition + noun (A–B)

What would you ask? Use the word in brackets with the correct preposition.
You may also need to use *the* or *your*.
▶ Ask if you can book a cabin before you travel. (advance)
Can *I book a cabin in advance*?
1 Ask if you can pay in notes. (cash)
Can ....
2 Ask if the information is current. (date)
Is ....
3 Ask your friend if he dropped the ball deliberately. (purpose)
Did ....
4 Ask if there is anything to watch tonight. (television)
Is ....
5 Ask your teacher if he or she will be here on the last day of July. (end)
Will ....
6 Ask Melanie if she thinks nuclear power is a good idea. (opinion)
Is ....
7 Ask Nick if he is selling his car. (sale)
Is ....
8 Ask Sarah if she approves of the plan in general. (whole)
Do ....

3 Transport (C)

Complete the conversation. Put in *by, in* or *on*.
Sarah: It's a long way to Glasgow. Why don't you go (▶) *on* the train?
Mark: I don't know. I think I'd rather go (1) .... car.
Sarah: How far is your hotel from the station?
Mark: Oh, it's only five minutes (2) .... foot, but with all my luggage,
I'd probably go (3) .... a taxi.
Sarah: Well, why not? It's less tiring going (4) .... train, isn't it?
Mark: I could go (5) .... air. That would be quickest.

124 Noun + preposition, e.g. **trouble with**

A Introduction

Read this true story about a prison escape.

> Prisoners at a jail in Iowa in the US were trying to think of a **way of** escaping. At last they found an **answer to** their problem. They told the governor about their **interest in** drama and their **need for** creative activities. They put in a **request for** some tunnel-digging equipment for a play about coalminers. They knew that the governor felt **sympathy for** his prisoners and wanted a good **relationship with** them, but they weren't surprised when he said no. But later, when the prisoners mentioned the **importance of** physical fitness, the governor agreed to let them use a trampoline. Their **skill at** trampolining was put to good use when six prisoners bounced over the prison wall and escaped.

Some nouns can have a preposition after them, e.g. **way of, answer to, interest in**.
The preposition often has a phrase with a noun after it.
   the answer **to the problem**   their interest **in drama**
And the preposition can sometimes have an ing-form after it.
   a way **of escaping**   their skill **at trampolining**

B Noun + preposition

Here are some more examples.

your **ability in** maths	an **example of** this	your **opinion of** the film
a cheap **alternative to** leather	some **experience of** selling	the **price of** food
an **attack on** the government	an **expert on** computers	the **reason for** the delay
my **attitude to/towards** him	no **hope of** winning	**respect for** the environment
a **belief in** God	an **invitation to** a party	a **student of** chemistry
the **cause of** the accident	some **knowledge of** Italian	a **substitute for** meat
the **cost of** living	a **lack of** money	**success at** golf/**in** my search
some **damage to** the car	something the **matter with** you	a **tax on** alcohol
a **difficulty over/with** visas	a new **method of** storing data	having **trouble with** my teeth

C Connection, difference; increase, reduction, etc

One thing has a link <u>with</u> another.	There is a link <u>between</u> two things.
a **connection with** another crime	a **connection between** the two crimes
Matthew's **relationship with** Emma	the **relationship between** Matthew and Emma
the **contrast with** yesterday's weather	the **contrast/difference between** town and country

Look at these words for increases and decreases. We use **in** before the thing that is increasing or decreasing and **of** before the amount of the increase or decrease.

an **increase/rise in** the price	an **increase/rise of** £10
a **reduction/fall in** the number of unemployed	a **reduction/fall of** 3%

D Need, wish, etc

Nouns meaning 'need', 'wish' or 'request' can have **for** after them.
   There's a **need for** more houses.   There was no **demand for** the product.
Here are some examples: **appetite for, application for, demand for, desire for, need for, order for, preference for, request for, taste for, wish for**

124 Exercises

1 Noun + preposition (A–B)

Complete the conversation. Put in *at*, *in* or *of*.
Daniel: What's the job you've applied for?
Vicky: It's with a travel company. But the advert says that you need some experience (▶) *of* work in tourism. I haven't got that. And I don't think my knowledge (1) .... foreign languages will be good enough. I'm having no success at all (2) .... my attempts to get a job.
Daniel: What about your interest (3) .... computers? And your skill (4) .... typing? That's the sort of thing employers are looking for.

2 Noun + preposition (A–B)

Complete the sentences. Use a preposition after these nouns:
answer, cause, damage, difficulty, invitation, matter, tax, way
▶ I've had an *invitation to* Laura's barbecue.
1 The accident caused some .... the car.
2 I'm trying to think of the best .... getting this piano upstairs.
3 I can't think of an .... the problem, I'm afraid.
4 The .... the accident is still unknown.
5 The government has introduced a new .... luxury goods.
6 Unfortunately there was some .... the arrangements.
7 The television won't come on. What's the .... it?

3 Noun + preposition (B–C)

Complete the advertisement for a supermarket. Put in *between, for, in, of* or *with*.

Why not shop at Greenway Supermarket? You'll find the cost (▶) *of* your weekly shopping is much lower. There's quite a contrast (1) .... other stores. Here's one example (2) .... this: from today many of our products have a price reduction (3) .... five per cent! But this is not the only reason (4) .... Greenway's success. We're proud of our good relationship (5) .... our customers. We believe there is simply no substitute (6) .... quality. And there is no lack (7) .... choice at Greenway. That's the difference (8) .... Greenway and ordinary stores.

4 Noun + preposition (A–D)

What are they saying? Read about each situation and complete the sentence.
▶ A motorist has rung the garage and requested a breakdown truck.
   Mechanic: I've just had a *request for a breakdown truck*.
1 Claude can answer all the quiz questions.
   Claude: I can tell you the ....
2 Matthew doesn't know any French.
   Matthew: Unfortunately I have no ....
3 The Prime Minister greatly desires progress.
   Prime Minister: I have a great ....
4 Vicky thinks the two colours are the same.
   Vicky: I can't see any ....
5 Most people say they prefer Zedco products.
   Zedco: Most people express a ....

125 Adjective + preposition, e.g. **proud of**

A Introduction

Matthew: Why are you **angry with** me, Emma?
Emma: I'm **tired of** talking to myself. You never listen. I get **annoyed at** the way you behave.
Matthew: Sorry, but I have to go now or I'll be **late for** the basketball game.
Emma: You aren't **interested in** us, are you? You never worry about our relationship, do you?

Some adjectives can have a preposition after them, e.g. **angry with**, **tired of**, **late for**.
The preposition often has a phrase with a noun or pronoun after it.
  annoyed **at the way** you behave   late **for the game**   angry **with me**
The preposition can sometimes have an ing-form after it.
  tired **of talking** to myself

B Feelings

Here are some examples of adjective + preposition which are to do with feelings.

afraid of the dark
amazed at/by the changes
ashamed of myself
bored with doing nothing
disappointed with/about the poor figures
eager for action

excited about the holiday
fed up with waiting
fond of my sister
happy about/with the arrangements
keen on sport
nervous of flying

proud of our work
satisfied with the result
shocked at/by the violence
surprised at/by the reaction
tired of housework
worried about money

Compare these examples.

> I'm **sorry about** the mistake.
> We were **angry at/about** the delay.
> We were **annoyed at/about** the delay.
> I was **pleased about** winning.
> Vicky is **anxious about** her exam.
>
> I feel **sorry for** poor Melanie.
> Sarah was **angry with** Henry.
> Emma was **annoyed with** Matthew.
> The winner was **pleased with** himself.
> People are **anxious for** news.

C Good, bad, etc

To talk about a person's ability, we use **good at**, **bad at**, etc.
  good at tennis   **brilliant at** crosswords   **bad at** games   **hopeless at** cooking
To talk about whether something makes you healthy or ill, we use **good for** and **bad for**.
  Oranges are **good for** you.   Smoking is **bad for** you.
For behaviour towards another person, we use **good to**, **kind to**, **nice to**, **polite to** and **rude to**.
  My friends have been **good to** me.   You were very **rude to** the waitress.

D Other adjectives

Here are some more expressions with other adjectives.

accustomed to the noise
aware of the facts
capable of looking after myself
different from our usual route
  (see page 381)
famous for her film roles

fit for work
full of water
guilty of murder
involved in a project
prepared for action
ready for the big day

responsible for running a business
safe from attack
the *same as* before
similar to my idea
typical of David
used to the traffic

▷ 71 **Afraid, anxious, ashamed, interested, sorry**   ▷ 72 **Used to**

125 Exercises

1 Feelings (A–B)
Say what these people's feelings are. Use the adjectives in brackets and a preposition.
▶ The children are leaving on a trip to the zoo. (excited)
They're *excited about the trip to the zoo.*
1 Vicky doesn't like the dark. (afraid)
She's ....
2 Nick was watching a video, but he's going to switch it off. (bored)
He's ....
3 Emma is reading about computers. (interested)
She's ....
4 Mark has just heard some news that he didn't expect. (surprised)
He's ....
5 United have won a victory. (proud)
They're ....
6 Olivia's children are being very silly. (annoyed)
She's ....
7 The Zedco staff don't think their pay increase is big enough. (not satisfied)
....

2 Good, bad, etc (C)
Complete the conversation. Put in *at, for* or *to*.
Sarah: You were very rude (▶) *to* Henry when you said he needs to lose weight.
Claire: Well, it's true. Exercise would be good (1) .... him. He started jogging and then gave it up.
Sarah: Yes, but we can't all be good (2) .... taking physical exercise.
Claire: Anyone can do a bit of jogging. You don't have to be brilliant (3) .... it.
And eating so much must be bad (4) .... you.
Sarah: Well, you could have been more polite.
Claire: Sorry. I'm not very good (5) .... saying the right thing.
I'll try to be nice (6) .... him next time I see him.

3 Other adjectives (A, D)
Complete these paragraphs from a letter Emma has received from her brother. Use these adjectives and put a preposition after each one: aware, <u>different</u>, famous, full, interested, late, ready, responsible, similar, <u>used</u>

Everything was strange here at first because this new job is (▶) *different from* any I've had before. But I've got (▶) *used to* it now, and I'm really enjoying it. I'm mainly (1) .... controlling the costs of the project. The work is quite hard, and I must say I feel (2) .... a holiday. The company expect people to do overtime. I wasn't (3) .... that before I arrived because they hadn't told me at the interview, but I don't mind.

I've got a nice flat, which is very (4) .... the one I had in London.
The only difference is that my flat here is (5) .... horrible old furniture.
I keep falling over it! I live right by the harbour. It's a pity
I've never been (6) .... boats, because this is a good place for sailing.
The noise of the motor boats wakes me up every morning, so I'm never
(7) .... work. The area is (8) .... its seafood, which
is great, because I love eating fish, as you know.

Test 21 Prepositions (Units 118–125)

Test 21A

Write the sentences correctly.
▶ ~~I'll see you at Monday.~~
   I'll see you on Monday.
1 ~~The doctor has been working since twelve hours.~~
2 ~~We had a great time in the disco.~~
3 ~~The woman was getting from the car.~~
4 ~~The players had numbers at their shirts.~~
5 ~~The new manager takes over at two weeks' time.~~
6 ~~Anna drove at the garage to get some petrol.~~
7 ~~We were sitting in the back of the room.~~

Test 21B

Read Polly's postcard and write the missing words. Use one word only in each space. Sometimes more than one answer is correct.

This is our first real holiday (▶) *for* ages, and I'm enjoying it tremendously. I love being (1) .... an island. We arrived here almost a week (2) ...., and I can't believe the time is going so fast. We finally completed the journey here (3) .... Friday evening (4) .... about eleven o'clock. The journey wasn't too bad, but we had to wait ages (5) .... the airport for our flight.

Our apartment here is fine. It's (6) .... the top floor. The beach isn't far away – we can walk there (7) .... five minutes. The only problem is that we have to get (8) .... a busy main road, which can be difficult.

We don't do much (9) .... the day, but we go out every evening. Last night's disco went on very late, and today we slept (10) .... eleven.

Test 21C

Some of these sentences are correct, and some have a word which should not be there. If the sentence is correct, put a tick (✓). If it is incorrect, cross the unnecessary word out of the sentence and write it in the space.
▶ The cat was sitting on top of the shed.   ✓
▶ Coventry is near ~~by~~ Birmingham.   *by*
1 Luckily our train arrived on the time.   ....
2 People were running away from the gunman.   ....
3 It sounds as if the company is in trouble.   ....
4 The car was in the front of a bus.   ....
5 There's a meeting on next Tuesday.   ....
6 Lisa drew a plan on the back of an envelope.   ....
7 I'll be exhausted by the time I get home.   ....

Test 21

Test 21D

Decide which word is correct.
▶ I saw a really funny programme *on* television.   a) at b) from c) in d) on
1 You can see all the information .... the screen.   a) at b) in c) inside d) on
2 Are these pictures .... sale?   a) at b) for c) in d) to
3 Could you let me know .... Friday at the latest?   a) by b) to c) up to d) until
4 The audience clapped .... the end of the show.   a) at b) for c) in d) to
5 I've lived here .... last year.   a) after b) by c) for d) since
6 What's the matter .... your car?   a) by b) for c) on d) with
7 We could see the balloon high .... the town.   a) above b) on c) onto d) up
8 There was a fall .... ten per cent in prices.   a) at b) by c) in d) of
9 The house was burgled .... we were out.   a) at b) during c) time d) while
10 What's the difference .... a boat and a ship?   a) between b) from c) under d) with
11 Rupert's new car looks more .... an aeroplane.   a) as b) like c) near d) similar
12 We're all bored .... this game.   a) about b) at c) for d) with
13 I can't find my keys. I had them a minute ....   a) ago b) before c) behind d) back
14 We get lots of requests .... help.   a) at b) for c) of d) on
15 The babysitter will stay there .... we get home.   a) by b) for c) to d) until
16 I'm going to be late .... the meeting.   a) at b) for c) in d) to
17 We do most of our business .... summer.   a) along b) at c) in d) on
18 The job is similar .... my old one.   a) as b) at c) to d) with

Test 21E

Complete the second sentence so that it has a similar meaning to the first. Use the word in brackets.
▶ This is the Glasgow train. (going)
This train is going to Glasgow.
1 Scott is a resident of Washington. (lives)
   ....
2 I'm travelling to Italy as part of my job. (business)
   ....
3 Friday morning is a busy time for me. (I'm)
   ....
4 They started playing an hour ago. (been)
   ....
5 Jonathan can play tennis very well. (good)
   ....
6 I'm rather busy now. (moment)
   ....
7 We took a plane to Budapest. (air)
   ....
8 Nigel passes the newsagent's every day. (goes)
   ....
9 The company is planning to reduce the workforce. (reduction)
   ....
10 We got to our guest-house early enough for a meal. (time)
   ....

126 Prepositional verbs, e.g. **wait for**

A Introduction

A prepositional verb is a verb + preposition.
*I'm **waiting for** you.*   *The dog **belongs to** our neighbours.*
The preposition always goes before the object.
NOT *I'm waiting you for.*
In questions the preposition usually goes at the end of the sentence (see Unit 38).
Who are you waiting for?

Some verbs can go with a number of different prepositions.
*I'm **looking at** these photos. They're really good.*   *I'm **looking for** my ticket. I can't find it anywhere.*
*I'm **looking after** the children while their parents are out.*   *The police are **looking into** the matter.*

B Some common prepositional verbs

Here are some more examples.
*Yes, I **agree with** you.*   *Tom's neighbours **apologized for** the noise.*
*I **approve of** the new scheme. I think it's a good idea.*
*Have you **applied for** the job?*   *The patient **asked for** a glass of water.*
*Do you **believe in** God?*   *I'm sorry, but I don't **care about** your problems.*
*Lots of people **care for** elderly relatives.* (= look after)
*I didn't **care for** the film.* (= like)   *Please **concentrate on** your work.*
*The US **consists of** fifty states.*   *I can **deal with** any enquiries.*
*Claire finally **decided on** a holiday in Turkey.*
*Whether we go out will **depend on** the weather.*   *I **feel like** a drink.* (= want)
*Everyone **laughed at** the joke.*   *I was **listening to** the radio.*
*Did you **pay for** the coffee?*   *You can't **rely on** the weather forecast.*
*I'll **see to** the matter at once.*   *Vicky **suffers from** headaches.*

We do not normally use a preposition after these verbs:
answer, approach, control, demand, enter, expect, leave, reach, request
*The President is **entering** the building.* NOT *He is entering into the building.*

C About, of and to

We can use **about** after many verbs. Here are some of them:
ask, complain, dream, enquire, hear, know, learn, protest, speak, talk, think, wonder
*Did you **hear about** the accident?*   *Mark was **talking about** golf.*
We do not use **about** after **discuss**.
*We **discussed** the problem.* NOT *We discussed about the problem.*

Note the meaning of **dream of**, **hear of** and **think of**.
*I'd never tell you a lie. I wouldn't **dream of** it.*
*Who's Ron Mason? ~ I don't know. I've never **heard of** him.*
*Did you like the play? What did you **think of** it?*

We can **apologize to**, **complain to**, **talk to** and **write to** a person.
*I'm **writing to** my sister.*   *We **talked to** Natasha about classical music.*
We do not use **to** after **phone**.
*I'm **phoning** the office.* NOT *I'm phoning to the office.*

▷ 70 Verb + preposition + ing-form

126 Exercises

1 Prepositions with **look** (A)

Complete the conversation between Laura and her friend Olivia. Put in *after, at, for* and *into*.

Laura: Did you say you were looking (▶) *for* an au pair?
Olivia: Yes, I was just looking (1) .... this advertisement.
   We need someone to look (2) .... our children.
Laura: Do you have to pay an au pair?
Olivia: I'm not sure. I'll have to look (3) .... how it all works.

2 Some common prepositional verbs (B)

This is part of a letter that Melanie has received from an old friend. Put in these verbs and add a preposition after each one: *agree, applied, ask, care, caring, concentrate, decided, pay, suffering*

I'm working in a hospital now. I (▶) *applied for* a nurse's job last July and started in August. I don't earn much money, and I even had to (1) .... my uniform out of my own money. Perhaps I should (2) .... a pay rise. But I don't really (3) .... the money. The work is the important thing. Of course it's very hard work (4) .... the patients, and at the moment I'm (5) .... backache. But I knew it would be like this when I (6) .... a career in nursing. I just try to forget all the problems and (7) .... the job. I think it's a worthwhile thing to do, and I'm sure you (8) .... me.

3 Some common prepositional verbs (B)

Put in the verbs and add a preposition if necessary.

Mark and Sarah had accepted an invitation to Mike and Harriet's party. Sarah had to stay late at work to (▶) *see to* (see) one or two things. Her boss really (1) .... (relies) her. It's usually Sarah who (2) .... (deals) all the little problems. Sarah didn't really (3) .... (feel) going to a party but thought she ought to keep Mark company. She decided to go straight to the party instead of going home first. She (4) .... (reached) the house just after nine. Mark was sitting in his car outside waiting for her. He was (5) .... (listening) the radio. Sarah (6) .... (apologized) being late. At the party Mark talked to a strange woman who (7) .... (believed) ghosts. Sarah met a man who kept (8) .... (laughing) his own jokes. She managed to get away from him but couldn't avoid a woman who wanted to (9) .... (discuss) house prices. Mark and Sarah (10) .... (left) the party early and drove home feeling exhausted.

4 **About, of** and **to** (C)

Complete the conversation. Put in *about, of* or *to*.

David: Did you hear about my experience at the Quick Burger café?
Harriet: No. And I've never heard (▶) *of* the Quick Burger café.
David: Oh, it's near the station. I was just talking (1) .... Melanie about it. They took at least twenty minutes to bring me a burger. I don't call that quick. I complained (2) .... the waitress, and she poured a can of cola over me.
Harriet: Really? She must have had a bad day.
David: The manager wasn't there, so I've written (3) .... him to complain (4) .... the service. It was terrible. I wouldn't go there if I were you.
Harriet: I wouldn't dream (5) .... going there. I hate those burger places.

127 Verb + object + preposition

A Introduction

We can use some verbs in the structure: verb + object + preposition.

	VERB	OBJECT	PREPOSITION	
People	**admired**	Cleopatra	**for**	her beauty.
The trees	**protect**	the garden	**from**	the wind.

In the passive, the preposition comes after the verb.
　　Cleopatra was **admired for** her beauty.　　The garden is **protected from** the wind.

B Verb + object + preposition

Here are some more examples.
　　Tom **accused** Nick **of** cheating at cards.　　Can I **add** something **to** your list?
　　You should never **aim/point** a gun **at** someone.
　　The player was **arrested/punished for** hitting an opponent.　　Let's **ask** someone **for** directions.
　　The passengers **blamed/criticized** the airline **for** the delay.
　　I'll have to **borrow** the money **from** my parents.
　　If you **compare** these figures **with/to** last year, you can see the improvement.
　　I **congratulated** Andrew **on** his excellent exam results.
　　Melanie **cut/divided/split** the pudding **into** four portions.
　　The cameras **discourage/prevent** motorists **from** speeding.
　　You should **insure** your camera **against** theft. It might get stolen.
　　Harriet has **invited** us **to** a party.　　I **prefer** hot weather **to** cold. I hate the cold.
　　The hotel **provided/supplied** us **with** a packed lunch.　　Most people **regard** Picasso **as** a great artist.
　　The two men **robbed** the woman **of** her savings. They **stole** £2,000 **from** her.
　　The restaurant was full. We **shared** a table **with** a young Swedish couple.
　　Mike doesn't **spend** much money **on** clothes.
　　Zedco **suspected** one of their managers **of** selling commercial secrets.
　　Don't forget to **thank** Tom **for** his help.　　Victor **translated** the letter **into** English.

C About, of and to

We can use **about** with **tell** and **ask**.
　　Did I **tell** you **about** my operation?　　**Ask** your travel agent **about** cheap flights.
With **inform** we can use **about** or **of**.
　　You should **inform** everyone **about/of** the decision.

Look at these examples with **warn**.
　　A sign **warned** motorists **about/of** the danger. (warn **of/about** a danger)
　　A sign **warned** motorists **about** the hole in the road. (warn **about** something that might be dangerous)
With **remind**, there is a difference in meaning between **about** and **of**.
　　Emma **reminded** me **about** my appointment. (= Emma told me not to forget.)
　　Emma **reminds** me **of** my sister. (= Emma is like my sister.)

We can **write**, **describe** or **explain** something **to** a person.
　　I've **written** several letters **to** the company.　　The woman **described** her attacker **to** the police.

▷ 3 **Give something to someone**　▷ 126 **Wait for, belong to**, etc

127 Exercises

1 Verb + object + preposition (B)
This is a sports commentary at the Olympic Games.
Put in the correct prepositions, e.g. *for, from*.

So Australia's Steve Brearley wins the gold medal ahead of Germany's Klaus Schliemann and Ivan Podorosky of Bulgaria. They're just congratulating Brearley (▶) *on* his victory. His speed over the first kilometre split the runners (1) .... two groups, and in the end it was a race between the three leaders. Brearley prevented Schliemann (2) .... overtaking him in a sprint finish. I've always regarded Brearley (3) .... a great athlete, and look how well he's done today. I would even compare him (4) .... the great Emil Kristo himself. There's no doubt now that Brearley will be invited (5) .... Oslo for the next World Championships. So the Australian runner adds another medal (6) .... his collection. And Australia are doing really well in the medals table. In fact, they share second place (7) .... the United States.

2 Verb + object + preposition (B)
People are saying some surprising things.
Complete the replies using a verb + object + preposition.

▶ Andrew: I've bought a lot of books. I've spent £300.
   Emma: What? Have you really *spent £300 on books*?
1 Jessica: I don't like wine. I prefer water.
   Daniel: I don't believe that. Do you really ....
2 Melanie: You heard about David's accident. Well, he's blaming Tom.
   Rita: But why? Why is he ....
3 Henry: I gave Claire a present, but she didn't thank me.
   Sarah: Did you say she didn't ....
4 Tom: The police say it's murder. They're accusing the head teacher.
   Rita: What evidence do they have? How can they ....
5 Vicky: We had no towels. The hotel didn't provide them.
   Rachel: Really? Why didn't they ....
6 Natasha: It's my sister's wedding today, but she didn't invite me.
   Emma: What! Do you mean she didn't ....
7 Nick: The team won a great victory, but no one congratulated them.
   Trevor: Oh? And why didn't anyone ....
8 David: A man pointed a gun. Melanie was terrified.
   Harriet: You mean someone ....

3 About, of and to (C)
Put in *about, of* or *to*.

▶ The interviewer asked Mrs Miles *about* her parachute jump.
1 I've told the police .... people throwing stones at our windows.
2 That man over there reminds me .... someone I know.
3 The man explained .... the court that he had some personal problems.
4 Vicky is writing a letter .... her friends in Toronto.
5 There was a poster warning young people .... the dangers of drugs.
6 Melanie had to remind Nick .... the money he owed her.
7 We would like to inform our customers .... a number of improvements in the service we offer.

128 Phrasal verbs (1)

A Introduction

A phrasal verb is a verb + adverb, e.g. **come in**, **sit down**, **take off**. There are very many phrasal verbs in English.

Here are some adverbs which are used in phrasal verbs:
about, along, around, away, back, behind, by, down, forward, in, off, on, out, over, round, through, up

Some of these words can also be prepositions.
For prepositional verbs see Unit 126.

B Understanding phrasal verbs

Some phrasal verbs are easy to understand.
*Tom asked Melanie to **come in**.*   *The man in front **turned round** and stared at me.*
The meanings are clear if you know the words **come, in, turn** and **round**.

But many phrasal verbs are idiomatic. The verb + adverb has a special meaning.
*Fortunately the plan **came off**.* (= succeeded)
*Why did you **turn down** such a good offer?* (= refuse)
*I can't **make out** if it's a man or a woman over there.* (= see clearly)

Sometimes a phrasal verb has the same meaning as a one-word verb.

find out = discover	*leave out* = omit	*send out* = distribute
go back = return	*make up* = invent (a story)	*throw away* = discard
go on = continue	*put off* = postpone	*turn up* = arrive

The phrasal verb is usually more informal than the one-word verb.

C Word order with phrasal verbs

When a phrasal verb has an object, the object can go either before or after the adverb.

	VERB	OBJECT	ADVERB			VERB	ADVERB	OBJECT
Melanie	*took*	*her coat*	*off.*	OR	*Melanie*	*took*	*off*	*her coat.*
I	*wrote*	*the number*	*down.*	OR	*I*	*wrote*	*down*	*the number.*
Who	*let*	*the cat*	*out?*	OR	*Who*	*let*	*out*	*the cat?*

A long object goes after the adverb.
*The gang have **carried out** a number of bank raids in the last few months.*
*Why don't you **try on** that dress in the window?*

A pronoun (e.g. **it, them**) always goes before the adverb.
*Melanie felt hot in her coat, so she **took it off**.*
NOT *She took off it.*
*There have been a number of raids. The police know who **carried them out**.*
NOT *The police know who carried out them.*

308   VERBS WITH PREPOSITIONS AND ADVERBS

128 Exercises

1 Understanding phrasal verbs (A–B)

Work out the meaning of these phrasal verbs and put them in the right sentences:
come back, come in, cut out, fall over, get on, give away, go away, let in, lie down, pay back, stay in, take back
(Use a dictionary if you need to.)

▶ Hello. Nice to see you. *Come in* and sit down.
▶ I didn't have a key, but luckily someone was there to *let* me *in*.
1. Can't we go out somewhere? I don't want to .... all evening.
2. Could you lend me ten pounds? I'll .... you .... on Friday.
3. The pavement is very icy. Be careful you don't ....
4. I was feeling so tired I had to .... on the bed for a while.
5. There was an article in the newspaper that I wanted to .... and keep.
6. Mark's gone out, and I don't know when he's going to ....
7. The driver unlocked the coach so that the passengers were able to ....
8. I'll have to .... these books .... to the library.
9. Your brother was being a nuisance, so I told him to ....
10. In order to get publicity, the company decided to .... some of the new sweets free to children.

2 One-word verb and phrasal verb (B)

Put in a phrasal verb that means the same as the verb in brackets. Use the correct form of the phrasal verb.
Rachel: I've (▶) *found out* (discovered) what the problem is with the exam.
Vicky: Oh, good. Tell me.
Rachel: When they printed the papers, they (1) .... (omitted) a page. No one noticed until the papers had all been (2) .... (distributed).
Now they'll have to (3) .... (discard) all the papers and
(4) .... (postpone) the exam.
Vicky: Are you sure you haven't (5) .... (invented) this whole story?
Rachel: It's true, I tell you. And isn't it good news?
Vicky: I don't know about that. It means we'll have to (6) .... (continue) revising.

3 Word order with phrasal verbs (C)

Complete the sentences by putting in the phrasal verbs. Some of the spaces you have to leave empty. Sometimes more than one answer is correct.
▶ The sweater was full of holes, so I *threw* it *away* (threw away).
▶ I've *put up* (put up) that picture we bought last week.
1. There's always litter here. No one ever .... it .... (pick up).
2. It's quite cold now. I think I'll .... my coat .... (put on).
3. I haven't heard from Rita lately. I might .... her .... (ring up).
4. Daniel has to go into college to .... his project .... (hand in).
5. I can't remember the address. I wish I'd .... it .... (write down).
6. Nick is trying to .... all the money he's just lost .... (win back).
7. I'm not going to have time to .... these dishes .... (wash up).
8. If you don't know the number, you can .... it .... (look up) in the phone book.
9. There was an accident which .... all the traffic coming into town .... (held up).
10. The words 'expect' and 'except' are so similar that I keep .... them .... (mix up).

129 Phrasal verbs (2)

A Everyday situations

Here are some phrasal verbs in everyday situations.
Come on, we're going now.
Trevor **dug up** an old coin in the garden.
You have to **fill in** your name and address.
How did you **get on** in the test?
I usually **get up** late on Sundays.
I'm **going out** for the evening.
Melanie poured tea for the guests and **handed** the cakes **round**.
Hurry up. We haven't got much time.
David hit his head on a lamppost and **knocked** himself **out**.
Mark **picked up** the cassette and put it in the player.
You have to **plug** the machine **in** first.
I'm going to **throw** these old clothes **away**.
We were too tired to **wash up** after the meal.
Sarah **woke up** suddenly in the night.

Look out! It's *boiling over*.

B Phrasal verbs and one-word verbs

Here are some phrasal verbs with the same meaning as a one-word verb (see also Unit 128B).
They're going to **bring in** a new law against drinking and driving. (= introduce)
How did the argument **come about**? (= happen)
Emma isn't speaking to Matthew. They've **fallen out**. (= quarrelled)
We've **fixed up** a meeting for next Tuesday. (= arranged)
Trevor **gave up** playing football years ago. (= stopped)
I had a pain in my arm, but it's **gone away**. (= disappeared)
We heard the bomb **go off** five miles away. (= explode)
The traffic was **held up** by road works. (= delayed)
The United Nations was **set up** to settle conflicts peacefully. (= established)
I'm trying to **work out** how much money I've spent. (= calculate)

C Business situations

Here are some examples of phrasal verbs in business situations.
If we're spending too much money, we'll have to **cut back**. (= spend less)
Our lawyers will **draw up** a new contract. (= write)
We mustn't **fall behind** in the race to develop new products. (= be slower than others)
The two sides were close to an agreement, but it **fell through**. (= didn't happen)
The company **fought off** a takeover by ICM Computers. (= managed to stop)
I tried to ring Santiago, but I couldn't **get through**. (= make contact)
The company has **laid off** two hundred workers because of a lack of new orders.
The computer will **print out** the details.
The consultants **put forward** a proposal to reorganize the company. (= suggested)
I'll get the information for you. Can I **ring you back** in half an hour? (= phone again)
Sarah paid a visit to the client to try to **sort out** the difficulties. (= put right)
The company boss has **stepped down** after ten years in charge. (= left the job)
We are **taking on** the challenge of expanding overseas. (= accepting)
Large companies sometimes **take over** smaller ones. (= take control of)

129 Exercises

1 Phrasal verbs in everyday situations (A)

Look at the pictures and say what is happening.
Use these phrasal verbs: *dig up, pick up, plug in, throw away, wash up*
Use these objects: *the armchair, litter, the plates, the road, the television*

▶ *They're throwing the armchair away.*
1 .... 3 ....
2 .... 4 ....

2 Phrasal verbs and one-word verbs (B)

Rewrite the sentences replacing each underlined verb with a phrasal verb.
▶ We're trying to arrange a holiday together.
  We're trying to fix up a holiday together.
1 Nick says he's stopped smoking.
  ....
2 How did the accident happen?
  ....
3 I think Matthew and Emma have quarrelled.
  ....
4 The problem isn't going to just disappear.
  ....
5 The government is introducing a new tax on computers.
  ....
6 Zedco want to establish a new sales office in Germany.
  ....

3 Business situations (C)

Complete the news article about Zedco. Put in these words: *fallen behind, fell through, fight off, laying off, put forward, sort out, step down, taking over, taken on*

Zedco Chief Executive Barry Douglas has (▶) *put forward* a new plan designed to
(1) .... the company's problems. It is only twelve months since Zedco tried to
strengthen its position by (2) .... Alpha Plastics. But the deal
(3) ...., and Alpha managed to (4) .... Zedco's attempts to
take control. Since then Zedco has performed poorly and has (5) .... in the race for
market share. Managing Director James Ironside has had to (6) ...., and Barry
Douglas has (7) .... the task of rescuing the company. There are fears that the new
plan will mean (8) .... staff in order to reduce expenditure.

130 Phrasal verbs (3)

A Introduction

Our advertising campaign has pushed sales **up**. I can show you on the screen. I'll just switch the computer **on**.

Here **up** has the sense of 'increasing', and **on** has the sense of 'connected'.

B Adverb meanings

Look at these adverbs and their meanings.
Remember that an adverb can have a number of different meanings.

down = becoming less
  turn **down** the music
  bring **down** the cost of living
down = completely to the ground
  knock a house **down**
  cut **down** a tree
down = stopping completely
  the car broke **down**
  a factory closing **down**
down = on paper
  copy **down** the words
  write **down** the message
  note **down** the details
off = away, departing
  set **off** on a journey
  jump in the car and drive **off**
  see Emma **off** at the station
  the plane took **off**
  the pain is wearing **off**
off = disconnected
  switch **off** the heater
  cut **off** our electricity
  the caller rang **off**
on = connected
  switch **on** the kettle
  turn **on** the TV
  leave the lights **on** all night
on = wearing
  put a coat **on**
  try the sweater **on**

on = continuing
  carry **on** working
  drive **on** a bit further
  hang **on**/hold **on** a minute
out = away, disappearing
  wash **out** the dirt
  cross **out** a mistake
  blow **out** the candle
out = to different people
  hand **out** free tickets
  share **out** the winnings
out = aloud
  read **out** the article
  call **out** anxiously
out = from start to finish
  write **out** the whole list
  work **out** the answer
over = from start to finish
  check your work **over**
  think the problem **over**
up = increasing
  prices are going **up**
  put **up** taxes
  speak **up** so we can hear
up = completely
  eat **up** these chocolates
  fill **up** with petrol
  count **up** the money
  tear **up** the paper

130 Exercises

1 Adverb meanings (B)

Look back at B and then write the meaning of the underlined words in these sentences.
- ▶ I must get these ideas <u>down</u> in writing.   *on paper*
1. Daniel finished all the cake <u>up</u>. ....
2. I'm writing in pencil so I can rub <u>out</u> my mistakes. ....
3. Vicky didn't answer. She just went <u>on</u> reading. ....
4. I'll just read <u>over</u> what I've written. ....
5. A woman in the audience shouted something <u>out</u>. ....
6. The water was turned <u>off</u> for about an hour today. ....
7. Nick's aggressive manner frightens people <u>off</u>. ....
8. The company wants to keep its costs <u>down</u>. ....
9. The embassy was burnt <u>down</u> by terrorists. ....
10. Someone will have to type all these figures <u>out</u>. ....
11. Social workers were giving <u>out</u> soup to the hungry. ....
12. Luckily Zedco's sales figures are moving <u>up</u> again. ....
13. The man was tall and dark. He had a blue jacket <u>on</u>. ....
14. Business is so bad that many firms have shut <u>down</u>. ....

2 Adverb meanings (B)

Put in the correct adverb.
- ▶ Melanie: Everything is so expensive. Prices seem to be going *up* all the time.
  David: Yes, and the government is supposed to be bringing inflation *down*.
1. Laura: You shouldn't leave the television .... all night.
   Trevor: Sorry, I forgot. I usually turn it ....
2. Vicky: I've written the wrong word here.
   Rachel: Well, rub it ....
   Vicky: I can't. It's in biro. I'll have to write the whole thing .... again.
3. Sarah: They're going to pull .... this beautiful old building.
   Mark: I know. Some protesters were handing .... leaflets about it.
4. Emma: Hold .... a minute. I thought I heard someone call ....
   Matthew: I think you must have imagined it.

3 Adverb meanings (B)

What are they saying? Put in the phrasal verbs.

- ▶ I'm afraid the car has *broken down*
1. Why don't you .... this coat?
2. Look, the plane is ....
3. I can't hear. Please ....
4. We're just .... on holiday.

131 Verb + adverb + preposition

A Simple meanings

Look at these examples.

	VERB	ADVERB	PREPOSITION	
So you've	come	in	from	the cold.
The old man	fell	down	on	the pavement.
I couldn't	get	through	to	directory enquiries.
David decided to	get	up	onto	the roof.
It was nice to	go	out	into	the fresh air.
We	look	out	over	the sea.
Everyone	looked	up	at	the aeroplane.
Vicky	ran	away	from	the fire.

B Idiomatic meanings

A verb + adverb + preposition often has a special, idiomatic meaning which isn't clear from the individual words. Look at these examples.

Tom often **calls in on/drops in on** us without warning. (= pays short visits)
You go on ahead. I'll soon **catch up with** you. (= reach the same place as)
The police are going to **clamp down on** drug dealers. (= take strong action against)
I'm afraid we've **come up against** another difficulty. (= be stopped by)
Did Claire's trip **come up to/live up to** her expectations? (= Was it as good as she expected?)
The country is **crying out for** a new leader. (= in great need of)
We need to **cut back on** our spending. (= reduce)
I'm trying to lose weight. I have to **cut down on** puddings. (= reduce)
They should **do away with** these useless traditions. (= abolish)
You've got to **face up to** your responsibilities. You can't just ignore them. (= not avoid)
If plan A doesn't work, we've got plan B to **fall back on**. (= use if necessary)
I'm tired, Mark. I don't really **feel up to** going out. (= have enough energy for)
We can't go on holiday together if your dates don't **fit in with** mine. (= go together with)
The thief managed to **get away with** about £2,000 in cash. (= steal and take away)
The goods are damaged. We'll have to **get on to** our suppliers. (= contact)
You haven't packed your suitcase yet. You'd better **get on with** it. (= start, continue)
Mark doesn't really **get on with** Alan. They're always arguing. (= have a good relationship with)
I have lots of little jobs to do, but I can never **get round to** actually doing them. (= find the right time for)
I can't make a promise and then **go back on** it, can I? (= break, fail to keep)
Matthew has decided to **go in for** the ten-mile 'Fun Run' this year. (= enter, compete in)
Most of the audience had left in the interval, but the actors decided to **go on with** the show. (= continue)
If you **hold on to** the rope, you'll be perfectly safe. (= keep your hands around)
Daniel was walking so fast I couldn't **keep up with** him. (= go as fast as)
I'm **looking forward to** the trip. (= thinking ahead with pleasure about)
If you're going barefoot, **look out for/watch out for** broken glass. (= be careful about)
I got some money from the insurance company, but nothing could **make up for** losing my wedding ring. (= compensate for)
I'm not going to **put up with** this nonsense. (= tolerate)
We've **run out of** milk, I'm afraid. (= We have none left.)
Are you going to **send away for** your free gift? (= write to ask for)

131 Exercises

1 Simple meanings (A)

Put in these words: *away from, down on, in from, out into, through to, up at, up onto*

▶ To reach the light bulb, Trevor had to get *up onto* the table.
1. Nick hurt himself when he was skating. He fell .... the ice.
2. It was a very long tunnel, but we finally came .... the sunshine.
3. Wondering if it was going to rain, Vicky looked .... the clouds.
4. People were running .... the gunman as fast as they could.
5. I'm trying to phone my secretary, but I can't get .... the office.
6. When I've come .... the cold, I just want to sit by the fire.

2 Idiomatic meanings (B)

Put in a verb + adverb + preposition which means the same as the expression in brackets.

▶ I'm afraid this product doesn't *live up to* (be as good as) the claims made in the advertisement.
1. I'll just call at the garage. I don't want to .... (have none left) petrol.
2. If you want a catalogue, I'll .... (write to ask for) one.
3. We'd better .... (be careful about) sheep in the road.
4. I .... (think ahead with pleasure about) seeing you again soon, Emma.
5. The teacher was dictating so fast we couldn't .... (go as fast as) her.
6. Why should we have to .... (tolerate) this awful noise?
7. It's half past twelve. I'd better .... (start) making lunch.
8. Do you think the committee will .... (change) their earlier decision?
9. There was a problem with the cheque, so I decided to .... (contact) my bank immediately.
10. I always like to .... (enter) quiz competitions.
11. I'm trying to .... (reduce) the amount of coffee I drink.
12. I might lose my job. And I haven't got any savings to .... (use if necessary).
13. I've been meaning to reply to Rachel's letter, but I haven't managed to .... (find the right time for) it yet.
14. An apology alone cannot .... (compensate for) all the inconvenience.

3 Idiomatic meanings (B)

What might you say in these situations? Use the words in brackets.

▶ You're tired. You can't go jogging. (don't feel up)
I don't feel up to jogging.
1. You like Melanie. The two of you are very friendly. (I get)

2. You might go and see David. It would be a short visit. (might drop)

3. You don't mind what you do. You'll do the same as everyone else. (I'll fit)

4. You are too slow. Matthew is too far ahead of you. (can't catch up)

5. The sunny weather is nice. Last week was terrible. (is making up)

Test 22   Verbs with prepositions and adverbs (Units 126–131)

Test 22A
Put the words in the right order to form a statement.
▶ I won't forget the titles of the books. down / I've / them / written
   I've written them down.
1. I'll give you the money. for / I / must / my ticket / pay

2. I have to look smart. going to / I'm / on / put / that expensive grey coat I bought

3. Anna rang. invited / lunch / she's / to / us

4. Peter's got the photos. at / he's / looking / them

5. I wasn't allowed to go. from / leaving / me / prevented / the police

6. This programme is boring. going to / I'm / it / off / turn

Test 22B
Decide which word is correct.
▶ I'm not speaking to Oliver. I've fallen *out* with him.
   a) away   b) back   c) out   d) through
1. Everyone complained .... the awful food.
   a) about   b) for   c) on   d) over
2. You don't need this word. You should cross it ....
   a) down   b) out   c) over   d) up
3. It's late. How much longer are you going to go .... working?
   a) along   b) on   c) through   d) with
4. My shoes are dirty. I'd better take them .... before I come in.
   a) away   b) off   c) on   d) up
5. The bus journey costs more now. They've put the fares ....
   a) down   b) out   c) over   d) up
6. We all laughed .... the cartoon.
   a) at   b) for   c) on   d) to
7. We'd all decided to go on holiday together, but the plan fell ...., I'm afraid.
   a) away   b) back   c) out   d) through
8. I suppose you're being nice to make .... the awful way you behaved yesterday.
   a) away of   b) down on   c) in with   d) up for

Test 22C
Write the correct sentence.
▶ Could you be a little quieter, please? ~~I'm trying to concentrate at my work.~~
   I'm trying to concentrate on my work.
1. You haven't answered all the questions. ~~You've left one away.~~

2. Where is Bigbury? ~~I've never heard about it.~~

Test 22

3   The children were frightened of the dog. ~~They ran out of it.~~
    ....

4   Michelle has got the job. ~~You must congratulate her for her success.~~
    ....

5   My sister is in computers. ~~She's going to set out her own company.~~
    ....

6   I like Peter. ~~He reminds me about an old school friend of mine.~~
    ....

7   Adrian has a suggestion. ~~He wants to put it ahead at the meeting.~~
    ....

Test 22D

Read the story and write the missing words. Use one word only in each space.

This true story is about a policeman in New York City who had a wife he cared (▶) *for* very much. I don't know if you regard New York City (1) .... a dangerous place, but the hero of our story certainly did, and he warned his wife (2) .... the danger of walking the streets alone and the need to (3) .... out for muggers. But as he also believed (4) .... being prepared for the worst, he bought a can of gas that would protect his wife (5) .... muggers. It certainly seemed worth spending a few dollars (6) .... The idea is that you point the thing (7) .... your attacker and spray him with the gas, which knocks him (8) .... On the day he bought the gas, the policeman and his wife had arranged to go (9) .... for the evening. So he was looking (10) .... to giving her the can later on. When he got home from work, he had a bath and then sprayed some deodorant on himself. He knew nothing more until he (11) .... up in hospital the next day. He had picked (12) .... the wrong can and sprayed himself with the gas.

Test 22E

Complete the second sentence so that it has a similar meaning to the first. Use the word in brackets.
▶ I'm trying to find my diary. (looking)
   I'm looking for my diary.
1 You're too young to stop working. (give)
   ....
2 This bag is Janet's. (belongs)
   ....
3 Everyone continued working as usual. (carried)
   ....
4 They talked about the plan. (discussed)
   ....
5 I haven't got any money left. (run)
   ....
6 I told the police what the problem was. (explained)
   ....
7 I wouldn't tolerate such terrible conditions. (put)
   ....
8 They'll have to postpone the game. (off)
   ....

132 Direct speech and reported speech

A Direct speech
Look at these examples of direct speech.

Trevor: **I'm tired.**

Wasn't it Greta Garbo who said, **'I want to be alone'**?

'But I don't know Elaine,' *replied Claire.*

We can show that words are direct speech by putting them in quotation marks (' '). See page 373. Sometimes the words are put after the speaker's name, in the script of a play or film, for example. In a picture we can put the words in a speech bubble.

B Reported speech
In reported speech we give the meaning of what was said rather than the exact words.

Trevor says **he's tired**.

Wasn't it Greta Garbo who said **that she wanted to be alone**?

Claire replied **that she didn't know Elaine**.

The actress Melissa Livingstone and supermarket owner Ron Mason have announced that they are getting married next month. Melissa is sure they will be happy together, she told reporters.

In reported speech we often change the actual words, e.g. *'I'm tired'* → **he's tired**.
Sometimes the verb tense changes, e.g. *I want* → *she wanted* (see Unit 134).

In reporting we use verbs such as **announce, answer, explain, mention, promise, reply, say, suggest, tell, warn**. The most common of these are **say** and **tell** (see C). We can also report thoughts.
   We **think** the meal was expensive.   Nick **knew** Rita wanted to be with someone else.

When we report statements, we often use **that**, but we can sometimes leave it out.
   You promised **(that)** *you wouldn't be late.*   *Sarah was saying* **(that)** *there's a problem.*

C Tell or say?

TELL	SAY

We use **tell** if we want to mention the hearer (the person spoken to).
   Sarah's boss **told her** *she could leave early.*
   NOT *Sarah's boss told she could leave early.*
   Daniel **tells me** *he's ready.*
We use **tell** without an indirect object (e.g. **her, me**) only in the expressions **tell a story, tell the truth** and **tell a lie**.
	When we do not mention the hearer, we use **say**.
	   Sarah's boss **said** *she could leave early.*
	   NOT *Sarah's boss said her she could leave early.*
	   Daniel **says** *he's ready.*
	We sometimes use **to** after **say**, especially when the words are not reported.
	   The boss wanted to **say** *something* **to** *Sarah.*
	   What did Matthew **say to** *you?*

318   REPORTED SPEECH

132 Exercises

1 Reported speech (B)

Why are these people at the doctor's? What do they say is wrong with them?

▶ I get pains in my leg.

1 I can't sleep.

2 I've hurt my back.

3 I feel sick all the time.

4 I fell over and hurt myself.

▶ She says *she gets pains in her leg.*
1 She says ....
2 He says ....
3 ....
4 ....

2 Reported speech (B)

Who said what? Match the words to the people and report what they said.
If you can't match them, look at the answers at the bottom of the page.

- ▶ Mrs Thatcher   a) 'All the world's a stage.'
- 1 Stokeley Carmichael b) 'Black is beautiful.'
- 2 Galileo   c) 'Big Brother is watching you.'
- 3 Shakespeare   d) 'There is no such thing as society.'
- 4 George Orwell   e) 'The earth moves round the sun.'

▶ *Mrs Thatcher said that there is no such thing as society.*
1 ....
2 ....
3 ....
4 ....

3 Tell or say? (C)

Put in *tell* or *say*.

▶ All the experts *say* the earth is getting warmer.
▶ Did you *tell* Mark and Sarah how to find our house?
1 The Sales Manager is going to .... everyone about the meeting.
2 Vicky, why don't you just .... what the matter is?
3 They .... they're going to build a new Disney World here.
4 What did Natasha .... about her holiday plans?
5 Could you .... me the way to the train station, please?
6 The company should .... its employees what's going on.
7 You shouldn't .... lies, you know, Matthew.
8 Did you .... anything to Melanie about the barbecue?

Answers: 1 b)   2 e)   3 a)   4 c)

133 Reported speech: person, place and time

A Introduction

It's Friday afternoon. David is at Tom's flat. Tom has decided to have a party for all his friends.

A few minutes later Nick has arrived at the flat. Now David is reporting what Tom said. So instead of Tom's words **I'm having**, David says **he's having**.

The next day David is talking to Harriet. Now David is in a different place from where Tom first told him about the party. So instead of **here**, he says **at his flat**. And a day has passed since he first heard about it. It is now the day of the party. So instead of **tomorrow evening**, David says **this evening**.

B Changes in reported speech

Changes from direct speech to reported speech depend on changes in the situation.
We may have to make changes when we are reporting something another person has said, or when we report it in a different place or at a different time. Here are some typical changes.

Person:	I	→	he/she
	my	→	his/her
Place:	here	→	there, at the flat
Time:	now	→	then, at the time
	today	→	that day, on Monday, etc
	yesterday	→	the day before, the previous day
	tomorrow	→	the next/following day, on Saturday, etc
	this week	→	that week
	last week	→	the week before, the previous week
	an hour ago	→	an hour before/earlier

133 Exercises

1 Changes in reported speech (A–B)
Read what each person says and then complete the sentences.
▶ Vicky: Daniel told me on Friday that he'd had a job interview the previous day.
   Daniel had a job interview on *Thursday*.
1 Trevor: Laura tells me I need a haircut.
   .... needs a haircut.
2 Claire: My brother told me in 1997 that he expected to become Manager the following year.
   Claire's brother expected that he would become Manager in ....
3 Alice: I wanted to see Mark in April, but he said he was very busy that month.
   Mark was very busy in ....
4 Harriet: I saw Nick last week. He said he'd given up smoking the week before.
   Nick gave up smoking .... ago.

2 Changes of person (A–B)
Put in the missing words.

3 Changes of place and time (A–B)
Put in *here, that day, the day before, the next day, the week before*.
▶ Rachel (a week ago):   I'm taking my driving test tomorrow.
   You (today):   When I saw Rachel, she said she was taking her driving test *the next day*.
1 Emma (two days ago):   I've only had this new computer since yesterday.
   You (today):   Emma said she'd only had the new computer since ....
2 Matthew (a week ago):   I'm meeting a friend at the station later today.
   You (today):   Matthew said he was meeting a friend at the station later ....
3 Mark (in the street):   I'll see you in the office.
   You (in the office):   Mark said he would see me ....
4 Sarah (a month ago):   The conference was last week.
   You (today):   Sarah told me the conference had taken place ....

134 Reported speech: the tense change

A When do we change the tense?

After a past-tense verb (e.g. **said**), there is often a tense change.
  'It really **is** cold today.' → Vicky said it **was** cold.

If the statement is still up to date when we report it, then we have a choice.
We can either leave the tense the same, or we can change it.
  You said you **like/liked** chocolate.   Claire told me her father **owns/owned** a racehorse.
  Sarah said she**'s going/she was** going to Rome in April.
We can say that Sarah <u>is</u> going to Rome because it <u>is</u> still true that she will go there.

If the statement is no longer up to date, then we change the tense.
  Claire once told me that her father **owned** a racehorse. (He may no longer own one.)
  Sarah said she **was** going to Rome in April. (Now it is May.)
Now Sarah's trip is over, so it is no longer true that she <u>is</u> going to Rome.

We usually change the tense if we think the statement is untrue or may be untrue.
  You said you **liked** chocolate, but you aren't eating any.
  The Prime Minister claimed that the government **had** made the right decision.

B Is → was, like → liked, etc

Look at these examples of the tense change.

DIRECT SPEECH		REPORTED SPEECH
'Andrew **is** working.'	→	Jessica said Andrew **was** working.
'The windows **aren't** locked.'	→	Mark told me the windows **weren't** locked.
'I**'ve** fixed the shelves.'	→	Trevor said he**'d** fixed the shelves.
'It**'s been** raining.'	→	We noticed it **had been** raining.
'We**'ve** got plenty of time.'	→	Rachel insisted they **had** plenty of time.
'We **like** the flat.'	→	The couple said they **liked** the flat.

If the verb phrase is more than one word (e.g. **is working**), then the first word changes,
e.g. **is** working → **was** working, **have** fixed → **had** fixed, **don't** know → **didn't** know.
If the verb is already in the past tense, then it can stay the same or change to the past perfect.

'We **came** by car.'	→	They said they **came**/they **had come** by car.
'Sorry. I **wasn't** listening.'	→	I admitted I **wasn't** listening/**hadn't been** listening.

If the verb is past perfect, it stays the same.

'My money **had run** out.'	→	Daniel said his money **had run** out.

C Modal verbs: can → could, etc

Can, **may** and **will** change to **could**, **might** and **would**.

'You **can** sit over there.'	→	The steward said we **could** sit here.
'I **may** go to Bali again.'	→	Claire said she **might** go to Bali again.
'I**'ll** help if you like.'	→	Tom said he **would** help.

Could, **might**, **ought to**, **should** and **would** stay the same. But **must** can change to **have to**.

'Sarah **would** love a holiday.'	→	Mark thought Sarah **would** love a holiday.
'I **must** finish this report.'	→	Sarah said she **must** finish/**had to** finish the report.

322 REPORTED SPEECH

134 Exercises

1 When do we change the tense? (A)

Put in *is* or *was*. Sometimes both are possible.
▶ I heard today that the house *is* for sale. I wonder who will buy it.
▶ I saw David yesterday. He said he *was* on his way to visit his sister.
1 This wallet is made of plastic not leather. Why did you tell me it .... leather?
2 We had to hurry yesterday morning. Just as we arrived at the station, we heard an announcement that the train .... about to leave.
3 I saw Emma just now. She said her tooth .... still aching.
4 I'm surprised Matthew lost. I thought he .... much better at tennis than Daniel.
5 When he spoke to reporters yesterday, Mr Douglas said that Zedco .... now in a much better financial position.

2 The tense change (B)

Complete the replies. The second speaker is surprised at what he or she hears.
▶ Matthew: Emma and I are getting married.
  Rachel: Really? But you said last week *you weren't getting married.*
▶ Rita: I like pop music more than classical music.
  Laura: I'm sure you told me *you liked classical music best.*
1 Vicky: I haven't finished my project.
  Emma: Haven't you? I thought you said ....
2 Rachel: I'm on a diet.
  Natasha: But you told me ....
3 Andrew: I enjoy parties.
  Daniel: Surely I remember you saying ....
4 Matthew: I'm applying for the job.
  Rachel: I thought you told me ....

3 The tense change (B–C)

A comedy show called 'Don't Look Now!' has just closed after five years in London's West End. Here's what the critics said when it opened five years ago.

▶ 'It's a marvellous show.' *The Daily Mail*
▶ 'You'll love it.' *The Guardian*
1 'The production is brilliant.' *The Sunday Times*
2 'I can't remember a funnier show.' *Edward Devine*
3 'It made me laugh.' *Robert Walsh*
4 'You must see it.' *The Evening Standard*
5 'It will be a great success.' *The Telegraph*
6 'You might die laughing.' *The Express*
7 'It's the funniest show I've ever seen.' *Susan Proctor*
8 'You shouldn't miss it.' *Time Out*

Now report what the critics said.
▶ *The Daily Mail said it was a marvellous show.*
▶ *The Guardian said people would love it.*
1 ....
2 ....
3 ....
4 ....
5 ....
6 ....
7 ....
8 ....

135 Reported questions

A Wh-questions

We can report questions with verbs like **ask**, **wonder** or **want to know**. Look first at these wh-questions.

DIRECT QUESTION	REPORTED QUESTION
'**When** did you start acting, Melissa?' →	Guy **asked** Melissa **when** she started acting.
'**What**'s the time?' →	I just **asked what** the time is.
'**Which** way is the post office?' →	Someone **wants to know which** way the post office is.
'**How** can we find out?' →	I was **wondering how** we can find out.
'**Where** can we eat?' →	They're **asking where** they can eat.

Wh-questions have a word like **when**, **what**, **which** or **how** both in direct speech and in reported speech.

B Yes/no questions

DIRECT QUESTION	REPORTED QUESTION
'Has the taxi arrived yet?' ~ 'No, not yet.' →	Someone was **wondering if/whether** the taxi has arrived yet.
'Can we take photos?' ~ 'Yes, of course.' →	The visitors **want to know if/whether** they can take photos.
'Is there a café nearby?' ~ 'No.' →	Daniel **asked if/whether** there was a café nearby.

Reported yes/no questions have **if** or **whether**.

C Word order

In a reported question the subject comes before the verb, as in a statement.
  Guy asked Melissa when **she started** acting.
  NOT Guy asked Melissa when did she start acting.
  Someone was wondering if **the taxi has** arrived yet.
  NOT Someone was wondering if has the taxi arrived yet.

D Asking for information

To ask politely for information, we sometimes use a reported question after a phrase like
Could you tell me …? or **Do you know** …?
  Could you tell me what time the concert starts?
  Do you know if there's a public phone in the building?
  Have you any idea how much a taxi would cost?
Note the word order **a taxi would cost** (see C).

E The tense change: **is** → **was**, etc

In reported speech there are often changes to the tense, to pronouns and so on.
This depends on changes to the situation since the words were spoken.
For details see Units 133 and 134. Here are some examples of the tense change.

'What's the problem?' →	We asked what the problem **was**.
'How much money **have** you got, Vicky?' →	I was wondering how much money Vicky **had**.
'**Does** Nick **need** a lift?' →	Tom asked if Nick **needed** a lift.
'**Can** you type?' →	They asked me if I **could** type.

324 REPORTED SPEECH

135 Exercises

1 Reported questions (A–C)

These people are at the tourist information centre. What do they want to know?

▶ *She wants to know what the most interesting sights are.*
▶ *He wants to know if the centre has got a town plan.*
1 ....
2 ....
3 ....
4 ....

2 Asking for information (D)

You need information. Ask for it using *Could you tell me …?* or *Do you know …?*
▶ Where are the toilets? (tell)   *Could you tell me where the toilets are?*
1 Can I park here? (know)   ....
2 How long does the film last? (tell) ....
3 How often do the buses run? (know)   ....
4 Are we allowed to smoke? (know)   ....
5 What time is the flight? (tell)   ....
6 How much does a ticket cost? (tell) ....

3 The tense change (E)

Barry Douglas, Zedco Chief Executive, is talking to a reporter about his business career.
He can still remember his first job interview after leaving school.

Interviewer:	Barry:
▶ 'Where do you live?'	The interviewer asked me *where I lived*.
▶ 'Have you worked before?'	She asked me *if I had worked before*.
1 'Why do you want the job?'	She wanted to know ....
2 'How did you hear about it?'	I remember she asked ....
3 'Are you fit?'	She wondered ....
4 'Can you work on Saturdays?'	Then she asked me ....
5 'How will you travel to work?'	She wanted to know ....
6 'Have you got a bicycle?'	And she asked me ....
7 'How much do you hope to earn?'	She also asked ....
8 'When can you start?'	And finally she asked ....

136 Reported requests, offers, etc

A Reported orders and requests

We can use the structure **tell/ask someone to do something**.

DIRECT SPEECH	REPORTED SPEECH
'Please move this car.' →	A policeman **told me to move** the car.
'You really must be careful.' →	Melanie is always **telling David to be** careful.
'Would you mind turning the music down?' →	We **asked our neighbours to turn** the music down.

The negative is **tell/ask someone not to do something**.

DIRECT SPEECH	REPORTED SPEECH
'You mustn't leave the door unlocked.' →	Mr Atkins **told Mark not to leave** the door unlocked.
'Please don't wear those boots in the house.' →	I **asked you not to wear** those boots in the house.

We can also use the structure **ask to do something**.

'Can I see your ticket, please?' →	The inspector **asked to see** my ticket.

We use **ask for** when someone asks to have something.

'Can I have some brochures, please?' →	I **asked** (the travel agent) **for** some brochures.

It is also possible to report an order or request like this.
> A policeman told me (that) I had to move the car.
> We asked our neighbours if they would mind turning the music down.

B Reported offers, suggestions, etc

We can use **agree, offer, promise, refuse** and **threaten** with a to-infinitive.

DIRECT SPEECH	REPORTED SPEECH
'We'll pay for the damage.' →	We **offered to pay** for the damage.
'I'll definitely finish it by the end of next week.' →	You **promised to finish** the work by the end of this week.

We can also use an object + to-infinitive after **advise, invite, remind** and **warn**.

'I think you should take a taxi.' →	Mark **advised us to take** a taxi.
'Don't forget to ring me.' →	I **reminded David to ring** me.

We can use an ing-form after **admit, apologize for, insist on** and **suggest**.

'I really must have a rest.' →	Emma **insisted on having** a rest
'Shall we go to a restaurant?' →	Claire **suggested going** to a restaurant.

C Admit that, insist that, etc

We can use a clause with **that** after **admit, advise, agree, insist, promise, remind, suggest** and **warn**.
> Trevor **admitted (that)** he had forgotten the shopping.
> Claire **insisted (that)** we all went round to her flat for coffee.
> You **promised (that)** you would finish the work by the end of this week.
> I **warned you (that)** Nick's dog is very fierce.

▷ 62 Verb + to-infinitive/ing-form ▷ 65 Verb + object + to-infinitive

136 Exercises

1 Tell/ask someone to do something (A)

Trevor isn't feeling very happy. Everyone has been telling him what to do. Report the orders and requests.

▶ His mother: Can you dig my garden, please, Trevor?
His mother asked him to dig her garden.

1 The doctor: You must take more exercise.
   ....

2 His boss: Would you mind not playing computer games in the office?
   ....

3 A traffic warden: You can't park your car in the High Street.
   ....

4 Laura: Could you put some shelves up, please, Trevor?
   ....

2 Reported offers, suggestions, etc (B)

Complete the sentences. Report what was said.

▶ Would you like to stay for lunch, Claire?
▶ All right. I won't talk about football.
1 You ought to take a break, Andrew.
2 I'm sorry I forgot the shopping.
3 Why don't we sing a few songs?
4 You're going to post the letter, don't forget, Vicky.
5 Yes, I made a mistake.
6 Laura! Don't touch the electric wires!

▶ Sarah invited *Claire to stay for lunch.*
▶ Tom agreed *not to talk about football.*
1 Matthew advised ....
2 Mike apologized ....
3 Tom suggested ....
4 Rachel reminded ....
5 Mr Atkins admitted ....
6 Trevor warned ....

3 Admit that, insist that, etc (C)

Combine each pair of sentences using *that*.

▶ The roads were dangerous. The police warned us.
   The police warned us that the roads were dangerous.

1 Everything will be ready on time. The builders have promised.
   ....

2 We have to check the figures carefully. The boss insists.
   ....

3 Tom's story wasn't completely true. He's admitted it.
   ....

4 Emma's train was about to leave. Matthew reminded her.
   ....

Test 23 Reported speech (Units 132–136)

Test 23A

Some of these sentences are correct, and some have a word which should not be there. If the sentence is correct, put a tick (✓). If it is incorrect, cross the unnecessary word out of the sentence and write it in the space.

▶ You promised you wouldn't be late.   ✓
▶ Susan thought 'That I can't understand what's happening.'   that
1 Do you know me what time the coach leaves?   ....
2 Robert wanted to know if did the price included breakfast.   ....
3 Anna insisted on showing us her photos.   ....
4 Someone asked us whether that we had eaten lunch.   ....
5 Nancy told me she had started the job the week before.   ....
6 Nigel said me he wanted to come with us.   ....
7 My friend said she did liked her new flat.   ....
8 Martin asked us for not to wake the baby.   ....

Test 23B

Decide which word is correct.

▶ What did that man say *to you*?
  a) at you   b) for you   c) to you   d) you
1 I rang my friend in Australia yesterday, and she said it .... raining there.
  a) is   b) should be   c) to be   d) was
2 The last time I saw Jonathan, he looked very relaxed. He explained that he'd been on holiday the .... week.
  a) earlier   b) following   c) next   d) previous
3 I wonder .... the tickets are on sale yet.
  a) what   b) when   c) where   d) whether
4 I told you .... switch off the computer, didn't I?
  a) don't   b) not   c) not to   d) to not
5 Someone .... me there's been an accident on the motorway.
  a) asked   b) said   c) spoke   d) told
6 When I rang Tessa some time last week, she said she was busy .... day.
  a) that   b) the   c) then   d) this
7 When he was at Oliver's flat yesterday, Martin asked if he .... use the phone.
  a) can   b) could   c) may   d) must
8 Judy .... going for a walk, but no one else wanted to.
  a) admitted   b) offered   c) promised   d) suggested

Test 23C

Read the news report and write the missing words. Use one word only in each space. Sometimes there is more than one possible answer.

Police have warned people (▶) *to* watch out for two men who have tricked their way into an old woman's home and stolen money. The men called on Mrs Iris Raine and said (1) .... were from the water company and wanted to check (2) .... her water was OK. They asked if (3) .... would mind letting them into her house. The woman didn't ask (4) .... see their identity cards. She said she (5) .... know about any problem with the water.

328 REPORTED SPEECH

The men explained that they (6) .... just discovered the problem but that it was very simple and (7) .... take long to check. The woman asked (8) .... the service was free, and they said yes. They (9) .... to know where the water tank was. While one man ran water in the kitchen, the other went upstairs and took several hundred pounds from a drawer in a bedroom. The men then left saying that they would return the (10) .... day to have another look.

Test 23D

Complete each sentence by reporting what was said to you yesterday.
Use *said* and change the tense in the reported speech.

▶ Polly: I'm really tired.
When I saw Polly yesterday, *she said she was really tired.*

1 Tessa: I feel quite excited.
When I saw Tessa yesterday, ...

2 Nigel: I can't remember the code word.
When I saw Nigel yesterday, ...

3 Robert: I won't be at the next meeting.
When I saw Robert yesterday, ...

4 The twins: We've got a problem.
When I saw the twins yesterday, ...

5 Michelle: I've been swimming.
When I saw Michelle yesterday, ...

6 Your friends: We would like to be in the show.
When I saw my friends yesterday, ...

7 Adrian: I don't need any help.
When I saw Adrian yesterday, ...

8 Susan: My sister is coming to see me.
When I saw Susan yesterday, ...

Test 23E

Report the sentences. They were all spoken last week. Use the verbs in brackets.

▶ Anna to Janet: Don't forget to sign the form. (remind)
Anna reminded Janet to sign the form.

▶ Robert: What time will the office close this evening? (ask)
Robert asked what time the office would close that evening.

1 A policeman to Christopher: Stop shouting. (tell)
....

2 Tessa: It was me. I ate all the cake yesterday. (admit)
....

3 Adrian: I'm sorry I was rude. (apologize)
....

4 Simon to Susan: Would you like to join me for lunch? (invite)
....

5 Martin to Nancy: Did someone ring you an hour ago? (ask)
....

6 Peter: I really must leave. (insist)
....

137 Relative clauses with **who, which** and **that**

A Introduction

Emma: I saw Natalie the other day.
Melanie: Natalie? The girl **who plays the piano**?
Emma: No, that's Natasha. Natalie is the student **who dropped out of college**, the one **who never did any studying**. She's working in Davidson's now, the shop **that sells very expensive clothes**.

The relative clauses in this conversation identify which person or thing we are talking about. The clause **who plays the piano** tells us which girl Melanie means. The clause **that sells very expensive clothes** tells us which shop Emma means.

Sometimes we can use an adjective or a phrase to identify someone or something.
Adjective: the **tall** girl   the **new** student   the **red** car
Phrase: the man **in the suit**   the shop **on the corner**   the woman **with red hair**
But when we need a longer explanation, we can use a relative clause.
Relative clause: the woman **who gets up early**   the car **that broke down**

B Who, which and that

The relative pronouns **who**, **which** and **that** go after the noun and at the beginning of the relative clause.

Who refers to people.
  Nick is the **man who** owns that enormous dog.   I don't like **people who** tell jokes all the time.
  The little **girl who** sat next to me on the coach ate sweets the whole way.
  Sarah is pretty annoyed with the **person who** stole her mobile phone.
We can also use **that**, but it is less usual.
  Jake is the **man that** plays the guitar.
  The **woman that** lived here before us is a romantic novelist.

That and **which** refer to things. **That** is more usual than **which**, especially in conversation.
  The **car that** won the race looked very futuristic, didn't it?
  They've recaptured all the **animals that** escaped from the zoo.
  The children saw the actual **spacecraft that** landed on the moon.

Which can be a little formal.
  There are several **restaurants which** do Sunday lunches.
  Is Zedco the **company which** was taken over last year?

We do not use another pronoun like **he** or **it** with the relative pronoun.
  NOT ~~the man who he owns that enormous dog~~
  NOT ~~the actual spacecraft that it landed on the moon~~

In all these sentences **who**, **which** and **that** are the subject of the relative clause.
For **who**, **which** and **that** as object, see Units 138 and 139.

330   RELATIVE CLAUSES

137 Exercises

1 Identifying (A)

Look at the information and identify which one is meant.
Use the shortest way of identifying where possible, e.g. *the tall boy*, not *the boy who is tall*.

▶ the boy (he is tall) → *the tall boy*
▶ the man (he has a beard) → *the man with a beard*
▶ the woman (she plays golf) → *the woman who plays golf*
1 the young man (he is at the door) → ....
2 the man (he plays his stereo at night) → ....
3 the woman (she is very thin) → ....
4 the girl (she has green eyes) → ....
5 the young woman (she is in the office) → ....
6 the man (he drives a taxi) → ....
7 the young man (he is smart) → ....
8 the student (she failed all her exams) → ....

2 Who, which and that (B)

Complete the conversation. Put in *who, which* or *that*. There is always more than one possible answer.
Emma: Shall we have something to eat?
Matthew: Yes, but not here. I don't like cafés (▶) *that* don't have chairs. I'm not one of those people (▶) *who* can eat standing up.
Emma: There's another restaurant over there.
Matthew: It looks expensive, one of those places (1) .... charge very high prices. The only customers (2) .... can afford to eat there are business executives (3) .... get their expenses paid. Anyway, I can't see a menu. I'm not going into a restaurant (4) .... doesn't display a menu.
Emma: We just passed a café (5) .... does snacks.
Matthew: Oh, I didn't like the look of that.
Emma: You're one of those people (6) .... are never satisfied, aren't you?

3 Relative clauses (A–B)

Combine the information to make news items. Make the sentence in brackets
into a relative clause with *who* or *which*. Start each sentence with *the*, e.g. *The man …*

▶ A man has gone to prison. (He shot two policemen.)
  The man who shot two policemen has gone to prison.
1 A bomb caused a lot of damage. (It went off this morning.)
  ....
2 A scientist has won the Nobel Prize. (He discovered a new planet.)
  ....
3 A footballer has been banned from playing again. (He took drugs.)
  ....
4 A little girl has been found safe and well. (She had been missing since Tuesday.)
  ....
5 A company has laid off thousands of workers. (It owns Greenway Supermarkets.)
  ....
6 An old lady now wants to swim the English Channel. (She did a parachute jump.)
  ....

138 The relative pronoun as object

A Subject and object

Harriet is showing David her holiday photos.
Harriet: *That's an old castle **that we visited** on holiday. And those are some people **we met**, a couple **who were staying at the campsite**.*
David: *Mm. They look very friendly.*

A relative pronoun such as **who** or **that** can be the subject of a relative clause.

Harriet talked to a couple **who** *were staying at the camp-site.*
(**They** were staying at the camp-site.)

The postcard **that** *came this morning was from Harriet.*
(**It** came this morning.)

A relative pronoun can also be the object of a relative clause.

Mike and Harriet are visiting a woman **who** *they met on holiday.*
(They met **her** on holiday.)

The old castle **that** *we visited was really interesting.*
(We visited **it**.)

We do not use another pronoun like **her** or **it** with the relative pronoun.
NOT *a woman who they met her* NOT *the old castle that we visited it*

B Leaving out the relative pronoun

We can leave out the relative pronoun when it is the object of the relative clause. We do this especially in spoken English. Compare these examples.

WITH OBJECT PRONOUN	WITHOUT OBJECT PRONOUN
The man **who Vicky saw** at the concert is Sarah's boss.	The man **Vicky saw** at the concert is Sarah's boss.
That's an old castle **that we visited**.	That's an old castle **we visited**.

Here are some more examples of relative clauses without an object pronoun.
*We don't know the name of the person **the police are questioning**.*
*The cakes **Melanie baked** were delicious.*
*That jacket **you're wearing** is falling to pieces, Mike.*

Remember that we cannot leave out a pronoun when it is the subject of a relative clause.
*The man **who** spoke to Vicky is Sarah's boss.*

C Who and whom

In formal English, **whom** is sometimes used when the object of the relative clause is a person.
*The person **who/whom** the police were questioning has now been released.*
But in conversation **whom** is not very common.

138 Exercises

1 Subject and object (A)

Comment on the conversations. Add a sentence with *who* or *that* as the subject of the underlined part.
► She's Tom's new secretary. ~ Who is? ~ That girl. She just said hello.
That's right. The *girl who just said hello is Tom's new secretary.*
1 The dog has been rescued. ~ What dog? ~ It fell down a hole.
Haven't you heard? The ....
2 The story was untrue. ~ What story? ~ You know. It upset everyone.
Yes, the ....
3 He's a film producer. ~ Who is? ~ That man. He interviewed Natasha.
That's what I heard. The ....

Now comment on these conversations. Add a sentence with *who* or *that* as the object of the underlined part.
4 The accident wasn't very serious. ~ What accident? ~ Oh, Daniel saw it.
Yes, the ....
5 He's a millionaire. ~ Who is? ~ That man. Claire knows him.
It's true. The ....
6 The vase was extremely valuable. ~ What vase? ~ You know. David broke it.
That's right. The ....
7 It's really nice. ~ What is? ~ The jacket. Melanie wore it at the party.
Yes, it is. The ....

2 Leaving out the relative pronoun (B)

Complete the script for these TV advertisements. Use a relative clause without a pronoun.
► Fresho soap. Beautiful people use it. *It's the soap beautiful people use.*
1 An Everyman car. You can afford it. ....
2 'Hijack'. People want to see this film. ....
3 Greenway Supermarket. You can trust it. ....
4 'Cool' magazine. Young people read it. ....
5 Jupiter chocolates. You'll love them. ....

3 Leaving out the relative pronoun (B)

Look carefully at these sentences. Are they correct without a relative pronoun? Where you see ★, you may need to put in *who, which* or *that*. Write the sentences and put in a pronoun only if you have to.
► The man ★ paid for the meal was a friend of Tom's.
The man who paid for the meal was a friend of Tom's.
► The meeting ★ Mark had to attend went on for three hours.
The meeting Mark had to attend went on for three hours.
1 Somewhere I've got a photo of the mountain ★ we climbed.
....
2 The man ★ repaired my car is a real expert.
....
3 The detective lost sight of the man ★ he was following.
....
4 I thought I recognized the assistant ★ served us.
....
5 I'm afraid the numbers ★ I chose didn't win a prize.
....

139 Prepositions in relative clauses

A Introduction

A relative pronoun (e.g. **that**) can be the object of a preposition (e.g. **for**).

This is the bus | that | I've been waiting **for**.
I've been waiting **for** | the bus.

The restaurant | that | we normally go **to** is closed today.
We normally go **to** | the restaurant.

In informal spoken English we normally put the preposition at the end of the relative clause. Compare the word order.

STATEMENT	RELATIVE CLAUSE
I've been waiting for the bus.	*the bus that I've been waiting for*
We go to the restaurant.	*the restaurant that we go to*

We do not use another pronoun like **it** or **her** after the preposition.
  NOT *the restaurant that we go to it*   NOT *someone who I work with her*

B Leaving out the pronoun

We often leave out the relative pronoun when it is the object of a preposition.

WITH OBJECT PRONOUN	WITHOUT OBJECT PRONOUN
*The bus **that** I'm waiting **for** is late.*	*The bus I'm waiting **for** is late.*
*Is this the article **which** you were interested **in**?*	*Is this the article you were interested **in**?*
*That's the man **who** I was talking **about**.*	*That's the man I was talking **about**.*

Here are some more examples of relative clauses without an object pronoun.
  *I can't remember the name of the hotel **we stayed at**.*
  *This is the colour **we've finally decided on**.*
  *The shop **I got my stereo from** has lots of bargains.*

C A preposition at the beginning

These examples are typical of formal English.
  *Was that the restaurant **to which** you normally go?*
  *Electronics is a subject **about which** I know very little.*
  *The Sales Manager is the person **from whom** I obtained the figures.*
Here the preposition comes at the beginning of the relative clause, before **which** or **whom**.

We cannot put a preposition before **that** or **who**.
  a subject (that) I know little about NOT *a subject about that I know little*
  the person (who) I got the figures from NOT *the person from who I got the figures*

▷ 138C **Whom**

139 Exercises

1 A preposition at the end (A–B)
What are they saying? Put in sentences with a preposition at the end.

▶ (Mark has been looking for this letter.) *This is the letter I've been looking for.*
1 (Rachel was talking about that film.) ....
2 (Laura has decided on this wallpaper.) ....
3 (Matthew played tennis with that man.) ....
4 (David fell down those steps.) ....

2 A preposition at the end (A–B)
Match the phrases and write the definitions. Put the preposition at the end of the relative clause.

▶ a kitchen   a cupboard   you hit nails with it
1 a hammer   the person   you keep valuable things in it
2 your destination   a piece of furniture   you cook in it
3 a safe   the place   you can either sit or sleep on it
4 your opponent   a room   you're going to it
5 a sofa bed   a tool   you're playing against them

▶ *A kitchen is a room you cook in.*
1 ....
2 ....
3 ....
4 ....
5 ....

3 A preposition at the beginning (C)
It's election time. All the politicians are arguing.
Rewrite the first sentence using a preposition at the beginning of a relative clause.

▶ I cannot agree with that statement. I hope I've made that clear.
That is a statement with which I cannot agree.
1 Our party believes in that idea. I say this from the bottom of my heart. ....
....
2 I am strongly opposed to that policy. And I am not afraid to say so. ....
....
3 No one cares about these people. They are the forgotten people. ....
....
4 Your party should be ashamed of those mistakes. And everyone knows that. ....
....
5 The government is now dealing with that problem. How many times do I have to tell you?
....

140 Relative structures with **whose**, **what** and **it**

A Whose

Vicky: *What I'd really like is a job in television.*
Daniel: *The other day I met a man **whose sister** works in television.*
Vicky: *Who? What's her name?*
Daniel: *Oh, I don't know. She's the woman **whose car** Tom crashed into.*

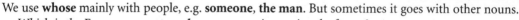

Here **whose sister** means his sister (the sister of the man Daniel met), and **whose car** means her car (the car belonging to the woman). Here are some more examples.

*Someone **whose bicycle** had been stolen was reporting it to the police.*
*Wayne Johnson is the man **whose goal** won the game for United.*

We use **whose** mainly with people, e.g. **someone**, **the man**. But sometimes it goes with other nouns.

*Which is the European **country whose** economy is growing the fastest?*
*Round the corner was a **building whose** windows were all broken.*
*Melanie was looking after a **dog whose** leg had been broken in an accident.*

B What

We use the relative pronoun **what** without a noun in front of it.

*The shop didn't have **what** I wanted.* (= the thing that I wanted)
***What** we saw gave us quite a shock.* (= the thing that we saw)

We can also use **what** to give emphasis to a word or phrase, to make it more important. Compare these examples.

NEUTRAL	EMPHATIC
Rachel's stereo kept me awake.	**What** kept me awake was **Rachel's stereo**.
Vicky is looking for a job in television.	**What** Vicky is looking for is **a job in television**.
I want to make a fresh start.	**What** I want to do is **make a fresh start**.
They booked a holiday together.	**What** they did was **book a holiday together**.

C It

We also use **it** + **be** + a relative clause to give emphasis.

NEUTRAL	EMPHATIC
Tom had an accident.	**It was Tom** who had an accident (not David).
The computer gives me a headache.	**It's the computer** that gives me a headache.
I'm eating chocolate cake.	**It's chocolate cake** (that) I'm eating.
Mike's uncle died on Thursday.	**It was on Thursday** that Mike's uncle died.

We must put in a pronoun when it is the subject of the relative clause (e.g. **who** had an accident). If it is the object (e.g. **that** I'm eating), then we can leave it out (see Unit 138B).

140 Exercises

1 Who or whose? (A)

You are reading a crime story. One of these people has murdered the industrialist Colin Howard. Look at the detective's notes and write a sentence about each person. Use a relative clause with *who* or *whose*.

▶ George Paxton, company director – he had an argument with Colin
   George is the company director who had an argument with Colin.
▶ Vera Stokes, politician – her sister once worked for Colin
   Vera is the politician whose sister once worked for Colin.
1 Felix Reeves, journalist – his tape recorder was stolen
   ....
2 Graham Wilshaw, architect – he knew Colin at school
   ....
3 Rex Carter, farmer – Colin bought his land
   ....
4 Norman Bridge, lawyer – he looked after Colin's interests
   ....
5 Sonia Goldman, house guest – her fingerprints were on the door handle
   ....

2 What (B)

Zedco Chief Executive Barry Douglas is telling a group of managers how to run a business successfully. He emphasizes the underlined words using *what*.

▶ You must pay attention to <u>the details</u>.
   What you must pay attention to are the details.
1 You have to think about <u>your profit</u>.
   ....
2 You must know <u>the needs of your customers</u>.
   ....
3 You should work towards <u>a realistic target</u>.
   ....
4 You need to <u>plan ahead</u>.
   ....

3 It (C)

Quiz champion Claude Jennings is answering some questions.
Look at each question and answer and write a sentence with *it* + *be* + a relative clause.

▶ Who invented radio? ~ Marconi.
   It was Marconi who *invented radio.*
1 When did Columbus sail to America? ~ In 1492.
   It was in 1492 that ....
2 What does Tiger Woods play? ~ Golf.
   It's ....
3 Where did the Olympic Games first take place? ~ In Greece.
   ....
4 Which is nearest the sun, Venus or Mercury? ~ Mercury.
   ....

141 The use of relative clauses

A Introduction

There are two kinds of relative clause. Compare this conversation and newspaper report.

Laura: *Art Golding has died.*
Trevor: *Who?*
Laura: *You know. The film star **who played the ship's captain in 'Iceberg'.***
Trevor: *I don't think I've seen that.*
Laura: *Yes, you have. It's the film **we saw on TV the other night.***

ART GOLDING DIES

The actor Art Golding, who starred in films such as 'Tornado' and 'Iceberg', has died after a long illness. He was seventy-eight. Art Golding's most famous role was as the scientist in the film 'Supernova', which broke all box-office records.

The clauses in this conversation identify which film star and which film Laura means. They are called identifying clauses.

The clauses in this report add information about Art Golding and about 'Supernova'. They are called adding clauses, or sometimes non-identifying clauses.

B Identifying clauses and adding clauses

IDENTIFYING	ADDING
*The man **who lives next door to Melanie** is rather strange.*	*Jake, **who lives next door to Melanie**, is rather strange.*
*The river **which flows through Hereford** is the Wye.*	*The Wye **(which flows through Hereford)** is a beautiful river.*
*The picture **which was damaged** is worth thousands of pounds.*	*This famous picture – **which was damaged during the war** – is worth thousands of pounds.*
These clauses identify which thing the speaker is talking about. The clause **who lives next door to Melanie** tells us which man. The clause **which flows through Hereford** tells us which river. Without the relative clause the sentence would be incomplete. **The man is rather strange** makes sense only if we know which man.	These clauses add extra information about something which is already identified. The clause **who lives next door to Melanie** adds information about Jake. But we can say the sentence on its own without the relative clause. **Jake is rather strange** makes sense because the name **Jake** identifies who we are talking about.
An identifying clause does not have commas around it.	An adding clause has commas around it. Instead of commas, we can use brackets ( ) or dashes – –. If the adding clause is at the end of the sentence, we need only one comma or dash. *That's Jake, who lives next door.*
Most relative clauses are identifying. We use them both in speech and in writing.	Adding clauses can be rather formal. We use them mainly in writing. They are common in news reports. In speech we often use two short sentences. *Jake lives next door to Melanie. He's rather strange.*

▷ 137A Identifying clauses ▷ 142A Pronouns in identifying and adding clauses

338 RELATIVE CLAUSES

141 Exercises

1 Adding clauses (A)

Match the parts and write sentences with an adding clause. Use *who* or *which*.

▶	The Grand Canyon	He was in prison for 27 years.	He was one of the Beatles.
1	Nelson Mandela	He was killed in 1980.	He became President of South Africa.
2	John Lennon	It is 140 million miles away.	It is one of the wonders of the world.
3	The Titanic	It is over 200 miles long.	It is known as the red planet.
4	Queen Victoria	It sank in 1912.	It stood for 28 years.
5	Mars	It was built in 1961.	It was supposed to be unsinkable.
6	The Berlin Wall	She came to the throne in 1837.	She ruled over the British Empire.

▶ *The Grand Canyon, which is over 200 miles long, is one of the wonders of the world.*
1 ....
2 ....
3 ....
4 ....
5 ....
6 ....

2 Identifying or adding? (B)

Read the news article and then say what each relative clause does.
Does it tell us which one, or does it add information?

The play (▶) <u>that the students put on last week</u> was Oscar Wilde's 'The Importance of Being Earnest',
(▶) <u>which was written in 1895</u>. The college theatre, (1) <u>which holds over 400 people</u>, was unfortunately
only half full for the Friday evening performance. However, the people (2) <u>who bothered to attend</u> must
have been glad they did. Lucy Kellett, (3) <u>who played Lady Bracknell</u>, was magnificent. Unfortunately the
young man (4) <u>who played John Worthing</u> forgot his lines twice, but that did not spoil the evening,
(5) <u>which was a great success</u>.

▶ *It tells us which play.*
▶ *It adds information about 'The Importance of Being Earnest'.*
1 ....
2 ....
3 ....
4 ....
5 ....

3 Commas in relative clauses (B)

Put in the relative clauses. You may also need to put in one or two commas.
▶ (that Claire drives) This car is a lot cheaper than the one *that Claire drives*
▶ (who has twins) Olivia, *who has twins*, often needs a babysitter.
1 (who took Rita to the party) The person .... was Tom.
2 (who has a bad temper) Henry .... shouted at the waiter.
3 (which Tom supports) The team .... is United.
4 (who is afraid of heights) We all climbed up except Vicky ....
5 (which is on the tenth floor) My new flat .... has a terrific view.
6 (she bought the sofa from) Sarah can't remember the name of the shop ....

142 Relative pronouns and relative adverbs

A Pronouns in identifying and adding clauses

There are two kinds of relative clause: identifying and adding (see Unit 141).
Look at the pronouns in these examples.

IDENTIFYING	ADDING
I'm sure I know the person **who** served us.	Natalie, **who** served us, is a friend of Emma's.
The pop singer **whom** Guy invited onto his chat show never turned up.	Arlene Black, **whom** Guy invited onto his chat show, never turned up.
The woman **whose** flat was burgled spent the night at a friend's house.	Natasha, **whose** flat was burgled, spent the night at a friend's house.
Towns **which/that** attract tourists are usually crowded in the summer.	Oxford, **which** attracts many tourists, is often crowded in the summer.
In an identifying clause we can use **who, whom, whose, which** or **that**.	In an adding clause we can use **who, whom, whose** or **which**. We do NOT use **that**.

B Leaving out the pronoun

Sometimes we can leave the pronoun out of an identifying clause (see Unit 138B).	We cannot leave the pronoun out of an adding clause.
The woman (**who**) you met yesterday works in advertising.	Sarah, **whom** you met yesterday, works in advertising.
Have you seen the book (**that**) I was reading?	That book 'Brighton Rock', **which** I was reading, is really good.
Laura couldn't find the box (**that**) she kept her photos **in**.	Laura had a wooden box, **in which** she kept her photos OR **which** she kept her photos **in**.

C The relative adverbs **where**, **when** and **why**

Look at these examples.
> This is the place **where** the accident happened.
> Do you remember the day **when** we moved the piano upstairs?
> The reason **why** Nick came was that he wanted to see Rita.

We can leave out **when** or **why**, or we can use **that**.
> Do you remember the day (**that**) we moved the piano upstairs?
> The reason (**that**) Nick came was that he wanted to see Rita.

There are also adding clauses with **where** and **when**.
> We went to the Riverside Restaurant, **where** I once had lunch with Henry.
> Mark likes to travel at night, **when** the roads are quiet.

D A special use of **which**

In an adding clause, we can use **which** relating to a whole sentence, not just to a noun.
> It rained all night, **which** was good for the garden.

Here **which** means 'the fact that it rained all night'.

Here are some more examples.
> David helped me clear up, **which** was very kind of him.
> Sarah had to work late again, **which** annoyed Mark.
> Tom pushed Nick into the swimming-pool, **which** seemed to amuse everyone.

340 RELATIVE CLAUSES

142 Exercises

1 Who, whom, whose, which, where and why (A, C)

Complete this advertisement. Put in *who, whom, whose, which, where* or *why*.

The town of Keswick, (▶) *which* lies at the heart of the Lake District, is the perfect place for a holiday, and the Derwent Hotel, (1) .... overlooks the town, is the perfect place to stay. Robin and Wendy Jackson, (2) .... bought this small hotel three years ago, have already won an excellent reputation. Robin, (3) .... cooking is one of the reasons (4) .... the Derwent is so popular, was once Young Chef of the Year. The comfort of the guests, (5) .... the owners treat almost as members of the family, always comes first. Peter Ustinov, (6) .... once stayed at the hotel, described it as 'marvellous'. And the Lake District, (7) .... has so much wonderful scenery and (8) .... the poet Wordsworth lived, will not disappoint you.

2 Identifying clauses and adding clauses (A–C)

Put in the relative clauses. Sometimes there is more than one possible answer.
- ▶ Someone knows all about it – the secretary.
  The person *who knows all about it* is the secretary.
1. Zedco has 10,000 employees. It's an international company.
   Zedco, ..., is an international company.
2. Vicky's name was missed off the list, so she wasn't very pleased.
   Vicky, ..., wasn't very pleased.
3. Laura painted a picture, and it's being shown in an exhibition.
   The picture .... is being shown in an exhibition.
4. We're all looking forward to a concert. It's next Saturday.
   The concert .... is next Saturday.
5. One week Mike and Harriet went camping. It was the wettest of the year.
   The week .... was the wettest of the year.
6. Aunt Joan is a bit deaf, so she didn't hear the phone.
   Aunt Joan, ..., didn't hear the phone.
7. You'll meet Henry tomorrow. He's also a member of the board.
   Henry, ..., is also a member of the board.
8. I'll see you near the post office. We met there the other day.
   I'll see you near the post office, ...

3 A special use of which (D)

Match the sentence pairs and join them with *which*.
- ▶ My phone is out of order.   It means he can't get about very easily.
1. Rachel's mother paid for the meal.   It's made her very depressed.
2. My brother is disabled.   That was rather careless of you.
3. You left the keys in the car.   That caused a traffic jam.
4. Vicky didn't get the job.   It's a real nuisance.
5. The police blocked off the road.   That was very kind of her.
- ▶ *My phone is out of order, which is a real nuisance.*
1. ....
2. ....
3. ....
4. ....
5. ....

143 Relative clauses: participle and to-infinitive

A Relative clauses with a participle

Read this news report about an accident.

> Several people were injured this morning when a lorry **carrying concrete pipes** overturned in the centre of town and hit two cars. Ambulances **called to the scene** took a long time to get through the rush hour traffic. The accident happened in Alfred Road, where road repairs are under way. People who saw the accident say that the lorry hit the cars after it swerved to avoid a pile of stones **left in the road**. The traffic chaos **caused by the accident** has meant long delays for people **travelling to work**.

Carrying concrete pipes, called to the scene, etc are relative clauses: they relate to a noun. **Carrying concrete pipes** tells us something about **a lorry**.

We can form these clauses with an active participle, e.g. **carrying**, or a passive participle, e.g. **called**. The participles can refer to the present or the past.

ACTIVE	PASSIVE
There are delays this morning for people **travelling** to work. (= people **who are travelling** to work) A lorry **carrying** concrete pipes has overturned. (= a lorry **which was carrying** pipes) the path **leading** to the church (= the path **which leads/led** to the church)	I have a message for people **delayed** by the traffic chaos. (= people **who are being delayed**) We noticed a pile of stones **left** in the road. (= stones **which had been left** there) food **sold** in supermarkets (= food **which is/was sold** in supermarkets)
The active participle means the same as a pronoun + a continuous verb, e.g. **which is/was carrying**, or a pronoun + a simple verb, e.g. **which leads/led**.	The passive participle means the same as a pronoun + a passive verb, e.g. **which is/was sold**.
But we do NOT use the active participle for a single action in the past. The police want to interview people **who saw** the accident. NOT *people seeing the accident*	

B Relative clauses with a to-infinitive

Look at this structure with the to-infinitive.
> New Zealand was the **first** country **to give** women the vote.
> (= the first country which gave women the vote)
> Melanie was the **only** person **to write** a letter of thanks.
> (= the only person who wrote a letter of thanks)

Here are some more examples.
> The guest on our show is the **youngest** golfer **to win** the Open.
> Emma Thompson is the **most famous** actress **to appear** on stage here.

We can use a to-infinitive with these words: **first, second**, etc; **next** and **last**; **only**; and superlatives, e.g. **youngest, most famous**.

We can leave out the noun (except after **only**) if the meaning is clear.
> The captain was the **last to leave** the sinking ship.

143 Exercises

1 Relative clauses with a participle (A)

Complete the definitions. Put in an active or passive participle of these verbs:
add, arrive, block, <u>own</u>, play, <u>take</u>, tell, watch, wear

▶ A competitor is someone *taking* part in a competition.
▶ Your property is everything *owned* by you.
1 Baseball is a game .... mainly in the US.
2 A wrist-watch is a watch .... on your wrist.
3 A latecomer is a person .... late.
4 An instruction is a statement .... you what to do.
5 A spectator is someone .... a game or an event.
6 An extension is a new part .... on to a building.
7 An obstacle is something .... your way.

2 Relative clauses with a participle (A)

Write each news item as one sentence. Change the part in brackets into a clause with an active participle (e.g. *costing*) or a passive participle (e.g. *found*).

▶ A new motorway is planned. (It will cost £500 million.)
A new motorway *costing £500 million is planned.*
▶ Some weapons belong to the IRA. (They were found at a flat in Bristol.)
Some weapons *found at a flat in Bristol belong to the IRA.*
1 Families have been evicted. (They were living in an empty office building.)
Families ....
2 A chemical company has gone bankrupt. (It employed 4,000 people.)
A chemical company ....
3 A bridge has been declared unsafe. (It was built only two years ago.)
A bridge ....
4 People have marched to London. (They are protesting against pollution.)
....
5 Tennis fans have been queuing all night at Wimbledon. (They hope to buy tickets.)
....
6 A new drug may give us eternal youth. (It was developed at a British university.)
....

3 Relative clauses with a to-infinitive (B)

Comment on each situation. Use the to-infinitive structure.

▶ David offered his help. No one else did.
David was *the only person to offer his help.*
1 Olivia's daughter swam a length of the pool. No other girl as young as her did that.
Olivia's daughter was ....
2 The secretaries got a pay rise. No one else did.
The secretaries were ....
3 The pilot left the aircraft. Everyone else had left before him.
....
4 Mrs Harper became Managing Director. No other woman had done that before.
....
5 Daniel applied for the job. No other candidate as suitable as him applied.
....

Test 24 Relative clauses (Units 137–143)

Test 24A

Decide which word or phrase is correct.
▶ *What* I really need is a long holiday.
   a) that b) what c) which d) who
1 At last I've found the information that I was looking ....
   a) for b) for it c) for that d) it
2 Everyone .... the building was searched by the police.
   a) enter b) entered c) entering d) enters
3 The plane .... has just taken off is an hour late.
   a) it b) what c) which d) who
4 I had just one reply. Abco was the .... company to reply to my letter.
   a) last b) most c) only d) second
5 My friend Nigel, ... works in the City, earns much more than I do.
   a) that b) which c) who d) whose
6 Martin is someone with .... I usually agree.
   a) him b) that c) who d) whom
7 I'd like to see the photo ....
   a) took b) you took it c) that you took d) that you took it
8 Atlanta is the city .... the Olympic Games were held in 1996.
   a) that b) when c) where d) which
9 It rained all the time, ... was a great pity.
   a) that b) what c) which d) who
10 We passed shops .... windows were decorated for Christmas.
   a) the b) their c) which d) whose

Test 24B

Each of these sentences has a mistake in it. Write the correct sentence.
▶ ~~I've found the magazine who was missing.~~
   I've found the magazine that was missing.
1 ~~This isn't the train on that I normally travel.~~
   ....
2 ~~The letter that I opened it wasn't for me.~~
   ....
3 ~~The reason because I didn't know was that no one had told me.~~
   ....
4 ~~That we should do is ring the police.~~
   ....
5 ~~I didn't know the name of the man helped me.~~
   ....
6 ~~Rupert knows the family who's house is for sale.~~
   ....
7 ~~Einstein who failed his university entrance exam discovered relativity.~~
   ....
8 ~~The person we talked to were very friendly.~~
   ....
9 ~~It's the President makes the important decisions.~~
   ....

Test 24

10 ~~I can't find my diary, what is a real nuisance.~~

11 ~~Outside the door was a pair of boots covering in mud.~~

12 ~~Lake Superior, that lies on the US-Canadian border, is the largest lake in North America.~~

Test 24C

Complete the story about a thief's punishment. Write the missing words. Use one word only in each space.

This is a true story (▶) *which* is supposed to have happened somewhere in the US. A man (1) .... was accused of housebreaking appeared in court. He had put his arm through the window of a house and stolen some money (2) .... was lying on a table inside. The argument (3) .... the man's lawyer put forward wasn't very impressive. He said that (4) .... was the man's arm (5) .... had committed the crime and not the man himself. 'You cannot punish a man for (6) .... his arm has done,' said the lawyer. Now the judge in (7) .... court the man was appearing wanted to show how stupid the lawyer's argument was. Instead of finding the man guilty, he found the man's arm guilty and sent it to prison. 'He can go with his arm or not, as he chooses,' the judge added, (8) .... made everyone laugh. But (9) .... the judge didn't know was that the man had an artificial arm. He took the arm off, gave it to the judge – (10) .... could hardly believe his eyes – and walked out of the court.

Test 24D

Combine the two sentences into one.
▶ That man was Anna's brother. He just walked past.
 The man *who just walked past was* Anna's brother.
1 The plane was twenty-five years old. It crashed.
 The plane .... twenty-five years old.
2 One day Tessa was ill in bed. Martin rang.
 The day .... ill in bed.
3 Our offices are in Queen Street. They are new.
 Our .... in Queen Street.
4 Some documents have been found. They were stolen from a car.
 The documents .... found.
5 That map is out of date. You were looking at it.
 The map .... out of date.
6 The King's Theatre is in the centre of town. It dates from 1896.
 The King's .... in the centre of town.
7 A woman was terribly upset. Her dog was run over.
 The woman .... terribly upset.
8 Janet solved the puzzle. She did it before everyone else.
 Janet was .... the puzzle.
9 A man was standing outside the building. He was selling newspapers.
 A man .... outside the building.
10 The talk was very interesting. Judy gave it.
 The talk .... very interesting.
11 The house is empty now. I used to live there.
 The house .... is empty now.

144 Conditionals (1)

A Introduction

Vicky and Rachel are talking about possible future actions. They may catch the bus, or they may miss it.

B Type 1: If we hurry, we'll catch the bus

IF-CLAUSE		MAIN CLAUSE	
if	Present simple		**will**
If we	**hurry**,	we	'll catch the bus.
If we	**miss** it,	there	'll be another one.
If it	**doesn't rain**,	we	'll be having a picnic.
If I	**don't practise** my golf,	I	**won't** get any better.

The verb in the if-clause (e.g. **hurry**) is in the present simple, not the future.
  NOT *If we'll hurry, we'll catch the bus.*
But we can use **will** in the if-clause when we make a request.
  *If you**'ll** just wait a moment, I'll find someone to help you.* (= Please wait a moment ...)

We can use the present continuous (e.g. **are doing**) or the present perfect (e.g. **have done**) in the if-clause.
  *If we**'re expecting** visitors, the flat will need a good clean.*
  *If you**'ve finished** with the computer, I'll put it away.*

The main clause often has **will**. But we can use other modal verbs (e.g. **can**).
  *If you haven't got a television, you **can't** watch it, can you?*
  *If Henry jogs regularly, he **might** lose weight.*
  *If Matthew is going to a job interview, he **should** wear a tie.*

The if-clause usually comes first, but it can come after the main clause.
  ***If** I hear any news, I'll phone you./I'll phone you **if** I hear any news.*

C More uses of type 1

We can use type 1 conditionals in offers and suggestions.
  If you need a ticket, I can get you one.   *If you feel like seeing the sights, we can take a bus tour.*
We can also use them in warnings and threats.
  If you go on like this, you'll make yourself ill.   *If you don't apologize, I'll never speak to you again.*

D If you heat water, it boils

We sometimes use the present simple in both clauses.
  *If you **heat** water, it **boils**.*   *If Daniel **has** any money, he **spends** it.*
  *If you **press** this switch, the computer **comes** on.*
This means that one thing always follows automatically from another.
Pressing the switch always results in the computer coming on.

346 CONDITIONALS AND WISH

144 Exercises

1 Type 1 (A–C)

Read the conversation and then choose the correct forms.
Rachel: Have you heard about the pop festival?
Vicky: Yes, (▶) it's/it'll be good if Express are playing. They're a great band.
Rachel: Will you be able to go, Nick?
Nick: If (1) I ask/I'll ask my boss, he'll give me some time off work, I expect.
Vicky: How are we going to get there?
Rachel: Well, if (2) there are/there'll be enough people, we can hire a minibus.
Vicky: I won't be going if (3) it's/it'll be too expensive.
Rachel: It (4) isn't costing/won't cost much if we all (5) share/will share the cost.
Nick: If (6) I see/I'll see the others later on tonight, (7) I ask/I'll ask them if they want to go.

2 Type 1 (A–C)

Comment on the situations. Use *if* + the present tense + *will/can*.
▶ It might rain. If it does, everyone can eat inside.
   If it rains, everyone can eat inside.
▶ The children mustn't go near Nick's dog. It'll bite them.
   If the children go near Nick's dog, it'll bite them.
1 Rachel might fail her driving test. But she can take it again.
   ....
2 United might lose. If they do, Tom will be upset.
   ....
3 The office may be closed. In that case Mark won't be able to get in.
   ....
4 Nick may arrive a bit early. If he does, he can help Tom to get things ready.
   ....
5 The party might go on all night. If it does, no one will want to do any work tomorrow.
   ....
6 Emma may miss the train. But she can get the next one.
   ....
7 Is Matthew going to enter the race? He'll probably win it.
   ....

3 Present simple in both clauses (D)

Match the sentences and join them with *if*.
▶ You lose your credit card.   I can't sleep.
1 You get promoted.   You get a warning letter.
2 I drink coffee late at night.   You have to ring the bank.
3 You don't pay the bill.   Your salary goes up.
4 I try to run fast.   The alarm goes off.
5 Someone enters the building.   I get out of breath.
▶ *If you lose your credit card, you have to ring the bank.*
1 ....
2 ....
3 ....
4 ....
5 ....

145 Conditionals (2)

A Introduction

Rachel: *Would you like some cake, Jessica?*
Jessica: *No thanks. **If I ate** cake, I'd get fat.*
Rachel: *But it's delicious.*
Jessica: *It looks delicious. **If I had** your figure, I'd eat the whole lot.*

I ate cake and *I had your figure* are imaginary or unreal situations. Jessica isn't going to eat the cake, and she hasn't got a figure like Rachel's.

B Type 2: **If I ate cake, I'd get fat**

IF-CLAUSE		MAIN CLAUSE	
if	Past simple		**would**
If I	**ate** *cake,*	*I*	**'d get** *fat.*
If I	**had** *your figure,*	*I*	**'d eat** *the whole lot.*
If we	**didn't have** *a car,*	*we*	**'d find** *it difficult to get about.*
If Rachel	**got** *up earlier,*	*she*	**wouldn't** *always be late.*

Note the past simple (e.g. **ate**). We do not use **would** in the if-clause. NOT *If I'd eat cake.*
But we can use **would** in the if-clause when we make a request.
  If you'd like to come this way, the doctor will see you now. (= Please come this way ...)

As well as the past simple we can use the past continuous (e.g. **was doing**) in the if-clause.
  *If Rachel **was playing** her stereo, it wouldn't be so quiet in here.*
In a type 2 if-clause we sometimes use **were** instead of **was**, especially in the clause **if I were you**.
  *If Rachel **were playing** her stereo, it wouldn't be so quiet in here.*
  *If I **were** you, I'd ask a lawyer for some advice.*

The main clause often has **would**. We can also use **could** or **might**.
  *If we had a calculator, we **could** work this out a lot quicker.*
  *If Rachel worked harder, she **might** do even better at her studies.*

The if-clause usually comes first, but it can come after the main clause.
  ***If** I knew, I'd tell you./I'd tell you **if** I knew.*

C Type 1 and type 2

Compare these examples.
  Type 1: *If you **have** a lie-down, you'll feel better.* (see Unit 144B)
  Type 2: *If I **had** a million pounds, I'd probably buy a yacht.*

The present tense (**have**) refers to a possible future action, something which may or may not happen. The past tense (**had**) refers to something unreal. *If I had a million pounds* means that I haven't really got a million pounds, but I am imagining that I have. Compare these examples.
  Type 1: *If we **take** the car, we'll have to pay for parking.*
  Type 2: *If we **took** the car, we'd have to pay for parking.*
Here both sentences refer to a possible future action. But in the type 2 conditional, the action is less probable. *If we took the car* may mean that we have decided not to take it.

We can use type 2 conditionals in offers and suggestions.
  *If you **needed** a ticket, I could get you one.*
  *If you **felt** like seeing the sights, we could take a bus tour.*
Type 2 is less direct than type 1 (Unit 144C). The speaker is less sure that you want to see the sights.

145 Exercises

1 Type 2 (A–B)

Comment on these situations. Use a type 2 conditional with *would* or *could*.

▶ Andrew is such a boring person because he works all the time.
   You know, *if Andrew didn't work all the time, he wouldn't be such a boring person.*
▶ You can't take a photo because you haven't got your camera.
   How annoying. *If I had my camera, I could take a photo.*
1 You can't look the word up because you haven't got a dictionary.
   I'm sorry. ....
2 You don't write to your friends because you're so busy.
   I've got so much to do. ....
3 You can't play tennis because your back is aching.
   It's a nuisance. ....
4 Claire won't speak to Henry because she is angry with him.
   Of course, ...
5 Nick can't find the way because he hasn't got a map.
   Nick's lost, but ....
6 David has so many accidents because he's so clumsy.
   You know, ...

2 Type 1 and type 2 (A–C)

Complete the conversation. Put in the correct form of the verb. You may need to use *will* or *would*.

Matthew: I haven't forgotten your birthday, you know. If you like, (▶) *I'll book* (I / book) a table for Thursday at our favourite restaurant.
Emma: My birthday is on Wednesday, Matthew. You're playing basketball then, aren't you? If you cared for me, (1) .... (you / not / play) basketball on my birthday.
Matthew: What's the difference? If (2) .... (we / go) out on Thursday, it'll be just the same. If (3) .... (I / not / play), I'd be letting the team down.
Emma: Yes, I suppose (4) .... (it / be) a disaster if you missed one game. Well, if (5) .... (you / think) more of your friends than you do of me, you can forget the whole thing.
Matthew: I just don't understand you sometimes, Emma.
Emma: If (6) .... (you / think) about it, you'd understand. And I think (7) .... (it / be) better if we forgot all about my birthday.
Matthew: Don't be silly, Emma. If you get into one of your bad moods,
   (8) .... (it / not / do) any good.
Emma: If you were interested in my feelings, (9) .... (I / not / get) into a bad mood.

3 Type 1 and type 2 (C)

What does the if-clause mean? Write a sentence with *isn't* or *might*.

▶ If this room was tidy, I could find things.   *The room isn't tidy.*
▶ If we're late tonight, we can get a taxi.   *We might be late tonight.*
1 If the phone was working, I could call you.   ....
2 If it rains, can you bring the washing in?   ....
3 If Mike was here, he'd know what to do.   ....
4 If this spoon was silver, it would be worth a lot. ....
5 If Sarah calls, can you say I'll ring back?   ....

146 Conditionals (3)

A Introduction

David: How was your camping holiday?
Mike: Well, it **would have** been all right if it **hadn't rained** all the time.
Harriet: *If we'd gone* two weeks earlier, *we'd have* had better weather.

If it hadn't rained and *if we'd gone two weeks earlier* are imaginary situations in the past.
It did rain, and they didn't go two weeks earlier.

B Type 3: If we had gone earlier, we would have had better weather

IF-CLAUSE		MAIN CLAUSE	
if	Past perfect		would have
If we	'd gone earlier,	we	'd have had better weather.
If Matthew	had phoned her,	Emma	wouldn't have been so annoyed.
If you	hadn't made that mistake,	you	'd have passed your test.
If David	had been more careful,	he	wouldn't have fallen.

Note the verb in the past perfect (e.g. **had been**). We do not use **would** in the if-clause.
NOT *If David would have been more careful, he would have fallen.*

The main clause often has **would have**. We can also use **could have** or **might have**.
If I'd had my mobile yesterday, I could have contacted you.
We just caught the train. If we'd stopped to buy a paper, we might have missed it.

The short form **'d** can be either **had** or **would**.
If you'd rung me, I'd have come to see you. (= If you **had** rung me, I **would** have come to see you.)

C The use of type 3

We use type 3 conditionals to talk about things in the past happening differently from the way they really happened. This sometimes means criticizing people or pointing out their mistakes.
If you'd been a bit more careful, you wouldn't have cut yourself.
If Matthew had set his alarm clock, he wouldn't have overslept.
We can also use this structure to express regret about the past.
If I hadn't fallen ill and missed the interview, I might have got the job.

D Type 2 and type 3

Compare these examples.
Type 2: *If you **planned** things properly, you **wouldn't** get into a mess.* (You don't plan.)
Type 3: *If you **had planned** things properly, you **wouldn't have** got into a mess.* (You didn't plan.)
We can mix types 2 and 3.
*If you **had planned** things at the start, we **wouldn't** be in this mess now.*
*If you **hadn't left** all these dirty dishes, the place **would** look a bit tidier.*
*If Matthew **was** more sensible, he **would have** worn a suit to the interview.*
*If I **didn't have** all this work to do, I **would have** gone out for the day.*

146 Exercises

1 Type 3 (A–C)

Complete the conversation. Put in the correct form of the verb. Use the past perfect or *would have*.

Nick: United didn't play very well today.
Tom: We were awful. But if Hacker (▶) *had taken* (take) that easy chance, (▶) *we would have won* (we / win).
Nick: We didn't deserve to win. It (1) .... (be) pretty unfair if Rangers (2) .... (lose).
Tom: Hacker was dreadful. My grandmother (3) .... (score) if (4) .... (she / be) in that position.
Nick: And if Burley (5) .... (not / be) asleep, he (6) .... (not / give) a goal away.
Tom: If Johnson (7) .... (not / be) injured when we needed him most, (8) .... (it / be) different.
Nick: Yes, (9) .... (we / beat) them if (10) .... (he / be) fit.

2 Type 3 (A–C)

Comment on each situation using a type 3 conditional with *if*. Use *would have, could have* or *might have*.

▶ In a bookshop yesterday Daniel saw a book he really wanted. The only problem was that he didn't have any money.   *Daniel would have bought the book if he had had any money.*
▶ Rita often goes to concerts at the town hall, although not to every one. There was one on Saturday, but she didn't know about it.   *Rita might have gone to the concert if she had known about it.*
1 On Sunday the guests had to have their lunch inside. Unfortunately it wasn't warm enough to have it outside. ....
2 There was a bomb scare last Tuesday. Sarah wanted to fly to Rome, but she wasn't able to. The airport was closed. ....
3 Laura has only met Nick once, and it's possible she wouldn't recognize him. He passed her yesterday, but he had a crash-helmet on. ....
4 Sarah has been quite busy, and she hasn't watered her plants for some time. As a result, they've died. ....
5 Nick likes ice hockey, but he didn't have a ticket to the game last week, so unfortunately he wasn't able to get in. ....

3 Type 2 and type 3 (D)

Complete the conversations. Put in the correct form of the verb.
Use the past simple, the past perfect, *would*, or *would have*.

▶ Mike: You look tired.
  Harriet: Well, if *you hadn't woken* (you / not / wake) me up in the middle of the night, *I wouldn't be* (I / not be) so tired.
1 Rita: Is Trevor a practical person?
  Laura: Trevor? No, he isn't. If .... (he / be) practical, ... (he / put) those shelves up a bit quicker. It took him ages.
2 Tom: Why are you sitting in the dark?
  David: Let's just say that if .... (I / pay) my electricity bill last month, ... (I / not be) in the dark now.
3 Matthew: Why are you so angry with me? All I did yesterday was play basketball.
  Emma: If .... (you / love) me, ... (you / not / leave) me here all alone on my birthday.

147 Review of conditionals

A Types 1, 2 and 3

BEFORE THE GAME   AFTER THE GAME

There are three main types of conditional. Study the examples.
Type 1: **if** ... the present simple ... **will/can/might**, etc
   If we win today, we'll go to the top of the league. (We may win, or we may not.)
Type 2: **if** ... the past simple ... **would/could/might**
   If Johnson was in the team, I'd feel more confident. (Johnson isn't in the team.)
Type 3: **if** ... the past perfect ... **would have/could have/might have**
   If Johnson had played, we'd have won. (Johnson didn't play.)

Here are some more examples with different verb forms.
Type 1   *If I'm going shopping, I'll need some money.*
         If the party has finished, we might be able to get some sleep.
         You should stay in bed if you feel unwell.
Type 2   *If I didn't like this pudding, I wouldn't eat it.*
         If the video recorder was working, we could watch a film.
         The alarm might go off if we tried to get in through a window.
Type 3   *If we'd dropped the piano, it would have been a disaster.*
         If Vicky had come to the theme park with us last week, she might have enjoyed it.
         We could have given you a lift if we'd known you were coming this way.

B Other conditional sentences

As well as the three main types, there are other types of conditional sentence.
For example, we can use two present-tense verbs (see Unit 144D).
   If you ring this number, no one answers.

We can also use a present-tense verb and an imperative.
   If you need any help, just ask.   *If you drink, don't drive.*

We can use **be going to**.
   If it's going to rain, I'd better take an umbrella.
   If they try to cut down the trees, there's going to be a big protest.

We can mix types 2 and 3 (see Unit 146D).
   If Matthew had booked a table, we wouldn't be standing here in a queue.
   If you needed help, you should have asked me.

352   CONDITIONALS AND WISH

147 Exercises

1 Types 1, 2 and 3 (A)

Match the sentences and join them with *if*. Say what type they are.

▶ I went to bed earlier.　　　　　　　　　I'll try to follow them.
1 The twins had worn different clothes.　You might not be warm enough.
2 You tell me what the instructions say.　I wouldn't have bought it.
3 People used public transport.　　　　　I wouldn't sleep.
4 You don't wear a sweater.　　　　　　　There'd be less pollution.
5 I hadn't seen the product advertised.　We could have told them apart.

▶ *If I went to bed earlier, I wouldn't sleep.*　　　　　　　　　　　　　　type 2
1 ....
2 ....
3 ....
4 ....
5 ....

2 Types 1, 2 and 3 (A)

Adam is a music student. He rents a room from Mr Day. Put in the correct forms.
Mr Day:　Can't you stop playing that trumpet? You're making an awful noise.
Adam:　　Well, if (▶) *I don't practise* (I / not practise), I won't pass my exam.
Mr Day:　But why at night? It's half past twelve. If (1) .... (you / play) it in the daytime, (2) .... (I / not / hear) you because I'd be at work. If (3) .... (you / tell) me about this trumpet when you first came here, (4) .... (I / not / let) you have the room. I'm afraid it's becoming a nuisance. If (5) .... (you / not / play) so loud, (6) .... (it / not / be) so bad.
Adam:　　I'm sorry, but you can't play a trumpet quietly.
Mr Day:　If (7) .... (I / realize) a year ago what you were going to do, then (8) .... (I / throw) you out long ago. If (9) .... (you / go) on making this noise at night, (10) .... (I / have) to complain to your college.

3 Conditionals (A–B)

What might you say in these situations? Use a conditional sentence.
▶ You think Emma should book a seat on the train. The alternative is having to stand.
　If Emma doesn't book a seat on the train, she'll have to stand.
1 You didn't know how unpopular Jason was when you invited him to your party.
　..
2 Warn your friend not to put too many tins into the plastic bag or it'll break.
　..
3 You haven't got a pen, so you can't write down the address.
　..
4 You should have started your project earlier. You're so far behind now.
　..
5 Your friend might need some help. If so, tell her to give you a ring.
　..
6 The automatic result of the door opening is the fan coming on.
　..

148 If, when, unless and in case

A Present simple for the future
Look at these examples.
> You'll be tired tomorrow **if** you **stay** up late.   Tell me **when** the water **boils**.
> I won't do anything **unless** you **agree**.   Write the name down **in case** you **forget** it.

We use the present simple for the future after linking words such as **if**, **when**, **unless** and **in case** (see also Units 27 and 144B).

B If or when?

If you hear any news, can you ring me immediately? (You <u>might</u> hear some news.)	*When you hear some news, can you ring me immediately?* (You <u>will</u> hear some news.)
I'll probably go for a walk later on if it stays fine. (It <u>might</u> stay fine.)	*I'll make myself an omelette when I get home tonight.* (I <u>will</u> get home tonight.)
We use **if** for something that we think might happen.	We use **when** for something that we know will happen.
We use **if** (not **when**) for something impossible or imaginary. *If I were you, I'd refuse.*	

We can use either **if** or **when** in contexts where they mean 'every time'.

If you run, you use up energy.	*When you run, you use up energy.*

C If and unless
If ... not means the same as **unless**.

I can't see if I don't wear glasses.	=	*I can't see unless I wear glasses.*
The doctor will be here if she isn't called to an emergency.	=	*The doctor will be here unless she's called to an emergency.*
If you can't pay your bills, you'll have to leave.	=	***Unless** you can pay your bills, you'll have to leave.*
I wouldn't say that if I didn't believe it.	=	*I wouldn't say that **unless** I believed it.*

D In case
Look at these examples.
> Take a sandwich with you **in case** you get hungry.
> I'd better reserve a seat today **in case** the train is full tomorrow.
> Laura took two photos **in case** one of them didn't come out.

We use **in case** to talk about doing something to avoid a possible problem later on.
(For American English, see page 381.)

Compare **if** and **in case**.

*I'll bring in the washing **if** it rains.* (= I'll bring it in at the time it starts raining.)	*I'll bring in the washing **in case** it rains.* (= I'll bring it in now because it might rain later.)

148 Exercises

1 If or when? (B)

Look at the information in brackets and complete the sentences using *if* or *when* and a verb in the present simple.
- ▶ (I may see Tom tonight.) *If I see Tom,* I'll tell him the news.
- ▶ (Melanie is coming soon.) *When Melanie comes,* can you let her in, please?
1. (The alarm will ring soon.) .... we all have to leave the building.
2. (I might feel better tomorrow.) .... I'll probably go back to work.
3. (This film finishes at ten.) .... I'll stop the video.
4. (The plan may not work.) .... we'll have to think of something else.

2 If and unless (C)

Complete the sentences using *unless* and the information in brackets.
- ▶ You won't get there in time *unless you hurry.* (if you don't hurry)
1. We can't have a picnic .... (if it isn't a nice day)
2. Don't leave the TV on .... (if you aren't watching it)
3. We can't do the job .... (if we don't get help)
4. I wouldn't have bought the picture .... (if I didn't like it)

3 If and unless (C)

Which word makes more sense? Put in *if* or *unless*.
- ▶ Rachel will be pleased *if* she passes her driving test.
- ▶ The bus won't stop *unless* you ring the bell.
1. I can't read your letters .... you type them.
2. Emma will be upset .... she doesn't get the job.
3. You can't go into the reception .... you've got a ticket.
4. Don't bother to ring me .... it's important.

4 In case (D)

What could you say in these situations? Use *in case*.
- ▶ You think Vicky had better take a coat. It might get cold.
  You to Vicky: *You'd better take a coat in case it gets cold.*
1. You think you and Mark had better book a table. The restaurant might be busy.
   You to Mark: ....
2. You think Claire ought to insure her jewellery. It might get stolen.
   You to Claire: ....
3. You'll leave David your phone number. He might want to contact you.
   You to David: ....

5 If, when, unless and in case (B–D)

Jake lives next door to Melanie. Complete their conversation. Put in *if*, *when* (x2), *unless* or *in case*.
Jake: A man is delivering a washing-machine this morning, but I have to go to work. I won't be here (▶) *when* he calls. Could you let him in for me, please, (1) .... you're terribly busy?
Melanie: Oh, that's no problem.
Jake: Oh, thanks. (2) .... you could do that, I'd be really grateful. I'll leave a message on his answerphone. And (3) .... he doesn't get the message, I'll put a note on the door, just to make sure. He'll see it (4) .... he comes.

149 Wish and if only

A Introduction

We can use **I wish** or **if only** to express a wish. Jessica wishes she was slimmer.
If only is stronger and more emphatic than **wish**.

We can use a clause with **if only** on its own, or we can add another clause.
If only I wasn't so fat.   *If only I wasn't so fat, I would be able to get into these trousers.*

B Wish ... would

Look at these examples.
*I wish you **would** put those shelves up soon.*
*Tom wishes his neighbours **wouldn't** make so much noise.*
*If only you'**d** try to keep the place tidy.*
Wish/If only ... would expresses a wish for something to happen, or to stop happening.

C Wish ... the past

Look at these examples.
*I wish I **lived** in a big city. It's so boring in the country.*
*We all wish we **had** more money, don't we?*   *If only I **was** taller, I might be better at basketball.*
Wish and **if only** with a past-tense verb express a wish for things to be different.

We can use **were** instead of **was** (see also Unit 145B).
*If only I **were** taller, I might be better at basketball.*

We cannot use **would** in these sentences, but we can use **could**.
*I wish I **could** sing (but I can't).*   *I feel so helpless. If only I **could** speak the language.*

Compare **wish** with **would** and with the past.
*I wish something exciting **would** happen.* (I wish for an action in the future.)
*I wish my life **was** more interesting.* (My life isn't interesting.)

D Wish ... the past perfect

We use **wish** and **if only** with the past perfect to express a wish about the past.
*I wish you **had told** me about the dance. I would have gone.*
*I wish I'**d got** up earlier. I'm behind with everything today.*
*I wish you **hadn't lost** that photo. It was a really good one.*
*If only David **had been** a bit more careful, he'd have been all right.*

We do not use **would have** for the past, but we can use **could have**.
*I wish I **could have** been at the wedding, but I was in New York.*

149 Exercises

1 Wish ... would (B)

What might you say in these situations? Begin *I wish* …
▶ to someone who never answers your e-mails
  I wish you'd answer my e-mails.
▶ to someone who makes rude remarks about you
  I wish you wouldn't make rude remarks about me.
1 to someone who won't hurry up
2 to someone who never does the washing-up
3 to someone who isn't telling you the whole story
4 to someone who blows cigarette smoke in your face
5 to someone who won't tell you what he's thinking

2 Wish ... the past (C)

Vicky is fed up. What is she saying? Use *I wish* or *if only*.
▶ (She can't think straight.) *I wish I could think straight.*
1 (She is so tired.)
2 (She gets headaches.)
3 (Her work isn't going well.)
4 (She can't concentrate.)
5 (Life is so complicated.)

3 Wish ... the past perfect (D)

Complete the sentences. Use these words: *accepted, caught, found, played, saved, stayed*
▶ I spent all my money. I wish now that *I had saved it.*
1 I missed the train. I really wish
2 Rita left the party early. Nick wishes
3 Emma refused the offer. But her parents wish
4 I looked everywhere for the key. I wish
5 The injured player could only watch. He wishes

4 Wish and if only (B–D)

Complete the conversation.
Claire: Oh, Henry. You're giving me another present. It's very sweet of you,
         but I wish (▶) *you wouldn't give me* so many presents.
Henry: Claire, I've been thinking. I shouldn't have asked you to marry me.
         I wish now that (1) ....
Claire: Now you're talking nonsense. I wish (2) ...., Henry.
Henry: I'm not a young man, am I? Of course I wish (3) ....
Claire: Why don't you listen? If only (4) .... to me just this once.
Henry: Why couldn't we have met twenty years ago? I wish (5) .... you then.
Claire: Henry, twenty years ago I was just starting school.

Test 25 Conditionals and **wish** (Units 144–149)

Test 25A

Complete the news report about a protest against a new road. Put in the correct form of the verbs. Sometimes you need *will* or *would*.

Yesterday protesters managed to hold up work on the Oldbury bypass. Protest leader Alison Compton defended the action by members of the Green World group. 'If we don't protest, soon (▶) *there'll be* (there / be) no countryside left,' she told reporters. The bypass is now well behind schedule, and if the protesters had not held up the work so often, (1) .... (it / open) two months ago. 'If these fields (2) .... (disappear), we'll never see them again,' said Ms Compton. 'Why can't we use public transport? If more people (3) .... (travel) on buses and trains, we wouldn't need new roads. If the motor car had never existed, the world (4) .... (be) a more pleasant place today.'

But many people in Oldbury want their new bypass. 'If (5) .... (they / not build) it soon, the traffic jams in the town will get worse,' said Asif Mohammed, whose house is beside the busy A34. 'We just can't leave things as they are. If things remained the same, people's health (6) .... (suffer) even more from all the pollution here. It's terrible. If we don't get the traffic out of the town, (7) .... (I / go) mad. If (8) .... (I / know) earlier how bad this problem would get, (9) .... (I / move) out years ago. But now it has become impossible to sell this house because of the traffic. The government waited too long. If (10) .... (they / do) something sooner, there would be less traffic today.' And the protest is making the new road even more expensive. 'If this goes on, (11) .... (there / not / be) enough money left to finish the road,' says the Transport Minister.

Test 25B

Look at the answers below and write the correct answer in each space.
▶ A: There's always something going wrong with this car.
  B: If you had any sense, you'd *have sold* it long ago.
  a) be selling b) have sold c) sell d) sold
1 A: It's a pity the lake wasn't frozen yesterday.
  B: Yes, it is. If it .... frozen, we could have gone skating.
  a) had been b) was c) would be d) would have been
2 A: Haven't you got enough money for a holiday?
  B: Oh yes. I've got some saved up .... I suddenly need it.
  a) if b) in case c) that d) unless
3 A: What are you going to do next year?
  B: I wish I .... the answer to that question.
  a) knew b) know c) could know d) would know
4 A: These figures are too complicated to work out in your head.
  B: Yes, if .... we had a calculator.
  a) better b) only c) really d) that
5 A: What are you doing later this afternoon?
  B: Oh, ... the game finishes, I'll go home, I expect.
  a) if b) in case c) unless d) when
6 A: Do you think I should take the job?
  B: You shouldn't do anything .... you think it's the right thing to do.
  a) if b) in case c) unless d) when

Test 25

Test 25C

Write a second sentence so that it has a similar meaning to the first. Begin with *If* ...
▶ I haven't got a key, so I can't get in.
 If I had a key, I could get in.
1 You talk about football and I'm going to be very bored.

2 The baby didn't cry, so we had a good sleep.

3 You may want a chat, so just give me a ring.

4 Nigel hasn't got satellite TV, so he can't watch the game.

5 You go away and I'll miss you.

6 I'm not rich or I'd have given up working long ago.

7 We should have bought that picture five years ago because it would be quite valuable now.

8 Throw a stone into water and it sinks.

Test 25D

Write the sentences correctly.
▶ There aren't any eggs. ~~If we have some eggs, I could make an omelette.~~
 If we had some eggs, I could make an omelette.
1 The weather doesn't look very good. ~~If it'll rain, I'll stay here.~~

2 The programme is starting soon. ~~Can you tell me if it starts?~~

3 Could you just listen? ~~I didn't need to repeat things all the time if you listened.~~

4 It's a simple law of science. ~~If air will get warmer, it rises.~~

5 There's only one key. ~~I'd better get another one made if I lose it.~~

6 We were really late. ~~I wish we left home earlier.~~

7 I hope the parcel comes today. ~~If it won't arrive today, we'll have to complain.~~

8 That radio is on loud. ~~I wish someone turns it down.~~

9 We must do something. ~~Until we act quickly, it'll be too late.~~

10 Of course Martin was angry. ~~But he hadn't been angry if you hadn't damaged his stereo.~~

150 But, although and in spite of

A Introduction

This is a news report about Zedco.

> This year's figures show that Zedco has become profitable and is now doing well **in spite of** its recent problems. **Although** Chief Executive Barry Douglas has not been in charge for long, there has already been a dramatic upturn. **Even though** there have been very few job losses at the company, Douglas has managed to reduce costs. Nothing is certain of course, **but** Zedco can now look forward to a brighter future.

The linking words **in spite of**, **although**, etc express the idea of a contrast.
For example, there is a contrast between Zedco's profits now and its recent problems.

B But and although

We can join two sentences with **but**.
> The café was crowded, **but** we found a table.   Nick has a car, **but** he doesn't often drive it.

We can also use **although**.
> **Although** the café was crowded, we found a table.   **Although** Nick has a car, he doesn't often drive it.

The clause with **although** can come at the end.
> We found a table, **although** the café was crowded.

C Though and even though

Though is informal. It means the same as **although**.
> **Though/Although** I liked the sweater, I decided not to buy it.

We can also use **though** at the end of a sentence.
> I liked the sweater. I decided not to buy it, **though**.

Even though is stronger, more emphatic than **although**.
> Matthew looked quite fresh, **even though** he'd been playing squash.
> **Even though** you dislike Jessica, you should try to be nice to her.

D In spite of and despite

We use **in spite of** before a noun or before the ing-form of a verb.
> Kitty wanted to report on the war **in spite of** the danger.
> Mark went on working **in spite of** feeling unwell.

We use **despite** in exactly the same way as **in spite of** and with the same meaning.
> She wanted to go **despite** the danger.   He went on working **despite** feeling unwell.

E In spite of and although

IN SPITE OF	ALTHOUGH
I'm no better **in spite of** the pills/**in spite of** taking the pills.	I'm no better, **although** I've taken the pills.
Laura wants to fly **in spite of** her fear/**in spite of** feeling afraid.	Laura wants to fly, **although** she feels afraid.
NOT *in spite of she feels afraid*	

We can use **in spite of the fact (that)** in the same way as **although**.
> I'm no better **in spite of the fact that** I've taken the pills.

▷ page 372 Punctuation

150 Exercises

1 But (B)

Complete each sentence with *but* and one of these clauses:
it didn't break, it's really quite modern, no one laughed, she turned it down
▶ I dropped the dish, *but it didn't break.*
1 The house looks old, ...
2 Emma was offered a job, ...
3 The joke was funny, ...

2 Although (B)

Rewrite the sentences in Exercise 1 using *although*.
▶ *Although I dropped the dish, it didn't break.*
1 ....
2 ....
3 ....

3 In spite of and although (E)

Put in *although* or *in spite of*.
▶ My sister got the job, *although* she didn't expect to.
1 .... I told the absolute truth, no one would believe me.
2 Daniel forgot his passport .... having it on his list.
3 .... it was sunny, it was quite a cold day.
4 The goods were never delivered .... the promise we had received.
5 Henry asked Claire to marry him .... the fact that he's a lot older than her.

4 But, although, even though, in spite of and despite (A–E)

Complete the report by putting in the correct linking words. There is always more than one possible answer.
(▶) *Although* the ground was very wet, it was decided to go ahead with United's game against City. United were 1–0 winners (1) .... not playing very well. (2) .... the poor conditions, City played some attractive football, (3) .... they just couldn't score. (4) .... they lost, their fans gave them a big cheer.

5 Although, even though, in spite of and despite (A–E)

Join each pair of sentences. Be careful where you put the words in brackets.
▶ Nick used to smoke. He seems to be in good health. (although)
   Although Nick used to smoke, he seems to be in good health.
▶ I couldn't sleep. I was tired. (despite)
   I couldn't sleep despite being tired.
1 Trevor didn't notice the sign. It was right in front of him. (even though)
   ....
2 Matthew doesn't know any French. It was one of his school subjects. (although)
   ....
3 Henry's friend is a millionaire. He hates spending money. (despite)
   ....
4 We couldn't get tickets. We queued for an hour. (in spite of)
   ....

151 To, in order to, so that and for

A Introduction

We use **to**, **in order to**, **so that** and **for** to express purpose, to say why we do things.
The purpose of stopping is to buy a newspaper.

B To

We can use the to-infinitive to express purpose.
  Melanie was hurrying **to catch** her bus.   Most people work **to earn** money.
  I rang **to find** out the train times.   We went to the library **to get** some books.

C In order to and so as to

In order to and **so as to** are more formal than **to**.
  The government took these measures **in order to** reduce crime.
  The staff are working at weekends **so as to** complete the project in time.
We can use the negative **in order not to** or **so as not to**.
  Melanie was hurrying **in order not to** miss her bus.
  The staff are working at weekends **so as not to** delay the project any further.
We cannot use **not to** on its own.
  She was hurrying **to catch** her bus. NOT *She was hurrying not to miss her bus.*

D So that

Look at this example.
  I'll post the card today **so that it gets** there on Daniel's birthday.
After **so that** we use a subject and verb, e.g. **it gets**.
We often use **will** or **can** for a present purpose and **would** or **could** for a past purpose.
  I'll give you a map **so that** you **can** find/you'll find the way all right.
  I gave Nick a map **so that** he **could** find/**would** be able to find the way all right.

E To or for?

We can use **for** with a noun to say why we do something.
  The whole family have gone out **for** a bike ride.   Why don't you come over **for** coffee?
To talk about the purpose of a <u>thing</u>, we use either a to-infinitive or **for** + an ing-form.
  This heater is **to keep/for keeping** the plants warm in winter.
  This machine is used **to cut/for cutting** plastic.
But we do not use **for** + an ing-form to talk about a specific action.
  I put the heater on **to keep** the plants warm. NOT *I put the heater on for keeping the plants warm.*

151 Exercises

1 To (B)

Complete each sentence using *to* and these words:
cash a cheque, finance her studies, go to sleep, hear the football results, look smart
▶ Laura went to the bank *to cash a cheque.*
1. Mrs Miles sometimes takes a pill ....
2. Tom turned on the radio ....
3. Just this once Mike is going to wear a suit ....
4. Jessica is borrowing some money ....

2 In order to and so as to (C)

Alan works for Zedco. He wants to succeed in business, so he is listening to a talk on the subject. Here is what the speaker is showing the audience.

	ACTION		PURPOSE
▶	study the market	→	be more successful
1	get to work earlier	→	impress the boss
2	work harder	→	achieve more
3	take risks	→	be a winner
4	think positively	→	not miss any opportunities

Say what Alan is going to do. Use either *in order to* or *so as to*. Both are correct.
▶ *He's going to study the market in order to be more successful.*
1. ....
2. ....
3. ....
4. ....

3 To, for and so that (B, D, E)

Comment on what each person says. Use the word in brackets.
▶ Ilona: I'm learning English. I want to get a better job. (to)
 Ilona is learning English to get a better job.
▶ Claude: I study encyclopedias. Then I can answer quiz questions. (so that)
 Claude studies encyclopedias so that he can answer quiz questions.
▶ Vicky: I'm saving up. I'm planning a holiday. (for)
 Vicky is saving up for a holiday.
1. Nick: I keep a dog. It guards the house. (to)
 ....
2. David: I'm going to be very careful. Then I won't have an accident. (so that)
 ....
3. Jessica: I'm going on a diet. I want to lose weight. (to)
 ....
4. Trevor: I often switch off the heating. It saves money. (to)
 ....
5. Sarah: I had to go to Birmingham. I had a business meeting. (for)
 ....
6. Emma: I wore boots because I didn't want my feet to get wet. (so that)
 ....

LINKING WORDS 363

152 Review of linking words

A Time words

Look at these examples with **when, while, as soon as**, etc.
> My leg hurts **when** I walk.
> (**when** I walk = **at the time** I walk)
> Mark heard the news on the radio **as/while** he was driving home.
> (**as/while** he was driving = **during the time** he was driving)
> We're going to tidy up **after** everyone's gone.
> (**after** everyone's gone = **later than** everyone goes)
> **As soon as** Laura had left the house, it started to rain.
> (**as soon as** she had left = **immediately after** she had left)
> I must get to the post office **before** it closes.
> (**before** it closes = **earlier than** it closes)
> You have to wait **until** the light changes to green.
> (**until** it changes = **up to the time** it changes)
> David hasn't been able to work **since** he broke his leg.
> (**since** he broke his leg = **from the time** he broke his leg)

Remember that we use the present simple for future time after **when**, etc.
We say *before it **closes**, until it **changes***, etc (see Unit 27).

B If, unless and in case

We use these words to express a condition (see Unit 148).
> Rachel might buy a car **if** she passes her test.
> (She may or may not pass her test.)
> You won't learn to use a keyboard properly **unless** you practise.
> (**unless** you practise = **if** you **don't** practise)
> We'd better allow plenty of time for the journey **in case** there are traffic hold-ups.
> (**in case** there are hold-ups = **because** there may be hold-ups)

C But, although and in spite of

We use these words to express the idea of a contrast (see Unit 150).
> The jacket was nice, **but** it was too small for me.
> **Although** the forecast said it would rain, it turned out to be a beautiful day.
> We still haven't got a sponsor **in spite of** writing/**in spite of the fact that** we've written to dozens of companies.

D Because and so

We use **because** to express the reason for something and **so** to express the result of something.
> I turned the heating on **because** it was cold.
> Henry started jogging **because** his doctor told him to.
> It was cold, **so** I turned the heating on.
> The stereo didn't work, **so** Vicky took it back to the shop.

E To, in order to and so that

We use these words to express purpose (see Unit 151).
> Sarah went to Birmingham **to** meet a client.
> We're having to borrow money **in order to** pay our bills.
> I took the bread out of the freezer **so that** it would defrost.

152 Exercises

1 Time words (A)

Arlene Black's new CD is now available in the shops. Write the titles of her songs.
Use these words instead of the ones in brackets: *as soon as, before, since, when, while, until*

▶ Think of me (during the time) I'm away   Think of me while I'm away
1. I'll try to be a good person (up to the day) I die ....
2. I hear music (at the time) I see you ....
3. Come back (earlier than) I forget you ....
4. I've been sad (from the time) you left me ....
5. I fell ill (immediately after) we ate fish. ....

2 Linking words (B–E)

Put in these words: *although, because, but, if, in case, in order to, in spite of, so, so that, unless*
▶ Olivia booked a babysitter *so that* she could go out for the evening.
1. .... it was late, Nick didn't seem in a hurry to leave.
2. They put video cameras in shops .... stop people stealing things.
3. We decided not to go out for a meal .... we were simply too tired.
4. .... you're ready, we can start now.
5. Our room was very small, ... we didn't really mind.
6. No one was watching the television, ... I switched it off.
7. You can't drive a car .... you've got a licence.
8. .... having absolutely no talent, Guy became a popular TV personality and chat show host.
9. I think my answers are right, but can I just check them with yours .... I've made a mistake?

3 Linking words (A–E)

Complete the conversation. Choose the correct linking word.

Daniel: What are you going to do (▶) <u>after</u>/<s>before</s> you finish college, Rachel?
Rachel: Vicky and I will be off to the States (1) <u>as soon as/in spite of</u> this term is over. We're going to travel around, and we may go to Canada (2) <u>so that/to</u> see some friends of Vicky's. We've been thinking about nothing else (3) <u>since/until</u> we bought our plane tickets.
Daniel: It sounds great. How are you getting around in the States?
Rachel: By Greyhound bus. I know it takes longer than flying, (4) <u>but/in spite of</u> it'll be more interesting. We fly to LA and then we're taking the bus to New York. We're going to buy a special ticket (5) <u>in order/so that</u> we can go anywhere we like on the way.
Daniel: Yes, it's better by bus (6) <u>because/unless</u> you can stop off at interesting places.
Rachel: Of course the bus will probably be tiring.
Daniel: Maybe you should take plenty of money (7) <u>if/in case</u> you decide to fly instead.
Rachel: I'll have to be careful with my money. I'm hoping to stay out there (8) <u>unless/until</u> I have to come back and start my job in September. I'm really looking forward to the trip, (9) <u>although/because</u> I'll be sad to leave here. And what about you? What are you doing this summer?
Daniel: I'd go away somewhere (10) <u>if/in case</u> I could afford to. But I'm working. I've got no money, (11) <u>because/so</u> I'll have to earn some.
Rachel: Have you really got no money (12) <u>although/in spite of</u> the fact that you've had a part-time job this term?
Daniel: You know me, Rachel. If I've got money, I spend it.

153 Links across sentences

A Introduction

Rita: You go to United's games, don't you, Tom? You watch them on TV, **too**.

Tom: Well, I'm a fan. It's wonderful when United win. **On the other hand**, it's terrible when they lose.

Rita: Why not have a change? **After all**, there are other things in life.

Tom: Such as?

Rita: There's music, **for example**. Why don't you go to a concert some time?

Tom: But I don't like classical music.

Look at the words and phrases **too**, **on the other hand**, **after all** and **for example**. They all make a link with an earlier sentence. When Rita says *There's music, for example*, she is giving an example of *other things in life*, which she has already mentioned.

B Words and phrases meaning 'and', 'but' and 'so'

'And': Sarah often works late. She works on Saturdays sometimes, **too/as well**.
Sarah often works late. She **also** works on Saturdays sometimes.
Arlene Black has a yacht and a helicopter. **In addition**, she has five cars.
I'm not inviting my cousin – I don't like him. **Besides**, he didn't invite me to his party.
The buildings are in a very poor condition. **Furthermore**, there is no money to repair them.

'But': I haven't been very well recently. **Still**, it could be worse.
Nick is looking for Rita. Rita, **however**, is busy working with Jessica.
Everyone thought that Emma should accept the offer. **Nevertheless/All the same**, she turned it down.
I don't want to be late for the meeting. **On the other hand**, I don't want to get there too early.

'So': The holiday had been a complete disaster. We **therefore** decided to fly home early if we could.
Someone switched the freezer off. **Consequently/As a result**, all the food was spoilt.

Some of these words and phrases are rather formal and typical of written English. They are **consequently**, **furthermore**, **however**, **in addition**, **nevertheless** and **therefore**.

C Other linking words and phrases

Rephrasing: Jessica isn't the most popular person around here. **In other words**, no one likes her.
Correcting yourself: We play basketball. **I mean/Or rather** volleyball.
Contradicting: Sarah isn't lazy. **On the contrary**, she works extremely hard.
Picking up a topic: I like Natasha. I went on holiday with her. ~ **Talking of** holidays, what are your plans for this year?
Changing the subject: It's a lovely day, isn't it? ~ Yes, beautiful. **By the way**, have you seen Melanie?
Supporting a statement: We don't need to drive to the club, do we? **After all**, it's only about 200 metres from here.
Dismissing something: I'm not sure a thank-you letter is really necessary. **Anyway**, I can't be bothered to write one.
Giving an example: Yes, I do think Henry is rude. He shouts at waiters, **for example/for instance**.

153 Exercises

1 Words and phrases meaning 'and', 'but' and 'so' (B)

What do the underlined words mean? Write *and*, *but* or *so*.

▶ Daniel's suitcase got left behind. He got it back in the end, <u>however</u>. = *but*
1. I'm too tired to go for a walk. <u>Besides</u>, it looks like rain. = ...
2. The road was under water. The police <u>therefore</u> closed it to traffic. = ...
3. We took lots of photos. We videoed the speeches <u>as well</u>. = ...
4. It was a terrible journey. <u>Still</u>, we got there safely in the end. = ...
5. A strike by air traffic controllers has begun. Many flights have <u>consequently</u> been cancelled. = ...
6. The company has spent millions on computers. <u>Nevertheless</u>, it does not seem to have become more efficient. = ...

2 Links across sentences (B–C)

Complete this letter to a local newspaper. Choose the correct word or phrase.

There's been a lot of talk about a 'spaceship' seen over the town at about eleven o'clock on Friday night. (▶) <u>As a result</u>/<s>Nevertheless</s>, hundreds of enthusiastic sky-watchers have arrived in town, hoping that it will return. But was it really a spaceship? About twenty people say they saw it. (1) <u>Consequently/Furthermore</u>, there is a photograph which is supposed to show the object in the sky. We know, (2) <u>however/as a result</u>, that trick photos are easy to produce. (3) <u>By the way/In other words</u>, it is almost certainly a fake. But it would be wrong to treat the whole thing as a joke. (4) <u>All the same/On the contrary</u>, all such reports should be carefully investigated. (5) <u>After all/Anyway</u>, the arrival of a spacecraft from another world would indeed be a serious matter. But usually there is a more simple explanation. Many supposed spaceships turn out to be weather balloons, (6) <u>for example/or rather</u>. A similar mistake probably lies behind the belief that someone from another world really did pay us a visit last Friday.

3 Links across sentences (C)

What would you say? Give your answer using a linking word or phrase.

▶ Support Emma's opinion: she might not get another offer.
   Emma: You're right. Maybe I should accept the offer.
           After all, you might not get another one.

1. Rephrase what Rita is saying: she doesn't want to see Nick.
   Rita: I don't know if I'll have time to see Nick.
           ....

2. Change the subject and ask what the time is.
   Tom: I hope Wayne Johnson will be fit to play for United on Saturday.
           ....

3. Dismiss the idea of buying a sweater: they haven't got one in your size.
   Daniel: I'm not sure if that sweater really suits you.
           ....

4. Mention Sarah as an example.
   Claire: Lots of our friends have mobile phones, don't they?
           ....

5. Contradict what Nick says.
   Nick: Sorry. I persuaded you to see that film and you hated it, didn't you?
           ....

Appendix 1: Word formation

A Introduction

Look at these examples.
> Lots of people believe that God **exists**.
> Lots of people believe in the **existence** of God.

Exist is a verb and **existence** is a noun. The word **existence** has two parts: **exist** and **ence**. We call **ence** a 'suffix'. We add it to end of the verb **exist** to form a noun.

We can also use suffixes to form verbs, adjectives and adverbs.
> The system is being **modernized**. (= made modern)
> I grew up in an **industrial** town. (= a town where there is a lot of industry)
> The man was behaving **strangely**. (= in a strange way)

There are many different suffixes, such as **ence**, **ize**, **al**, **ly**, **tion** and **ment**. Some of them can be used to form many different words. For example, there are a lot of nouns ending in **tion**: **action, education, explanation, information, instruction**, etc. There are no exact rules about which suffix you can add to which word. Adding a suffix can also involve other changes to the form of a word.
> industry → industrial   repeat → repetition   science → scientist.

Now look at these examples.
> They're going to **play** the match on Wednesday.
> They're going to **replay** the match on Wednesday.

We can add **re** to the beginning of the verb **play**. We call **re** a 'prefix'. A prefix adds something to the meaning of a word. The verb **replay** means 'play again'. We can also add prefixes to nouns and adjectives. See G and H.

B Noun suffixes

ment	the prospects for **employment**	reach an **agreement**
ion/tion/sion	take part in a **discussion**	increase steel **production** ask for **permission**
ation/ition	an **invitation** to a party	people's **opposition** to the idea
ence/ance	a **preference** for houses rather than flats	a **distance** of ten miles
ty/ity	no **certainty** that we shall succeed	keep the door locked for **security**
ness	people's **willingness** to help	recovering from an **illness**
ing	enter a **building**	reach an **understanding**

C Nouns for people

er/or	the **driver** of the car a newspaper **editor**
ist	a place full of **tourists** a **scientist** doing an experiment
ant/ent	an **assistant** to help with my work **students** at the university
an/ian	**Republicans** and Democrats the **electrician** rewiring the house
ee	an **employee** of the company (= someone employed)
	notes for **examinees** (= people taking an exam)

We also use **er** for things, especially machines.
> a hair-**dryer**   a food **mixer**   a cassette **player**

D Verb suffixes

Many verbs are formed by adding **ize** or **ise** to an adjective. Some are formed by adding **en**.
> **ize**   European safety rules are being **standardized**.   They **privatized** the company.
> **en**   They're **widening** the road here.   Meeting you has really **brightened** my day.

E Adjective suffixes

Most of these adjectives are formed from nouns.

al	a **professional** musician	Britain's **coastal** waters
ic	a **metallic** sound	a **scientific** inquiry
ive	an **informative** guidebook	an offer **exclusive** to our readers
ful	a **successful** career	feeling **hopeful** about the future
less	feeling **hopeless** about the future (= without hope)	**powerless** to do anything about it
ous	guilty of **dangerous** driving	**luxurious** holiday apartments
y	a **rocky** path	the **salty** taste of sea water
ly ▷109A	a **friendly** smile	a very **lively** person
able/ible	an **acceptable** error (= an error that can be accepted)	a **comprehensible** explanation
	a **valuable** painting (= worth a lot of money)	a **comfortable** chair

F Adverbs

ly ▷108   *He looked around **nervously**.*   *I moved here quite **recently**.*

G Some common prefixes

anti (= against)	**anti-roads** protestors	**anti-government** troops
inter (= between)	an **international** match	**interstate** highways in the US
mini (= small)	a **minicomputer**	the **minibar** in your hotel room
mis (= wrongly)	**mishear** what someone says	**miscalculate** the amount
multi (= many)	**multicoloured** lights	a **multimillionaire**
over (= too much)	too fond of **overeating**	**overcrowded** roads
post (= after)	the **post-war** world	a **postgraduate** student
pre (= before)	**pre-match** entertainment	in **prehistoric** times
re (= again)	a **reunion** of old friends	**reread** a favourite book
semi (= half)	**semi-skilled** work	sitting in a **semicircle**
super (= big)	a huge new **superstore**	a **supertanker** carrying oil
under (= too little)	thin and **underweight**	**underpaid** work

H Negative prefixes

We can also use a prefix to form an opposite. For example, the opposite of **clear** is **unclear** (= not clear). **Un** is the most common negative prefix.

dis	a **dishonest** way to behave	can't help being **disorganized**	**dislike** the idea
	disappear from the scene	a **disadvantage** of the plan	
il (+ l)	an **illegal** drug	an **illiberal** attitude	
im (+ m or p)	an **impossible** task	an **impolite** question	
in	an **indirect** route	the **invisible** man	a great **injustice**
ir (+ r)	an **irregular** shape	an **irrelevant** remark	
non	**non-alcoholic** drinks	a **non-stop** flight	
un	an **uncomfortable** chair	an **unusual** event	an **undated** letter
	uncertain what to do	**unpack** your suitcase	**unzip** the bag

Appendix 2: The spelling of endings

A Plural nouns

We add **s** to a noun to form the plural.
a car → two cars   *a name → some names*

1. After **s**, **sh**, **ch** and **x** we add **es** /ɪz/.
   glass → glasses   *dish → dishes*
   match → matches   *box → boxes*

2. A few nouns ending in **o** have **es**.
   heroes   potatoes   tomatoes
   But most have **s**.
   discos   kilos   photos   pianos
   radios   stereos   studios   zoos

3. When a noun ends in a consonant + **y**, the **y** changes to **ies**.
   penny → pennies   *story → stories*
   We do not change **y** after a vowel.
   day → days   *journey → journeys*

B The present simple s ending

In the third person singular, a present simple verb ends in **s**. (See Unit 5B.)
I know → he knows   *I work → she works*

1. After **s**, **sh**, **ch** and **x** we add **es** /ɪz/.
   pass → passes   *wash → washes*
   catch → catches   *mix → mixes*

2. Some verbs ending in **o** have **es**.
   go → goes /gəʊz/   *do → does* /dʌz/

3. When a verb ends in a consonant + **y**, the **y** changes to **ies**.
   hurry → hurries   *copy → copies*
   We do not change **y** after a vowel.
   stay → stays   *enjoy → enjoys*

C The ed ending

Most verbs have **ed** in the past tense. (See Unit 8B.) Most past participles also end in **ed**. (See Unit 11B.)
look → looked   *call → called*

1. If the verb ends in **e**, we add **d**.
   hope → hoped   *save → saved*

2. When a verb ends in a consonant + **y**, the **y** changes to **ied**.
   hurry → hurried   *copy → copied*

3. Sometimes we double a final consonant. This happens when a one-syllable verb ends with one vowel and one consonant, e.g. **beg**, **plan**.
   beg → begged   *plan → planned*
   For more details about doubling, see G.

D The ing-form

1. We normally leave out **e** when we add **ing** to a verb.
   take → taking   *drive → driving*
   But we keep a double **e** before **ing**.
   see → seeing   *agree → agreeing*

2. When a verb ends in **ie**, it changes to **ying**.
   die → dying   *lie → lying*
   But **y** does not change.
   hurry → hurrying

3. Sometimes we double a final consonant. This happens when a one-syllable verb ends with one vowel and one consonant, e.g. **win**, **put**.
   win → winning   *put → putting*
   For more details about doubling, see G.

E Adverbs

We form many adverbs from an adjective + **ly**.
slow → slowly   *calm → calmly*

1. We do not leave out **e** before **ly**.
   safe → safely   *strange → strangely*
   But there are a few exceptions.
   due → duly   *true → truly*
   whole → wholly

2. When an adjective ends in a consonant + **y**, the **y** changes to **ily**.
   angry → angrily   *happy → happily*
   An exception is *shy → shyly*.

3. When an adjective ends in a consonant + **le**, the **e** changes to **y**.
   probable → probably   *sensible → sensibly*

4. When an adjective ends in **ic**, we add **ally**.
   automatic → automatically /ɔːtəˈmætɪkli/
   romantic → romantically /rəʊˈmæntɪkli/
   But there is one exception.
   public → publicly

F The comparison of adjectives

We form the comparative and superlative of short adjectives with **er** and **est**. See Unit 110.
  old → older, oldest
  quick → quicker, quickest

1 If the adjective ends in **e**, we add **r** and **st**.
  late → later, latest   fine → finer, finest

2 When an adjective ends in a consonant + **y**, the **y** changes to **ier** or **iest**.
  heavy → heavier, heaviest
  lucky → luckier, luckiest

3 Sometimes we double a final consonant. This happens when a one-syllable adjective ends with one vowel and one consonant, e.g. *big*, *flat*.
  big → bigger, biggest   flat → flatter, flattest
  For more details about doubling, see G.

G The doubling of consonants

1 When we add **ed**, **ing**, **er** or **est** to a word, we sometimes double a final consonant. This happens when a one-syllable word ends with one vowel and one consonant, e.g. *stop*, *get*, *thin*, *sad*.
  stop → stopped   get → getting
  thin → thinner   sad → saddest

2 We do not double **y**, **w** or **x**.
  play → played   new → newest
  fax → faxing
  We do not double when there are two consonants.
  ask → asking   short → shortest
  rich → richer
  And we do not double when there are two vowels.
  seem → seemed   shout → shouting
  fair → fairest

3 The rule about doubling is also true for words of more than one syllable (e.g. *permit* = per + mit), but only if the last syllable is stressed.
  per'mit → per'mitted
  pre'fer → pre'ferring
  We do not usually double a consonant when the syllable is unstressed.
  'open → opened   'enter → entering
  An exception is that in British English l is usually doubled, even if the syllable is unstressed.
  travel → travelled (US: traveled)

Appendix 3: Punctuation

A Full stop (.), question mark (?) and exclamation mark (!)

A sentence ends with one of these punctuation marks.
- Full stop: *It's cold today.*   *The office was closed.*   *Please be careful.*
- Question mark: *Who's that?*   *Did you see the show?*   *Could you wait, please?*
- Exclamation mark: *Oh, no! I don't believe it!*

In the US a full stop is called a 'period'.

B Semi-colon (;)

We can use a semi-colon between two separate statements which are linked in meaning.
   Melanie is a very kind person; she visits David in hospital every day.
We could also use a full stop here.

C Colon (:)

We can use a colon before an explanation or before a list.
   Vicky felt nervous: she hated the dark.
   There wasn't much in the fridge: a couple of sausages, some butter, half a bottle of milk.

D Dash (–)

A dash is rather informal. It is sometimes used instead of a colon or a semi-colon.
   I'm having a great time – there's lots to do here.
   Vicky felt nervous – she hated the dark.

E Comma (,)

We often use a comma when we link two statements with **and**, **but** or **or**.
   Daniel was tired, and his feet were hurting.   *It's a really good camera, but I can't afford it.*
Note the two subjects in each sentence: *Daniel... his feet* and *It... I*. When there is only one subject, we do not use a comma.
   Daniel sat down and took his shoes off.

We can also use a comma when a sentence has a linking word like **when** or **although**.
   When the office is busy, Sarah has to work late.
For commas with relative clauses, see Unit 141.

Sometimes a comma can separate off an adverb or a phrase.
   Sarah, unfortunately, has to work late.   *On busy days, Sarah has to work late.*
Here the commas separate off *on busy days* and *unfortunately*.

The rules about commas are not very exact. In general, commas are more likely around longer phrases. With a short phrase there is often no comma.
   On busy days Sarah has to work late.   *Sometimes she has to work late.*

It is less usual to separate off something at the end of the sentence.
   Sarah has to work late when the office is busy.   *She stayed late to get the work done.*
We do not usually put a comma before **to** expressing purpose.

We also use commas in a list of more than two. The last two are linked by **and**, often without a comma.
   I went out with Rachel, Vicky, Emma and Matthew.

F Quotation marks (' ')

We put direct speech in quotation marks.
>   *Laura said, 'You haven't put those shelves up yet.'*   *'I haven't had time,' replied Trevor.*

We normally use a comma to separate the direct speech from the rest of the sentence. The comma comes before the quotation mark. Quotation marks are also called 'quotes' or 'inverted commas'.

Double quotation marks are sometimes used.
>   *Laura said, "You haven't put those shelves up yet."*

We can put quotation marks around titles.
>   *Do you watch that American comedy series called 'Roseanne'?*

We often use quotation marks when we mention a word or phrase.
>   *What does 'punctuation' mean?*   *Rap music is also called 'hip hop'.*

G Hyphen (-)

We sometimes use hyphens in these structures.
>   Compound noun: *eating ice-cream*
>   Compound expression before a noun: *an oven-ready meal*
>   Noun formed from a phrasal verb: *ready for take-off*
>   Noun + ing-form: *interested in rock-climbing*
>   Before the last word of a compound number: *a hundred and twenty-six people*
>   After some prefixes: *anti-aircraft guns*
>   Letter + noun: *sending an e-mail*

The rules about hyphens are not very exact. For example, you may see a compound noun written as **phonecard**, **phone-card** or **phone card**. Hyphens are not very frequent in British English, and they are used even less in American English. If you are unsure, it is usually safer to write two separate words.

H Apostrophe (')

Look at these examples.
>   *Today we're going for a drive in the country.*   *Everyone is looking at Nick's car.*

We use an apostrophe (') in short forms, when there is a missing letter, e.g. **we're** (= we are). See Unit 32.
We also use an apostrophe with **s** to form the possessive of a noun, e.g. **Nick's car**. See Unit 93.

I Capital letters

There are two capital letters (big letters) in this sentence.
>   *The boss said **I** could leave early.*

We use a capital letter at the beginning of a sentence and for the word **I**.

We also use a capital letter to begin the names of people, places, companies, etc.
>   *Mark and Sarah*   *New Orleans*   *the High Street*   *Somerset House*   *General Motors*

This includes the names of books, films, magazines, etc. All the important words start with a capital letter.
>   *The Spy Who Loved Me*   *Four Weddings and a Funeral*   *Newsweek*

We also use a capital letter for days of the week, months of the year, holidays and festivals, historical times, nationalities and most abbreviations.
>   *Monday*   *August*   *Easter*   *the New Year*   *the Industrial Revolution*
>   some *Italian* wine   the **UN** (= the United Nations)

APPENDIX 3: PUNCTUATION   373

Appendix 4: Pronunciation

A Key to phonetic symbols

VOWELS				CONSONANTS					
iː	tea	ʌ	cup	p	put	f	first	h	house
i	happy	ɜː	bird	b	best	v	van	m	must
ɪ	sit	ə	away	t	tell	θ	three	n	next
e	ten	eɪ	pay	d	day	ð	this	ŋ	song
æ	sad	əʊ	so	k	cat	s	sell	l	love
ɑː	car	aɪ	cry	g	good	z	zoo	r	rest
ɒ	dog	aʊ	now	tʃ	cheese	ʃ	ship	j	you
ɔː	ball	ɔɪ	boy	dʒ	just	ʒ	pleasure	w	will
ʊ	book	ɪə	dear						
u	actual	eə	chair						
uː	fool	ʊə	sure						

B Stress

In books about English, the symbol ' is used before a stressed syllable, the part of the word which is spoken with greater force.

   midnight /ˈmɪdnaɪt/   *about* /əˈbaʊt/   *exercise* /ˈeksəsaɪz/   *belonging* /bɪˈlɒŋɪŋ/

Here the syllables **mid**, **bout**, **ex** and **long** are stressed. It is important to get the stress on the right part of the word. Stressing a word incorrectly can make it difficult to understand.

Now look at these two sentences.
   We want to **protest** /prəˈtest/ *against experiments on live animals.*
   We want to make a **protest** /ˈprəʊtest/ *against experiments on live animals.*

Protest as a verb is stressed on the second syllable. As a noun it is stressed on the first syllable. There are a number of words like this, e.g. **conflict, contrast, export, import, increase, insult, produce, progress, protest, record, suspect, transfer, transport.** Sometimes a change of stress means a change of vowel sound.
   Verbs: *produce* /prəˈdjuːs/, *progress* /prəˈgres/, *record* /rɪˈkɔːd/
   Nouns: *produce* /ˈprɒdjuːs/, *progress* /ˈprəʊgres/, *record* /ˈrekɔːd/

We also use stress to show which are the important words in a sentence.
   'Claire's got a 'lovely 'flat. She 'bought it last 'year. It's 'right in the 'centre of 'town.

Here the important words are **Claire, lovely, flat** and so on. We do not usually stress 'grammatical words' like **a, she, the** and **of**.

C Intonation

The voice usually falls or rises on the most important word in the sentence. This word is usually at or near the end of the sentence.
   Claire's got a lovely ↘ flat.
Here the voice falls when saying **flat**, which is the key word.

The symbol ↘ is used for a falling intonation and ↗ for a rising intonation.
   Everything is more or less ↘ ready. (a statement)
   Everything is more or less ↗ ready? (a question)
The voice usually goes down in a statement and up in a yes/no question. In general, a fall means that what we say is complete. A rise means that what we say is incomplete, or it needs an answer. See also Unit 42 for intonation in question tags.

The voice often rises in the first part of a sentence and falls at the end.
   If you don't ↗ mind, I ought to be ↘ going.

There is always a fall or rise on the important part of the message. Which word is the key word depends on the meaning. Compare these examples.
   My friend is a bit upset. She's just failed her ↘ exam.
   I passed my exam last summer, but my friend has just ↘ failed hers.
   Lots of people have failed their exams. My ↘ friend has just failed.

D Voicing

Sounds can be voiced or voiceless. Voiced sounds are like those you make when you sing. All the vowels are voiced and some of the consonants. Voiceless sounds are like those you make when you whisper. Some of the consonants are voiceless. Compare these sounds.

VOICED		VOICELESS	
/b/	bill	/p/	pill
/d/	down	/t/	town
/g/	gold	/k/	cold
/z/	prize	/s/	price

The voiceless sounds are /p/, /t/, /k/, /f/, /θ/, /s/, /ʃ/, /tʃ/ and /h/.

E The **s** ending

We sometimes add the ending **s** or **es** to a word. For example we can do this to form the plural or the possessive of a noun.
   some chairs   the bushes   Mark's car   the woman's name
We can also add **s** or **es** to a verb.
   It looks nice and sunny.   Tom watches the football on Saturday afternoons.

The pronunciation of **s/es** depends on the sound which is before it. The ending is pronounced /s/ after a voiceless sound, /z/ after a voiced sound, and /ɪz/ after a sibilant sound.

Voiceless + /s/	shops /ps/	gets /ts/	takes /ks/
Voiced + /z/	jobs /bz/	hides /dz/	bags /gz/
	Laura's /əz/	days /eɪz/	knows /əʊz/
Sibilant + /ɪz/	buses /sɪz/	loses /zɪz/	crashes /ʃɪz/

For voiced and voiceless sounds see D. The sibilant sounds are /s/, /z/, /ʃ/, /ʒ/, /tʃ/ and /dʒ/.

F The **ed** ending

We add **ed** or **d** to a regular verb to form the past tense or past participle.
   *We all **walked** home.   They've **closed** the gates.*

The pronunciation of **ed** depends on the sound coming before it. The ending is pronounced /t/ after a voiceless sound, /d/ after a voiced sound, and /ɪd/ after /t/ or /d/.

Voiceless + /t/	hoped /pt/	worked /kt/	increased /st/
Voiced + /d/	robbed /bd/	begged /gd/	raised /zd/
	played /eɪd/	allowed /aʊd/	cared /eəd/
/t/ or /d/ + /ɪd/	wanted /tɪd/	landed /dɪd/	

For voiced and voiceless sounds see D.

G Weak forms

We are using a weak form when we pronounce **is** as /s/ rather than /ɪz/, or we pronounce **from** as /frəm/ rather than /frɒm/. Normally a word like **is** or **from** is not stressed, and so we can use a weak form. (For written short forms see Unit 32.)

	STRONG FORM	WEAK FORM		STRONG FORM	WEAK FORM
a	/eɪ/	/ə/	is	/ɪz/	/z/ or /s/
am	/æm/	/əm/ or /m/	me	/miː/	/mi/
an	/æn/	/ən/	must	/mʌst/	/məst/ or /məs/
and	/ænd/	/ənd/, /ən/ or /n/	of	/ɒv/	/əv/ or /v/
are	/ɑː(r)/	/ə(r)/	shall	/ʃæl/	/ʃəl/ or /ʃl/
as	/æz/	/əz/	she	/ʃiː/	/ʃi/
at	/æt/	/ət/	should	/ʃʊd/	/ʃəd/
be	/biː/	/bi/	some	/sʌm/	/səm/ or /sm/
been	/biːn/	/bɪn/	than	/ðæn/	/ðən/
can	/kæn/	/kən/	that	/ðæt/	/ðət/
could	/kʊd/	/kəd/	the	/ðiː/	/ði/ or /ðə/
do	/duː/	/du/ or /də/	them	/ðem/	/ðəm/ or /əm/
for	/fɔː(r)/	/fə(r)/	there	/ðeə(r)/	/ðə(r)/
from	/frɒm/	/frəm/	to	/tuː/	/tu/ or /tə/
had	/hæd/	/həd/, /əd/ or /d/	was	/wɒz/	/wəz/
has	/hæz/	/həz/, /əz/ or /z/	we	/wiː/	/wi/
have	/hæv/	/həv/, /əv/ or /v/	were	/wɜː(r)/	/wə(r)/
he	/hiː/	/hi/ or /i/	will	/wɪl/	/l/
her	/hɜː(r)/	/hə(r)/ or /ə(r)/	would	/wʊd/	/wəd/, /əd/ or /d/
him	/hɪm/	/ɪm/	you	/juː/	/ju/
his	/hɪz/	/ɪz/	your	/jɔː(r)/	/jə(r)/

Notes on weak forms

1 (r) means that an r-sound is pronounced before a vowel. In the phrase **for a minute**, the words **for a** are pronounced /fərə/.

2 **A, an** and **the** are normally spoken in their weak form.

3 **Some** does not have a weak form when it means 'some but not all'. See Unit 96A.

4 **That** normally has a weak form when it is a linking word, e.g. *I knew **that** /ðət/ it was true*. It does not have a weak form when it means something at a distance from the speaker, e.g. *Look at **that** /ðæt/ car*. (See Unit 91.)

5 **There** normally has a weak form in a sentence like **There's** /ðəz/ *a bookshop in town*. (See Unit 99.) It does not have a weak form when it means 'in that place', e.g. *The bookshop is over **there** /ðeə/*.

6 A verb does not have a weak form in a short answer with **yes**.
   *Are you tired? ~ Yes, **I am** /æm/*.

Appendix 5: American English

The differences between British and American English are mainly matters of pronunciation and vocabulary. There are also a few spelling differences such as British **centre** and **colour** and American **center** and **color**. There are some grammatical differences. Although they are not very great, those points that are most relevant to learners of English are explained here.

A Seem, look, etc

Compare these examples.

BRITISH

In British English there can be a noun (e.g. **pilot**) after **appear**, **feel**, **look**, **seem** and **sound**.
She **seemed (to be)** a good pilot.

It **looks (to be)** a lovely evening.

I **felt** a fool.

AMERICAN

Americans do not say *She seemed a good pilot.* They use **to be** or **like** after these verbs.
She **seemed to be** a good pilot.
OR She **seemed like** a good pilot.
It **looks to be** a lovely evening.
OR It **looks like** a lovely evening.
I **felt like** a fool.

B Present perfect and past simple (Units 11–15)

The British use the present perfect for recent actions, and especially with **just**, **already** and **yet**.
Bob **has washed** the dishes, look.

We've already **eaten** our lunch.

I've just **seen** Elaine.

Have you **corrected** your work yet?

The British normally use the present perfect with **ever** and **never**, not the past simple.

Have you ever **played** cricket?

The child **has** never **seen** snow before.

Americans can use either the present perfect or the past simple in these sentences.
Bob **has washed** the dishes, look.
OR Bob **washed** the dishes, look.
We've already **eaten** our lunch.
OR We already **ate** our lunch.
I've just **seen** Elaine.
OR I just **saw** Elaine.
Have you **corrected** your work yet?
OR **Did** you **correct** your work yet?
Americans normally use the past simple with **ever** and **never**, but the present perfect is possible.
Did you ever **play** baseball?
OR **Have** you ever **played** baseball?
The child never **saw** snow before.
OR The child **has** never **seen** snow before.

C Shall (Unit 23D)

The British use **will** for the future, but they can also use **shall** in the first person.
I **will**/I **shall** be here tomorrow.
We **will**/We **shall** contact you.

Americans do not normally use **shall** for the future.
I **will** be here tomorrow.
We **will** contact you.

The British use **shall** to make an offer. **Shall** I make the coffee?	Americans normally use **should**. **Should** I make the coffee?
The British can use **Shall we** …? for a suggestion. **Shall** we go for a walk?	Americans do not normally use **shall** in suggestions. **How about** a walk? **Would you like** to take a walk?

D Got and gotten

Both **have** and **have got** are used in Britain and in the US.
  He **has** a lot of money./He's **got** a lot of money. (= He is rich.)

The British do not use **gotten**. He's **made** a lot of money from his business activities. Your driving has **got** better.	In the US, **have gotten** expresses an action. He's **gotten/made** a lot of money from his business activities. Americans also use **gotten** meaning 'become'. Your driving has **gotten** better.

E Negatives and questions with have (Unit 31)

In Britain there are two different structures. I **haven't (got)** enough time. OR I **don't have** enough time. **Has** Carol **got** a computer? OR **Does** Carol **have** a computer?	Americans normally use the auxiliary **do**. I **don't have** enough time. **Does** Carol **have** a computer?

In the past tense, **did** is usual in both countries.
  We **didn't have** tickets.

F Emphatic do (Unit 33C)

The British can use **do** with an imperative for emphasis. Have a piece of cake. OR **Do** have a piece of cake.	**Do** with an imperative is less common in the US. Have a piece of cake.

G Do for an action

The British can use **do** to refer to an action already mentioned. I don't practise as often as I should (**do**). You'd better take your pill. ~ I already have (**done**).	Americans do not use **do** in this way. I don't practice as often as I should. You'd better take your pill. ~ I already have.

H Question tags (Unit 42)

Both the British and the Americans can use question tags when talking about facts.

*Blackpool is in Lancashire, **isn't it**?*   *Las Vegas is in Nevada, **isn't it**?*

But in general Americans use tags much less often than the British. They do not use tags to persuade or to argue. A sentence like *You aren't listening to me, are you?* is British but not American. But Americans often use **right?** and **OK?** as tags.

*I'll bring the luggage in, **shall I**?*   *I'll bring the baggage in, **OK**?*

I Can't and mustn't (Unit 46C)

| The British use **can't** to say that something is impossible.
*I rang, but there's no reply. They **can't** be at home.* | Americans can also use **mustn't** to say that something is impossible.
*I called, but there's no reply. They **can't** be home./They **mustn't** be home.* |

J Needn't and don't need to (Unit 48)

| The British can use either form.
*You **needn't** see the inspector.*
OR *You **don't need** to see the inspector.* | Americans do not normally use **needn't**.
*You **don't need** to see the inspector.* |

K Group nouns (Unit 81B)

| In Britain a group noun can usually take either a singular or a plural verb.
*The crowd **was/were** getting restless.*
*Sweden **plays/play** Germany tomorrow.* | In the US a group noun takes a singular verb.
*The crowd **was** getting restless.*
*Sweden **plays** Germany tomorrow.* |

L The (Unit 86C and 87A)

| The British use **the** with a musical instrument.
*I can play **the** piano.* | Americans can leave out **the**.
*I can play piano/play **the** piano.* |

| The British say **in hospital**.
*My sister is still **in hospital**.* | Americans say **in the hospital**.
*My sister is still **in the hospital**.* |

M Numbers

| The British use **and** between **hundred** and the rest of the number.
*six hundred **and** twenty* | Americans can leave out **and**.
six hundred twenty
OR *six hundred **and** twenty* |

N Dates

There are a number of different ways of writing and saying dates, but these are the most common.

BRITISH	AMERICAN
23 June 'the twenty-third of June' 'June the twenty-third'	June 23 'June twenty-third'

The British write 23.6.98, and Americans write 6.23.98.

O You and one (Unit 98C)

The British use **you** for people in general, including the speaker. In more formal English they can use **one**. *You/One can't be too careful.*	Americans use **you** for people in general. **One** is unusual. *You can't be too careful.*

P Somewhere and someplace (Unit 103)

In informal American English, **everyplace**, **someplace**, **anyplace** and **no place** can be used as well as **everywhere**, **somewhere**, etc.

*Let's find **somewhere** to eat.*	*Let's find **somewhere/someplace** to eat.*

Q Adjectives and adverbs (Unit 108)

In informal speech we can sometimes use an adjective form instead of an adverb. Americans do this more than the British.

*We had some **really** nice weather.*	*We had some **really** nice/some **real** nice weather.*
*It **certainly** doesn't make things any easier.*	*It **certainly/sure** doesn't make things any easier.*

R Prepositions (Units 118–126)

There are some differences in prepositions.

BRITISH	AMERICAN
round/around the village **towards/toward** the west looking **out of** the window **outside** the town	**around** the village **toward** the west looking **out** the window/**out of** the window **outside** the town/**outside of** the town

In American English there is a special use of **through** as a preposition of time.

*He'll be on the road **from** Tuesday **to/till** Friday.* *They will stay in Brighton **until** the end of April.*	*He'll be on the road (**from**) Tuesday **through** Friday.* *They will stay in Miami **through** April.*

Note the prepositions after **different**.

BRITISH	AMERICAN
This cup is different **from/to** the others.	This cup is different **from/than** the others.

Compare these expressions.

BRITISH	AMERICAN
in Bond Street	**on** Fifth Avenue
at the weekend, **at** weekends	**on** the weekend, **on** weekends
stay **at** home	stay home
a player **in** the team	a player **on** the team
ten minutes **past** four	ten minutes **past/after** four
twenty **to** seven	twenty **to/of** seven
write **to** me	write **me**/write **to** me
talk **to** someone	talk **to/with** someone
meet someone	meet **with** someone

S In case (Unit 148D)

In case can have different meanings.

BRITISH	AMERICAN
Take an umbrella **in case** it rains. (= because it may rain)	**In case** you're sick, you should call the office. (= if you're sick)

T Go and ...

Americans can leave out **and** from this structure.

I'll go **and** buy the tickets.	I'll go buy/I'll go **and** buy the tickets.

U The subjunctive

We can use expressions like **I suggest that** ... and **It's important that** ... to talk about what we want to happen. Look at these examples.

BRITISH	AMERICAN
Tim's parents have suggested that he **gets** a job/that he **should** get a job. It's important that everything **goes**/everything **should** go according to plan.	Tim's parents have suggested that he **get** a job. It's important that everything **go** according to plan.

The British normally use the present simple or **should**. (They use the subjunctive only in formal English.)

Americans normally use a form called the 'subjunctive', e.g. **get**, **go**.

V Irregular verbs

In the past tense some verbs can have either an irregular **t** ending or the regular **ed** ending. These verbs are **burn**, **learn**, **smell**, **spell**, **spill** and **spoil**.

The British prefer the **t** ending, although **ed** is also possible.	Americans normally use the **ed** ending.
They **burnt/burned** the old sofa. You've **spelt/spelled** this word wrong.	They **burned** the old sofa. You've **spelled** this word wrong.

But we say e.g. *a slice of **burnt** toast* in both British and American English.

In Britain the verbs **dream**, **lean** and **leap** can be regular, or they can have a **t** ending.

*I **dreamt/dreamed** about you.*	*I **dreamed** about you.*

These three forms ending in **t** have the vowel sound /e/. For example, **dreamt** is pronounced /dremt/, and **dreamed** is pronounced /driːmd/.

The verb **dive** is regular in Britain but can be irregular in the US.

*Craig **dived** into the water.*	*Craig **dived/dove** into the water.*

Dived is pronounced /daɪvd/, and **dove** is pronounced /dəʊv/.

Appendix 6: Irregular verbs

VERB	PAST TENSE	PAST/PASSIVE PARTICIPLE
arise	arose	arisen
be	was, were	been
bear	bore	borne
beat	beat	beaten
become	became	become
begin	began	begun
bend	bent	bent
bet	bet	bet
		betted
bind	bound	bound
bite	bit	bitten
		bit
bleed	bled	bled
blow	blew	blown
break	broke	broken
breed	bred	bred
bring	brought	brought
broadcast	broadcast	broadcast
build	built	built
burn	burnt	burnt
	burned	burned
burst	burst	burst
buy	bought	bought
catch	caught	caught
choose	chose	chosen
come	came	come
cost	cost	cost
creep	crept	crept
cut	cut	cut
deal /di:l/	dealt /delt/	dealt /delt/
dig	dug	dug
dive	dived	dived
	dove (US)	
do	did	done
draw	drew	drawn
dream /dri:m/	dreamt /dremt/	dreamt /dremt/
	dreamed	dreamed
drink	drank	drunk
drive	drove	driven
eat /i:t/	ate /et/	eaten /'i:tn/
fall	fell	fallen
feed	fed	fed
feel	felt	felt
fight	fought	fought

VERB	PAST TENSE	PAST/PASSIVE PARTICIPLE
find	found	found
flee	fled	fled
fly	flew	flown
forbid	forbad(e) /fə'bæd/	forbidden
forget	forgot	forgotten
forgive	forgave	forgiven
freeze	froze	frozen
get	got	got
		gotten (US)
give	gave	given
go	went	gone
grind	ground	ground
grow	grew	grown
hang	hung	hung
have	had	had
hear /hɪə/	heard /hɜːd/	heard /hɜːd/
hide	hid	hidden
hit	hit	hit
hold	held	held
hurt	hurt	hurt
keep	kept	kept
kneel	knelt	knelt
know	knew	known
lay	laid	laid
lead	led	led
lean /li:n/	leant /lent/	leant /lent/
	leaned	leaned
leap /li:p/	leapt /lept/	leapt /lept/
	leaped	leaped
learn	learnt	learnt
	learned	learned
leave	left	left
lend	lent	lent
let	let	let
lie	lay	lain
light	lit	lit
	lighted	lighted
lose	lost	lost
make	made	made
mean /mi:n/	meant /ment/	meant /ment/
meet	met	met
mow	mowed	mown
		mowed

VERB	PAST TENSE	PAST/PASSIVE PARTICIPLE
pay	paid	paid
put	put	put
read /riːd/	read /red/	read /red/
ride	rode	ridden
ring	rang	rung
rise	rose	risen
run	ran	run
say /seɪ/	said /sed/	said /sed/
see	saw	seen
seek	sought	sought
sell	sold	sold
send	sent	sent
set	set	set
sew	sewed	sewn
		sewed
shake	shook	shaken
shine	shone	shone
shoot	shot	shot
show	showed	shown
		showed
shrink	shrank	shrunk
	shrunk	
shut	shut	shut
sing	sang	sung
sink	sank	sunk
sit	sat	sat
sleep	slept	slept
slide	slid	slid
smell	smelt	smelt
	smelled	smelled
speak	spoke	spoken
speed	sped	sped
	speeded	speeded
spell	spelt	spelt
	spelled	spelled
spend	spent	spent
spill	spilt	spilt
	spilled	spilled
spin	spun	spun
spit	spat	spat
split	split	split
spoil	spoilt	spoilt
	spoiled	spoiled
spread	spread	spread
spring	sprang	sprung

VERB	PAST TENSE	PAST/PASSIVE PARTICIPLE
stand	stood	stood
steal	stole	stolen
stick	stuck	stuck
sting	stung	stung
stink	stank	stunk
	stunk	
stride	strode	stridden
strike	struck	struck
swear	swore	sworn
sweep	swept	swept
swim	swam	swum
swing	swung	swung
take	took	taken
teach	taught	taught
tear	tore	torn
tell	told	told
think	thought	thought
throw	threw	thrown
tread	trod	trodden
understand	understood	understood
wake	woke	woken
	waked	waked
wear	wore	worn
weave	wove	woven
	weaved	weaved
weep	wept	wept
win	won	won
wind	wound	wound
write	wrote	written

The verbs in this list are also irregular when they have a prefix, e.g. **overtake – overtook – overtaken**, **foretell – foretold – foretold**.

A few verbs have irregular present simple forms:

VERB	PRESENT SIMPLE
be	I **am**; you/we/they **are**; he/she/it **is**
do	he/she/it **does** /dʌz/
go	he/she/it **goes** /gəʊz/
have	he/she/it **has**
say	he/she/it **says** /sez/

For **burnt/burned, dreamt/dreamed**, etc in British and American English see page 382. For **gotten** see page 378.

Key to the starting test

The number after the answer tells you which unit of the book has information and practice on that grammar point.

1	c)	3	35	c)	49, 53	69	b)	106
2	c)	4, 6	36	b)	54	70	a)	108
3	d)	5, 6	37	b)	55, 56	71	d)	109
4	a)	7	38	b)	57	72	b)	110, 111
5	a)	8	39	b)	58	73	d)	112
6	d)	9	40	d)	60, 62	74	b)	113
7	c)	9, 10	41	b)	61, 62	75	c)	114
8	d)	11	42	c)	64	76	d)	115
9	b)	12, 13	43	c)	65	77	c)	118
10	d)	14	44	d)	66	78	d)	119
11	b)	15	45	b)	68	79	c)	120
12	d)	16	46	b)	70	80	c)	121
13	d)	17	47	b)	72	81	a)	123
14	a)	18, 19	48	b)	73	82	c)	124, 125
15	a)	20	49	d)	74	83	d)	126, 127
16	b)	23	50	c)	76, 77	84	d)	128–130
17	b)	24, 25	51	a)	78	85	d)	131
18	d)	26	52	c)	80	86	c)	132
19	c)	27	53	d)	81	87	a)	133
20	b)	28	54	d)	83, 84	88	c)	134
21	d)	31	55	a)	86	89	d)	136
22	b)	33	56	b)	87	90	d)	137
23	a)	34, 36	57	c)	89	91	b)	139
24	c)	37	58	c)	90	92	c)	140
25	c)	38	59	c)	91	93	c)	141, 142
26	b)	40	60	d)	92	94	b)	143
27	d)	41	61	b)	94	95	a)	144, 147
28	d)	42	62	d)	95	96	b)	145, 147
29	c)	43	63	d)	96	97	d)	146, 147
30	d)	44	64	d)	99	98	d)	149
31	b)	46	65	a)	100, 101	99	d)	150
32	c)	47	66	b)	102	100	d)	151
33	a)	48	67	c)	103			
34	b)	51, 52	68	a)	105			

Key to the exercises

Unit 1

1
1. determiner
2. verb
3. pronoun
4. adverb
5. pronoun
6. verb
7. adjective
8. preposition
9. linking word
10. adverb
11. determiner
12. adjective
13. linking word
14. noun

2
Verb: is, loves
Noun: Claire, café
Adjective: wonderful, old, romantic
Adverb: madly, unfortunately, rather
Preposition: of, for, at
Determiner: a, their, some
Pronoun: He, her, they
Linking word: and, but, so

3
1. verb
2. noun
3. adjective
4. verb
5. noun
6. verb
7. verb
8. noun
9. adjective
10. verb

Unit 2

1
1. subject
2. verb
3. complement
4. adverbial
5. object
6. complement

2 1 e) 2 a) 3 c) 4 d)

3
1. Tom likes football.
2. David had an accident.
3. We moved the piano.
4. Harriet is a tall woman.
5. Everyone sat on the floor.
6. Mike's friends gave him some help.

4
1. also, with several young people
2. first, in 1994
3. naturally, without help
4. fortunately, from the National Lottery

Unit 3

1
1. David gave Melanie a sweater.
2. Laura gave Trevor a scarf.
3. Emma gave Matthew a tennis racket.
4. Henry gave Claire a necklace.

2
1. sold her bike to her sister.
2. told the joke to all his friends.
3. gave her neighbour some help.
4. wrote her teacher a letter.

3 1 for 2 to 3 to 4 for 5 for 6 to

4
1. them to the bottle bank.
2. me a job.
3. them to the police.
4. you my umbrella.

Unit 4

1
1. They're/They are playing basketball.
2. She's/She is taking a photo.
3. He's/He is painting a picture.
4. They're/They are carrying a parcel.

2
1. are trying
2. are you finding
3. is helping
4. We're/We are getting
5. We aren't spending
6. It isn't taking
7. are you waiting
8. I'm/I am correcting

3
1. it's/it is raining.
2. I'm/I am working.
3. you're/you are sitting on my coat.
4. I'm/I am writing an important letter.
5. I'm/I am getting/feeling better.

Unit 5

1
1. a feeling
2. a repeated action
3. a fact
4. a fact
5. a thought
6. a feeling
7. a repeated action
8. a thought

2
1. doesn't speak
2. walk
3. needs
4. love
5. doesn't eat
6. don't look
7. doesn't work
8. don't like
9. wins
10. don't own

3
1. I go
2. comes
3. we travel
4. don't you come
5. doesn't make
6. do you take
7. I love
8. does it cost
9. I don't know
10. that doesn't matter
11. I don't want
12. Does that annoy
13. it doesn't annoy
14. find

Unit 6

1
1. He's/He is talking
2. I think
3. they're/they are discussing
4. Are you looking
5. Do you know
6. works
7. She doesn't work
8. You know
9. I give
10. she gives
11. She lives
12. It saves
13. I agree
14. I'm/I am wasting

2
1. It's/It is snowing, It's/It is coming
2. I start, I'm/I am starting
3. I'm/I am going, I drive
4. rises, we're/we are travelling
5. I'm/I am writing, I promise
6. I want, I'm/I am saving

3
1. she always takes
2. She's/She is always missing
3. do you always go
4. They're/They are always arguing.

Unit 7

1
1. state
2. action
3. state
4. action
5. state

2
1. I think
2. I have
3. it didn't fit
4. I see
5. you're having
6. you're thinking
7. I come
8. It weighed

3
1. are being
2. 's/is
3. 're being/are being
4. 're/are
5. 's being/is being

4
1. And I've still got a chance to win.
2. It's too expensive to buy.
3. It uses so much petrol.
4. I think it's going to be perfect for me.
5. I've never wanted to change it.

Unit 8

1
1. She swam in the sea.
2. She had a picnic.
3. She played volleyball.
4. She went out dancing.

2
1. were
2. started
3. saw
4. called
5. tried
6. was
7. arrived
8. fought
9. brought
10. entered
11. found

3
1. We didn't try
2. did you see
3. I didn't know
4. did you go
5. I didn't like
6. did Sarah enjoy
7. I didn't want

Unit 9

1
1. were watching television
2. were dancing in the street
3. was driving his taxi
4. was writing an essay

2
1. were you doing
2. I was taking
3. She was coming
4. I was going
5. You weren't looking
6. you were going

3
1. I was making phone calls all evening.
2. I was waiting in the rain for half an hour.
3. I was making sandwiches all afternoon.
4. I was sitting in a traffic jam for two hours.
5. My neighbour was playing loud music all night.

Unit 10

1
1. He sat down on a chair while I was painting it.
2. As he was running for a bus, he collided with a lamppost.
3. His hair caught fire when he was cooking chips.
4. When he was holding a beautiful vase, he suddenly dropped it.
5. He was sitting in the garden when a wasp stung him on the nose.

2
1. We lost
2. it came
3. was coming
4. went
5. fell
6. were playing
7. I was working
8. I lost
9. I got
10. did

3
1. The train was waiting when we arrived at the station.
2. I was reading a library book when I found a £10 note in it.
3. Sarah had an electric shock when she touched the wire.
4. When the doors opened, the crowd rushed in.
5. When the campers woke, they saw that the sun was shining.

Unit 11

1
1. She's/She has repaired it.
2. I've/I have opened the window.
3. They've/They have arrived.
4. He's/He has moved it.
5. We've/We have watched all these.

2
1. He's/He has broken his leg.
2. They've/They have built a house.
3. They've/They have seen a film.
4. She's/She has caught a fish.

3
1. I haven't done
2. hasn't made
3. You haven't put
4. I've/I have hurt
5. you've/you have had
6. have you put
7. It's/It has disappeared
8. I've/I have looked
9. have you done
10. I've/I have painted
11. I've/I have cleaned
12. We've/We have made
13. has that brush gone
14. you've/you have left

Unit 12

1
1. just tidied it.
2. He's/He has just made some/it.
3. I've/I have just eaten it.
4. she's/she has just checked them.
5. I've/I have just rung her.

2
1. I haven't started it yet.
2. I've/I have just seen Andrew
3. he's/he has already done
4. I haven't finished my plan yet.
5. You've/You have already begun
6. We've/We have already spent
7. I haven't done any real work yet
8. I've/I have just realized
9. I've/I have just decided

3
1. He hasn't had any fun for a long time.
2. He's/He has had a cold for a week.
3. He hasn't seen his friends for ages.
4. He hasn't done any sport since last year.
5. He's/He has been busy with his studies for months.

4
1. rung her since
2. seen them for
3. watched one for
4. had one since
5. played (it) since

Unit 13

1 1 been 2 been 3 gone

2
1. Have you ever been to San Francisco?
   No, I've never been to San Francisco
   I've been to Los Angeles.
2. Have you ever played basketball?
   No, I've never played basketball
   I've played volleyball.
3. Have you ever seen/read (the play) 'Hamlet'?
   No, I've never read/seen 'Hamlet'
   I've read/seen 'Macbeth'.

3
1. the second time I've lost my bank card.
2. This is the third time the washing-machine has broken down.
3. This is the first time I've been in/to England.
4. This is the second time I've stayed in this hotel.
5. This is (about) the fifth time I've missed the bus.

4
1. I haven't seen her today.
2. we haven't been there this weekend.
3. we haven't had one this term.
4. has rung this evening.

Unit 14

1
1. have arrived
2. repaired
3. I've/I have lost
4. has started
5. ran
6. earned
7. We planted
8. have gone
9. has turned
10. I phoned
11. I've/I have made
12. broke

2
1. The train drivers have gone on strike. They **stopped** work(ing) at twelve o'clock.
2. The Queen has arrived in Toronto. She flew **there in** an RAF aircraft.
3. Two men have escaped from Parkhurst Prison. **They** got away during the night.
4. The actor Howard Bates has died in a car accident. His car crashed into a wall.
5. Linda Jones has won the women's marathon. She ran it in 2 hours 27 minutes.

3
1. haven't taken a photo since
2. weeks since I last saw
3. was the last time we played
4. haven't eaten anything for

Unit 15

1
1. has stood
2. was
3. stayed
4. 've/have lived
5. 've/have known
6. were

2 1 b) 2 b) 3 a)

3
1. this, last
2. today, yesterday
3. last, this
4. this, yesterday

4
1. What's/What has happened
2. He's/He has had
3. He fell
4. broke
5. did it happen
6. told
7. You knew
8. you didn't tell
9. I didn't see
10. I haven't seen
11. He's/He has had
12. He did

Unit 16

1
1. have you been doing
2. She's/She has been helping
3. have you been studying
4. I've/I have been trying
5. it's/it has been getting

2
1. they've/they have been arguing
2. he's/he has been cooking
3. he's/he has been driving
4. He's/He has been waiting

3
1. Matthew has been swimming for an hour.
2. My friends have been travelling (around the world) for three months.
3. Mark has been working for ten hours.
4. Melanie and Rita have been talking for forty minutes.
5. How long have you been reading the/that/your book?

Unit 17

1
1. 's/has left, He's/He has been cleaning, he's/he has finished
2. I've/I have been working, You've/You have done
3. I've/I have heard, have you been doing, We've/We have done

2
1. How many miles have you walked?
2. How long have they/the workmen been digging up the road?
3. How many photos have you taken?
4. How long has it been raining?

3
1. I've/I have been clearing
2. I've/I have found
3. You've/You have been sitting
4. I've/I have been watching
5. You've/You have been
6. I've/I have had
7. They've/They have been
8. I've/I have never had

Unit 18

1 1 b) 2 a) 3 a) 4 b)

2
1. The train had just gone.
2. The rain had stopped.
3. I'd/I had forgotten my ticket.
4. They'd/They had stolen it a week before.
5. I hadn't seen her for ages.
6. I'd/I had just cleaned it.
7. I'd/I had already eaten my sandwiches.

3
1. had left
2. 've/have finished
3. 've/have eaten
4. 'd/had ordered
5. 've/have made
6. had told
7. 'd had/had had
8. 's/has started
9. 've/have turned
10. 'd/had made

Unit 19

1 1 a) 2 a) 3 b) 4 a)

2
1. When Nick had saved enough money, he bought a motor bike.
2. Mark put all the dishes away when he'd/he had dried them.
3. When I'd/I had looked both ways, I pulled out into the road.
4. The golfers went into the clubhouse when they'd/they had played the last hole.

3
1. had decided
2. We were waiting
3. I realized
4. I'd/I had forgotten
5. It was
6. I hurried
7. rang
8. They were working
9. heard
10. They found
11. drove
12. I met
13. We had
14. I'd/I had said
15. I ran
16. I got
17. were sitting
18. they saw
19. started

Unit 20

1
1. I'd/I had been working
2. I hadn't been looking
3. she'd/she had been dealing
4. I'd/I had been waiting
5. I'd/I had been reading

2
1. She'd/She had been crying.
2. He'd/He had been driving too fast.
3. They'd/They had been playing with matches.
4. He'd/He had been standing under a tree.

3
1. had been watching
2. 'd/had been playing, hadn't won
3. 'd/had been walking, 'd/had walked
4. 'd/had stopped, was smoking
5. has been aching
6. was lying, 'd/had bought, 'd/had been reading

Unit 21

1
1. She uses it
2. She's/She has lost it
3. We're/We are getting them
4. She's/She is enjoying it
5. I hate it
6. I've/I have checked them
7. They play it
8. You haven't watered them

2
1. I haven't seen you for months.
2. I'm/I am waiting for a (phone) call.
3. I like your (new) jacket.
4. It's/It has been snowing since yesterday.

3 1 a) 2 b) 3 a) 4 b) 5 a) 6 b)

4
1. I've/I have been working
2. she went
3. You've/You have been writing
4. They moved
5. he stopped, I was waiting

5
1. you know
2. David told
3. haven't been
4. I started
5. have you sold
6. I've been learning
7. had
8. I've had
9. I don't often drive
10. I don't like
11. I ride
12. bought
13. was working
14. I'd been doing
15. I'd earned

6
1. I'm/I am speaking
2. knows
3. had heard
4. he'd/he had been taking (Also possible: he's/he has been taking)
5. he's/he has answered
6. he arrived
7. were waiting
8. has been reading

Unit 22

1
1. I'll be leaving here at the end of the month.
2. Luckily they'll find a flat for me.
3. The training programme finishes next summer.
4. They'll decide about that next year.

2
1. future 4. future
2. future 5. present
3. future

3 1 a) 2 a) 3 b) 4 b) 5 a)

Unit 23

1
1. future 4. decision
2. decision 5. future
3. future

2
1. I'll answer it/the phone.
2. I'll have (the) chicken (, please).
3. I'll carry the/your bag (for you).
4. I'll post it/the letter (for you),

3
1. Tom will watch the match.
2. Harriet's party will be fun.
3. Trevor won't put up the shelves.
4. Laura will be annoyed.
5. Andrew will study all weekend.
6. Rachel won't do any work.

4
1. will 4. will
2. Shall 5. will
3. will 6. Shall

Unit 24

1
1. He's/He is going to light the firework.
2. She's/She is going to hit the ball.
3. They're/They are going to catch a bus.
4. She's/She is going to answer the phone.

2
1. I'm/I am going to lend
2. He's/He is going to take
3. It's/It is going to be
4. is he going to keep
5. are we going to get
6. He's/He is going to have
7. We're/We are going to get
8. it isn't going to get

3
1. I'm/I am going to get wet.
2. I'm/I am going to be sick.
3. I'm/I am going to lose.
4. It's/It is going to crash!
5. It isn't going to stop.

Unit 25

1
1. 's/is going to read
2. 'll have
3. 'll video
4. are you going to buy

2
1. It's/It is going to attack us/me.
2. aliens will land on the earth in the next ten years.
3. she's/she is going to get married.
4. I'll invite her for a meal.

3
1. We're/We are going to build
2. will be (Also possible: is going to be)
3. will like (Also possible: are going to like)
4. will be (Also possible: are going to be)
5. We aren't going to cut (Also possible: We won't cut)
6. We're/We are going to have
7. will be (Also possible: is going to be)
8. We're/We are going to stop (Also possible: We will stop)

Unit 26

1
1. future 4. future
2. future 5. present
3. present

2
1. She's/She is working on Saturday.
2. She's/She is flying to Cairo on 15 May.
3. He's/He is seeing his boss at four o'clock this afternoon.
4. They're/They are playing tennis tomorrow afternoon.

3
1. I'm/I am going 5. I'm/I am going
2. He's/He is staying 6. finishes
3. gets 7. we're/we are going
4. are you doing

4
1. 's/is about to win 4. 're/are about to move
2. are to go 5. are to take
3. is to visit

Unit 27

1
1. When Mark sees the boss, he's/he is going to discuss his problem.
2. When Rachel uses the computer (later), she's/she is going to send an e-mail.
3. When Tom visits David in hospital, he's/he is going to tell him about United's win.
4. When Matthew's/Matthew is in town tomorrow, he might buy some new trainers.

2
1. you need
2. you get
3. I hire
4. it'll/it will be
5. I'll/I will get
6. there's/there is
7. I arrive
8. I'll/I will ring
9. I'll/I will be
10. I hear
11. I'm/I am
12. I'll/I will lie
13. I go
14. You'll/You will be
15. you don't get

3
1. You shouldn't decide until you've/you have thought about it (first).
2. I'll think of you next week when I'm/I am lying on the beach.
3. We ought to/We can leave as soon as I've/I have paid the bill.
4. We can discuss it (later) while we're/we are sitting on the plane together.
5. You can use the computer when I've/I have finished with it.

Unit 28

1
1. I'll/I will be earning
2. I'll/I will be doing
3. will you be doing
4. I'll/I will be giving
5. who'll/who will be doing
6. you'll/you will be playing

2
1. I'll/I will be seeing her
2. I'll/I will be going there next summer
3. I'll/I will be playing (it/badminton) next weekend.
4. I'll/I will be having lunch/it in the canteen tomorrow. OR I'll/I will be having lunch/it there tomorrow.

3
1. Will you be going to the library today?
2. Will you be writing to Vicky soon?
3. Will you be using your calculator this afternoon?
4. Will you be seeing Daniel tomorrow?
5. Will you be driving to the festival?
6. Will you be phoning your sister soon?

Unit 29

1
1. I'll/I will have had
2. I'll/I will have been the subject of a TV documentary
3. I'll/I will have become world-famous
4. I'll/I will have made millions of pounds from my pictures

2
1. twenty
2. She will/She'll have travelled two hundred miles.
3. He will/He'll have done a/one hundred and fifty (press-ups).

3
1. were going to go
2. was going to pick
3. were going to see

4
1. I was going to paint the door, but I didn't feel **very** well.
2. I was going to repair the lamp, but I forgot.
3. I was going to wallpaper the bedroom, but I **didn't** have time.

Unit 30

1
1. It will/It'll be
2. who will/who'll answer OR who will/who'll be answering
3. will be answering
4. he'll/he will still be giving
5. he'll/he will have replied
6. he won't/will not be eating OR he won't/will not eat
7. will be
8. he'll/he will have earned
9. we'll/we will be returning OR we'll/we will return
10. he'll/he will have got

2
1. 'm/am going to get up early tomorrow.
2. arrives at ten thirty.
3. I'm/I am seeing my bank manager tomorrow.
4. I'm/I am about to go out.
5. There's/There is going to be trouble.

3
1. I'm/I am spending OR I'm/I am going to spend
2. I'm/I am going to look OR I'll/I will be looking
3. That'll/That will be OR That's/That is going to be
4. I'll/I will be OR I'm/I am going to be
5. Are you staying/Are you going to stay OR Will you be staying/Will you stay
6. I'm/I am staying OR I'm/I am going to stay OR I'll/I will be staying
7. I'm/I am going to see OR I'm/I am seeing OR I'll/I will be seeing OR I'll/I will see
8. I'm/I am going OR I'll/I will be going
9. we might see OR we'll/we will probably see OR we're/we are probably going to see
10. do you leave OR are you leaving OR will you be leaving
11. is
12. I'll/I will see

Unit 31

1
1. She's/She has got a map. OR She has a map.
2. He hasn't got an umbrella. OR He doesn't have an umbrella.
3. They've/They have got a rabbit. OR They have a rabbit.
4. They haven't got a car. OR They don't have a car.

2
1. Has … got
2. hasn't got
3. didn't have
4. didn't have
5. haven't got

3
1. played
2. drinks
3. spent
4. received

4
1 we're/we are having
2 you've/you have got OR you have
3 it hasn't got OR it doesn't have
4 Did you have
5 I had
6 Have you got OR Do you have
7 have
8 I didn't have

Unit 32

1
1 It's a difficult problem.
2 I've seen the results.
3 I don't have any information.
4 We haven't reached a decision.
5 I'm very excited about it.
6 You needn't decide now.
7 It isn't yet certain. OR It's not yet certain.
8 We'll be pleased to see you.
9 Don't worry.
10 I'd like to buy a new computer.
11 We're willing to help.
12 We won't know the result for some time.

2
1 Where's, It's
2 don't, isn't OR 's not
3 What's, He's

3
1 I would like a coffee, please.
2 There has been an accident.
3 That is correct.
4 I had seen the film before.
5 Who has got the key?
6 We would have stopped if we had seen you.

Unit 33

1
1 I am smiling.
2 I do like my new portrait.
3 It is foggy today.
4 Yes, I did remember the water.

2
1 it did cost   4 I did go
2 you do look   5 they do quarrel
3 it does stop

3
1 I did finish the crossword today.
2 my room does need tidying up.
3 I do find the work difficult.
4 I did want to give the course up.
5 Do have a chocolate.
6 this place does depress me.

Unit 34

1
1 offering
2 making a suggestion
3 asking for information
4 requesting
5 inviting
6 asking for information
7 asking permission

2
1 Are you a rich man?
2 Are quizzes your only hobby?
3 Did you work hard at school?
4 Have you got/Do you have any other interests?
5 Is it an interesting life?
6 Does your wife ask you quiz questions?
7 Do you answer questions in your dreams?

3
1 Are you going to America?
2 Does Laura play tennis?
3 Did you enjoy your holiday?
4 Shall we (both) go for a walk?
5 Will you be at the club tonight?
6 Is the train on time?
7 Do Mike and Harriet go camping?
8 Could I/Can I/May I borrow your squash racket?
9 Have you got/Do you have a motor bike?

Unit 35

1
1 Yes, I can   5 No, they aren't
2 Yes, it is   6 Yes, I do
3 No, he hasn't   7 No, he isn't
4 Yes, I did   8 No, I haven't

2
1 No, we won't   5 Yes, she does
2 Yes, I did   6 No, we aren't
3 Yes, she has   7 No, we can't
4 No, I didn't   8 No, I'm/I am not

3 1 b) 2 b) 3 b) 4 a) 5 b) 6 a) 7 b) 8 b)

Unit 36

1
1 What's/What is the date (today)?
2 When does the course finish?
3 Who have you invited (to your party)?
4 How can I/we get tickets (to the concert)?
5 Where are we going to have lunch? OR Where shall we have lunch?

2
1 Where   6 How far
2 How many   7 How often
3 When   8 What kind
4 Who   9 How long
5 What

3
1. where do you record
2. How many programmes have you done?
3. How much money do you earn?
4. When did you start acting?
5. What are your plans for the future?

Unit 37

1
1. a) Rita b) Rita   2 a) Mark b) a bus
3. a) a/the lorry b) a/the car

2
1. Who is/Who's having a party?
2. What were you reading?
3. What have you learnt?
4. what should we do?
5. Who is/Who's looking for me?
6. Who are you looking for?
7. What is she planning?
8. Who has/Who's moved in next door?
9. What is/What's worrying you?
10. Who do you want to meet?

3
1. photos can I keep?
2. flowers look lovely?
3. (money) went missing?
4. house did you pass (earlier)?
5. children has the doctor got?/does the doctor have?
6. (money) do doctors earn?
7. uncle has died?
8. wife is coming (later)?

Unit 38

1
1. What are you looking at?
2. What are you talking about?
3. What are you waiting for?
4. What are you pointing at?

2
1. What are you ashamed of?
2. What is she famous for?
3. What is he going to complain about?
4. What is she going to be late for?
5. What do you feel nervous about?

3
1. What   6. for
2. for   7. What
3. What   8. like
4. like   9. how
5. what

Unit 39

1
1. Which flight did you take?
2. Which hotel did you stay at?
3. What music do you like?
4. What magazine did you buy?
5. What company do you work for?
6. What language are you learning?

2
1. Which   4. What
2. Which   5. Which
3. What

3
1. Who   4. What
2. Which   5. Which
3. What   6. Who

Unit 40

1
1. wasn't   5. has
2. had   6. didn't know
3. don't know   7. isn't
4. didn't land

2
1. can't   5. wasn't
2. doesn't   6. isn't
3. didn't   7. don't
4. weren't   8. haven't

3
1. doesn't get headaches.
2. can't relax.
3. didn't miss a lecture.
4. isn't a nervous person.
5. doesn't lose things.
6. wasn't a happy child.
7. hasn't decided on a career.

4
1. no   4. no
2. no   5. No
3. not   6. not

Unit 41

1
1. Can't you drive, Melanie?
2. Won't you be at the disco, Rachel?
3. Haven't you got/Don't you have a television, Nick?

2
1. Don't you feel well? OR Aren't you feeling well?
2. Haven't they arrived yet?
3. Didn't she say hello?
4. Can't you swim?

3
1 No 2 Yes 3 Yes 4 No

4
1. Why didn't the staff know what to do?
2. Why couldn't they stop the ride?
3. Why aren't they trained in first aid?
4. Why wasn't the ambulance called immediately?
5. Why didn't the doctor have a mobile phone?

Unit 42

1
1. a comment   3. a question
2. a comment   4. a question

2
1. isn't it?   5. don't they?
2. are there?   6. can't we?
3. aren't you?   7. was it?
4. didn't you?

3
1. don't you?   5. does it?
2. haven't I?   6. is there?
3. aren't you?   7. can you?
4. do you?

4
1 Let's listen to some music, shall we?
2 Don't do anything silly, will you?
3 You haven't got a train timetable, have you?
4 Pass me the salt, can you?/could you? OR You couldn't pass me the salt, could you?

Unit 43

1
1 neither am I
2 Neither can I
3 so am I
4 so do I
5 Neither have I
6 so would I

2
1 neither does Emma.
2 so has Emma.
3 neither can Mark.
4 neither is Melanie.
5 so does Emma.
6 so does Claire.

3
1 I don't expect so
2 I suppose so
3 I hope not
4 I don't think so
5 I'm afraid not

Unit 44

1
1 She can't play the violin.
2 He can climb trees.
3 She can juggle.
4 They can't lift the weights.

2
1 I can walk
  (Also possible: I'm able to walk)
2 I can go/I'll be able to go
3 to be able to get
4 been able to do

3 1 c) 2 a)

4
1 was able to
2 could
3 could/was able to
4 were able to
5 couldn't/wasn't able to

Unit 45

1 (*Can*, *could* and *may* are all possible.)
1 Can I borrow your calculator?
2 May I join you?
3 Could I look at your notes?

2
1 You can have a picnic.
2 You can't drop litter.
3 You can turn left.
4 You can't play ball games/football.
5 You can't smoke.

3
1 I wasn't allowed to have
2 we're/we are allowed to have
3 we're/we are allowed to do
4 we'll/we will be allowed to hold

4
1 Am I allowed to
2 May I
3 Am I allowed to
4 Am I allowed to
5 May I

Unit 46

1 (*May* and *might* are both possible.)
1 she might be
2 She may be
3 She might be sitting
4 She may be having
5 You might find
6 She might know

2
1 He may/might win.
2 I may/might have one.
3 We may/might get one.
4 She may/might be late.
5 They may/might be visiting me.

3
1 mightn't
2 mightn't
3 couldn't
4 couldn't
5 mightn't

4
1 can't
2 must
3 might
4 can't
5 might
6 must

Unit 47

1
1 I had to pay, did you have to pay
2 You have to slam, You'll have to fix
3 do you have to take, I'll have to take
4 We had to move, We didn't have to look, We've/We have had to do
5 has to start, does he have to get

2
1 You must get to work on time.
2 has to keep his dog under control.
3 You must listen carefully.
4 visitors have to report to the security officer.

3
1 must
2 has to
3 have to
4 must
5 have to
6 must
7 must

Unit 48

1
1 must, mustn't, needn't
2 mustn't, must
3 mustn't, needn't
4 mustn't, must, needn't

2
1 didn't have to wait ages to cross the road.
2 don't have to work long hours.
3 doesn't have to work in a factory.
4 didn't have to lock their doors.
5 don't have to wash their clothes by hand.

3
1 we didn't need to borrow any money.
2 I needn't have bothered.
3 We needn't have left/We didn't need to leave so early.
4 I didn't need to pay to go in.
5 you needn't have tipped/you didn't need to tip the waiter.

unit 49

1
1. shouldn't
2. ought
3. should
4. shouldn't
5. should
6. oughtn't

2
1. We'd better wait (for Rachel).
2. You'd better lock it/lock your bike.
3. I'd better tidy my room.
4. You'd better not drive/We'd better not go too fast.
5. We'd better do some revision.

3
1. I'm/I am supposed to take two before meals.
2. They're/They are supposed to report to the police.
3. You're/You are supposed to stand in a queue.
4. They aren't supposed to watch it.

4
1. We had/We'd better hurry. (Also possible: We should hurry./We ought to hurry.)
2. We had/We'd better not be OR We oughtn't to be/We shouldn't be
3. should arrive/ought to arrive
4. You shouldn't take/You oughtn't to take
5. We aren't supposed to get

Unit 50

1
1. Can I have a fork, please?
2. Could I have a towel, please?
3. Would you mind answering the phone?

2
1. must
2. have
3. like
4. want
5. Can/Could
6. Would
7. wonder
8. Can/Could

3
1. Can I have a receipt, please?/Can you give me a receipt, please?
2. Could you tell me the time, please?
3. Can you help me, please?
4. Could I have a bag, please?/Could you give me a bag, please?
5. Would you mind clearing a space (on the table), please?
6. Could I speak to the manager, please?

Unit 51

1
1. Shall we stop for a minute?
2. Would you like a game?
3. I'll post that letter for you.

2
1. Shall
2. Shall
3. could
4. Would
5. Will
6. Would

3
1. Would you like a cup of tea? OR Will/Won't you have a cup of tea?
2. What shall/can/should I say in my letter?
3. Let's have/We could have a cup of coffee. OR Shall we have a cup of coffee?
4. I'll/I can walk home with you. OR Shall/Can I walk home with you?
5. Would you like to visit me one weekend? (Also possible: Will/Won't you visit me one weekend?)

Unit 52

1
1. will
2. won't
3. would
4. will
5. would
6. wouldn't
7. would

2
1. will help
2. wouldn't let
3. will give
4. won't go
5. would like
6. wouldn't open
7. won't stand

3
1. Shall we go to the swimming-pool?
2. I won't take any risks.
3. I'd/I would like a shower (, please).
4. You shouldn't decide in a hurry.
5. (I think) the world will end in the year 3000.

Unit 53

1
1 b) 2 a) 3 b)

2
1. They shouldn't have left/oughtn't to have left litter everywhere.
2. She should say/ought to say hello to people.
3. He shouldn't have been/oughtn't to have been late for the interview.
4. She should have looked./She ought to have looked.

3
1. he shouldn't have left
2. might have taken
3. You must have been
4. he can't have rung

4
1. someone must have posted it.
2. she may/might not have heard the alarm.
3. he shouldn't have driven/oughtn't to have driven at 100 miles an hour/so fast.
4. He can't/couldn't have failed the exam.

Unit 54

1
1. Dinner is being served.
2. Some houses are being built.
3. The seals are being fed.
4. A flag is being raised.

2
1. is owned
2. was being used
3. was bought
4. hadn't been looked
5. has been done
6. is used

3
1. will be done/are going to be done
2. will ... be called
3. can't be bought
4. should be sold

4
1. got hurt
2. get lost
3. get broken
4. got divorced

Unit 55

1
1. swept
2. burst
3. were rescued
4. received
5. reached
6. were blocked
7. were brought
8. is being done
9. said

2
1. my brother
2. The water
3. terrorists
4. the alarm
5. The guide
6. The dog

3
1. was won by Claude Jennings.
2. did a parachute jump last week.
3. been attacked by a bull.
4. being built.
5. likes Jessica.
6. been thrown away.
7. been kidnapped by Martians.
8. was seen by five people.

Unit 56

1
1. was taken
2. was done
3. was interviewed by a very nice young police officer
4. fingerprints were found (by detectives)
5. burglar was identified (by the police computer).
6. has been arrested
7. (he) is being questioned
8. jewellery hasn't been found

2
1. didn't produce many cars for sale.
2. production was started by a German called Karl Benz.
3. is now seen as the father of the motor car.

3
1. People should use them/bicycles for short journeys.
2. someone has discovered a new source of energy?
3. they're/they are going to knock it down/knock down this building.
4. you shouldn't keep them/eggs in a freezer.
5. people put it/litter in the bin?

Unit 57

1
1. New employees are given special training.
2. Extra payments are given to staff who perform well.
3. Most employees are offered company shares.
4. All Zedco staff are allowed six weeks' holiday.
5. A full salary is paid to women who leave to have children.

2
1. expected that the soap opera 'Round the Corner' will end next year.
2. It is supposed that the footballer Wayne Johnson is earning £10 million a year.
3. It is believed that the Prime Minister and his wife have separated.

3
1. is expected to end next year.
2. The footballer Wayne Johnson is supposed to be earning £10 million a year.
3. The Prime Minister and his wife are believed to have separated.

Unit 58

1
1. had his car repaired.
2. is having her photo taken.
3. had his windows cleaned.
4. is having her eyes tested.

2
1. David (has) had his arm bandaged.
2. Daniel is going to have his tooth filled.
3. Laura is having her photos developed.

3
1. did you get your arm bandaged, David?
2. did you get your tooth filled, Daniel?
3. did you get your photos developed, Laura?

4
1. Tom had his car stolen from outside his house.
2. Rita had her rent increased by ten per cent.
3. David has had his electricity cut off.

Unit 59

1
1. He is afraid of being sent away.
2. He doesn't want to be misunderstood.
3. He hopes to be offered a job.
4. He doesn't mind being paid low wages at first.
5. He is willing to be re-trained.
6. He would like to be given a chance.

2
1. being used
2. working
3. to be treated
4. to give
5. to be invited
6. being taken

3
1. to write
2. to be tidied
3. hoovering/to be hoovered
4. to do
5. ironing/to be ironed
6. to finish
7. missing
8. to be handed
9. to be
10. being told

Unit 60

1
1. Trevor promised to put up the shelves/to put the shelves up (soon).
2. Claire decided to buy both the dresses.
3. Melanie offered to cook the meal.
4. Tom threatened to shoot Nick's dog/the dog.

2
1. They seem to believe
2. it seems to have improved
3. She doesn't seem to like
4. He seems to be working
5. He doesn't seem to have made
   (Also possible: He seems not to have made)

3
1. to hang   4. to invite
2. to come   5. to take
3. to be having   6. to have left

Unit 61

1
1. I've/I have given up trying. OR I gave up trying.
2. I can't imagine being
3. I enjoy watching it on TV.
4. suggested having a party.

2
1. can't stand lying
2. couldn't/can't resist having
3. couldn't face doing
4. can't help feeling

3
1. trying   5. getting
2. walking   6. changing
3. ringing   7. missing
4. waiting   8. discussing

Unit 62

1
1. to get   6. to go
2. to leave   7. to hire
3. staying   8. driving
4. sitting   9. to spend
5. touring   10. taking

2
1. taking   6. to repair
2. losing   7. waiting
3. to insist   8. to have
4. arguing   9. to accept
5. to be   10. saying

3
1. I don't mind asking to see the manager.
2. Matthew admitted promising to go to Scotland.
3. the band happened to finish playing.

Unit 63

1
1. I'd like to buy this tin.
2. I like driving this car.
3. I'd like to see the manager.
4. I like chasing rabbits.

2
1. he loves watching/to watch
2. I wouldn't like to work
3. I'd like to see
4. I'd prefer to come/go
5. I hate queuing
6. He doesn't like cooking
7. I'd love to fly
8. I like to have

3
1. to drive/driving   3. to go/going
2. to make   4. to search

Unit 64

1
1. mentioning   5. to lock
2. agreeing   6. looking
3. to call   7. to look
4. to lock

2
1. running   6. to tell
2. to make   7. to disappoint
3. spending   8. phoning
4. watching   9. to explain
5. to work   10. going

3
1. Harriet didn't even try to move the piano.
2. Mike will never forget seeing a spaceship.
3. The walls need painting.
4. Natasha didn't mean to be unkind to Jessica.
5. Andrew went on studying through the night.
6. Mark stopped to make a phone call.

Unit 65

1
1. Guy invited Kitty to come on his chat show.
2. Sarah reminded Mark to get the theatre tickets.
3. The dentist told Daniel to give up eating sweets.
4. The police ordered the gunman to come out with his hands up.

2
1. don't want her to do a parachute jump
2. doesn't want him to lose his job
3. would like/'d like her to go (on holiday) with them

3
1. The police must stop the suspects leaving the country.
2. The President didn't expect Congress to oppose him.
3. The terrorists forced the hostages to lie down.
4. The government doesn't mind the pound falling in value.

4
1. to travel   3. to use
2. buying   4. to take

Unit 66

1
1. He can't think what to say.
2. They're not sure/They aren't sure where to go.
3. She doesn't know how to stop.

2
1. what to expect   4. what to do
2. where to go   5. who to contact
3. how to find

3
1. whether to do
2. how much (money) to spend
3. whether to join
4. which route to take
5. which (lottery numbers) to choose

Unit 67

1
1. simple to use the computer.
2. difficult to understand the handbook.
3. It's easy to run any kind of software.
4. It's absolutely fascinating to explore the world of Compex.
5. Are you ready to try the ultimate computer experience?

2
1. is very simple to use.
2. isn't difficult to understand.
3. Any kind of software is easy to run.
4. The world of Compex is absolutely fascinating to explore.

3
1. it's/it is likely to be pretty crowded.
2. she's/she is certain to be there.
3. you're/you are unlikely to find it. OR you'll be unlikely to find it.

4 1 of 2 for 3 of 4 of 5 for

Unit 68

1
1. (just) can't wait for it to arrive.
2. It would be a mistake for him to marry her.
3. It's important for advertisements to tell the truth.

2
1. There's a fun pool for children to swim in.
2. There are quiet areas for you to relax in.
3. There are regular shows for you to enjoy.
4. There's a giant roller-coaster for you to ride on (if you dare).

3
1. It's/It is too high for her to reach.
2. It's/It is too difficult for us to understand.
3. It wasn't loud enough for them/everyone to hear.
4. It wasn't hot enough for him to drink.

4
1. difficult for the town to attract new industry.
2. very generous of the council to give the land to Sanko.
3. is eager for production to begin soon.

Unit 69

1
1. have something to eat.
2. nice to have a rest.
3. wants Rita to speak to him.
4. Daniel doesn't know how to repair the video.
5. Claire and her sister have decided to go to Bali.
6. Melanie has gone to the hospital to visit David.
7. (Unfortunately) Vicky has to do some studying.
8. It's important for Sarah to ring the office.

2
1. see/read
2. drive/go
3. cry/weep
4. lie/sit/stay
5. snow
6. see/visit

3
1. to visit   8. look
2. to see   9. get
3. to have   10. to leave
4. buy   11. to change
5. to read   12. forget
6. read   13. to get
7. feel

Unit 70

1
1. of buying   3. on buying
2. for breaking   4. like arguing

2
1. blamed Trevor for forgetting the tickets.
2. succeeded in saving the driver's life.
3. The customers complained about not receiving the goods.
4. Emma has accused Matthew of breaking his promise.
5. Melanie is insisting on cooking a meal for David.
6. A new traffic scheme has stopped cars from going into the town centre.
7. Everyone congratulated Claude on winning the quiz competition.
8. Some football fans were arrested for attacking a policeman.

3
1. about seeing   5. from doing
2. about/at getting   6. like writing
3. on travelling   7. with doing
4. for not writing   8. of/about going

Unit 71

1
1. of falling   3. to move
2. of dropping them

2
1. Nick was afraid to jump.
2. Daniel was afraid to argue with the policeman.
3. Matthew is afraid of getting sunburnt.

3
1. to buy   4. to read
2. of getting   5. to book
3. of being

4
1. about being so rude
2. about losing my temper
3. to interrupt you

Unit 72

1
1. We used to like   4. did you use to help
2. used to be   5. I used to look
3. we didn't use to have

2
1. 's/is used to flying planes.
2. used to play badminton.
3. 's/is used to climbing mountains.

3
1. to living   5. to drinking
2. to stop   6. to being
3. to work   7. to have
4. to be

Unit 73

1
1. by staying up all night.
2. on waking (in the morning).
3. without using a calculator.
4. for carrying the food.
5. in spite of having it on his list.
6. as well as doing the typing.

2
1. before signing
2. after eating
3. Before leaving
4. after using
5. before changing
6. before opening

3
1. He thought carefully before deciding to buy it.
2. He bought the shop despite having little money of his own.
3. He became successful by giving the customers what they wanted.
4. He put the profit back into the business instead of spending it on himself.
5. He was happy when running his own business.
6. He fell ill as a result of working too hard.
7. He has made a lot of money since buying his first shop ten years ago.

Unit 74

1
1. I saw him take it.
2. I watched him leave (the restaurant).
3. I heard him drive away.

2
1. I can hear it ringing.
2. I can see her waving.
3. I can hear them barking.
4. I can smell it burning.

3
1. She felt the building shake.
2. He heard people shouting.
3. She could hear an alarm ringing.
4. They saw the police arrive.
5. He saw a woman crying.

Unit 75

1
1. broke his leg skiing.
2. cut his finger opening a tin.
3. injured her toe running.
4. hurt his back lifting weights.

2
1. Taking a gun out of the drawer, he put it in his briefcase. (Also possible: Having taken a gun …)
2. Having left the office, he (then) had to wait a while for the lift.
3. Reaching the ground floor, he hurried outside to a taxi. (Also possible: Having reached the ground floor …)
4. Pulling out a gun, the taxi driver shot Mitchell. (Also possible: Having pulled out a gun …)

3
1. Having studied the map, Trevor knew which way to go.
2. Feeling cold, Harriet turned on the heating.
3. Not knowing French, Daniel found it hard to communicate.
4. Having finished the book, Andrew took it back to the library.

Unit 76

1
1. uncountable
2. countable
3. countable
4. uncountable
5. uncountable
6. uncountable
7. countable
8. countable

2
1. some biscuits
2. a light bulb
3. some wine
4. some mineral water
5. a banana
6. some soap
7. a lemon
8. some butter
9. some eggs

3
1. a computer
2. essays
3. hours
4. many
5. money
6. food
7. much
8. a job
9. some
10. a few
11. pictures

Unit 77

1
1. a jar of jam
2. a box of matches
3. two loaves of bread
4. a bar of chocolate
5. five kilos of potatoes
6. a box/packet of breakfast cereal
7. two bottles of mineral water
8. a tube of toothpaste

2
1. some
2. some
3. some
4. a
5. some
6. some
7. a
8. some

3
1. beautiful scenery
2. good weather
3. a meal
4. fun
5. an awful journey

Unit 78

1
1. sport
2. some potatoes
3. painting
4. a noise
5. cheese
6. a conversation
7. some chicken
8. war
9. life
10. some egg

2
1. some business
2. an iron
3. a glass, a light
4. a business, some time
5. some experience, an experience

3	1	time	4	a paper	**4**	1	team is	5	police are
	2	an experience	5	an orange		2	choir are	6	cattle are
	3	a painting	6	fruits		3	crew are	7	population is
						4	orchestra is		

Unit 79

1
1. is
2. are
3. look
4. are
5. has
6. costs
7. have
8. weren't

2
1. was
2. were
3. was
4. were
5. were
6. were
7. was
8. was/were

3
1. is
2. isn't
3. are
4. work
5. have
6. is
7. is
8. has

4
1. Fifteen miles is a long walk.
2. Eight students are travelling on the bus.
3. Three people were waiting for the museum to open.
4. Twenty kilos is the baggage allowance.

Unit 80

1
1. thanks
2. damages
3. pain
4. belongings
5. saving
6. goods
7. damage
8. savings
9. pains

2
1. mathematics/maths
2. history
3. athletics
4. economics
5. geography

3
1. are
2. is
3. were
4. seem
5. is
6. was
7. were

4
1. was
2. outskirts
3. headquarters
4. savings
5. damage
6. aren't
7. crossroads
8. is
9. gives

Unit 81

1
1. don't
2. go
3. is
4. fit
5. look
6. suit
7. some
8. a

2
1. some
2. pairs
3. pair
4. some

3
1. are
2. have
3. know
4. are
5. want
6. has

Unit 82

1
1. a tennis-racket/a tennis racket
2. a television camera
3. an alarm clock
4. a motor cycle
5. a luggage trolley

2
1. Have you got any cotton shirts?
2. What shall I do with this lemonade bottle?
3. Have you got a shopping bag?
4. Is there a shoe shop near here?
5. I'd like a corner table, please.
6. I'll need some climbing boots.
7. Are you a computer operator?

3
1. a stone wall
2. a tourist information centre
3. a bath-towel/a bath towel
4. working clothes
5. a city centre office block
6. a sales graph
7. a credit card
8. a horse-race/a horse race
9. the Marketing Director
10. a weekend bicycle tour

Unit 83

1
1. a
2. the
3. a
4. the
5. The
6. the
7. the
8. a
9. The
10. the
11. the
12. the
13. the
14. a
15. the
16. the
17. an
18. the
19. the
20. the

2
1. Matthew won the race easily.
2. Suddenly a child ran into the road.
3. She was watching a film on television.
4. The bus was half an hour late.
5. The camera videoed the thief.

3
1. a, the, the
2. a, the, a
3. the, the
4. a, the, The
5. a, the
6. a, the
7. a, the

Unit 84

1
1. an, the
2. The, a
3. The, an
4. an, the
5. a, the
6. the, a

2
1. a, a
2. a, a, the, a
3. the, a
4. a, the, an, the
5. the, a, the, the, a, The, a
6. the, a, a, the, the

3
1. a DJ
2. a VIP
3. an IRA member
4. a PC
5. an LA suburb
6. a UFO
7. an AGM
8. an MP

Unit 85

1
1. some luggage
2. some flowers
3. a cat
4. some birds
5. some fruit

2 1 a 2 One 3 One 4 a

3
1. A violin is a musical instrument.
2. A queue is a line of people.
3. An atlas is a book of maps.
4. A spade is a tool for digging.

4
1. some nuts
2. mineral water
3. some clothes
4. lovely bread
5. (university) students

Unit 86

1
1. He likes chips.
2. She likes dogs.
3. He likes art.
4. She likes chemistry.

2
1. dogs, the dogs
2. cars, pollution, cars, aeroplanes, the pollution
3. the birds, birds, wildlife
4. history, the history, museums, old buildings

3
1. the atom
2. football
3. the guitar
4. television
5. the telescope

Unit 87

1
1. church, the church
2. the cinema, the pub
3. hospital (In American English: the hospital), the hospital
4. school, college

2
1. college
2. the cinema
3. the station
4. sea
5. home
6. bed
7. work
8. the church
9. prison

3
1. at home
2. in bed
3. to the hospital
4. to church
5. to work
6. to the library
7. in prison
8. at college
9. in the factory

Unit 88

1
1. Thanksgiving, November
2. the weekend, Saturday
3. Christmas, a white Christmas
4. the summer, 1997
5. the afternoon, the year
6. night, the dark, the day

2
1. breakfast
2. lunch
3. the lunch
4. the dinner
5. a marvellous meal

3
1. breakfast
2. midnight
3. Christmas
4. Wednesday
5. the morning
6. night
7. the day
8. Wednesday
9. the Wednesday
10. February

Unit 89

1
1. a very grand hotel
2. quite a tiring journey
3. a really big flat
4. quite a nice meal

2 1 so 2 such 3 such 4 so 5 such 6 so

3
1. The piano was so heavy (that) Mike and Harriet couldn't move it.
2. Tom was so annoyed about United losing (that) he wouldn't speak to anyone.
3. The band was such a big attraction (that) all the tickets sold out.
4. Vicky had such a lot of work to do (that) she was sure she'd never finish it.
5. The party made such a (lot of) noise/so much noise (that) it kept all the neighbours awake.

4 1 what 2 What a 3 What

Unit 90

1
1. Lake Michigan
2. Italy
3. The Andes
4. The United Kingdom
5. Tasmania
6. the West Indies
7. The River Nile
8. Brussels
9. the North

2
1. the Thames
2. Hyde Park
3. Heathrow Airport
4. Trafalgar Square
5. Westminster Bridge
6. the Houses of Parliament
7. Buckingham Palace
8. West London
9. The M1 motorway
10. The Ritz

3
1. New York
2. the Statue of Liberty
3. Central Park
4. the Metropolitan Museum of Art
5. Broadway
6. Macy's
7. Washington Square
8. New York University
9. the Paramount
10. Broadway

4
1. the Little Theatre
2. Kingston House
3. Wood Lane
4. the High Street
5. the Royal Hotel

5
1. is in George Street.
2. The Odeon Cinema is in the Avenue.
3. The Clarendon Art Gallery is in Newton Lane.
4. King Edward College is in College Road.
5. St John's Church is in South Street.
6. Webster's department store is in the High Street.
7. The Bristol Hotel is in Westville Way.

6
1. A day at Blenheim Palace
2. A train journey in North Wales
3. A tour of the White House
4. A beach on the Riviera
5. A shopping trip to Harrods
6. A small town in France
7. A trip across the Severn Bridge
8. A walk around Lake Windermere
9. A visit to Tower Bridge
10. A journey across the Rockies
11. A look around the National Gallery
12. A boat trip along the Oxford Canal

Unit 91

1

	Near	Further away
Singular		that
Plural	these	those

2
1. these flowers
2. this parcel
3. those trees
4. that dog

3
1. That
2. these
3. this
4. this
5. those
6. that
7. This
8. this, That
9. These

Unit 92

1
1. our
2. his
3. his
4. their
5. yours
6. mine
7. hers
8. her

2 1 its 2 it's 3 it's 4 its

3
1. the
2. her
3. the (Also possible: her)
4. their
5. your, your

4
1. Harriet introduced me to a friend of hers.
2. They've got their own pool.
3. It's a favourite hobby of mine.
4. I've got some CDs of his.
5. I'd like my own room.

Unit 93

1
1. the boy's bike
2. the girls' tent
3. the children's skateboards
4. the girl's cat
5. the boys' trophies

2
1. the twins'
2. Luke's
3. Jason's
4. Debbie's
5. her children's
6. the Lanskys'
7. Olivia's

3
1. Mr Hillman's Gun
2. The Smell of Blood
3. The Terrorist's Car
4. The Middle of the Night
5. The Death of Someone Important
6. The Gangsters' Money

4
1. yesterday's paper
2. (a) five minutes' rest
3. this month's special offer
4. in a week's time

Unit 94

1
1. She's/She has got some cats.
2. He hasn't got any petrol.
3. He's/He has got some poison.

2
1. any
2. any
3. some
4. some
5. some
6. any

3
1. some, anything
2. someone, any/some
3. anyone (Also possible: someone), any
4. something, some

4
1. anyone
2. any bus
3. any colour
4. anything
5. any day

Unit 95

1
1. She hasn't had many lessons yet.
2. I'll have to make a lot (of it).
3. I haven't got much energy.
4. Maybe you should add a little water/a few drops of water.
5. We've invited lots of friends/a lot of friends.

2
1. a lot of
2. many/a lot of
3. many
4. a lot of
5. much/a lot of
6. many/a lot of
7. much

3
1. few
2. little
3. a little
4. a few
5. little
6. a few

4
1. much
2. little
3. much
4. many
5. few
6. little

Unit 96

1
1. Some of them
2. most of them
3. Half of them
4. All of them
5. some of them
6. None of them

2
1. She got some of them right.
2. He got most of them right.
3. He got all of them right.
4. She got none of them right.

3
1. most people
2. No student/No students
3. Most of the money
4. All cars
5. All fruit/Most fruit
6. All (of) the lights

Unit 97

1
1. each
2. each/every
3. every
4. each/every
5. every

2
1. all day/the whole day
2. all night/the whole night
3. every morning
4. all morning/the whole morning
5. all day/the whole day
6. every time

3
1. One of them has a separate restaurant.
2. Both of them serve bar snacks.
3. One of them has a family room.
4. Neither of them allows/allow pub games.
5. Neither of them has/have live music.
6. One of them has a non-smoking area.

4
1. Neither
2. either
3. each (Also possible: every)
4. every
5. whole

Unit 98

1
1. the dress
2. Laura
3. the jeans
4. Rita
5. Rita and Melanie
6. Rita
7. Mike and Harriet
8. Tom

2
1. he
2. them
3. us/me
4. her
5. she
6. she
7. them
8. she
9. They
10. you
11. him
12. he
13. you/we
14. him

3
1. We
2. you, us
3. it, it, her, She
4. Me, it
5. she, her
6. I, you, them, they

4 1 You 2 They 3 You 4 they

Unit 99

1
1. There's/There is a balloon in the sky.
2. There are some boxes on the car.
3. There's/There is an elephant in the garden.

2
1. There's/There is, There'll be
2. are there, There's/There has been OR There was
3. there was, There ... have been

3
1. It was very cheap.
2. It was Vicky.
3. It's/It is a nuisance.
4. It's/It is very warm.
5. It's/It is important to keep it somewhere safe.

4
1. There
2. It
3. There, It
4. there, it
5. It, there, It, there

Unit 100

1
1. 's/is looking at herself (in the mirror).
2. 're/are introducing themselves.
3. He's/He is teaching himself Arabic.
4. She's/She is drying herself (on/with a towel).

2 1 yourself 2 ourselves 3 itself

3
1. you
2. him
3. himself
4. her
5. yourself

4
1. feel
2. help yourselves
3. remember
4. worry
5. relax

Unit 101

1
1. He cleans them himself.
2. I bake it myself.
3. They grow them themselves.
4. We decorated it ourselves.
5. He types them himself.
6. I develop them myself.

2
1. herself
2. itself
3. himself
4. themselves
5. yourselves

3
1 They're/They are always thinking about each other.
2 They've/They have got lots of photos of each other.
3 They enjoy each other's company.
4 They're/They are crazy about films.

4
1 each other 4 ourselves
2 each other 5 themselves
3 themselves 6 each other

Unit 102

1
1 a smart one or a casual one, a casual one
2 a big one or a small one, A big one
3 A white one or a brown one, A brown one
4 an ordinary one or an electric one, an ordinary one

2
1 I haven't got one.
2 I must get some new ones.
3 Have you seen this one?
4 I've hired one.
5 Can't you find any nice ones?
6 The one in the car is better.

3
1 one 4 them
2 it 5 some
3 one

Unit 103

1
1 everyone/everybody, no one/nobody
2 someone/somebody, something
3 somewhere, Someone/somebody
4 everywhere, nothing

2
1 someone 4 anywhere
2 anyone 5 anything
3 somewhere 6 something

3
1 his 3 likes, they
2 it 4 has, their

4
1 I once met someone famous.
2 Someone's car is blocking me in.
3 I've got something else/something different to tell you.
4 We know everyone's opinions/opinion.
5 Everyone else except you is going.
6 Nothing exciting ever happens here.

Unit 104

1
1 modern chairs 4 classical music
2 a black cat 5 an old car
3 solar power 6 a tall building

2 pleasant, ideal, quiet, short, popular, lovely, friendly, helpful, good, marvellous, excellent, local

3
1 The world is asleep
2 My chief desire
3 My heart is content
4 The main thing to remember
5 The night is alive

6 Inner secrets
7 The only girl for me

Unit 105

1
1 a small white car
2 an attractive old building
3 an expensive wooden garden seat
4 a famous Italian opera singer

2
1 a lovely old glass vase
2 an attractive wall mirror
3 a modern office desk
4 red metal kitchen chairs
5 a splendid old model boat
6 valuable Australian postage stamps
7 a small wooden coffee table

3
1 This is a powerful Japanese business computer.
2 This is an excellent small electric fire.
3 This is a big new chocolate bar.
4 This is a terrific American television comedy.
5 These are stylish aluminium garage doors.
6 These are wonderful modern sports shoes.
7 This is a very good German mobile phone.

Unit 106

1
1 the hungry 4 the unemployed
2 the homeless 5 the old
3 the sick

2
1 We live near a special school for the deaf.
2 The old soldiers were holding a service for the dead.
3 The government should do more for the poor.
4 I'm doing a course on caring for the mentally handicapped.

3
1 The sick 5 the old people
2 the young people 6 The homeless
3 the unemployed 7 the deaf
4 the poor

Unit 107

1
1 exhausted 3 fascinating
2 interested 4 exciting

2
1 surprised 4 confusing
2 disappointing 5 bored
3 puzzled 6 interesting

3
1 relaxing 5 fascinating
2 annoyed 6 thrilling
3 amused 7 exhausting
4 interested

Unit 108

1
1 brightly 6 safely
2 patiently 7 fluently
3 immediately 8 carefully
4 punctually 9 quietly
5 secretly

2
1. angrily
2. happily
3. automatically
4. publicly
5. enthusiastically
6. reasonably
7. securely

3
1. United won the game easily.
2. I've/I have checked the figures carefully.
3. Your dog barked at me very fiercely.
4. It's/It is raining quite heavily (here).

4
1. dark
2. terribly
3. badly
4. suddenly
5. quietly
6. unhappy
7. sadly
8. curious
9. foolishly

Unit 109

1
1. adjective
2. adjective
3. adverb
4. adjective
5. adverb
6. adverb

2
1. hardly
2. nearly
3. long
4. late
5. fast
6. hard
7. wrong
8. straight

3
1. bad
2. good
3. badly
4. well
5. ill

4
1. badly
2. good
3. fast
4. long
5. hardly
6. nearly
7. hard
8. lately
9. likely

Unit 110

1
1. are more interesting
2. is higher
3. is more beautiful

2
1. richest
2. most modern
3. greatest
4. most exciting
5. most popular
6. most successful
7. most attractive
8. happiest

3
1. happier
2. faster
3. more helpful
4. lovelier
5. bigger
6. more restful
7. more modern

4
1. more smartly
2. longer
3. more often
4. more carefully
5. earlier
6. louder/more loudly

5
1. worst
2. better
3. worse
4. best
5. furthest

6 1 least 2 less 3 more 4 Most

7
1. happier
2. smallest
3. best
4. shorter
5. most important
6. older
7. more exciting
8. most
9. wetter
10. lower
11. worse

Unit 111

1
1. The church is older than the library.
2. Matthew is stronger than Daniel.
3. Harriet is taller than Mike.
4. Claire is more popular than Andrew.
4. Mark's car is bigger than Sarah's.

2
1. Friday is the busiest day
2. The Metropole is the nicest hotel in (the) town.
3. This watch is one of the cheapest (watches) you can buy.
4. This Beatles album is the best (one) they ever made.
5. Alan is the most successful salesman in the company.

3
1. Plastic isn't as strong as metal.
2. The stool isn't as comfortable as the armchair.
3. Swimming isn't as exciting as surfing.
4. The post isn't as quick as e-mail.

4 1 me 2 I am 3 me 4 he has

Unit 112

1
1. less painful
2. less busy
3. less convenient
4. less attractive
5. less seriously
6. less optimistic

2
1. Yesterday was a lot colder than today.
2. My coat is a bit longer than is fashionable.
3. I left work slightly earlier than usual this afternoon.
4. The shop is much more expensive than the supermarket.
5. Is the new machine any more reliable than the old one?

3
1. more and more difficult
2. more and more complicated
3. more and more
4. longer and longer
5. worse and worse

4
1. the quieter the roads (are).
2. the wider the choice (is).
3. the more confused I get.
4. the more fluently you can speak.
5. the more crowded the beaches get.

Unit 113

1
1. outside
2. Perhaps
3. always
4. Obviously
5. silently
6. hard

2
1. mid
2. end
3. front
4. mid
5. mid
6. mid
7. end
8. front
9. mid
10. mid

3
1. clearly crossed
2. will probably rain
3. didn't fully understand
4. are usually
5. occasionally visited it/ visited it occasionally
6. were soon working
7. has obviously forgotten

4
1. It usually rains when David is on holiday.
2. Rita's friend visits her most weekends.
3. Mark gets a pay rise every year.
4. Rachel never checks her work.

5
1. I've always known your secret.
2. We certainly can't afford a new car. (Also possible: Certainly we can't afford a new car.)
3. The tourists didn't walk far.
4. Tom cut the paper carefully./Tom carefully cut the paper.
5. Natasha can also play the violin. (Also possible: Natasha can play the violin also.)
6. I read the newspaper most days./Most days I read the newspaper.

6
1. peacefully at his home
2. through the streets yesterday
3. to Greece last year
4. there in June

7
1. We had a lovely time in the country.
2. We arrived home safely at about eight.
3. You must come and visit us before too long. (Also possible: Before too long you must come and visit us.)
4. It's always nice to see you and Tony.
5. Maybe you'll be able to come in the New Year./You'll be able to come in the New Year maybe. (Also possible: You'll maybe be able to come in the New Year.)
6. We'll see you sometime.

Unit 114

1
1. still, yet
2. still, already
3. yet, still

2
1. I already owe Emma £20.
2. We've already spent all our money./We've spent all our money already.
3. But it still looks dirty. (Also possible: But it looks dirty still.)
4. We haven't seen them yet. (Also possible: We haven't yet seen them.)
5. I still can't understand the rules.

3
1. They/Children don't play there any more
2. they/boats still come along the river
3. it/the view isn't beautiful any more
4. it's/it is still our home (Also possible: it's/it is our home still)

4
1. no longer
2. yet
3. any more
4. already

Unit 115

1
1. She's very busy.
2. She's a bit thirsty.
3. He's very strong.
4. He's extremely happy.

2
1. very
2. quite
3. a bit
4. very
5. a bit
6. quite

3
1. That radio is a bit loud.
2. I quite like my new job.
3. Why don't you slow down a little?
4. The rain completely spoilt our day./The rain spoilt our day completely.
5. We did the job fairly quickly.
6. I feel a lot better now.
7. We enjoyed the concert very much. (Also possible: We very much enjoyed the concert.)
8. My arms ached terribly.

4
1. absolutely
2. really
3. very much
4. extremely
5. very
6. totally
7. very

Unit 116

1
1. quite
2. late
3. easy
4. quite
5. bright

2
1. rather better
2. rather noisy
3. rather/quite busy
4. quite popular

3
1. It's/It is rather/quite complicated.
2. My car is quite big.
3. it went on rather longer than I expected.
4. I made it quite quickly.

4
1. completely ridiculous
2. fairly difficult
3. completely different
4. fairly surprised
5. fairly useful
6. completely certain

406 KEY TO THE EXERCISES

Unit 117

1
1. The plane is too low.
2. The gate isn't wide enough.
3. The water isn't warm enough.

2
1. sweet enough.
2. too expensive.
3. enough rain.
4. clearly enough.
5. too many mistakes.
6. too much traffic.
7. too complicated.
8. enough food

3
1. It's too wet for a picnic/too wet to have a picnic.
2. I/We haven't got enough chairs for all my/our guests.
3. I had too much equipment to carry.
4. (I think) Natasha is good enough to be a professional musician.

Unit 118

1
1. up
2. in/inside
3. above/over
4. along (Also possible: down)
5. by/beside/next to
6. around/round
7. in front of
8. away from/out of

2
1. behind, through, below
2. past, down, opposite

3
1. opposite
2. between
3. opposite
4. between
5. next to

4
1. under
2. up
3. on
4. around
5. into
6. out of

5
1. to
2. outside
3. in/into
4. past/by
5. off
6. on
7. through
8. near
9. among

Unit 119

1
1. He's/He is on the roof.
2. They're/They are at the disco.
3. He's/He is in the bath.
4. She's/She is at the lights

2
1. at the petrol station
2. at the zoo
3. in the theatre
4. in the restaurant
5. at the station

3 1 in 2 on 3 in 4 at 5 at
6 at 7 on 8 on 9 in 10 at

Unit 120

1
1. In 1961.
2. On 22 November 1963.
3. At 12.30.

2
1. ✗
2. on
3. ✗
4. in
5. at
6. on
7. in
8. in
9. on
10. at

3
1. in time
2. on time
3. in time
4. on time

4 1 at, on 2 at, in 3 on, in 4 in, in

Unit 121

1 1 since 2 for 3 since 4 for

2
1. He's/He has been in bed for three days.
2. They've/They have been in the garden since breakfast.
3. He's/He has been at his desk since nine o'clock.
4. She's/She has been on the road for five hours.

3
1. since four o'clock
2. ten years ago
3. since Monday/ since then
4. for six weeks
5. for three years
6. eight months ago
7. for three weeks

4 1 before 2 ago 3 before

Unit 122

1 1 while 2 while 3 during 4 while

2 1 by 2 until 3 until 4 by 5 by

3 1 as 2 like 3 as 4 like

4 1 as 2 as if 3 as 4 as if

5
1. By the time I arrived at your flat, you'd/you had left.
2. Rita went to the party with Tom, as you predicted.
3. I saw your sister while I was shopping in London.
4. You can keep the book until you've/you have finished it OR you finish it.

Unit 123

1
1. in
2. from
3. in
4. by
5. in
6. on
7. on
8. in
9. by
10. on
11. In
12. on, on

2
1. I pay in cash?
2. the information up to date?
3. you drop the ball on purpose?
4. there anything (to watch) on television tonight?
5. you be here at the end of July?
6. nuclear power a good idea in your opinion?
7. your car for sale?
8. you approve of the plan on the whole?

3 1 by 2 on 3 in 4 by 5 by

Unit 124

1
1. of
2. in
3. in
4. at (Also possible: in)

2
1. damage to
2. way of
3. answer to
4. cause of
5. tax on
6. difficulty with
7. matter with

3
1. with
2. of
3. of
4. for
5. with
6. for
7. of
8. between

4
1. answers to all the (quiz) questions
2. knowledge of French
3. desire for progress
4. difference between the (two) colours
5. preference for our/Zedco products

Unit 125

1
1. afraid of the dark.
2. bored with the video.
3. interested in computers.
4. surprised at/by the news.
5. proud of the/their victory.
6. annoyed with her/the children.
7. They're not/They aren't satisfied with their pay increase.

2 1 for 2 at 3 at 4 for 5 at 6 to

3
1. responsible for
2. ready for
3. aware of
4. similar to
5. full of
6. interested in
7. late for
8. famous for

Unit 126

1 1 at 2 after 3 into

2
1. pay for
2. ask for
3. care about
4. caring for
5. suffering from
6. decided on
7. concentrate on
8. agree with

3
1. relies on
2. deals with
3. feel like
4. reached
5. listening to
6. apologized for
7. believed in
8. laughing at
9. discuss
10. left

4 1 to 2 to 3 to 4 about 5 of

Unit 127

1
1. into
2. from
3. as
4. with/to
5. to
6. to
7. with

2
1. prefer water to wine?
2. blaming Tom for the/his accident?
3. thank you for the/her present?
4. accuse him/the head teacher of murder?
5. provide you with towels?
   (Also possible: provide towels for you?)
6. invite you to her wedding?
7. congratulate them on the/their (great) victory?
8. pointed a gun at Melanie?

3
1. about
2. of
3. to
4. to
5. about/of
6. about
7. about/of

Unit 128

1
1. stay in
2. pay ... back
3. fall over
4. lie down
5. cut out
6. come back
7. get on
8. take ... back
9. go away
10. give away

2
1. left out
2. sent out
3. throw away
4. put off
5. made up
6. go on /carry on

3
1. picks ... up
2. put on/put ... on
3. ring ... up
4. hand in/hand ... in
5. written ... down
6. win back
7. wash up/wash ... up
8. look ... up
9. held up
10. mixing ... up

Unit 129

1
1. She's picking litter up./She's picking up litter.
2. They're digging the road up./They're digging up the road.
3. He's washing the plates up./He's washing up the plates.
4. She's plugging the television in./She's plugging in the television.

2
1. Nick says he's/he has given up smoking.
2. How did the accident come about?
3. I think Matthew and Emma have fallen out.
4. The problem isn't going to just go away.
5. The government is bringing in a new tax on computers.
6. Zedco want to set up a new sales office in Germany.

3
1. sort out
2. taking over
3. fell through
4. fight off
5. fallen behind
6. step down
7. taken on
8. laying off

Unit 130

1
1. completely
2. away/disappearing
3. continuing
4. from start to finish
5. aloud
6. disconnected
7. away/departing
8. becoming less
9. completely to the ground
10. from start to finish
11. to different people
12. increasing
13. wearing
14. stopping completely

2
1. on, off
2. out, out
3. down, out
4. on, out

3
1. try on
2. taking off
3. speak up
4. setting off

Unit 131

1
1. down on
2. out into
3. up at
4. away from
5. through to
6. in from

2
1. run out of
2. send away for
3. look/watch out for
4. look forward to
5. keep up with
6. put up with
7. get on with
8. go back on
9. get on to
10. go in for
11. cut down on
12. fall back on
13. get round to
14. make up for

3
1. I get on (well) with Melanie./Melanie and I get on (well).
2. I might drop in on David.
3. I'll fit in with everyone else.
4. I can't catch up (with) Matthew.
5. The sunny weather is making up for last week.

Unit 132

1
1. she can't sleep.
2. he's/he has hurt his back.
3. She says she feels sick all the time.
4. He says he fell over and hurt himself.

2
1. Stokeley Carmichael said (that) black is beautiful.
2. Galileo said (that) the earth moves round the sun.
3. Shakespeare said (that) all the world's a stage.
4. George Orwell said (that) Big Brother is watching you.

3
1. tell
2. say
3. say
4. say
5. tell
6. tell
7. tell
8. say

Unit 133

1
1. Trevor
2. 1998
3. April
4. (about) two weeks

2
1. you
2. he, your
3. he, your book.

3
1. the day before/the previous day
2. that day
3. here
4. the week before/the previous week

Unit 134

1
1. was
2. was
3. is (Also possible: was)
4. was
5. was (Also possible: is)

2
1. you had finished it/your project.
2. you weren't on a diet.
3. you didn't enjoy them/parties.
4. you weren't applying for it/the job.

3
1. The Sunday Times said the production was brilliant.
2. Edward Devine said he couldn't remember a funnier show.
3. Robert Walsh said it (had) made him laugh.
4. The Evening Standard said you/people had to see it. (Also possible: The Evening Standard said you/people must see it.)
5. The Telegraph said it would be a great success.
6. The Express said you/people might die laughing.
7. Susan Proctor said it was the funniest show she'd/she had ever seen.
8. Time Out said you/people shouldn't miss it.

Unit 135

1
1. She wants to know how she can find out about the area.
2. He wants to know if/whether there are any guided tours.
3. They want to know where they can stay.
4. They want to know what shows there are.

2
1. Do you know if I can park here?
2. Could you tell me how long the film lasts?
3. Do you know how often the buses run?
4. Do you know if we are/we're allowed to smoke?
5. Could you tell me what time the flight is?
6. Could you tell me how much a ticket costs?

3
1. why I wanted the job.
2. how I (had) heard about it.
3. if/whether I was fit.
4. if/whether I could work on Saturdays.
5. how I would/I'd travel to work.
6. if/whether I had (got) a bicycle.
7. how much I hoped to earn.
8. when I could start.

Unit 136

1
1. The doctor told him to take more exercise.
2. His boss asked/told him not to play computer games in the office.
3. A traffic warden told him not to park his car in the High Street.
4. Laura asked him to put some shelves up.

2
1. Andrew to take a break.
2. for forgetting the shopping.
3. singing a few songs.
4. Vicky to post a/the letter.
5. making a mistake.
6. Laura not to touch the electric wires.

3
1. The builders have promised that everything will be ready on time.
2. The boss insists that we (have to) check the figures carefully.
3. Tom has admitted that his story wasn't completely true.
4. Matthew reminded Emma that her train was about to leave.

Unit 137

1
1. the young man at the door
2. the man who plays his stereo at night
3. the very thin woman
4. the girl with green eyes (Also possible: the green-eyed girl)
5. the young woman in the office
6. the man who drives a taxi
7. the smart young man
8. the student who failed all her exams

2
1. that/which
2. who/that
3. who/that
4. that/which
5. that/which
6. who/that

3
1. The bomb which went off this morning caused a lot of damage.
2. The scientist who discovered a new planet has won the Nobel Prize.
3. The footballer who took drugs has been banned from playing again.
4. The little girl who had been missing since Thursday has been found safe and well.
5. The company which owns Greenway Supermarkets has laid off thousands of workers.
6. The old lady who did a parachute jump now wants to swim the English Channel.

Unit 138

1
1. dog that fell down a hole has been rescued.
2. story that upset everyone was untrue.
3. man who interviewed Natasha is a film producer.
4. accident that Daniel saw wasn't very serious.
5. man who/that Claire knows is a millionaire.
6. vase that David broke was extremely valuable.
7. jacket Melanie wore at the party is really nice.

2
1. It's/It is the car you can afford.
2. It's/It is the film people want to see.
3. It's/It is the supermarket you can trust.
4. It's/It is the magazine young people read.
5. They're/They are the chocolates you'll love.

3
1. Somewhere I've got a photo of the mountain we climbed.
2. The man who/that repaired my car is a real expert.
3. The detective lost sight of the man he was following.
4. I thought I recognized the assistant who/that served us.
5. I'm afraid the numbers I chose didn't win a prize.

Unit 139

1
1. That's/That is the film (that/which) I was talking about.
2. This is the wallpaper (that/which) I've/I have decided on.
3. That's/That is the man (who/that) I played tennis with.
4. Those are the steps (that/which) I fell down.

2
1. A hammer is a tool (that/which) you hit nails with.
2. Your destination is the place (that/which) you're/you are going to.
3. A safe is a cupboard (that/which) you keep valuable things in.
4. Your opponent is the person (who/that) you're/you are playing against.
5. A sofa bed is a piece of furniture you can either sit or sleep on.

3
1. That is an idea in which our party believes.
2. That is a policy to which I am strongly opposed.
3. These are people about whom no one cares.
4. Those are mistakes of which your party should be ashamed.
5. That is a problem with which the government is now dealing.

Unit 140

1
1. Felix Reeves is the journalist whose tape recorder was stolen.
2. Graham Wilshaw is the architect who knew Colin at school.
3. Rex Carter is the farmer whose land Colin bought.
4. Norman Bridge is the lawyer who looked after Colin's interests.
5. Sonia Goldman is the house guest whose fingerprints were on the door handle.

2
1. What you have to think about is your profit.
2. What you must know are the needs of your customers.
3. What you should work towards is a realistic target.
4. What you need to do is (to) plan ahead.

3
1. Columbus sailed to America.
2. golf that Tiger Woods plays.
3. It was in Greece that the Olympic Games first took place.
4. It's/It is Mercury that is nearest the sun.

Unit 141

1
1. Nelson Mandela, who was in prison for 27 years, became President of South Africa.
2. John Lennon, who was killed in 1980, was one of the Beatles.
3. The Titanic, which sank in 1912, was supposed to be unsinkable.
4. Queen Victoria, who came to the throne in 1837, ruled over the British Empire.
5. Mars, which is 140 million miles away, is known as the red planet.
6. The Berlin Wall, which was built in 1961, stood for 28 years.

2
1. It adds information about the college theatre.
2. It tells us which people.
3. It adds information about Lucy Kellett.
4. It tells us which young man.
5. It adds information about the evening.

3
1. who took Rita to the party
2. , who has a bad temper,
3. which Tom supports
4. , who is afraid of heights.
5. , which is on the tenth floor,
6. she bought the sofa from

Unit 142

1
1	which	5	whom/who
2	who	6	who
3	whose	7	which
4	why	8	where

2
1. which has ten thousand employees
2. whose name was missed off the list
3. (that/which) Laura painted
4. (that/which) we're/we are all looking forward to OR to which we're/we are all looking forward
5. (that/when) Mike and Harriet went camping
6. who is a bit deaf
7. whom/who you'll meet tomorrow
8. where we met the other day

3
1. Rachel's mother paid for the meal, which was very kind of her.
2. My brother is disabled, which means he can't get about very easily.
3. You left the keys in the car, which was rather careless of you.
4. Vicky didn't get the job, which has made her very depressed.
5. The police blocked off the road, which caused a traffic jam.

Unit 143

1
1	played	5	watching
2	worn	6	added
3	arriving	7	blocking
4	telling		

2
1. living in an empty office building have been evicted.
2. employing four thousand people has gone bankrupt.
3. built only two years ago has been declared unsafe.
4. People protesting against pollution have marched to London.
5. Tennis fans hoping to buy tickets have been queuing all night at Wimbledon.
6. A new drug developed at a British university may give us eternal youth.

3
1. the youngest girl to swim a length of the pool.
2. the only people to get a pay rise.
3. The pilot was the last person to leave the aircraft.
4. Mrs Harper was the first woman to become Managing Director.
5. Daniel was the most suitable candidate to apply for the job.

Unit 144

1
1	I ask	5	share
2	there are	6	I see
3	it's	7	I'll ask
4	won't cost		

2
1. If Rachel fails her driving test, she can take it again.
2. If United lose, Tom will be upset.
3. If the office is closed, Mark won't be able to get in.
4. If Nick arrives a bit early, he can help Tom to get things ready.
5. If the party goes on all night, no one will want to do any work tomorrow.
6. If Emma misses the train, she can get the next one.
7. If Matthew enters the race, he'll probably win it.

3
1. If you get promoted, your salary goes up.
2. If I drink coffee late at night, I can't sleep.
3. If you don't pay the bill, you get a warning letter.
4. If I try to run fast, I get out of breath.
5. If someone enters the building, the alarm goes off.

Unit 145

1
1. If I had a dictionary, I could look the word up.
2. If I wasn't so busy, I'd/I would write to my friends.
3. If my back wasn't aching, I could play tennis.
4. if Claire was not angry with Henry, she'd/she would speak to him.
5. if he had a map, he could find the way.
6. if he/David wasn't so clumsy, he wouldn't have so many accidents.

2
1. you wouldn't play
2. we go
3. I didn't play
4. it'd be/it would be
5. you think
6. you thought
7. it'd be/it would be
8. it won't do
9. I wouldn't get

3
1. The phone isn't working.
2. It might rain.
3. Mike isn't here.
4. The/This spoon isn't silver.
5. Sarah might call.

Unit 146

1
1. would have been
2. had lost
3. would have scored
4. she'd been/she had been
5. hadn't been
6. wouldn't have given
7. hadn't been
8. it would have been
9. we'd have beaten/we would have beaten
10. he'd been/he had been

2
1. The guests could/would have had their lunch outside if it had been warm enough/if it hadn't been so cold.
2. Sarah could/would have flown to Rome if the airport hadn't been closed/had been open.
3. Laura might have recognized Nick if he hadn't had a crash-helmet on.
4. Sarah's plants wouldn't have died/might not have died if she'd/she had watered them.
5. Nick could/would have got in (to the ice hockey game) if he'd/he had had a ticket.

3
1. he was/were, he'd/he would have put
2. I'd/I had paid, I wouldn't be
3. you loved, you wouldn't have left

Unit 147

1
1. If the twins had worn different clothes, we could have told them apart. type 3
2. If you tell me what the instructions say, I'll try to follow them. type 1
3. If people used public transport, there'd be less pollution. type 2
4. If you don't wear a sweater, you might not be warm enough. type 1
5. If I hadn't seen the product advertised, I wouldn't have bought it. type 3

2
1. you played
2. I wouldn't/couldn't hear
3. you'd/you had told
4. I wouldn't have let
5. you didn't play
6. it wouldn't be/it might not be
7. I'd/I had realized
8. I would have thrown
9. you go
10. I'll have

3
1. If I'd/I had known how unpopular Jason was, I wouldn't have invited him (to my party).
2. If you put too many tins into the plastic bag, it'll break.
3. If I had a pen, I could write down the address.
4. If I'd/I had started my project earlier, I wouldn't be so far behind (now).
5. If you need some/any help, give me a ring.
6. If the door opens, the fan comes on.

Unit 148

1
1. When the alarm rings,
2. If I feel better tomorrow,
3. When this film finishes,
4. If the plan doesn't work,

2
1. unless it's/it is a nice day.
2. unless you're/you are watching it.
3. unless we get help.
4. unless I liked it.

3 1 unless 2 if 3 unless 4 unless

4
1. We'd/We had better book a table in case the restaurant is busy.
2. You ought to insure your jewellery in case it gets stolen.
3. I'll leave you my phone number in case you want to contact me.

5 1 unless 2 If 3 in case 4 when

Unit 149

1
1. I wish you'd/you would hurry up.
2. I wish you'd/you would do the washing-up.
3. I wish you'd/you would tell me the whole story.
4. I wish you wouldn't blow cigarette smoke in my face.
5. I wish you'd/you would tell me what you're thinking.

2
1. I wish/If only I wasn't so tired.
2. I wish/If only I didn't get (these) headaches.
3. I wish/If only my work was going well/better.
4. I wish/If only I could concentrate.
5. I wish/If only life wasn't so complicated.

3
1. I'd/I had caught it.
2. she'd/she had stayed (there).
3. she'd/she had accepted it.
4. I'd/I had found it. OR I could have found it.
5. he could have played

4
1. I hadn't asked you (to marry me)
2. you wouldn't talk nonsense
3. I was a young man
4. you would/you'd listen
5. I'd/I had met you OR I could have met you

Unit 150

1
1. but it's really quite modern.
2. but she turned it down.
3. but no one laughed.

2
1. Although the house looks old, it's really quite modern.
2. Although Emma was offered a job, she turned it down.
3. Although the joke was funny, no one laughed.

3
1. Although
2. in spite of
3. Although
4. in spite of
5. in spite of

4
1. in spite of/despite
2. In spite of/Despite
3. but/although/though
4. Even though/Although/Though

5
1. Trevor didn't notice the sign even though it was right in front of him.
2. Matthew doesn't know any French although it was one of his school subjects.
3. Despite being a millionaire, Henry's friend hates spending money.
4. We couldn't get tickets in spite of queuing for an hour.

Unit 151

1
1. to go to sleep.
2. to hear the football results.
3. to look smart.
4. to finance her studies.

2
1. He's/He is going to get to work earlier in order to/so as to impress the boss.
2. He's/He is going to work harder in order to/so as to achieve more.
3. He's/He is going to take risks in order to/so as to be a winner.
4. He's/He is going to think positively in order not to/so as not to miss any opportunities.

3
1. Nick keeps a dog to guard the house.
2. David is going to be very careful so that he doesn't/won't have an accident.
3. Jessica is going on a diet to lose weight.
4. Trevor often switches off the heating to save money.
5. Sarah had to go to Birmingham for a business meeting.
6. Emma wore boots so that her feet wouldn't get wet.

Unit 152

1
1. I'll be a good person until I die
2. I hear music when I see you
3. Come back before I forget you
4. I've been sad since you left me
5. I fell ill as soon as we ate fish

2
1. Although   6. so
2. in order to   7. unless
3. because   8. In spite of
4. If   9. in case
5. but

3
1. as soon as   7. in case
2. to   8. until
3. since   9. although
4. but   10. if
5. so that   11. so
6. because   12. in spite of

Unit 153

1
1. and   4. but
2. so   5. so
3. and   6. but

2
1. Furthermore   4. On the contrary
2. however   5. After all
3. In other words   6. for example

3
1. In other words, you don't want to see him.
2. By the way, what's the time/what time is it?
3. Anyway, they haven't got one in my size.
4. Sarah ('s got one/has one), for example.
5. On the contrary, I loved/liked it.

Key to the tests

The number after the answer tells you which unit of the book has information and practice on that grammar point. The letter after the number tells you which section of the unit to look at.

Test 1

1A
1. aren't 4B
2. does 5C
3. Do 5C
4. don't 5C
5. are 4B
6. doesn't 5C
7. isn't 4B

1B
1. is 4B
2. do 5C
3. sitting 4B
4. don't 5C
5. doesn't 5C,7A
6. go 5A-B
7. being 7B
8. get 5B
9. gets 5B
10. means 5B,7A
11. always 6D
12. costing 4B,7C

1C
1. The girls are playing tennis at the moment. 4B
2. Both my brothers like sport. 5B
3. Anna is wearing her new coat today. 4B
4. What colour do you like best? 5C
5. My suitcase weighs ten kilos. 7B
6. At the moment I'm staying at a hotel. 6C
7. Robert catches the same bus every morning. 5B
8. What does this word here mean? 5C, 6B

1D
1. I'm thinking 7B, cost 7C, It's/It is getting 4C
2. look 7B, they don't fit 7B, I don't know 7B
3. are you doing 6A, I'm/I am weighing 7B, I need 7A
4. I think 7B, is going 6A, I agree 5A
5. I like 7C, Are you enjoying 7C, I'm/I am loving 7C
6. I'm/I am always falling 6D, do you go 6A, it doesn't make 6A
7. I'm living 6C, I'm looking 4C, I promise 5A
8. do you want 6B, I don't understand 6B, you're/you are being 7B

Test 2

2A
1. left 8B
2. were 8B
3. died 8D
4. had 8B
5. didn't like 8C
6. went 8D
7. happened 8B
8. wasn't 8C
9. knew 8D

2B
1. I was wearing my old coat. 9B, 9C
2. We were (both) on holiday. 8B
3. I didn't make a mistake. 8C
4. The boys were playing (a game of) cards. 9B, 9C
5. I didn't know about the change of plan. 8C, 8D
6. My friend won the competition. 8B
7. Did the Romans build this wall? 8C

2C
1. shining 9A
2. was 9B
3. wasn't 9B
4. didn't 8C
5. hated/detested 8B,8D
6. walked/went 8B, 8D
7. were 9B
8. sat 8B, 8D
9. had 8B, 8D
10. was 9B
11. took 8B, 8D
12. didn't 8C
13. wanted/hoped/had/intended 8B, 8D
14. When 10B
15. was 8B

2D
1. It was peaceful and the birds were singing. 9B
2. I was washing my hair when the phone rang. 10B
3. You didn't come to the club last night. 8C
4. It took ages to get home. 8B
5. We tried to keep quiet because the baby was sleeping. 9B
6. As I was watching him, the man suddenly ran away. 10B
7. We passed a petrol-station two minutes ago. 8B
8. Everything seemed OK. 10A
9. Where did you buy that bag? 8C
10. When I heard the alarm, I left the room immediately. 10B

2E
1. was lying 10B, rang 10B, stopped 10A
2. was 10A, left 10B, was falling 10C
3. came 10A, seemed 10A, enjoyed 10A
4. saw 10B, was standing 10B, had 10A
5. opened 10B, fell 10B
6. was walking 10B, felt 10B, didn't know 10A
7. were going 10A, heard 10A, drove 10A
8. happened 10A, was driving 10A, saw 10A

Test 3

3A
1. washed 11B
2. eaten 11D
3. opened 11B
4. written 11C
5. made 11C
6. had 11C
7. scored 11B
8. landed 11A
9. broken 11D
10. been 11C
11. sold 11C
12. finished 11B

3B
1. 's/has opened 11B
2. 's/has drawn 11C
3. 's/has broken 11C
4. have won 11C
5. 've/have drunk/finished 11C, 11B
6. 've/have washed/cleaned 11B
7. 've/have learnt/learned 11C, 11B
8. have arrived/come 11B, 11C
9. haven't finished 12A

3C
1. already 12A
2. yet 12A
3. been 13A
4. ever 13B
5. this 13D
6. long 12B
7. gone 13A
8. since 12B
9. time 13C
10. never 13B

3D
1. have 14A
2. ✔ 14A
3. have 14C
4. ✔ 14C
5. ✔ 14A
6. has 14A
7. ✔ 14A
8. ✔ 14A
9. has 14B
10. have 14B

3E
1. went 14C
2. 've/have never seen 15B
3. did 14C
4. has won 14A
5. worked 15A
6. did you get 15C
7. has been 15B
8. has come 14A
9. did you get 14C
10. haven't ridden 14C
11. was 15B
12. Have you ever baked 15B
13. was 15A
14. rang 14B
15. Have you seen 15C
16. 've/have been 15A

Test 4

4A
1. been 16B
2. I've 18C
3. were 19C
4. been 20B
5. hadn't 18C
6. Have 18C
7. was 19B
8. went 19B
9. I've 16B

4B
1. The doctor has been working since six o'clock. 16C
2. Rupert had forgotten his credit card. 18A
3. I didn't want to go until I'd/I had taken a photo. 19D
4. Nancy has written the report. 17A
5. I've/I have been waiting in the queue (for) forty minutes (so far). 16C
6. When we arrived, everyone was dancing. 19C
7. I've had/I have had the computer for four years. 17B
8. When we were having/eating lunch, there was a knock at the door. 19C
9. Nigel felt sick because he'd/he had eaten too many cakes. 20C

4C
1. I'd/I had been on holiday. 19D
2. I've/I have been playing badminton. 16C
3. I'd had/I had had a shock. 17A
4. How long have you been working? 16D
5. Lots of people were walking along the street outside. 19B
6. She's/She has been practising her English since last summer. 16C
7. I've/I have passed my exam. 17A
8. She'd/She had been lying in the sun for too long. 20C
9. But the coach had already gone. 18A

4D
1. I've/I have finished 18C
2. have we been waiting 17A, We've/We have been 17B
3. we'd/we had drunk, she hurried 19D
4. I was having, I heard 19C
5. have you been doing 16D, We've/We have done 17A
6. she'd/she had been crying 20C, she'd had/she had had 18A
7. heard, threw 19D

Test 5

5A
1. I'm/I am living 21B, I've/I have found 21C
2. I think, it belongs 21B
3. I'm/I am using 21B, I want 21B, I've/I have started 21C
4. You leave 21B, I've had/I have had 21D, I've/I have been rushing 21D

5B
1. heard 21E
2. thought 21E
3. was 21E
4. called/rang/phoned 21F
5. stopped 21F
6. was 21E
7. had 21F
8. knocked 21F
9. got/come 21F
10. been 21G

5C
1. It's/It has been raining for ten hours. 21D
2. I think it's the right thing to do. 21B
3. We've moved our/the sofa. 21C
4. I was having/eating (some/my) breakfast when Susan rang. 21E
5. They always play badminton on Tuesday. 21B

5D
1. I was looking 21E
2. I'm going 21B
3. I've been trying 21D
4. I'd spent 21F
5. They opened 21C

5E
1. ✔ 21B
2. been 21G
3. was 21E
4. are 21B
5. have 21C
6. ✔ 21G
7. been 21D
8. ✔ 21F

5F
1. failed 21C
2. lives 21B
3. left 21C
4. had made 21G
5. were walking 21E
6. saw 21E
7. has seen 21D
8. hadn't arrived 21F
9. had been waiting 21G/were waiting 21E
10. have been trying/have tried 21D
11. have had 21D
12. are taking 21B
13. believe 21B
14. want 21B

Test 6

6A
1. going 24A
2. will 23B (Also possible: won't)
3. see 27A
4. not 23C
5. to 26C
6. Shall 23D
7. is 24B
8. getting 26A
9. has 27C
10. about (Also possible: going/ready)

6B
1. What time does it get to London? 26B
2. I'll tell her when I see her this evening. 27A
3. He's about to fall asleep. 26C
4. We're/We are meeting in town later. OR We're/We are going to meet in town later. 26A
5. I'll send you a postcard. 23B
6. I can read a book while I'm waiting. 27C
7. I'm/I am going to lie down. 24A
8. All your friends will be there. 23D
9. No one can go into the building until the police have searched it. 27C

6C
1. will 25A
2. is 27A
3. will 25A
4. going 24A
5. to 24B
6. have 27C
7. will 25A
8. having/holding 26A
9. starts/begins 26B
10. will 25A

6D
1. leaves 26B
2. I'm going to apply 25A
3. I'll help 25B
4. it's about to open 26C
5. I go 27A
6. Are you doing 26A

6E
1. I'm/I am going to have a rest. 24A
2. (The) term starts on 6 September. 26B
3. There will be a world war in five years' time. 23B
4. Judy and I are/We're playing tennis tomorrow. 26A
5. Prices will probably fall. 25C
   (Also possible: Prices are probably going to fall.)
6. The car is/We're going to crash! 24C

Test 7

7A
1. going 24C
2. be 28C
3. will 23A
4. don't 26B
5. was 29B
6. are 26A
7. to 24B
8. about 26C

7B
1. is 26B
2. ✔ 26C
3. be 23C
4. for 26C
5. ✔ 28C
6. ✔ 29B
7. will 27B
8. to 29A

7C
1. 'll/will be having 28B
2. was going to drive 29B
3. 'll/will be working 28B
4. 'll/will have done 29A
5. were going to buy 29B
6. 'll/will have had 29A

7D
1. I'm/I am going 26A OR I'm/I am going to go 24A
2. I'm/I am leaving 26A OR I leave 26B OR I'm going to leave 24A
3. I'm/I am visiting 26A OR I'm/I am going to visit 24A
4. That'll/That will be 25A
5. starts 26B/is starting 26A
6. you get 27B
7. I'll/I will send 23B

7E
1. We'll wait for you. 23B
2. This train stops at Bath. 26B
3. My friend was going to meet us. 29B
4. Adrian is having a job interview on 17 October. 26A
5. We'll/We will have finished our meal by eight o'clock. 29A
6. I might go on the trip. 30C
7. The fire is about to go out. 26C

7F
1. I'm going to move 24A
2. I'll take 23B
3. we're going 26A
4. He's going to jump 24C
5. I'll be using 28C

Test 8

8A
1. Where have you been? 36B
2. Do you sell postcards? 34B
3. Who does this calculator belong to? 39A
4. How long are you staying here? 36C
5. What is your new office like? 38B
6. Which of the flights are full? 39B
7. What time does the carnival start? 36C
8. What holiday has Nancy decided on? 38A

8B
1. How old 36C
2. What colour 36C
3. Whose 37B
4. How much 36C
5. Which 39A
6. What kind 36C
7. Who 39B
8. How 38B
9. How far 36C
10. How often 36C
11. What 39A

8C
1. Are you a student here? 34B
2. How many cakes have you eaten? 37B
3. Did you enjoy your walk? 34B
4. Where have your friends gone? 36B
5. What kind of music do you like? 36C
6. Does Peter play tennis? 34B
7. What are you talking about? 38A
8. What has happened? 37A

8D
1. Where did you buy your coat? 36B
2. Can Amy swim? 34B
3. Which band do you like best? 37B
4. Who am I speaking to? 38A
5. How much do video recorders cost? 36C
6. May/Can I come in (, please)? 34A
7. How long does the journey take? 36B
8. What did you lock the door for? 38B
9. What happens next? 37A
10. Shall we (all) go out together? 34A

8E
1. How many cars have the Smiths got/do the Smiths have? 36C
2. Where does Janet work? 36B
3. Why is Andrea learning English? 36A
4. What was the film like? 38B
5. When will the meeting take place? 36B
6. Who switched off the computer? 37A
7. Whose burglar alarm was ringing? 37B
8. Who did Anna go to the dance with? 38A

Test 9

9A
1. Who's 37A
2. don't 42B
3. not 40B
4. has 35B
5. Haven't 41B
6. so 43B
7. they 42B
8. Which 39B
9. don't 40B
10. neither 42A
11. doesn't 41B
12. Let's 42C

9B
1. Where do you live? 36B
2. What are you thinking about? 38A
3. Would you like to come to my room? 34A
4. Didn't you watch the football match on television? 41C
5. May I take a photo (, please)? 34A
6. Have you seen Polly? 34B
7. How many letters have you written? 37B
8. Who is/Who's coming to your party? 37A
9. How often does Martin cook? 36C
10. What will the weather be (like) tomorrow? 38B

9C
1. No, it hasn't. 35B
2. No, I hate it./Yes, I love it. 41D
3. Yes, I expect so. 43B
4. It isn't very nice, is it? 42B
5. Yes, please. 35C
6. So am I./I am too. 43A
7. I hope not. 43B
8. Neither did the second. 43A

9D
1. How old are you? 36C
2. Did you go to college? 34B
3. What are your interests? 39A
4. Which company do you work for? 38A
5. What don't you like about your job? 41E

9E
1. doesn't 40B
2. course 35C
3. neither/nor 43A
4. No 41D
5. for 38B
6. did 42B
7. won't 35B
8. not 43B
9. will 42C
10. far 36C
11. so 43B
12. don't 41E
13. Which 39A
14. so 43A
15. hasn't 41E
16. Which 40B

Test 10

10A
1. mustn't 48A
2. Would 51C
3. might 46B
4. would 52A
5. needn't 48A
6. Shall 51B
7. had 49C
8. wouldn't 52C

10B
1. ✔ 51C
2. ✔ 47A
3. to 44C
4. for 50A
5. be 46A
6. ✔ 52A
7. been 53B
8. ✔ 49D
9. ✔ 48B
10. be 45C

10C
1. We ought to be careful. 49B
2. I was able to finish all my work. 44C
3. It must have been a terrible experience for you. 53D
4. Players aren't allowed/are not allowed to have a drink. 45C
5. You'd/You had better sit down. 49C
6. The report has to be on my desk tomorrow morning. 47A
7. Joanne mightn't have/might not have received my message. 53C
8. Martin can't be jogging in this weather. 46C
9. Tessa would like a cup of coffee. 52B
10. Nancy didn't need to clean the flat. 48C

10D
1. asking permission 45A
2. giving an order 50B
3. asking for advice 49B
4. inviting 51C
5. offering to help 51B
6. making a suggestion 51A
7. refusing permission 45B
8. making a request 50A
9. expressing a wish 47B

10E
1. have/need 48B
2. may/might (Also possible: could) 46A
3. has 47A
4. can 44A
5. allowed 45C
6. supposed 49D
7. shouldn't 49B (Also possible: mustn't 48A)
8. able 44B

Test 11

11A
1. The film may be banned. 54C
2. Nancy was offered a pay increase. 57A
3. The mistakes need correcting/need to be corrected. 59B
4. The situation was reported to be under control. 57C
5. The new drug is being tested. 54B
6. The machine hasn't been used for ages. 55B

KEY TO THE TESTS 417

11B
1. is 54B
2. by 55B
3. be 54C/get 54D
4. were 54B
5. it 57B
6. been 54B
7. have 58B
8. to 57C
9. being 59A

11C
1. The song was sung by Pavarotti. 55B
2. Nigel had his passport stolen. 58D
3. Doctors are paid a lot of money. 57A
4. I hope to be interviewed for the job. 59A
5. The floor was being cleaned. 54B
6. Judy is having her car repaired. 58B
7. Tessa got lost. 54D
8. It was agreed that the plan should go ahead. 57B
9. When did you get your kitchen decorated? 58C
10. Exercise is said to be good for you. 57C

11D
1. b) 55A
2. b) 55A
3. a) 55A
4. a) 55A
5. b) 55A

11E
1. The story was written by Agatha Christie. 55B
2. Baseball is played at this stadium. 54B
3. This shirt needs ironing/needs to be ironed. 59B
4. I got my hair cut yesterday. 58C
5. It is believed that there is going to be a war. 57B
6. My parents got divorced last year. 54D
7. I've got a report to write. 59B
8. The winner was given a prize. 57A
9. This man on TV is supposed to be the tallest person in the world. 57C

Test 12

12A
1. to organize 62B
2. wearing 62B
3. to approve 62B
4. to be 62B
5. reminding 62B
6. to be 62B
7. working 62B
8. to buy 62B
9. waiting 62B

12B
1. We must avoid wasting so much time. 61A
2. Sometimes a country refuses to take part in the Olympics. 62B
3. I'd/I would like to see the Rocky Mountains some day. 63B
4. I meant to give Judy a nice welcome yesterday. 64E
5. I always like to see my doctor once a year. 63A
6. The buses usually stop running before midnight. 64D
7. I can't face getting up at five tomorrow. 61C
8. Last year we made an agreement to work together. 60D
9. Yesterday you promised to carry on shooting the film. 62B
10. My father seems to be getting better now. 60B

12C
1. wait 62C
2. to 60A
3. seeing/meeting 61A
4. would 63B
5. need 64G (Also possible: have/ought)
6. not 61A
7. help 61C (Also possible: stop 64D)
8. to 62D
9. on 61D

12D
1. We've finished decorating the flat. 61A
2. I regret saying what I did. 63B
3. Tessa decided not to go to work. 60A
4. Do you mind helping me? 61B
5. I'm beginning to get worried. 63C
6. I can't afford to buy a new car. 60A
7. I hope to avoid making things worse. 62E
8. Peter seems to have gone away already. 60B

12E
1. The children couldn't wait to see their presents. 62C
2. I can't stand getting up in the dark. 61C
3. I happened to see your brother yesterday. 62D
4. The shop tends to open ten minutes late. 60C
5. Do you fancy going for a walk? 62C
6. The police carried on watching the house. 61D
7. I'll/I will never forget seeing Nelson Mandela. 64A

Test 13

13A
1. for 67B
2. in 75A
3. ✔ 70C
4. ✔ 66C
5. ✔ 65D
6. to 69B(3)
7. enough 68C
8. for 74C
9. them 67C
10. ✔ 73B

13B
1. to get 71B
2. making 70B
3. reaching 70B
4. running 65D
5. dreaming 73A
6. to happen 65C
7. ordering 73B
8. to follow 68B
9. to be 67D
10. to do 65B
11. respect 69B(3)
12. to do 65B
13. buying 65E
14. order 69B(2)

13C
1. We saw Rupert looking in a shop window. 74A
2. I remember the clown falling over. 65D
3. Tessa wasn't sure which way to go. 66C
4. The porter just stood there expecting a tip. 75A
5. How about going to the barbecue? 73B
6. Susan is used to (always) living in the country. 72B
7. I'm afraid of hurting myself. 71A
8. Christopher apologized for forgetting to pay. 70B
9. The food was too cold for Michelle to eat. 68C
10. It was silly of Polly to give away the secret. 67E
    (Also possible: Polly was silly to give away the secret.)

13D
1. after 73C
2. to 65B
3. used 72A
4. to 71B
5. having/eating 70B
6. of 67E
7. to 68D
8. to 72B
9. how 66B
10. of 71A
11. for 68A
12. by 73B
13. Having 75B
14. put 74D

13E 1 breaking 70C, knock 74D
2 to see 69A(8), to forget 68D
3 doing 73C, to write 69A(2)
4 to bother 71C, to ask 66B
5 to play 72A, watch 69B(2)

Test 14

14A 1 a 77B
2 ✔ 76A
3 ✔ 77B
4 a 76A
5 ✔ 77B
6 some 77A
7 an 78C
8 an 78C

14B 1 much 76C
2 clothes 80A
3 pairs 81A
4 fun 76A
5 is/was 79E
6 saving 80A
7 doesn't 79C
8 was 79A
9 was 79A
10 piece/slice 78A

14C 1 Every window was broken. 79B
2 My earnings aren't enough to live on. 80A
3 There was litter everywhere. 77B
4 We went to the hotel to get some food. 76A
5 Judy bought a pair of binoculars. 81A
6 I need a new cheque book. 82B
7 I'll have a glass of orange juice, please. 78C
8 The reporter needed two pieces/bits/items of information. 77B

14D 1 We can't sit here because the grass is wet. 79A
2 Do you want (some) butter on your bread? 76A
3 All my belongings were stolen. 80A
4 Do you have any information about hotels? 77B
5 The police are questioning two men. 81C
6 Can we have two coffees/two cups of coffee, please? 78D
7 The news isn't very good, I'm afraid. 80B
8 I just want to go into this shoe shop. 82B
9 It's only a short journey by train. 79B

14E 1 wears 79B
2 a piece of advice 77B
3 the football match 82A
4 customs 80A
5 are 81B
6 many 76C
7 is 79E
8 these glasses 81A
9 steelworks 80C
10 any 77B
11 meat 76A
12 were 80A
13 A noise 78B
14 were 81C
15 is 79C
16 light 78C
17 sports club 82B
18 means 80C
19 woods 78D
20 has 79B

Test 15

15A 1 a 83B
2 the 84C
3 the 88B
4 The 83B
5 the 90E
6 a 85C
7 The 83B
8 the 83B
9 the 84B
10 the 83B
11 a 89B
12 a 83B
13 one 85B
14 the 83B
15 The 83B

15B 1 work 87B
2 quite a difficult 89B
3 Golf 86B
4 School 87A
5 a really nice 89B
6 some photos 85D
7 the violin 86C
8 breakfast 84F
9 an X-ray 84D
10 the radio 86C
11 the environment 84B
12 such terrible 89C

15C 1 ✘ 86B
2 a 89B
3 ✘ 88B
4 an 84D
5 a 83B
6 the 90C
7 ✘ 90F
8 a 83B
9 ✘ 88D
10 some 85D/the 83B (Also possible: ✘)
11 a 83B
12 a 84C
13 one 85B
14 a 83B (Also possible: one)
15 the 83B
16 What 89D (Also possible: Such)
17 so 89C
18 the 84C

15D 1 ✔ 87B
2 ✔ 88F
3 The 86B
4 the 89D
5 ✔ 85D
6 the 88E
7 ✔ 87A
8 A 85B
9 ✔ 89C
10 ✔ 90J
11 ✔ 86C

15E 1 a beautiful city 84C
2 The weather 84B
3 Easter 88C
4 Princes Street 90G
5 the Royal Scottish Museum 90I
6 the Highlands 90D
7 mountains 86B
8 a thing 89C
9 the sea 87B
10 Corfu 90B
11 some sunshine 85D (Also possible: sunshine)
12 beach holidays 88B

Test 16

16A 1 b) 97B
2 b) 93A
3 a) 92D
4 a) 95C
5 b) 97C
6 c) 94A

KEY TO THE TESTS   419

16B
1. either 97C
2. Someone 94B
3. these 91A
4. a few 95C
5. Some 96A
6. People's 93A
7. that 91B
8. Polly's 92E

16C
1. a 95C
2. mine 92A
3. of 92E
4. many 95B
5. anyone 94B
6. None 96D
7. all 96B
8. lot 95A
9. whole 97B

16D
1. That was a very good idea of yours. 92E
2. You've got a lot of books, haven't you? 95A
3. I don't know the time of the meeting. 93B
4. Nigel has hurt his leg. 92C
5. All (of) the rooms in the house were cold. 96B
6. Wear anything - it doesn't matter what. 94C
7. Each of the four doors was locked. 97A
8. I live my life, and my sister lives hers. 92A
9. Both socks/Both the socks/Both of the socks have got holes in them. 97C
10. Here's a copy of this week's magazine. 93C
11. This sweater is losing its colour. 92B
12. I want some paper, but there's none in here. 96D

16E
1. I've lived here most of my life. 96B
2. Every hotel was full. 97A
3. The house on the corner is bigger than ours. 92A
4. I've forgotten the name of my doctor. 93A
5. We have had/We've had little warning of the changes. 95C
6. So many people have applied for the job. 95B
7. I met an old boyfriend of yours at a party. 92E
8. Neither of the chairs is/are comfortable. 97C
9. My holiday starts in ten days' time. 93C

Test 17

17A
1. himself 100C
2. They 98B
3. We 98B
4. them 98B
5. us 98B
6. themselves 100D
7. It 99B
8. They 98C
9. ourselves 98D
10. her 98B
11. me 98B

17B
1. yourself 100C
2. it 99B
3. some 102C
4. us 100C
5. Me 98B
6. ones 102B
7. there 99A
8. each other's 101B
9. else 103D

17C
1. one 102C
2. everyone/everybody 103A
3. herself 100C
4. one 102B
5. It 99B
6. something 103A
7. one 102C
8. You 98C
9. ourselves 101A

17D
1. one 102C
2. himself 100D
3. something 103A
4. it 99B
5. her 98B
6. There 99A
7. everyone/everybody 103C
8. it 99B
9. there 99A
10. each 101B
11. them 98B
12. him 98B

17E
1. There's/There is a train leaving in ten minutes. 99C
2. I think someone is/someone's coming up the stairs. 103C
3. Let's meet at eight o'clock, shall we? 100E
4. We haven't got a camcorder, but we'd like one. 102C
5. Let's do something different/something else today. 103D
6. They are/They're going to build a new motorway through here. 98C
7. I'm afraid I haven't done anything all day. 103B
8. Everyone enjoyed themselves at the barbecue. 100B, 100D
9. If you're buying a loaf, get a nice fresh one. 102B
10. I've looked everywhere for my credit card. 103A
11. The two friends still see each other/see one another occasionally. 101B

Test 18

18A
1. freely 109C
2. The young man 106C
3. hungry 104B
4. thoughtfully 108C
5. right 109B
6. fascinating 107B
7. similar 104C
8. well 109D
9. the disabled 106B
10. confused 107B
11. scientifically 108B
12. frightened 104C

18B
1. This is a nice place. 104B
2. I can't find the large biscuit tin. 105B
3. Tessa behaved in a silly way. 109A
4. Your coffee is getting cold. 104B
5. They live in a lovely old stone house. 105C
6. This hospital is for the mentally ill. 106B

18C
1. expensive 104B
2. nice 104B
3. surprised 107B
4. carefully 108A
5. amusing 107B
6. elderly 109A
7. friendly 109A
8. free 109C

18D
1. The drink tasted strange. 108C
2. Obviously, the sick need to be looked after. 106A
3. The dog was asleep. 104C
4. The young woman spoke politely. 108A
5. The train arrived late. 109C
6. The film ends dramatically. 108B
7. Polly shouted angrily. 108B
8. Billiards is an indoor game. 104C
9. The clown was amusing. 107B
(Also possible: People found the clown amusing.)
10. There was hardly any time left. 109C

18E
1. I tasted the soup carefully. 108C
2. ✔ 105C
3. Are the children asleep? 104C
4. It's a school for the deaf/for deaf people. 106C
5. It's a nice new leather jacket. 105C
6. The rich are/Rich people are very lucky. 106A
7. ✔ 109D
8. He used a thick green paper towel. 105C
9. ✔ 106A
10. The course I started was boring./I was bored with the course I started. 107B
11. I often talk to the two old people/men/women next door. 106C
12. The smoke rose high into the air. 109C
13. ✔ 104B
14. We felt disappointed when we lost. 107B
15. Everyone seemed very nervous. 108C
16. Tessa drives too fast. 109B
17. ✔ 107B

Test 19

19A
1. more intelligent 110B
2. cleaner 110B
3. thinner 110C
4. more carefully 110D
5. worse 110E
6. later 110C
7. longer 110D
8. more useful 110B
9. sooner 110D
10. busier 110C
11. more annoyed 110B
12. more nervous 110B

19B
1. funniest 110C
2. most horrible 110B
3. most recent 110B
4. largest 110C
5. most boring 110B
6. farthest/furthest 110E
7. most helpful 110B
8. most modern 110B
9. earliest 110D
10. saddest 110C

19C
1. ✔ 111D
2. the 111B
3. ✔ 111C
4. a 112B
5. so 112D
6. ✔ 111B
7. most 110A
8. ✔ 111E
9. of 111C
10. more 112C

19D
1. nicer 111B
2. as 111D
3. least 112A
4. than me 111E
5. in 111C
6. bit 112B
7. as 111D
8. the easier 112D

19E
1. is bigger than the living-room 111B
2. fitter than I am 110C, 111B
3. is as big as 111D
4. just get higher and higher 112C
5. is more expensive than 110A, 111B
6. is the least difficult 112A
7. more and more excited 112C
8. most romantic story I've ever 111C

Test 20

20A
1. I quite like old cowboy films. 115C
2. Have you finished this magazine yet? 114B
3. This coat is too big. 117B
4. Have the children already had their tea?/Have the children had their tea already? 114C
5. You certainly don't look ill. 113G
6. We don't go out much. 115D
7. I think everyone works fairly hard. 115B
8. I still don't know the date of the meeting. 114C
9. The others are just getting ready. 113B
10. I have to go to work on Saturdays./On Saturdays I have to go to work. 113H

20B
1. This game is rather silly. 115B
2. I've already paid the bill./I've paid the bill already. 114C
3. The alarm isn't loud enough. 117B
4. Jonathan passed the test easily./Jonathan easily passed the test. 113C
5. The children play cards a lot. 115C
6. They didn't sell enough tickets. 117B
7. You ask too many questions. 117B
8. I'm not a member of the club any more. 114D
9. It's warm enough to sit outside. 117C

20C
1. yet 114B
2. still 114C
3. rather 116C
4. enough 117B
5. many 117B
6. to 117C
7. any 114D
8. no 114D
9. bit 115A
10. soon 113E

20D
1. I didn't sleep very well last night./Last night I didn't sleep very well. 113E
2. I think I need to rest a little. 115C
3. I don't work for the company any longer. 114D
4. The article is fairly interesting. 115A
5. Tessa locked the door carefully./Tessa carefully locked the door. 113C
6. You aren't tall enough to play basketball. 117B
7. We went to town yesterday./Yesterday we went to town. 113H
8. I like this music very much./I very much like this music. 115D

20E
1. We go to the cinema a lot. 115C
2. Adrian always wears jeans. 113F
3. These shoes aren't big enough. 117A
4. I no longer live in Birmingham. 114D
5. Polly spent too much money in the sales. 117B

Test 21

21A
1. The doctor has been working for twelve hours. 121B
2. We had a great time at the disco. 119B
3. The woman was getting out of the car. 118A
4. The players had numbers on their shirts. 119A
5. The new manager takes over in two weeks' time. 120C
6. Anna drove to the garage to get some petrol. 118B
7. We were sitting at the back of the room. 119C

21B
1. on 119C
2. ago 121C
3. on 120A
4. at 120A/by 122B
5. at 119C
6. on 119A
7. in 120C
8. across 118A
9. during 122A/in
10. until/till 122B

21C
1. the 120B
2. ✔ 118A
3. ✔ 122C
4. the 118A
5. on 120A
6. ✔ 119C
7. ✔ 122B

21D
1. on 119C
2. for 123A
3. by 122B
4. at 123B
5. since 121B
6. with 124B
7. above 118A
8. of 124C
9. while 122A
10. between 124C
11. like 122C
12. with 125B
13. ago 121C
14. for 124D
15. until 122B
16. for 125A
17. in 120A
18. to 125D

21E
1. Scott lives in Washington. 119A
2. I'm travelling to Italy on business. 120A
3. I'm busy on Friday morning. 120A
4. They've/They have been playing (for) an hour. 121A
5. Jonathan is very good at tennis. 125C
6. I'm rather busy at the moment. 120A
7. We went/travelled to Budapest by air. 123C
8. Nigel goes past the newsagent's every day. 118A
9. The company is planning (to make) a reduction in the workforce. 124C
10. We got to our guest house in time for a meal. 120B

Test 22

22A
1. I must pay for my ticket. 126B
2. I'm going to put on that expensive grey coat I bought. 128C
3. She's invited us to lunch. 127B
4. He's looking at them. 126A
5. The police prevented me from leaving. 127C
6. I'm going to turn it off. 128C

22B
1. about 126C
2. out 130B
3. on 128B
4. off 128C
5. up 130B
6. at 126B
7. through 129C
8. up for 131B

22C
1. You've left one out. 128B
2. I've never heard of it. 126C
3. They ran away from it. 131A
4. You must congratulate her on her success. 127B
5. She's going to set up her own company. 129B
6. He reminds me of an old schoool friend of mine. 127C
7. He wants to put it forward at the meeting. 129C

22D
1. as 127B
2. about/of 127C
3. look/watch 131B
4. in 126B
5. from 127A
6. on 127B
7. at 127B
8. out 129A (Also possible: over)
9. out 125A
10. forward 131B
11. woke 129A
12. up 129A

22E
1. You're too young to give up working. 129B
2. This bag belongs to Janet. 126A
3. Everyone carried on working as usual. 130B
4. They discussed the plan. 126C
5. I've/I have run out of money. 131B
6. I explained the problem to the police./I explained to the police what the problem was. 127C
7. I wouldn't put up with such terrible conditions. 131B
8. They'll have to put off the game/put the game off. 128B

Test 23

23A
1. me 135D
2. did 135C
3. ✔ 136B
4. that 135B
5. ✔ 133B
6. me 132C
7. did 134B
8. for 136A

23B
1. was 134B
2. previous 133B
3. whether 135B
4. not to 136A
5. told 132C
6. that 133B
7. could 134C
8. suggested 136B

23C
1. they 133B
2. that/if/whether 132B
3. she 133B
4. to 132A
5. didn't 134B
6. had 134B
7. wouldn't/didn't 134C
8. if/whether 135B
9. wanted/needed/had 135A
10. next/following/same 134B

23D
1 she said she felt quite excited. 133B, 134B
2 he said he couldn't remember the code word. 133B, 134C
3 he said he wouldn't be at the next meeting. 133B, 134C
4 they said they had/they'd got a problem. 133B, 134B
5 she said she'd been swimming/she had been swimming. 133B, 134B
6 they said they would like to be in the show. 133B, 134C
7 he said he didn't need any help. 133B, 134B
8 she said her sister was coming to see her. 133B, 134B

23E
1 A policeman told Christopher to stop shouting. 136A
2 Tessa admitted eating all the cake/having eaten all the cake the day before/the previous day. 133B, 136B
3 Adrian apologized for being rude/for having been rude. 136B
4 Simon invited Susan to join him for lunch. 133B, 136B
5 Martin asked Nancy if/whether someone rang her/someone had rung her an hour before. 133B, 135B
6 Peter insisted on leaving. 136B

Test 24

24A
1 for 139A
2 entering 143A
3 which 136B
4 only 143B
5 who 142A
6 whom 139C
7 that you took 138A
8 where 142C
9 which 142D
10 whose 140A

24B
1 This isn't the train on which I normally travel. 139C / This isn't the train (that/which) I normally travel on. 139B
2 The letter that I opened wasn't for me. 137B
3 The reason (why/that) I didn't know was that no one had told me. 142C
4 What we should do is ring the police. 140B
5 I didn't know the name of the man who/that helped me. 138B
6 Rupert knows the family whose house is for sale. 140A
7 Einstein, who failed his university entrance exam, discovered relativity. 141B
8 The person we talked to was very friendly./138B The people we talked to were very friendly.
9 It's the President who makes the important decisions. 140C
10 I can't find my diary, which is a real nuisance. 142D
11 Outside the door was a pair of boots covered in mud. 143A
12 Lake Superior, which lies on the US-Canadian border, is the largest lake in North America. 142A

24C
1 who 133B (Also possible: that)
2 that/which 133B
3 that/which 135A
4 it 136C
5 that/which 133B
6 what 136B
7 whose 136A
8 which 138D
9 what 136B
10 who 138A

24D
1 that/which crashed was 137B/, which crashed, was 142A
2 (when/that) Martin rang (,) Tessa was 142C
3 new offices are 133A/offices, which are new, are 142A
4 stolen from a car have been 143A / that/which were stolen from a car have been 137B
5 (that/which) you were looking at is 139A–B
6 Theatre, which dates from 1896, is 142A
7 whose dog was run over was 140A
8 the first (person) to solve 143B/the first (person) who solved 137B
9 selling newspapers was standing 143A / who was selling newspapers was standing 137B
10 (that/which) Judy gave was 138A–B/, which Judy gave, was 142A
11 where I used to live is 142C/(that/which) I used to live in 139A–B/in which I used to live 139C

Test 25

25A
1 it would have opened 146B
2 disappear 144B
3 travelled 145B
4 would be 147B
5 they don't build 144B
6 would suffer 145B
7 I'll go 144B/I'm going to go 147B
8 I'd/I had known 146B
9 I'd/I would have moved 146B
10 they'd/they had done 147B
11 there won't be/there might not be 144B

25B
1 had been 146B
2 in case 148D
3 knew 149C
4 only 149A
5 when 148B
6 unless 148C

25C 1 If you talk about football, I'm going to be very bored. 147B
2 If the baby had cried, we wouldn't have had a good sleep. 146B
3 If you want a chat, just give me a ring. 147B
4 If Nigel had satellite TV, he could watch/would be able to watch the game. 145B
5 If you go away, I'll miss you. 144B
6 If I was/were rich, I'd/I would have given up working long ago. 146D
7 If we'd/we had bought that picture five years ago, it would be quite valuable now. 146D
8 If you throw a stone into water, it sinks. OR If you throw a stone into water, it'll/it will sink. 144D

25D 1 If it rains, I'll stay here. 144B
2 Can you tell me when it starts? 148B
3 I wouldn't need to repeat things all the time if you listened. 145B
4 If air gets warmer, it rises. 144D
5 I'd better get another one made in case I lose it. 148D
6 I wish we'd/we had left home earlier. 149D
7 If it doesn't arrive today, we'll have to complain. 144B
8 I wish someone would turn it down. 149B
9 Unless we act quickly, it'll be too late. 148C
10 But he wouldn't have been angry if you hadn't damaged his stereo. 146B

Index

The numbers in this index are unit numbers unless they have the letter 'p' for 'page'.

'negative questions 41' means that you can read about negative questions in Unit 41.

'**was able to** 44C' means that you can find out about *was able to* in Unit 44 part C.

'**someplace** p 380' means that you can find this word on page 380.

Aa

a 83–5, Test 15 p 214
   and **one** 85B
   a potato or *potato*? 78
   quite a 89B
a bit 115
   + comparative 112B
a few 95
a little 95
   + comparative 112B
a lot + comparative 112B
a lot of 95
   agreement 79C
a number of 79C
ability: **can, be able to** 44
able to 44
about after a verb 126C, 127C
about to 26C
action verbs 7
active and passive 55–6
adding relative clauses 141–2
adjectives 104–9, Test 18 p 258
   word order 104B, 105
   adjective or adverb? 108–9, p 380
   comparative and superlative 110–12
   the old, the rich 106
   after **everyone** etc 103D
   suffixes p 369
   ending in **ing/ed** 107
   + **one/ones** 102
   + to-infinitive 67
   + preposition 125
   + preposition + ing-form 70D
adverbs 113–17, Test 18 p 258, Test 20 p 282
   word order 113
   adverb or adjective? 108–9, p 380
   ly ending p 371
   comparative and superlative 110D
   of manner 108, 113D
   of frequency 113F
   of place and time 113E
   of degree 115
   sentence adverbs 113G
   in phrasal verbs 128–31
adverbials 2
advice 77B
afraid
   + **so** 43B
   + to-infinitive or ing-form 71A
agent with **by** 55
ago 121C
agreement 79, Test 14 p 194
all 96
   with a singular verb 79B
allow with a to-infinitive or ing-form 65E
allowed to 45
already 114
   with the present perfect 12A
   in American English p 377
also 113G, 153B
although 150
always
   with the present continuous and simple 6D
American English p 377–82
amount + singular verb 79E
an 84D
   see also **a**
and
   faster and faster 112C
   go and buy p 381
answering questions 34A, 35, 41D
anxious + to-infinitive or ing-form 71B
any 94
   + comparative 112B
any longer 114D
any more 114D
any of 79D
anyone, anything, etc 94B, 103
apostrophe p 373
   in a possessive form 93
   in a short form 32A
appear + to-infinitive 60B
articles 83–90
   see also **a** and **the**
as
   in comparisons 111D
   and **like** 122C
   linking word 152A
   with the past continuous 10B
as if 122C
as soon as 152A
as well 113G, 153B
ashamed + to-infinitive or ing-form 71B
asking for advice 49B, 52D
asking for information 135D
at
   place 118, 119
   time 120
   at the end 123B
   good at 125C

Bb

badly 109D
be
   simple and continuous 7B
   past simple 8B
   present perfect 11C
   + to-infinitive 59B
be able to 44
be about to 26C
be allowed to 45
be going to 24
   and **will** 25
   past tense 29B
be supposed to 49D, 57C
be to 26C
be used to 72B
because 152D
bed and **the bed** 87B
been to and **gone to** 13A
before
   linking word 152A
   with the past perfect 121D
   + ing-form 73C
begin + to-infinitive or ing-form 63C
being done 59
believe so 43B
best 110E
better 110E
   had better 49C, 69B
between 118
   link between 124C
bit of 77B
   see also **a bit**

both 97C
bother + to-infinitive or ing-form 63C
British and American English p 377–82
but 150B
by
  place 118A
  time 122B
  by car 123C
  + agent 55B, 56A
  + ing-form 73B

Cc

can
  ability 44
  permission 45
  requests 50
  offers 51B
  asking for a suggestion 51A
cannot 44A
can't
  ability 44A
  refusing permission 45B
  certainty 46C
  in questions 41C
can't have done 53D
can't help + ing-form 61C
can't wait + to-infinitive 62C
capital letter p 373
carry on + ing-form 61D
cattle 81C
certain + to-infinitive 67D
certainly 113G
certainty: **must, can't** 46C
changes in reported speech 133–4
church and **the church** 87A
clothes 80A
collective nouns see group nouns
colons p 372
commas p 372
  around a relative clause 141B
comparative 110–12, Test 19 p 268
  spelling p 371
comparison of adverbs 110D
complement 2A
compound nouns 82
conditionals 144–8, Test 25 p 358
conjunctions see linking words
consonant doubling p 371
contracted forms see short forms

could
  ability 44C
  permission 45
  possibility 46
  requests 50
  suggestions 51A
could have done 53
couldn't
  ability 44C
  impossibility 46B
countable and uncountable nouns 76–8

Dd

'd (short form) 32C
dashes p 372
dates p 380
decisions 25B, 52C
defining relative clauses 141–2
definite article see **the**
demonstratives (**this** etc) 91
despite 150D
determiners 91–7, Test 16 p 230
did
  in the past simple 8C, 34B, 36B, 43A
  emphatic 33
didn't 8C, 40B
didn't need to 48B
different + preposition p 381
direct and indirect objects 3
direct speech 132A, p 373
do
  in the present simple 5, 34B, 36B, 43A
  emphatic 33, p 378
  as I should (do) p 378
does
  in the present simple 5, 34B, 36B, 43A
  emphatic 33
doesn't 5, 40B
don't
  in the present simple 5, 40B
  with an imperative 50A
don't have to 48B
don't need to 48B
dove p 382
doubling of consonants p 371
down in a phrasal verb 130B
during 122A

Ee

each 97A
  + **one** 102B
  with a singular verb 79B
each other 101B
early 109B
ed-adjective 107
ed ending 8B
  pronunciation p 375
  spelling p 370
either 97C
either of + singular/plural verb 79D
elder, eldest 110E
else 103D
emphatic form 33
emphatic pronouns 101
empty subjects 56B
end position 113H
endings of words p 368–71
  spelling p 370–1
enough 117
  with **for** and a to-infinitive 68C
er, est ending 110
  spelling p 371
even though 150C
ever with the present perfect or past simple 13B, 15B, p 377
every 97A
  + **one** 102B
  with a singular verb 79B
everyone, everything, etc 103
exclamation marks p 372
exclamations with **what** 89D
expect so 43B

Ff

fail + to-infinitive 60C
fancy + ing-form 62C
far + comparative 112B
farther, farthest 110E
fast 109
few 95
for
  and **since** 121
  with the present perfect 12B, 14C, 121B
  with the present perfect continuous 16D
  expressing purpose 73B, 151E
  buy it for you 3B
  a need for 124D

good for you 125C
　with a to-infinitive 68
　with **too** and **enough** 117C
forget + to-infinitive or ing-form 64A
free, freely 109C
friendly 109A
front position 113A
full stops p 372
further, furthest 110E
future 22–30, Test 6 p 68, Test 7 p 76
future continuous 28
future passive 54C
future perfect 29A

Gg

general meaning of **a** and **the** 85C
gerund see ing-form
get
　passive auxiliary 54D
　get dressed etc 54D
　get something done 58C
get used to 72B
go on + to-infinitive or ing-form 64F
going to (future) see **be going to**
gone to and **been to** 13A
good and **well** 109D
good + preposition 125C
got 31
gotten p 378
group nouns 81B, p 379
guess so 43B

Hh

had 31
had been doing 20
had better 49C, 69B
had done 18
had got 31B
had to 47
half 96B
happen + to-infinitive 62D
hard, hardly 109
has 31
has been doing 16
has done 11
has to 47
have 31
　action verb 31C
　have something done 58

have and **have got** 31
　in American English p 378
have been doing 16
have done 11
have got 31
have got to 47C
have something done 58
have to 47, 48B
having done 75
he 98
help + infinitive 69C
her 92, 98
hers 92
herself 100, 101
high, highly 109C
him 98
himself 100, 101
his 92
home and **the home** 87B
hope so 43B
hospital and **the hospital** 87A
how 38B
how about + ing-form 73B
how long with the perfect 12B, 16D
how many/much 37B, 95B
hyphens p 373

Ii

I (pronoun) 98
identifying relative clauses 141–2
idioms
　phrasal verbs 128–31
　preposition + noun 123
　prepositional verbs 126
　with reflexive pronouns 100E
if 144–9, 152B
　or **when**? 148B
　in reported questions 135B
　with **any** 94A
if only 149
imperative 50B
　invitations 51C
　offers 51B
　with **do** 33C, p 378
　question tags 42C
in
　place 118B, 119
　time 120
　transport 123C
　in the end, in the way 123B
　increase in 124C

　after a superlative 111C
in case 148D, 152B
　in American English p 381
in order to 151C
in spite of 150
indefinite article see **a**
indirect object 3
　passive structure 57A
indirect speech 132–6
　see also reported speech
infinitive 60–9, see also to-infinitive
　with and without **to** 69
　see it happen 74
information 77B
ing-adjective 107
ing-form 61–5, 70–5, Test 13 p 178, Test 12 p 154
　spelling p 370
　passive 59
　perfect 75
　or to-infinitive 62–5, 71–2, 74
　after a preposition 70, 73
　after an adjective + preposition 70D
　after a linking word 73C
　after a verb 61–2
　after a verb + object 65
　after a verb + preposition 70
　in relative clauses 143A
　see it happening 74
　+ noun 82D
　other structures 75
intend + to-infinitive or ing-form 63C
intentions 25B
interested
　and **interesting** 107
　+ to-infinitive or ing-form 71B
into 118B
intonation p 374-5
　in question tags 42A
inverted commas p 373
invitations 51C
irregular comparative and superlative forms 110E
irregular verbs p 383–4
　in American English p 382
is done see passive
it 98
　and **one** 102C
　and **there** 99
　+ **be** + adjective + to-infinitive 67B

+ **be** + relative clause 140C
it is said that ... 57B
item of 77B
its 92
itself 100, 101

Jj

just
with the present perfect 12A, p 377

Kk

keep (on) + ing-form 61D
key to phonetic symbols p 374
key to symbols p vii

Ll

last
with the past simple 14C, 15C
lately 109C
with the present perfect continuous 16D
leaving out a relative pronoun 138B, 139B
leaving out **the** 86–8, p 379
least 110F, 112A
less 110F, 112A
less and less 112C
let with an infinitive 69B
let's 51A
with a question tag 42C
like
+ to-infinitive or ing-form 63A
would like to 50A
and **as** 122C
likely + to-infinitive 67D
linking verb + adjective 108C
linking words 150–3
+ ing-form 73
links across sentences 153
little 95, see also **a little**
'll (short form) 23
lots of 95, see also **a lot of**
love + to-infinitive or ing-form 63A
ly ending 108–9, p 371

Mm

make with an infinitive 69B
manage + to-infinitive 60C

many 95
mass noun see uncountable noun
may
permission 45
possibility 46
may have done 53
me 98
than me 111E
mean + to-infinitive or ing-form 64D
means 80C
mid position 113B
might 46
might have done 53
mind 50A
+ ing-form 61B
mine 92
modal verbs 44–53, Test 10 p 128
passive 54C
with the perfect 53
in reported speech 134C
in conditionals 144–7
more 110
more and more 112C
most 96B, 110
much 95, 115D
+ comparative 112B
musical instruments with **the** 86C, p 379
must
certainty 46C
necessity 47
must have done 53D
mustn't 48A, p 379
my 92
myself 100, 101

Nn

names of places and **the** 90
near, nearly 109C
necessity: **must, have to, needn't** 47–8
need + to-infinitive or ing-form 64G
needn't 48, p 379
needn't have done 48C
needs doing 59B, 64G
negative prefixes p 369
negative questions 41
Why don't we ...? 5A
negative statements 40, Test 9 p 106
neither 97C
+ **of** 79D

neither do I 43A
never with the present perfect and past simple 13B, 15B, p 377
news 77B, 80B
next to 118
no
and **not** 40C
+ noun 40C, 96D
no bigger 112B
in short answers 35
after a question tag 42B
after a negative question 41D
no longer 114D
no one, nothing, etc 103
non-identifying relative clauses 141–2
none 79D, 96D
nor 43A
not 40
I hope not 43B
nouns 76–82, Test 14 p 194
countable and uncountable 76–8
possessive form 93
plural p 370
singular or plural? 80
suffixes p 368
+ noun 82
+ preposition 124
+ to-infinitive 60D
n't 32B, 40
number of 79C
numbers (in American English) p 379

Oo

object 2
direct and indirect 3
of a relative clause 138
object pronouns 98
of
the name of the boy 93
the history of Ireland 86B
a friend of mine 92E
carton of milk 77
cup of tea and *teacup* 82C
most of, some of 96
each of, both of 97
dream of 126C
increase of 124C
warn me of 127C
after a superlative 111C
+ object + to-infinitive 68D

off in a phrasal verb 130B
offers 51B, 52D
   reported 136B
   in conditionals 144B, 145C
on
   place 118B, 119
   time 120
   transport 123C
   on the way 123B
   + ing-form 53B
   in a phrasal verb 130
on top of 118A
one
   and **a/an** 85B
   one of + singular verb 79C
   and **ones** 102
   meaning people in general 56B, 98C, p 380
one another 101B
ones 102
onto 118B
opposite 118
opposites p 369
order of adjectives 105
order of words see word order
ought to 49B
ought to have done 53E
our, ours 92
ourselves 100, 101
out 118A
   in American English p 380
   in a phrasal verb 130B
over in a phrasal verb 130B
own (*my own*) 92D

Pp

pair nouns 81A
pair of 81A
participles
   used as adjectives 107
   with **see, hear** 74
   in relative clauses 143A
   other structures 75
   see also past/passive participle
parts of speech 1
passive 54–9, Test 11 p 142
   verb forms 54
   to-infinitive and ing-form 59
   past and perfect tenses 8–21, Test 4 p 48
past continuous 9, Test 2 p 24

and past simple 10, 19C, 21E
and past perfect continuous 20D
past/passive participle
   in the perfect 11
   in the passive 54
   irregular p 383–4
   see also participle
past perfect 18
   and past simple 19D, 21F
   and past perfect continuous 20C, 21G
   and present perfect 18C
   in reported speech 134B
   in conditionals 146
   after **wish** 149
past perfect continuous 20, 21G
past simple 8, Test 2 p 24
   and present perfect 14–15, 21C, Test 3 p 36
   and past continuous 10, 19C, 21E
   and past perfect 19D, 21F
   in conditionals 145
   after **wish** 149
   irregular p 383–4
   in American English p 377
past tense in reported speech 134
people 81C
   empty subject 56B
perfect after modal verbs 53
perfect and past tenses 8–21, Test 4 p 48
perfect ing-form 75
permission: **can, may,** etc 45
personal pronouns 98
phonetic symbols p 374
phrasal verbs 128–31, Test 22 p 316
phrases of time
   without **a/an** or **the** 88
   with a possessive form (*last week's news*) 93C
piece of 77
place names and **the** 90
plural nouns and **the** 86
plural of nouns p 370
plural-only nouns 80A
police 81C, 84B
position of adverbs 113
possessive forms
   my etc 92
   of noun 93
   of **someone** etc 103D
possibility: **may, might, could** 46

predictions 25C, 52A
prefer + to-infinitive or ing-form 63A
prefixes p 369
prepositions 118–27, Test 21 p 302
   of place 118–19
   of time 120–1
   in wh-questions 38
   in relative clauses 139
   after an adjective 125
   after a noun 124
   after a verb 126
   after a verb + adverb 131
   after a verb + object 127
   + noun without **the** 88
   + object pronoun 98B
   + reflexive pronoun 100C
   + ing-form 70, 73
   in American English p 380–1
prepositional verbs 126–7, Test 22 p 316
present continuous 4
   and present simple 6, 21B, Test 1 p 16
   for the future 26
   for the future after a linking word 27C
present perfect 11–13
   and past simple 14–15, 21C, Test 3 p 36
   and past perfect 18C
   and present perfect continuous 17, 21D
   for the future after a linking word 27C
   in American English p 377
present perfect continuous 16
   and present perfect simple 17, 21D
   and past perfect continuous 20D
present simple 5
   and present continuous 6, 21B, Test 1 p 16
   for the future 26
   for the future after a linking word 27
   in conditionals 144
present tenses for the future 26
prison and the prison 87A
probably 113G
pronouns 98–103, Test 17 p 244
   personal 98
   reflexive 100
   relative 137–42

after **give** 3C
after **than** 111E
with a phrasal verb 128C
prove + to-infinitive 62D
punctuation p 372–3
purpose 151

Qq

quantifiers 94–7
questions 34, 36, 41, Test 8 p 96,
    Test 9 p 106
  yes/no questions 34
  wh-questions 36
  reported 135
question marks p 372
question phrases 36C
question tags 42
  in American English p 379
question words 36–9
  with a short form 32B
  + to-infinitive 66
quite 115
  + **a** 89A
  and **rather** 116
quotation marks p 373

Rr

rather 89B, 115
  and **quite** 116
  + comparative 112B
  would rather 69B
really 115C
recently 16D
reflexive pronouns 100
refusals 52C
regret + to-infinitive or ing-form 64B
relative adverbs 142C
relative clauses 137–43, Test 24 p 344
  identifying and adding 141–2
  pronoun as object 138
  without a pronoun 138B, 139B
  with a preposition 139
  after a superlative 111C
  participle clauses 143A
  to-infinitive clauses 143B
remember + to-infinitive or ing-form 64A
remind about/of 127C
reported speech 132–6,
    Test 23 p 238

questions 135
  orders and requests 136A
requests 50
  with a question tag 42C
  reported 136A
Review units
  past simple, continuous and perfect 19
  present and past tenses 21
  future 30
  conditionals 147
  linking words 152

Ss

's
  possessive form 93
  short form 32C
s ending
  plural p 370
  in the present simple 5B, p 370
  pronunciation p 375
same as 111D
say
  and **tell** 132C
  it is said that ... 57B
  he is said to ... 57B
school and **the school** 87A
sea and **the sea** 87B
see it happen/happening 74
seem
  + to-infinitive 60B
  in American English p 377
semi-colons p 372
sentence adverbs 113G
sentence structure 2
shall 52D
  future 23D
  offers 51B, 52D
  suggestions 51A, 52D
  in American English p 377–8
she 98
short answers 35
short forms 32
should 49B, 51A, 52D, p 381
  instead of **would** 52A
should have done 53E
simple past see past simple
simple present see present simple
singular or plural noun? 80
singular or plural verb? 79

since
  and **for** 121
  with the present perfect 12B, 14C, 121B
  with the present perfect continuous 16D
  linking word 152A
  + ing-form 73C
so
  + adjective 89C
  in comparisons 111D
  so do I 43A
  I think so 43B
  linking word 152D
so as to 151C
so that 151D
some 85, 96B
  and **any** 94
someone, something, etc 94B, 103
someplace p 380
somewhere 94B, 103, p 380
sorry + to-infinitive or ing-form 71C
spelling of endings p 370–1
start + to-infinitive or ing-form 63C
starting test p viii-xiii
state verbs 7
still
  adverb 114
  linking word 153B
stop + to-infinitive or ing-form 64D
stress p 374
  with **quite** 116B
structure of sentences 2
subject 2A
  in the passive 55–7
subject/object questions 37
subject pronouns 98
subject-verb agreement 79
subjunctive p 381
such a 89C
suffixes p 368–9
suggest (that) 65E
suggestions 41E, 51A, 52D, 73B
  reported 136B
  in conditionals 144B, 145C
superlative 110–12, Test 19 p 268
  + **one/ones** 102B
  + to-infinitive 143B
suppose so 43B
supposed to 49D, 57C
sure + to-infinitive 67D

Tt

t (past tense ending) p 382
tag questions see question tags
tell and **say** 132C
tend + to-infinitive 60C
tense changes in reported speech 134
tenses of the verb 4–30, Test 5 p 54
    passive 54
Tests
    A/an and **the**: Test 15 p 214
    Adjectives and adverbs:
        Test 18 p 258
    Adverbs and word order:
        Test 20 p 282
    Comparative and superlative:
        Test 19 p 268
    Conditionals and **wish**:
        Test 25 p 358
    Future: Test 6 p 68, Test 7 p 76
    Infinitive and ing-form:
        Test 13 p 178
    Modal verbs: Test 10 p 128
    Nouns and agreement:
        Test 14 p 194
    Passive: Test 11 p 142
    Past and perfect tenses: Test 4 p 48
    Past simple and past continuous:
        Test 2 p 24
    Prepositions: Test 21 p 302
    Present and past tenses: Test 5 p 54
    Present perfect and past simple:
        Test 3 p 36
    Present tenses: Test 1 p 16
    Pronouns: Test 17 p 244
    Questions: Test 8 p 96
    Questions, negatives and answers:
        Test 9 p 106
    Relative clauses: Test 24 p 344
    Reported speech: Test 23 p 328
    This, my, some, a lot of, all, etc:
        Test 16 p 230
    Verb + to-infinitive or ing-form:
        Test 12 p 154
    Verbs with prepositions and
        adverbs: Test 22 p 316
than 111
that 91
    relative pronoun 137–9
the 83–4, 86–7, Test 15 p 214
    cars or *the cars?* 86
    school or *the school?* 87, p 379
    the old, the rich 106
    in place names 90
    + **one** 102B
    with musical instruments 86C,
        p 379
    + superlative 111C
    the faster the better 112D
their, theirs 92
    with **everyone, someone** 103C
them 98
themselves 100, 101
    and *each other* 101B
there
    there is and *it is* 99
    with a to-infinitive 59B
these 91
they 98
    meaning people in general 56B,
        98C
think so 43B
this 91
    this one 102B
    this week etc with the present
        perfect and past simple 13D, 15C
those 91
though 150C
through 118A
    time p 380
till see **until**
time
    first time etc with the present
        perfect 13C
    time phrases 120
        without **a/an** or **the** 88
        with a possessive form (*last week's
            news*) 93C
    time words, e.g. **when, as** 152A
to 118
    give it to you 3B
    write to 126C, 127C
    good to me 125C
    see also to-infinitive
to be done 59
to-infinitive 60–9, Test 13 p 178,
    Test 12 p 154
    or ing-form 62–5, 71–2, 74
    passive 59
    expressing purpose 151B
    in relative clauses 143B
    in reported offers etc 136B
    after an adjective 67
    after a noun 60D
    after a question word 66
    after a verb 60, 62
    after a passive verb 57C
    after a verb + object 65
    after **for/of** + object 68
today with the present perfect and
    past simple 13D, 15C
too (*too big*)117
    with **for** and a to-infinitive 68C
too (= also) 113G, 153B
too many, too much 117B
town and **the town** 87B
try + to-infinitive or ing-form 64C
turn out + to-infinitive 62D
two adverbs together 115B
two nouns together 82

Uu

uncountable nouns 76–8
unless 148C, 152B
until
    and **by** 122B
    linking word 152A
    in American English p 380
up in a phrasal verb 130
us 98
used to do/doing 72

Vv

verb structures
    verb + to-infinitive 60, 62,
        Test 12 p 154
    verb + ing-form 61–2,
        Test 12 p 154
    verb + object + to-infinitive or
        ing-form 65
    verb + preposition 126,
        Test 22 p 316
    verb + preposition + ing-form 70
    verb + object + preposition 127
    verb + adverb (phrasal verb)
        128–31, Test 22 p 316
    verb + adverb + preposition 131
verb suffixes p 369
verb tenses 4–30, Test 5 p 54
    passive 54
verbs without a reflexive pronoun
    100E
very 115
very much 115D
voicing p 375

Ww

want + object + to-infinitive 65C
was 8
was able to 44C
was allowed to 45C
was doing 9
was done see passive
was going to 29B
we 98
weak forms p 376
well 109D
were 8
were doing 9
wh-questions 36
   with a preposition 38
what
   question word 37, 39
   in exclamations 89D
   relative pronoun 140B
what a 89D
what about + ing-form 73B
what ... for/like 38B
when
   question word 36
   linking word 152A
   with past tenses 10B
   + ing-form 73C
   or **if?** 148B
   relative adverb 142C
where
   question word 36
   relative adverb 142C
whether
   in a reported question 135B
   + to-infinitive 66C
which
   and **who, what** 39
   as subject/object 37B
   relative pronoun 137, 142D

while 122A
   linking word 152A
   with the past continuous 10B
   + ing-form 73C
who
   and **what, which** 39
   as subject/object 37
   relative pronoun 137–9
whole 97B
whom 138C
whose
   question word 37B
   in relative clause 140A
why
   question word 36
   relative adverb 142C
will 52
   future 22C, 23
   and *be going to* 25
   in conditionals 144
   invitations 51C
   offers 51B
will be able to 44B
will be allowed to 45C
will be doing 28
will be done 54C
will have done 29A
wish 149
with (*link with*) 124C
won't
   future 23C
   offers 51B
   invitations 51C
   refusals 52C
word classes 1
word formation p 368–9
word order
   sentence structure 2
   questions 34, 36, 38
   reported questions 135C

   adjectives 104B, 105
   adverbs 113
   with phrasal verbs 128C
   prepositions in relative clauses 139
work and **the work** 87B
worse, worst 110E
would 52
   in conditionals 145–6
   after **wish** 149
would like 52B
   offers 51B
   invitations 51C
   requests 50A, 50C
   + to-infinitive 63B
   + object + to-infinitive 65C
would rather 69B
wouldn't for a refusal 52C

Yy

yes
   short answers 35
   after a negative question 41D
   after a question tag 42B
yes/no questions 34
   negative 41C
yet 114
   with the present perfect 12A
   in American English p 377
you 98
   people in general 56B, 98C, p 380
your, yours 92
yourself, yourselves 100, 101